Eighteenth-Century Critical Essays

Eighteenth-Century Critical Essays

EDITED BY

SCOTT ELLEDGE

VOLUME II

Cornell University Press

ITHACA, NEW YORK

This work has been brought to
publication with the assistance of
a grant from the Ford Foundation.

© 1961 by Cornell University

CORNELL UNIVERSITY PRESS

First published 1961
Second printing 1966

Library of Congress Catalog Card Number: 61-7868

PRINTED IN THE UNITED STATES OF AMERICA
BY VALLEY OFFSET, INC.

For LIANE

CONTENTS

Volume I

Contents   xiii

Eighteenth-Century Critical Essays

SAMUEL JOHNSON ✍

The Rambler[1] (1750-1752)

No. 4, March 31, 1750
[The Moral Duty of Novelists][2]

> *Simul et jucunda et idonea dicere vitae.*
> —Hor. [*Ars poet.* 334]
>
> And join both profit and delight in one.—Creech[3]

The works of fiction with which the present generation seems more particularly delighted are such as exhibit life in its true state, diversified only by accidents that daily happen in the world, and influenced by passions and qualities which are really to be found in conversing with mankind.

This kind of writing may be termed not improperly the comedy of romance, and is to be conducted nearly by the rules of comic poetry. Its province is to bring about natural events by easy means and to keep up curiosity without the help of wonder; it is therefore precluded from the machines and expedients of the heroic romance, and can neither employ giants to snatch away a lady from the nuptial rites nor knights to bring her back from captivity; it can neither bewilder its personages in deserts nor lodge them in imaginary castles.

I remember a remark made by Scaliger upon Pontanus,[4] that all his writings are filled with the same images and that if you take from him his lilies and his roses, his satyrs and his dryads, he will have nothing left that can be called poetry. In like manner almost all the fictions of the last age will vanish if you deprive them of a hermit and a wood, a battle and a shipwreck.

Why this wild strain of imagination found reception so long in polite and learned ages it is not easy to conceive, but we cannot wonder that, while readers could be procured, the authors were willing to continue it, for when a man had by practice gained some fluency of language, he had no further care than to retire to his closet, let loose his invention, and heat his mind with incredibilities; a book was thus produced without fear of criticism, without the toil of study, without knowledge of nature or acquaintance with life.

The task of our present writers is very different; it requires, together with that learning which is to be gained from books, that experience which can never be attained by solitary diligence but must arise from general converse and accurate observation of the living world. Their performances have, as Horace expresses it, *plus oneris quanto veniae minus*,[5] little indulgence, and therefore more difficulty. They are engaged in portraits of which everyone knows the original and can detect any deviation from exactness of resemblance. Other writings are safe, except from the malice of learning, but these are in danger from every common reader, as the slipper ill executed was censured by a shoemaker who happened to stop in his way at the Venus of Apelles.[6]

But the danger of not being approved as just copiers of human manners is not the most important concern that an author of this sort ought to have before him. These books are written chiefly to the young, the ignorant, and the idle, to whom they serve as lectures of conduct and introductions into life. They are the entertainment of minds unfurnished with ideas and therefore easily susceptible of impressions, not fixed by principles and therefore easily following the current of fancy, not informed by experience and consequently open to every false suggestion and partial account.

That the highest degree of reverence should be paid to youth and that nothing indecent should be suffered to approach their eyes or ears are precepts extorted by sense and virtue from an ancient writer by no means eminent for chastity of thought.[7] The same kind, though not the same degree of caution, is required in everything which is laid before them, to secure them from unjust prejudices, perverse opinions, and incongruous combinations of images.

In the romances formerly written, every transaction and sentiment was so remote from all that passes among men that the reader was in very little danger of making any applications to himself. The virtues and crimes were equally beyond his sphere of activity, and he amused himself with heroes and with traitors, deliverers and persecutors, as with beings of another species, whose actions were regulated upon motives of their own and who had neither faults nor excellencies in common with himself.

But when an adventurer is leveled with the rest of the world and acts in such scenes of the universal drama as may be the lot of any other man, young spectators fix their eyes upon him with closer attention and hope by observing his behavior and success to regulate their own practices when they shall be engaged in the like part.

For this reason these familiar histories may perhaps be made of greater use than the solemnities of professed morality, and convey the knowledge of vice and virtue with more efficacy than axioms and definitions. But if the power of example is so great as to take possession of the memory by a kind of violence, and produce effects almost without the intervention of the will, care ought to be taken that, when the choice is unrestrained, the best examples only should be exhibited, and that which is likely to operate so strongly should not be mischievous or uncertain in its effects.

The chief advantage which these fictions have over real life is that their authors are at liberty, though not to invent, yet to select objects and to cull from the mass of mankind those individuals upon which the attention ought most to be employed, as a diamond, though it cannot be made, may be polished by art and placed in such a situation as to display that luster which before was buried among common stones.

It is justly considered as the greatest excellency of art to imitate nature, but it is necessary to distinguish those parts of nature which are most proper for imitation. Greater care is still required in representing life, which is so often discolored by passion or deformed by wickedness. If the world be promiscuously described, I cannot see of what use it can be to read the account or why it may not be as safe to turn the eye immediately upon mankind, as upon a mirror which shows all that presents itself without discrimination.

It is therefore not a sufficient vindication of a character that it is drawn as it appears, for many characters ought never to be drawn; nor of a narrative, that the train of events is agreeable to observation and experience, for that observation which is called knowledge of the world will be found much more frequently to make men cunning than good. The purpose of these writings is surely not only to show mankind, but to provide that they may be seen hereafter with less hazard; to teach the means of avoiding the snares which are laid by Treachery for Innocence, without infusing any wish for that superiority with which the betrayer flatters his vanity; to give the power of counteracting fraud, without the temptation to practice it; to initiate youth by mock encounters in the art of necessary defense; and to increase prudence without impairing virtue.

Many writers for the sake of following nature so mingle good and bad qualities in their principal personages that they are both equally conspicuous, and as we accompany them through their adventures with delight, and are led by degrees to interest ourselves in their favor, we lose the abhorrence of their faults because they do not hinder our pleasure, or, perhaps, regard them with some kindness for being united with so much merit.

There have been men indeed splendidly wicked whose endowments threw a brightness on their crimes and whom scarce any villainy made perfectly detestable, because they never could be wholly divested of their excellencies; but such have been in all ages the great corrupters of the world, and their resemblance ought no more to be preserved than the art of murdering without pain.

Some have advanced, without due attention to the consequences of this notion, that certain virtues have their correspondent faults and therefore that to exhibit either apart is to deviate from probability. Thus men are observed by Swift to be "grateful in the same degree as they are resentful." This principle, with others of the same kind, supposes man to act from a brute impulse and pursue a certain degree of inclination without any choice of the object, for otherwise, though it should be allowed that gratitude and resentment arise from the same constitution of the passions, it follows not that they will be equally indulged when reason is consulted; yet unless that consequence be admitted, this sagacious maxim becomes an empty sound, without any relation to practice or to life.

Nor is it evident that even the first motions to these effects are always in the same proportion. For pride, which produces quickness of resentment, will frequently obstruct gratitude by unwillingness to admit that inferiority which obligation implies; and it is very unlikely that he who cannot think he receives a favor will ever acknowledge or repay it.

It is of the utmost importance to mankind that positions of this tendency should be laid open and confuted, for while men consider good and evil as springing from the same root, they will spare the one for the sake of the other, and in judging, if not of others at least of themselves, will be apt to estimate their virtues by their vices. To this fatal error all those will contribute who confound the colors of right and wrong, and instead of helping to settle their boundaries, mix them with so much art that no common mind is able to disunite them.

In narratives where historical veracity has no place I cannot discover why there should not be exhibited the most perfect idea of virtue, of virtue not angelical, nor above probability, for what we cannot credit we shall never imitate, but the highest and purest that humanity can reach, which, exercised in such trials as the various revolutions of things shall bring upon it, may, by conquering some calamities and enduring others, teach us what we may hope and what we can perform. Vice (for vice is necessary to be shown) should always disgust, nor should the graces of gaiety or the dignity of courage be so united with it as to reconcile it to the mind. Wherever it appears, it should raise hatred by the malignity of its practices, and contempt by the meanness of its stratagems, for while it is supported by either parts or spirit, it will be seldom heartily abhorred. The Roman tyrant was content to be hated if he was but feared, and there are thousands of the readers of romances willing to be thought wicked if they may be allowed to be wits. It is therefore to be steadily inculcated that virtue is the highest proof of understanding and the only solid basis of greatness, and that vice is the natural consequence of narrow thoughts, that it begins in mistake and ends in ignominy.

No. 36, July 21, 1750   [Pastoral Poetry, I][8]

'Αμ' ἕποντο νομῆες
τερπόμενοι σύριγξι· δόλον δ' οὔτι προνόησαν.
                                —HOMER [*Iliad* xviii. 525]

Piping on their reeds the shepherds go,
Nor fear an ambush, nor suspect a foe.—POPE

There is scarcely any species of poetry that has allured more readers or excited more writers than the pastoral. It is generally pleasing, because it entertains the mind with representations of scenes familiar to almost every imagination, and of which all can equally judge whether they are well described. It exhibits a life to which we have been always accustomed to associate peace and leisure and innocence, and therefore we readily set open the heart for the admission of its images, which contribute to drive away cares and perturbations, and suffer ourselves without resistance to be transported to Elysian regions, where we are to meet with nothing but joy and plenty and contentment—where every gale whispers pleasure, and every shade promises repose.

It has been maintained by some who love to talk of what they do not know that pastoral is the most ancient poetry; and, indeed, since it is probable that poetry is nearly of the same antiquity with rational nature, and since the life of the first men was certainly rural, we may reasonably conjecture that as their ideas would necessarily be borrowed from those objects with which they were acquainted, their composures, being filled chiefly with such thoughts on the visible creation as must occur to the first observers, were pastoral hymns, like those which Milton introduces the original pair singing in the day of innocence to the praise of their Maker.[9]

For the same reason that pastoral poetry was the first employment of the human imagination, it is generally the first literary amusement of our minds. We have seen fields and meadows and groves from the time that our eyes opened upon life, and are pleased with birds and brooks and breezes much earlier than we engage among the actions and passions of mankind. We are therefore delighted with rural pictures because we know the original at an age when our curiosity can be very little awakened by descriptions of courts which we never beheld or representations of passion which we never felt.

The satisfaction received from this kind of writing not only begins early but lasts long; we do not, as we advance into the intellectual world, throw it away among other childish amusements and pastimes, but willingly return to it in any hour of indolence and relaxation. For the images of true pastoral have always the power of exciting delight, because the works of nature, from which they are drawn, have always the same order and beauty, and continue to force themselves upon our thoughts, being at once obvious to the most careless regard and more than adequate to the strongest reason and severest contemplation. Our inclination to stillness and tranquillity is seldom much lessened by long knowledge of the busy and tumultuary part of the world. In childhood we turn our thoughts to the country as to the region of pleasure; we recur to it in old age as a port of rest, and perhaps with that secondary and adventitious gladness which every man feels on reviewing those places or recollecting those occurrences that contributed to his youthful enjoyments and bring him back to the prime of life, when the world was gay with the bloom of novelty, when mirth wantoned at his side, and hope sparkled before him.

The sense of this universal pleasure has invited "numbers without number" to try their skill in pastoral performances, in which they have generally succeeded after the manner of other imitators, transmitting the same images in the same combination from one to another, till he that reads the title of a poem may guess at the whole series of the composition; nor will a man, after the perusal of thousands of these performances, find his knowledge enlarged with a single view of nature not produced before, or his imagination amused with any new application of those views to moral purposes.

The range of pastoral is indeed narrow, for though nature itself, philosophically considered, be inexhaustible, yet its general effects on the eye and on the ear are uniform and incapable of much variety of description. Poetry cannot dwell upon the minuter distinctions by which one species differs from another without departing from that simplicity of grandeur which fills the imagination, nor dissect the latent qualities of things without losing its general power of gratifying every mind by recalling its conceptions.[10] However, as each age makes some discoveries and those discoveries are by degrees generally known, as new plants or modes of culture are introduced and by little and little become common, pastoral might receive from time to time small augmentations, and exhibit, once in a century, a scene somewhat varied.

But pastoral subjects have been often, like others, taken into the hands of those that were not qualified to adorn them—men to whom the face of nature was so little known that they have drawn it only after their own imagination and changed or distorted her features that their portraits might appear something more than servile copies from their predecessors.

Not only the images of rural life but the occasions on which they can be properly produced are few and general. The state of a man confined to the employments and pleasures of the country is so little diversified, and exposed to so few of those accidents which produce perplexities, terrors, and surprises in more complicated transactions, that he can be shown but seldom in such circumstances as attract curiosity. His ambition is without policy, and his love without intrigue. He has no complaints to make of his rival but that he is richer than himself, nor any disasters to lament but a cruel mistress or a bad harvest.

The conviction of the necessity of some new source of pleasure induced Sannazarius [11] to remove the scene from the fields to the sea, to substitute fishermen for shepherds, and derive his sentiments from the piscatory life; for which he has been censured by succeeding critics because the sea is an object of terror and by no means proper to amuse the mind and lay the passions asleep. Against this objection he might be defended by the established maxim that the poet has a right to select his images, and is no more obliged to show the sea in a storm than the land under an inundation, but may display all the pleasures and conceal the dangers of the water, as he may lay his shepherd under a shady beech without giving him an ague or letting a wild beast loose upon him.

There are, however, two defects in the piscatory eclogue which perhaps cannot be supplied. The sea, though in hot countries it is considered by those who live, like Sannazarius, upon the coast as a place of pleasure and diversion, has notwithstanding much less variety than the land and therefore will be sooner exhausted by a descriptive writer. When he has once shown the sun rising or setting upon it, curled its waters with the vernal breeze, rolled the waves in gentle succession to the shore, and enumerated the fish sporting in the shallows, he has nothing remaining but what is common to all other poetry, the complaint of a nymph for a drowned lover, or the indignation of a fisher that his oysters are refused and Mycon's accepted.

Another obstacle to the general reception of this kind of poetry is the ignorance of maritime pleasures in which the greater part of mankind must always live. To all the inland inhabitants of every region, the sea is only known as an immense diffusion of waters over which men pass from one country to another and in which life is frequently lost. They have, therefore, no opportunity of tracing in their own thoughts the descriptions of winding shores and calm bays, nor can look on the poem in which they are mentioned with other sensations than on a sea chart or the metrical geography of Dionysius. [12]

This defect Sannazarius was hindered from perceiving by writing in a learned language to readers generally acquainted with the works of nature, but if he had made his attempt in any vulgar tongue, he would soon have discovered how vainly he had endeavored to make that loved which was not understood.

I am afraid it will not be found easy to improve the pastorals of antiquity by any great additions or diversifications. Our descriptions may indeed differ from those of Virgil, as an English from an Italian summer, and, in some respects, as modern from ancient life; but as nature is in both countries nearly the same, and as poetry has to do rather with the passions of men, which are uniform, than their customs, which are changeable, the varieties which time or place can furnish will be inconsiderable; and I shall endeavor to show in the next paper how little the latter ages have contributed to the improvement of the rustic muse.

No. 37, July 24, 1750   [Pastoral Poetry, II]

Canto, quae solitus, si quando armenta vocabat
Amphion Dircaeus.—Virg. [*Ecl.* II. 23]

Such strains I sing as once Amphion play'd,
When list'ning flocks the powerful call obey'd.
                              —Elphinston

In writing or judging of pastoral poetry, neither the authors nor critics of latter times seem to have paid sufficient regard to the originals left us by antiquity but have entangled themselves with unnecessary difficulties by advancing principles which, having no foundation in the nature of things, are wholly to be rejected from a species of composition in which, above all others, mere nature is to be regarded.

It is therefore necessary to inquire after some more distinct and exact idea of this kind of writing. This may, I think, be easily found in the pastorals of Virgil, from whose opinion it will not appear very safe to depart if we consider that every advantage of nature and of fortune concurred to complete his productions, that he was born with great accuracy and severity of judgment, enlightened with all the learning of one of the brightest ages and embellished with the elegance of the Roman court, that he employed his powers rather in improving than inventing and therefore must have endeavored to recompense the want of novelty by exactness, that, taking Theocritus for his original, he found pastoral far advanced towards perfection, and that, having so great a rival, he must have proceeded with uncommon caution.[13]

If we search the writings of Virgil for the true definition of a pastoral, it will be found "a poem in which any action or passion is represented by its effects upon a country life." Whatsoever, therefore, may according to the common course of things happen in the country may afford a subject for a pastoral poet.

In this definition it will immediately occur to those who are versed in the writings of the modern critics that there is no mention of the golden age. I cannot, indeed, easily discover why it is thought necessary to refer descriptions of a rural state to remote times, nor can I perceive that any writer has consistently preserved the Arcadian manners and sentiments. The only reason that I have read on which this rule has been founded is that according to the customs of modern life it is improbable that shepherds should be capable of harmonious numbers or delicate sentiments, and therefore the reader must exalt his ideas of the pastoral character by carrying his thoughts back to the age in which the care of herds and flocks was the employment of the wisest and greatest men.

These reasoners seem to have been led into their hypothesis by considering pastoral, not in general as a representation of rural nature, and consequently as exhibiting the ideas and sentiments of those, whoever they are, to whom the country affords pleasure or employment, but simply as a dialogue or narrative of men actually tending sheep and busied in the lowest and most laborious offices; from whence they very readily concluded, since characters must necessarily be preserved, that either the sentiments must sink to the level of the speakers, or the speakers must be raised to the height of the sentiments.

In consequence of these original errors a thousand precepts have been given, which have only contributed to perplex and to confound. Some have thought it necessary that the imaginary manners of the golden age should be universally preserved and have therefore believed that nothing more could be admitted in pastoral than lilies and roses, and rocks and streams, among which are heard the gentle whispers of chaste fondness, or the soft complaints of amorous impatience. In pastoral, as in other writings, chastity of sentiment ought doubtless to be observed and purity of manners to be represented, not because the poet is confined to the images of the golden age, but because, having the subject in his own choice, he ought always to consult the interest of virtue.

These advocates for the golden age lay down other principles not very consistent with their general plan, for they tell us that to support the character of the shepherd it is proper that all refinement should be avoided, and that some slight instances of ignorance should be interspersed. Thus the shepherd in Virgil is supposed to have forgot the name of Anaximander, and in Pope the term *zodiac* is too hard for a rustic apprehension.[14] But if we place our shepherds in their primitive condition, we may give them learning among their other qualifications; and if we suffer them to allude at all to things of later existence, which, perhaps, cannot with any great propriety be allowed, there can be no danger of making them speak with too much accuracy, since they conversed with divinities and transmitted to succeeding ages the arts of life.

Other writers, having the mean and despicable condition of a shepherd always before them, conceive it necessary to degrade the language of pastoral by obsolete terms and rustic words, which they very learnedly call Doric, without reflecting that they thus become authors of a mingled dialect which no human being ever could have spoken, that they may as well refine the speech as the sentiments of their personages, and that none of the inconsistencies which they endeavor to avoid is greater than that of joining elegance of thought with coarseness of diction. Spenser begins one of his pastorals with studied barbarity:

> Diggon Davie, I bid her good-day:
> Or, Diggon her is, or I missay.
>
> *Dig.* Her was her while it was day-light,
> But now her is a most wretched wight.[15]

What will the reader imagine to be the subject on which speakers like these exercise their eloquence? Will he not be somewhat disappointed when he finds them met together to condemn the corruptions of the church of Rome? Surely, at the same time that a shepherd learns theology he may gain some acquaintance with his native language.

Pastoral admits of all ranks of persons because persons of all ranks inhabit the country. It excludes not, therefore, on account of the characters necessary to be introduced any elevation or delicacy of sentiment; those ideas only are improper which, not owing their original to rural objects, are not pastoral. Such is the exclamation in Virgil:

> Nunc scio quid sit Amor. duris in cotibus illum
> aut Tmaros aut Rhodope aut extremi Garamantes
> nec generis nostri puerum nec sanguinis edunt.
>   —VIRG. [*Ecl.* VIII. 43]

> I know thee, Love! in desarts thou wert bred,
> And at the dugs of savage tigers fed;
> Alien of birth, usurper of the plains!—DRYDEN

which Pope, endeavoring to copy, has carried to still greater impropriety:

> I know thee, love, wild as the raging main,
> More fierce than tigers on the Lybian plain;
> Thou wert from Etna's burning entrails torn,
> Begot in tempests, and in thunders born! [16]

Sentiments like these, as they have no ground in nature, are indeed of little value in any poem, but in pastoral they are particularly liable to censure because it wants that exaltation above common life which in tragic or heroic writings often reconciles us to bold flights and daring figures.

Pastoral, being the "representation of an action or passion by its effects upon a country life," has nothing peculiar but its confinement to rural imagery, without which it ceases to be pastoral. This is its true characteristic, and this it cannot lose by any dignity of sentiment or beauty of diction. The "Pollio" of Virgil, with all its elevation, is a composition truly bucolic, though rejected by the critics, for all the images are either taken from the country or from the religion of the age common to all parts of the empire.

The "Silenus" is indeed of a more disputable kind because, though the scene lies in the country, the song, being religious and historical, had been no less adapted to any other audience or place. Neither can it well be defended as a fiction, for the introduction of a god seems to imply the golden age; and yet he alludes to many subsequent transactions and mentions Gallus, the poet's contemporary.

It seems necessary to the perfection of this poem that the occasion which is supposed to produce it be at least not inconsistent with a country life or less likely to interest those who have retired into places of solitude and quiet than the more busy part of mankind. It is therefore improper to give the title of a pastoral to verses in which the speakers, after the slight mention of their flocks, fall to complaints of errors in the church and corruptions in the government, or to lamentations of the death of some illustrious person whom when once the poet has called a shepherd he has no longer any labor upon his hands but can make the clouds weep and lilies wither and the sheep hang their heads, without art or learning, genius or study.

It is part of Claudian's character of his rustic that he computes his time, not by the succession of consuls, but of harvests.[17] Those who pass their days in retreats distant from the theaters of business are always least likely to hurry their imagination with public affairs.

The facility of treating actions or events in the pastoral style has incited many writers from whom more judgment might have been expected to put the sorrow or the joy which the occasion required into the mouth of Daphne or of Thyrsis, and as one absurdity may naturally be expected to make way for another, they have written with an utter disregard both of life and nature, and filled their productions with mythological allusions, with incredible fictions, and with sentiments which neither passion nor reason could have dictated since the change which religion has made in the whole system of the world.

No. 86, January 12, 1751
[Milton's Versification, I][18]

> *Legitimumque sonum digitis callemus et aure.*
> —HOR. [*Ars poet.* 274]

By fingers, or by ear, we numbers scan.—ELPHINSTON

One of the ancients has observed that the burden of government is increased upon princes by the virtues of their immediate predecessors. It is indeed always dangerous to be placed in a state of unavoidable comparison with excellence, and the danger is still greater when that excellence is consecrated by death, when envy and interest cease to act against it, and those passions by which it was at first vilified and opposed now stand in its defense and turn their vehemence against honest emulation.

He that succeeds a celebrated writer has the same difficulties to encounter: he stands under the shade of exalted merit and is hindered from rising to his natural height by the interception of those beams which should invigorate and quicken him. He applies to that attention which is already engaged and unwilling to be drawn off from certain satisfaction, or perhaps to an attention already wearied and not to be recalled to the same object. One of the old poets congratulates himself that he has the untrodden regions of Parnassus before him and that his garland will be gathered from plantations which no writer had yet culled.[19] But the imitator treads a beaten walk and, with all his diligence, can only hope to find a few flowers or branches untouched by his predecessor, the refuse of contempt or the omissions of negligence. The Macedonian conqueror, when he was once invited to hear a man that sung like a nightingale, replied with contempt that "he had heard the nightingale herself"; and the same treatment must every man expect whose praise is that he imitates another.

Yet in the midst of these discouraging reflections I am about to offer to my reader some observations upon *Paradise Lost,* and hope that, however I may fall below the illustrious writer that has so long dictated to the commonwealth of learning, my attempt may not be wholly useless.[20] There are in every age new errors to be rectified and new prejudices to be opposed. False taste is always busy to mislead those that are entering upon the regions of learning, and the traveler uncertain of his way and forsaken by the sun will be pleased to see a fainter orb arise on the horizon that may rescue him from total darkness though with weak and borrowed luster.

Addison, though he has considered this poem under most of the general topics of criticism, has barely touched upon the versification, not probably because he thought the art of numbers unworthy of his notice, for he knew with how minute attention the ancient critics considered the disposition of syllables and had himself given hopes of some metrical observations upon the great Roman poet.[21] But being the first who undertook to display the beauties and point out the defects of Milton, he had many objects at once before him and passed willingly over those which were most barren of ideas and required labor rather than genius.

Yet versification, or the art of modulating his numbers, is indispensably necessary to a poet. Every other power by which the understanding is enlightened or the imagination enchanted may be exercised in prose. But the poet has this peculiar superiority, that to all the powers which the perfection of every other composition can require he adds the faculty of joining music with reason and of acting at once upon the senses and the passions. I suppose there are few who do not feel themselves touched by poetical melody and who will not confess that they are more or less moved by the same thoughts as they are conveyed by different sounds, and more affected by the same words in one order than in another. The perception of harmony is indeed conferred upon men in degrees very unequal, but there are none who do not perceive it or to whom a regular series of proportionate sounds cannot give delight.

In treating on the versification of Milton, I am desirous to be generally understood and shall therefore studiously decline the dialect of grammarians, though, indeed, it is always difficult and sometimes scarcely possible to deliver the precepts of an art without the terms by which the peculiar ideas of that art are expressed and which had not been invented but because the language already in use was insufficient. If, therefore, I shall seem sometimes obscure, may it be imputed to this voluntary interdiction and to a desire of avoiding that offense which is always given by unusual words.

The heroic measure of the English language may be properly considered as pure or mixed. It is pure when the accent rests upon every second syllable through the whole line.

> Courage uncertain dangers may abate,
> But whó can beár th'appróach of cértain fáte.
> —DRYDEN [*Tyrannic Love*, IV, i]

> Here Love his golden shafts imploys, here lights
> His cónstant Lámp, and wáves his púrple wíngs,
> Reigns here and revels; not in the bought smile
> Of Hárlots, lóveless, jóyless, únindéar'd.
> —MILTON [*P.L.*, IV, 763]

The accent may be observed in the second line of Dryden and the second and fourth of Milton to repose upon every second syllable.

The repetition of this sound or percussion at equal times is the most complete harmony of which a single verse is capable and should therefore be exactly kept in distichs, and generally in the last line of a paragraph, that the ear may rest without any sense of imperfection.

But to preserve the same series of sounds untransposed in a long composition is not only very difficult but tiresome and disgusting, for we are soon wearied with the perpetual recurrence of the same cadence. Necessity has therefore enforced the mixed measure, in which some variation of the accents is allowed; this, though it always injures the harmony of the line considered by itself, yet compensates the loss by relieving us from the continual tyranny of the same sound and makes us more sensible of the harmony of the pure measure.

Of these mixed numbers every poet affords us innumerable instances, and Milton seldom has two pure lines together, as will appear if any of his paragraphs be read with attention merely to the music:

> Thus at thir shady Lodge arriv'd, both stood,
> Both turn'd, and under op'n Sky ador'd
> The God that made both Sky, Air, Earth, and Heav'n
> Which they beheld, the Moon's resplendent Globe
> *And starry Pole; Thou also mad'st the Night,*
> Maker Omnipotent, and thou the Day,
> Which we in our appointed work imploy'd
> Have finisht happy in our mutual help
> *And mutual love, the Crown of all our bliss*
> Ordain'd by thee, and this delicious place
> For us too large, where thy abundance wants
> Partakers, and uncropt falls to the ground.
> But thou hast promis'd from us two a Race
> To fill the Earth, who shall with us extol
> Thy goodness infinite, both when we wake,
> And when we seek, as now, thy gift of sleep.
>
> [*P.L.,* IV, 720]

In this passage it will be at first observed that all the lines are not equally harmonious, and upon a nearer examination it will be found that only the fifth and ninth lines are regular, and the rest are more or less licentious with respect to the accent. In some the accent is equally upon two syllables together, and in both strong, as:

> Thus at their shady Lodge arriv'd, *both stood,*
> *Both turn'd,* and under op'n Sky ador'd
> The God that made both Sky, *Air, Earth,* and Heav'n.

In others the accent is equally upon two syllables, but upon both weak:

> A Race
> To fill the Earth, who shall with us extol
> Thy goodness *infinite,* both when we wake,
> *And when* we seek, as now, thy gift of sleep.

In the first pair of syllables the accent may deviate from the rigor of exactness without any unpleasing diminution of harmony, as may be observed in the lines already cited, and more remarkably in this:

> Thou also mad'st the Night,
> *Maker* Omnipotent! and thou the Day.

But excepting in the first pair of syllables, which may be considered as arbitrary, a poet who, not having the invention or knowledge of Milton, has more need to allure his audience by musical cadences should seldom suffer more than one aberration from the rule in any single verse.

There are two lines in this passage more remarkably unharmonious:

> This delicious place
> For us too large, *where thy* abundance wants
> Partakers, and uncropt *falls to* the ground.

Here the third pair of syllables in the first, and fourth pair in the second verse have their accents retrograde or inverted, the first syllable being strong or acute, and the second weak. The detriment which the measure suffers by this inversion of the accents is sometimes less perceptible when the verses are carried one into another, but is remarkably striking in this place, where the vicious verse concludes a period, and is yet more offensive in rhyme, when we regularly attend to the flow of every single line. This will appear by reading a couplet in which Cowley, an author not sufficiently studious of harmony, has committed the same fault:

> His harmless Life
> Does with substantial Blessedness abound,
> And the soft Wings of Peace *cover* him round.[22]

In these lines the law of meter is very grossly violated by mingling combinations of sound directly opposite to each other, as Milton expresses it in his sonnet,[23] by "committing short and long," and setting one part of the measure at variance with the rest. The ancients, who had a language more capable of variety than ours, had two kinds of verse, the iambic, consisting of short and long syllables alternately, from which our heroic measure is derived, and the trochaic, consisting in a like alternation of long and short. These were considered as opposites, and conveyed the contrary images of speed and slowness; to confound them, therefore, as in these lines, is to deviate from the established practice. But where the senses are to judge, authority is not necessary: the ear is sufficient to detect dissonance; nor should I have brought auxiliaries on such an occasion against any name but that of Milton.

No. 88, January 19, 1751
[Milton's Versification, II]

Cum tabulis animum censoris sumet honesti;
audebit, quaecumque parum splendoris habebunt
et sine pondere erunt et honore indigna ferentur,
verba movere loco, quamvis invita recedant
et versentur adhuc intra penetralia Vestae.
—Hor. [Epist. II. ii. 110]

But he that hath a curious piece design'd,
When he begins must take a censor's mind,
Severe and honest; and what words appear
Too light and trivial, or too weak to bear
The weighty sense, nor worth the reader's care,
Shake off; though stubborn, they are loth to move,
And though we. fancy, dearly though we love.—Creech

"There is no reputation for genius," says Quintilian, "to be gained by writing on things which, however necessary, have little splendor or show. The height of a building attracts the eye, but the foundations lie without regard. Yet since there is not any way to the top of science but from the lowest parts, I shall think nothing unconnected with the art of oratory which he that wants cannot be an orator." [24]

Confirmed and animated by this illustrious precedent, I shall continue my inquiries into Milton's art of versification, since, however minute the employment may appear of analyzing lines into syllables, and whatever ridicule may be incurred by a solemn deliberation upon accents and pauses, it is certain that without this petty knowledge no man can be a poet, and that from the proper disposition of single sounds results that harmony that adds force to reason and gives grace to sublimity, that shackles attention, and governs passions.

That verse may be melodious and pleasing it is necessary not only that the words be so ranged as that the accent may fall on its proper place, but that the syllables themselves be so chosen as to flow smoothly into one another. This is to be effected by a proportionate mixture of vowels and consonants and by tempering the mute consonants with liquids and semivowels. The Hebrew grammarians have observed that it is impossible to pronounce two consonants without the intervention of a vowel or without some emission of the breath between one and the other; this is longer and more perceptible as the sounds of the consonants are less harmonically conjoined, and by consequence the flow of the verse is longer interrupted.

It is pronounced by Dryden that a line of monosyllables is almost always harsh.[25] This, with regard to our language, is evidently true, not because monosyllables cannot compose harmony, but because our monosyllables, being of Teutonic original, or formed by contraction, commonly begin and end with consonants, as:

> Every lower faculty
> *Of sense, whereby they hear, see, smell, touch, taste.*
> [*P.L.*, V, 410]

The difference of harmony arising principally from the collocation of vowels and consonants will be sufficiently conceived by attending to the following passages:

> Immortal *Amarant* . . . there grows,
> And flow'rs aloft shading the Fount of Life,
> And where the river of Bliss through midst of Heav'n
> *Rolls o'er Elysian Flow'rs her Amber stream;*
> With these that never fade the Spirits elect
> *Bind thir resplendent locks inwreath'd with beams.* [III, 353]

The same comparison that I propose to be made between the fourth and sixth verses of this passage may be repeated between the last lines of the following quotations:

> Underfoot the Violet,
> Crocus, and Hyacinth, with rich inlay
> *Broider'd the ground, more colour'd than with stone*
> Of costliest Emblem. [IV, 700]

> Here in close recess
> With Flowers, Garlands, and sweet-smelling Herbs
> Espoused *Eve* deckt first her Nuptial Bed,
> *And heav'nly Quires the Hymenaean sung.* [IV, 708]

Milton, whose ear had been accustomed not only to the music of the ancient tongues, which, however vitiated by our pronunciation, excel all that are now in use, but to the softness of the Italian, the most mellifluous of all modern poetry, seems fully convinced of the unfitness of our language for smooth versification, and is therefore pleased with an opportunity of calling in a softer word to his assistance; for this reason, and I believe for this only, he sometimes indulges himself in a long series of proper names, and introduces them where they add little but music to his poem:

> The richer seat
> Of *Atabalipa,* and yet unspoil'd
> *Guiana,* whose great City *Geryon's* Sons
> Call *El Dorado.* [XI, 408]

> The Moon . . . the *Tuscan* Artist views
> At Ev'ning from the top of *Fesole*
> Or in *Valdarno,* to descry new Lands. [I, 287]

He has, indeed, been more attentive to his syllables than to his accents, and does not often offend by collisions of consonants, or openings of vowels upon each other, at least not more often than other writers who have had less important or complicated subjects to take off their care from the cadence of their lines.

The great peculiarity of Milton's versification, compared with that of later poets, is the elision of one vowel before another, or the suppression of the last syllable of a word ending with a vowel when a vowel begins the following word, as:

> Knowledge . . .
> Oppresses else with Surfeit, and soon turns
> Wisdom to Fol*ly,* as Nourishment to Wind. [VII, 126]

This licence, though now disused in English poetry, was practiced by our old writers, and is allowed in many other languages ancient and modern, and therefore the critics on *Paradise Lost* have, without much deliberation, commended Milton for continuing it. But one language cannot communicate its rules to another. We have already tried and rejected the hexameter of the ancients, the double close of the Italians, and the Alexandrine of the French; and the elision of vowels, however graceful it may seem to other nations, may be very unsuitable to the genius of the English tongue.

There is reason to believe that we have negligently lost part of our vowels and that the silent *e* which our ancestors added to most of our monosyllables was once vocal. By this detruncation of our syllables, our language is overstocked with consonants, and it is more necessary to add vowels to the beginning of words than to cut them off from the end.

Milton, therefore, seems to have somewhat mistaken the nature of our language, of which the chief defect is ruggedness and asperity, and has left our harsh cadences yet harsher. But his elisions are not all equally to be censured; in some syllables they may be allowed, and perhaps in a few may be safely imitated. The abscission of a vowel is undoubtedly vicious when it is strongly sounded, and makes, with its associate consonant, a full and audible syllable:

> What he gives
>
> .   .   .   .   .
>
> Spiritual, may of purest Spirits be found
> *No* ingrateful food: and food alike those pure
> Intelligential substances require. [V, 404]
>
> Fruit . . . *Hesperian* Fables true
> If true, here *only,* and of delicious taste. [IV, 249]
>
> . . . Ev'ning now approach'd
> (For wee have *also* our Ev'ning and our Morn). [V, 627]
>
> Of guests he makes them slaves
> Inhospita*bly,* and kills thir infant Males. [XII, 167]
>
> And vital vir*tue* infus'd, and vital warmth
> Throughout the fluid Mass. [VII, 236]
>
> God made *thee* of choice his own, and of his own
> To serve him. [X, 766]

I believe every reader will agree that in all those passages, though not equally in all, the music is injured, and in some the meaning obscured. There are other lines in which the vowel is cut off, but it is so faintly pronounced in common speech that the loss of it in poetry is scarcely perceived, and therefore such compliance with the measure may be allowed:

> Nature breeds
> Perverse, all monstrous, all prodigious things,
> Abomina*ble,* inuttera*ble,* and worse
> Than Fables yet have feign'd. [II, 624]

> From the shore
> They view'd the vast immeasura*ble* Abyss. [VII, 210]

> Impenetra*ble,* impal'd with circling fire. [II, 647]

> To none communica*ble* in Earth or Heaven. [VII, 124]

Yet even these contractions increase the roughness of a language too rough already, and though in long poems they may be sometimes suffered, it never can be faulty to forbear them.

Milton frequently uses in his poems the hypermetrical or redundant line of eleven syllables:

> Thus it shall befall
> Him who to worth in Women overtrust*ing*
> Lets her Will rule. [IX, 1182]

> I also err'd in overmuch admir*ing.* [IX, 1178]

Verses of this kind occur almost in every page, but though they are not unpleasing or dissonant, they ought not to be admitted into heroic poetry, since the narrow limits of our language allow us no other distinction of epic and tragic measures than is afforded by the liberty of changing at will the terminations of the dramatic lines and bringing them by that relaxation of metrical rigor nearer to prose.

No. 90, January 26, 1751
[Milton's Versification, III]

In tenui labor.—Virg. [*Geor.* IV. 6]

What toil in slender things!

It is very difficult to write on the minuter parts of literature without failing either to please or instruct. Too much nicety of detail disgusts the greatest part of readers, and to throw a multitude of particulars under general heads and lay down rules of extensive comprehension is to common understandings of little use. They who undertake these subjects are therefore always in danger, as one or other inconvenience arises to their imagination, of frighting us with rugged science or amusing us with empty sound.

In criticizing the work of Milton, there is, indeed, opportunity to intersperse passages that can hardly fail to relieve the languors of attention, and since in examining the variety and choice of the pauses with which he has diversified his numbers it will be necessary to exhibit the lines in which they are to be found, perhaps the remarks may be well compensated by the examples, and the irksomeness of grammatical disquisitions somewhat alleviated.

Milton formed his scheme of versification by the poets of Greece and Rome, whom he proposed to himself for his models, so far as the difference of his language from theirs would permit the imitation. There are, indeed, many inconveniences inseparable from our heroic measure compared with that of Homer and Virgil—inconveniences which it is no reproach to Milton not to have overcome, because they are in their own nature insuperable, but against which he has struggled with so much art and diligence that he may at least be said to have deserved success.

The hexameter of the ancients may be considered as consisting of fifteen syllables, so melodiously disposed that, as everyone knows who has examined the poetical authors, very pleasing and sonorous lyric measures are formed from the fragments of the heroic. It is, indeed, scarce possible to break them in such a manner but that *invenias etiam disjecti membra poetae,*[26] some harmony will still remain, and the due proportions of sound will always be discovered. This measure therefore allowed great variety of pauses and great liberties of connecting one verse with another, because wherever the line was interrupted, either part singly was musical. But the ancients seem to have confined this privilege to hexameters, for in their other measures, though frequently longer than the English heroic, those who wrote after the refinements of versification venture so seldom to change their pauses that every variation may be supposed rather a compliance with necessity than the choice of judgment.

Milton was constrained within the narrow limits of a measure not very harmonious in the utmost perfection; the single parts, therefore, into which it was to be sometimes broken by pauses were in danger of losing the very form of verse. This has, perhaps, notwithstanding all his care, sometimes happened.

As harmony is the end of poetical measures, no part of a verse

ought to be so separated from the rest as not to remain still more
harmonious than prose, or to show by the disposition of the tones
that it is part of a verse. This rule in the old hexameter might be
easily observed, but in English it will very frequently be in danger
of violation, for the order and regularity of accents cannot well be
perceived in a succession of fewer than three syllables, which will
confine the English poet to only five pauses, it being supposed that
when he connects one line with another, he should never make a
full pause at less distance than that of three syllables from the beginning or end of a verse.

That this rule should be universally and indispensably established
perhaps cannot be granted; something may be allowed to variety,
and something to the adaptation of the numbers to the subject; but
it will be found generally necessary, and the ear will seldom fail to
suffer by its neglect.

Thus when a single syllable is cut off from the rest, it must either
be united to the line with which the sense connects it or be sounded
alone. If it be united to the other line, it corrupts its harmony; if
disjoined, it must stand alone, and with regard to music be superfluous, for there is no harmony in a single sound, because it has no
proportion to another:

> Hypocrites austerely talk,
>
> .   .   .   .   .
>
> Defaming as impure what God declares
> *Pure,* and commands to some, leaves free to all.
>
> [*P.L.*, IV, 744]

When two syllables likewise are abscinded from the rest, they
evidently want some associate sounds to make them harmonious:

> Eyes . . . more wakeful than to drowse,
> Charm'd with *Arcadian* Pipe, the Pastoral Reed
> Of *Hermes,* or his opiate Rod. *Meanwhile*
> To resalute the World with sacred Light
> *Leucothea* wak'd. [XI, 130]
>
> He ended, and the Son gave signal high
> To the bright Minister that watch'd, *hee blew*
> His Trumpet. [XI, 72]
>
> First in his East the glorious Lamp was seen,
> Regent of Day, and all th' Horizon round
> Invested with bright Rays, jocund to run

His Longitude through Heav'n's high road: *the gray*
Dawn, and the *Pleiades* before him danc'd
Shedding sweet influence. [VII, 370]

The same defect is perceived in the following lines, where the pause is at the second syllable from the beginning:

The Race
Of that wild Rout that tore the *Thracian* Bard
In *Rhodope,* where Woods and Rocks had Ears
To rapture, till the savage clamor drown'd
Both Harp and Voice; nor could the Muse defend
Her *Son.* So fail not thou, who thee implores. [VII, 33]

When the pause is upon the third syllable or the seventh, the harmony is better preserved, but as the third and seventh are weak syllables, the period leaves the ear unsatisfied and in expectation of the remaining part of the verse:

He with his horrid crew
Lay vanquisht, rolling in the fiery Gulf
Confounded though immor*tal:* But his doom
Reserv'd him to more wrath; for now the thought
Both of lost happiness and lasting pain
Torments *him.* [I, 51]

God . . . with frequent intercourse
Thither will send his winged Messengers
On errands of supernal Grace. So sung
The glorious Train ascend*ing.* [VII, 569]

It may be, I think, established as a rule that a pause which concludes a period should be made for the most part upon a strong syllable, as the fourth and sixth, but those pauses which only suspend the sense may be placed upon the weaker. Thus the rest in the third line of the first passage satisfies the ear better than in the fourth, and the close of the second quotation better than of the third.

The evil soon
Driv'n [27] back redounded as a flood on those
From whom it *sprung,* impossible to mix
With *Blessedness.* [VII, 56]

What we by day
Lop overgrown, or prune, or prop, or bind,
One night or two with wanton growth derides,
Tending to *wild.* [IX, 209]

> These paths and Bowers doubt not but our joint hands
> Will keep from Wilderness with ease, as wide
> As we need walk, till younger hands ere long
> Assist *us*. [IX, 244]

The rest in the fifth place has the same inconvenience as in the seventh and third, that the syllable is weak:

> Beast now with Beast gan war, and Fowl with Fowl,
> And Fish with Fish; to graze the Herb all leaving,
> Devour'd each *other;* nor stood much in awe
> Of Man, but fled *him,* or with count'nance grim
> Glar'd on him pas*sing*. [X, 710]

The noblest and most majestic pauses which our versification admits are upon the fourth and sixth syllables, which are both strongly sounded in a pure and regular verse, and at either of which the line is so divided that both members participate of harmony:

> But now at last the sacred influence
> Of light *appears,* and from the walls of Heav'n
> Shoots far into the bosom of dim Night
> A glimmering *dawn;* here Nature first begins
> Her fardest verge, and *Chaos* to retire. [II, 1034]

But far above all others, if I can give any credit to my own ear, is the rest upon the sixth syllable, which taking in a complete compass of sound, such as is sufficient to constitute one of our lyric measures, makes a full and solemn close. Some passages which conclude at this stop I could never read without some strong emotions of delight or admiration:

> Before the Hills appear'd, or Fountain flow'd,
> Thou with Eternal Wisdom didst converse,
> Wisdom thy Sister, and with her didst play
> In presence of th' Almighty Father, pleas'd
> With thy Celestial *Song*. [VII, 8]

> Or other Worlds they seem'd, or happy Iles,
> Like those *Hesperian* Gardens fam'd of old,
> Fortunate Fields, and Groves and flow'ry Vales,
> Thrice happy Iles, but who dwelt happy there
> He stay'd not to *enquire*. [III, 567]

> Hee blew
> His Trumpet, heard in *Oreb* since perhaps

When God descended, and perhaps once more
To sound at general *Doom*. [XI, 73]

If the poetry of Milton be examined with regard to the pauses and flow of his verses into each other, it will appear that he has performed all that our language would admit, and the comparison of his numbers with those who have cultivated the same manner of writing will show that he excelled as much in the lower as the higher parts of his art and that his skill in harmony was not less than his invention or his learning.

No. 92, February 2, 1751
[Sound and Sense]

Iam nunc minaci murmure cornuum
perstringis auris, iam litui strepunt.
                    —Hor. [*Carm.* II. i. 17]

Lo! now the clarion's voice I hear,
Its threat'ning murmurs pierce mine ear,
And in thy lines with brazen breath
The trumpet sounds the charge of death.—Francis

It has been long observed that the idea of beauty is vague and undefined, different in different minds, and diversified by time or place. It has been a term hitherto used to signify that which pleases us we know not why, and in our approbation of which we can justify ourselves only by the concurrence of numbers, without much power of enforcing our opinion upon others by any argument but example and authority. It is, indeed, so little subject to the examinations of reason that Pascal supposes it to end where demonstration begins, and maintains that without incongruity and absurdity we cannot speak of "geometrical beauty." [28]

To trace all the sources of that various pleasure which we ascribe to the agency of beauty or to disentangle all the perceptions involved in its idea would, perhaps, require a very great part of the life of an Aristotle or Plato. It is, however, in many cases apparent that this quality is merely relative and comparative; that we pronounce things beautiful because they have something which we agree, for whatever reason, to call beauty, in a greater degree than we have been accustomed to find it in other things of the same kind; and that we transfer the epithet as our knowledge increases, and appropriate it to higher excellence when higher excellence comes within our view.

Much of the beauty of writing is of this kind, and therefore Boileau justly remarks that the books which have stood the test of time and been admired through all the changes which the mind of man has suffered from the various revolutions of knowledge and the prevalence of contrary customs have a better claim to our regard than any modern can boast, because the long continuance of their reputation proves that they are adequate to our faculties and agreeable to nature.

It is, however, the task of criticism to establish principles, to improve opinion into knowledge, and to distinguish those means of pleasing which depend upon known causes and rational deduction from the nameless and inexplicable elegancies which appeal wholly to the fancy, from which we feel delight but know not how they produce it, and which may well be termed the enchantresses of the soul. Criticism reduces those regions of literature under the dominion of science which have hitherto known only the anarchy of ignorance, the caprices of fancy, and the tyranny of prescription.

There is nothing in the art of versifying so much exposed to the power of imagination as the accommodation of the sound to the sense, or the representation of particular images by the flow of the verse in which they are expressed. Every student has innumerable passages in which he, and perhaps he alone, discovers such resemblances, and since the attention of the present race of poetical readers seems particularly turned upon this species of elegance, I shall endeavor to examine how much these conformities have been observed by the poets or directed by the critics, how far they can be established upon nature and reason, and on what occasions they have been practiced by Milton.

Homer, the father of all poetical beauty, has been particularly celebrated by Dionysius of Halicarnassus as "he that of all the poets exhibited the greatest variety of sound, for there are," says he, "innumerable passages in which length of time, bulk of body, extremity of passion, and stillness of repose, or in which, on the contrary, brevity, speed, and eagerness are evidently marked out by the sound of the syllables. Thus the anguish and slow pace with which the blind Polypheme groped out with his hands the entrance of his cave are perceived in the cadence of the verses which describe it:

> Κύκλωψ δὲ στενάχων τε καὶ ὠδίνων ὀδύνῃσι
> χερσὶ ψηλαφόων." [*Odyssey* ix. 415]

Meantime the Cyclop raging with his wound,
Spreads his wide arms, and searches round and round.
—POPE

The critic then proceeds to show that the efforts of Achilles struggling in his armor against the current of a river, sometimes resisting and sometimes yielding, may be perceived in the elisions of the syllables, the slow succession of the feet, and the strength of the consonants:

> Δεινὸν δ' ἀμφ' Ἀχιλῆα κυκώμενον ἵστατο κῦμα
> ὤθει δ' ἐν σάκεϊ πίπτων ῥόος· οὐδὲ πόδεσσιν
> εἶχε στηρίξασθαι. [*Iliad* xxi. 240]

So oft the surge, in wat'ry mountains spread,
Beats on his back, or bursts upon his head,
Yet, dauntless still, the adverse flood he braves,
And still indignant bounds above the waves
Tir'd by the tides, his knees relax with toil;
Wash'd from beneath him, slides the slimy soil.—POPE

When Homer describes the crush of men dashed against a rock, he collects the most unpleasing and harsh sounds:

> Σὺν δὲ δύω μάρψας ὥστε σκύλακας ποτὶ γαίῃ
> κόπτ'· ἐκ δ' ἐγκέφαλος χαμάδις ῥέε δεῦε δὲ γαῖαν. [*Odyssey* ix. 289]

His bloody hand
Snatch'd two, unhappy! of my martial band,
And dash'd like dogs against the stony floor:
The pavement swims with brains and mingled gore.
—POPE

And when he would place before the eyes something dreadful and astonishing, he makes choice of the strongest vowels, and the letters of most difficult utterance.

> Τῇ δ' ἐπι μὲν Γοργὼ βλοσυρῶπις ἐστεφάνωτο
> δεινὸν δερκομένη, περὶ δὲ Δεῖμός τε Φόβος τε. [*Iliad* xi. 36]

Tremendous Gorgon frown'd upon its field,
And circling terrors fill'd th' expressive shield.—POPE

Many other examples Dionysius produces, but these will sufficiently show that either he was fanciful or we have lost the genuine
pronunciation, for I know not whether in any one of these instances
such similitude can be discovered. It seems, indeed, probable that
the veneration with which Homer was read produced many supposi-
titious beauties, for though it is certain that the sound of many of
his verses very justly corresponds with the things expressed, yet when
the force of his imagination, which gave him full possession of every
object, is considered, together with the flexibility of his language,
of which the syllables might be often contracted or dilated at pleasure, it will seem unlikely that such conformity should happen less
frequently even without design.

It is not, however, to be doubted that Virgil, who wrote amidst
the light of criticism, and who owed so much of his success to art
and labor, endeavored among other excellencies to exhibit this
similitude; nor has he been less happy in this than in the other graces
of versification. This felicity of his numbers was at the revival of
learning displayed with great elegance by Vida in his art of poetry. . . .[29]

From the Italian gardens Pope seems to have transplanted this
flower, the growth of happier climates, into a soil less adapted to its
nature, and less favorable to its increase:

> Soft is the strain when Zephyr gently blows,
> And the smooth stream in smoother numbers flows;
> But when loud surges lash the sounding shore,
> The hoarse rough verse should like the torrent roar:
> When Ajax strives some rock's vast weight to throw,
> The line too labours, and the words move slow:
> Not so, when swift Camilla scours the plain,
> Flies o'er th' unbending corn, and skims along the main.
>
> [*E.C.*, 364]

From these lines, labored with great attention and celebrated by a
rival wit,[30] may be judged what can be expected from the most
diligent endeavors after this imagery of sound. The verse intended to
represent the whisper of the vernal breeze must be confessed not
much to excel in softness or volubility, and the smooth stream runs
with a perpetual clash of jarring consonants. The noise and turbulence of the torrent is, indeed, distinctly imaged, for it requires very
little skill to make our language rough, but in the lines which mention the effort of Ajax there is no particular heaviness, obstruction,

or delay. The swiftness of Camilla is rather contrasted than exemplified; why the verse should be lengthened to express speed will not easily be discovered. In the dactyls used for that purpose by the ancients two short syllables were pronounced with such rapidity as to be equal only to one long; they, therefore, naturally exhibit the act of passing through a long space in a short time. But the Alexandrine, by its pause in the midst, is a tardy and stately measure; and the word *unbending,* one of the most sluggish and slow which our language affords, cannot much accelerate its motion.

These rules and these examples have taught our present critics to inquire very studiously and minutely into sounds and cadences. It is, therefore, useful to examine with what skill they have proceeded, what discoveries they have made, and whether any rules can be established which may guide us hereafter in such researches.

No. 93, February 5, 1751
[The Prejudices of Critics] [31]

Experiar quid concedatur in illos
quorum Flaminia tegitur cinis atque Latina.
—Juv. [*Sat.* I. 170]

More safely truth to urge her claim presumes,
On names now found alone on books and tombs.

There are few books on which more time is spent by young students than on treatises which deliver the characters of authors, nor any which oftener deceive the expectation of the reader or fill his mind with more opinions which the progress of his studies and the increase of his knowledge oblige him to resign.

Baillet has introduced his collection of the decisions of the learned by an enumeration of the prejudices which mislead the critic and raise the passions in rebellion against the judgment.[32] His catalogue, though large, is imperfect. And who can hope to complete it? The beauties of writing have been observed to be often such as cannot in the present state of human knowledge be evinced by evidence or drawn out into demonstrations; they are therefore wholly subject to the imagination and do not force their effects upon a mind pre-occupied by unfavorable sentiments nor overcome the counteraction of a false principle or of stubborn partiality.

To convince any man against his will is hard, but to please him against his will is justly pronounced by Dryden to be above the reach of human abilities. Interest and passion will hold out long against the closest siege of diagrams and syllogisms, but they are absolutely impregnable to imagery and sentiment, and will forever bid defiance to the most powerful strains of Virgil or Homer, though they may give way in time to the batteries of Euclid or Archimedes.

In trusting, therefore, to the sentence of a critic, we are in danger not only from that vanity which exalts writers too often to the dignity of teaching what they are yet to learn, from that negligence which sometimes steals upon the most vigilant caution, and that fallibility to which the condition of nature has subjected every human under-standing, but from a thousand extrinsic and accidental causes, from everything which can excite kindness or malevolence, veneration or contempt.

Many of those who have determined with great boldness upon the various degrees of literary merit may be justly suspected of having passed sentence, as Seneca remarks of Claudius,

> Una tantum parte audita,
> saepe et nulla,[33]

without much knowledge of the cause before them; for it will not easily be imagined of Langbaine, Borrichius, or Rapin [34] that they had very accurately perused all the books which they praise or cen-sure, or that even if nature and learning had qualified them for judges, they could read forever with the attention necessary to just criticism. Such performances, however, are not wholly without their use, for they are commonly just echoes to the voice of fame, and transmit the general suffrage of mankind when they have no particu-lar motives to suppress it.

Critics, like all the rest of mankind, are very frequently misled by interest. The bigotry with which editors regard the authors whom they illustrate or correct has been generally remarked. Dryden was known to have written most of his critical dissertations only to recom-mend the works upon which he then happened to be employed, and Addison is suspected to have denied the expediency of poetical justice because his own Cato was condemned to perish in a good cause.[35]

There are prejudices which authors not otherwise weak or corrupt have indulged without scruple, and perhaps some of them are so complicated with our natural affections that they cannot easily be disentangled from the heart. Scarce any can hear with impartiality a comparison between the writers of his own and another country, and though it cannot, I think, be charged equally on all nations that they are blinded with this literary patriotism, yet there are none that do not look upon their authors with the fondness of affinity, and esteem them as well for the place of their birth as for their knowledge or their wit. There is, therefore, seldom much respect due to comparative criticism when the competitors are of different countries, unless the judge is of a nation equally indifferent to both. The Italians could not for a long time believe that there was any learning beyond the mountains, and the French seem generally persuaded that there are no wits or reasoners equal to their own. I can scarcely conceive that if Scaliger had not considered himself as allied to Virgil by being born in the same country, he would have found his works so much superior to those of Homer or have thought the controversy worthy of so much zeal, vehemence, and acrimony.

There is, indeed, one prejudice and only one by which it may be doubted whether it is any dishonor to be sometimes misguided. Criticism has so often given occasion to the envious and ill-natured of gratifying their malignity that some have thought it necessary to recommend the virtue of candor without restriction and to preclude all future liberty of censure. Writers possessed with this opinion are continually enforcing civility and decency, recommending to critics the proper diffidence of themselves and inculcating the veneration due to celebrated names.

I am not of opinion that these professed enemies of arrogance and severity have much more benevolence or modesty than the rest of mankind or that they feel in their own hearts any other intention than to distinguish themselves by their softness and delicacy. Some are modest because they are timorous, and some are lavish of praise because they hope to be repaid.

There is indeed some tenderness due to living writers when they attack none of those truths which are of importance to the happiness of mankind and have committed no other offense than that of betraying their own ignorance or dulness. I should think it cruelty to crush an insect who had provoked me only by buzzing in my ear and would not willingly interrupt the dream of harmless stupidity or destroy the jest which makes its author laugh. Yet I am far from thinking this tenderness universally necessary, for he that writes may be considered as a kind of general challenger whom everyone has a right to attack, since he quits the common rank of life, steps forward beyond the lists, and offers his merit to the public judgment. To commence author is to claim praise, and no man can justly aspire to honor but at the hazard of disgrace.

But whatever be decided concerning contemporaries, whom he that knows the treachery of the human heart and considers how often we gratify our own pride or envy under the appearance of contending for elegance and propriety will find himself not much inclined to disturb, there can surely be no exemptions pleaded to secure them from criticism who can no longer suffer by reproach and of whom nothing now remains but their writings and their names. Upon these authors the critic is undoubtedly at full liberty to exercise the strictest severity, since he endangers only his own fame and, like Aeneas when he drew his sword in the infernal regions, encounters phantoms which cannot be wounded. He may indeed pay some regard to established reputation, but he can by that show of reverence consult only his own security, for all other motives are now at an end.

The faults of a writer of acknowledged excellence are more dangerous because the influence of his example is more extensive, and the interest of learning requires that they should be discovered and stigmatized before they have the sanction of antiquity conferred upon them and become precedents of indisputable authority.

It has, indeed, been advanced by Addison as one of the characteristics of a true critic that he points out beauties rather than faults.[36] But it is rather natural to a man of learning and genius to apply himself chiefly to the study of writers who have more beauties than faults to be displayed, for the duty of criticism is neither to depreciate nor dignify by partial representations, but to hold out the light of reason, whatever it may discover, and to promulgate the determination of truth, whatever she shall dictate.

No. 94, February 9, 1751
[Sound and Sense in Milton]

> *Bonus atque fidus*
> *iudex . . . per obstantes catervas*
> *explicuit sua victor arma.*—Hor. [*Carm.* IV. ix. 40]
>
> Perpetual magistrate is he
>   Who keeps strict justice full in sight;
> Who bids the crowd at awful distance gaze,
>   And virtue's arms victoriously displays.—Francis

The resemblance of poetic numbers to the subject which they mention or describe may be considered as general or particular: as consisting in the flow and structure of a whole passage taken together, or as comprised in the sound of some emphatical and descriptive words or in the cadence and harmony of single verses.

The general resemblance of the sound to the sense is to be found in every language which admits of poetry, in every author whose force of fancy enables him to impress images strongly on his own mind, and whose choice and variety of language readily supplies him with just representations. To such a writer it is natural to change his measures with his subject, even without any effort of the understanding or intervention of the judgment. To revolve jollity and mirth necessarily tunes the voice of a poet to gay and sprightly notes as it fires his eye with vivacity, and reflection on gloomy situations and disastrous events will sadden his numbers as it will cloud his countenance. But in such passages there is only the similitude of pleasure to pleasure and of grief to grief, without any immediate application to particular images. The same flow of joyous versification will celebrate the jollity of marriage and the exultation of triumph, and the same languor of melody will suit the complaints of an absent lover, as of a conquered king.

It is scarcely to be doubted that on many occasions we make the music which we imagine ourselves to hear, that we modulate the poem by our own disposition, and ascribe to the numbers the effects of the sense. We may observe in life that it is not easy to deliver a pleasing message in an unpleasing manner, and that we readily associate beauty and deformity with those whom for any reason we love or hate. Yet it would be too daring to declare that all the celebrated adaptations of harmony are chimerical, that Homer had no extraordinary attention to the melody of his verse when he described a nuptial festivity:

Νύμφας δ' ἐκ θαλάμων δαΐδων ὕπο λαμπομενάων
ἠγίνεον ἀνὰ ἄστυ, πολὺς δ' ὑμέναιος ὀρώρει. [*Iliad* xviii. 492]

Here sacred pomp and genial feast delight,
And solemn dance, and hymeneal rite;
Along the street the new-made brides are led,
With torches flaming, to the nuptial bed;
The youthful dancers in a circle bound
To the soft flute, and cittern's silver sound.—POPE

that Vida was merely fanciful when he supposed Virgil endeavoring to represent by uncommon sweetness of numbers the adventitious beauty of Aeneas:

Os, humerosque deo similis: namque ipsa decoram
Caesariem nato genetrix, lumenque juventae
purpureum, et laetos oculis afflarat honores. [*Aeneid* i. 589]

The Trojan chief appeared in open sight,
August in visage, and serenely bright.
His mother goddess, with her hands divine,
Had formed his curling locks, and made his temples shine;
And giv'n his rolling eyes a sparkling grace,
And breath'd a youthful vigour on his face.—Dryden

or that Milton did not intend to exemplify the harmony which he mentions:

Fountains and yee, that warble, as ye flow,
Melodious murmurs, warbling tune his praise.
                                    [*P.L.*, V, 195]

That Milton understood the force of sounds well adjusted and knew the compass and variety of the ancient measures cannot be doubted, since he was both a musician and a critic; but he seems to have considered these conformities of cadence as either not often attainable in our language or as petty excellencies unworthy of his ambition, for it will not be found that he has always assigned the same cast of numbers to the same subjects. He has given in two passages very minute descriptions of angelic beauty, but though the images are nearly the same, the numbers will be found upon comparison very different:

> And now a stripling Cherub he appears,
> Not of the prime, yet such as in his face
> Youth smil'd Celestial, and to every Limb
> *Suitable grace diffus'd, so well he feign'd;*
> Under a Coronet his flowing hair
> *In curls on either cheek play'd, wings he wore*
> *Of many a colour'd plume sprinkl'd with Gold.* [III, 636]

Some of the lines of this description are remarkably defective in harmony and therefore by no means correspondent with that symmetrical elegance and easy grace which they are intended to exhibit. The failure, however, is fully compensated by the representation of Raphael, which equally delights the ear and imagination:

> A Seraph wing'd; six wings he wore, to shade
> His lineaments Divine; the pair that clad
> Each shoulder broad, came mantling o'er his breast
> With regal Ornament; the middle pair
> Girt like a Starry Zone his waste, and round
> Skirted his loins and thighs with downy Gold,
> And colours dipt in Heav'n; the third his feet
> Shadow'd from either heel with feather'd mail
> Sky-tinctur'd grain. Like *Maia's* son he stood,
> And shook his Plumes, that Heav'nly fragrance fill'd
> The circuit wide. [V, 277]

The adumbration of particular and distinct images by an exact and perceptible resemblance of sound is sometimes studied, and sometimes casual. Every language has many words formed in imitation of the noises which they signify. Such are *stridor, balo,* and *beatus* in Latin, and in English, *to growl, to buzz, to hiss,* and *to jar.* Words of this kind give to a verse the proper similitude of sound without much labor of the writer, and such happiness is therefore to be attributed rather to fortune than skill; yet they are sometimes combined with great propriety, and undeniably contribute to enforce the impression of the idea. We hear the passing arrow in this line of Virgil:

> Effugit *horrendum stridens* adducta sagitta.
>
> > [*Aeneid* ix. 632]
>
> Th'impetuous arrow whizzes on the wing.—Pope

and the creaking of hell-gates in the description by Milton:

> Op'n fly
> With impetuous recoil and jarring sound
> Th'infernal doors, and on thir hinges grate
> Harsh Thunder. [II, 879]

But many beauties of this kind, which the moderns and perhaps the ancients have observed, seem to be the product of blind reverence acting upon fancy. Dionysius himself tells us that the sound of Homer's verses sometimes exhibits the idea of corporeal bulk. Is not this a discovery nearly approaching to that of the blind man who after a long inquiry into the nature of the scarlet color found that it represented nothing so much as the clangor of a trumpet? [37] The representative power of poetic harmony consists of sound and measure, of the force of the syllables singly considered, and of the time in which they are pronounced. Sound can resemble nothing but sound, and time can measure nothing but motion and duration.

The critics, however, have struck out other similitudes, nor is there any irregularity of numbers which credulous admiration cannot discover to be eminently beautiful. Thus the propriety of each of these lines has been celebrated by writers whose opinion the world has reason to regard:

> Vertitur interea caelum, et ruit oceano nox. [*Aeneid* ii. 250]
>
> Meantime the rapid heav'ns rowl'd down the light
> And on the shaded ocean rush'd the night.—DRYDEN
>
> Sternitur exanimisque tremens procumbit humi bos.
> [*Aeneid* v. 481]
>
> Down drops the beast, nor needs a second wound;
> But sprawls in pangs of death, and spurns the ground.
> —DRYDEN
>
> Parturiunt montes, nascetur ridiculus mus. [*Ars poet.* 139]
> The mountains labour, and a mouse is born.—ROSCOMMON

If all these observations are just, there must be some remarkable conformity between the sudden succession of night to day, the fall of an ox under a blow, and the birth of a mouse from a mountain, since we are told of all these images that they are very strongly impressed by the same form and termination of the verse.

We may, however, without giving way to enthusiasm admit that some beauties of this kind may be produced. A sudden stop at an unusual syllable may image the cessation of action or the pause of discourse, and Milton has very happily imitated the repetitions of an echo:

> I fled, and cri'd out *Death;*
> Hell trembl'd at the hideous Name, and sigh'd
> From all her Caves, and back resounded *Death.*
>
> [*P.L.*, II, 787]

The measure or time of pronouncing may be varied so as very strongly to represent not only the modes of external motion but the quick or slow succession of ideas, and consequently the passions of the mind. This at least was the power of the spondaic and dactylic harmony, but our language can reach no eminent diversities of sound. We can indeed, sometimes, by encumbering and retarding the line, show the difficulty of a progress made by strong efforts and with frequent interruptions, or mark a slow and heavy motion. Thus Milton has imaged the toil of Satan struggling through chaos:

> So he with difficulty and labour hard
> Mov'd on, with difficulty and labour hee. [II, 1021]

Thus he has described the leviathans or whales:

> Wallowing unwieldy, enormous in thir Gait. [VII, 411]

But he has at other times neglected such representations, as may be observed in the volubility and levity of these lines, which express an action tardy and reluctant:

> Descent and fall
> To us is adverse. Who but felt of late
> When the fierce Foe hung on our brok'n Rear
> Insulting, and pursu'd us through the Deep,
> With what compulsion and laborious flight
> We sunk thus low? Th' ascent is easy then. [II, 76]

In another place he describes the gentle glide of ebbing waters in a line remarkably rough and halting:

> Tripping ebb, that stole
> With soft foot towards the deep, who now had stopt
> His Sluices. [XI, 847]

It is not, indeed, to be expected that the sound should always assist the meaning, but it ought never to counteract it; and therefore

Milton has here certainly committed a fault like that of the player who looked on the earth when he implored the heavens, and to the heavens when he addressed the earth.

Those who are determined to find in Milton an assemblage of all the excellencies which have ennobled all other poets will perhaps be offended that I do not celebrate his versification in higher terms, for there are readers who discover that in this passage,

> So stretcht out huge in length the Arch-fiend lay, [I, 209]

a *long* form is described in a *long* line; but the truth is that length of body is only mentioned in a *slow* line, to which it has only the resemblance of time to space, of an hour to a Maypole.

The same turn of ingenuity might perform wonders upon the description of the ark:

> Then from the Mountain hewing Timber tall,
> Began to build a Vessel of huge bulk,
> Measur'd by Cubit, length, and breadth, and highth.
>
> > [XI, 728]

In these lines the poet apparently designs to fix the attention upon bulk, but this is effected by the enumeration, not by the measure; for what analogy can there be between modulations of sound and corporeal dimensions?

Milton, indeed, seems only to have regarded this species of embellishment so far as not to reject it when it came unsought, which would often happen to a mind so vigorous, employed upon a subject so various and extensive. He had, indeed, a greater and a nobler work to perform; a single sentiment of moral or of religious truth, a single image of life or nature, would have been cheaply lost for a thousand echoes of the cadence to the sense; and he who had undertaken to "vindicate the ways of God to man" might have been accused of neglecting his cause, had he lavished much of his attention upon syllables and sounds.

No. 121, May 14, 1751 [Imitation] [38]

O imitatores, servum pecus!
—Hor. [*Epist.* I. xix. 19]

Away, ye imitators, servile herd!—Elphinston

I have been informed by a letter from one of the universities that among the youth from whom the next swarm of reasoners is to learn philosophy, and the next flight of beauties to hear elegies and sonnets, there are many who instead of endeavoring by books and meditation to form their own opinions content themselves with the secondary knowledge which a convenient bench in a coffee-house can supply, and without any examination or distinction adopt the criticisms and remarks which happen to drop from those who have risen by merit or fortune to reputation and authority.

These humble retailers of knowledge my correspondent stigmatizes with the name of *Echoes* and seems desirous that they should be made ashamed of lazy submission, and animated to attempts after new discoveries and original sentiments.

It is very natural for young men to be vehement, acrimonious, and severe. For, as they seldom comprehend at once all those consequences of a position or perceive the difficulties by which cooler and more experienced reasoners are restrained from confidence, they form their conclusions with great precipitance. Seeing nothing that can darken or embarrass the question, they expect to find their own opinion universally prevalent, and are inclined to impute uncertainty and hesitation to want of honesty rather than of knowledge. I may, perhaps, therefore be reproached by my lively correspondent when it shall be found that I have no inclination to persecute these collectors of fortuitous knowledge with the severity required; yet, as I am now too old to be much pained by hasty censure, I shall not be afraid of taking into protection those whom I think condemned without a sufficient knowledge of their cause.

He that adopts the sentiments of another whom he has reason to believe wiser than himself is only to be blamed when he claims the honors which are not due but to the author, and endeavors to deceive the world into praise and veneration. For to learn is the proper business of youth, and whether we increase our knowledge by books or by conversation, we are equally indebted to foreign assistance.

The greater part of students are not born with abilities to construct systems or advance knowledge, nor can have any hope beyond that of becoming intelligent hearers in the schools of art, of being able to comprehend what others discover, and to remember what others teach. Even those to whom Providence hath allotted greater strength of understanding can expect only to improve a single science. In every other part of learning they must be content to follow opinions which they are not able to examine, and even in that which they claim as peculiarly their own can seldom add more than some small particle of knowledge to the hereditary stock devolved to them from ancient times, the collective labor of a thousand intellects.

In science, which, being fixed and limited, admits of no other variety than such as arises from new methods of distribution or new arts of illustration, the necessity of following the traces of our predecessors is indisputably evident, but there appears no reason why imagination should be subject to the same restraint. It might be conceived that of those who profess to forsake the narrow paths of truth everyone may deviate towards a different point, since though rectitude is uniform and fixed, obliquity may be infinitely diversified. The roads of science are narrow, so that they who travel them must either follow or meet one another, but in the boundless regions of possibility which fiction claims for her dominion, there are surely a thousand recesses unexplored, a thousand flowers unplucked, a thousand fountains unexhausted, combinations of imagery yet unobserved, and races of ideal inhabitants not hitherto described.

Yet, whatever hope may persuade or reason evince, experience can boast of very few additions to ancient fable. The wars of Troy and the travels of Ulysses have furnished almost all succeeding poets with incidents, characters, and sentiments. The Romans are confessed to have attempted little more than to display in their own tongue the inventions of the Greeks. There is in all their writings such a perpetual recurrence of allusions to the tales of the fabulous age that they must be confessed often to want that power of giving pleasure which novelty supplies, nor can we wonder that they excelled so much in the graces of diction, when we consider how rarely they were employed in search of new thoughts.

The warmest admirers of the great Mantuan poet can extol him for little more than the skill with which he has, by making his hero both a traveler and a warrior, united the beauties of the *Iliad* and *Odyssey* in one composition; yet his judgment was perhaps sometimes overborne by his avarice of the Homeric treasures, and for fear of suffering a sparkling ornament to be lost, he has inserted it where it cannot shine with its original splendor.

When Ulysses visited the infernal regions, he found among the heroes that perished at Troy his competitor Ajax, who, when the arms of Achilles were adjudged to Ulysses, died by his own hand in the madness of disappointment. He still appeared to resent, as on earth, his loss and disgrace. Ulysses endeavored to pacify him with praises and submission, but Ajax walked away without reply. This passage has always been considered as eminently beautiful, because Ajax the haughty chief, the unlettered soldier, of unshaken courage, of immovable constancy, but without the power of recommending his own virtues by eloquence or enforcing his assertions by any other argument than the sword, had no way of making his anger known but by gloomy sullenness and dumb ferocity.[39] His hatred of a man whom he conceived to have defeated him only by volubility of tongue was therefore naturally shown by silence more contemptuous and piercing than any words that so rude an orator could have found, and by which he gave his enemy no opportunity of exerting the only power in which he was superior.

When Aeneas is sent by Virgil to the shades, he meets Dido, the queen of Carthage, whom his perfidy had hurried to the grave; he accosts her with tenderness and excuses, but the lady turns away, like Ajax, in mute disdain.[40] She turns away like Ajax, but she resembles him in none of those qualities which give either dignity or propriety to silence. She might, without any departure from the tenor of her conduct, have burst out like other injured women, into clamor, reproach, and denunciation, but Virgil had his imagination full of Ajax, and therefore could not prevail on himself to teach Dido any other mode of resentment.

If Virgil could be thus seduced by imitation, there will be little hope that common wits should escape, and accordingly we find that besides the universal and acknowledged practice of copying the ancients, there has prevailed in every age a particular species of fiction. At one time all truth was conveyed in allegory; at another nothing was seen but in a vision; at one period all the poets followed sheep, and every event produced a pastoral; at another they busied themselves wholly in giving directions to a painter.

It is, indeed, easy to conceive why any fashion should become popular by which idleness is favored and imbecility assisted, but surely no man of genius can much applaud himself for repeating a tale with which the audience is already tired, and which could bring no honor to any but its inventor.

There are, I think, two schemes of writing on which the laborious wits of the present time employ their faculties. One is the adaptation of sense to all the rhymes which our language can supply to some word that makes the burden of the stanza, but this, as it has been only used in a kind of amorous burlesque, can scarcely be censured with much acrimony. The other is the imitation of Spenser, which by the influence of some men of learning and genius seems likely to gain upon the age and therefore deserves to be more attentively considered.

To imitate the fictions and sentiments of Spenser can incur no reproach, for allegory is perhaps one of the most pleasing vehicles of instruction. But I am very far from extending the same respect to his diction or his stanza. His style was in his own time allowed to be vicious, so darkened with old words and peculiarities of phrase and so remote from common use that Jonson boldly pronounces him "to have written no language." [41] His stanza is at once difficult and unpleasing, tiresome to the ear by its uniformity, and to the attention by its length. It was at first formed in imitation of the Italian poets, without due regard to the genius of our language. The Italians have little variety of terminations, and were forced to contrive such a stanza as might admit the greatest number of similar rhymes, but our words end with so much diversity that it is seldom convenient for us to bring more than two of the same sound together. If it be justly observed by Milton that rhyme obliges poets to express their thoughts in improper terms,[42] these improprieties must always be multiplied as the difficulty of rhyme is increased by long concatenations.

The imitators of Spenser are, indeed, not very rigid censors of themselves, for they seem to conclude that when they have disfigured their lines with a few obsolete syllables, they have accomplished their design, without considering that they ought not only to admit old words but to avoid new. The laws of imitation are broken by every word introduced since the time of Spenser, as the character of Hector is violated by quoting Aristotle in the play.[43] It would indeed be difficult to exclude from a long poem all modern phrases, though it is easy to sprinkle it with gleanings of antiquity. Perhaps, however, the style of Spenser might by long labor be justly copied, but life is surely given us for higher purposes than to gather what our ancestors have wisely thrown away and to learn what is of no value but because it has been forgotten.

No. 125, May 28, 1751
[Inappropriate Comedy][44]

> *Descriptas servare vices operumque colores*
> *cur ego si nequeo ignoroque poeta salutor.*
> —HOR. [*Ars poet.* 86]

> But if, through weakness, or my want of art,
> I can't to every different style impart
> The proper strokes and colors it may claim,
> Why am I honor'd with a poet's name?—FRANCIS

It is one of the maxims of the civil law that "definitions are hazardous." Things modified by human understandings, subject to varieties of complications, and changeable as experience advances knowledge or accident influences caprice, are scarcely to be included in any standing form of expression, because they are always suffering some alteration of their state. Definition is, indeed, not the province of man; everything is set above or below our faculties. The works and operations of nature are too great in their extent or too much diffused in their relations, and the performances of art too inconstant and uncertain, to be reduced to any determinate idea. It is impossible to impress upon our minds an adequate and just representation of an object so great that we can never take it into our view or so mutable that it is always changing under our eye and has already lost its form while we are laboring to conceive it.

Definitions have not been less difficult or uncertain in criticism than in law. Imagination, a licentious and vagrant faculty, unsusceptible of limitations and impatient of restraint, has always endeavored to baffle the logician, to perplex the confines of distinction, and burst the enclosures of regularity.[45] There is therefore scarcely any species of writing of which we can tell what is its essence and what are its constituents; every new genius produces some innovation which, when invented and approved, subverts the rules which the practice of foregoing authors had established.

Comedy has been particularly unpropitious to definers, for though perhaps they might properly have contented themselves with declaring it to be "such a dramatic representation of human life as may excite mirth," they have embarrassed their definition with the means by which the comic writers attain their end, without considering that the various methods of exhilarating their audience, not being limited by nature, cannot be comprised in precept. Thus, some make comedy a representation of mean, and others of bad, men; some think that its essence consists in the unimportance, others in the fictitiousness, of the transaction. But any man's reflections will inform him that every dramatic composition which raises mirth is comic, and that to raise mirth it is by no means universally necessary that the personages should be either mean or corrupt, nor always requisite that the action should be trivial, nor ever that it should be fictitious.

If the two kinds of dramatic poetry had been defined only by their effects upon the mind, some absurdities might perhaps have been prevented with which the compositions of our greatest poets are disgraced, who for want of some settled ideas and accurate distinctions have unhappily confounded tragic with comic sentiments. They seem to have thought that as the meanness of personages constituted comedy, their greatness was sufficient to form a tragedy, and that nothing was necessary but that they should crowd the scene with monarchs and generals and guards and make them talk at certain intervals of the downfall of kingdoms and the rout of armies. They have not considered that thoughts or incidents in themselves ridiculous grow still more grotesque by the solemnity of such characters, that reason and nature are uniform and inflexible, and that what is despicable and absurd will not by any association with splendid titles become rational or great; that the most important affairs by an intermixture of an unseasonable levity may be made contemptible, and that the robes of royalty can give no dignity to nonsense or to folly.

"Comedy," says Horace, "sometimes raises her voice," [46] and tragedy may likewise on proper occasions abate her dignity; but as the comic personages can only depart from their familiarity of style when the more violent passions are put in motion, the heroes and queens of tragedy should never descend to trifle but in the hours of ease and intermissions of danger. Yet in the tragedy of *Don Sebastian*,[47] when the King of Portugal is in the hands of his enemy, and having just drawn the lot by which he is condemned to die, breaks out into a wild boast that his dust shall take possession of Afric, the dialogue proceeds thus between the captive and his conqueror:

> *Muley Moluch.* What shall I do to conquer thee?
> *Seb.* Impossible!
> Souls know no conquerors.
> *M. Mol.* I'll show thee for a monster thro' my Afric.
> *Seb.* No, thou canst only show me for a man:
> Afric is stor'd with monsters; man's a prodigy
> Thy subjects have not seen.
> *M. Mol.* Thou talk'st as if
> Still at the head of battle.
> *Seb.* Thou mistak'st,
> For there I would not talk.
> *Benducar, the Minister.* Sure he would sleep. [I, i.]

This conversation, with the sly remark of the minister, can only be found not to be comic, because it wants the probability necessary to representations of common life and degenerates too much towards buffoonery and farce.

The same play affords a smart return of the general to the Emperor, who, enforcing his orders for the death of Sebastian, vents his impatience in this abrupt threat:

> No more replies,
> But see thou dost it: or . . . .

To which Dorax answers,

> Choke in that threat; I can say "or" as loud. [III, i]

A thousand instances of such impropriety might be produced were not one scene in *Aureng-Zebe* sufficient to exemplify it. Indamora, a captive queen, having Aureng-Zebe for her lover, employs Arimant, to whose charge she had been entrusted and whom she had made sensible of her charms, to carry a message to his rival.

Arimant, *with a letter in his hand;* Indamora.

> *Arim.* And I the messenger to him from you?
> Your empire you to tyranny pursue:

You lay commands, both cruel and unjust,
To serve my rival, and betray my trust.
   Ind. You first betray'd your trust in loving me,
And should not I my own advantage see?
Serving my love, you may my friendship gain,
You know the rest of your pretences vain.
You must, my Arimant, you must be kind:
'Tis in your nature, and your noble mind.
   Arim. I'll to the King, and strait my trust resign.
   Ind. His trust you may, but you shall never mine.
Heav'n made you love me for no other end,
But to become my confident and friend;
As such, I keep no secret from your sight,
And therefore make you judge how ill I write;
Read it, and tell me freely then your mind:
If 'tis indited as I meant it, kind.
   Arim. [*Reading*] *I ask not Heav'n my freedom to restore,*
But only for your sake—I'll read no more;
And yet I must—
[*Reading*] *Less for my own, than for your sorrow sad*—
Another line, like this, would make me mad—
Heav'n! she goes on—yet more—and yet more kind!
      [*As reading*]
Each sentence is a dagger to my mind.
See me this night—
Thank fortune, who did such a friend provide,
For faithful Arimant shall be your guide.
Not only to be made an instrument,
But pre-engaged without my own consent!
   Ind. Unknown t'engage you still augments my score,
And gives you scope of meriting the more.
   Arim. The best of men
Some interest in their actions must confess;
None merit, but in hope they may possess.
The fatal paper rather let me tear,
Than, like Bellerophon, my own sentence bear.
   Ind. You may; but 'twill not be your best advice:
'Twill only give me pains of writing twice.
You know you must obey me, soon or late:
Why should you vainly struggle with your fate?
   Arim. I thank thee, Heav'n, thou hast been wond'rous kind!
Why am I thus to slavery design'd,

And yet am cheated with a freeborn mind?
Or make thy orders with my reason suit,
Or let me live by sense a glorious brute—
(*She frowns*)
You frown, and I obey with speed, before
That dreadful sentence comes, *See me no more.* [III, i]

In this scene every circumstance concurs to turn tragedy to farce. The wild absurdity of the expedient, the contemptible subjection of the lover, the folly of obliging him to read the letter only because it ought to have been concealed from him, the frequent interruptions of amorous impatience, the faint expostulations of a voluntary slave, the imperious haughtiness of a tyrant without power, and the deep reflection of the yielding rebel upon fate and freewill, and his wise wish to lose his reason as soon as he finds himself about to do what he cannot persuade his reason to approve are surely sufficient to awaken the most torpid risibility.

There is scarce any tragedy of the last century which has not debased its most important incidents and polluted its most serious interlocutions with buffoonery and meanness. But though perhaps it cannot be pretended that the present age has added much to the force and efficacy of the drama, it has at least been able to escape many faults which either ignorance had overlooked or indulgence had licensed. The later tragedies indeed have faults of another kind, perhaps more destructive to delight, though less open to censure. That perpetual tumor of phrase with which every thought is now expressed by every personage, the paucity of adventures which regularity admits, and the unvaried equality of flowing dialogue has taken away from our present writers almost all that dominion over the passions which was the boast of their predecessors. Yet they may at least claim this commendation, that they avoid gross faults and that if they cannot often move terror or pity, they are always careful not to provoke laughter.

No. 139, July 16, 1751   [*Samson Agonistes*, I][48]

Sit quodvis, simplex dumtaxat et unum.
—HOR. [*Ars poet.* 23]

Let ev'ry piece be simple and be one.

It is required by Aristotle to the perfection of a tragedy, and is equally necessary to every other species of regular composition, that it should have a beginning, a middle, and an end. "The beginning," says he, "is that which has nothing necessarily previous, but to which that which follows is naturally consequent; the end, on the contrary, is that which by necessity, or at least, according to the common course of things, succeeds something else, but which implies nothing consequent to itself; the middle is connected on one side to something that naturally goes before, and on the other to something that naturally follows it."

Such is the rule laid down by this great critic for the disposition of the different parts of a well-constituted fable. It must begin where it may be made intelligible without introduction, and end where the mind is left in repose, without expectation of any farther event. The intermediate passages must join the last effect to the first cause by a regular and unbroken concatenation; nothing must be, therefore, inserted which does not apparently arise from something foregoing and properly make way for something that succeeds it.

This precept is to be understood in its rigor only with respect to great and essential events, and cannot be extended in the same force to minuter circumstances and arbitrary decorations, which yet are more happy as they contribute more to the main design; for it is always a proof of extensive thought and accurate circumspection to promote various purposes by the same act, and the idea of an ornament admits use, though it seems to exclude necessity.

Whoever purposes, as it is expressed by Milton, "to build the lofty rhyme," must acquaint himself with this law of poetical architecture and take care that his edifice be solid as well as beautiful, that nothing stand single or independent so as that it may be taken away without injuring the rest, but that from the foundation to the pinnacles one part rest firm upon another.

This regular and consequential distribution is among common authors frequently neglected, but the failures of those whose example can have no influence may be safely overlooked; nor is it of much use to recall obscure and unregarded names to memory for the sake of sporting with their infamy. But if there be any writer whose genius can embellish impropriety and whose authority can make error venerable, his works are the proper objects of critical inquisition.[49] To expunge faults where there are no excellencies is a task equally useless with that of the chemist who employs the arts of separation and refinement upon ore in which no precious metal is contained to reward his operations.

The tragedy of *Samson Agonistes* has been celebrated as the second work of the great author of *Paradise Lost,* and opposed with all the confidence of triumph to the dramatic performances of other nations. It contains, indeed, just sentiments, maxims of wisdom, and oracles of piety, and many passages written with the ancient spirit of choral poetry, in which there is a just and pleasing mixture of Seneca's moral declamation with the wild enthusiasm of the Greek writers. It is, therefore, worthy of examination, whether a performance thus illuminated with genius and enriched with learning is composed according to the indispensable laws of Aristotelian criticism, and, omitting at present all other considerations, whether it contains a beginning, a middle, and an end.

The beginning is undoubtedly beautiful and proper, opening with a graceful abruptness, and proceeding naturally to a mournful recital of facts necessary to be known:

> *Samson.* A little onward lend thy guiding hand
> To these dark steps, a little further on;
> For yonder bank hath choice of Sun or shade,
> There I am wont to sit, when any chance
> Relieves me from my task of servile toil,
> Daily in common Prison else enjoin'd me.
>
> .   .   .   .   .
>
> O wherefore was my birth from Heaven foretold
> Twice by an Angel?
>
> .   .   .   .   .
>
> Why was my breeding order'd and prescrib'd
> As of a person separate to God,
> Design'd for great exploits, if I must die
> Betray'd, Captiv'd, and both my Eyes put out?
>
> .   .   .   .   .

Whom have I to complain of but myself?
Who this high gift of strength committed to me,
In what part log'd, how easily bereft me,
Under the Seal of silence could not keep,
But weakly to a woman must reveal it.

His soliloquy is interrupted by a chorus or company of men of his
own tribe, who condole his miseries, extenuate his fault, and conclude with a solemn vindication of divine justice. So that at the
conclusion of the first act there is no design laid, no discovery made,
nor any disposition formed towards the subsequent event.

In the second act, Manoah, the father of Samson, comes to seek
his son and, being shown him by the chorus, breaks out into lamentations of his misery and comparisons of his present with his former
state, representing to him the ignominy which his religion suffers
by the festival this day celebrated in honor of Dagon, to whom the
idolaters ascribed his overthrow:

Thou bear'st
Enough, and more the burden of that fault;
Bitterly hast thou paid, and still art paying
That rigid score. A worse thing yet remains.
This day the *Philistines* a popular Feast
Here celebrate in *Gaza;* and proclaim
Great Pomp, and Sacrifice, and Praises loud
To *Dagon,* as their God who hath deliver'd
Thee, *Samson,* bound and blind into thir hands,
Them out of thine, who slew'st them many a slain. [430]

Samson, touched with this reproach, makes a reply equally peni-
tential and pious, which his father considers as the effusion of
prophetic confidence:

Samson.   He, be sure,
Will not connive, or linger, thus provok'd,
But will arise and his great name assert:
Dagon must stoop, and shall e're long receive
Such a discomfit, as shall quite despoil him
Of all these boasted Trophies won on me. . . .
    Man.   With cause this hope relieves thee, and these words
I as a Prophecy receive; for God,
Nothing more certain, will not long defer
To vindicate the glory of his name. [465]

This part of the dialogue, as it might tend to animate or exasperate Samson, cannot, I think, be censured as wholly superfluous but the succeeding dispute, in which Samson contends to die, and which his father breaks off that he may go to solicit his release, is only valuable for its own beauties and has no tendency to introduce anything that follows it.

The next event of the drama is the arrival of Dalilah, with all her graces, artifices, and allurements. This produces a dialogue in a very high degree elegant and instructive, from which she retires after she has exhausted her persuasions and is no more seen or heard of, nor has her visit any effect but that of raising the character of Samson.

In the fourth act enters Harapha, the giant of Gath, whose name had never been mentioned before, and who has now no other motive of coming than to see the man whose strength and actions are so loudly celebrated:

> *Harapha.*   Much have I heard
> Of thy prodigious might, and feats perform'd
> Incredible to me, in this displeas'd,
> That I was never present on the place
> Of those encounters where we might have tried
> Each other's force in camp or listed field:
> And now am come to see of whom such noise
> Hath walk'd about, and each limb to survey,
> If thy appearance answer loud report. [1082]

Samson challenges him to the combat, and after an interchange of reproaches, elevated by repeated defiance on one side, and embittered by contemptuous insults on the other, Harapha retires. We then hear it determined by Samson and the chorus that no consequence, good or bad, will proceed from their interview:

> *Chorus.*   He will directly to the Lords, I fear,
> And with malicious counsel stir them up
> Some way or other yet further to afflict thee.
> *Samson.*   He must allege some cause, and offer'd fight
> Will not dare mention, lest a question rise
> Whether he durst accept the offer or not,
> And that he durst not plain enough appear'd. [1250]

At last, in the fifth act, appears a messenger from the lords assembled at the festival of Dagon, with a summons by which Samson is required to come and entertain them with some proof of his strength. Samson after a short expostulation dismisses him with a firm and resolute refusal, but during the absence of the messenger, having awhile defended the propriety of his conduct, he at last declares himself moved by a secret impulse to comply and utters some dark presages of a great event to be brought to pass by his agency under the direction of Providence:

> *Samson.* Be of good courage, I begin to feel
> Some rousing motions in me which dispose
> To something extraordinary my thoughts.
> I with this Messenger will go along,
> Nothing to do, be sure, that may dishonour
> Our Law, or stain my vow of *Nazarite.*
> If there be aught of presage in the mind,
> This day will be remarkable in my life
> By some great act, or of my days the last. [1381]

While Samson is conducted off by the messenger, his father returns with hopes of success in his solicitation, upon which he confers with the chorus till their dialogue is interrupted, first by a shout of triumph, and afterwards by screams of horror and agony. As they stand deliberating where they shall be secure, a man who had been present at the show enters and relates how Samson, having prevailed on his guide to suffer him to lean against the main pillars of the theatrical edifice, tore down the roof upon the spectators and himself:

> Those two massy Pillars
> With horrible convulsion to and fro,
> He tugg'd, he shook, till down they came and drew
> The whole roof after them with burst of thunder
> Upon the heads of all who sat beneath. . . .
> *Samson* with these immixt, inevitably
> Pull'd down the same destruction on himself. [1648]

This is undoubtedly a just and regular catastrophe, and the poem, therefore, has a beginning and an end which Aristotle himself could not have disapproved; but it must be allowed to want a middle, since nothing passes between the first act and the last that either hastens or delays the death of Samson. The whole drama, if its superfluities were cut off, would scarcely fill a single act; yet this is the tragedy which ignorance has admired, and bigotry applauded.

No. 140, July 20, 1751   [*Samson Agonistes*, II]

Quis tam Lucili fautor inepte est,
ut non hoc fateatur?—Hor. [*Serm.* I. x. 2]

What doating bigot, to his faults so blind,
As not to grant me this, can Milton find?

It is common, says Bacon, to desire the end without enduring the means.[50] Every member of society feels and acknowledges the necessity of detecting crimes, yet scarce any degree of virtue or reputation is able to secure an informer from public hatred. The learned world has always admitted the usefulness of critical disquisitions; yet he that attempts to show, however modestly, the failures of a celebrated writer shall surely irritate his admirers and incur the imputation of envy, captiousness, and malignity.

With this danger full in my view, I shall proceed to examine the sentiments of Milton's tragedy, which, though much less liable to censure than the disposition of his plan, are, like those of other writers, sometimes exposed to just exception for want of care, or want of discernment.

Sentiments are proper and improper as they consist more or less with the character and circumstances of the person to whom they are attributed, with the rules of the composition in which they are found, or with the settled and unalterable nature of things.

It is common among the tragic poets to introduce their persons alluding to events or opinions of which they could not possibly have any knowledge. The barbarians of remote or newly discovered regions often display their skill in European learning. The god of love is mentioned in *Tamerlane* with all the familiarity of a Roman epigrammatist;[51] and a late writer has put Harvey's doctrine of the circulation of the blood into the mouth of a Turkish statesman who lived near two centuries before it was known even to philosophers or anatomists.[52]

Milton's learning, which acquainted him with the manners of the ancient eastern nations, and his invention, which required no assistance from the common cant of poetry, have preserved him from frequent outrages of local or chronological propriety. Yet he

has mentioned Chalybean steel, of which it is not very likely that
his chorus should have heard, and has made *Alp* the general name
of a mountain in a region where the Alps could scarcely be known:

> [No] medicinal liquor can assuage,
> Nor breath of Vernal Air from snowy *Alp*. [627]

He has taught Samson the tales of Circe and the Sirens, at which he
apparently hints in his colloquy with Dalilah:

> I know thy trains
> Though dearly to my cost, thy gins and toils;
> Thy fair enchanted cup, and warbling charms
> No more on me have power. [932]

But the grossest error of this kind is the solemn introduction of
the phoenix in the last scene, which is faulty, not only as it is incongruous to the personage to whom it is ascribed, but as it is so
evidently contrary to reason and nature that it ought never to be
mentioned but as a fable in any serious poem:

> Virtue giv'n for lost,
> Deprest, and overthrown, as seem'd,
> Like that self-begott'n bird
> In the *Arabian* woods embost,
> That no second knows nor third,
> And lay erewhile a Holocaust,
> From out her ashy womb now teem'd,
> Revives, reflourishes, then vigorous most
> When most unactive deem'd,
> And though her body die, her fame survives,
> A secular bird ages of lives. [1697]

Another species of impropriety is the unsuitableness of thoughts
to the general character of the poem. The seriousness and solemnity
of tragedy necessarily rejects all pointed or epigrammatical expressions, all remote conceits and opposition of ideas. Samson's complaint
is therefore too elaborate to be natural:

> As in the land of darkness yet in light,
> To live a life half dead, a living death,
> And buried; but O yet more miserable!
> Myself, my Sepulcher, a moving Grave,
> Buried, yet not exempt
> By privilege of death and burial
> From worst of other evils, pains and wrongs. [99]

All allusions to low and trivial objects with which contempt is usually associated are doubtless unsuitable to a species of composition which ought to be always awful, though not always magnificent. The remark, therefore, of the chorus on good and bad news seems to want elevation:

> *Manoah.*   A little stay will bring some notice hither.
> *Chor.*   Of good or bad so great, of bad the sooner;
> For evil news *rides post,* while good news *baits.* [1536]

But of all meanness, that has least to plead which is produced by mere verbal conceits, which, depending only upon sounds, lose their existence by the change of a syllable. Of this kind is the following dialogue:

> *Chor.*   But had we best retire? I see a *storm.*
> *Sams.*   Fair days have oft contracted wind and rain.
> *Chor.*   But this another kind of tempest brings.
> *Sams.*   Be less abstruse, my ridling days are past.
> *Chor.*   Look now for no enchanting voice, nor fear
> The bait of honied words; a rougher tongue
> Draws hitherward; I know him by his stride,
> The giant *Harapha.* [1061]

And yet more despicable are the lines in which Manoah's paternal kindness is commended by the chorus:

> Fathers are wont to *lay up* for thir Sons,
> Thou for thy Son art bent to *lay out* all. [1485]

Samson's complaint of the inconveniencies of imprisonment is not wholly without verbal quaintness:

> I a Prisoner chain'd, scarce freely draw
> The air imprison'd also, close and damp. [7]

From the sentiments we may properly descend to the consideration of the language, which in imitation of the ancients is through the whole dialogue remarkably simple and unadorned, seldom heightened by epithets, or varied by figures; yet sometimes metaphors find admission, even where their consistency is not accurately preserved. Thus Samson confounds loquacity with a shipwreck:

> How could I once look up, or heave the head,
> Who like a foolish *Pilot* have *shipwrack't*

> My *Vessel* trusted to me from above,
> Gloriously *rigg'd;* and for a word, a tear,
> Fool, have *divulg'd* the *secret gift* of God
> To a deceitful Woman? [197]

And the chorus talks of adding fuel to flame in a report:

> He's gone, and who knows how he may *report*
> Thy *words* by *adding fuel* to the *flame?* [1350]

The versification is in the dialogue much more smooth and harmonious than in the parts allotted to the chorus, which are often so harsh and dissonant as scarce to preserve, whether the lines end with or without rhymes, any appearance of metrical regularity:

> Or do my eyes misrepresent? Can this be hee,
> That Heroic, that Renown'd,
> Irresistible *Samson?* whom unarm'd
> No strength of man, or fiercest wild beast could withstand;
> Who tore the Lion, as the Lion tears the Kid. [124]

Since I have thus pointed out the faults of Milton, critical integrity requires that I should endeavor to display his excellencies, though they will not easily be discovered in short quotations, because they consist in the justness of diffuse reasonings, or in the contexture and method of continued dialogues, this play having none of those descriptions, similes, or splendid sentences with which other tragedies are so lavishly adorned.

Yet some passages may be selected which seem to deserve particular notice, either as containing sentiments of passion, representations of life, precepts of conduct, or sallies of imagination. It is not easy to give a stronger representation of the weariness of despondency than in the words of Samson to his father:

> I feel my genial spirits droop,
> My hopes all flat, nature within me seems
> In all her functions weary of herself;
> My race of glory run, and race of shame,
> And I shall shortly be with them that rest. [594]

The reply of Samson to the flattering Dalilah affords a just and striking description of the stratagems and allurements of feminine hypocrisy:

> These are thy wonted arts,
> And arts of every woman false like thee,

> To break all faith, all vows, deceive, betray,
> Then as repentant to submit, beseech,
> And reconcilement move with feign'd remorse,
> Confess and promise wonders in her change,
> Not truly penitent, but chief to try
> Her husband, how far urg'd his patience bears,
> His virtue or weakness which way to assail:
> Then with more cautious and instructed skill
> Again transgresses, and again submits. [748]

When Samson has refused to make himself a spectacle at the feast of Dagon, he first justifies his behavior to the chorus, who charge him with having served the Philistines by a very just distinction; and then destroys the common excuse of cowardice and servility, which always confound temptation with compulsion:

> *Chor.*   Yet with this strength thou serv'st the *Philistines.*
>
> .   .   .   .   .
>
> *Sams.*   Not in thir Idol-Worship, but by labour
> Honest and lawful to deserve my food
> Of those who have me in their civil power.
>   *Chor.*   Where the heart joins not, outward acts defile not.
>   *Sams.*   Where outward force constrains, the sentence holds;
> But who constrains me to the Temple of *Dagon,*
> Not dragging? the *Philistian* Lords command.
> Commands are no constraints. If I obey them,
> I do it freely; venturing to displease
> God for the fear of Man, and Man prefer,
> Set God behind. [1363]

The complaint of blindness which Samson pours out at the beginning of the tragedy is equally addressed to the passions and the fancy. The enumeration of his miseries is succeeded by a very pleasing train of poetical images, and concluded by such expostulations and wishes as reason too often submits to learn from despair.

> O first created Beam, and thou great Word,
> Let there be light, and light was over all;
> Why am I thus bereav'd thy prime decree?
> The Sun to me is dark
> And silent as the Moon,
> When she deserts the night
> Hid in her vacant interlunar cave.
> Since light so necessary is to life,

And almost life it self, if it be true
That light is in the Soul,
She all in every part; why was the sight
To such a tender ball as th' eye confin'd?
So obvious and so easy to be quench't,
And not as feeling through all parts diffus'd,
That she might look at will through every pore? [83]

Such are the faults and such the beauties of *Samson Agonistes*, which I have shown with no other purpose than to promote the knowledge of true criticism. The everlasting verdure of Milton's laurels has nothing to fear from the blasts of malignity, nor can my attempt produce any other effect than to strengthen their shoots by lopping their luxuriance.

No. 156, September 14, 1751
[The Rules, I]⁵³

Numquam aliud natura aliud sapientia dicit.
—Juv. [*Sat.* XIV. 321]

For Wisdom ever echoes Nature's voice.

Every government, say the politicians, is perpetually degenerating towards corruption, from which it must be rescued at certain periods by the resuscitation of its first principles and the reestablishment of its original constitution. Every animal body, according to the methodic physicians, is by the predominance of some exuberant quality continually declining towards disease and death, which must be obviated by a seasonable reduction of the peccant humor to the just equipoise which health requires.

In the same manner the studies of mankind, all at least which, not being subject to rigorous demonstration, admit the influence of fancy and caprice, are perpetually tending to error and confusion. Of the great principles of truth which the first speculatists discovered, the simplicity is embarrassed by ambitious additions or the evidence obscured by inaccurate argumentation, and as they descend from one succession of writers to another, like light transmitted from room to room, they lose their strength and splendor and fade at last in total evanescence.

The systems of learning therefore must be sometimes reviewed, complications analyzed into principles, and knowledge disentangled from opinion. It is not always possible without a close inspection to separate the genuine shoots of consequential reasoning which grow out of some radical postulate from the branches which art has engrafted on it. The accidental prescriptions of authority, when time has procured them veneration, are often confounded with the laws of nature, and those rules are supposed coeval with reason of which the first rise cannot be discovered.

Criticism has sometimes permitted fancy to dictate the laws by which fancy ought to be restrained, and fallacy to perplex the principles by which fallacy is to be detected; her superintendence of others has betrayed her to negligence of herself, and like the ancient Scythians, by extending her conquests over distant regions, she has left her throne vacant to her slaves.

Among the laws of which the desire of extending authority or ardor of promoting knowledge has prompted the prescription, all which writers have received had not the same original right to our regard. Some are to be considered as fundamental and indispensable, others only as useful and convenient; some as dictated by reason and necessity, others as enacted by despotic antiquity; some as invincibly supported by their conformity to the order of nature and operations of the intellect, others as formed by accident or instituted by example and therefore always liable to dispute and alteration.

That many rules have been advanced without consulting nature or reason we cannot but suspect when we find it peremptorily decreed by the ancient masters that "only three speaking personages should appear at once upon the stage," a law which, as the variety and intricacy of modern plays has made it impossible to be observed, we now violate without scruple and, as experience proves, without inconvenience.

The original of this precept was merely accidental. Tragedy was a monody or solitary song in honor of Bacchus, improved afterwards into a dialogue by the addition of another speaker; but the ancients, remembering that the tragedy was at first pronounced only by one, durst not for some time venture beyond two; at last, when custom and impunity had made them daring, they extended their liberty to the admission of three, but restrained themselves by a critical edict from further exorbitance.

By what accident the number of acts was limited to five I know not that any author has informed us, but certainly it is not determined by any necessity arising either from the nature of action or propriety of exhibition. An act is only the representation of such a part of the business of the play as proceeds in an unbroken tenor, or without any intermediate pause. Nothing is more evident than that of every real, and by consequence of every dramatic, action the intervals may be more or fewer than five, and indeed the rule is upon the English stage every day broken in effect without any other mischief than that which arises from an absurd endeavor to observe it in appearance. For whenever the scene is shifted the act ceases, since some time is necessarily supposed to elapse while the personages of the drama change their place.

With no greater right to our obedience have the critics confined the dramatic action to a certain number of hours. Probability requires that the time of action should approach somewhat nearly to that of exhibition, and those plays will always be thought most happily conducted which crowd the greatest variety into the least space. But since it will frequently happen that some delusion must be admitted, I know not where the limits of imagination can be fixed. It is rarely observed that minds not prepossessed by mechanical criticism feel any offence from the extension of the intervals between the acts, nor can I conceive it absurd or impossible that he who can multiply three hours into twelve or twenty-four might image with equal ease a greater number.

I know not whether he that professes to regard no other laws than those of nature will not be inclined to receive tragi-comedy to his protection, whom, however generally condemned, her own laurels have hitherto shaded from the fulminations of criticism. For what is there in the mingled drama which impartial reason can condemn? The connection of important with trivial incidents, since it is not only common but perpetual in the world, may surely be allowed upon the stage, which pretends only to be the mirror of life. The impropriety of suppressing passions before we have raised them to the intended agitation and of diverting the expectation from an event which we keep suspended only to raise it may indeed be speciously urged. But will not experience show this objection to be rather subtle than just? Is it not certain that the tragic and comic affections have been moved alternately with equal force and that no plays have oftener filled the eye with tears and the breast with palpitation than those which are variegated with interludes of mirth?

I do not, however, think it safe to judge of works of genius merely by the event. These resistless vicissitudes of the heart, this alternate prevalence of merriment and solemnity, may sometimes be more properly ascribed to the vigor of the writer than the justness of the design; and instead of vindicating tragi-comedy by the success of Shakespeare, we ought perhaps to pay new honors to that transcendant and unbounded genius that could preside over the passions in sport, who to actuate the affections needed not the slow gradation of common means but could fill the heart with instantaneous jollity or sorrow and vary our disposition as he changed his scenes. Perhaps the effects even of Shakespeare's poetry might have been yet greater had he not counteracted himself, and we might have been more interested in the distresses of his heroes had we not been so frequently diverted by the jokes of his buffoons.

There are other rules more fixed and obligatory. It is necessary that of every play the chief action should be single, for since a play represents some transaction through its regular maturation to its final event, two transactions equally important must evidently constitute two plays.

As the design of a tragedy is to instruct by moving the passions, it must always have a hero, a personage apparently and incontestably superior to the rest, upon whom the attention may be fixed and the anxiety suspended. For though of two persons opposing each other with equal abilities and equal virtue the auditor will indeed inevitably in time choose his favorite, yet as that choice must be without any cogency of conviction, the hopes or fears which it raises will be faint and languid. Of two heroes acting in confederacy against a common enemy, the virtues or dangers will give little emotion, because each claims our concern with the same right, and the heart lies at rest between equal motives.

It ought to be the first endeavor of a writer to distinguish nature from custom, or that which is established because it is right from that which is right only because it is established, that he may neither violate essential principles by a desire of novelty nor debar himself from the attainment of beauties within his view by a needless fear of breaking rules which no literary dictator had authority to enact.

No. 158, September 21, 1751
[The Rules, II]

Grammatici certant et adhuc sub judice lis est.
—Hor. [*Ars poet.* 78]

Critics yet contend,
And of their vain disputings find no end.—Francis

Criticism, though dignified from the earliest ages by the labors of men eminent for knowledge and sagacity, and since the revival of polite literature, the favorite study of European scholars, has not yet attained the certainty and stability of science. The rules hitherto received are seldom drawn from any settled principle or self-evident postulate or adapted to the natural and invariable constitution of things, but will be found upon examination the arbitrary edicts of legislators authorized only by themselves, who, out of various means by which the same end may be attained, selected such as happened to occur to their own reflection and then, by a law which idleness and timidity were too willing to obey, prohibited new experiments of wit, restrained fancy from the indulgence of her innate inclination to hazard and adventure, and condemned all future flights of genius to pursue the path of the Meonian eagle.

This authority may be more justly opposed as it is apparently derived from them whom they endeavor to control, for we owe few of the rules of writing to the acuteness of critics, who have generally no other merit than that of having read the works of great authors with attention; they have observed the arrangement of their matter or the graces of their expression and then expected honor and reverence for precepts which they never could have invented; so that practice has introduced rules rather then rules have directed practice.

For this reason the laws of every species of writing have been settled by the ideas of him who first raised it to reputation, without inquiry whether his performances were not yet susceptible of improvement. The excellencies and faults of celebrated writers have been equally recommended to posterity, and so far has blind reverence prevailed that even the number of their books has been thought worthy of imitation.

The imagination of the first authors of lyric poetry was vehement and rapid, and their knowledge various and extensive. Living in an age when science had been little cultivated and when the minds of their auditors, not being accustomed to accurate inspection, were easily dazzled by glaring ideas, they applied themselves to instruct rather by short sentences and striking thoughts than by regular argumentation; and finding attention more successfully excited by sudden sallies and unexpected exclamations than by the more artful and placid beauties of methodical deduction, they loosed their genius to its own course, passed from one sentiment to another without expressing the intermediate ideas, and roved at large over the ideal world with such lightness and agility that their footsteps are scarcely to be traced.

From the accidental peculiarity of the ancient writers the critics deduce the rules of lyric poetry, which they have set free from all the laws by which other compositions are confined and allow to neglect the niceties of transition, to start into remote digressions, and to wander without restraint from one scene of imagery to another.

A writer of later times has, by the vivacity of his essays, reconciled mankind to the same licentiousness in short dissertations, and he, therefore, who wants skill to form a plan or diligence to pursue it needs only entitle his performance an essay to acquire the right of heaping together the collections of half his life, without order, coherence, or propriety.[54]

In writing, as in life, faults are endured without disgust when they are associated with transcendent merit, and may be sometimes recommended to weak judgments by the luster which they obtain from their union with excellence, but it is the business of those who presume to superintend the taste or morals of mankind to separate delusive combinations and distinguish that which may be praised from that which can only be excused. As vices never promote happiness, though when overpowered by more active and more numerous virtues they cannot totally destroy it, so confusion and irregularity produce no beauty, though they cannot always obstruct the brightness of genius and learning. To proceed from one truth to another and connect distant propositions by regular consequences is the great prerogative of man. Independent and unconnected sentiments flashing upon the mind in quick succession may for a time delight by their novelty; yet they differ from systematical reasoning as single notes from harmony, as glances of lightning from the radiance of the sun.

When rules are thus drawn rather from precedents than reason, there is danger not only from the faults of an author but from the errors of those who criticize his works, since they may often mislead their pupils by false representations, as the Ciceronians of the sixteenth century were betrayed into barbarisms by corrupt copies of their darling writer.

It is established at present that the proemial lines of a poem, in which the general subject is proposed, must be void of glitter and embellishment. "The first lines of *Paradise Lost*," says Addison, "are perhaps as plain, simple, and unadorned as any of the whole poem, in which particular the author has conformed himself to the example of Homer and the precept of Horace." [55]

This observation seems to have been made by an implicit adoption of the common opinion without consideration either of the precept or example. Had Horace been consulted, he would have been found to direct only what should be comprised in the proposition, not how it should be expressed, and to have commended Homer in opposition to a meaner poet, not for the gradual elevation of his diction, but the judicious expansion of his plan, for displaying unpromised events, not for producing unexpected elegancies.

> Speciosa dehinc miracula promat
> Antiphaten Scyllamque et cum Cyclope Charybdim.
>
> [*Ars poet.* 144]

> But from a cloud of smoke he breaks to light,
> And pours his specious miracles to sight;
> Antiphates his hideous feast devours,
> Charybdis barks, and Polyphemus roars.—Francis

If the exordial verses of Homer be compared with the rest of the poem, they will not appear remarkable for plainness or simplicity, but rather eminently adorned and illuminated.

> Ἄνδρα μοι ἔννεπε, μοῦσα, πολύτροπον, ὃς μάλα πολλὰ
> πλάγχθη, ἐπεὶ Τροίης ἱερὸν πτολίεθρον ἔπερσεν,
> πολλῶν δ' ἀνθρώπων ἴδεν ἄστεα καὶ νόον ἔγνω·
> πολλὰ δ' ὅγ' ἐν πόντῳ πάθεν ἄλγεα ὃν κατὰ θυμόν,
> ἀρνύμενος ἥν τε ψυχὴν καὶ νόστον ἑταίρων.
> ἀλλ' οὐδ' ὣς ἑτάρους ἐρρύσατο ἱέμενός περ·
> αὐτῶν γὰρ σφετέρῃσιν ἀτασθαλίῃσιν ὄλοντο,
> νήπιοι, οἳ κατὰ βοῦς Ὑπερίονος Ἠελίοιο
> ἤσθιον· αὐτὰρ ὁ τοῖσιν ἀφείλετο νόστιμον ἦμαρ.
> τῶν ἁμόθεν γε, θεὰ θύγατερ Διός, εἰπὲ καὶ ἡμῖν.

The man for wisdom's various arts renown'd,
Long exercis'd in woes, O Muse! resound;
Who, when his arms had wrought the destin'd fall
Of sacred Troy, and raz'd her heav'n-built wall,
Wand'ring from clime to clime, observant stray'd,
Their manners noted, and their states survey'd.
On stormy seas unnumber'd toils he bore,
Safe with his friends to gain his natal shore:
Vain toils! their impious folly dared to prey
On herds devoted to the god of day;
The god vindictive doom'd them never more
(Ah, men unbless'd!) to touch that natal shore.
Oh, snatch some portion of these acts from fate,
Celestial Muse! and to our world relate.—POPE

The first verses of the *Iliad* are in like manner particularly splendid, and the proposition of the *Aeneid* closes with dignity and magnificence not often to be found even in the poetry of Virgil.

The intent of the introduction is to raise expectation and suspend it; something therefore must be discovered, and something concealed; and the poet, while the fertility of his invention is yet unknown, may properly recommend himself by the grace of his language.

He that reveals too much or promises too little, he that never irritates the intellectual appetite, or that immediately satiates it, equally defeats his own purpose. It is necessary to the pleasure of the reader that the events should not be anticipated, and how then can his attention be invited but by grandeur of expression?

The Idler (1758-1760) [56]

No. 60, June 9, 1759 [Dick Minim, I]

Criticism is a study by which men grow important and formidable at a very small expense. The power of invention has been conferred by nature upon few, and the labor of learning those sciences which may by mere labor be obtained is too great to be willingly endured; but every man can exert such judgment as he has upon the works of others, and he whom nature has made weak and idleness keeps ignorant may yet support his vanity by the name of a critic.

I hope it will give comfort to great numbers who are passing through the world in obscurity, when I inform them how easily distinction may be obtained. All the other powers of literature are coy and haughty; they must be long courted, and at last are not always gained; but Criticism is a goddess easy of access and forward of advance, who will meet the slow and encourage the timorous; the want of meaning she supplies with words, and the want of spirit she recompenses with malignity.

This profession has one recommendation peculiar to itself, that it gives vent to malignity without real mischief. No genius was ever blasted by the breath of critics. The poison which if confined would have burst the heart fumes away in empty hisses, and malice is set at ease with very little danger to merit. The critic is the only man whose triumph is without another's pain, and whose greatness does not rise upon another's ruin.

To a study at once so easy and so reputable, so malicious and so harmless, it cannot be necessary to invite my readers by a long or labored exhortation; it is sufficient, since all would be critics if they could, to show by one eminent example that all can be critics if they will.

Dick Minim, after the common course of puerile studies, in which he was no great proficient, was put apprentice to a brewer, with whom he had lived two years when his uncle died in the City and left him a large fortune in the stocks. Dick had for six months before used the company of the lower players, of whom he had learned to scorn a trade, and being now at liberty to follow his genius, he resolved to be a man of wit and humor. That he might be properly initiated in his new character, he frequented the coffeehouses near the theaters, where he listened very diligently day after day to those who talked of language and sentiments, and unities and catastrophes, till by slow degrees he began to think that he understood something of the stage, and hoped in time to talk himself.

But he did not trust so much to natural sagacity as wholly to neglect the help of books. When the theaters were shut, he retired to Richmond with a few select writers,[57] whose opinions he impressed upon his memory by unwearied diligence, and when he returned with other wits to the town, was able to tell, in very proper phrases, that the chief business of art is to copy nature; that a perfect writer is not to be expected, because genius decays as judgment increases; that the great art is the art of blotting; and that according to the rule of Horace every piece should be kept nine years.

Of the great authors he now began to display the characters, laying down as a universal position that all had beauties and defects. His opinion was that Shakespeare, committing himself wholly to the impulse of nature, wanted that correctness which learning would have given him, and that Jonson, trusting to learning, did not sufficiently cast his eye on nature. He blamed the stanza of Spenser, and could not bear the hexameters of Sidney. Denham and Waller he held the first reformers of English numbers, and thought that if Waller could have obtained the strength of Denham, or Denham the sweetness of Waller, there had been nothing wanting to complete a poet. He often expressed his commiseration of Dryden's poverty, and his indignation at the age which suffered him to write for bread; he repeated with rapture the first lines of *All for Love,* but wondered at the corruption of taste which could bear anything so unnatural as rhyming tragedies. In Otway he found uncommon powers of moving the passions but was disgusted by his general negligence, and blamed him for making a conspirator his hero; and never concluded his disquisition without remarking how happily the sound of the clock is made to alarm the audience. Southerne would have been his favorite but that he mixes comic with tragic scenes, intercepts the natural course of the passions, and fills the mind with a wild confusion of mirth and melancholy. The versification of Rowe he thought too melodious for the stage and too little varied in different passions. He made it the great fault of Congreve that all his persons were wits and that he always wrote with more art than nature. He considered *Cato* rather as a poem than a play and allowed Addison to be the complete master of allegory and grave humor, but paid no great deference to him as a critic. He thought the chief merit of Prior was in his easy tales and lighter poems, though he allowed that his *Solomon* had many noble sentiments elegantly expressed. In Swift he discovered an inimitable vein of irony and an easiness which all would hope and few would attain. Pope he was inclined to degrade from a poet to a versifier, and thought his numbers rather luscious than sweet. He often lamented the neglect of *Phaedra and Hippolytus,*[58] and wished to see the stage under better regulations.

These assertions passed commonly uncontradicted; and if now

and then an opponent started up, he was quickly repressed by the suffrages of the company, and Minim went away from every dispute with elation of heart and increase of confidence.

He now grew conscious of his abilities and began to talk of the present state of dramatic poetry; wondered what was become of the comic genius which supplied our ancestors with wit and pleasantry, and why no writer could be found that durst now venture beyond a farce. He saw no reason for thinking that the vein of humor was exhausted, since we live in a country where liberty suffers every character to spread itself to its utmost bulk, and which therefore produces more originals than all the rest of the world together. Of tragedy he concluded business to be the soul, and yet often hinted that love predominates too much upon the modern stage.

He was now an acknowledged critic and had his own seat in the coffeehouse and headed a party in the pit. Minim has more vanity than ill nature and seldom desires to do much mischief; he will perhaps murmur a little in the ear of him that sits next him, but endeavors to influence the audience to favor, by clapping when an actor exclaims "Ye Gods!" or laments the misery of his country.

By degrees he was admitted to rehearsals, and many of his friends are of opinion that our present poets are indebted to him for their happiest thoughts; by his contrivance the bell was rung twice in *Barbarossa*,[59] and by his persuasion the author of *Cleone*[60] concluded his play without a couplet; for what can be more absurd, said Minim, than that part of a play should be rhymed, and part written in blank verse? And by what acquisition of faculties is the speaker who never could find rhymes before enabled to rhyme at the conclusion of an act?

He is the great investigator of hidden beauties and is particularly delighted when he finds "the sound an echo to the sense." He has read all our poets with particular attention to this delicacy of versification and wonders at the supineness with which their works have been hitherto perused, so that no man has found the sound of a drum in this distich,

> When pulpit, drum ecclesiastic,
> Was beat with fist instead of a stick; [*Hudibras*, I, i,11]

and that the wonderful lines upon honor and a bubble have hitherto passed without notice,

> Honor is like the glassy bubble,
> Which costs philosophers such trouble;
> Where one part cracked, the whole does fly,
> And wits are cracked to find out why. [II, ii, 385]

In these verses, says Minim, we have two striking accommodations of the sound to the sense. It is impossible to utter the two lines emphatically without an act like that which they describe; *bubble* and *trouble* causing a momentary inflation of the cheeks by the retention of the breath, which is afterwards forcibly emitted, as in the practice of "blowing bubbles." But the greatest excellence is in the third line, which is "cracked" in the middle to express a crack, and then shivers into monosyllables. Yet has this diamond lain neglected with common stones, and among the innumerable admirers of *Hudibras* the observation of this superlative passage has been reserved for the sagacity of Minim.

No. 61, June 16, 1759   [Dick Minim, II]

Mr. Minim had now advanced himself to the zenith of critical reputation; when he was in the pit, every eye in the boxes was fixed upon him; when he entered his coffeehouse, he was surrounded by circles of candidates, who passed their novitiate of literature under his tuition; his opinion was asked by all who had no opinion of their own and yet loved to debate and decide; and no composition was supposed to pass in safety to posterity till it had been secured by Minim's approbation.

Minim professes great admiration of the wisdom and munificence by which the academies of the continent were raised, and often wishes for some standard of taste, for some tribunal, to which merit may appeal from caprice, prejudice, and malignity. He has formed a plan for an academy of criticism, where every work of imagination may be read before it is printed, and which shall authoritatively direct the theaters what pieces to receive or reject, to exclude or to revive.

Such an institution would, in Dick's opinion, spread the fame of English literature over Europe and make London the metropolis of elegance and politeness, the place to which the learned and ingenious of all countries would repair for instruction and improvement, and where nothing would any longer be applauded or endured that was not conformed to the nicest rules and finished with the highest elegance.

Till some happy conjunction of the planets shall dispose our princes or ministers to make themselves immortal by such an academy, Minim contents himself to preside four nights in a week in a critical society selected by himself, where he is heard without contradiction, and whence his judgment is disseminated through the great vulgar and the small.

When he is placed in the chair of criticism, he declares loudly for the noble simplicity of our ancestors, in opposition to petty refinements and ornamental luxuriance. Sometimes he is sunk in despair and perceives false delicacy daily gaining ground, and sometimes brightens his countenance with a gleam of hope and predicts the revival of the true sublime. He then fulminates his loudest censures against the monkish barbarity of rhyme, wonders how beings that pretend to reason can be pleased with one line always ending like another, tells how unjustly and unnaturally sense is sacrificed to sound, how often the best thoughts are mangled by the necessity of confining or extending them to the dimensions of a couplet, and rejoices that genius has in our days shaken off the shackles which had encumbered it so long. Yet he allows that rhyme may sometimes be borne if the lines be often broken and the pauses judiciously diversified.[61]

From blank verse he makes an easy transition to Milton, whom he produces as an example of the slow advance of lasting reputation. Milton is the only writer whose books Minim can read forever without weariness. What cause it is that exempts this pleasure from satiety he has long and diligently inquired, and believes it to consist in the perpetual variation of the numbers, by which the ear is gratified and the attention awakened. The lines that are commonly thought rugged and unmusical he conceives to have been written to temper the melodious luxury of the rest or to express things by a proper cadence, for he scarcely finds a verse that has not this favorite beauty. He declares that he could shiver in a hothouse when he reads that

> the ground
> Burns frore, and cold performs th' effect of Fire;
>
> [*P.L.*, II, 594]

and that when Milton bewails his blindness, the verse

So thick a drop serene has quench'd these orbs, [III, 25] [62]

has, he knows not how, something that strikes him with an obscure sensation like that which he fancies would be felt from the sound of darkness.

Minim is not so confident of his rules of judgment as not very eagerly to catch new light from the name of the author. He is commonly so prudent as to spare those whom he cannot resist, unless, as will sometimes happen, he finds the public combined against them. But a fresh pretender to fame he is strongly inclined to censure, till his own honor requires that he commend him. Till he knows the success of a composition, he entrenches himself in general terms; there are some new thoughts and beautiful passages, but there is likewise much which he would have advised the author to expunge. He has several favorite epithets, of which he has never settled the meaning, but which are very commodiously applied to books which he has not read, or cannot understand. One is *manly*, another is *dry*, another *stiff*, and another *flimsy;* sometimes he discovers delicacy of style, and sometimes meets with *strange expressions.*

He is never so great or so happy as when a youth of promising parts is brought to receive his directions for the prosecution of his studies. He then puts on a very serious air; he advises the pupil to read none but the best authors, and when he finds one congenial to his own mind, to study his beauties but avoid his faults, and when he sits down to write, to consider how his favorite author would think at the present time on the present occasion. He exhorts him to catch those moments when he finds his thoughts expanded and his genius exalted, but to take care lest imagination hurry him beyond the bounds of nature. He holds diligence the mother of success, yet enjoins him, with great earnestness, not to read more than he can digest, and not to confuse his mind by pursuing studies of contrary tendencies. He tells him that every man has his genius and that Cicero could never be a poet. The boy retires illuminated, resolves to follow his genius, and to think how Milton would have thought; and Minim feasts upon his own beneficence till another day brings another pupil.

No. 77, October 6, 1759   [Easy Poetry] [63]

Easy poetry is universally admired, but I know not whether any rule has yet been fixed by which it may be decided when poetry can be properly called easy. Horace has told us that it is such as "every reader hopes to equal but after long labor finds unattainable." [64] This is a very loose description, in which only the effect is noted; the qualities which produce this effect remain to be investigated.

Easy poetry is that in which natural thoughts are expressed without violence to the language. The discriminating character of ease consists principally in the diction, for all true poetry requires that the sentiments be natural. Language suffers violence by harsh or by daring figures, by transposition, by unusual acceptations of words, and by any licence which would be avoided by a writer of prose. Where any artifice appears in the construction of the verse, that verse is no longer easy. Any epithet which can be ejected without diminution of the sense, any curious iteration of the same word, and all unusual though not ungrammatical structure of speech destroy the grace of easy poetry.

The first lines of Pope's *Iliad* afford examples of many licences which an easy writer must decline:

> *Achilles' wrath,* to Greece the *direful spring*
> Of woes unnumber'd, *heav'nly* Goddess sing,
> The wrath which *hurl'd* to Pluto's *gloomy reign*
> The souls of *mighty* chiefs untimely slain.

In the first couplet the language is distorted by inversions, clogged with superfluities, and clouded by a harsh metaphor; and in the second there are two words used in an uncommon sense, and two epithets inserted only to lengthen the line; all these practices may in a long work easily be pardoned, but they always produce some degree of obscurity and ruggedness.

Easy poetry has been so long excluded by ambition of ornament and luxuriance of imagery that its nature seems now to be forgotten. Affectation, however opposite to ease, is sometimes mistaken for it, and those who aspire to gentle elegance collect female phrases and fashionable barbarisms and imagine that style to be easy which custom has made familiar. Such was the idea of the poet who wrote the following verses to a "Countess Cutting Paper":

> *Pallas* grew *vap'rish once and odd;*
>   She would not *do the least right thing*
> Either for Goddess or for God,
>   Nor work, nor play, nor paint, nor sing.
>
> *Jove* frown'd and "Use (he cry'd) those eyes
>   "So skillful, and those hands so taper;
> "Do something exquisite and wise"—
>   She bowed, obey'd him, and cut paper.
>
> This vexing him who gave her birth,
>   Thought by all heav'n a *burning shame,*
> *What does she next,* but bids on earth
>   Her *Burlington* do just the same?
>
> *Pallas,* you give yourself *strange airs;*
>   But sure you'll find it hard to spoil
> The sense and taste of one that bears
>   The names of *Savile* and of *Boyle.*
>
> Alas! one bad example shown,
>   How quickly all the sex pursue!
> See, madam! see, the arts o'erthrown
>   Between *John Overton* and *you.*[65]

It is the prerogative of easy poetry to be understood as long as the language lasts, but modes of speech which owe their prevalence only to modish folly or to the eminence of those that use them die away with their inventors, and their meaning in a few years is no longer known.

Easy poetry is commonly sought in petty compositions upon minute subjects, but ease, though it excludes pomp, will admit greatness. Many lines in Cato's soliloquy are at once easy and sublime:

> 'Tis the Divinity that stirs within us;
> 'Tis heav'n itself that points out an hereafter,
> And intimates eternity to man.
> . . . If there's a pow'r above us,
> And that there is all Nature cries aloud
> Through all her works, he must delight in virtue,
> And that which he delights in must be happy. [V. i. 7]

Nor is ease more contrary to wit than to sublimity; the celebrated stanza of Cowley, on a lady elaborately dressed, loses nothing of its freedom by the spirit of the sentiment:

> Th' adorning thee with so much art
> Is but a barb'rous skill,
> 'Tis like the pois'ning of a dart
> Too apt before to kill.[66]

Cowley seems to have possessed the power of writing easily beyond any other of our poets; yet his pursuit of remote thoughts led him often into harshness of expression. Waller often attempted but seldom attained it, for he is too frequently driven into transpositions. The poets from the time of Dryden have gradually advanced in embellishment, and consequently departed from simplicity and ease.

To require from any author many pieces of easy poetry would be indeed to oppress him with too hard a task. It is less difficult to write a volume of lines swelled with epithets, brightened by figures, and stiffened by transpositions than to produce a few couplets graced only by naked elegance and simple purity, which require so much care and skill that I doubt whether any of our authors has yet been able for twenty lines together nicely to observe the true definition of easy poetry.

Preface to *The Plays of William Shakespeare* (1765)[67]

That praises are without reason lavished on the dead and that the honors due only to excellence are paid to antiquity is a complaint likely to be always continued by those who, being able to add nothing to truth, hope for eminence from the heresies of paradox, or those who, being forced by disappointment upon consolatory expedients, are willing to hope from posterity what the present age refuses, and flatter themselves that the regard which is yet denied by envy will be at last bestowed by time.[68]

Antiquity, like every other quality that attracts the notice of mankind, has undoubtedly votaries that reverence it, not from reason, but from prejudice. Some seem to admire indiscriminately whatever has been long preserved, without considering that time has sometimes co-operated with chance; all perhaps are more willing to honor past than present excellence; and the mind contemplates genius through the shades of age as the eye surveys the sun through artificial opacity. The great contention of criticism is to find the faults of the moderns and the beauties of the ancients.[69] While an author is yet living we estimate his powers by his worst performance, and when he is dead we rate them by his best.

To works, however, of which the excellence is not absolute and definite but gradual and comparative, to works not raised upon principles demonstrative and scientific, but appealing wholly to observation and experience, no other test can be applied than length of duration and continuance of esteem. What mankind have long possessed they have often examined and compared, and if they persist to value the possession, it is because frequent comparisons have confirmed opinion in its favor. As among the works of nature no man can properly call a river deep or a mountain high without the knowledge of many mountains and many rivers, so in the productions of genius nothing can be styled excellent till it has been compared with other works of the same kind. Demonstration immediately displays its power and has nothing to hope or fear from the flux of years, but works tentative and experimental must be estimated by their proportion to the general and collective ability of man as it is discovered in a long succession of endeavors. Of the first building that was raised it might be with certainty determined that it was round or square, but whether it was spacious or lofty must have been referred to time. The Pythagorean scale of numbers was at once discovered to be perfect,[70] but the poems of Homer we yet know not to transcend the common limits of human intelligence but by remarking that nation after nation and century after century has been able to do little more than transpose his incidents, new name his characters, and paraphrase his sentiments.

The reverence due to writings that have long subsisted arises, therefore, not from any credulous confidence in the superior wisdom of past ages or gloomy persuasion of the degeneracy of mankind, but is the consequence of acknowledged and indubitable positions, that what has been longest known has been most considered, and what is most considered is best understood.

The poet of whose works I have undertaken the revision may now begin to assume the dignity of an ancient and claim the privilege of established fame and prescriptive veneration. He has long outlived his century, the term commonly fixed as the test of literary merit.[71] Whatever advantages he might once derive from personal allusions, local customs, or temporary opinions have for many years been lost, and every topic of merriment or motive of sorrow which the modes of artificial life afforded him now only obscure the scenes which they once illuminated. The effects of favor and competition are at an end; the tradition of his friendships and his enmities has perished; his works support no opinion with arguments, nor supply any faction with invectives; they can neither indulge vanity nor gratify malignity, but are read without any other reason than the desire of pleasure, and are therefore praised only as pleasure is obtained; yet, thus unassisted by interest or passion, they have passed through variations of taste and changes of manners and, as they devolved from one generation to another, have received new honors at every transmission.

But because human judgment, though it be gradually gaining upon certainty, never becomes infallible, and approbation, though long continued, may yet be only the approbation of prejudice or fashion, it is proper to inquire by what peculiarities of excellence Shakespeare has gained and kept the favor of his countrymen.

Nothing can please many and please long but just representations of general nature. Particular manners can be known to few, and therefore few only can judge how nearly they are copied. The irregular combinations of fanciful invention may delight a while by that novelty of which the common satiety of life sends us all in quest, but the pleasures of sudden wonder are soon exhausted, and the mind can only repose on the stability of truth.

Shakespeare is above all writers, at least above all modern writers, the poet of nature, the poet that holds up to his readers a faithful mirror of manners and of life. His characters are not modified by the customs of particular places, unpracticed by the rest of the world; by the peculiarities of studies or professions, which can operate but upon small numbers; or by the accidents of transient fashions or temporary opinions. They are the genuine progeny of common humanity such as the world will always supply and observation will always find. His persons act and speak by the influence of those general passions and principles by which all minds are agitated and the whole system of life is continued in motion. In the writings of other poets a character is too often an individual; in those of Shakespeare it is commonly a species.

It is from this wide extension of design that so much instruction is derived. It is this which fills the plays of Shakespeare with practical axioms and domestic wisdom. It was said of Euripides that every verse was a precept,[72] and it may be said of Shakespeare that from his works may be collected a system of civil and economical prudence. Yet his real power is not shown in the splendor of particular passages but by the progress of his fable and the tenor of his dialogue, and he that tries to recommend him by select quotations will succeed like the pedant in Hierocles,[73] who, when he offered his house to sale, carried a brick in his pocket as a specimen.

It will not easily be imagined how much Shakespeare excels in accommodating his sentiments to real life but by comparing him with other authors. It was observed of the ancient schools of declamation that the more diligently they were frequented, the more was the student disqualified for the world, because he found nothing there which he should ever meet in any other place. The same remark may be applied to every stage but that of Shakespeare. The theater, when it is under any other direction, is peopled by such characters as were never seen, conversing in a language which was never heard, upon topics which will never arise in the commerce of mankind. But the dialogue of this author is often so evidently determined by the incident which produces it and is pursued with so much ease and simplicity that it seems scarcely to claim the merit of fiction, but to have been gleaned by diligent selection out of common conversation and common occurrences.

Upon every other stage the universal agent is love, by whose power all good and evil is distributed, and every action quickened or retarded.[74] To bring a lover, a lady, and a rival into the fable, to entangle them in contradictory obligations, perplex them with oppositions of interest, and harass them with violence of desires inconsistent with each other, to make them meet in rapture and part in agony, to fill their mouths with hyperbolical joy and outrageous sorrow, to distress them as nothing human ever was distressed, to deliver them as nothing human ever was delivered is the business of a modern dramatist. For this, probability is violated, life is misrepresented, and language is depraved. But love is only one of many passions, and as it has no great influence upon the sum of life, it has little operation in the dramas of a poet who caught his ideas from the living world and exhibited only what he saw before him. He knew that any other passion, as it was regular or exorbitant, was a cause of happiness or calamity.

Characters thus ample and general were not easily discriminated and preserved; yet perhaps no poet ever kept his personages more distinct from each other.[75] I will not say with Pope that every speech may be assigned to the proper speaker,[76] because many speeches there are which have nothing characteristical; but perhaps, though some may be equally adapted to every person, it will be difficult to find any that can be properly transferred from the present possessor to another claimant. The choice is right when there is reason for choice.

Other dramatists can only gain attention by hyperbolical or aggravated characters, by fabulous and unexampled excellence or depravity, as the writers of barbarous romances invigorated the reader by a giant and a dwarf, and he that should form his expectations of human affairs from the play or from the tale would be equally deceived. Shakespeare has no heroes; his scenes are occupied only by men who act and speak as the reader thinks that he should himself have spoken or acted on the same occasion. Even where the agency is supernatural, the dialogue is level with life. Other writers disguise the most natural passions and most frequent incidents, so that he who contemplates them in the book will not know them in the world; Shakespeare approximates the remote and familiarizes the wonderful; the event which he represents will not happen, but if it were possible, its effects would probably be such as he has assigned; and it may be said that he has not only shown human nature as it acts in real exigences, but as it would be found in trials to which it cannot be exposed.[77]

This, therefore, is the praise of Shakespeare, that his drama is the mirror of life, that he who has mazed his imagination in following the phantoms which other writers raise up before him may here be cured of his delirious ecstasies by reading human sentiments in human language, by scenes from which a hermit may estimate the transactions of the world and a confessor predict the progress of the passions.

His adherence to general nature has exposed him to the censure of critics who form their judgments upon narrower principles. Dennis and Rymer think his Romans not sufficiently Roman, and

Voltaire censures his kings as not completely royal.[78] Dennis is offended that Menenius, a senator of Rome, should play the buffoon, and Voltaire perhaps thinks decency violated when the Danish usurper is represented as a drunkard. But Shakespeare always makes nature predominate over accident, and if he preserves the essential character, is not very careful of distinctions superinduced and adventitious. His story requires Romans or kings, but he thinks only on men. He knew that Rome, like every other city, had men of all dispositions, and wanting a buffoon, he went into the senate-house for that which the senate-house would certainly have afforded him. He was inclined to show a usurper and a murderer not only odious but despicable; he therefore added drunkenness to his other qualities, knowing that kings love wine like other men and that wine exerts its natural power upon kings. These are the petty cavils of petty minds; a poet overlooks the casual distinction of country and condition, as a painter, satisfied with the figure, neglects the drapery.[79]

The censure which he has incurred by mixing comic and tragic scenes, as it extends to all his works, deserves more consideration.[80] Let the fact be first stated, and then examined.

Shakespeare's plays are not in the rigorous and critical sense either tragedies or comedies, but compositions of a distinct kind, exhibiting the real state of sublunary nature, which partakes of good and evil, joy and sorrow, mingled with endless variety of proportion and innumerable modes of combination, and expressing the course of the world, in which the loss of one is the gain of another, in which, at the same time, the reveler is hasting to his wine and the mourner burying his friend, in which the malignity of one is sometimes defeated by the frolic of another, and many mischiefs and many benefits are done and hindered without design.

Out of this chaos of mingled purposes and casualties the ancient poets, according to the laws which custom had prescribed, selected some the crimes of men, and some their absurdities; some the momentous vicissitudes of life, and some the lighter occurrences; some the terrors of distress, and some the gaieties of prosperity. Thus rose the two modes of imitation known by the names of *tragedy* and *comedy,* compositions intended to promote different ends by contrary means, and considered as so little allied that I do not recollect among the Greeks or Romans a single writer who attempted both.[81]

Shakespeare has united the powers of exciting laughter and sorrow not only in one mind, but in one composition. Almost all his plays are divided between serious and ludicrous characters, and, in the successive evolutions of the design, sometimes produce seriousness and sorrow, and sometimes levity and laughter.

That this is a practice contrary to the rules of criticism will be readily allowed, but there is always an appeal open from criticism to nature. The end of writing is to instruct; the end of poetry is to instruct by pleasing. That the mingled drama may convey all the instruction of tragedy or comedy cannot be denied, because it includes both in its alternations of exhibition, and approaches nearer than either to the appearance of life, by showing how great machinations and slender designs may promote or obviate one another, and the high and the low co-operate in the general system by unavoidable concatenation.

It is objected that by this change of scenes the passions are interrupted in their progression and that the principal event, being not advanced by a due gradation of preparatory incidents, wants at last the power to move, which constitutes the perfection of dramatic poetry. This reasoning is so specious that it is received as true even by those who in daily experience feel it to be false. The interchanges of mingled scenes seldom fail to produce the intended vicissitudes of passion. Fiction cannot move so much but that the attention may be easily transferred, and though it must be allowed that pleasing melancholy be sometimes interrupted by unwelcome levity, yet let it be considered likewise that melancholy is often not pleasing and that the disturbance of one man may be the relief of another, that different auditors have different habitudes, and that, upon the whole, all pleasure consists in variety.[82]

The players [83] who in their edition divided our author's works into comedies, histories, and tragedies seem not to have distinguished the three kinds by any very exact or definite ideas.

An action which ended happily to the principal persons, however serious or distressful through its intermediate incidents, in their opinion constituted a comedy. This idea of a comedy continued long amongst us, and plays were written which, by changing the catastrophe, were tragedies today and comedies tomorrow.

Tragedy was not in those times a poem of more general dignity or elevation than comedy; it required only a calamitous conclusion, with which the common criticism of that age was satisfied, whatever lighter pleasure it afforded in its progress.

History was a series of actions with no other than chronological succession, independent on each other, and without any tendency to introduce or regulate the conclusion. It is not always very nicely distinguished from tragedy.[84] There is not much nearer approach to unity of action in the tragedy of *Antony and Cleopatra* than in the history of *Richard the Second*. But a history might be continued through many plays; as it had no plan, it had no limits.

Through all these denominations of the drama, Shakespeare's mode of composition is the same: an interchange of seriousness and merriment, by which the mind is softened at one time and exhilarated at another. But whatever be his purpose, whether to gladden or depress, or to conduct the story without vehemence or emotion through tracts of easy and familiar dialogue, he never fails to attain his purpose; as he commands us, we laugh or mourn, or sit silent with quiet expectation, in tranquillity without indifference.

When Shakespeare's plan is understood, most of the criticisms of Rymer and Voltaire vanish away. The play of *Hamlet* is opened, without impropriety, by two sentinels; Iago bellows at Brabantio's window, without injury to the scheme of the play, though in terms which a modern audience would not easily endure; the character of Polonius is seasonable and useful; and the Grave-diggers themselves may be heard with applause.[85]

Shakespeare engaged in dramatic poetry with the world open before him; the rules of the ancients were yet known to few; the public judgment was unformed; he had no example of such fame as might force him upon imitation, nor critics of such authority as might restrain his extravagance. He therefore indulged his natural disposition, and his disposition, as Rymer has remarked, led him to comedy.[86] In tragedy he often writes with great appearance of toil and study what is written at last with little felicity; but in his comic scenes he seems to produce without labor what no labor can improve. In tragedy he is always struggling after some occasion to be comic, but in comedy he seems to repose, or to luxuriate, as in a mode of thinking congenial to his nature. In his tragic scenes there is always something wanting, but his comedy often surpasses expectation or desire. His comedy pleases by the thoughts and the language, and his tragedy for the greater part by incident and action. His tragedy seems to be skill, his comedy to be instinct.[87]

The force of his comic scenes has suffered little diminution from the changes made by a century and a half in manners or in words. As his personages act upon principles arising from genuine passion, very little modified by particular forms, their pleasures and vexations are communicable to all times and to all places; they are natural, and therefore durable; the adventitious peculiarities of personal habits are only superficial dyes, bright and pleasing for a little while, yet soon fading to a dim tinct, without any remains of former luster; but the discriminations of true passion are the colors of nature; they pervade the whole mass and can only perish with the body that exhibits them. The accidental compositions of heterogeneous modes are dissolved by the chance which combined them, but the uniform simplicity of primitive qualities neither admits increase, nor suffers decay. The sand heaped by one flood is scattered by another, but the rock always continues in its place. The stream of time, which is continually washing the dissoluble fabrics of other poets, passes without injury by the adamant of Shakespeare.

If there be, what I believe there is, in every nation, a style which never becomes obsolete, a certain mode of phraseology so consonant and congenial to the analogy and principles of its respective language as to remain settled and unaltered, this style is probably to be sought in the common intercourse of life, among those who speak only to be understood, without ambition of elegance. The polite are always catching modish innovations, and the learned depart from established forms of speech in hope of finding or making better; those who wish for distinction forsake the vulgar, when the vulgar is right; but there is a conversation above grossness and below refinement, where propriety resides, and where this poet seems to have gathered his comic dialogue. He is therefore more agreeable to the ears of the present age than any other author equally remote, and among his other excellencies deserves to be studied as one of the original masters of our language.

These observations are to be considered not as unexceptionably constant, but as containing general and predominant truth. Shakespeare's familiar dialogue is affirmed to be smooth and clear, yet not wholly without ruggedness or difficulty, as a country may be eminently fruitful though it has spots unfit for cultivation. His characters are praised as natural though their sentiments are sometimes forced and their actions improbable, as the earth upon the whole is spherical though its surface is varied with protuberances and cavities.

Shakespeare with his excellencies has likewise faults, and faults sufficient to obscure and overwhelm any other merit. I shall show them in the proportion in which they appear to me, without envious malignity or superstitious veneration. No question can be more innocently discussed than a dead poet's pretensions to renown, and little regard is due to that bigotry which sets candor higher than truth.

His first defect is that to which may be imputed most of the evil in books or in men. He sacrifices virtue to convenience, and is so much more careful to please than to instruct that he seems to write without any moral purpose. From his writings, indeed, a system of social duty may be selected, for he that thinks reasonably must think morally; but his precepts and axioms drop casually from him; he makes no just distribution of good or evil nor is always careful to show in the virtuous a disapprobation of the wicked; he carries his persons indifferently through right and wrong and at the close dismisses them without further care and leaves their examples to operate by chance.[88] This fault the barbarity of his age cannot extenuate, for it is always a writer's duty to make the world better, and justice is a virtue independent on time or place.[89]

The plots are often so loosely formed that a very slight consideration may improve them, and so carelessly pursued that he seems not always fully to comprehend his own design. He omits opportunities of instructing or delighting which the train of his story seems to force upon him, and apparently rejects those exhibitions which would be more affecting, for the sake of those which are more easy.[90]

It may be observed that in many of his plays the latter part is evidently neglected. When he found himself near the end of his work and in view of his reward, he shortened the labor to snatch the profit. He therefore remits his efforts where he should most vigorously exert them, and his catastrophe is improbably produced or imperfectly represented.[91]

He had no regard to distinction of time or place, but gives to one age or nation, without scruple, the customs, institutions, and opinions of another, at the expense not only of likelihood but of possibility. These faults Pope has endeavored, with more zeal than judgment, to transfer to his imagined interpolators.[92] We need not wonder to find Hector quoting Aristotle, when we see the loves of Theseus and Hippolyta combined with the Gothic mythology of fairies. Shakespeare, indeed, was not the only violator of chronology, for in the same age Sidney, who wanted not the advantages of learning, has in his *Arcadia* confounded the pastoral with the feudal times, the days of innocence, quiet, and security, with those of turbulence, violence, and adventure.

In his comic scenes he is seldom very successful when he engages his characters in reciprocations of smartness and contests of sarcasm; their jests are commonly gross, and their pleasantry licentious; neither his gentlemen nor his ladies have much delicacy, nor are sufficiently distinguished from his clowns by any appearance of refined manners. Whether he represented the real conversation of his time is not easy to determine; the reign of Elizabeth is commonly supposed to have been a time of stateliness, formality, and reserve, yet perhaps the relaxations of that severity were not very elegant. There must, however, have been always some modes of gaiety preferable to others, and a writer ought to choose the best.

In tragedy his performance seems constantly to be worse as his labor is more. The effusions of passion which exigence forces out are for the most part striking and energetic, but whenever he solicits his invention or strains his faculties, the offspring of his throes is tumor, meanness, tediousness, and obscurity.[93]

In narration he affects a disproportionate pomp of diction and a wearisome train of circumlocution, and tells the incident imperfectly in many words which might have been more plainly delivered in few. Narration in dramatic poetry is naturally tedious, as it is unanimated and inactive, and obstructs the progress of the action; it should therefore always be rapid, and enlivened by frequent interruption. Shakespeare found it an encumbrance, and instead of lightening it by brevity, endeavored to recommend it by dignity and splendor.

His declamations or set speeches are commonly cold and weak, for his power was the power of nature; when he endeavored, like other tragic writers, to catch opportunities of amplification and, instead of inquiring what the occasion demanded, to show how much his stores of knowledge could supply, he seldom escapes without the pity or resentment of his reader.

It is incident to him to be now and then entangled with an unwieldy sentiment which he cannot well express and will not reject; he struggles with it a while, and if it continues stubborn, comprises it in words such as occur and leaves it to be disentangled and evolved by those who have more leisure to bestow upon it.

Not that always where the language is intricate the thought is subtle, or the image always great where the line is bulky; the equality of words to things is very often neglected, and trivial sentiments and vulgar ideas disappoint the attention, to which they are recommended by sonorous epithets and swelling figures.

But the admirers of this great poet have most reason to complain when he approaches nearest to his highest excellence and seems fully resolved to sink them in dejection and mollify them with tender emotions by the fall of greatness, the danger of innocence, or the crosses of love. What he does best he soon ceases to do. He is not long soft and pathetic without some idle conceit or contemptible equivocation.[94] He no sooner begins to move than he counteracts himself, and terror and pity, as they are rising in the mind, are checked and blasted by sudden frigidity.

A quibble is to Shakespeare what luminous vapors are to the traveler: he follows it at all adventures; it is sure to lead him out of his way, and sure to engulf him in the mire. It has some malignant power over his mind, and its fascinations are irresistible. Whatever be the dignity or profundity of his disquisition, whether he be enlarging knowledge or exalting affection, whether he be amusing attention with incidents, or enchaining it in suspense, let but a quibble spring up before him, and he leaves his work unfinished. A quibble is the golden apple for which he will always turn aside from his career or stoop from his elevation. A quibble, poor and barren as it is, gave him such delight that he was content to purchase it by the sacrifice of reason, propriety, and truth. A quibble was to him the fatal Cleopatra for which he lost the world, and was content to lose it.

It will be thought strange that in enumerating the defects of this writer I have not yet mentioned his neglect of the unities, his violation of those laws which have been instituted and established by the joint authority of poets and of critics.[95]

For his other deviations from the art of writing I resign him to critical justice without making any other demand in his favor than that which must be indulged to all human excellence: that his virtues be rated with his failings. But from the censure which this irregularity may bring upon him I shall, with due reverence to that learning which I must oppose, adventure to try how I can defend him.

His histories, being neither tragedies nor comedies, are not subject to any of their laws; nothing more is necessary to all the praise which they expect than that the changes of action be so prepared as to be understood, that the incidents be various and affecting, and the characters consistent, natural, and distinct. No other unity is intended, and therefore none is to be sought.

In his other works he has well enough preserved the unity of action. He has not, indeed, an intrigue regularly perplexed and regularly unraveled; he does not endeavor to hide his design only to discover it, for this is seldom the order of real events, and Shakespeare is the poet of nature. But his plan has commonly what Aristotle requires, a beginning, a middle, and an end; one event is concatenated with another, and the conclusion follows by easy consequence. There are perhaps some incidents that might be spared, as in other poets there is much talk that only fills up time upon the stage; but the general system makes gradual advances, and the end of the play is the end of expectation.

To the unities of time and place he has shown no regard, and perhaps a nearer view of the principles on which they stand will diminish their value and withdraw from them the veneration which from the time of Corneille they have very generally received, by discovering that they have given more trouble to the poet than pleasure to the auditor.[96]

The necessity of observing the unities of time and place arises from the supposed necessity of making the drama credible. The critics hold it impossible that an action of months or years can be possibly believed to pass in three hours, or that the spectator can suppose himself to sit in the theater while ambassadors go and return between distant kings, while armies are levied and towns besieged, while an exile wanders and returns, or till he whom they saw courting his mistress shall lament the untimely fall of his son. The mind revolts from evident falsehood, and fiction loses its force when it departs from the resemblance of reality.

From the narrow limitation of time necessarily arises the contraction of place. The spectator who knows that he saw the first act at Alexandria cannot suppose that he sees the next at Rome, at a distance to which not the dragons of Medea could in so short a time have transported him; he knows with certainty that he has not changed his place, and he knows that place cannot change itself, that what was a house cannot become a plain, that what was Thebes can never be Persepolis.

Such is the triumphant language with which a critic exults over the misery of an irregular poet, and exults commonly without resistance or reply. It is time therefore to tell him by the authority of Shakespeare that he assumes as an unquestionable principle a position which, while his breath is forming it into words, his understanding pronounces to be false. It is false that any representation is mistaken for reality, that any dramatic fable in its materiality was ever credible, or, for a single moment, was ever credited.

The objection arising from the impossibility of passing the first hour at Alexandria and the next at Rome supposes that, when the play opens, the spectator really imagines himself at Alexandria and believes that his walk to the theater has been a voyage to Egypt and that he lives in the days of Antony and Cleopatra. Surely he that imagines this may imagine more. He that can take the stage at one time for the palace of the Ptolemies may take it in half an hour for the promontory of Actium. Delusion, if delusion be admitted, has no certain limitation; if the spectator can be once persuaded that his old acquaintance are Alexander and Caesar, that a room illuminated with candles is the plain of Pharsalia or the bank of Granicus, he is in a state of elevation above the reach of reason or of truth, and from the heights of empyrean poetry may despise the circumscriptions of terrestrial nature. There is no reason why a mind thus wandering in ecstasy whould count the clock, or why an hour should not be a century in that calenture of the brains that can make the stage a field.

The truth is that the spectators are always in their senses, and know, from the first act to the last, that the stage is only a stage and that the players are only players. They come to hear a certain number of lines recited with just gesture and elegant modulation. The lines relate to some action, and an action must be in some place; but the different actions that complete a story may be in places very remote from each other, and where is the absurdity of allowing that space to represent first Athens and then Sicily which was always known to be neither Sicily nor Athens, but a modern theater?

By supposition, as place is introduced, time may be extended; the time required by the fable elapses for the most part between the acts; for of so much of the action as is represented the real and poetical duration is the same. If in the first act preparations for war against Mithridates are represented to be made in Rome, the event of the war may, without absurdity, be represented in the catastrophe as happening in Pontus; we know that there is neither war nor preparation for war; we know that we are neither in Rome nor Pontus, that neither Mithridates nor Lucullus are before us. The drama exhibits successive imitations of successive actions, and why may not the second imitation represent an action that happened years after the first if it be so connected with it that nothing but time can be supposed to intervene? Time is, of all modes of existence, most obsequious to the imagination; a lapse of years is as easily conceived as a passage of hours. In contemplation we easily contract the time of real actions, and therefore willingly permit it to be contracted when we only see their imitations.

It will be asked how the drama moves if it is not credited. It is credited with all the credit due to a drama. It is credited, whenever it moves, as a just picture of a real original, as representing to the auditor what he would himself feel if he were to do or suffer what is there feigned to be suffered or to be done. The reflection that strikes the heart is not that the evils before us are real evils, but that they are evils to which we ourselves may be exposed. If there be any fallacy, it is not that we fancy the players, but that we fancy ourselves unhappy for a moment; but we rather lament the possibility than suppose the presence of misery, as a mother weeps over her babe when she remembers that death may take it from her. The delight of tragedy proceeds from our consciousness of fiction; if we thought murders and treasons real, they would please no more.

Imitations produce pain or pleasure, not because they are mistaken for realities, but because they bring realities to mind. When the imagination is recreated by a painted landscape, the trees are not supposed capable to give us shade, or the fountains coolness, but we consider how we should be pleased with such fountains playing beside us and such woods waving over us. We are agitated in reading the history of *Henry the Fifth;* yet no man takes his book for the field of Agincourt. A dramatic exhibition is a book recited with concomitants that increase or diminish its effect. Familiar comedy is often more powerful on the theater than in the page;

imperial tragedy is always less. The humor of Petruchio may be heightened by grimace, but what voice or what gesture can hope to add dignity or force to the soliloquy of Cato?

A play read affects the mind like a play acted. It is therefore evident that the action is not supposed to be real, and it follows that between the acts a longer or shorter time may be allowed to pass and that no more account of space or duration is to be taken by the auditor of a drama than by the reader of a narrative, before whom may pass in an hour the life of a hero or the revolutions of an empire.

Whether Shakespeare knew the unities and rejected them by design or deviated from them by happy ignorance it is, I think, impossible to decide and useless to inquire. We may reasonably suppose that, when he rose to notice, he did not want the counsels and admonitions of scholars and critics and that he at last deliberately persisted in a practice which he might have begun by chance. As nothing is essential to the fable but unity of action, and as the unities of time and place arise evidently from false assumptions and, by circumscribing the extent of the drama, lessen its variety, I cannot think it much to be lamented that they were not known by him, or not observed. Nor if such another poet could arise, should I very vehemently reproach him that his first act passed at Venice, and his next in Cyprus. Such violations of rules merely positive become the comprehensive genius of Shakespeare, and such censures are suitable to the minute and slender criticism of Voltaire:

> Non usque adeo permiscuit imis
> Longus summa dies, ut non, si voce Metelli
> Servantur leges, malint a Cæsare tolli.[97]

Yet when I speak thus slightly of dramatic rules, I cannot but recollect how much wit and learning may be produced against me; before such authorities I am afraid to stand, not that I think the present question one of those that are to be decided by mere authority, but because it is to be suspected that these precepts have not been so easily received but for better reasons than I have yet been able to find. The result of my inquiries, in which it would be ludicrous to boast of impartiality, is that the unities of time and place are not essential to a just drama, that though they may sometimes conduce to pleasure, they are always to be sacrificed to the nobler beauties of variety and instruction, and that a play written with nice observation of critical rules is to be contemplated as an elaborate curiosity, as the product of superfluous and ostentatious art, by which is shown rather what is possible than what is necessary.

He that without diminution of any other excellence shall preserve all the unities unbroken deserves the like applause with the architect who shall display all the orders of architecture in a citadel without any deduction from its strength; but the principal beauty of a citadel is to exclude the enemy, and the greatest graces of a play are to copy nature and instruct life.

Perhaps what I have here not dogmatically but deliberatively written may recall the principles of the drama to a new examination. I am almost frighted at my own temerity, and when I estimate the fame and the strength of those that maintain the contrary opinion, am ready to sink down in reverential silence, as Æneas withdrew from the defense of Troy when he saw Neptune shaking the wall and Juno heading the besiegers.

Those whom my arguments cannot persuade to give their approbation to the judgment of Shakespeare will easily, if they consider the condition of his life, make some allowance for his ignorance.

Every man's performances, to be rightly estimated, must be compared with the state of the age in which he lived and with his own particular opportunities, and though to the reader a book be not worse or better for the circumstances of the author, yet as there is always a silent reference of human works to human abilities, and as the inquiry how far man may extend his designs or how high he may rate his native force is of far greater dignity than in what rank we shall place any particular performance, curiosity is always busy to discover the instruments, as well as to survey the workmanship, to know how much is to be ascribed to original powers, and how much to casual and adventitious help. The palaces of Peru or Mexico were certainly mean and incommodious habitations if compared to the houses of European monarchs; yet who could forbear to view them with astonishment who remembered that they were built without the use of iron?

The English nation in the time of Shakespeare was yet struggling to emerge from barbarity. The philology of Italy had been transplanted hither in the reign of Henry the Eighth, and the learned languages had been successfully cultivated by Lilly, Linacre, and

More; by Pole, Cheke, and Gardiner; and afterwards by Smith, Clerk, Haddon, and Ascham.[98] Greek was now taught to boys in the principal schools, and those who united elegance with learning, read with great diligence the Italian and Spanish poets. But literature was yet confined to professed scholars, or to men and women of high rank. The public was gross and dark, and to be able to read and write was an accomplishment still valued for its rarity.

Nations, like individuals, have their infancy. A people newly awakened to literary curiosity, being yet unacquainted with the true state of things, knows not how to judge of that which is proposed as its resemblance. Whatever is remote from common appearances is always welcome to vulgar, as to childish, credulity; and of a country unenlightened by learning, the whole people is the vulgar.[99] The study of those who then aspired to plebeian learning was laid out upon adventures, giants, dragons, and enchantments. *The Death of Arthur* was the favorite volume.[100]

The mind which has feasted on the luxurious wonders of fiction has no taste of the insipidity of truth. A play which imitated only the common occurrences of the world would upon the admirers of *Palmerin* and *Guy of Warwick* have made little impression; [101] he that wrote for such an audience was under the necessity of looking round for strange events and fabulous transactions, and that incredibility by which maturer knowledge is offended was the chief recommendation of writings to unskillful curiosity.

Our author's plots are generally borrowed from novels, and it is reasonable to suppose that he chose the most popular, such as were read by many and related by more, for his audience could not have followed him through the intricacies of the drama had they not held the thread of the story in their hands.

The stories which we now find only in remoter authors were in his time accessible and familiar. The fable of *As You Like It,* which is supposed to be copied from Chaucer's *Gamelyn,* was a little pamphlet of those times,[102] and old Mr. Cibber [103] remembered the tale of Hamlet in plain English prose, which the critics have now to seek in Saxo Grammaticus.

His English histories he took from English chronicles and English ballads,[104] and as the ancient writers were made known to his countrymen by versions, they supplied him with new subjects; he dilated some of Plutarch's lives into plays, when they had been translated by North.[105]

His plots, whether historical or fabulous, are always crowded with incidents, by which the attention of a rude people was more easily caught than by sentiment or argumentation, and such is the power of the marvelous, even over those who despise it, that every man finds his mind more strongly seized by the tragedies of Shakespeare than of any other writer; others please us by particular speeches, but he always makes us anxious for the event, and has perhaps excelled all but Homer in securing the first purpose of a writer, by exciting restless and unquenchable curiosity and compelling him that reads his work to read it through.

The shows and bustle with which his plays abound have the same original. As knowledge advances, pleasure passes from the eye to the ear, but returns, as it declines, from the ear to the eye. Those to whom our author's labors were exhibited had more skill in pomps or processions than in poetical language and perhaps wanted some visible and discriminated events as comments on the dialogue. He knew how he should most please, and whether his practice is more agreeable to nature, or whether his example has prejudiced the nation, we still find that on our stage something must be done as well as said, and inactive declamation is very coldly heard, however musical or elegant, passionate or sublime.

Voltaire expresses his wonder that our author's extravagancies are endured by a nation which has seen the tragedy of *Cato*.[106] Let him be answered that Addison speaks the language of poets, and Shakespeare of men. We find in *Cato* innumerable beauties which enamor us of its author, but we see nothing that acquaints us with human sentiments or human actions; we place it with the fairest and the noblest progeny which judgment propagates by conjunction with learning, but *Othello* is the vigorous and vivacious offspring of observation impregnated by genius. *Cato* affords a splendid exhibition of artificial and fictitious manners and delivers just and noble sentiments in diction easy, elevated and harmonious, but its hopes and fears communicate no vibration to the heart; the composition refers us only to the writer; we pronounce the name of Cato, but we think on Addison.[107]

The work of a correct and regular writer is a garden accurately formed and diligently planted, varied with shades, and scented with flowers; the composition of Shakespeare is a forest, in which oaks extend their branches, and pines tower in the air, interspersed sometimes with weeds and brambles, and sometimes giving shelter to myrtles and to roses; filling the eye with awful pomp, and gratifying the mind with endless diversity.[108] Other poets display cabinets of precious rarities, minutely finished, wrought into shape, and polished unto brightness. Shakespeare opens a mine which contains gold and diamonds in unexhaustible plenty, though clouded by incrustations, debased by impurities, and mingled with a mass of meaner minerals.

It has been much disputed whether Shakespeare owed his excellence to his own native force, or whether he had the common helps of scholastic education, the precepts of critical science, and the examples of ancient authors.

There has always prevailed a tradition that Shakespeare wanted learning, that he had no regular education nor much skill in the dead languages. Jonson, his friend, affirms that "he had small Latin, and less Greek," [109] who, besides that he had no imaginable temptation to falsehood, wrote at a time when the character and acquisitions of Shakespeare were known to multitudes. His evidence ought therefore to decide the controversy unless some testimony of equal force could be opposed.

Some have imagined that they have discovered deep learning in many imitations of old writers, but the examples which I have known urged were drawn from books translated in his time or were such easy coincidencies of thought as will happen to all who consider the same subjects or such remarks on life or axioms of morality as float in conversation and are transmitted through the world in proverbial sentences.[110]

I have found it remarked that in this important sentence, "Go before, I'll follow," we read a translation of, *I prae, sequar.*[111] I have been told that when Caliban, after a pleasing dream, says, "I cry'd to sleep again," the author imitates Anacreon, who had, like every other man, the same wish on the same occasion.

There are a few passages which may pass for imitations, but so few that the exception only confirms the rule; he obtained them from accidental quotations or by oral communication, and as he used what he had, would have used more if he had obtained it.

The *Comedy of Errors* is confessedly taken from the *Menaechmi* of Plautus, from the only play of Plautus which was then in English. What can be more probable than that he who copied that would have copied more but that those which were not translated were inaccessible? [112]

Whether he knew the modern languages is uncertain. That his plays have some French scenes proves but little; he might easily procure them to be written, and probably, even though he had known the language in the common degree, he could not have written it without assistance. In the story of *Romeo and Juliet* he is observed to have followed the English translation where it deviates from the Italian, but this, on the other part, proves nothing against his knowledge of the original. He was to copy, not what he knew himself, but what was known to his audience.

It is most likely that he had learned Latin sufficiently to make him acquainted with construction, but that he never advanced to an easy perusal of the Roman authors. Concerning his skill in modern languages I can find no sufficient ground of determination, but as no imitations of French or Italian authors have been discovered, though the Italian poetry was then high in esteem, I am inclined to believe that he read little more than English and chose for his fables only such tales as he found translated.

That much knowledge is scattered over his works is very justly observed by Pope,[113] but it is often such knowledge as books did not supply. He that will understand Shakespeare must not be content to study him in the closet; he must look for his meaning sometimes among the sports of the field, and sometimes among the manufactures of the shop.

There is, however, proof enough that he was a very diligent reader, nor was our language then so indigent of books but that he might very liberally indulge his curiosity without excursion into foreign literature. Many of the Roman authors were translated, and some of the Greek; the reformation had filled the kingdom with theological learning; most of the topics of human disquisition had found English writers; and poetry had been cultivated, not only with diligence, but success. This was a stock of knowledge sufficient for a mind so capable of appropriating and improving it.

But the greater part of his excellence was the product of his own genius. He found the English stage in a state of the utmost rudeness; [114] no essays either in tragedy or comedy had appeared from which it could be discovered to what degree of delight either one or other might be carried. Neither character nor dialogue were yet understood. Shakespeare may be truly said to have introduced them both amongst us and, in some of his happier scenes, to have carried them both to the utmost height.

By what gradations of improvement he proceeded is not easily known, for the chronology of his works is yet unsettled. Rowe is of opinion that "perhaps we are not to look for his beginning, like those of other writers, in his least perfect works; art had so little, and nature so large a share in what he did, that for aught I know," says he, "the performances of his youth, as they were the most vigorous, were the best." [115] But the power of nature is only the power of using to any certain purpose the materials which diligence procures, or opportunity supplies. Nature gives no man knowledge, and when images are collected by study and experience, can only assist in combining or applying them. Shakespeare, however favored by nature, could impart only what he had learned, and as he must increase his ideas, like other mortals, by gradual acquisition, he, like them, grew wiser as he grew older, could display life better as he knew it more, and instruct with more efficacy as he was himself more amply instructed.

There is a vigilance of observation and accuracy of distinction which books and precepts cannot confer; from this almost all original and native excellence proceeds. Shakespeare must have looked upon mankind with perspicacity, in the highest degree curious and attentive. Other writers borrow their characters from preceding writers and diversify them only by the accidental appendages of present manners; the dress is a little varied, but the body is the same.[116] Our author had both matter and form to provide, for except the characters of Chaucer, to whom I think he is not much indebted, there were no writers in English, and perhaps not many in other modern languages, which showed life in its native colors.

The contest about the original benevolence or malignity of man had not yet commenced.[117] Speculation had not yet attempted to analyze the mind, to trace the passions to their sources, to unfold the seminal principles of vice and virtue, or sound the depths of the heart for the motives of action. All those inquiries which from that time that human nature became the fashionable study have been made, sometimes with nice discernment, but often with idle subtility, were yet unattempted. The tales with which the infancy of learning was satisfied exhibited only the superficial appearances of action, related the events but omitted the causes, and were formed for such as delighted in wonders rather than in truth. Mankind was not then to be studied in the closet; he that would know the world was under the necessity of gleaning his own remarks by mingling as he could in its business and amusements.

Boyle congratulated himself upon his high birth because it favored his curiosity by facilitating his access.[118] Shakespeare had no such advantage; he came to London a needy adventurer and lived for a time by very mean employments. Many works of genius and learning have been performed in states of life that appear very little favorable to thought or to inquiry—so many that he who considers them is inclined to think that he sees enterprise and perserverance predominating over all external agency and bidding help and hindrance vanish before them. The genius of Shakespeare was not to be depressed by the weight of poverty nor limited by the narrow conversation to which men in want are inevitably condemned; the incumbrances of his fortune were shaken from his mind "as dewdrops from a lion's mane." [119]

Though he had so many difficulties to encounter and so little assistance to surmount them, he has been able to obtain an exact knowledge of many modes of life and many casts of native dispositions, to vary them with great multiplicity, to mark them by nice distinctions, and to show them in full view by proper combinations. In this part of his performances he had none to imitate, but has himself been imitated by all succeeding writers, and it may be doubted whether from all his successors more maxims of theoretical knowledge or more rules of practical prudence can be collected than he alone has given to his country.

Nor was his attention confined to the actions of men; he was an exact surveyor of the inanimate world; his descriptions have always some peculiarities, gathered by contemplating things as they really exist. It may be observed that the oldest poets of many nations preserve their reputation and that the following generations of wit, after a short celebrity, sink into oblivion. The first, whoever they be, must take their sentiments and descriptions immediately from knowledge; the resemblance is therefore just, their descriptions are verified by every eye, and their sentiments acknowledged by every breast. Those whom their fame invites to the same studies copy partly them and partly nature, till the books of one age gain such authority as to stand in the place of nature to another, and imitation, always deviating a little, becomes at last capricious and casual. Shakespeare, whether life or nature be his subject, shows plainly that he has seen with his own eyes; he gives the image which he receives, not weakened or distorted by the intervention of any other mind; the ignorant feel his representations to be just, and the learned see that they are complete.

Perhaps it would not be easy to find any author except Homer who invented so much as Shakespeare, who so much advanced the studies which he cultivated, or effused so much novelty upon his age or country.[120] The form, the characters, the language, and the shows of the English drama are his. "He seems," says Dennis, "to have been the very original of our English tragical harmony, that is, the harmony of blank verse, diversified often by dissyllable and trissyllable terminations. For the diversity distinguishes it from heroic harmony and, by bringing it nearer to common use, makes it more proper to gain attention, and more fit for action and dialogue. Such verse we make when we are writing prose; we make such verse in common conversation." [121]

I know not whether this praise is rigorously just. The dissyllable termination, which the critic rightly appropriates to the drama, is to be found, though I think not in *Gorboduc,* which is confessedly before our author, yet in *Hieronimo,* of which the date is not certain but which there is reason to believe at least as old as his earliest plays. This, however, is certain, that he is the first who taught either tragedy or comedy to please, there being no theatrical piece of any older writer of which the name is known, except to antiquaries and collectors of books, which are sought because they are scarce, and would not have been scarce had they been much esteemed.

To him we must ascribe the praise, unless Spenser may divide it with him, of having first discovered to how much smoothness and harmony the English language could be softened. He has speeches, perhaps sometimes scenes, which have all the delicacy of Rowe, without his effeminacy. He endeavors indeed commonly to strike by the force and vigor of his dialogue, but he never executes his purpose better than when he tries to soothe by softness.

Yet it must be at last confessed that as we owe everything to him, he owes something to us; that if much of his praise is paid by perception and judgment, much is likewise given by custom and veneration. We fix our eyes upon his graces and turn them from his deformities, and endure in him what we should in another loath or despise. If we endured without praising, respect for the father of our drama might excuse us, but I have seen in the book of some modern critic[122] a collection of anomalies which show that he has corrupted language by every mode of depravation, but which his admirer has accumulated as a monument of honor.

He has scenes of undoubted and perpetual excellence, but perhaps not one play which, if it were now exhibited as the work of a contemporary writer, would be heard to the conclusion. I am indeed far from thinking that his works were wrought to his own ideas of perfection; when they were such as would satisfy the audience, they satisfied the writer. It is seldom that authors, though more studious of fame than Shakespeare, rise much above the standard of their own age; to add a little to what is best will always be sufficient for present praise, and those who find themselves exalted into fame are willing to credit their encomiasts and to spare the labor of contending with themselves.

It does not appear that Shakespeare thought his works worthy of posterity, that he levied any ideal tribute upon future times or had any further prospect than of present popularity and present profit. When his plays had been acted, his hope was at an end; he solicited no addition of honor from the reader. He therefore made no scruple to repeat the same jests in many dialogues or to entangle different plots by the same knot of perplexity, which may be at least forgiven him by those who recollect that of Congreve's four comedies two are concluded by a marriage in a mask, by a deception which perhaps never happened and which, whether likely or not, he did not invent.

So careless was this great poet of future fame that, though he retired to ease and plenty while he was yet little "declined into the vale of years," [123] before he could be disgusted with fatigue or disabled by infirmity, he made no collection of his works nor desired to rescue those that had been already published from the depravations that obscured them, or secure to the rest a better destiny by giving them to the world in their genuine state.

Of the plays which bear the name of Shakespeare in the late editions, the greater part were not published till about seven years after his death, and the few which appeared in his life are apparently thrust into the world without the care of the author, and therefore probably without his knowledge.

Of all the publishers, clandestine or professed, the negligence and unskillfulness has by the late revisers been sufficiently shown. The faults of all are indeed numerous and gross and have not only corrupted many passages perhaps beyond recovery but have brought others into suspicion which are only obscured by obsolete phraseology or by the writer's unskillfulness and affectation. To alter is more easy than to explain, and temerity is a more common quality than diligence. Those who saw that they must employ conjecture to a certain degree were willing to indulge it a little further. Had the author published his own works, we should have sat quietly down to disentangle his intricacies and clear his obscurities; but now we tear what we cannot loose, and eject what we happen not to understand.

The faults are more than could have happened without the concurrence of many causes. The style of Shakespeare was in itself ungrammatical, perplexed, and obscure; his works were transcribed for the players by those who may be supposed to have seldom understood them; they were transmitted by copiers equally unskillful, who still multiplied errors; they were perhaps sometimes mutilated by the actors for the sake of shortening the speeches; and were at last printed without correction of the press.[124]

In this state they remained, not as Dr. Warburton supposes, because they were unregarded, but because the editor's art was not yet applied to modern languages, and our ancestors were accustomed to so much negligence of English printers that they could very patiently endure it. At last an edition was undertaken by Rowe, not because a poet was to be published by a poet (for Rowe seems to have thought very little on correction or explanation), but that our author's works might appear like those of his fraternity, with the appendages of a life and recommendatory preface.[125] Rowe has been clamorously blamed for not performing what he did not undertake, and it is time that justice be done him by confessing that though he seems to have had no thought of corruption beyond the printer's errors, yet he has made many emendations, if they were not made before, which his successors have received without acknowledgment and which, if they had produced them, would have filled pages and pages with censures of the stupidity by which the faults were committed, with displays of the absurdities which they involved, with ostentatious expositions of the new reading, and self-congratulations on the happiness of discovering it.

As of the other editors I have preserved the prefaces, I have likewise borrowed the author's life from Rowe, though not written with much elegance or spirit; it relates, however, what is now to be known, and therefore deserves to pass through all succeeding publications.

The nation had been for many years content enough with Mr. Rowe's performance, when Mr. Pope made them acquainted with the true state of Shakespeare's text, showed that it was extremely corrupt, and gave reason to hope that there were means of reforming it. He collated the old copies, which none had thought to examine before, and restored many lines to their integrity; but by a very compendious criticism he rejected whatever he disliked, and thought more of amputation than of cure.

I know not why he is commended by Dr. Warburton for distinguishing the genuine from the spurious plays. In this choice he exerted no judgment of his own; the plays which he received were given by Heming and Condell, the first editors, and those which he rejected, though according to the licentiousness of the press in those times they were printed during Shakespeare's life with his name, had been omitted by his friends, and were never added to his works before the edition of 1664, from which they were copied by the later printers.

This was a work which Pope seems to have thought unworthy of his abilities, being not able to suppress his contempt of "the dull duty of an editor." He understood but half his undertaking. The duty of a collator is indeed dull, yet like other tedious tasks, is very necessary; but an emendatory critic would ill discharge his duty, without qualities very different from dulness. In perusing a corrupted piece, he must have before him all possibilities of meaning, with all possibilities of expression. Such must be his comprehension of thought, and such his copiousness of language. Out of many readings possible he must be able to select that which best suits with the state, opinions, and modes of language prevailing in every age, and with his author's particular cast of thought and turn of expression. Such must be his knowledge, and such his taste. Conjectural criticism demands more than humanity possesses, and he that exercises it with most praise has very frequent need of indulgence. Let us now be told no more of the dull duty of an editor.

Confidence is the common consequence of success. They whose excellence of any kind has been loudly celebrated are ready to conclude that their powers are universal. Pope's edition fell below his own expectations, and he was so much offended when he was found to have left anything for others to do that he passed the latter part of his life in a state of hostility with verbal criticism.

I have retained all his notes, that no fragment of so great a writer may be lost; his preface, valuable alike for elegance of composition and justness of remark, and containing a general criticism on his author so extensive that little can be added and so exact that little can be disputed, every editor has an interest to suppress, but that every reader would demand its insertion.

Pope was succeeded by Theobald, a man of narrow comprehension and small acquisitions, with no native and intrinsic splendor of genius, with little of the artificial light of learning, but zealous for minute accuracy, and not negligent in pursuing it. He collated the ancient copies and rectified many errors. A man so anxiously scrupulous might have been expected to do more, but what little he did was commonly right.

In his reports of copies and editions he is not to be trusted without examination. He speaks sometimes indefinitely of copies when he has only one. In his enumeration of editions he mentions the two first folios as of high, and the third folio as of middle, authority, but the truth is that the first is equivalent to all others and that the rest only deviate from it by the printer's negligence. Whoever has any of the folios has all, excepting those diversities which mere reiteration of editions will produce. I collated them all at the beginning, but afterwards used only the first.

Of his notes I have generally retained those which he retained himself in his second edition, except when they were confuted by subsequent annotators or were too minute to merit preservation. I have sometimes adopted his restoration of a comma without inserting the panegyric in which he celebrated himself for his achievement. The exuberant excrescence of his diction I have often lopped, his triumphant exultations over Pope and Rowe I have sometimes suppressed, and his contemptible ostentation I have frequently concealed; but I have in some places shown him as he would have shown himself, for the reader's diversion, that the inflated emptiness of some notes may justify or excuse the contraction of the rest.

Theobald, thus weak and ignorant, thus mean and faithless, thus petulant and ostentatious, by the good luck of having Pope for his enemy, has escaped, and escaped alone, with reputation from this undertaking. So willingly does the world support those who solicit favor against those who command reverence, and so easily is he praised whom no man can envy.

Our author fell then into the hands of Sir Thomas Hanmer, the Oxford editor, a man, in my opinion, eminently qualified by nature for such studies. He had what is the first requisite to emendatory criticism, that intuition by which the poet's intention is immediately discovered and that dexterity of intellect which dispatches its work by the easiest means. He had undoubtedly read much; his acquaintance with customs, opinions, and traditions seems to have been large; and he is often learned without show. He seldom passes what he does not understand without an attempt to find or to make a meaning, and sometimes hastily makes what a little more attention would have found. He is solicitous to reduce to grammar what he could not be sure that his author intended to be grammatical. Shakespeare regarded more the series of ideas than of words, and his language, not being designed for the reader's desk, was all that he desired it to be if it conveyed his meaning to the audience.

Hanmer's care of the meter has been too violently censured. He found the measure reformed in so many passages by the silent labors of some editors, with the silent acquiescence of the rest, that he thought himself allowed to extend a little further the license which had already been carried so far without reprehension; and of his corrections in general it must be confessed that they are often just, and made commonly with the least possible violation of the text.

But by inserting his emendations, whether invented or borrowed, into the page, without any notice of varying copies, he has appropriated the labor of his predecessors and made his own edition of little authority. His confidence, indeed, both in himself and others, was too great; he supposes all to be right that was done by Pope and Theobald; he seems not to suspect a critic of fallibility, and it was but reasonable that he should claim what he so liberally granted.

As he never writes without careful inquiry and diligent consideration, I have received all his notes, and believe that every reader will wish for more.

Of the last editor it is more difficult to speak.[126] Respect is due to high place, tenderness to living reputation, and veneration to genius and learning; but he cannot be justly offended at that liberty of which he has himself so frequently given an example, nor very solicitous what is thought of notes which he ought never to have considered as part of his serious employments and which,

I suppose, since the ardor of composition is remitted, he no longer numbers among his happy effusions.

The original and predominant error of his commentary is acquiescence in his first thoughts, that precipitation which is produced by consciousness of quick discernment, and that confidence which presumes to do by surveying the surface what labor only can perform by penetrating the bottom. His notes exhibit sometimes perverse interpretations, and sometimes improbable conjectures; he at one time gives the author more profundity of meaning than the sentence admits, and at another discovers absurdities where the sense is plain to every other reader. But his emendations are likewise often happy and just, and his interpretation of obscure passages learned and sagacious.

Of his notes, I have commonly rejected those against which the general voice of the public has exclaimed, or which their own incongruity immediately condemns, and which, I suppose, the author himself would desire to be forgotten. Of the rest, to part I have given the highest approbation by inserting the offered reading in the text; part I have left to the judgment of the reader, as doubtful, though specious; and part I have censured without reserve, but I am sure without bitterness of malice, and I hope, without wantonness of insult.

It is no pleasure to me, in revising my volumes, to observe how much paper is wasted in confutation. Whoever considers the revolutions of learning and the various questions of greater or less importance upon which wit and reason have exercised their powers must lament the unsuccessfulness of inquiry and the slow advances of truth when he reflects that great part of the labor of every writer is only the destruction of those that went before him. The first care of the builder of a new system is to demolish the fabrics which are standing. The chief desire of him that comments an author is to show how much other commentators have corrupted and obscured him. The opinions prevalent in one age as truths above the reach of controversy are confuted and rejected in another, and rise again to reception in remoter times. Thus the human mind is kept in motion without progress. Thus sometimes truth and error, and sometimes contrarieties of error, take each other's place by reciprocal invasion. The tide of seeming knowledge which is poured over one generation retires and leaves another naked and barren; the sudden meteors of intelligence which for a while appear to shoot their beams into the regions of obscurity, on a sudden withdraw their luster and leave mortals again to grope their way.

These elevations and depressions of renown and the contradictions to which all improvers of knowledge must forever be exposed, since they are not escaped by the highest and brightest of mankind, may surely be endured with patience by critics and annotators, who can rank themselves but as the satellites of their authors. How canst thou beg for life, says Homer's hero to his captive, when thou knowest that thou art now to suffer only what must another day be suffered by Achilles?

Dr. Warburton had a name sufficient to confer celebrity on those who could exalt themselves into antagonists, and his notes have raised a clamor too loud to be distinct. His chief assailants are the authors of *The Canons of Criticism* and of *The Revisal of Shakespeare's Text*,[127] of whom one ridicules his errors with airy petulance, suitable enough to the levity of the controversy; the other attacks them with gloomy malignity, as if he were dragging to justice an assassin or incendiary. The one stings like a fly, sucks a little blood, takes a gay flutter, and returns for more; the other bites like a viper and would be glad to leave inflammations and gangrene behind him. When I think on one, with his confederates, I remember the danger of Coriolanus, who was afraid that "girls with spits, and boys with stones, should slay him in puny battle"; [128] when the other crosses my imagination, I remember the prodigy in Macbeth,

> A falcon tow'ring in his pride of place,
> Was by a mousing owl hawk'd at and kill'd. [II, iv, 12]

Let me however do them justice. One is a wit, and one a scholar. They have both shown acuteness sufficient in the discovery of faults and have both advanced some probable interpretations of obscure passages, but when they aspire to conjecture and emendation, it appears how falsely we all estimate our own abilities, and the little which they have been able to perform might have taught them more candor to the endeavors of others.

Before Dr. Warburton's edition, *Critical observations on Shakespeare* had been published by Mr. Upton, a man skilled in languages and acquainted with books, but who seems to have had no great vigor of genius or nicety of taste. Many of his explanations are curious and useful, but he likewise, though he professed to oppose the licentious confidence of editors and adhere to the old copies, is unable to restrain the rage of emendation, though his ardor is ill seconded by his skill. Every cold empiric, when his heart is expanded by a successful experiment, swells into a theorist, and the laborious collator at some unlucky moment frolics in conjecture.

Critical, Historical and Explanatory Notes have been likewise published upon Shakespeare by Dr. Grey, whose diligent perusal of the old English writers has enabled him to make some useful observations. What he undertook he has well enough performed, but as he neither attempts judicial nor emendatory criticism, he employs rather his memory than his sagacity. It were to be wished that all would endeavor to imitate his modesty who have not been able to surpass his knowledge.

I can say with great sincerity of all my predecessors what I hope will hereafter be said of me, that not one has left Shakespeare without improvement, nor is there one to whom I have not been indebted for assistance and information. Whatever I have taken from them it was my intention to refer to its original author, and it is certain that what I have not given to another I believed when I wrote it to be my own. In some perhaps I have been anticipated, but if I am ever found to encroach upon the remarks of any other commentator, I am willing that the honor, be it more or less, should be transferred to the first claimant, for his right, and his alone, stands above dispute; the second can prove his pretensions only to himself, nor can himself always distinguish invention, with sufficient certainty, from recollection.

They have all been treated by me with candor, which they have not been careful of observing to one another. It is not easy to discover from what cause the acrimony of a scholiast can naturally proceed. The subjects to be discussed by him are of very small importance; they involve neither property nor liberty; nor favor the interest of sect or party. The various readings of copies and different interpretations of a passage seem to be questions that might exercise the wit without engaging the passions. But, whether it be that "small things make mean men proud," [129] and vanity catches small occasions, or that all contrariety of opinion, even in those that can defend it no longer, makes proud men angry, there is often found in commentaries a spontaneous strain of invective and contempt more eager and venomous than is vented by the most furious controvertist in politics against those whom he is hired to defame.

Perhaps the lightness of the matter may conduce to the vehemence of the agency; when the truth to be investigated is so near to inexistence as to escape attention, its bulk is to be enlarged by rage and exclamation. That to which all would be indifferent in its original state may attract notice when the fate of a name is appended to it. A commentator has indeed great temptations to supply by turbulence what he wants of dignity, to beat his little gold to a spacious surface, to work that to foam which no art or diligence can exalt to spirit.

The notes which I have borrowed or written are either illustrative, by which difficulties are explained; or judicial, by which faults and beauties are remarked; or emendatory, by which depravations are corrected.

The explanations transcribed from others, if I do not subjoin any other interpretation, I suppose commonly to be right—at least I intend by acquiescence to confess that I have nothing better to propose.

After the labors of all the editors, I found many passages which apeared to me likely to obstruct the greater number of readers and thought it my duty to facilitate their passage. It is impossible for an expositor not to write too little for some and too much for others. He can only judge what is necessary by his own experience, and how long soever he may deliberate, will at last explain many lines which the learned will think impossible to be mistaken, and omit many for which the ignorant will want his help. These are censures merely relative, and must be quietly endured. I have endeavored to be neither superfluously copious nor scrupulously reserved, and hope that I have made my author's meaning accessible to many who before were frighted from perusing him, and contributed something to the public by diffusing innocent and rational pleasure.

The complete explanation of an author not systematic and consequential, but desultory and vagrant, abounding in casual allusions and light hints, is not to be expected from any single scholiast. All personal reflections, when names are suppressed, must be in a few years irrecoverably obliterated, and customs too minute to attract the notice of law, such as modes of dress, formalities of conversation, rules of visits, disposition of furniture, and practices of ceremony, which naturally find places in familiar dialogue, are so fugitive and unsubstantial that they are not easily retained or recovered. What can be known will be collected by chance from the recesses of obscure and obsolete papers, perused commonly with some other view. Of this knowledge every man has some, and none has much; but when an author has engaged the public attention, those who can add anything to his illustration communicate their discoveries, and time produces what had eluded diligence.

To time I have been obliged to resign many passages which, though I did not understand them, will perhaps hereafter be explained, having, I hope, illustrated some which others have neglected or mistaken, sometimes by short remarks, or marginal directions, such as every editor has added at his will, and often by comments more laborious than the matter will seem to deserve; but that which is most difficult is not always most important, and to an editor nothing is a trifle by which his author is obscured.

The poetical beauties or defects I have not been very diligent to observe. Some plays have more, and some fewer judicial observations, not in proportion to their difference of merit, but because I gave this part of my design to chance and to caprice. The 'reader, I believe, is seldom pleased to find his opinion anticipated; it is natural to delight more in what we find or make than in what we receive. Judgment, like other faculties, is improved by practice, and its advancement is hindered by submission to dictatorial decisions, as the memory grows torpid by the use of a table-book. Some initiation is however necessary; of all skill, part is infused by precept, and part is obtained by habit; I have therefore shown so much as may enable the candidate of criticism to discover the rest.

To the end of most plays I have added short strictures, containing a general censure of faults or praise of excellence, in which I know not how much I have concurred with the current opinion; but I have not, by any affectation of singularity, deviated from it. Nothing is minutely and particularly examined, and therefore it is to be supposed that in the plays which are condemned there is much to be praised, and in those which are praised much to be condemned.

The part of criticism in which the whole succession of editors has labored with the greatest diligence, which has occasioned the most arrogant ostentation and excited the keenest acrimony, is the emendation of corrupted passages, to which the public attention, having been first drawn by the violence of the contention between Pope and Theobald, has been continued by the persecution which, with a kind of conspiracy, has been since raised against all the publishers of Shakespeare.

That many passages have passed in a state of depravation through all the editions is indubitably certain; of these the restoration is only to be attempted by collation of copies or sagacity of conjecture. The collator's province is safe and easy, the conjecturer's perilous and difficult. Yet as the greater part of the plays are extant only in one copy, the peril must not be avoided, nor the difficulty refused.

Of the readings which this emulation of amendment has hitherto produced, some from the labors of every publisher I have advanced into the text; those are to be considered as in my opinion sufficiently supported; some I have rejected without mention, as evidently erroneous; some I have left in the notes without censure or approbation, as resting in equipoise between objection and defense; and some which seemed specious but not right I have inserted with a subsequent animadversion.

Having classed the observations of others, I was at last to try what I could substitute for their mistakes and how I could supply their omissions. I collated such copies as I could procure, and wished for more, but have not found the collectors of these rarities very communicative.[130] Of the editions which chance or kindness put into my hands I have given an enumeration, that I may not be blamed for neglecting what I had not the power to do.

By examining the old copies, I soon found that the later publishers, with all their boasts of diligence, suffered many passages to stand unauthorized and contented themselves with Rowe's regulation of the text, even where they knew it to be arbitrary and with a little consideration might have found it to be wrong. Some of these alterations are only the ejection of a word for one that appeared to him more elegant or more intelligible. These corruptions I have often silently rectified, for the history of our language and the true force of our words can only be preserved by keeping the text of authors free from adulteration. Others, and those very frequent, smoothed the cadence or regulated the measure; on these I have not exercised the same rigor; if only a word was transposed, or a particle inserted or omitted, I have sometimes suffered the line to stand, for the inconstancy of the copies is such as that some liberties may be easily permitted. But this practice I have not suffered to proceed far, having restored the primitive diction wherever it could for any reason be preferred.

The emendations which comparison of copies supplied I have inserted in the text, sometimes, where the improvement was slight, without notice, and sometimes with an account of the reasons of the change.

Conjecture, though it be sometimes unavoidable, I have not wantonly nor licentiously indulged. It has been my settled principle that the reading of the ancient books is probably true and therefore is not to be disturbed for the sake of elegance, perspicuity, or mere improvement of the sense. For though much credit is not due to the fidelity, nor any to the judgment of the first publishers, yet they who had the copy before their eyes were more likely to read it right than we who read it only by imagination. But it is evident that they have often made strange mistakes by ignorance or negligence and that therefore something may be properly attempted by criticism, keeping the middle way between presumption and timidity.

Such criticism I have attempted to practice, and where any passage appeared inextricably perplexed, have endeavored to discover how it may be recalled to sense with least violence. But my first labor is always to turn the old text on every side and try if there be any interstice through which light can find its way; [131] nor would Huetius[132] himself condemn me as refusing the trouble of research for the ambition of alteration. In this modest industry I have not been unsuccessful. I have rescued many lines from the violations of temerity and secured many scenes from the inroads of correction. I have adopted the Roman sentiment that it is more honorable to save a citizen than to kill an enemy, and have been more careful to protect than to attack.

I have preserved the common distribution of the plays into acts, though I believe it to be in almost all the plays void of authority. Some of those which are divided in the later editions have no division in the first folio and some that are divided in the folio have no division in the preceding copies. The settled mode of the theater requires four intervals in the play, but few, if any, of our author's compositions can be properly distributed in that manner. An act is so much of the drama as passes without intervention of time or change of place. A pause makes a new act. In every real, and therefore in every imitative action, the intervals may be more or fewer, the restriction of five acts being accidental and arbitrary. This Shakespeare knew, and this he practiced; his plays were written and at first printed in one unbroken continuity and ought now to be exhibited with short pauses, interposed as often as the scene is changed or any considerable time is required to pass. This method would at once quell a thousand absurdities.

In restoring the author's works to their integrity, I have considered the punctuation as wholly in my power, for what could be their care of colons and commas who corrupted words and sentences. Whatever could be done by adjusting points is therefore silently performed, in some plays with much diligence, in others with less; it is hard to keep a busy eye steadily fixed upon evanescent atoms, or a discursive mind upon evanescent truth.

The same liberty has been taken with a few particles or other words of slight effect. I have sometimes inserted or omitted them without notice. I have done that sometimes which the other editors have done always and which indeed the state of the text may sufficiently justify.

The greater part of readers, instead of blaming us for passing trifles, will wonder that on mere trifles so much labor is expended, with such importance of debate and such solemnity of diction. To these I answer with confidence that they are judging of an art which they do not understand; yet cannot much reproach them with their ignorance, nor promise that they would become in general, by learning criticism, more useful, happier, or wiser.

As I practiced conjecture more, I learned to trust it less, and after I had printed a few plays, resolved to insert none of my own readings in the text. Upon this caution I now congratulate myself, for every day increases my doubt of my emendations.

Since I have confined my imagination to the margin, it must not be considered as very reprehensible if I have suffered it to play some freaks in its own dominion. There is no danger in conjecture if it be proposed as conjecture, and while the text remains uninjured, those changes may be safely offered which are not considered even by him that offers them as necessary or safe.

If my readings are of little value, they have not been ostentatiously displayed or importunately obtruded. I could have written longer notes, for the art of writing notes is not of difficult attainment. The work is performed, first, by railing at the stupidity, negligence, ignorance, and asinine tastelessness of the former editors, and showing, from all that goes before and all that follows, the inelegance and absurdity of the old reading; then, by proposing something which to superficial readers would seem specious but which the editor rejects with indignation; then, by producing the true reading, with a long paraphrase, and concluding with loud acclamations on the discovery and a sober wish for the advancement and prosperity of genuine criticism.

All this may be done, and perhaps done sometimes without impropriety. But I have always suspected that the reading is right which requires many words to prove it wrong; and the emendation wrong, that cannot without so much labor appear to be right. The justness of a happy restoration strikes at once, and the moral precept may be well applied to criticism, *quod dubitas ne feceris.*

To dread the shore which he sees spread with wrecks is natural to the sailor. I had before my eye so many critical adventures ended in miscarriage that caution was forced upon me. I encountered in every page Wit struggling with its own sophistry, and Learning confused by the multiplicity of its views. I was forced to censure those whom I admired, and could not but reflect, while I was dispossessing their emendations, how soon the same fate might happen to my own and how many of the readings which I have corrected may be by some other editor defended and established:

> Critics, I saw, that other's names efface,
> And fix their own, with labour, in the place;
> Their own, like others, soon their place resign'd,
> Or disappear'd, and left the first behind.—Pope [133]

That a conjectural critic should often be mistaken cannot be wonderful, either to others or himself, if it be considered that in his art there is no system, no principal and axiomatical truth that regulates subordinate positions. His chance of error is renewed at every attempt; an oblique view of the passage, a slight misapprehension of a phrase, a casual inattention to the parts connected, is sufficient to make him not only fail, but fail ridiculously; and when he succeeds best, he produces perhaps but one reading of many probable, and he that suggests another will always be able to dispute his claims.

It is an unhappy state in which danger is hid under pleasure. The allurements of emendation are scarcely resistible. Conjecture has all the joy and all the pride of invention, and he that has once started a happy change is too much delighted to consider what objections may rise against it.

Yet conjectural criticism has been of great use in the learned world, nor is it my intention to depreciate a study that has exercised so many mighty minds from the revival of learning to our own age, from the Bishop of Aleria [134] to English Bentley.[135] The critics on ancient authors have, in the exercise of their sagacity, many assistances which the editor of Shakespeare is condemned to want. They are employed upon grammatical and settled languages, whose construction contributes so much to perspicuity that Homer has fewer passages unintelligible than Chaucer. The words have not only a known regimen, but invariable quantities, which direct and confine the choice. There are commonly more manuscripts than one, and they do not often conspire in the same mistakes. Yet Scaliger could confess to Salmasius how little satisfaction his emendations gave him.[136] *Illudunt nobis conjecturæ nostræ, quarum nos pudet, posteaquam in meliores codices incidimus.*[137] And Lipsius [138] could complain, that critics were making faults by trying to remove them, *Ut olim vitiis, ita nunc remediis laboratur.*[139] And indeed, where mere conjecture is to be used, the emendations of Scaliger and Lipsius, notwithstanding their wonderful sagacity and erudition, are often vague and disputable, like mine or Theobald's.

Perhaps I may not be more censured for doing wrong than for doing little, for raising in the public expectations which at last I have not answered. The expectation of ignorance is indefinite, and that of knowledge is often tyrannical. It is hard to satisfy those who know not what to demand or those who demand by design what they think impossible to be done. I have indeed disappointed no opinion more than my own; yet I have endeavored to perform my task with no slight solicitude. Not a single passage in the whole work has appeared to me corrupt which I have not attempted to restore; or obscure, which I have not endeavored to illustrate. In many I have failed like others, and from many, after all my efforts, I have retreated and confessed the repulse. I have not passed over with affected superiority what is equally difficult to the reader and to myself, but where I could not instruct him, have owned my ignorance. I might easily have accumulated a mass of seeming learning upon easy scenes, but it ought not to be imputed to negligence that, where nothing was necessary, nothing has been done, or that where others have said enough, I have said no more.

Notes are often necessary, but they are necessary evils. Let him that is yet unacquainted with the powers of Shakespeare and who desires to feel the highest pleasure that the drama can give read every play from the first scene to the last, with utter negligence of all his commentators. When his fancy is once on the wing, let it not stoop at correction or explanation. When his attention is strongly engaged, let it disdain alike to turn aside to the name of Theobald and of Pope. Let him read on through brightness and obscurity, through integrity and corruption; let him preserve his comprehension of the dialogue and his interest in the fable. And when the pleasures of novelty have ceased, let him attempt exactness, and read the commentators.

Particular passages are cleared by notes, but the general effect of the work is weakened. The mind is refrigerated by interruption; the thoughts are diverted from the principal subject; the reader is weary, he suspects not why, and at last throws away the book which he has too diligently studied.

Parts are not to be examined till the whole has been surveyed; there is a kind of intellectual remoteness necessary for the comprehension of any great work in its full design and its true proportions; a close approach shows the smaller niceties, but the beauty of the whole is discerned no longer.

It is not very grateful to consider how little the succession of editors has added to this author's power of pleasing. He was read, admired, studied, and imitated while he was yet deformed with all the improprieties which ignorance and neglect could accumulate upon him, while the reading was yet not rectified, nor his allusions understood; yet then did Dryden pronounce "that Shakespeare was the man who of all modern and perhaps ancient poets had the largest and most comprehensive soul. All the images of Nature were still present to him, and he drew them not laboriously, but luckily; when he describes anything, you more than see it, you feel it too. Those who accuse him to have wanted learning, give him the greater commendation: he was naturally learned; he needed not the spectacles of books to read Nature; he looked inwards, and found her there. I cannot say he is everywhere alike; were he so, I should do him injury to compare him with the greatest of mankind. He is many times flat and insipid, his comic wit degenerating into clenches, his serious swelling into bombast. But he is always great when some great occasion is presented to him. No man can say he ever had a fit subject for his wit and did not then raise himself as high above the rest of poets,

Quantum lenta solent inter viburna cupressi." [140]

It is to be lamented that such a writer should want a commentary, that his language should become obsolete, or his sentiments obscure. But it is vain to carry wishes beyond the condition of human things; that which must happen to all has happened to Shakespeare, by accident and time; and more than has been suffered by any other writer since the use of types has been suffered by him through his own negligence of fame, or perhaps by that superiority of mind which despised its own performances when it compared them with its powers, and judged those works unworthy to be preserved which the critics of following ages were to contend for the fame of restoring and explaining.

Among these candidates of inferior fame, I am now to stand the judgment of the public, and wish that I could confidently produce my commentary as equal to the encouragement which I have had the honor of receiving. Every work of this kind is by its nature deficient, and I should feel little solicitude about the sentence, were it to be pronounced only by the skillful and the learned.

ROBERT LOWTH ✍

Lectures on the Sacred Poetry of the Hebrews (1753; trans., 1787)

Lecture XIV, "Of the Sublime in General, and of Sublimity of Expression in Particular"

In what manner the word *mashal* implies the idea of Sublimity.—Sublimity of language and sentiment.—On what account the poetic diction of the Hebrews, either considered in itself, or compared with prose composition, merits an appellation expressive of sublimity.—The sublimity of the poetic diction arises from the passions.—How far the poetic diction differs from the prose among the Hebrews.—Certain forms of poetic diction and construction exemplified from Job, chap. iii.

Having, in the preceding lectures, given my sentiments at large on the nature of the figurative style, on its use and application in poetry, and particularly in the poetry of the Hebrews, I proceed to treat of the sublimity of the sacred poets, a subject which has been already illustrated by many examples quoted upon other occasions, but which, since we have admitted it as a third characteristic of the poetic style, now requires to be distinctly explained. We have already seen that this is implied in one of the senses of the word *mashal,* it being expressive of power or supreme authority, and when applied to style seems particularly to intimate something eminent or energetic, excellent or important. This is certainly understood in the phrase "to take (or lift) up his parable," that is, to express a great or lofty sentiment. The very first instance in which the phrase occurs will serve as an example in point. For in this manner Balaam "took up," as our translation renders it, "his parable, and said:"

> From Aram I am brought by Balak,
> By the king of Moab from the mountains of the East:
> Come, curse me, Jacob;
> And come, execrate Israel.
> How shall I curse whom God hath not cursed?
> And how shall I execrate whom God hath not execrated?
> For from the tops of the rocks I see him,
> And from the hills I behold him;
> Lo! the people, who shall dwell alone,
> Nor shall number themselves among the nations!
> Who shall count the dust of Jacob?
> Or the number of the fourth of Israel?
> Let my soul die the death of the righteous,
> And let my end be as his. [Numbers 23:7–10]

Let us now consider on what account this address of the prophet is entitled *mashal*. The sentences are indeed accurately distributed in parallelisms, as may be discovered even in the translation, which has not entirely obscured the elegance of the arrangement; and compositions in this form, we have already remarked, are commonly classed among the proverbs and adages which are properly called *mashalim,* though perhaps they entertain nothing of a proverbial or didactic nature. But if we attentively consider this very passage, or others introduced by the same form of expression, we shall find in all of them either an extraordinary variety of figure and imagery or an elevation of style and sentiment, or perhaps a union of all these excellencies, which will induce us to conclude that something more is meant by the term to which I am alluding than the bare merit of a sententious neatness. If again we examine the same passage in another point of view, we shall discover in it little or nothing of the figurative kind, at least according to our ideas or according to that acceptation of the word *mashal* which denotes figurative language; there is evidently nothing in it of the mystical kind, nothing allegorical, no pomp of imagery, no comparison, and in fourteen verses but a single metaphor; as far, therefore, as figurative language is a characteristic of the parobolical style, this is no instance of it. We must then admit the word *parable,* when applied to this passage, to be expressive of those exalted sentiments, that spirit of sublimity, that energy and enthusiasm, with which the answer of the prophet is animated. By this example I wished to explain on what reasons I was induced to suppose that the term *mashal,* as well from its proper power or meaning as from its usual acceptation, involves an idea of sublimity, and that the Hebrew poetry expresses in its very name and title the particular quality in which it so greatly excels the poetry of all other nations.

The word *sublimity* I wish in this place to be understood in its most extensive sense. I speak not merely of that sublimity which exhibits great objects with a magnificent display of imagery and diction, but that force of composition, whatever it be, which strikes and overpowers the mind, which excites the passions, and which expresses ideas at once with perspicuity and elevation, not solicitous whether the language be plain or ornamented, refined or familiar. In this use of the word I copy Longinus, the most accomplished author on this subject, whether we consider his precepts or his example.

The sublime consists either in language or sentiment, or more frequently in a union of both, since they reciprocally assist each other and since there is a necessary and indissoluble connection between them; this, however, will not prevent our considering them apart with convenience and advantage. The first object, therefore, which presents itself for our investigation is upon what grounds the poetic diction of the Hebrews, whether considered in itself or in comparison with prose composition, is deserving of an appellation immediately expressive of sublimity?

The poetry of every language has a style and form of expression peculiar to itself: forcible, magnificent, and sonorous; the words pompous and energetic; the composition singular and artificial; the whole form and complexion different from what we meet with in common life, and frequently (as with a noble indignation) breaking down the boundaries by which the popular dialect is confined. The language of reason is cool, temperate, rather humble than elevated, well arranged and perspicuous, with an evident care and anxiety lest anything should escape which might appear perplexed or obscure. The language of the passions is totally different: the conceptions burst out into a turbid stream, expressive in a manner of the internal conflict; the more vehement break out in hasty confusion; they catch (without search or study) whatever is impetuous, vivid, or energetic. In a word, reason speaks literally, the passions poetically. The mind, with whatever passion it be agitated, remains fixed upon the object that excited it, and while it is earnest to display it, is not satisfied with a plain and exact description but adopts one agreeable to its own sensations, splendid or gloomy, jocund or unpleasant. For the passions are naturally inclined to amplification; they wonderfully magnify and exaggerate whatever dwells upon the mind, and labor to express it in animated, bold, and magnificent terms. This they commonly effect by two different methods, partly by illustrating the subject with splendid imagery, and partly by employing new and extraordinary forms of expression, which are indeed possessed of great force and efficacy in this respect especially, that they in some degree imitate or represent the present habit and state of the soul. Hence those theories of rhetoricians which they have so pompously detailed, attributing that to art which above all things is due to nature alone:

> For nature to each change of fortune forms
> The secret soul, and all its passions warms;
> Transports to rage, dilates the heart with mirth,
> Wrings the sad soul, and bends it down to earth.
> The tongue these various movements must express.
>
> [Horace, *Art of Poetry*, 155]

A principle which prevades all poetry may easily be conceived to prevail, even in a high degree, in the poetry of the Hebrews. Indeed, we have already seen how daring these writers are in the selection of their imagery, how forcible in the application of it, and what elegance, splendor, and sublimity they have by these means been enabled to infuse into their compositions. With respect to the diction also we have had an opportunity of remarking the peculiar force and dignity of their poetic dialect, as well as the artificial distribution of the sentences, which appears to have been originally closely connected with the metrical arrangement, though the latter be now totally lost. We are, therefore, in the next place, to consider whether there be any other remarkable qualities in the poetical language of the Hebrews which serve to distinguish it from prose composition.

It is impossible to conceive anything more simple and unadorned than the common language of the Hebrews. It is plain, correct, chaste, and temperate; the words are uncommon neither in their meaning nor application; there is no appearance of study, nor even of the least attention to the harmony of the periods. The order of the words is generally regular and uniform. The verb is the first word in the sentence; the noun, which is the agent, immediately succeeds, and the other words follow in their natural order. Each circumstance is exhibited at a single effort, without the least perplexity or confusion of the different parts, and what is remarkable, by the help of a simple particle the whole is connected from the beginning to the end in a continued series, so that nothing appears inconsistent, abrupt, or confused. The whole composition, in fine, is disposed in such an order, and so connected by the continued succession of the different parts, as to demonstrate clearly the regular state of the author and to exhibit the image of a sedate and tranquil mind. But in the Hebrew poetry the case is different, in part at least if not in the whole. The free spirit is hurried along and has neither leisure nor inclination to descend to those minute and frigid attentions. Frequently, instead of disguising the secret feelings of the author, it lays them quite open to public view; and the veil being, as it were, suddenly removed, all the affections and emotions of the soul, its sudden impulses, its hasty sallies and irregularities, are conspicuously displayed.

Should the curious inquirer be desirous of more perfect information upon this subject, he may satisfy himself, I apprehend, with no great labor or difficulty. Let him take the book of Job; let him read the historical proem of that book; let him proceed to the metrical parts; and let him diligently attend to the first speech of Job. He will, I dare believe, confess that, when arrived at the metrical part, he feels as if he were reading another language, and is surprised at a dissimilarity in the style of the two passages much greater than between that of Livy and Virgil, or even Herodotus and Homer. Nor indeed could the fact be otherwise, according to the nature of things, since in the latter passage the most exquisite pathos is displayed, such indeed as has not been exceeded, and scarcely equalled, by any effort of the Muses. Not only the force, the beauty, the sublimity of the sentiments are unrivalled, but such is the character of the diction in general, so vivid is the expression, so interesting the assemblage of objects, so close and connected the sentences, so animated and passionate the whole arrangement that the Hebrew literature itself contains nothing more poetical. The greater part of these beauties are so obvious that they cannot possibly escape the eye of a diligent reader; there are some, however, which, depending chiefly upon the arrangement and construction, are of a more abstruse nature. It also sometimes happens that those beauties which may be easily conceived are very difficult to be explained. While we simply contemplate them, they appear sufficiently manifest; if we approach nearer, and attempt to touch and handle them, they vanish and escape. Since, however, it would not be consistent with my duty on the present occasion to pass them by totally unregarded, I shall rely, Gentlemen, upon your accustomed candor, while I attempt to render, if possible, some of these elegancies more obvious and familiar.

The first thing that arrests the attention of the reader in this passage is the violent sorrow of Job, which bursts forth on a sudden and flows from his heart, where it had long been confined and suppressed:

> Let the day perish, I was born in it; (i.e. in
>   which I was born)
> And the night (which) said, A man is conceived. [3:3]

Observe here the concise and abrupt form of the first verse, and in the second the boldness of the figure and the still more abrupt conclusion. Let the reader then consider whether he could endure such a spirited, vehement, and perplexed form of expression in any prose composition, or even in verse, unless it were expressive of the deepest pathos. He will, nevertheless, I doubt not, acknowledge that the meaning of this sentence is extremely clear—so clear, indeed, that if any person should attempt to make it more copious and explanatory, he would render it less expressive of the mind and feelings of the speaker. It happens fortunately that we have an opportunity of making the experiment upon this very sentiment. There is a passage in Jeremiah so exactly similar that it might almost be imagined a direct imitation; the meaning is the same, nor is there any very great difference in the phraseology; but Jeremiah fills up the ellipses, smooths and harmonizes the rough and uncouth language of Job, and dilates a short distich into two equal distichs, consisting of somewhat longer verses, which is the measure he commonly makes use of:

> Cursed be the day on which I was born;
> The day on which my mother bare me, let it not be blessed.
> Cursed be the man who brought the news to my father,
> Saying, There is a male child born unto thee;
> Making him exceedingly glad. [20:14]

Thus it happens that the imprecation of Jeremiah has more in it of complaint than of indignation; it is milder, softer, and more plaintive, peculiarly calculated to excite pity, in moving which the great excellence of this prophet consists, while that of Job is more adapted to strike us with terror than to excite our compassion.

But to proceed. I shall not trouble you with a tedious discussion of those particulars which are sufficiently apparent: the crowded and abrupt sentences, which seem to have little connection, bursting from the glowing bosom with matchless force and impetuosity; the bold and magnificent expressions, which the eloquence of indignation pours forth, four instances of which occur in the space of twice as many verses, and which seem to be altogether poetical; two of them indeed are found continually in the poets, and in them only; the others are still more uncommon. Omitting these, therefore, the object which at present seems more worthy of examination is that redundancy of expression which, in a few lines, takes [the] place of the former excessive conciseness:

> That night—let darkness seize upon it.

In this also there is the strongest indication of passion and a perturbed mind. He doubtless intended at first to express himself in this manner:

> Be that night darkness—

But, in the very act of uttering it, he suddenly catches at an expression which appears more animated and energetic. I do not know that I can better illustrate this observation than by referring to a passage in Horace, in which a similar transition and redundancy falls from the indignant poet:

> He who—(bane of the fruitful earth!
> Curst was the hour that gave thee birth!)
> He—O vile, pernicious tree!
> Was surely curst who planted thee.
> Well may I think the parricide
> In blood his guilty soul had dy'd;
> Or plung'd his dagger in the breast,
> At midnight, of his sleeping guest;
> Or temper'd every baleful juice
> Which poisonous Colchian glebes produce;
> Or, if a blacker crime be known,
> That crime the wretch had made his own.
>
> [*Odes*, II, xiii, 1]

For undoubtedly the poet began as if he intended to pursue the subject in a regular order, and to finish the sentence in this form: "He who—planted thee; he was accessory to the murder of his parents, and sprinkled his chambers with the blood of his guest; he dealt in the poison of Colchis," etc.; but anger and vexation dissipated the order of his ideas and destroyed the construction of this sentence. But should some officious grammarian take in hand the passage (for this is a very diligent race of beings, and sometimes more than sufficiently exact and scrupulous) and attempt to restore it to its primitive purity and perfection, the whole grace and excellence of that beautiful exordium would be immediately annihilated, all the impetuosity and ardour would in a moment be extinguished. But to return to Job:

> Lo! that night, may it be fruitless!

He appears to have a direct picture or image of that night before his eyes and to point it out with his finger. "The doors of my womb" for "the doors of my mother's womb" is an elliptical form of expression, the meaning of which is easily cleared up, but which no person in a tranquil state of mind, and quite master of himself, would venture to employ. Not to detain you too long upon this subject, I shall produce only one passage more, which is about the conclusion of this animated speech:

> Wherefore should he give light to the miserable?
> And life to those who are in bitterness of soul?
> Who call aloud for death, but it cometh not;
> Who dig for it more than for hidden treasures;
> Who would rejoice even to exultation,
> And be in raptures, if they had found the grave.
> Well might it befit the man whose way is sheltered,
> And whom God hath surrounded with a hedge:
> But my groaning cometh like my daily food,
> And my roarings are poured out like water. [3:20–24]

The whole composition of this passage is admirable, and deserves a minute attention. "Wherefore should he give light to the miserable?" But who is the giver alluded to? Certainly God himself, whom Job has indeed in his mind, but it escaped his notice that no mention is made of him in the preceding lines. He seems to speak of the miserable in general, but by a violent and sudden transition he applies the whole to himself: "But my groaning cometh like my daily food." It is plain, therefore, that in all the preceding reflections he has himself only in view. He makes a transition from the singular to the plural, and back again, a remarkable amplification intervening, expressive of his desire of death, the force and boldness of which is incomparable. At last, as if suddenly recollecting himself, he returns to the former subject, which he had apparently quitted, and resumes the detail of his own misery. From these observations I think it will be manifest that the agitated and disordered state of the speaker's mind is not more evidently demonstrated by a happy boldness of sentiment and imagery and an uncommon force of language than by the very form, conduct, and arrangement of the whole.

The peculiar property which I have labored to demonstrate in this passage will, I apprehend, be found to prevail as a characteristic of the Hebrew poetry, making due allowance for different subjects and circumstances—I mean that vivid and ardent style which is so well calculated to display the emotions and passions of the mind. Hence the poetry of the Hebrews abounds with phrases and idioms totally unsuited to prose composition, and which frequently appear to us harsh and unusual (I had almost said unnatural and barbarous), which, however, are destitute neither of meaning nor of force, were we but sufficiently informed to judge of their true application. It will, however, be worth our while, perhaps, to make the experiment on some other passages of this nature and to try at least what can be done towards the further elucidation of this point.

Lecture XXXIII, "The Poem of Job Not a Perfect Drama"

The poem of Job commonly accounted dramatic and thought by many to be of the same kind with the Greek tragedy; this opinion examined. —A plot or fable essential to a regular drama; its definition and essential qualities according to Aristotle.—Demonstrated, that the poem of Job does not contain any plot; its form and design more fully explained. —Compared with the *Oedipus Tyrannus* of Sophocles; with the *Oedipus Coloneus;* and shown to differ entirely from both in form and manner.

—It is nevertheless a most beautiful and perfect performance in its kind; it approaches very near the form of a perfect drama, and for regularity in form and arrangement justly claims the first place among the poetical compositions of the Hebrews.

When I undertook the present investigation, my principal object was to enable us to form some definite opinion concerning the poem of Job and to assign it its proper place among the compositions of the Hebrew poets. This will possibly appear to some a superfluous and idle undertaking, as the point seems long since to have been finally determined, the majority of the critics having decidedly adjudged it to belong to the dramatic class. Since, however, the term *dramatic,* as I formerly had reason to remark, is in itself extremely ambiguous, the present disquisition will not be confined within the limits of a single question, for the first object of inquiry will necessarily be what idea is affixed to the appellation by those critics who term the book of Job a dramatic poem, and after we have determined this point (if it be possible to determine it, for they do not seem willing to be explicit), we may then with safety proceed to inquire whether, pursuant to that idea, the piece may be justly entitled to this appellation.

A poem is called dramatic either in consequence of its form, the form I mean of a perfect dialogue, which is sustained entirely by the characters or personages without the intervention of the poet (and this was the definition adopted by the ancient critics), or else, according to the more modern acceptation of the word, in consequence of a plot or fable being represented in it. If those who account the book of Job dramatic adhere to the former definition, I have little inclination to litigate the point (and indeed the object of the controversy would scarcely be worth the labor), though a critic, if disposed to be scrupulously exact, might insist that the work, upon the whole, is by no means a perfect dialogue, but consists of a mixture of the narrative and colloquial style, for the historical part, which is all composed in the person of the writer himself, is certainly to be accounted a part of the work itself considered as a whole. Since, however, on the other hand, the historical or narrative part is all evidently written in prose and seems to me to be substituted merely in the place of an argument or comment for the purpose of explaining the rest, and certainly does not constitute any part of the poem, since, moreover, those short sentences which serve to introduce the different speeches contain very little more than the names, I am willing to allow that the structure or form of this poem is on the whole dramatic. But this concession will, I fear, scarcely satisfy the critics in question, for they speak of the regular order and conduct of the piece, and of the dramatic catastrophe; they assert that the interposition of the Deity is a necessary part of the machinery of the fable; they even enumerate the acts and scenes, and use the very same language in all respects as if they spoke of a Greek tragedy, insomuch that when they term the poem of Job dramatic they seem to speak of that species of drama which was cultivated and improved in the theater of Athens. It appears therefore a fair object of inquiry whether the poem of Job be possessed of the peculiar properties of the Greek drama, and may with reason and justice be classed with the theatrical productions of that people.

We have already agreed that the greater and more perfect drama is peculiarly distinguished from the lesser and more common species inasmuch as it retains not only the dramatic form, or the perfect dialogue, but also exhibits some entire action, fable, or plot. And this is perfectly agreeable to the definition of Aristotle, for although he points out many parts or constituents in the composition of a tragedy, he assigns the first place to the plot or fable. This he says is the beginning, this the end; this is the most important part, the very soul of a tragedy, without which it is utterly undeserving of the name, and indeed cannot properly be said to exist. A plot or fable is the representation of an action or event, or of a series of events or incidents tending all to one point, which are detailed with a view to a particular object or conclusion. A tragedy, says the same author, is not a representation of men, but of actions, a picture of life, of prosperity and adversity: in other words, the business of the poem is not merely to exhibit manners only, nor does the most perfect representation of manners constitute a tragedy, for in reality a tragedy may exist with little or no display of manners or character; its business is to exhibit life and action, or some regular train of actions and events, on which depends the felicity or infelicity of the persons concerned. For human happiness or prosperity consists in action, and action is not a quality, but is the end of man. According to our manners we are denominated good or bad, but we are happy or unhappy, prosperous or unsuccessful, according to actions or events. Poets therefore do not form a plot or action merely for the sake of imitating manners or character, but manners and character are added to the plot, and for the sake of it are chiefly attended to. Thus far he has accurately drawn the line between the representation of action and that of manners. He adds, moreover, that unity is essential to a regular plot or action, and that it must be complete in itself, and of a proper length. But to comprehend more perfectly the nature of a plot or fable, it must be observed that there are two principal species, for they are either complex or simple; the former contains some unexpected vicissitude of fortune, such as the recognition of a person at first unknown, the recovery of a lost child, or a sudden change in the situation of the parties, or perhaps both; the latter contains nothing of the kind, but proceeds in one uniform and equal tenor. In every plot or fable, however, be it ever so simple, and though it contain nothing of the wonderful or unexpected, there is always a perplexity or embarrassment, as also a regular solution or catastrophe; the latter must proceed from the former, and indeed must depend upon it, which cannot be the case unless there be a certain order or connexion in the incidents and events which inclines them towards the same end and combines them all in one termination.

On fairly considering these circumstances, I have no hesitation in affirming that the poem of Job contains no plot or action whatever, not even of the most simple kind; it uniformly exhibits one constant state of things, not the smallest change of fortune taking place from the beginning to the end; and it contains merely a representation of those manners, passions, and sentiments which might actually be expected in such a situation. Job is represented as reduced from the summit of human prosperity to a condition the most miserable and afflicted; and the sentiments of both Job and his friends are exactly such as the occasion dictates. For here a new temptation falls upon him, by which the constancy of Job is put to the severest trial; and this circumstance it is that constitutes the principal subject of the poem. Job had, we find, endured the most grievous calamities, the loss of his wealth, the deprivation of his children, and the miserable union of poverty and disease, with so much fortitude and with so just a confidence in his own integrity that nothing could be extorted from him in the least inconsistent with the strictest reverence for the Divine Being; he is now put to the proof whether after enduring all this with firmness and resignation he can with equal patience endure to have his innocence and virtue (in which perhaps he had placed too much confidence) indirectly questioned, and even in plain terms arraigned. Job, now sinking under the weight of his misery, laments his condition with more vehemence than before. His friends reprove his impatience and drop some dark insinuations to the apparent disparagement of his virtue and integrity by entering into very copious declamations concerning the justice of God in proportioning his visitations to the crimes of men. Job is still more violently agitated, and his friends accuse him with less reserve. He appeals to God, and expostulates —with some degree of freedom. They urge and press him in the very heat of his passion, and by still more malignant accusations excite his indignation and his confidence, which were already too vehement. Elihu interposes as an arbiter of the controversy; he reproves the severe spirit of the friends, as well as the presumption of Job, who trusted too much in his own righteousness. Job receives his admonitions with mildness and temper, and being rendered more sedate by his expostulation, makes no reply, though the other appears frequently to expect it. When the Almighty, however, condescends to set before him his rashness, frailty, and ignorance, he submits in perfect humility and with sincere repentance. Here the temptation of Job concludes, in the course of which there was great reason to apprehend he would be totally vanquished. At the same time the poem necessarily terminates, the state of things still remaining without any change or vicissitude whatever. The poem indeed contains a great variety of sentiment, excellent representations of manners and character, remarkable efforts of passion, much important controversy; but no change of fortune, no novelty of incident, no plot, no action.

If indeed we rightly consider, we shall, I dare believe, find that the very nature of the subject excludes even the possibility of a plot or action. From that state of settled and unvarying misery in which Job is involved arises the doubt of his integrity and those insinuations and criminations which serve to exasperate him and by which he is stimulated to expostulate with God and to glory in his own righteousness. It was proper, therefore, that by a continuance of the same state and condition he should be recalled to a humble spirit and to a proper reverence for the Almighty Providence. For it would have been altogether contrary to what is called poetical justice if he had been restored to prosperity previous to his submission and penitence. The repentance of Job, however, we find concludes the poem. Nor was it at all necessary that the question concerning the divine justice should be resolved in the body of the work, either by the fortunate issue of the affairs of Job, or even by the explication of the divine intentions: this, in fact, was not the primary object, nor does it at all constitute the subject of the poem, but is subservient, or in a manner an appendage to it. The disputation which takes place upon this topic is no more than an instrument of temptation, and is introduced in order to explain the inmost sentiments of Job, and to lay open the latent pride that existed in his soul. The Almighty, therefore, when he addresses Job, pays little regard to this point, nor indeed was it necessary, for neither the nature nor the object of the poem required a defence of the Divine Providence, but merely a reprehension of the over-confidence of Job.

If indeed we suppose any change to have taken place in the state of affairs, the nature and subject of the poem will also be changed. If we connect with the poetical part either the former or the latter part of the history, or both, the subject will then be the display of a perfect example of patience in enduring the severest outward calamities and at length receiving an ample reward at the hands of the Almighty; from this, however, the universal tenor of the poem will be found greatly to differ. It will be found to exhibit rather the impatience of Job in bearing the reproaches and abuse of his pretended friends, and this appears to lead to the true object of the poem. For Job is irritated; he indulges his passion; he speaks too confidently of his own righteousness, and in too irreverent a style concerning the justice of God. In the end he is converted by the admonitions of Elihu and the reproofs of his omnipotent Creator. The true object of the poem appears, therefore, to be to demonstrate the necessity of humility, of trust in God, and of the profoundest reverence for the divine decrees, even in the holiest and most exalted characters.

Should it be objected that I have contended with a scrupulous perverseness concerning the meaning of a word, and should it after all be affirmed that this very temptation of Job, this dispute itself, possesses in some degree the form or appearance of an action, I am content to submit the trial to another issue, and to be judged by a fair investigation of the practice of the Greek poets upon similar occasions. There is no necessity to remind this assembly with how much art and design the fable or plot of the *Oedipus Tyrannus* of Sophocles appears to have been constructed, with what powers of imagination and judgment the process of the drama is conducted, and in what manner, by a regular succession of events, arising naturally from each other, the horrid secret is developed which, as soon as disclosed, precipitates the hero of the tragedy from the summit of human happiness into the lowest depths of misery and ruin. Let us only suppose Sophocles to have treated the same subject in a different manner, and to have formed a poem on that part of the story alone which is comprised in the last act. Here Oedipus would be indeed exhibited as an object of the most tender compassion; here would be a spacious field for the display of the most interesting and tragical affections; the fatal catastrophe would be deplored; the blindness, disgrace, exile of the hero would enhance the distress of the scene; and to the bitterness of present calamity would be added the still more bitter remembrance of the past. The poet might copiously display the sorrow and commiseration of his daughters, his detestation of himself and of all that belong to him, and more copiously, of those who had preserved him when exposed, who had supported and educated him: all these topics the poet has slightly touched upon in these lines,

> O curst Cithaeron! why didst thou receive me?
> Or when thou didst, how could'st thou not destroy me?

The succeeding passages are also extremely pathetic. These would easily admit of amplification, and when the ardor of grief was a little abated he might have added his vindication of himself, his asseverations of his innocence, his plea of ignorance and fatal necessity, and his impassioned exclamations against fortune and the gods. From all this might be constructed a poem, great, splendid, copious, diversified; and the subject would also furnish a topic of disputation not unlike that of Job. It might also assume in some measure the dramatic form; the same characters that appear in the tragedy might be introduced; it might possess the exact proportions and all the requisites of a drama, fable alone excepted, which indeed constitutes the very essence of a dramatic poem, and without which all other qualities are of no avail, for the Greeks would have called such a production a monody, or elegiac dialogue, or anything but a tragedy.

This opinion receives still further confirmation from the example and authority of Sophocles himself in another instance. For when he again introduces the same Oedipus upon the stage in another tragedy, though the groundwork of the piece be nearly that which we have been describing, the conduct of it is totally different. This piece is called *Oedipus Coloneus*. The plot or fable is quite simple, on which account it is a fairer object of comparison with the poem of Job than any the plot of which is more complex. Oedipus is introduced blind, exiled, and oppressed with misery; none of those circumstances above-mentioned have escaped the poet, such as the lamentation of his misery, the passionate exclamations against fate and the gods, and the vindication of his innocence. These, however, do not form the basis of the poem; they are introduced merely as circumstances which afford matter of amplification and which seem to flow from that elegant plot or action he has invented. Oedipus, led by his daughter, arrives at Colonus, there to die and be interred according to the admonition of the Oracle, for upon these circumstances the victory of the Athenians over the Thebans was made to depend. The place being accounted sacred, the Athenians are unwilling to receive him, but Theseus affords him refuge and protection. Another of his daughters is introduced, who informs him of the discord between her brothers, also that Creon is coming with an intention of bringing him back to his own country in pursuance of a decree of the Thebans. After this Creon arrives; he endeavors to persuade Oedipus to return to Thebes, and on his refusal, attempts to make use of violence. Theseus protects Oedipus, and in the meantime Polynices arrives, with a view of bringing over his father to his party in the war against the Thebans, this being the only condition on which he was to hope for victory. Oedipus refuses and execrates his son in the severest terms. In conclusion, the answer of the Oracle being communicated to Theseus, Oedipus dies, and is secretly buried there. In this manner is constructed a regular, perfect, and important action or plot, all the parts of which are connected together in one design, and tend exactly to the same conclusion, and in which are involved the fates of both Thebes and Athens. The manners, passions, characters, and sentiments, serve to adorn, but not to support the fable. Without any striking representation of these, the plot or action would still remain and would of itself sustain the tragedy, but if the action be removed, though all the rest remain, it is evident that the tragedy is totally annihilated.

From these observations it will, I think, be evident, that the poem of Job cannot properly be brought into comparison with either *Oedipus* of Sophocles, or with any other of the Greek tragedies. It will be evident, I think, that this poem ought not to be accounted of the same kind, nor can possibly be classed with them, unless the whole nature and form of either the Greek or the Hebrew poem be changed, or unless the plot or action be taken from the one or added to the other, for without this great essential no poem can indeed be accounted a perfect drama.

But though I have urged thus much against its claim to that title, let it not be understood that I wish to derogate from its merits. That censure will rather apply to those who by criticizing it according to foreign and improper rules would make that composition appear lame and imperfect which on the contrary is in its kind most beautiful and perfect. If indeed the extreme antiquity of this poem, the obscurity, and the difficulty that necessarily ensue from that circumstance be considered, and if allowance be made for the total want of plot and action, we shall have cause to wonder at the elegance and interest which we find in its form, conduct, and economy. The arrangement is perfectly regular, and every part is admirably adapted to its end and design. The antiquary or the critic who has been at the pains to trace the history of the Grecian drama from its first weak and imperfect efforts, and has carefully observed its tardy progress to perfection, will scarcely, I think, without astonishment contemplate a poem produced so many ages before, so elegant in its design, so regular in its structure, so animated, so affecting, so near to the true dramatic model, while, on the contrary, the united wisdom of Greece after ages of study was not able to produce anything approaching to perfection in this walk of poetry before the time of Aeschylus. But however this be— whatever rank may be assigned to Job in a comparison with the poets of Greece, to whom we must at least allow the merit of art and method—amongst the Hebrews it must certainly be allowed in this respect to be unrivaled. It is of little consequence whether it be esteemed a didactic or an ethic, a pathetic or dramatic poem; only let it be assigned a distinct and conspicuous station in the highest rank of the Hebrew poetry.

JOSEPH WARTON ✍

The Adventurer (1753)

No. 75, July 24, 1753 [The *Odyssey*, I]

> *Quid virtus et quid sapientia possit,*
> *Utile proposuit nobis exemplar Ulyssem.*
> —Hor. [*Epist.* I. ii. 17]
>
> To show what pious wisdom's power can do,
> The poet sets Ulysses in our view.—Francis

I have frequently wondered at the common practice of our instructors of youth in making their pupils far more intimately acquainted with the *Iliad* than with the *Odyssey* of Homer. This absurd custom, which seems to arise from the supposed superiority of the former poem, has inclined me to make some reflections on the excellence of the latter, a task I am the more readily induced to undertake as so little is performed in the dissertation prefixed by Broome to Pope's translation of this work, which one may venture to pronounce is confused, defective, and dull. Those who receive all their opinions in criticism from custom and authority and never dare to consult the decisions of reason and the voice of nature and truth must not accuse me of being affectedly paradoxical if I endeavor to maintain that the *Odyssey* excels the *Iliad* in many respects and that for several reasons young scholars should peruse it early and attentively.

The moral of this poem is more extensively useful than that of the *Iliad,* which, indeed, by displaying the dire effects of discord among rulers may rectify the conduct of princes and may be called "The Manual of Monarchs," whereas the patience, the prudence, the wisdom, the temperance, and fortitude of Ulysses afford a pattern

the utility of which is not confined within the compass of courts and
palaces, but descends and diffuses its influence over common life
and daily practice.¹ If the fairest examples ought to be placed
before us in an age prone to imitation, if patriotism be preferable
to implacability, if an eager desire to return to one's country and
family be more manly and noble than an eager desire to be
revenged of an enemy, then should our eyes rather be fixed on
Ulysses than Achilles. Unexperienced minds, too easily captivated
with the fire and fury of a gallant general, are apt to prefer courage
to constancy and firmness to humanity. We do not behold the
destroyers of peace and the murderers of mankind with the detestation due to their crimes because we have been inured almost
from our infancy to listen to the praises that have been wantonly
lavished on them by the most exquisite poetry. "The muses,"
to apply the words of an ancient lyric, "have concealed and
decorated the bloody sword with wreaths of myrtle." Let the *Iliad*
be ever ranked at the head of human compositions for its spirit
and sublimity, but let not the milder and, perhaps, more in-
sinuating and attractive beauties of the *Odyssey* be despised and
overlooked. In the one we are placed amidst the rage of storms and
tempests:

> Ὡς δ' ὑπὸ λαίλαπι πᾶσα κελαινὴ βέβριθε χθὼν
> ἤματ' ὀπωρινῷ, ὅτε λαβρότατον χέει ὕδωρ
> Ζεύς, ὅτε δή ῥ' ἄνδρεσσι κοτεσσάμενος χαλεπήνῃ.
>
> [*Iliad* xvi. 384]

> As when in autumn Jove his fury pours,
> And earth is loaden with incessant showers:
> From their deep beds he bids the rivers rise,
> And opens all the flood-gates of the skies.—POPE

In the other, all is tranquil and sedate, and calmly delightful:

> οὔτε ποτ' ὄμβρος,
> ἀλλ' αἰεὶ Ζεφύροιο λιγὺ πνείοντας ἀήτας
> Ὠκεανὸς ἀνίησιν ἀναψύχειν ἀνθρώπους. [*Odyssey* iv. 566]

> Stern winter smiles on that auspicious clime;
> The fields are florid with unfading prime:
> From the bleak pole no winds inclement blow,
> Mold the round hail, or flake the fleecy snow:
> But from the breezy deep, the blest inhale
> The fragrant murmurs of the western gale.—POPE

Accordingly, to distinguish the very different natures of these poems it was anciently the practice of those who publicly recited them to represent the *Iliad,* in allusion to the bloodshed it described, in a robe of scarlet; and the *Odyssey,* on account of the voyages it relates, in an azure vestment.

The predominant passion of Ulysses being the love of his country, for the sake of which he even refuses immortality, the poet has taken every occasion to display it in the liveliest and most striking colors. The first time we behold the hero we find him disconsolately sitting on the solitary shore, sighing to return to Ithaca, νόστον ὀδυρομένῳ, weeping incessantly, and still casting his eyes upon the sea, πόντον ἐπ᾽ ἀτρύγετον δερκέσκετο, δάκρυα λείβων [v.153,84]. "While a goddess," says Minerva at the very beginning of the poem, "by her power and her allurements detains him from Ithaca, he is dying with desire to see even so much as the smoke arise from his much-loved island." *Tarda fluunt ingrataque tempora!* [2] While the luxurious Phaeacians were enjoying a delicious banquet, he attended not to their mirth and music, for the time approached when he was to return to Ithaca; they had prepared a ship for him to set sail the very next morning, and the thoughts of his approaching happiness having engrossed all his soul,

> He sate, and ey'd the sun, and wish'd the night.

> δὴ γὰρ μενέαινε νέεσθαι. [xiii. 30]

To represent his impatience more strongly, the poet adds a most expressive simile, suited to the simplicity of ancient times: "The setting of the sun," says he, "was as welcome and grateful to Ulysses as it is to a well-labored plowman who earnestly waits for its decline that he may return to his supper, δόρπον ἐποίχεσθαι, while his weary knees are painful to him as he walks along."

> Βλάβεται δέ τε γούνατ᾽ ἰόντι. [xiii. 34]

"Notwithstanding all the pleasures and endearments I received from Calypso, yet," says our hero, "I perpetually bedewed with my tears the garments which this immortal beauty gave to me":

> εἵματα δ᾽ αἰεὶ
> δάκρυσι δεύεσκον τὰ μοὶ ἄμβροτα δῶκε Καλυψώ. [vii. 259]

We are presented in every page with fresh instances of this love of his country and his whole behavior convinces us:

ὡς οὐδὲν γλύκιον ἧς πατρίδος, οὐδὲ τοκήων. [ix. 34]

This generous sentiment runs like a golden vein throughout the whole poem. If this animating example were duly and deeply inculcated, how strong an impression would it necessarily make upon the yielding minds of youth when melted and mollified by the warmth of such exalted poetry!

Nor is the *Odyssey* less excellent and useful in the amiable pictures it affords of private affections and domestic tendernesses:

> And all the charities
> Of father, son, and brother.
> —MILTON [*P.L.*, IV, 756]

When Ulysses descends into the infernal regions, it is finely contrived that he should meet his aged mother Anticlea. After his first sorrow and surprise, he eagerly inquires into the causes of her death and adds, "Doth my father yet live? Does my son possess my dominions or does he groan under the tyranny of some usurper who thinks I shall never return? Is my wife still constant to my bed? Or hath some noble Grecian married her?" These questions are the very voice of nature and affection. Anticlea answers that "she herself died with grief for the loss of Ulysses, that Laertes languishes away life in solitude and sorrow for him, and that Penelope perpetually and inconsolably bewails his absence and sighs for his return."

When the hero, disguised like a stranger, has the first interview with his father, whom he finds diverting his cares with rural amusements in his little garden, he informs him that he had seen his son in his travels but now despairs of beholding him again. Upon this the sorrow of Laertes is inexpressible: Ulysses can counterfeit no longer, but exclaims ardently,

> I, I am he! O father rise! behold
> Thy son! [POPE, XXIV, 375]

And the discovery of himself to Telemachus, in the Sixteenth Book, in a speech of short and broken exclamations is equally tender and pathetic.

The duties of universal benevolence, of charity, and of hospitality, that unknown and unpracticed virtue, are perpetually inculcated with more emphasis and elegance than in any ancient philosopher, and I wish I could not add than in any modern. Ulysses meets with a friendly reception in all the various nations to which he is driven, who declare their inviolable obligations to protect and cherish the stranger and the wanderer. Above all, how amiable is the behavior of Eumeus to his unknown master, who asks for his charity! "It is not lawful for me," says the δῖον ὑφορβσος, "I dare not despise any stranger or indigent man, even if he were much meaner than thou appearest to be, for the poor and strangers are sent to us by Jupiter!" [xiv. 3] "Keep," says Epictetus, "continually in thy memory what Eumeus speaks in Homer to the disguised Ulysses." [3] I am sensible that many superficial French critics have endeavored to ridicule all that passes at the lodge of Eumeus as coarse and indelicate and below the dignity of epic poetry, but let them attend to the following observation of the greatest genius of their nation: "Since it is delightful," says Fénelon, "in one of Titian's landscapes to see the goats climbing up a hanging rock, or to behold in one of Teniers' pieces a country feast and rustic dances, it is no wonder that we are pleased with such natural descriptions as we find in the *Odyssey*. This simplicity of manners seems to recall the golden age. I am more pleased with honest Eumeus than with the polite heroes of *Clelia* or *Cleopatra*." [4]

The moral precepts with which every page of the *Odyssey* is pregnant are equally noble. Plato's wish is here accomplished, for we behold Virtue personally appearing to the sons of men in her most awful and most alluring charms.[5]

The remaining reasons why the *Odyssey* is equal if not superior to the *Iliad*, and why it is a poem most peculiarly proper for the perusal of youth are, because the great variety of events and scenes it contains interest and engage the attention more than the *Iliad*, because characters and images drawn from familiar life are more useful to the generality of readers and are also more difficult to be drawn, and because the conduct of this poem, considered as the most perfect of epopees, is more artful and judicious than that of the other. The discussion of these beauties will make the subject of some ensuing paper.

No. 80, August 11, 1753   [The *Odyssey*, II]

Non desunt crassi quidam, qui studiosos ab hujusmodi libris deterreant,
ceu poeticis, ut vocant, et ad morum integritatem officientibus. Ego
vero dignos censeo quos et omnibus in ludis praelegant adoloscentiae
literatores, et sibi legant relegantque senes.—ERASMUS

There are not wanting persons so dull and insensible as to deter students
from reading books of this kind, which, they say, are poetical and pernicious to the purity of morals; but I am of opinion that they are not only
worthy to be read by the instructors of youth in their schools but that
the old and experienced should again and again peruse them.

Greatness, novelty, and beauty are usually and justly reckoned
the three principal sources of the pleasures that strike the imagination. If the *Iliad* be allowed to abound in objects that may be
referred to the first species, yet the *Odyssey* may boast a greater
number of images that are beautiful and uncommon. The vast
variety of scenes perpetually shifting before us, the train of unexpected events, and the many sudden turns of fortune in this
diversified poem must more deeply engage the reader and keep his
attention more alive and active than the martial uniformity of
the *Iliad*. The continual glare of a single color that unchangeably
predominates throughout a whole piece is apt to dazzle and disgust
the eye of the beholder. I will not, indeed, presume to say with
Voltaire that among the greatest admirers of antiquity there is
scarce one to be found who could ever read the *Iliad* with that
eagerness and rapture which a woman feels when she peruses of the
novel of *Zayde*,[6] but will, however, venture to affirm that the
speciosa miracula of the *Odyssey* are better calculated to excite our
curiosity and wonder and to allure us forward with unextinguished
impatience to the catastrophe than the perpetual tumult and terror
that reign through the *Iliad*.

The boundless exuberance of his imagination, his unwearied
spirit and fire, ἀκάματον πῦρ, has enabled Homer to diversify the
descriptions of his battles with many circumstances of great variety;
sometimes by specifying the different characters, ages, professions,
or nations of his dying heroes; sometimes by describing different
kinds of wounds and deaths; and sometimes by tender and pathetic

strokes, which remind the reader of the aged parent who is fondly
expecting the return of his son just murdered, of the desolate
condition of the widows who will now be enslaved, and of the
children that will be dashed against the stones. But notwithstanding this delicate art and address in the poet, the subject remains
the same, and from this sameness, it will, I fear, grow tedious and
insipid to impartial readers. These small modifications and adjuncts
are not sufficiently efficacious to give the grace of novelty to repetition and to make tautology delightful; the battles are indeed nobly
and variously painted, yet still they are only battles. But when we
accompany Ulysses through the manifold perils he underwent by
sea and land and visit with him the strange nations to which the
anger of Neptune has driven him, all whose manners and customs
are described in the most lively and picturesque terms; when we
survey the wondrous monsters he encountered and escaped,

Antiphaten, Scyllamque, et cum Cyclope Charybdin; [7]

when we see him refuse the charms of Calypso and the cup of
Circe; when we descend with him into hell and hear him converse
with all the glorious heroes that assisted at the Trojan war; when
after struggling with ten thousand difficulties unforeseen and almost
unsurmountable he is at last restored to the peaceable possession of
his kingdom and his queen; when such objects as these are displayed, so new and so interesting; when all the descriptions,
incidents, scenes, and persons differ so widely from each other; then
it is that poetry becomes "a perpetual feast of nectared sweets," [8]
and a feast of such an exalted nature as to produce neither satiety or
disgust.

But besides its variety, the *Odyssey* is the most amusing and
entertaining of all other poems on account of the pictures it
preserves to us of ancient manners, customs, laws, and politics, and
of the domestic life of the heroic ages. The more any nation
becomes polished, the more the genuine feelings of nature are
disguised, and their manners are consequently less adapted to bear
a faithful description. Good breeding is founded on the dissimula-
tion or suppression of such sentiments as may probably provoke or
offend those with whom we converse. The little forms and ceremonies which have been introduced into civil life by the moderns
are not suited to the dignity and simplicity of the epic Muse. The
coronation feast of a European monarch would not shine half so

much in poetry as the simple supper prepared for Ulysses at the
Phaeacian court; the gardens of Alcinous are much fitter for description than those of Versailles; and Nausicaa, descending to the
river to wash her garments, and dancing afterwards upon the banks
with her fellow virgins like Diana amidst her nymphs,

ῥεῖά τ᾽ ἀριγνώτη πέλεται, καλαὶ δέ τε πᾶσαι, [vi. 108]

is a far more graceful figure than the most glittering lady in the
drawing room, with a complexion plastered to repair the vigils of
cards and a shape violated and destroyed by a stiff brocade and an
immeasurable hoop. The compliment also which Ulysses pays to
this innocent unadorned beauty, especially when he compares her
to a young palm tree of Delos, contains more gallantry and elegance
than the most applauded sonnet of the politest French marquis that
ever rhymed. However indelicate I may be esteemed, I freely confess
I had rather sit in the grotto of Calypso than in the most pompous
saloon of Louis XV. The tea and the card tables can be introduced
with propriety and success only in the mock-heroic, as they have
been very happily in the *Rape of the Lock,* but the present modes
of life must be forgotten when we attempt anything in the serious
or sublime poetry, for heroism disdains the luxurious refinements,
the false delicacy and state of modern ages. The primeval, I was
about to say patriarchal, simplicity of manners displayed in the
Odyssey is a perpetual source of true poetry, is inexpressibly pleasing to all who are uncorrupted by the business and the vanities of
life, and may therefore prove equally instructive and captivating to
younger readers.

It seems to be a tenet universally received among common critics
as certain and indisputable that images and characters of peaceful
and domestic life are not so difficult to be drawn as pictures of war
and fury. I own myself of a quite contrary opinion, and think the
description of Andromache parting with Hector in the *Iliad* and
the tender circumstance of the child Astyanax starting back from
his father's helmet and clinging to the bosom of his nurse are as
great efforts of the imagination of Homer as the dreadful picture of
Achilles fighting with the rivers or dragging the carcass of Hector
at his chariot wheels; the behavior of Hecuba, when she points to
the breast that had suckled her dear Hector, is as finely conceived as
the most gallant exploits of Diomede and Ajax. The natural is as
strong an evidence of true genius as the sublime. It is in such images

the *Odyssey* abounds, the superior utility of which, as they more nearly concern and more strongly affect us, need not be pointed out. Let Longinus admire the majesty of Neptune whirling his chariot over the deep, surrounded by sea monsters that gamboled before their king; the description of the dog Argus creeping to the feet of his master, whom he alone knew in his disguise, and expiring with joy for his return is so inexpressibly pathetic that it equals if not exceeds any of the magnificent and bolder images which that excellent critic hath produced in his treatise on the sublime. He justly commends the prayer of Ajax, who, when he was surrounded with a thick darkness that prevented the display of his prowess, begs of Jupiter only to remove the clouds that involved him, "and then," he says, "destroy me if thou wilt in the daylight," ἐν δὲ φάει καὶ ὄλεσσον.⁹ But surely the reflections which Ulysses makes to Amphinomus, the most virtuous of the suitors, concerning the misery and vanity of man will be found to deserve equal commendations if we consider their propriety, solemnity, and truth. Our hero, in the disguise of a beggar, had just been spurned at and ridiculed by the rest of the riotous lovers, but is kindly relieved by Amphinomus, whose behavior is finely contrasted to the brutality of his brethren. Upon which Ulysses says, "Hear me, O Amphinomus! and ponder the words I shall speak unto thee. Of all creatures that breathe or creep upon the earth, the most weak and impotent is man. For he never thinks that evil shall befall him at another season, while the Gods bestow on him strength and happiness. But when the immortal Gods afflict him with adversity, he bears it with unwillingness and repining. Such is the mind of the inhabitants of earth, that it changes as Jupiter sends happiness or misery. I once numbered myself among the happy and, elated with prosperity and pride and relying on my family and friends, committed many acts of injustice. But let no man be proud or unjust, but receive whatever gifts the Gods bestow on him with humility and silence" [xviii. 125]. I chose to translate this sententious passage as literally as possible, to preserve the air of its venerable simplicity and striking solemnity. If we recollect the speaker, and the occasion of the speech, we cannot fail of being deeply affected. Can we, therefore, forbear giving our assent to the truth of the title which Alcidamas, according to Aristotle in his *Rhetoric,* bestows on the *Odyssey,* who calls it "a beautiful mirror of human life," καλὸν ἀνθρωπίνου βίου κάτοπτρον. [iii. 3].

Homer, in the *Iliad*, resembles the river Nile when it descends in a cataract that deafens and astonishes the neighboring inhabitants. In the *Odyssey* he is still like the same Nile when its genial inundations gently diffuse fertility and fatness over the peaceful plains of Egypt.

No. 101, October 23, 1753   [Milton]

Est ubi peccat.—HOR. [*Epist.* II. i. 63]

To the Adventurer

SIR,

If we consider the high rank which Milton has deservedly obtained among our few English classics, we cannot wonder at the multitude of commentaries and criticisms of which he has been the subject. To these I have added some miscellaneous remarks, and if you should at first be inclined to reject them as trifling, you may, perhaps, determine to admit them when you reflect that they are new.

The description of Eden in the Fourth Book of the *Paradise Lost*, and the battle of the angels in the Sixth, are usually selected as the most striking examples of a florid and vigorous imagination, but it requires much greater strength of mind to form an assemblage of natural objects and range them with propriety and beauty than to bring together the greatest variety of the most splendid images without any regard to their use or congruity; as in painting, he who by the force of his imagination can delineate a landscape is deemed a greater master than he who by heaping rocks of coral upon tesselated pavements can only make absurdity splendid and dispose gaudy colors so as best to set off each other.

Sapphire fountains that rolling over orient pearl run nectar, roses without thorns, trees that bear fruit of vegetable gold and that weep odorous gums and balms [10] are easily feigned, but having no relative beauty as pictures of nature, nor any absolute excellence as derived from truth, they can only please those who when they read exercise no faculty but fancy and admire because they do not think.

If I shall not be thought to digress wholly from my subject, I would illustrate this remark by comparing two passages written by Milton and Fletcher on nearly the same subject. The spirit in *Comus* thus pays his address of thanks to the water nymph Sabrina,

> May thy brimmed waves for this,
> Their full tribute never miss
> From a thousand petty rills,
> That tumble down the snowy hills:
> Summer drouth, or singed air,
> Never scorch thy tresses fair;
> Nor wet *October's* torrent flood
> Thy molten chrystal fill with mud. [924]

Thus far the wishes are most proper for the welfare of a river goddess; the circumstance of summer not scorching her tresses is highly poetical and elegant, but what follows, though it is pompous and majestic, is unnatural and far fetched,

> May thy billows roll ashore
> The beryl, and the golden ore,
> May thy lofty head be crown'd
> With many a tower and terrace round;
> And here and there, thy banks upon,
> With Groves of myrrh and cinnamon! [931]

The circumstance in the third and forth lines is happily fancied, but what idea can the reader have of an English river rolling gold and the beryl ashore, or of groves of cinnamon growing on its banks? The images in the following passage of Fletcher are all simple and real, all appropriated and strictly natural,

> For thy kindness to me shown,
> Never from thy banks be blown
> Any tree, with windy force,
> Cross thy stream to stop thy course:
> May no beast that comes to drink,
> With his horns cast down thy brink:
> May none that for thy fish do look,
> Cut thy banks to dam thy brook;
> Barefoot may no neighbour wade
> In thy cool streams, wife or maid,
> When the spawn on stones do lie,
> To wash their hemp, and spoil the fry.[11]

The glaring picture of Paradise is not, in my opinion, so strong an evidence of Milton's force of imagination as his representation of Adam and Eve when they left it and of the passions with which they were agitated on that event.

Against his battle of the Angels I have the same objections as against his garden of Eden. He has endeavored to elevate his combatants by giving them the enormous stature of giants in romances, books of which he was known to be fond; and the prowess and behavior of Michael as much resemble the feats of Ariosto's knights as his two-handed sword does the weapons of chivalry. I think the sublimity of his genius much more visible in the first appearance of the fallen Angels, the debates of the infernal peers, the passage of Satan through the dominions of Chaos and his adventure with Sin and Death, the mission of Raphael to Adam, the conversations between Adam and his wife, the creation, the account which Adam gives of his first sensations and of the approach of Eve from the hand of her Creator, the whole behavior of Adam and Eve after the first transgression, and the prospect of the various states of the world and history of man, exhibited in vision to Adam.

In this vision, Milton judiciously represents Adam as ignorant of what disaster had befallen Abel when he was murdered by his brother, but during his conversation with Raphael, the poet seems to have forgotten this necessary and natural ignorance of the first man. How was it possible for Adam to discern what the Angel meant by "cubic phalanxes," by "planets of aspect malign," by "encamping on the foughten field," by "van and rear," by "standards and gonfalons and glittering tissues," by "the girding sword," by "embattled squadrons," "chariots," and "flaming arms and fiery steeds?" And although Adam possessed a superior degree of knowledge, yet doubtless he had not skill enough in chemistry to understand Raphael, who informed him that

> Sulphurous and Nitrous Foam
> They found, they mingl'd, and with subtle Art,
> Concocted and adusted, they reduc'd
> To blackest grain, and into store convey'd. [*P.L.*, VI, 512]

And surely the nature of cannon was not much explained to Adam, who neither knew or wanted the use of iron tools, by telling him that they resembled the hollow bodies of oak or fir,

> With branches lopt, in Wood or Mountain fell'd. [VI, 575]

He that never beheld the brute creation but in its pastimes and sports, must have greatly wondered when the Angel expressed the flight of the Satanic host by saying that they fled

> As a Herd
> Of Goats or timorous flock together throng'd. [VI, 856]

But as there are many exuberances in this poem, there appears to be also some defects. As the serpent was the instrument of the temptation, Milton minutely describes its beauty and allurements, and I have frequently wondered that he did not, for the same reason, give a more elaborate description of the tree of life, especially as he was remarkable for his knowledge and imitation of the Sacred Writings, and as the following passage in the *Revelations* afforded him a hint from which his creative fancy might have worked up a striking picture. "In the midst of the street of it, and on either side of the river, was there the tree of life; which bare twelve manner of fruits, and yielded her fruit every month: and the leaves of the tree were for the healing of the nations" [Rev. 22:2].

At the end of the Fourth Book, suspense and attention are excited to the utmost; a combat between Satan and the guardians of Eden is eagerly expected, and curiosity is impatient for the action and the catastrophe, but this horrid fray is prevented, expectation is cut off, and curiosity disappointed by an expedient which, though applauded by Addison and Pope and imitated from Homer and Virgil, will be deemed frigid and inartificial by all who judge from their own sensations and are not content to echo the decisions of others. The golden balances are held forth, "which," says the poet, "are yet seen betwixt Astrea and the Scorpion"; Satan looks up, and perceiving that his scale mounted aloft, departs with the shades of Night. To make such a use, at so critical a time, of Libra, a mere imaginary sign of the Zodiac, is scarcely justifiable in a poem founded on religious truth.

Among innumerable beauties in the *Paradise Lost,* I think the most transcendent is the speech of Satan at the beginning of the Ninth Book, in which his unextinguishable pride and fierce indignation against God and his envy towards Man are so blended with an involuntary approbation of goodness, and disdain of the meanness and baseness of his present undertaking, as to render it, on account of the propriety of its sentiments and its turns of passion, the most natural, most spirited, and truly dramatic speech that is, perhaps, to be found in any writer whether ancient or modern; and yet Mr. Addison has passed it over unpraised and unnoticed.

If an apology should be deemed necessary for the freedom here used with our inimitable bard, let me conclude in the words of Longinus: "Whoever was carefully to collect the blemishes of Homer, Demosthenes, Plato, and of other celebrated writers of the same rank, would find they bore not the least proportion to the sublimities and excellencies with which their works abound." [12]

I am, Sir
Your humble servant
PALAEOPHILUS

An Essay on the Genius and Writings of Pope (1756, 1782) [13]

To the Reverend Dr. Young, Rector of Welwyn, in Hertfordshire [14]

DEAR SIR,

Permit me to break into your retirement, the residence of virtue and literature, and to trouble you with a few reflections on the merits and real character of an admired author and on other collateral subjects of criticism that will naturally arise in the course of such an inquiry. No love of singularity, no affectation of paradoxical opinions, gave rise to the following work. I revere the memory of Pope, I respect and honor his abilities, but I do not think him at the head of his profession. In other words, in that species of poetry wherein Pope excelled he is superior to all mankind; and I only say that this species of poetry is not the most excellent one of the art.

We do not, it should seem, sufficiently attend to the difference there is betwixt a man of wit, a man of sense, and a true poet. Donne and Swift were undoubtedly men of wit and men of sense, but what traces have they left of pure poetry? It is remarkable that

Dryden says of Donne, "He was the greatest wit, though not the greatest poet, of this nation." [15] Fontenelle and La Motte are entitled to the former character, but what can they urge to gain the latter? Which of these characters is the most valuable and useful is entirely out of the question. All I plead for is to have their several provinces kept distinct from each other and to impress on the reader that a clear head and acute understanding are not sufficient alone to make a poet; that the most solid observations on human life expressed with the utmost elegance and brevity are morality, and not poetry; that the *Epistles* of Boileau in rhyme are no more poetical than the *Characters* of La Bruyère in prose; and that it is a creative and glowing *imagination, acer spiritus ac vis,*[16] and that alone, that can stamp a writer with this exalted and very uncommon character which so few possess and of which so few can properly judge.

For one person who can adequately relish and enjoy a work of imagination, twenty are to be found who can taste and judge of observations on familiar life and the manners of the age. The satires of Ariosto are more read than the *Orlando Furioso,* or even Dante. Are there so many cordial admirers of Spenser and Milton as of *Hudibras,* if we strike out of the number of these supposed admirers those who appear such out of fashion and not of feeling? Swift's "Rhapsody on Poetry" is far more popular than Akenside's noble "Ode to Lord Huntingdon." The epistles on the characters of men and women and your sprightly satires,[17] my good friend, are more frequently perused and quoted than "L'Allegro" and "Il Penseroso" of Milton. Had you written only these satires, you would, indeed, have gained the title of a man of wit and a man of sense, but, I am confident, would not insist on being denominated a poet merely on their account.

Non satis est puris versum perscribere verbis.[18]

It is amazing this matter should ever have been mistaken, when Horace has taken particular and repeated pains to settle and adjust the opinion in question. He has more than once disclaimed all right and title to the name of poet on the score of his ethic and satiric pieces.

Neque enim concludere versum
dixeris esse satis.[19]

are lines often repeated, but whose meaning is not extended and weighed as it ought to be. Nothing can be more judicious than the method he prescribes of trying whether any composition be essentially poetical or not, which is to drop entirely the measures and numbers and transpose and invert the order of the words, and in this unadorned manner to peruse the passage.[20] If there be really in it a true poetical spirit, all your inversions and transpositions will not disguise and extinguish it, but it will retain its luster like a diamond unset and thrown back into the rubbish of the mine. Let us make a little experiment on the following well-known lines:

Yes, you despise the man that is confined to books, who rails at humankind from his study, though what he learns he speaks, and may perhaps advance some general maxims or may be right by chance. The coxcomb bird, so grave and so talkative, that cries whore, knave, and cuckold from his cage, though he rightly call many a passenger, you hold him no philosopher. And yet, such is the fate of all extremes, men may be read too much, as well as books. We grow more partial, for the sake of the observer, to observations which we ourselves make; less so to written wisdom, because another's. Maxims are drawn from notions, and those from guess.[21]

What shall we say of this passage? Why, that it is most excellent sense, but just as poetical as the "Qui fit Maecenas" of the author who recommends this method of trial. Take ten lines of the *Iliad*, *Paradise Lost*, or even of the *Georgics* of Virgil, and see whether, by any process of critical chemistry, you can lower and reduce them to the tameness of prose. You will find that they will appear like Ulysses in his disguise of rags, still a hero, though lodged in the cottage of the herdsman Eumaeus.

The sublime and the pathetic are the two chief nerves of all genuine poesy. What is there transcendently sublime or pathetic in Pope? [22] In his works there is, indeed, *nihil inane, nihil arcessitum; puro tamen fonti quam magno flumini proprior,* as the excellent Quintilian remarks of Lysias.[23] And because I am, perhaps, unwilling [24] to speak out in plain English, I will adopt the following passage of Voltaire, which in my opinion as exactly characterizes Pope as it does his model Boileau, for whom it was originally designed:

Incapable peut-être du sublime qui élève l'âme, et du sentiment qui l'attendrit, mais fait pour éclairer ceux à qui la nature accorda l'un et l'autre, laborieux, sévère, précis, pur, harmonieux, il devint, enfin, le poète de la raison.[25]

Our English poets may, I think, be disposed in four different classes and degrees. In the first class I would place our only three sublime and pathetic poets: Spenser, Shakespeare, Milton.[26] In the second class should be ranked such as possessed the true poetical genius in a more moderate degree, but who had noble talents for moral, ethical, and panegyrical poesy.[27] At the head of these are Dryden, Prior, Addison, Cowley, Waller, Garth, Fenton, Gay, Denham, Parnell.[28] In the third class may be placed men of wit, of elegant taste, and lively fancy in describing familiar life, though not the higher scenes of poetry.[29] Here may be numbered Butler, Swift, Rochester, Donne, Dorset, Oldham.[30] In the fourth class the mere versifiers, however smooth and mellifluous some of them may be thought, should be disposed. Such as Pitt, Sandys, Fairfax, Broome, Buckingham, Lansdowne. This enumeration is not intended as a complete catalogue of writers, and in their proper order, but only to mark out briefly the different species of our celebrated authors.[31] In which of these classes Pope deserves to be placed the following work is intended to determine.

> *I am,* DEAR SIR,
> 1756.   *Your affectionate*
> *And faithful servant*

From Section I, "Of the Pastorals and *The Messiah*, an Eclogue" [32]

Princes and authors are seldom spoken of during their lives with justice and impartiality. Admiration and envy, their constant attendants, like two unskillful artists, are apt to overcharge their pieces with too great a quantity of light or of shade, and are disqualified happily to hit upon that middle color, that mixture of error and excellence which alone renders every representation of man just and natural. This, perhaps, may be one reason, among others, why we have never yet seen a fair and candid criticism on the character and merits of our last great poet, Mr. Pope. I have therefore thought that it would be no unpleasing amusement or uninstructive employment to examine at large, without blind panegyric or petulant invective, the writings of this English classic in the order in which they are arranged in the nine volumes of the elegant edition of Dr. Warburton. As I shall neither censure nor commend without alleging the reason on which my opinion is founded, I shall be entirely unmoved at the imputation of malignity or the clamors of popular prejudice.

It is somewhat strange that in the pastorals of a young poet there should not be found a single rural image that is new, but this, I am afraid, is the case in the pastorals before us. The ideas of Theocritus, Virgil, and Spenser are, indeed, here exhibited in language equally mellifluous and pure, but the descriptions and sentiments are trite and common.

That the design of pastoral poesy is to represent the undisturbed felicity of the golden age is an empty notion which, though supported by a Rapin and a Fontenelle,[33] I think all rational critics have agreed to extirpate and explode. But I do not remember that even these, or any critics, have remarked the circumstance that gave origin to the opinion that any golden age was intended. Theocritus, the father and the model of this enchanting species of composition, lived and wrote in Sicily. The climate of Sicily was delicious, and the face of the country various and beautiful; its valleys and its precipices, its grottoes and cascades were "sweetly interchanged," and its flowers and fruits were lavish and luscious. The poet described what he saw and felt, and had no need to have recourse to those artificial assemblages of pleasing objects which are not to be found in nature. The figs and the honey which he assigns as a reward to a victorious shepherd were in themselves exquisite, and are therefore assigned with great propriety; and the beauties of that luxurious landscape, so richly and circumstantially delineated in the close of the Seventh Idyllium, where all things smelled of summer and smelled of autumn,

$$\pi\acute{a}\nu\tau' \ \mathring{\omega}\sigma\delta\epsilon\nu \ \theta\acute{\epsilon}\rho\epsilon os \ \mu\acute{a}\lambda a \ \pi\acute{\iota}o\nu os, \ \mathring{\omega}\sigma\delta\epsilon \ \delta' \ o\pi\acute{\omega}\rho as\cdot \ [\text{vii. } 143]$$

were present and real. Succeeding writers, supposing these beauties too great and abundant to be real, referred them to the fictitious and imaginary scenes of a golden age.

A mixture of British and Grecian ideas may justly be deemed a blemish in the pastorals of Pope, and propriety is certainly violated when he couples Pactolus with Thames, and Windsor with Hybla. Complaints of "immoderate heat" and wishes to be conveyed to cooling caverns, when uttered by the inhabitants of Greece, have a decorum and consistency which they totally lose in the character of a British shepherd; and Theocritus, during the ardors of Sirius, must have heard the murmurings of a brook and the whispers of a pine with more home-felt pleasure than Pope could possibly experience upon the same occasion. We can never completely relish or adequately understand any author, especially any ancient, except we constantly keep in our eye his climate, his country, and his age. Pope himself informs us in a note that he judiciously omitted the following verse,

> And list'ning wolves grow milder as they hear,

on account of the absurdity, which Spenser overlooked, of introducing wolves into England. But on this principle, which is certainly a just one, may it not be asked why he should speak, the scene lying in Windsor Forest, of the "sultry Sirius," of the "grateful clusters" of grapes, of a pipe of reeds, the antique fistula, of thanking Ceres for a plentiful harvest, of the sacrifice of lambs, with many other instances that might be adduced to this purpose. That Pope, however, was sensible of the importance of adapting images to the scene of action is obvious from the following example of his judgment, for in translating

> Audiit *Eurotas,* jussitque ediscere *lauros,*

he has dexterously dropped the *laurels* appropriated to Eurotas, as he is speaking of the river Thames, and has rendered it,

> Thames heard the numbers as he flow'd along,
> And bade his *willows* learn the moving song.

In the passages which Pope has imitated from Theocritus and from his Latin translator, Virgil, he has merited but little applause. It may not be unentertaining to see how coldly and unpoetically Pope has copied the subsequent appeal to the nymphs on the death of Daphnis in comparison of Milton on "Lycidas," one of his juvenile, but one of his most exquisite pieces.[34]

> Πᾷ ποκ᾽ ἄρ ἦσθ᾽, ὅκα Δάφνις ἐτάκετο, πᾷ ποκα Νύμφαι;
> ἢ κατὰ Πηνειῶ καλὰ τέμπεα; ἢ κατὰ Πίνδω;

οὐ γὰρ δὴ ποταμοῖο μέγαν ῥόον εἶχετ' Ἀνάπω,
οὐδ' Αἴτνας σκοπιάν, οὐδ' Ἄκιδος ἱερὸν ὕδωρ. [i. 66]

Where stray ye, Muses! in what lawn or grove,
While your Alexis pines in hopeless love?
In those fair fields where sacred Isis glides,
Or else where Cam his winding vales divides?

[*Pastorals*, II, 23]

Where were ye Nymphs when the remorseless deep
Clos'd o'er the head of your lov'd *Lycidas?*
For neither were ye playing on the steep,
Where your old *Bards,* the famous *Druids,* lie,
Nor on the shaggy top of *Mona* high,
Nor yet where *Deva* spreads her wizard stream.

The mention of places remarkably romantic, the supposed habitation of druids, bards, and wizards, is far more pleasing to the imagination than the obvious introduction of Cam and Isis as seats of the Muses.

.   .   .   .   .   .

Upon the whole, the principal merit of the pastorals of Pope consists in their correct and musical versification, musical to a degree of which rhyme could hardly be thought capable, and in giving the first specimen of that harmony in English verse which is now become indispensably necessary, and which has so forcibly and universally influenced the public ear as to have rendered every moderate rhymer melodious. Pope lengthened the abruptness of Waller and at the same time contracted the exuberance of Dryden.

I remember to have been informed by an intimate friend of Pope that he had once laid a design of writing American eclogues. The subject would have been fruitful of the most poetical imagery and, if properly executed, would have rescued the author from the accusation here urged of having written eclogues without invention.

Our author, who had received an early tincture of religion, a reverence for which he preserved to the last, was with justice convinced that the scriptures of God contained not only the purest precepts of morality but the most elevated and sublime strokes of genuine poesy, strokes as much superior to anything heathenism can produce as is Jehovah to Jupiter. This is the case more particularly in the exalted prophecy of Isaiah, which Pope has so

successfully versified in an eclogue that incontestably surpasses the
Pollio of Virgil, although perhaps the dignity, the energy, and the
simplicity of the original are in a few passages weakened and
diminished by florid epithets and useless circumlocutions.

> See Nature hastes her earliest wreaths to bring,
> With all the incense of the breathing spring [*Messiah,* 23]

are lines which have too much prettiness and too modern an air.
The judicious addition of circumstances and adjuncts is what
renders poesy a more lively imitation of nature than prose. Pope has
been happy in introducing the following circumstance: The
prophet says, "The parched ground shall become a pool." Our
author expresses this idea by saying that the shepherd

> Shall start, amidst the thirsty wilds, to hear
> New falls of water murm'ring in his ear. [69]

A striking example of a similar beauty may be added from Thomson. Melisander, in the tragedy of *Agamemnon,* after telling us he
was conveyed in a vessel at midnight to the wildest of the Cyclades,
adds when the pitiless mariners had left him in that dreadful
solitude,

> I never heard
> A sound so dismal as their parting oars! [III, i]

On the other hand the prophet has been sometimes particular
when Pope has been only general:

Lift up thine eyes round about, and see: all they gather themselves together, they come to thee. . . . The multitude of camels shall cover
thee, the dromedaries of Midian and Ephah; all they from Sheba shall
come: they shall bring gold and incense; and they shall shew forth
the praises of the Lord. All the flocks of Kedar shall be gathered together unto thee, the rams of Nebaioth shall minister unto thee.
[Isaiah 60:4–7]

In imitating this passage, Pope has omitted the different beasts
that in so picturesque a manner characterize the different countries
which were to be gathered together on this important event, and
says only in undistinguishing terms:

> See, barb'rous nations at thy gates attend,
> Walk in thy light, and in thy temple bend!
> See thy bright altars throng'd with prostrate kings
> And heap'd with products of Sabaean springs! [91]

As prosperity and happiness are described in this eclogue by a combination of the most pleasing and agreeable objects, so misery and destruction are as forcibly delineated in the same Isaiah by the circumstances of distress and desolation that were to attend the fall of that magnificent city Babylon, and the latter is perhaps a more proper and interesting subject for poetry than the former, as such kinds of objects make the deepest impression on the mind, terror being a stronger sensation than joy.[35]

.   .   .   .   .

From Section II, "Of 'Windsor Forest' and Lyric Pieces"

.   .   .   .   .

It is one of the greatest and most pleasing arts of descriptive poetry to introduce moral sentences and instructions in an oblique and indirect manner in places where one naturally expects only painting and amusement. We have virtue, as Pope remarks, put upon us by surprise and are pleased to find a thing where we should never have looked to meet with it. I must do a pleasing English poet [36] the justice to observe that it is this particular art that is the very distinguishing excellence of *Cooper's Hill*, throughout which the descriptions of places and images raised by the poet are still tending to some hint or leading into some reflection upon moral life or political institution, much in the same manner as the real sight of such scenes and prospects is apt to give the mind a composed turn and incline it to thoughts and contemplations that have a relation to the object. This is the great charm of the incomparable *Elegy Written in a Country Churchyard.* Having mentioned the rustic monuments and simple epitaphs of the swains, the amiable poet falls into a very natural reflection:

> For who, to dumb forgetfulness a prey
> This pleasing anxious being e'er resign'd.
> Left the warm precincts of the cheerful day,
> Nor cast one longing, ling'ring look behind?

Of this art Pope has exhibited some specimens in the poem we are examining, but not so many as might be expected from a mind so strongly inclined to a moral way of writing. After speaking of hunting the hare, he immediately subjoins much in the spirit of Denham,

> Beasts urg'd by us their fellow-beasts pursue,
> And learn of man each other to undo. [123]

Where he is describing the tyrannies formerly exercised in this kingdom,

> Cities laid waste, they storm'd the dens and caves,

he instantly adds, with an indignation becoming a true lover of liberty,

> For wiser brutes were backward to be slaves. [50]

But I am afraid our author, in the following passage, has fallen into a fault rather uncommon in his writings, a reflection that is very farfetched and forced,

> Here waving groves a chequer'd scene display,
> And part admit, and part exclude the day;
> As some coy nymph her lover's warm address
> Nor quite indulges, nor can quite repress. [17]

Bouhours would rank this comparison among false thoughts and Italian conceits, such particularly as abound in the works of Marino.[37] The fallacy consists in giving design and artifice to the wood as well as to the coquette, and in putting the light of the sun and the warmth of a lover on a level.

A pathetic reflection properly introduced into a descriptive poem will have greater force and beauty and more deeply interest a reader than a moral one. When Pope, therefore, has described a pheasant shot, he breaks out into a very masterly exclamation,

> Ah! what avail his glossy, varying dyes,
> His purple crest, and scarlet-circled eyes,
> The vivid green his shining plumes unfold,
> His painted wings, and breast that flames with gold? [115]

This exquisite picture heightens the distress and powerfully excites the commiseration of the reader.[38] Under this head it would be unpardonable to omit a capital, and, I think, one of the most excellent examples extant of the beauty here intended, in the Third

Georgic of Virgil. The poet having mournfully described a steer struck with a pestilence and falling down dead in the middle of his work, artfully reminds us of his former services,

> Quid labor aut benefacta juvant? quid vomere terras
> invertisse graves? [525] [39]

This circumstance would have been sufficient, as it raised our pity from a motive of gratitude, but with this circumstance the tender Virgil was not content; what he adds, therefore, of the natural undeviating temperance of the animal, who cannot have contracted disease by excess and who for that reason deserved a better fate, is moving beyond compare:

> Atqui non Massica Bacchi
> munera, non illis epulae nocuere repostae
> frondibus, et victu pascuntur simplicis herbae;
> pocula sunt fontes liquidi, atque exercita cursu
> flumina, nec somnos abrumpit cura salubres.[40]

Of English poets perhaps none have excelled the ingenious Mr. Dyer in this oblique instruction, into which he frequently steals imperceptibly in his little descriptive poem entitled "Grongar Hill," where he disposes every object so as it may give occasion for some observation on human life. Denham himself is not superior to Mr. Dyer in this particular. After painting a landscape very extensive and diversified, he adds,

> Thus is Nature's vesture wrought,
> To instruct our wandering thought;
> Thus she dresses green and gay,
> To disperse our cares away.

Another view from this favorite spot gives him an opportunity for sliding into the following moralities:

> How close and small the hedges lie!
> What streaks of meadows cross the eye!
> A step, methinks, may pass the stream,
> So little distant dangers seem;
> So we mistake the Future's face,
> Ey'd through Hope's deluding glass.
> As yon summits, soft and fair,
> Clad in colours of the air,
> Which to those, who journey near,

> Barren, brown, and rough appear,
> Still we tread the same coarse way,
> The Present's still a cloudy day.[41]

The unexpected insertion of such reflections imparts to us the same pleasure that we feel when, in wandering through a wilderness or grove, we suddenly behold in the turning of the walk a statue of some virtue or muse.

It may be observed in general that description of the external beauties of nature is usually the first effort of a young genius before he hath studied manners and passions. Some of Milton's most early as well as most exquisite pieces are his "Lycidas," "L'Allegro," and "Il Penseroso"—if we may except his "Ode on the Nativity of Christ," which is, indeed, prior in the order of time, and in which a penetrating critic might have discovered the seeds of that boundless imagination which afterwards was to produce the *Paradise Lost*. This ode, which, by the way, is not sufficiently read nor admired, is also of the descriptive kind, but the objects of its description are great and striking to the imagination: the false deities of the heathen forsaking their temples on the birth of our Saviour, divination and oracles at an end—which facts, though perhaps not historically true, are poetically beautiful.

> The lonely mountains o'er,
> And the resounding shore,
>   A voice of weeping heard, and loud lament;
> From haunted spring, and dale
> Edg'd with poplar pale,
>   The parting Genius is with sighing sent,
> With flow'r-inwov'n tresses torn
> The Nymphs in twilight shade of tangled thickets mourn.

The lovers of poetry (and to such only I write) will not be displeased at my presenting them also with the following image, which is so strongly conceived that, methinks, I see at this instant the demon it represents:

> And Sullen *Moloch*, fled,
> Hath left in shadows dread
>   His burning Idol all of blackest hue;
> In vain with Cymbals' ring,
> They call the grisly king,
>   In dismal dance about the furnace blue; [42]

Attention is irresistibly awakened and engaged by that air of solemnity and enthusiasm that reigns in the following stanzas:

> The Oracles are dumb,
> No voice or hideous hum
>   Runs through the arched roof in words deceiving.
>
> No nightly trance, or breathed spell,
> Inspires the pale-ey'd Priest from the prophetic cell.

Such is the power of true poetry that one is almost inclined to believe the superstitions here alluded to to be real, and the succeeding circumstances make one start and look around.

> In consecrated Earth,
> And on the holy Hearth,
>   The *Lars,* and *Lemures* moan with midnight plaint;
> In Urns and Altars round,
> A drear and dying sound
>   Affrights the *Flamens* at their service quaint.

Methinks we behold the priests interrupted in the middle of the secret ceremonies they were performing "in their temples dim," gazing with ghastly eyes on each other, and terrified, and wondering from whence these aerial voices should proceed. I have dwelt chiefly on this ode as much less celebrated than "L'Allegro" and "Il Penseroso," which are now universally known, but which, by a strange fatality, lay in a sort of obscurity, the private enjoyment of a few curious readers, till they were set to admirable music by Mr. Handel. And, indeed, this volume of Milton's *Miscellaneous Poems* has not till very lately met with suitable regard.[43] Shall I offend any rational admirer of Pope by remarking that these juvenile descriptive poems of Milton, as well as his Latin elegies, are of a strain far more exalted than any the former author can boast? Let me add at the same time what justice obliges me to add, that they are far more incorrect. For in the very ode before us occur one or two passages that are puerile and affected to a degree not to be paralleled in the purer but less elevated compositions of Pope. The season being winter when Jesus was born, Milton says,

> Nature in awe to him
> Had doff't her gaudy trim,[44]

and afterwards observes, in a very epigrammatic and forced thought, unsuitable to the dignity of the subject and of the rest of the ode, that "she wooed the air to hide her guilty front with innocent snow,"

> And on her naked shame,
> Pollute with sinful blame,
>   The Saintly Veil of Maiden white to throw,
> Confounded, that her Maker's eyes
> Should look so near upon her foul deformities.

"It is enough," in the words of Voltaire, "to think one perceives some errors in this great genius, and it is a sort of consolation to a mind so bounded and limited as mine to be persuaded that the greatest men are sometimes deceived like the vulgar."

It would be unpardonable to conclude these remarks on descriptive poesy without taking notice of *The Seasons* of Thomson, who had peculiar and powerful talents for this species of composition. Let the reader, therefore, pardon a digression, if such it be, on his merits and character.

Thomson was blessed with a strong and copious fancy; he hath enriched poetry with a variety of new and original images which he painted from nature itself and from his own actual observations. His descriptions have, therefore, a distinctness and truth which are utterly wanting to those of poets who have only copied from each other and have never looked abroad on the objects themselves. Thomson was accustomed to wander away into the country for days and for weeks, attentive to "each rural sight, each rural sound," while many a poet who has dwelt for years in the Strand has attempted to describe fields and rivers and generally succeeded accordingly. Hence that nauseous repetition of the same circumstances; hence that disgusting impropriety of introducing what may be called a set of hereditary images without proper regard to the age or climate or occasion in which they were formerly used. Though the diction of *The Seasons* is sometimes harsh and inharmonious, and sometimes turgid and obscure, and though in many instances the numbers are not sufficiently diversified by different pauses, yet is this poem on the whole, from the numberless strokes of nature in which it abounds, one of the most captivating and amusing in our language, and which, as its beauties are not of a transitory kind, as depending on particular customs and manners, will ever be perused with delight. The scenes of Thomson are frequently as wild and romantic as those of Salvator Rosa, varied with precipices and torrents, and "castled cliffs" and deep valleys with piny mountains, and the gloomiest caverns. Innumerable are the little circumstances in his descriptions totally unobserved by all his predecessors. What poet hath ever taken notice of the leaf that, towards the end of autumn,

> Incessant rustles from the mournful grove,
> Oft startling such as studious walk below,
> And slowly circles through the waving air. [990]

or who, in speaking of a summer evening, hath ever mentioned "the quail that clamours for its running mate," or the following natural image at the same time of year?

> Wide o'er the thistly lawn, as swells the breeze,
> A whitening shower of vegetable down
> Amusive floats. [1658]

In what other poet do we find the silence and expectation that precedes an April shower insisted on, as in *Spring,* line 165. Or where,

> The stealing shower is scarce to patter heard
> By such as wander through the forest walks,
> Beneath the umbrageous multitude of leaves. [177]

How full, particular, and picturesque is this assemblage of circumstances that attend a very keen frost in a night of winter!

> Loud rings the frozen earth, and hard reflects
> A double noise; while, at his evening watch,
> The village-dog deters the nightly thief;
> The heifer lows; the distant waterfall
> Swells in the breeze; and with the hasty tread
> Of traveller the hollow-sounding plain
> Shakes from afar. [732]

In no one subject are common writers more confused and unmeaning than in their descriptions of rivers, which are generally said only to wind and to murmur, while their qualities and courses are seldom accurately marked. Examine the exactness of the ensuing description and consider what a perfect idea it communicates to the mind:

> Around the adjoining brook, that purls along
> The vocal grove, now fretting o'er a rock,

Now scarcely moving through a reedy pool,
Now starting to a sudden stream, and now
Gently diffused into a limpid plain,
A various group the herds and flocks compose,
Rural confusion! [480]

A group worthy the pencil of Giacomo da Bassano, and so minutely delineated that he might have worked from this sketch:

On the grassy bank
Some ruminating lie, while others stand'
Half in the flood and, often bending, sip
The circling surface. [486]

He adds that the ox, in the middle of them,

from his sides
The troublous insects lashes with his tail,
Returning still. [491]

a natural circumstance that, to the best of my remembrance, hath escaped even the natural Theocritus. Nor do I recollect that any poet hath been struck with the murmurs of the numberless insects that swarm abroad at the noon of a summer's day (as attendants of the evening, indeed, they have been mentioned):

Resounds the living surface of the ground:
Nor undelightful is the ceaseless hum
To him who muses through the woods at noon,
Or drowsy shepherd as he lies reclined,
With half-shut eyes. [281]

But the novelty and nature we admire in the descriptions of Thomson are by no means his only excellencies; he is equally to be praised for impressing on our minds the effects which the scene delineated would have on the present spectator or hearer. Thus, having spoken of the roaring of the savages in a wilderness of Africa, he introduces a captive, who, though just escaped from prison and slavery under the tyrant of Morocco, is so terrified and astonished at the dreadful uproar that "the wretch half wishes for his bonds again." Thus also having described a caravan lost and overwhelmed in one of those whirlwinds that so frequently agitate and lift up the whole sands of the desert, he finishes his picture by adding that:

> In Cairo's crowded streets
> The impatient merchant, wondering, waits in vain,
> And Mecca saddens at the long delay. [*Summer*, 977]

And thus, lastly, in describing the pestilence that destroyed the British troops at the siege of Carthagena, he has used a circumstance inimitably lively, picturesque, and striking to the imagination, for he says that the admiral not only heard the groans of the sick that echoed from ship to ship, but that he also pensively stood and listened at midnight to the dashing of the waters, occasioned by throwing the dead bodies into the sea:

> Heard, nightly plunged amid the sullen waves,
> The frequent corse. [1048]

A minute and particular enumeration of circumstances judiciously selected is what chiefly discriminates poetry from history and renders the former, for that reason, a more close and faithful representation of nature than the latter. And if our poets would accustom themselves to contemplate fully every object before they attempted to describe it, they would not fail of giving their readers more new and more complete images than they generally do.[45]

These observations on Thomson, which, however, would not have been so large if there had been already any considerable criticism on his character, might be still augmented by an examination and development of the beauties in the loves of the birds in *Spring*, line 580; a view of the torrid zone in *Summer*, line 632; the rise of fountains and rivers in *Autumn*, line 781; a man perishing in the snows, in *Winter*, line 276; the wolves descending from the Alps, and a view of winter within the polar circle, line 389; which are all of them highly finished originals, excepting a few of those blemishes intimated above. *Winter* is, in my apprehension, the most valuable of these four poems; the scenes of it, like those of "Il Penseroso" of Milton, being of that awful, solemn, and pensive kind on which a great genius best delights to dwell.

Pope, it seems, was of opinion that descriptive poetry is a composition as absurd as a feast made up of sauces, and I know many other persons that think meanly of it. I will not presume to say it is equal, either in dignity or utility, to those compositions that lay open the internal constitution of man and that imitate characters, manners, and sentiments. I may, however, remind such contemners of it that, in a sister art, landscape painting claims the very next rank to history painting, being ever preferred to single portraits, to pieces of still life, to droll figures, to fruit and flower pieces; that Titian thought it no diminution of his genius to spend much of his time in works of the former species, and that, if their principles lead them to condemn Thomson, they must also condemn the *Georgics* of Virgil and the greatest part of the noblest descriptive poem extant,, I mean that of Lucretius.

.   .   .   .   .

From Section III, "Of *The Essay on Criticism*"

.   .   .   .   .

> Those rules of old, discover'd, not devis'd,
> Are Nature still, but Nature methodiz'd:
> Nature, like Liberty, is but restrain'd
> By the same Laws which first herself ordain'd.
>
> [*Essay on Criticism*, I, 88]

The precepts of the art of poesy were posterior to practice; the rules of the epopea were all drawn from the *Iliad* and the *Odyssey*, and of tragedy from the *Oedipus* of Sophocles. A petulant rejection and an implicit veneration of the rules of the ancient critics are equally destructive of true taste. "It ought to be the first endeavor of a writer," says the excellent Rambler, "to distinguish nature from custom, or that which is established because it is right, from that which is right only because it is established, that he may neither violate essential principles by a desire of novelty, nor debar himself from the attainment of any beauties within his view by a needless fear of breaking rules where no literary dictator had authority to prescribe." [46]

This liberal and manly censure of critical bigotry extends not to those fundamental and indispensable rules which nature and necessity dictate and demand to be observed: such, for instance, as (in the higher kinds of poetry) that the action of the epopea be one, great, and entire; that the hero be eminently distinguished, move our concern, and deeply interest us; that the episodes arise easily out of the main fable; that the action commence as near the catastrophe as possible; and (in the drama) that no more events be crowded together than can be justly supposed to happen during the time of representation or to be transacted on one individual spot; and the like. But the absurdity here animadverted on is the scrupulous nicety of those who bind themselves to obey frivolous and unimportant laws: such as that an epic poem should consist not of less than twelve books; that it should end fortunately; that in the first book there should be no simile; that the exordium should be very simple and unadorned; that in a tragedy only three personages should appear at once upon the stage; and that every tragedy should consist of five acts, by the rigid observation of which last unnecessary precept the poet is deprived of using many a moving story that would furnish matter enough for three, perhaps, but not for five acts; with other rules of the like indifferent nature. For the rest, as Voltaire observes,[47] whether the action of an epopea be simple or complex, completed in a month or in a year, or a longer time; whether the scene be fixed on one spot, as in the *Iliad,* or that the hero voyages from sea to sea, as in the *Odyssey;* whether he be furious, like Achilles, or pious, like Aeneas; whether the action pass on land or sea, on the coast of Africa, as in the *Lusiads* of Camoëns, in America, as in the *Araucana* of Alonzo D'Ercilla, in heaven, in hell, beyond the limits of our world, as in the *Paradise Lost.* All these circumstances are of no consequence; the poem will be forever an epic poem, a heroic poem, at least till another new title be found proportioned to its merit. "If you scruple," says Addison, "to give the title of an epic poem to the *Paradise Lost* of Milton, call it, if you choose, a *divine* poem, give it whatever name you please, provided you confess that it is a work as admirable in its kind as the *Iliad.*" [48]

· · · · ·

So pleas'd at first the tow'ring Alps we try,
Mount o'er the vales, and seem to tread the sky;
Th' eternal snows appear already past,
And the first clouds and mountains seem the last:
But, those attain'd, we tremble to survey
The growing labours of the lengthen'd way;
Th' increasing prospect tires our wand'ring eyes;
Hills peep o'er hills, and Alps on Alps arise. [II, 25]

This comparison is frequently mentioned as an instance of the strength of fancy. The images, however, appear too general and indistinct, and the last line conveys no new idea to the mind. The following picture in Shaftesbury on the same sort of subject appears to be more full and striking:

Beneath the mountain's foot the rocky country rises into hills, a proper basis of the ponderous mass above, where huge embodied rocks lie piled on one another and seem to prop the high arch of heaven. See with what trembling steps poor mankind tread the narrow brink of the deep precipices! From whence with giddy horror they look down, mistrusting even the ground that bears them, whilst they hear the hollow sound of torrents underneath and see the ruin of the impending rock, with falling trees, which hang with their roots upwards and seem to draw more ruin after them. [*The Moralists*, III, i]

See the picturesque description of Hannibal passing the Alps in Livy, who is a great poet.[49]

. . . . .

> The mighty Stagyrite first left the shore,
> Spread all his sails, and durst the deeps explore;
> He steer'd securely, and discover'd far,
> Led by the light of the Mæonian star. [III, 86]

A noble and just character of the first and the best of critics! And sufficient to repress the fashionable and nauseous petulance of several impertinent moderns who have attempted to discredit this great and useful writer.[50] Whoever surveys the variety and perfection of his productions, all delivered in the chastest style, in the clearest order, and the most pregnant brevity, is amazed at the immensity of his genius. His *Logic*, however at present neglected for those redundant and verbose systems which took their rise from Locke's *Essay on the Human Understanding*, is a mighty effort of the mind, in which are discovered the principal sources of the art of reasoning and the dependencies of one thought on another, and where, by the different combinations he hath made of all the forms the understanding can assume in reasoning which he hath traced for it, he hath so closely confined it that it cannot depart from them without arguing inconsequentially. His *Physics* contain many useful observations, particularly his *History of Animals*, which Buffon highly praises, to assist him in which Alexander gave orders that creatures of different climates and countries should, at a great expense, be brought to him to pass under his inspection. His *Morals* are perhaps the purest system in antiquity. His *Politics* are a most valuable monument of the civil wisdom of the ancients, as they preserve to us the description of several governments, and particularly of Crete and Carthage, that otherwise would have been unknown. But of all his compositions his *Rhetoric* and *Poetics* are most excellent. No writer has shown a greater penetration into the recesses of the human heart than this philosopher in the second book of his *Rhetoric,* where he treats of the different manners and passions that distinguish each different age and condition of man, and from whence Horace plainly took his famous description in the *Art of Poetry.*[51] La Bruyère, La Rochefoucauld, and Montaigne himself are not to be compared to him in this respect. No succeeding writer on eloquence, not even Tully, has added anything new or important on this subject. His *Poetics,* which I suppose are here by Pope chiefly referred to, seem to have been written for the use of that prince with whose education Aristotle was honored, to give him a just taste in reading Homer and the tragedians, to judge properly of which was then thought no unnecessary accomplishment in the character of a prince. To attempt to understand poetry without having diligently digested this treatise would be as absurd and impossible as to pretend to a skill in geometry without having studied Euclid. The fourteenth, fifteenth, and sixteenth chapters, wherein he has pointed out the properest methods of exciting terror and pity, convince us that he was intimately acquainted with those objects which most forcibly affect the heart. The prime excellence of this precious treatise is the scholastic precision and philosophical closeness with which the subject is handled, without any address to the passions or imagination. It is to be lamented that the part of the *Poetics* in which he had given precepts for comedy did not likewise descend to posterity.

> Horace still charms with graceful negligence,
> And without method talks us into sense. [III, 94]

The vulgar notion that Horace's "Epistle to the Pisos" contains a complete art of poetry is totally groundless, it being solely confined to the state and defects of the Roman drama.[52] The transitions in the writings of Horace are some of them the most exquisite strokes of his art. Many of them pass at present unobserved, and that his contemporaries were equally blind to this beauty he himself complains, though with a seeming irony:

Cum lamentamur non apparere labores
nostros, et tenui deducta poemata filo.[53]

It seems also to be another common mistake that one of Horace's characteristics is the sublime, of which, indeed, he has given a very few strokes and those taken from Pindar and probably from Alcaeus. His excellence lay in exquisite observations on human life and in touching the foibles of mankind with delicacy and urbanity. It is easy to perceive this moral turn in all his compositions; the writer of the epistles is discerned in the odes. Elegance, not sublimity, was his grand characteristic. Horace is the most popular author of all antiquity. The reason is because he abounds in images drawn from familiar life and in remarks that "come home to men's business and bosoms." Hence he is more frequently quoted and alluded to than any poet of antiquity.

. . . . .

From the same foes, at last, both felt their doom,
And the same age saw Learning fall, and Rome. [III, 126]

It was the fate of Rome to have scarce an intermediate age or single period of time between the rise of arts and fall of liberty. No sooner had that nation begun to lose the roughness and barbarity of their manners and learn of Greece to form their heroes, their orators, and poets on a right model, than, by their unjust attempt upon the liberty of the world, they justly lost their own. With their liberty they lost not only their force of eloquence, but even their style and language itself. The poets who afterwards arose among them were mere unnatural and forced plants. Their two most finished, who came last and closed the scene, were plainly such as had seen the days of liberty and felt the sad effects of its departure.[54]

Shaftesbury proceeds to observe that when despotism was fully established, not a statue, picture, or medal, not a tolerable piece of architecture, afterwards appeared. And it was, I may add, the opinion of Longinus and Addison, who adopted it from him, that arbitrary governments were pernicious to the fine arts as well as to the sciences.[55] Modern history, however, has afforded an example to the contrary. Painting, sculpture, and music have been seen to arrive to a high perfection in Rome, notwithstanding the slavery and superstition that reign there; nay, superstition itself has been highly productive of these fine arts, for with what enthusiasm must a popish painter work for an altarpiece? There have been instances of painters who, before they began to work, have always received the sacrament. Neither Dante, Ariosto, nor Tasso flourished in free governments, and it seems chimerical to assert that Milton would never have written his *Paradise Lost* if he had not seen monarchy destroyed and the state thrown into disorder.[56] Michelangelo, Raphael, and Julio Romano lived in despotic states. The fine arts, in short, are naturally attendant upon power and luxury. But the sciences require unlimited freedom to raise them to their full vigor and growth. In a monarchy there may be poets, painters, and musicians; but orators, historians, and philosophers can exist in a republic alone.

.   .   .   .   .

And Boileau still in right of Horace sways. [III, 155]

May I be pardoned for declaring it as my opinion that Boileau's is the best art of poetry extant? The brevity of his precepts, enlivened by proper imagery, the justness of his metaphors, the harmony of his numbers as far as Alexandrine lines will admit, the exactness of his method, the perspicacity of his remarks, and the energy of his style, all duly considered, may render this opinion not unreasonable. It is scarcely to be conceived how much is comprehended in four short cantos.[57] He that has well digested these cannot be said to be ignorant of any important rule of poetry. The tale of the physician turning architect, in the fourth canto, is told with true pleasantry. It is to this work Boileau owes his immortality, which was of the highest utility to his nation in diffusing a just way of thinking and writing, banishing every species of false wit and introducing a general taste for the manly simplicity of the ancients, on whose writings this poet had formed his taste. Boileau's chief talent was the didactic. His fancy was not the predominant faculty of his mind. Fontenelle has thus characterized him:

Il était grand et excellent versificateur, pourvû cependent que cette louange se renferme dans ses beaux jours, dont la différence avec les autres est bien marquée; et faisait souvent dire "Hélas!" et "Hola!" mais il n'était pas grand poète, si l'on entend par ce mot, comme on le doit, celui qui fait, qui invent, qui crée.[58]

.   .   .   .   .

Such late was Walsh—the Muse's judge and friend.

[III, 170]

If Pope has here given too magnificent an eulogy to Walsh, it must be attributed to friendship rather than to judgment. Walsh was in general a flimsy and frigid writer. The Rambler calls his works pages of inanity.[59] His three letters to Pope, however, are well written. His remarks on the nature of pastoral poetry, on borrowing from the ancients, and against florid conceits, are worthy of perusal.[60] Pope owed much to Walsh. It was he who gave him a very important piece of advice in his early youth, for he used to tell our author that there was one way still left open for him by which he might excel any of his predecessors, which was by correctness, that though, indeed, we had several great poets, we as yet could boast of none that were perfectly correct, and that therefore he advised him to make this quality his particular study.

Correctness is a vague term, frequently used without meaning and precision. It is perpetually the nauseous cant of the French critics, and of their advocates and pupils, that the English writers are generally incorrect. If correctness implies an absence of petty faults, this perhaps may be granted. If it means that because their tragedians have avoided the irregularities of Shakespeare and have observed a juster economy in their fables, therefore the *Athalia,* for instance, is preferable to *Lear,* the notion is groundless and absurd. Though the *Henriade* [61] should be allowed to be free from any very gross absurdities, yet who will dare to rank it with the *Paradise Lost?* Some of their most perfect tragedies abound in faults as contrary to the nature of that species of poetry and as destructive of its end as the fools or grave-diggers of Shakespeare. That the French may boast some excellent critics, particularly Le Bossu, Boileau, Fénelon, and Brumoy, cannot be denied, but that these are sufficient to form a taste upon without having recourse to the genuine fountains of all polite literature, I mean the Grecian writers, no one but a superficial reader can allow.

I conclude these reflections with a remarkable fact. In no polished nation, after criticism has been much studied and the rules of writing established, has any very extraordinary work ever appeared. This has visibly been the case in Greece, in Rome, and in France after Aristotle, Horace, and Boileau had written their arts of poetry. In our own country, the rules of the drama, for instanace, were never more completely understood than at present, yet what uninteresting, though faultless, tragedies have we lately seen! So much better is our judgment than our execution. How to account for the fact here mentioned, adequately and justly, would be attended with all those difficulties that await discussions relative to the productions of the human mind and to the delicate and secret causes that influence them. Whether or no the natural powers be not confined and debilitated by that timidity and caution which is occasioned by a rigid regard to the dictates of art; or whether that philosophical, that geometrical and systematical spirit so much in vogue, which has spread itself from the sciences even into polite literature by consulting only reason, has not diminished and destroyed sentiment and made our poets write from and to the head rather than the heart; or whether, lastly, when just models from which the rules have necessarily been drawn have once appeared, succeeding writers, by vainly and ambitiously striving to surpass those just models, and to shine and surprise, do not become stiff, and forced, and affected in their thoughts and diction.[62]

. . . . .

From Section V, "Of 'The Elegy to the Memory of an Unfortunate Lady,' the Prologue to *Cato,* and the Epilogue to *Jane Shore"*

. . . . .

If this elegy be so excellent, it may be ascribed to this cause, that the occasion of it was real, for it is certainly an indisputable maxim that Nature is more powerful than fancy, that we can always feel more than we can imagine, and that the most artful fiction can give way to truth. When Polus, the celebrated actor, once affected his audience with more than ordinary emotions, it was *luctu et lamentis veris,* by bursting out into real cries and tears, for in personating Electra weeping over the supposed urn of her brother Orestes, he held in his hand the real ashes of his own son lately dead.[63] Events that have actually happened are, after all, the properest subjects for poetry. The best eclogue of Virgil,[64] the best ode of Horace,[65] are founded on real incidents. If we briefly cast our eyes over the most interesting and affecting stories, ancient or modern, we shall find that they are such as, however adorned and a little diversified, are yet grounded on true history and on real matters of fact. Such, for instance, among the ancients, are the stories of Joseph, of Oedipus, the Trojan War and its consequences, of Virginia and the Horatii; such, among the moderns, are the stories of King Lear, the Cid, Romeo and Juliet, and Oroonoko.[66] The series of events contained in these stories seem far to surpass the utmost powers of human imagination. In the best-conducted fiction some mark of improbability and incoherence will still appear.

I shall only add to these a tale literally true which the admirable Dante has introduced in his *Inferno* and which is not sufficiently known. I cannot recollect any passage in any writer whatever so truly pathetic. Ugolino, a Florentine count, is giving the description of his being imprisoned with his children by the Archbishop Ruggieri:

The hour approached when we expected to have something brought us to eat, but instead of seeing the food appear *I heard the doors of that horrible dungeon more closely barred.*[67] I beheld my little children in silence and could not weep. My heart was petrified! The little wretches wept, and my dear Anselm said, *"Tu guardi si, padre: che hai? Father, you look on us; what ails you?"* I could neither weep nor answer, and continued swallowed up in silent agony all that day and the following night, even till the dawn of day. As soon as a glimmering ray darted through the doleful prison, that I could view *again those four faces in which my own image was impressed, I gnawed both my hands* with grief and rage. My children, believing I did this through eagerness to eat, raising themselves suddenly up, said to me, *"My father, our torments would be less if you would allay the rage of your hunger upon us."* I restrained myself that I might not increase their misery. *We were all mute that day and the following.* Quel di, e l'altro, stemmo tutti muti. The fourth day being come,[68] Gaddo, falling extended at my feet, cried, *"Padre mio, che non m'ajuti! My father, why do you not help me?"* and died. The other three expired one after the other between the fifth and sixth day, famished, as thou seest me now. And I, *being seized with blindness,* began to go *groping upon them with my hands and feet,* and continued calling them by their *names three days* after they were dead. *E tre di li chiamai poiche fur morti;* then *hunger vanquished my grief.*[69]

If this inimitable description had been found in Homer, the Greek tragedies, or Virgil, how many commentaries and panegyrics would it have given rise to? What shall we say or think of the genius able to produce it? Perhaps the *Inferno* of Dante is the next composition to the *Iliad* in point of originality and sublimity. And with regard to the pathetic, let this tale stand a testimony of his abilities. For my own part, I truly believe it was never carried to a greater height. It is remarkable that Chaucer appears to have been particularly struck with this tale in Dante, having highly commended this "grete poete of Italie" for this narration, with a summary of which he concludes "The Monk's Tale." [70]

. . . . .

The tragedy of *Cato* itself is a glaring instance of the force of party; so sententious and declamatory a drama would never have met with such rapid and amazing success if every line and sentiment had not been particularly tortured and applied to recent events and the reigning disputes of the times. The purity and energy of the diction and the loftiness of the sentiments, copied in a great measure from Lucan, Tacitus, and Seneca the philosopher, merit approbation. But I have always thought that those pompous Roman sentiments are not so difficult to be produced as is vulgarly imagined, and which, indeed, dazzle only the vulgar. A stroke of nature is, in my opinion, worth a hundred such thoughts as

> When vice prevails, and impious men bear sway,
> The post of honour is a private station. [IV, iv, 141]

Cato is a fine dialogue on liberty and the love of one's country, but considered as a dramatic performance, nay, as a model of a just tragedy as some have affectedly represented it, it must be owned to want action and pathos, the two hinges, I presume, on which a just tragedy ought necessarily to turn, and without which it cannot subsist. It wants also character, although that be not so essentially necessary to a tragedy as action. Syphax, indeed, in his interview with Juba [II, v], bears some marks of a rough African; the speeches of the rest may be transferred to any of the personages concerned. The simile drawn from Mount Atlas and the description of the Numidian traveler smothered in the desert are, indeed, in character, but sufficiently obvious. How Addison could fall into the false and unnatural custom of ending his three first acts with similes is amazing in so chaste and correct a writer. The loves of Juba and Marcia, of Portius and Lucia, are vicious and insipid episodes, debase the dignity and destroy the unity of the fable.

One would imagine from the practice of our modern playwrights that love was the only passion capable of producing any great calamities in human life, for this passion has engrossed and been impertinently introduced into all subjects. In the *Cinna* of Corneille, which the Prince of Condé called "the breviary of kings," Maximus whines like a shepherd in the *Pastor Fido,* even in the midst of profound political reflections that equal those of Tacitus and Machiavelli, and while the most important event that could happen to the empire of the world was debating. In his imitation of the *Electra* of Sophocles, Crébillon has introduced a frigid love-intrigue. Achilles must be in love in the *Iphigenia* of Racine, and the rough Mithridates must be involved in this universal passion. A passion, however, it is that will always shine upon the stage where it is introduced as the chief subject, but not subordinate and secondary.[71] Thus, perhaps, there cannot be finer subjects for a drama than Phaedra, Romeo, Othello, and Monimia.[72] The whole distress in these pieces arises singly from this unfortunate passion carried to an extreme.[73] The greater passions were the constant subjects of the Grecian, the tenderer passions of the French and English theaters. Terror reigned in the former; pity occupies the latter. The moderns may yet boast of some pieces that are not emasculated with this epidemical effeminacy. Racine was at last convinced of its impropriety, and gave the public his admirable *Athalia,* in which were no parts commonly called by the French *d'amoreux* and *de l'amoreuse,* which parts were always given to their two capital actors. The *Merope, Mohamet,* and *Orestes* of Voltaire are likewise free from any ill-placed tenderness and romantic gallantry, for which he has merited the praises of the learned father Tournemine, in a letter to his friend father Brumoy (*Oeuvres de Voltaire* [Paris, 1828, IV, 356]). But *Lear* and *Macbeth* are also striking instances what interesting tragedies may be written without having recourse to a love story. It is pity that the tragedy of *Cato,* in which all the rules of the drama, as far as the mechanism of writing reaches, are observed, is not exact with respect to the unity of time. There was no occasion to extend the time of the fable longer than the mere representation takes up; all might have passed in the compass of three hours from the morning, with a description of which the play opens, if the poet in the fourth scene of the fifth act had not talked of the setting sun playing on the armor of the soldiers.

.   .   .   .   .

Whatever censures we have here too boldly, perhaps, ventured to deliver on the professed poetry of Addison, yet must we candidly own that in various parts of his prose essays are to be found many strokes of genuine and sublime poetry, many marks of a vigorous and exuberant imagination, particularly in the noble allegory of pain and pleasure, the vision of Mirza, the story of Maraton and Yaratilda, of Constantia and Theodosius, and the beautiful eastern tale of Abdullah and Balsora, and many others, together with several strokes in the essay on the pleasures of imagination.[74] It has been the lot of many great names not to have been able to express themselves with beauty and propriety in the fetters of verse in their respective languages, who have yet manifested the force, fertility, and creative power of a most poetic genius in prose.[75] This was the case of Plato, of Lucian, of Fénelon, of Sir Philip Sidney, and Dr. T. Burnet, who, in his *Theory of the Earth*,[76] has displayed an imagination very nearly equal to that of Milton:

> Mænia mundi
> discedunt! totum video per Inane geri res!

After all, the chief and characteristical excellency of Addison was his humor; for in humor no mortal has excelled him, except Molière. Witness the character of Sir Roger de Coverley, so original, so natural, and so inviolably preserved, particularly in the month which the Spectator spends at his hall in the country.[77] Witness also the *Drummer,* that excellent and neglected comedy, that just picture of life and real manners, where the poet never speaks in his own person or totally drops or forgets a character for the sake of introducing a brilliant simile or acute remark, where no train is laid for wit, no Jeremys or Bens are suffered to appear.[78]

The Epilogue to *Jane Shore* is the last piece that belongs to this section, the title of which by this time the reader may have possibly forgot. It is written with that air of gallantry and raillery which, by a strange perversion of taste, the audience expects in all epilogues to the most serious and pathetic pieces. To recommend cuckoldom and palliate adultery is their usual intent. I wonder Mrs. Oldfield was not suffered to speak it, for it is superior to that which was used on the occasion. In this taste Garrick has written some that abound in spirit and drollery. Rowe's genius [79] was rather delicate and soft than strong and pathetic; his compositions soothe us with a tranquil and tender sort of complacency, rather than cleave the heart with pangs of commiseration. His distresses are entirely founded on the passion of love. His diction is extremely elegant and chaste, and his versification [80] highly melodious. His plays are declamations rather than dialogues, and his characters are general and undistinguished from each other. Such a furious character as that of Bajazet [81] is easily drawn and, let me add, easily acted. There is a want of unity in the fable of *Tamerlane*. The death's head, dead body, and stage hung in mourning, in the *Fair Penitent,* are artificial and mechanical methods of affecting an audience. In a word, his plays are musical and pleasing poems, but inactive and unmoving tragedies. This of *Jane Shore* is, I think, the most interesting and affecting of any he has given us, but probability is sadly violated in it by the neglect of the unity of time. For a person to be supposed to be starved during the representation of five acts is a striking instance of the absurdity of this violation. In this piece, as in all of Rowe, are many florid speeches, utterly inconsistent with the state and situation of the distressful personages who speak them. When Shore first meets with her husband, she says,

> Art thou not risen by miracle from death?
> Thy shroud is fall'n from off thee, and the grave
> Was bid to give thee up, that thou might'st come
> The messenger of grace and goodness to me. [V, i, 339]

He has then added some lines, intolerably flowery and unnatural:

> Give me your drops, ye soft-descending rains,
> Give me your streams, ye never ceasing springs,
> That my sad eyes may still supply my duty,
> And feed an everlasting flood of sorrow.

This is of a far distant strain from those tender and simple exclamations she uses when her husband offers her some rich conserves:

> How can you be so good? [V, 1, 363]

And again,

>   Have you forgot
> The costly string of pearl you brought me home
> And tied about my neck? How could I leave you?

She continues to gaze on him with earnestness, and, instead of eating, as he entreats her, she observes:

> You're strangely alter'd—
> Say, gentle Bellmour, is he not? How pale
> Your visage is become? Your eyes are hollow;
> Nay, you are wrinkled too.

To which she instantly subjoins, struck with the idea that she herself was the unhappy cause of this alteration,

> Alas the day!
> My wretchedness has cost you many a tear
> And many a bitter pang, since last we parted.

What she answers to her husband, when he asks her movingly,

> Why dost thou fix thy dying eyes upon me
> With such an earnest, such a pitious look,
> As if thy heart was full of some sad meaning
> Thou could'st not speak! [V, i, 411]

is pathetic to a great degree.

> Forgive me!—but forgive me!

These few words far exceed the most pompous declamations of Cato. The interview betwixt Jane Shore and Alicia, in the middle of this act, is also very affecting, where the madness of Alicia is well painted. But of all representations of madness, that of Clementina, in *The History of Sir Charles Grandison,* is the most deeply interesting. I know not whether even the madness of Lear is wrought up and expressed by so many little strokes of nature and genuine passion. Shall I say it is pedantry [82] to prefer and compare the madness of Orestes in Euripides to this of Clementina?

It is probable that this is become the most popular and pleasing tragedy of all Rowe's works because it is founded on our own history. I cannot forbear wishing that our writers would more frequently search for subjects in the annals of England, which afford many striking and pathetic events proper for the stage. We have been too long attached to Grecian and Roman stories. In truth, the *domestica facta* are more interesting, as well as more useful: more interesting because we all think ourselves concerned in the actions and fates of our countrymen; more useful because the characters and manners bid the fairest to be true and natural when they are drawn from models with which we are exactly acquainted. The Turks, the Persians, and Americans of our poets, are, in reality, distinguished from Englishmen only by their turbans and feathers, and think and act as if they were born and educated within the bills of mortality. The historical plays of Shakespeare [83] are always particularly grateful to the spectator who loves to see and hear our own Harrys and Edwards better than all the Achilleses or Caesars [84] that ever existed. In the choice of a domestic story, however, much judgment and circumspection must be exerted to select one of the proper era, neither of too ancient or of too modern a date. The manners of times very ancient we shall be apt to falsify, as those of the Greeks and Romans. And recent èvents with which we are thoroughly acquainted are deprived of the power of impressing solemnity and awe by their notoriety and familiarity. Age softens and wears away all those disgracing and depreciating circumstances which attend modern transactions merely because they are modern. Lucan was much embarrassed by the proximity of the times he treated of. On this very account, as well as others, the best tragedy that could be possibly written on the murder of Charles I would be coldly received. Racine ventured to write on a recent history in his *Bajazet,* but would not have attempted it had he not thought that the distance of his hero's country repaired in some measure the nearness of the time in which he lived. *Major a longinquo reverentia.*[85]

·   ·   ·   ·   ·

From Section VI, "Of the 'Epistle of Sappho to Phaon,' and of 'Eloisa to Abelard' "

·   ·   ·   ·   ·

No part of this poem ["Eloisa to Abelard"], or indeed of any of Pope's productions, is so truly poetical and contains such strong painting as the passage to which we are now arrived—the description of the convent—where Pope's religion certainly aided his fancy. It is impossible to read it without being struck with a pensive pleasure and a sacred awe at the solemnity of the scene, so picturesque are the epithets.

> In these *lone* walls (their days eternal bound)
> These *moss-grown* domes with *spiry* turrets crown'd,
> Where *awful* arches make the noon-day night,
> And the *dim* windows shed a *solemn* light;
> Thy eyes diffus'd a reconciling ray. [141]

All the circumstances that can amuse and soothe the mind of a solitary are next enumerated in this expressive manner, and the reader that shall be disgusted at the length of the quotation, one might pronounce, has no taste either for painting or poetry:

> The darksome pines that o'er yon rocks reclin'd,
> Wave high, and murmur to the hollow wind;
> The wand'ring streams that shine between the hills,
> The grots that echo to the tinkling rills,
> The dying gales that pant upon the trees,[86]
> The lakes that quiver to the curling breeze;
> No more these scenes my meditation aid,
> Or lull to rest the visionary maid. [155]

The effect and influence of Melancholy, who is beautifully personified, on every object that occurs and on every part of the convent, cannot be too much applauded or too often read, as it is founded on nature and experience. That temper of mind casts a gloom on all things.

> But o'er the twilight groves and dusky caves,
> Long-sounding isles, and intermingled graves,
> Black Melancholy sits, and round her throws
> A death-like silence, and a dread repose;
> Her gloomy presence saddens all the scene,
> Shades ev'ry flower, and darkens ev'ry green,
> Deepens the murmur of the falling floods,
> And breathes a browner horror on the woods. [163]

The figurative expressions "throws" and "breathes" and "browner" horror are, I verily believe, some of the strongest and boldest in the English language. The image of the goddess Melancholy sitting over the convent and, as it were, expanding her dreadful wings over its whole circuit and diffusing her gloom all around it is truly sublime and strongly conceived.

.   .   .   .   .

From Section IX, "Of the *Essay on Man*"

If it be a true observation that for a poet to write happily and well he must have seen and felt what he describes and must draw from living models alone, and if modern times from their luxury and refinement afford not manners that will bear to be described,[87] it will then follow that those species of poetry bid fairest to succeed at present which treat of things, not men; which deliver doctrines, not display events. Of this sort is didactic and descriptive poetry. Accordingly, the moderns have produced many excellent pieces of this kind. We may mention the *Syphilis* of Fracastorius, the *Silkworms* and *Chess* of Vida, the *Ambra* of Politian, the *Agriculture* of Alamanni, the *Art of Poetry* of Boileau, the *Gardens* of Rapin, the *Cyder* of Philips, the *Chase* of Somerville, the *Pleasures of Imagination*, the *Art of Preserving Health*, the *Fleece*, the *Religion* of Racine the Younger, the elegant Latin poem of Browne on the immortality of the soul, the Latin poems of Stay and Boscovick, and the philosophical poem before us, to which, if we may judge from some beautiful fragments, we might have added Gray's didactic poem on education and government, had he lived to finish it; and the *English Garden* of Mr. Mason must not be omitted.[88]

The *Essay on Man* is as close a piece of argument, admitting its principles, as perhaps can be found in verse. Pope informs us in his first preface "that he chose his epistolary way of writing, notwithstanding his subject was high and of dignity, because of its being mixed with argument which of its nature approacheth to prose." He has not wandered into any useless digressions, has employed no fictions, no tale or story, and has relied chiefly on the poetry of his style for the purpose of interesting his readers. His style is concise and figurative, forcible and elegant. He has many metaphors and images artfully interspersed in the driest passages, which stood most in need of such ornaments. Nevertheless, there are too many lines in this performance plain and prosaic. The meaner the subject is of a preceptive poem, the more striking appears the art of the poet. It is even of use, perhaps, to choose a low subject. In this respect Virgil had the advantage over Lucretius. The latter, with all his vigor and sublimity of genius, could hardly satisfy and come up to the grandeur of his theme. Pope labors under the same difficulty.

If any beauty in this essay be uncommonly transcendent and peculiar, it is brevity of diction which, in a few instances, and those pardonable, has occasioned obscurity. It is hardly to be imagined how much sense, how much thinking, how much observation on human life is condensed together in a small compass. He was so accustomed to confine his thoughts in rhyme that he tells us he could express them more shortly this way than in prose itself. On its first publication Pope did not own it, and it was given by the public to Lord Paget, Dr. Young, Dr. Desaguliers,[89] and others. Even Swift seems to have been deceived. There is a remarkable passage in one of his letters:

I confess, I did never imagine you were so deep in morals or that so many new and excellent rules could be produced so advantageously and agreeably in that science from any one head. I confess in some places I was forced to read twice. I believe I told you before what the Duke of D—— said to me on that occasion, how a judge here, who knows you, told him that on the first reading those essays he was much pleased but found some lines a little dark; on the second most of them cleared up and his pleasure increased; on the third he had no doubt remaining and then he admired the whole.[90]

The subject of this essay is a vindication of providence in which the poet proposes to prove that of all possible systems, infinite wisdom has formed the best; that in such a system, coherence, union, subordination are necessary; and if so, that appearances of evil, both moral and natural, are also necessary and unavoidable; that the seeming defects and blemishes in the universe conspire to its general beauty; that as all parts in an animal are not eyes and as in a city, comedy, or picture, all ranks, characters, and colors are not equal or alike, even so, excesses and contrary qualities contribute to the proportion and harmony of the universal system; that it is not strange that we should not be able to discover perfection and order in every instance, because in an infinity of things mutually relative a mind which sees not infinitely can see nothing fully. This doctrine was inculcated by Plato and the Stoics, but more amply and particularly by the later Platonists, and by Antoninus and Simplicius.[91] In illustrating his subject Pope has been much more deeply indebted to the *Theodicée* of Leibnitz, to Archbishop King's *Origin of Evil*, and to the *Moralists* of Lord Shaftesbury, than to the philosophers above mentioned. The late Lord Bathurst repeatedly assured me that he had read the whole scheme of the *Essay on Man* in the handwriting of Bolingbroke and drawn up a series of propositions which Pope was to versify and illustrate, in doing which, our poet, it must be confessed, left several passages so expressed as to be favorable to fatalism and necessity, notwithstanding all the pains that can be taken and the turns that can be given to those passages to place them on the side of religion and make them coincide with the fundamental doctrines of revelation.

> Awake, my St. John! leave all meaner things
> To low ambition, and the pride of Kings.
> Let us (since life can little more supply
> Than just to look about us and to die)
> Expatiate free o'er all this scene of Man;
> A mighty maze! but not without a plan.

This opening is awful and commands the attention of the reader. The word *awake* has peculiar force and obliquely alludes to his noble friend's leaving his political for philosophical pursuits. May I venture to observe that the metaphors in the succeeding lines, drawn from the field sports of setting and shooting, seem below the dignity of the subject, especially,

> Eye Nature's walks, shoot Folly as it flies,
> And catch the Manners living as they rise.

> But vindicate the ways of God to Man.

This line is taken from Milton:

> And justify the ways of God to man [*sic*].

Pope seems to have hinted by this allusion to the *Paradise Lost* that he intended his poem for a defense of providence as well as Milton, but he took a very different method in pursuing that end and imagined that the goodness and justice of the Deity might be defended *without* having recourse to the doctrine of a future state and of the depraved state of man.

.   .   .   .   .

> The lamb thy riot dooms to bleed today,
> Had he thy Reason would he skip and play?
> Pleas'd to the last he crops the flow'ry food,
> And licks the hand just rais'd to shed his blood. [I, 81]

The tenderness of this striking image, and particularly the circumstance in the last line, has an artful effect in alleviating the dryness in the argumentative parts of the essay and interesting the reader.

> The soul uneasy, and confin'd from home,
> Rests and expatiates in a life to come. [I, 97]

In former editions it used to be printed *at home,* but this expression seeming to exclude a future existence (as to speak the plain truth it was intended to do) it was altered to *from home,* not only with great injury to the harmony of the line, but also to the reasoning of the context.

> Lo, the poor Indian! whose untutor'd mind
> Sees God in clouds, or hears him in the wind;
> His soul proud Science never taught to stray
> Far as the solar walk, or milky way;
> Yet simple Nature to his hope has giv'n,
> Behind the cloud-topt hill, an humbler heav'n;
> Some safer world in depth of woods embrac'd,
> Some happier island in the wat'ry waste,
> Where slaves once more their native land behold,
> No fiends torment, no Christians thirst for gold.
> To Be, contents his natural desire,
> He asks no Angel's wing, no Seraph's fire;
> But thinks, admitted to that equal sky,
> His faithful dog shall bear him company. [I, 99]

Pope has indulged himself in but few digressions in this piece; this is one of the most poetical. Representations of undisguised nature and artless innocence always amuse and delight. The simple notions which uncivilized nations entertain of a future state are many of them beautifully romantic and some of the best subjects for poetry. It has been questioned whether the circumstance of the dog, although striking at the first view, is introduced with propriety, as it is known that this animal is not a native of America. The notion of seeing God in clouds and hearing him in the wind cannot be enough applauded.

> From burning suns when livid deaths descend,
> When earthquakes swallow, or when tempests sweep
> Towns to one grave, whole nations to the deep? [I, 142]

I quote these lines as an example of energy of style and of Pope's manner of compressing together many images without confusion and without superfluous epithets. Substantives and verbs are the sinews of language.

.   .   .   .   .

All are but parts of one stupendous whole,
Whose body Nature is, and God the soul;
That chang'd thro' all, and yet in all the same;
Great in the earth as in th' aethereal frame;
Warms in the sun, refreshes in the breeze,
Glows in the stars, and blossoms in the trees;
Lives thro' all life, extends thro' all extent,
Spreads undivided, operates unspent;
Breathes in our soul, informs our mortal part,
As full, as perfect, in a hair as heart;
As full, as perfect, in vile Man that mourns,
As the rapt Seraph, that adores and burns:
To him on high, no low, no great, no small;
He fills, he bounds, connects, and equals all! [I, 267]

Whilst I am transcribing this exalted description of the omni-presence of the Deity, I feel myself almost tempted to retract an assertion in the beginning of this work that there is nothing transcendently sublime in Pope. These lines have all the energy and harmony that can be given to rhyme.

.   .   .   .   .

Who taught the nations of the field and wood
To shun their poison and to choose their food?
Prescient, the tides or tempests to withstand,
Build on the wave, or arch beneath the sand? [III, 99]

This passage is highly finished; such objects are more suited to the nature of poetry than abstract ideas. Every verb and epithet has here a descriptive force. We find more imagery from these lines to the end of the epistle than in any other parts of this essay. The origin of the connections in social life, the account of the state of nature, the rise and effects of superstition and tyranny, and the restoration of true religion and just government, all these ought to be mentioned as passages that deserve high applause, nay as some of the most exalted pieces of English poetry.

.   .   .   .   .

A better would you fix?
Then give Humility a coach and six. [IV, 169]

Worth makes the man, and want of it, the fellow,
The rest is all but leather or prunella. [IV, 203]

Not one looks backward, onward still he goes,
Yet ne'er looks forward further than his nose. [IV, 223]

To sigh for ribands if thou art so silly,
Mark how they grace Lord Umbra, or Sir Billy. [IV, 277]

In a work of so serious and severe a cast, in a work of reasoning, in a work of theology designed to explain the most interesting subject that can employ the mind of man, surely such strokes of levity, of satire, of ridicule, however poignant and witty, are ill placed and disgusting, are violations of that propriety which Pope in general so strictly observed. Lucretius preserves throughout the dignity he at first assumed; even his sarcasms and irony on the superstitions have something august and a noble haughtiness in them, as in particular where he asks how it comes to pass that Jupiter sometimes strikes his own temples with his thunderbolts, whether he employs himself in casting them in the deserts for the sake of exercising his arm, and why he hurls them in places where he cannot strike the guilty:

> Tum fulmina mittat; et aedes
> saepe suas disturbet, et in deserta recedens
> saeviat, exercens telum, quod saepe nocentes
> praeterit, exanimatque indignos, inque merentes.
>
> [II. 1101]

He has turned the insult into a magnificent image.

· · · · · ·

From Section X, "Of the 'Moral Essays in Five Epistles to Several Persons' "

The patrons and admirers of French literature usually extol those authors of that nation who have treated of life and manners, and five of them particularly are esteemed to be unrivaled: namely Montaigne, Charron, La Rochefoucauld, La Bruyère, and Pascal. These are supposed to have penetrated deeply into the most secret recesses of the human heart and to have discovered the various vices and vanities that lurk in it. I know not why the English should in this respect yield to their polite neighbors more than in any other. Bacon in his *Essays* and *Advancement of Learning,* Hobbes and Hume in their *Treatises,* Prior in his elegant and witty *Alma,* Richardson in his *Clarissa,* and Fielding in his *Tom Jones* (comic writers are not here included) have shown a profound knowledge of man, and many portraits of Addison may be compared with the most finished touches of La Bruyère. But the epistles we are now entering upon will place the matter beyond a dispute, for the French can boast of no author who has so much exhausted the science of morals as Pope has in these five epistles. They, indeed, contain all that is solid and valuable in the above-mentioned French writers, of whom our author was remarkably fond. But whatever observations he has borrowed from them he has made his own by the dexterity of his application.

.   .   .   .   .

> Like some lone Chartreux stands the good old Hall,
> Silence without, and Fasts within the wall;
> No rafter'd roofs with dance and tabor sound,
> No noontide-bell invites the country round;
> Tenants with sighs the smoakless tow'rs survey,
> And turn th' unwilling steeds another way:
> Benighted wanderers, the forest o'er,
> Curse the sav'd candle and unop'ning door;
> While the gaunt mastiff, growling at the gate,
> Affrights the beggar whom he longs to eat. [III, 187]

> In the worst inn's worst room, with mat half-hung,
> The floors of plaister, and the walls of dung,
> On once a flock-bed, but repair'd with straw,
> With tape-ty'd curtains, never meant to draw,
> The George and Garter dangling from that bed
> Where tawdry yellow strove with dirty red,
> Great Villiers lies. [III, 299]

The use, the force, and the excellence of language certainly consists in raising clear, complete, and circumstantial images and in turning readers into spectators. I have quoted the two preceding passages as eminent examples of this excellence, of all others the most essential in poetry. Every epithet here used paints its object and paints it distinctly. After having passed over the moat full of cresses, do you not actually find yourself in the middle court of this forlorn and solitary mansion overgrown with docks and nettles? And do you not hear the dog that is going to assault you? Among the other fortunate circumstances that attended Homer, it was not one of the least that he wrote before general and abstract terms were invented. Hence his Muse (like his own Helen, standing on the walls of Troy) points out every person and thing accurately and forcibly. All the views and prospects he lays before us appear as fully and perfectly to the eye as that which engaged the attention of Neptune when he was sitting

> ὑψοῦ 'επ' ἀκροτάτης κορυφῆς Σάμου ὑληέσσης
> Θρηϊκίης· ἔνθεν γὰρ ἐφαίνετο πᾶσα μὲν Ἴδη,
> φαίνετο δὲ Πριάμοιο πόλις καὶ νῆες Ἀχαιῶν.[92]

Those who are fond of generalities may think the number of natural little circumstances introduced in the beautiful narration of the expedition of Dolon and Diomede (Book X) too particular and trifling and below the dignity of epic poetry. But every reader of a just taste will always admire the minute description of the helmet and crest at verse the 257th, the clapping of the wings of the heron which they could not see, the squatting down among the dead bodies till Dolon has passed, Ulysses hissing to Diomede as a signal, the striking the horses with his bow because he had forgotten to bring his whip with him, and the innumerable circumstances which make this narration so lively, so dramatic, and so interesting. Half the *Iliad* and the *Odyssey* might be quoted as examples of this way of writing, so different from the unfinished, half-formed figures presented to us by many modern writers. How much is the pathetic heightened by Sophocles when, speaking of Deianira, determined to destroy herself and taking leave of her palace, he adds a circumstance that Voltaire would have disdained!

> Κλαῖε δ' ὀργάνων ὅτου
> ψαύσειεν οἷς ἐχρῆτο δειλαία πάρος · [93]

Among the Roman poets, Lucretius will furnish many instances of this sort of strong painting. Witness his portrait of a jealous man:

> Aut quod in ambiguo *verbum jaculata* reliquit;
>
> . . . . .
>
> aut nimium *jactare* oculos, aliumve *tueri*
> quod putat, in vultuque videt *vestigia* risus. [iv. 1137]

Of Iphigenia going to be sacrificed at the moment when

maestum ante aras astare parentem
sensit, et hunc propter ferrum *celare* ministros. [i. 89]

Of fear:

Sudoresque ita *palloremque* existere toto
corpore et *infringi* linguam vocemque aboriri:
caligare oculos; *sonere* suris; *succidere* artus. [iii. 154] [94]

.   .   .   .   .

Who hung with woods yon mountain's sultry brow?
From the dry rock who bade the waters flow?
Not to the skies in useless columns tost,
Or in proud falls magnificently lost,
But clear and artless, pouring thro' the plain
Health to the sick, and solace to the swain.
Whose Cause-way parts the vale with shady rows?
Whose Seats the weary Traveller repose?
Who taught that heav'n-directed spire to rise?
"The Man of Ross," each lisping babe replies.
Behold the Market-place with poor o'erspread!
The Man of Ross divides the weekly bread:
He feeds yon Alms-house, neat, but void of state,
Where Age and Want sit smiling at the gate:
Him portion'd maids, apprenticed orphans blest,
The young who labour, and the old who rest. [III, 253]

These lines which are eminently beautiful, particularly one of
the three last containing a fine prosopopoeia, have conferred immortality on a plain, worthy and useful citizen of Herefordshire,
Mr. John Kyrle, who spent his long life in advancing and contriv-
ing plans of public utility. The Howard of his time who deserves
to be celebrated more than all the heroes of Pindar. The particular
reason for which I quoted them was to observe the pleasing effect
that the use of common and familiar words and objects judiciously
managed produce in poetry. Such as are here the words *causeway,
seats, spire, market place, almshouse, apprenticed.* A fastidious
delicacy and a false refinement in order to avoid meanness have
deterred our writers from the introduction of such words, but
Dryden often hazarded it and gave by it a secret charm and a
natural air to his verses, well knowing of what consequence it was
sometimes to soften and subdue his tints and not to paint and
adorn every object he touched with perpetual pomp and unremitted
splendor.

. . . . .

You show us, Rome was glorious, not profuse,
And pompous buildings once were things of Use:
Yet shall (my Lord) your just, your noble rules
Fill half the land with Imitating Fools. [IV, 23]

Thus our author addresses the Earl of Burlington, who was then publishing the designs of Inigo Jones and the *Antiquities of Rome*, by Palladio.

Never was protection and great wealth [says an able judge of the subject] more generously and more judiciously diffused than by this great person, who had every quality of a genius and artist except envy. Though his own designs were more chaste and classic than Kent's, he entertained him in his house till his death, and was more studious to extend his friend's fame than his own. . . . As we have few samples of architecture more antique and imposing than the colonnade [within the court of his house in Piccadilly], I cannot help mentioning the effect it had on myself. I had not only never seen it, but had never heard of it, at least with any attention, when, soon after my return from Italy, I was invited to a ball at Burlington House. As I passed under the gate by night, it could not strike me. At daybreak, looking out of the window to see the sun rise, I was surprised with the vision of the colonnade that fronted me. It seemed one of those edifices in fairy tales that are raised by genii in a night's time.[95]

Pope, having appeared an excellent moralist in the foregoing epistles, in this appears to be as excellent a connoisseur,[96] and has given not only some of our first but our best rules and observations on architecture and gardening, but particularly on the latter of these useful and entertaining arts, on which he has dwelt more largely and with rather more knowledge of the subject. The following is copied verbatim from a little paper which he gave to Mr. Spence; [97]

Arts are taken from nature, and, after a thousand vain efforts for improvements, are best when they return to their first simplicity. A sketch or analysis of the first principles of each art, with their first consequences, might be a thing of most excellent service. Thus, for instance, all the rules of architecture [98] might be reducible to three or four heads: the justness of the openings, bearings upon bearings, the regularity of the pillars, etc. That which is not just in buildings is disagreeable to the eye (as a greater upon a lesser, etc.), and this may be called the reasoning of the eye.[99] In laying out a garden, the first and chief thing to be considered, is the genius of the place. Thus at Riskins, now called Piercy Lodge, Lord * * * should have raised two or three mounts, because his situation is all a plain, and nothing can please without variety.[100]

Mr. Walpole, in his elegant and entertaining *History of Modern Gardening,* has clearly proved that Kent was the artist to whom the English nation was chiefly indebted for diffusing a taste in laying out grounds, of which the French and Italians have no idea.[101] But he adds, much to the credit of our author, that Pope undoubtedly contributed to form Kent's taste. The design of the Prince of Wales's garden at Carleton House was evidently borrowed from the poet's at Twickenham. There was little affected modesty in the latter when he said, of all his works, he was most proud of his garden; and yet it was a singular effort of art and taste to impress so much variety and scenery on a spot of five acres. The passing through the gloom from the grotto to the opening day, the retiring and again assembling shades, the dusky groves, the larger lawn, and the solemnity of the termination at the cypresses that lead up to his mother's tomb, are managed with exquisite judgment, and though Lord Peterborough [102] assisted him

> To form his quincunx, and to rank his vines,[103]

those were not the most pleasing ingredients of his little perspective. I do not know whether the disposition of the garden at Rousham, laid out for General Dormer, and in my opinion the most engaging of all Kent's works, was not planned on the model of Mr. Pope's, at least in the opening and retiring "shades of Venus's Vale."

It ought to be observed that many years before this epistle was written, and before Kent was employed as an improver of grounds, even so early as the year 1713, Pope seems to have been the very first person that censured and ridiculed the formal French, Dutch, false and unnatural, mode in gardening, by a paper in the *Guardian,* Number 173, leveled against capricious operations of art and every species of verdant sculpture and inverted nature, which paper abounds with wit as well as taste, and ends with a ridiculous catalog of various figures cut in evergreens.[104] Neither do I think that these four lines in this epistle,

> Here Amphitrite sails thro' myrtle bow'rs;
> There Gladiators fight, or die in flow'rs;

Un-water'd see the drooping sea-horse mourn,
And swallows roost in Nilus' dusty Urn, [IV, 123]

do at all excel the following passage in his *Guardian:*

A citizen is no sooner proprietor of a couple of yews but he entertains thoughts of erecting them into giants, like those of Guildhall. I know an eminent cook who beautified his countryseat with a coronation dinner in greens, where you see the champion flourishing on horse-back at one end of the table, and the Queen in perpetual youth at the other.

But it was the vigorous and creative imagination of Milton, superior to the prejudices of his times,[105] that exhibited in his Eden the first hints and outlines of what a beautiful garden should be; for even his beloved Ariosto and Tasso, in their luxuriant pictures of the gardens of Alcina and Armida, showed they were not free from the unnatural and narrow taste of their countrymen; and even his master, Spenser, has an artificial fountain in the midst of his "bowre of bliss."

I cannot forbear taking occasion to remark in this place that in the sacred drama entitled *L'Adamo,* written and published at Milan in the year 1617, by Gio. Battista Andreini, a Florentine, which Milton certainly had read (and of which Voltaire has given so false and so imperfect an account in his *Essay on the Epic Poets*), the prints that are to represent Paradise are full of clipped hedges, square parterres, straight walks, trees uniformly lopped, regular knots and carpets of flowers, groves nodding at groves, marble fountains, and waterworks. And yet these prints were designed by Carlo Antonio Procaccini, a celebrated landscape painter of his time, and of the school of the Caracci; many of those works are still admired at Milan. To every scene of this drama is prefixed a print of this artist's designing. And, as the book is very curious and uncommon, I intend to give a specimen and analysis of it in the appendix to this volume.

It hence appears that this enchanting art of modern gardening, in which this kingdom claims a preference over every nation in Europe, chiefly owes its origin and its improvements to two great poets, Milton and Pope. May I be suffered to add, in behalf of a favorite author, and who would have been a first rate poet if his style had been equal to his conceptions, that the *Seasons* of

Thomson have been very instrumental in diffusing a general taste
for the beauties of nature and landscape? [106]

.   .   .   .   .

From Section XIV and Last, "Of some Imitations of Horace, the Miscellanies, Epitaphs, and Prose Works"

.   .   .   .   .

Thus have I endeavored to give a critical account, with freedom,
but it is hoped, with impartiality, of each of Pope's works, by which
review it will appear that the largest portion of them is of the
didactic, moral, and satiric kind, and consequently not of the most
poetic species of poetry: whence it is manifest that good sense and
judgment were his characteristical excellencies rather than fancy
and invention: not that the author of *The Rape of the Lock* and
Eloisa can be thought to want imagination, but because his imagination was not his predominant talent, because he indulged it not,
and because he gave not so many proofs of this talent as of the
other. This turn of mind led him to admire French models; he
studied Boileau attentively, formed himself upon him as Milton
formed himself upon the Grecian and Italian sons of fancy. He stuck
to describing modern manners, but those manners because they are
familiar, uniform, artificial, and polished, are, in their very nature,
unfit for any lofty effort of the Muse. He gradually became one of
the most correct, even, and exact poets that ever wrote, polishing
his pieces with a care and assiduity that no business or avocation
ever interrupted; so that if he does not frequently ravish and
transport his reader, yet he does not disgust him with unexpected
inequalities and absurd improprieties. Whatever poetical enthusiasm he actually possessed, he withheld and stifled. The perusal of
him affects not our minds with such strong emotions as we feel
from Homer and Milton, so that no man of a true poetical spirit
is master of himself while he reads them. Hence, he is a writer fit
for universal perusal, adapted to all ages and stations, for the old

and for the young, the man of business and the scholar. He who would think *The Fairy Queen, Palamon and Arcite, The Tempest,* or *Comus* childish and romantic might relish Pope. Surely it is no narrow and niggardly encomium to say he is the great poet of reason, the first of ethical authors in verse. And this species of writing is, after all, the surest road to an extensive reputation. It lies more level to the general capacities of men than the higher flights of more genuine poetry. We all remember when even a Churchill was more in vogue than a Gray. He that treats of fashionable follies and the topics of the day, that describes present persons and recent events, finds many readers whose understandings and whose passions he gratifies. The name of Chesterfield on one hand and of Walpole on the other failed not to make a poem bought up and talked of. And it cannot be doubted that the *Odes* of Horace which celebrated, and the *Satires* which ridiculed, well-known and real characters at Rome, were more eagerly read and more frequently cited than the *Aeneid* and the *Georgics* of Virgil.

Where, then, according to the question proposed at the beginning of this essay, shall we with justice be authorized to place our admired Pope? Not, assuredly, in the same rank with Spenser, Shakespeare, and Milton, however justly we may applaud the "Eloisa" and *Rape of the Lock;* but, considering the correctness, elegance, and utility of his works, the weight of sentiment, and the knowledge of man they contain, we may venture to assign him a place next to Milton and just above Dryden. Yet, to bring our minds steadily to make this decision, we must forget for a moment the divine "Music Ode" of Dryden, and may, perhaps, then be compelled to confess that though Dryden be the greater genius, yet Pope is the better artist.

The preference here given to Pope above other modern English poets, it must be remembered, is founded on the excellencies of his works in general, and taken all together, for there are parts and passages in other modern authors, in Young and in Thomson, for instance, equal to any of Pope, and he has written nothing in a strain so truly sublime as "The Bard," of Gray.

THOMAS WARTON ✿

Observations on the Fairy Queen (1754)

Section I, "Of the Plan and Conduct of the *Fairy Queen*"

When the works of Homer and of Aristotle began to be restored and studied in Italy, when the genuine and uncorrupted sources of ancient poetry and ancient criticism were opened, and every species of literature at last emerged from the depths of Gothic ignorance and barbarity, it might have been expected that, instead of the romantic manner of poetical composition introduced and established by the Provençal bards, a new and more legitimate taste of writing would have succeeded.[1] With these advantages it was reasonable to conclude that unnatural events, the machinations of imaginary beings, and adventures entertaining only as they were improbable would have given place to justness of thought and design, and to that decorum which nature dictated and which the example and the precept of antiquity had authorized. But it was a long time before such a change was effected. We find Ariosto, many years after the revival of letters, rejecting truth for magic, and preferring the ridiculous and incoherent excursions of Boiardo to the propriety and uniformity of the Grecian and Roman models. Nor did the restoration of ancient learning produce any effectual or immediate improvement in the state of criticism. Beni, one of the most celebrated critics of the sixteenth century, was still so infatuated with a fondness for the old Provençal vein that he ventured to write a regular dissertation in which he compares Ariosto with Homer.[2]

Trissino, who flourished a few years after Ariosto, had taste and boldness enough to publish an epic poem, written in professed imitation of the *Iliad*.[3] But this attempt met with little regard or applause for the reason on which its real merit was founded. It was rejected as an insipid and uninteresting performance, having few devils or enchantments to recommend it. To Trissino succeeded Tasso, who in his *Gierusaleme Liberata* took the ancients for his guides, but was still too sensible of the popular prejudice in favor of ideal beings and romantic adventures to neglect or omit them entirely. He had studied and acknowledged the beauties of classical purity. Yet he still kept his first and favorite acquaintance, the old Provençal poets, in his eyes, like his own Rinaldo, who after he had gazed on the diamond shield of truth, and with seeming resolution was actually departing from Armida and her enchanted gardens, could not help looking back upon them with some remains of fondness. Nor did Tasso's poem, though composed in some measure on a regular plan, give its author, among the Italians at least, any greater share of esteem and reputation on that account. Ariosto, with all his extravagancies, was still preferred. The superiority of the *Orlando Furioso* was at length established by a formal decree of the Academicians della Crusca, who amongst other literary debates held a solemn court of inquiry concerning the merit of both poems.

Such was the prevailing taste when [4] Spenser projected the *Fairy Queen,* a poem which, according to the practice of Ariosto, was to consist of allegories, enchantments, and romantic expeditions, conducted by knights, giants, magicians, and fictitious beings. It may be urged that Spenser made an unfortunate choice and discovered but little judgment in adopting Ariosto for his example rather than Tasso, who had so evidently exceeded his rival, at least in conduct and decorum.[5] But our author naturally followed the poem which was most celebrated and popular. For although the French critics universally gave the preference to Tasso, yet in Italy the partisans on the side of Ariosto were by far the most powerful, and consequently in England; for Italy in the age of Queen Elizabeth gave laws to our island in all matters of taste, as France has done ever since. At the same time it may be supposed that of the two Ariosto was Spenser's favorite, and that he was naturally biased to prefer that plan which would admit the most extensive range for his unlimited imagination. What was Spenser's particular plan in consequence of this choice, and how it was conducted, I now proceed to examine.

The poet supposes that the *Fairy Queen,* according to an established annual custom, held a magnificent feast which continued twelve days, on each of which, respectively, twelve several complaints are presented before her. Accordingly, in order to redress the injuries which were the occasion of these several complaints, she dispatches, with proper commissions, twelve different knights, each of which, in the particular adventure allotted to him, proves an example of some particular virtue, as of holiness, temperance, justice, chastity; and has one complete book assigned to him, of which he is the hero. But besides these twelve knights, severally exemplifying twelve moral virtues, the poet has constituted one principal knight or general hero, viz., Prince Arthur. This personage represents magnificence, a virtue which is supposed to be the perfection of all the rest. He moreover assists in every book, and the end of his actions is to discover and win Gloriana, or Glory. In a word, in this character the poet professes to portray "the image of a brave knight perfected in the twelve private moral virtues."

It is evident that our author in establishing one hero who, seeking and attaining one grand end, which is Gloriana, should exemplify one grand character—or a brave knight perfected in the twelve private moral virtues—copied the cast and construction of the ancient epic. But sensible as he was of the importance and expediency of the unity of the hero and of his design, he does not, in the meantime, seem convinced of the necessity of that unity of action by the means of which such a design should be properly accomplished. At least, he has not followed the method practiced by Homer and Virgil in conducting their respective heroes to the proposed end.

It may be asked with great propriety how does Arthur execute the grand, simple, and ultimate design intended by the poet? It may be answered, with some degree of plausibility, that by lending his respective assistance to each of the twelve knights who patronize the twelve virtues, in his allotted defense of each, Arthur approaches still nearer and nearer to Glory, till at last he gains a complete possession. But surely to assist is not a sufficient service. This secondary merit is inadequate to the reward. The poet ought to have made this "brave knight" the leading adventurer. Arthur should have been the principal agent in vindicating the cause of holiness, temperance, and the rest. If our hero had thus, in his own person, exerted himself in the protection of the twelve virtues, he might have been deservedly styled the perfect pattern of all, and consequently would have succeeded in the task assigned, the attainment of Glory. At present he is only a subordinate or accessory character. The difficulties and obstacles which we expect him to surmount in order to accomplish his final achievement are removed by others. It is not he who subdues the dragon, in the First Book, or quells the magician Busirane, in the Third. These are the victories of St. George and of Britomart. On the whole, the twelve knights do too much for Arthur to do anything, or at least, so much as may be reasonably required from the promised plan of the poet. While we are attending to the design of the hero of the book, we forget that of the hero of the poem. Dryden remarks, "We must do Spenser that justice to observe that magnanimity (magnificence), which is the true character of Prince Arthur, shines throughout the whole poem and succors the rest when they are in distress." [6] If the magnanimity of Arthur did, in reality, thus shine in every part of the poem with a superior and steady luster, our author would fairly stand acquitted. At present it bursts forth but seldom, in obscure and interrupted flashes. "To succor the rest when they are in distress" [7] is, as I have hinted, a circumstance of too little importance in the character of this universal champion. It is a service to be performed in the cause of the hero of the epic poem by some dependent or inferior chief, the business of a Gyas or a Cloanthus.

On the whole, we may observe that Spenser's adventures, separately taken as the subject of each single book, have not always a mutual dependence upon each other and consequently do not properly contribute to constitute one legitimate poem. Hughes, not considering this, has advanced a remark in commendation of Spenser's critical conduct which is indeed one of the most blameable parts of it. "If we consider the First Book as an entire work of itself, we shall find it to be no irregular contrivance. There is one principal action, which is completed in the twelfth canto, and the several incidents are proper, as they tend either to obstruct or promote it." [8]

As the heroic poem is required to be one whole, compounded of many various parts, relative and dependent, it is expedient that not one of those parts should be so regularly contrived, and so completely finished, as to become a whole of itself. For the mind, being once satisfied in arriving at the consummation of an orderly series of events, acquiesces in that satisfaction. Our attention and curiosity are in the midst diverted from pursuing, with due vigor, the final and general catastrophe. But while each part is left incomplete, if separated from the rest, the mind, still eager to gratify its expectations, is irresistibly and imperceptibly drawn from part to part till it receives a full and ultimate satisfaction from the accomplishment of one great event, which all those parts, following and illustrating each other, contributed to produce.

Our author was probably aware that by constituting twelve several adventures for twelve several heroes the want of a general connection would often appear. On this account, as I presume, he sometimes resumes and finishes in some distant book a tale formerly begun and left imperfect. But as numberless interruptions necessarily intervene, this proceeding often occasions infinite perplexity to the reader. And it seems to be for the same reason that after one of the twelve knights has achieved the adventure of his proper book, the poet introduces him in the next book acting perhaps in an inferior sphere and degraded to some less dangerous exploit. But this conduct is highly inartificial, for it destroys that repose which the mind feels after having accompanied a hero through manifold struggles and various distresses to success and victory. Besides, when we perceive him entering upon any less illustrious attempt, our former admiration is in some measure diminished. Having seen him complete some memorable conquest, we become interested in his honor, and are jealous concerning his future reputation. To attempt, and even to achieve, some petty posterior enterprise is to derogate from his dignity and to sully the transcendent luster of his former victories.

Spenser perhaps would have embarrassed himself and the reader less had he made every book one entire detached poem of twelve cantos, without any reference to the rest. Thus he would have written twelve different books, in each of which he might have completed the pattern of a particular virtue in twelve knights respectively. At present he has remarkably failed, in endeavoring to represent all the virtues exemplified in one. The poet might either have established twelve knights without an Arthur, or an Arthur without twelve knights. Upon supposition that Spenser was resolved to characterize the twelve moral virtues, the former plan perhaps would have been best; the latter is defective as it necessarily wants simplicity. It is an action consisting of twelve actions, all equally great and unconnected between themselves, and not compounded of one uninterrupted and coherent chain of incidents tending to the accomplishment of one design.

I have before remarked that Spenser intended to express the character of a hero perfected in the twelve moral virtues by representing him as assisting in the service of all till at last he becomes possessed of all. This plan, however injudicious, he certainly was obliged to observe. But in the Third Book, which is styled the Legend of Chastity, Prince Arthur does not so much as lend his assistance in the vindication of that virtue. He appears, indeed, but not as an agent, or even an auxiliary, in the adventure of the book.

Yet it must be confessed that there is something artificial in the poet's manner of varying from historical precision. This conduct is rationally illustrated by himself.[9] According to this plan, the reader would have been agreeably surprised in the last book when he came to discover that the series of adventures which he had just seen completed were undertaken at the command of the Fairy Queen and that the knights had severally set forward to the execution of them from her annual birthday festival. But Spenser, in most of the books, has injudiciously forestalled the first of these particulars, which certainly should have been concealed till the last book, not only that a needless repetition of the same thing might be prevented, but that an opportunity might be secured of striking the reader's mind with a circumstance new and unexpected.

But notwithstanding the plan and conduct of Spenser in the poem before us is highly exceptionable, yet we may venture to pronounce that the scholar has more merit than his master in this respect, and that the *Fairy Queen* is not so confused and irregular as the *Orlando Furioso*. There is indeed no general unity which prevails in the former: but, if we consider every book, or adventure, as a separate poem, we shall meet with so many distinct, however imperfect, unities, by which an attentive reader is less bewildered than in the maze of indigestion and incoherence of which the latter totally consists, where we seek in vain either for partial or universal integrity.

> Ut nec pes nec caput uni
> reddatur formae.[10]

Ariosto has his admirers, and most deservedly. Yet every classical, every reasonable critic must acknowledge that the poet's conception in celebrating the madness, or, in other words, describing the irrational acts, of a hero, implies extravagance and absurdity.[11] Orlando does not make his appearance till the Eighth Book, where he is placed in a situation not perfectly heroic. He is discovered to us in bed, desiring to sleep. His ultimate design is to find Angelica, but his pursuit of her is broken off in the Thirtieth Book, after which there are sixteen books in none of which Angelica has the least share. Other heroes are likewise engaged in the same pursuit. After reading the first stanza, we are inclined to think that the subject of the poem is the expedition of the Moors into France, under the emperor Agramante, to fight against Charlemagne; but this business is the most insignificant and inconsiderable part of it. Many of the heroes perform exploits equal, if not superior, to those of Orlando, particularly Ruggiero, who closes the poem with a grand and important achievement, the conquest and death of Rodomont. But this event is not the completion of a story carried on principally and perpetually through the work.

This spirited Italian [12] passes from one incident to another, and from region to region, with such incredible expedition and rapidity that one would think he was mounted upon his winged steed Ippogrifo. Within the compass of ten stanzas he is in England and the Hesperides, in the earth and the moon. He begins the history of a knight in Europe and suddenly breaks it off to resume the unfinished catastrophe of another in Asia. The reader's imagination is distracted and his attention harassed, amidst the multiplicity of tales, in the relation of which the poet is at the same instant equally engaged. To remedy this inconvenience, the compassionate expositors have affixed in some of the editions marginal hints, informing the bewildered reader in what book and stanza the poet intends to recommence an interrupted episode. This expedient reminds us of the awkward artifice practiced by the first painters.[13] However, it has proved the means of giving Ariosto's admirers a clear comprehension of his stories, which otherwise they could not have obtained without much difficulty. This poet is seldom read a second time in order—that is, by passing from the First Canto to the Second, and from the Second to the rest in succession—[but] by thus pursuing, without any regard to the proper course of the books and stanzas, the different tales, which, though all somewhere finished, yet are at present so mutually complicated that the incidents of one are perpetually clashing with those of another. The judicious Abbé Dubos observes happily enough that "Homer is a geometrician in comparison of Ariosto." [14] His miscellaneous contents cannot be better expressed than by the two first verses of his exordium:

> Le Donni, i Cavallìer, l'Arme, gli Amori,
> Le Cortegie, le' audaci Imprese, io canto.[15]

But it is absurd to think of judging either Ariosto or Spenser by precepts which they did not attend to. We who live in the days of writing by rule are apt to try every composition by those laws which we have been taught to think the sole criterion of excellence. Critical taste is universally diffused, and we require the same order and design which every modern performance is expected to have in poems where they never were regarded or intended. Spenser (and the same may be said of Ariosto) did not live in an age of planning. His poetry is the careless exuberance of a warm imagination and a strong sensibility. It was his business to engage the fancy and to interest the attention by bold and striking images,[16] in the formation and the disposition of which little labor or art was applied. The various and the marvellous were the chief sources of delight. Hence we find our author ransacking alike the regions of reality and romance, of truth and fiction, to find the proper decorations and furniture for his fairy structure. Born in such an age, Spenser wrote rapidly from his own feelings, which at the same time were naturally noble. Exactness in his poem would have been like the cornice which a painter introduced in the grotto of Calypso. Spenser's beauties are like the flowers in Paradise.

> Which not nice Art
> In Beds and curious Knots, but Nature boon
> Pour'd forth profuse on Hill and Dale and Plain,
> Both where the morning Sun first warmly smote
> The open field, and where the unpierc't shade
> Imbrown'd the noontide Bow'rs. [*Paradise Lost,* IV, 241] [17]

If the *Fairy Queen* be destitute of that arrangement and economy which epic severity requires, yet we scarcely regret the loss of these while their place is so amply supplied by something which more powerfully attracts us, something which engages the affections, the feelings of the heart, rather than the cold approbation of the head.

If there be any poem whose graces please because they are situated beyond the reach of art, and where the force and faculties of creative imagination delight because they are unassisted and unrestrained by those of deliberate judgment, it is this. In reading Spenser, if the critic is not satisfied, yet the reader is transported.

Section X, "Of Spenser's Allegorical Character"

In reading the works of a poet who lived in a remote age, it is necessary that we should look back upon the customs and manners which prevailed in that age. We should endeavor to place ourselves in the writer's situation and circumstances. Hence we shall become better enabled to discover how his turn of thinking and manner of composing were influenced by familiar appearances and established objects which are utterly different from those with which we are at present surrounded. For want of this caution too many readers view the knights and damsels, the tournaments and enchantments, of Spenser, with modern eyes, never considering that the encounters of chivalry subsisted in our author's age; that romances were then most eagerly and universally studied; and that consequently Spenser, from the fashion of the times, was induced to undertake a recital of chivalrous achievements and to become, in short, a *romantic* poet.

Spenser in this respect copied real manners no less than Homer. A sensible historian observes that "Homer copied true natural manners, which, however rough and uncultivated, will always form an agreeable and interesting picture. But the pencil of the English poet (Spenser) was employed in drawing the affectations, and conceits, and fopperies of chivalry." [18] This, however, was nothing more than an imitation of real life, as much, at least, as the plain descriptions in Homer, which corresponded to the simplicity of manners then subsisting in Greece. Spenser, in the address of the *Shepherd's Calendar* to Sir Philip Sidney, couples his patron's learning with his skill in chivalry, a topic of panegyric which would sound very odd in a modern dedication, especially before a set of pastorals. "To the noble and virtuous gentleman, most worthy of all titles, both of Learning and *Chivalry,* Master Philip Sydney."

> Go little book; thyself present,
> As child whose parent is unkent,
> To him that is the president
> Of nobleness and *Chivalry*.[19]

Nor is it sufficiently considered that a popular practice of Spenser's age contributed in a considerable degree to make him an allegorical poet. We should remember that in this age allegory was applied as the subject and foundation of public shows and spectacles, which were exhibited with a magnificence superior to that of former times. The virtues and vices, distinguished by their respective emblematical types, were frequently personified and represented by living actors. These figures bore a chief part in furnishing what they called pageants,[20] which were then the principal species of entertainment and were shown, not only in private or upon the stage, but very often in the open streets for solmnizing public occasions or celebrating any grand event. As a proof of what is here mentioned, I refer the reader to Holinshed's description of the *Show of Manhood and Desert*, exhibited at Norwich before Queen Elizabeth; [21] and more particularly to that historian's account of a turney performed by Fulke Greville, the Lords Arundell and Windsor, and Sir Philip Sidney, who are feigned to be the children of Desire, attempting to win the Fortress of Beauty.[22] In the composition of the last spectacle, no small share of poetical invention appears.

In the meantime, I do not deny that Spenser was, in great measure, tempted by the *Orlando Furioso* to write an allegorical poem. Yet it must still be acknowledged that Spenser's peculiar mode of allegorizing seems to have been dictated by those spectacles rather than by the fictions of Ariosto. In fact, Ariosto's species of allegory does not so properly consist in impersonating the virtues, vices, and affections of the mind as in the adumbration of moral doctrine under the actions of men and women.[23] On this plan Spenser's allegories are sometimes formed, as in the First Book, where the Red Cross Knight or a True Christian, defeats the wiles of Archimago, or the Devil, etc. etc. These indeed are fictitious personages, but he proves himself a much more ingenious allegorist where his imagination bodies forth unsubstantial things, turns them to shape, and marks out the nature, powers, and effects of that which is ideal and abstracted, by visible and external symbols, as in his delineations of Fear, Despair, Fancy, Envy, and the like. Ariosto gives us but few symbolical beings of this sort, for a picturesque invention was by no means his talent, while those few which we find in his poem are seldom drawn with that characteristical fullness and significant expression so striking in the fantastic portraits of Spenser. And that Spenser painted these figures in so distinct and animated a style, may we not partly account for it from this cause: that he had been long habituated to the sight of these emblematical personages, visibly decorated with their proper attributes, and actually endued with speech, motion, and life?

As a more convincing argument in favor of this hypothesis, I shall remark that Spenser expressly denominates his most exquisite group of allegorical figures the "Mask of Cupid." [24] Thus, without recurring to conjecture, his own words [25] evidently demonstrate that he sometimes had representations of this sort in his eye. He tells us moreover that these figures were

> a jolly company,
> In manner of a maske, enranged orderly. [III, xii, 5]

In his introduction to this group, it is manifest that he drew from another allegoric spectacle of that age called the "dumb show," [26] which was wont to be exhibited before every act of a tragedy:

> 3
> And forth issewd, as on the ready flore
> Of some Theatre, a graue personage,
> That in his hand a branch of laurell bore,
> With comely haueour, and count'nance sage,
> Yclad in costly garments, fit for tragicke Stage.

> 4
> Proceeding to the midst, he still did stand,
> As if in mind he somewhat had to say;
> And to the vulgar beckning with his hand,
> In signe of silence, as to heare a play,
> By liuely actions he gan bewray
> Some argument of matter passioned;
> Which doen, he backe retyred soft away,
> And passing by, his name discouered,
> *Ease*, on his robe in golden letters cyphered.

He afterwards styles these figures "maskers":

6

The whiles the maskers marched forth in trim aray.

7

The first was *Fancy,* like a louely boy,
Of rare aspect.

From what has been said, I would not have it objected that I have intended to arraign the powers of our author's invention, or insinuated that he servilely copied such representations. All I have endeavored to prove is that Spenser was not only better qualified to delineate fictions of this sort because they were the real objects of his sight,[27] but as all men are influenced by what they see, that he was prompted and induced to delineate them because he saw them, especially as they were so much the delight of his age.

Instead of entering into a critical examination of Spenser's manner of allegorizing, and of the poetical conduct of his allegories, which has been done with an equally judicious and ingenious discernment by Mr. Spence,[28] I shall observe that our author frequently introduces an allegory under which no meaning is couched; viz., II, ix, 21. Alma is the mind, and her castle, the body. The tongue is the porter of this castle, the nose the portcullis, and the mouth the porch, about the inside of which are placed twice sixteen warders clad in white, which are the teeth; these Alma passes by, who rise up, and do obeisance to her (St. 26). But how can the teeth be said to rise up and bow to the mind? Spenser here forgot that he was allegorizing, and speaks as if he was describing, without any latent meaning, a real queen, with twice sixteen real warders, who as such, might, with no impropriety, be said to rise and bow to their queen. Many instances of his confounding allegory with reality occur through this whole canto and the two next—particularly where he is describing the kitchen of this castle, which is the belly, he gives us a formal description of such a kitchen as was to be seen in his time in castles and great houses, by no means expressive of the thing intended. Again, the occult meaning of his bringing Scudamore to the house of Care (IV, v, 32) clashes with what he had before told us. By this allegory of Scudamore coming to Care's house, it should be *understood* that Scudamore, from a happy, passed into a miserable state. For we may reasonably suppose that before he came to Care's house, he was unacquainted with Care, whereas the poet had before represented him as involved in extreme misery. It would be tedious, by an allegation of particular examples, to demonstrate how frequently his allegories are mere descriptions, and that taken in their literal sense they contain an improper, or no, signification. I shall, however, mention one. The Blatant Beast is said to break into the monasteries, to rob their chancels, cast down the desks of the monks, deface the altars, and destroy the images found in their churches. By the Blatant Beast is understood Scandal, and by the havoc just mentioned as effected by it is implied the suppression of religious houses and popish superstition. But how can this be properly said to have been brought about by scandal? And how could Spenser in particular, with any consistency say this, who was, as appears by his pastorals, a friend to the reformation, as was his heroine Elizabeth?

But there is another capital fault in our author's allegories which does not immediately fall under the stated rules of criticism. "Painters," says a French writer,

ought to employ their allegories in religious pictures with much greater reserve than in profane pieces. They may, indeed, in such subjects as do not represent the mysteries and miracles of our religion, make use of an allegorical composition, the action whereof shall be expressive of some truth that cannot be represented otherwise, either in painting or sculpture. I agree therefore to let them draw Faith and Hope supporting a dying person, and Religion in deep affliction at the feet of a deceased prelate. But I am of opinion that artists who treat of the miracles and dogmas of our religion are allowed no kind of allegorical composition. . . . The facts whereon our religion is built, and the doctrine it delivers, are subjects in which the painter's imagination has no liberty to sport.[29]

The conduct which this author blames is practiced by Spenser, with this difference only, that the painters here condemned are supposed to adapt human allegory to divine mystery, whereas Spenser has mingled divine mystery with human allegory. Such a practice as this tends not only to confound sacred and profane subjects, but to place the licentious sallies of imagination upon a level with the dictates of divine inspiration—to debase the truth and dignity of heavenly things by making Christian allegory subservient to the purposes of romantic fiction.

This fault our author, through a defect of judgment rather than a contempt of religion, has most glaringly committed throughout his whole First Book, where the imaginary instruments and expedients of romance are perpetually interwoven with the mysteries contained in the Book of Revelations. Duessa, who is formed upon the idea of a romantic enchantress, is gorgeously arrayed in gold and purple, presented with a triple crown [30] by the giant Orgoglio, and seated by him on a monstrous seven-headed dragon (I, vii, 16), whose tail reaches to the skies and throws down the stars (18), she bearing a golden cup in her hand (I, viii, 25). This is the scarlet whore and the red dragon in the Revelations. "Behold a great red dragon, having seven heads, and ten horns, and seven crowns upon his heads; and his tail drew the third part of the stars of heaven, and did cast them to earth" (12:3,4). Again, "I saw a woman sit upon a scarlet-colored beast, full of names of blasphemy, having seven heads, and ten horns; and the woman was arrayed in purple and scarlet color, and decked with gold, and precious stones, and pearls, having a golden cup in her hands, full of abomination, and filthiness of her fornication" (7:3,4).

In Orgoglio's castle, which is described as very magnificent, Prince Arthur discovers:

> An Altare caru'd with cunning imagery,
> On which true Christians bloud was often spilt,
> And holy Martyrs often doen to dye,
> With cruell malice and strong tyranny:
> Whose blessed sprites, from vnderneath the stone
> To God for vengeance cryde continually. [I, viii, 36]

The inspired author of the above-named book mentions the same of what he saw in heaven. "I saw under the altar the souls of them that were slain for the word of God, and for the testimony which they held; and they cried with a loud voice, how long, O Lord, holy and true, dost thou not judge, and avenge our blood on them that dwell on earth?" (6:9,10.)

A hermit points out to the Red Cross Knight the New Jerusalem (I, x, 53), which an angel discovers to St. John (xxi, 10, etc.). This prospect is taken, says the poet, from a mountain more lofty than either the Mount of Olives or Parnassus. These two comparisons thus impertinently linked together strongly remind us of the absurdity now spoken of, the mixture of divine truth and profane invention, and naturally lead us to reflect on the difference between the oracles uttered from the former and the fictions of those who dreamed on the latter.

Spenser, in the visionary dominions of Una's father, has planted the Tree of Life and of Knowledge; from the first of the trees, he says, a well flowed, whose waters contained a most salutary virtue, and which the dragon could not approach. Thus in the same scripture: "He showed me a pure river of water of life, clear as crystal, proceeding out of the throne of God, and of the lamb. In the midst of the street of it, and on either side of the river, was there the Tree of Life" (22:1,2). The circumstance, in particular, of the dragon not being able to approach this water is literally adopted from romance, as has been before observed. Thus also by the steps and fictions of romance we are conducted to the death of the dragon who besieged the parents of Una, by which is figured the destruction of the old serpent mentioned in the *Apocalypse*.

The extravagancies of pagan mythology are not improperly introduced into a poem of this sort, as they are acknowledged falsities, or at best, if expressive of any moral truth, no more than the inventions of men. But the poet that applies the visions of God in such a manner is guilty of an impropriety which, I fear, amounts to an impiety.

If we take a retrospect of English poetry from the age of Spenser, we shall find that it principally consisted in visions and allegories. Fancy was a greater friend to the dark ages, as they are called, than is commonly supposed. Our writers caught this vein from the Provençal poets.[31] There are indeed the writings of some English poets now remaining who wrote before Gower or Chaucer. But these are merely chroniclers in rhyme, and seem to have left us the last dregs of that sort of composition which was practiced by the British bards: for instance, the *Chronicle* of Robert of Gloucester, who wrote, according to his account, about the year 1280.[32] The most ancient allegorical poem which I have seen in our language is a manuscript vision, in the Bodleian Library, written in the reign of Edward II by Adam Davie.[33] It is in the short verse of the old metrical romance. However, Gower and Chaucer were justly reputed the first English poets, because they were the first, of any note at least, who introduced *invention* into our poetry, the first who "moralized their song" and strove to render virtue more amiable by clothing her in the veil of fiction. Chaucer, it must be acknowledged, deserves to be placed the first in time of our English poets on another account: his admirable artifice in painting the familiar manners, which none before him had ever attempted in the most imperfect degree; and it should be remembered to his immortal honor that he was the first writer who gave the English nation in their own language an idea of *humor*. About the same time flourished an allegorical satyrist, the author of *Piers Plowman's Visions*. To these succeeded Lydgate, who from his principal performances, the *Fall of Princes* [34] and *Story of Thebes,* more properly may be classed among the legendary poets, although the first of these is in great measure a series of visions. But we have of this author two poems, viz., *The Temple of Glass,* and the *Dance of Death,*[35] besides several other pieces, chiefly in manuscript, professedly written in this species. Lydgate has received numberless encomiums from our old English poets, which he merited more from his language than his imagination. Lydgate is an unanimated writer, yet he made considerable improvements in the rude state of English versification, and is perhaps the first of our poets whom common readers can peruse with little hesitation and difficulty. He was followed by Hardyng, who wrote a chronicle in verse of all the English kings from Brutus, the favorite subject of the British bards or poetical genealogists,[36] down to the reign of Edward IV, in whose reign he lived.[37] This piece is often commended and quoted by our most learned antiquaries. But the poet is lost in the historian; care in collecting and truth in relating events are incompatible with the sallies of invention. So frigid and prosaic a performance, after such promising improvements, seemed to indicate that poetry was relapsing into its primitive barbarism and that the rudeness of Robert of Gloucester would be soon reinstated in the place of Chaucer's judgment and imagination.

However, in the reign of Henry VII this interval of darkness was happily removed by Stephen Hawes, a name generally unknown and not mentioned by any compiler of the lives of English poets. This author was at this period the restorer of invention, which seems to have suffered a gradual degeneracy from the days of Chaucer. He not only revived but improved the ancient allegoric vein which Hardyng had almost entirely banished. Instead of that dryness of description, so remarkably disgusting in many of his predecessors, we are by this poet often entertained with the luxuriant effusions of Spenser. Hawes refined Lydgate's versification and gave it sentiment and imagination, added new graces to the seven-lined stanza which Chaucer and Gower had adopted from the Italian, and to sum up all, was the first of our poets who decorated invention with perspicuous and harmonious numbers. The title of his principal performance is almost as obscure as his name, viz. *The history of* GRAUNDE AMOURE *and* LA BEL PUCEL, *called the* PASTIME OF PLEASURE; *containing the knowledge of the seven sciences, and the course of man's life in this world. Invented by Stephen Hawes, groom of King Henry the Seventh his chamber.*[38] Henry VII is said to have preferred Hawes to this station, chiefly on account of his extraordinary memory, for he could repeat by heart most of the English poets, especially Lydgate.[39] This reign produced another allegorical poem, entitled the *Ship of Fools*. It was translated from the High Dutch,[40] and professes to ridicule the vices and absurdities of all ranks of men. The language is tolerably pure, but it has nothing of the invention and pleasantry which the plan seems to promise, neither of which, however, could be expected if we consider its original.

In the reign of Henry VIII classical literature began to be received and studied in England, and the writings of the ancients were cultivated with true taste and erudition by Sir Thomas More, Colet, Ascham, Leland, Cheke, and other illustrious rivals in polished composition. Erasmus was entertained and patronized by the king and nobility; and the Greek language, that inestimable repository of genuine elegance and sublimity, was taught and admired. In this age flourished John Skelton, who, notwithstanding the great and new lights with which he was surrounded, contributed nothing to what his ancestors had left him, nor do I perceive that his versification is in any degree more refined than that of one of his immediate predecessors, Hawes. Indeed, one would hardly suspect that he wrote in the same age with his elegant contemporaries Surrey and Wyatt.[41] His best pieces are written in the allegorical manner, and are his [*Garland*] *of Laurel*, and *Bouge of Court*. But the genius of Skelton seems little better qualified for picturesque than satirical poetry. In the one he wants invention, grace, and dignity; in the other, wit and good manners.[42]

I should be guilty of injustice to a nation which amid a variety of disadvantages has kept a constant pace with England in the progress of literature if I neglected to mention in this general review two Scottish poets who flourished about this period. Sir

David Lindsay and Sir William Dunbar, the former of which in his *Dream,* and other pieces, and the latter in his "Golden Terge," or "Shield," appear to have been animated with the noblest spirit of allegoric fiction.

Soon afterwards appeared a series of poems entitled *The Mirror of Magistrates,* formed upon a dramatic [43] plan, and capable of admitting some of the most affecting pathetical strokes. But these pieces, however honored with the commendation of Sidney, seem to be little better than a biographical detail.[44] There is one poem indeed, among the rest, which exhibits a group of imaginary personages so beautifully drawn that in all probability they contributed to direct, at least to stimulate, Spenser's imagination in the construction of the like representations. Thus much may be truly said, that Sackville's Induction approaches nearer to the *Fairy Queen* in the richness of allegoric description than any previous or succeeding poem.

After the *Fairy Queen,* allegory began to decline, and by degrees gave place to a species of poetry whose images were of the metaphysical and abstracted kind.[45] This fashion evidently took its rise from the predominant studies of the times, in which the disquisitions of school divinity and the perplexed subtilities of philosophic disputation became the principal pursuits of the learned.

> Then Una Fair gan drop her princely mien.[46]

James I is contemptuously called a pedantic monarch. But surely nothing could be more serviceable to the interests of learning at its infancy than this supposed foible. "To stick the doctor's chair into the throne" was to patronize the literature of the times. In a more enlightened age, the same attention to letters and love of scholars might have produced proportionable effects on sciences of real utility. This cast of mind in the King, however indulged in some cases to an ostentatious affectation, was at least innocent.[47]

Allegory, notwithstanding, unexpectedly rekindled some faint sparks of its native splendor in *The Purple Island* [48] of Fletcher, with whom it almost as soon disappeared, when a poetry succeeded in which imagination gave way to correctness, sublimity of description to delicacy of sentiment, and majestic imagery to conceit and epigram. Poets began now to be more attentive to words than to things and objects. The nicer beauties of happy expression were preferred to the daring strokes of great conception. Satire, that bane of the sublime, was imported from France.[49] The muses were debauched at court, and polite life and familiar manners became their only themes.[50] The simple dignity of Milton was either entirely neglected or mistaken for bombast and insipidity by the refined readers of the dissolute age, whose taste and morals were equally vitiated.[51]

From this detail it will appear that allegorical poetry through many gradations at last received its ultimate consummation in the *Fairy Queen*. Under this consideration, therefore, I hope what I have here collected on this subject will not seem too great a deviation from the main subject of the present section, which I conclude with the just and pertinent sentiments of the Abbé Dubos, on allegorical action. The passage, though properly respecting dramatic poets, is equally applicable to the action of the *Fairy Queen*.

It is impossible for a piece whose subject is an allegorical action to interest us very much. Those which writers of approved wit and talents have hazarded in this kind have not succeeded so well as others, where they have been disposed to be less ingenious and to treat historically their subject.—Our heart requires truth even in fiction itself, and when it is presented with an allegorical fiction, it cannot determine itself, if I may be allowed the expression, to enter into the *sentiments* of those chimerical personages. . . . A theatrical piece, were it to speak only to the *mind*, would never be capable of engaging our attention through the whole performance. We may therefore apply the words of Lactantius upon this occasion. "Poetic licence has its bounds, beyond which you are not permitted to carry your fiction. A poet's art consists in making a good representation of things that might have really happened, and embellishing them with elegant images. *Totum autem, quod referas, fingere, id est ineptum esse et mendacem, potius quam poetam.*" [52]

Postscript

At the close of this work I shall beg leave to subjoin an apology for the manner in which it has been conducted and executed.

I presume it will be objected that these remarks would have appeared with greater propriety connected with Spenser's text and arranged according to their respective references; at least it may be urged that such a plan would have prevented much unnecessary transcription. But I was dissuaded from this method by two reasons. The first is that these "Observations," thus reduced to general heads, form a series of distinct essays on Spenser, and exhibit a course of systematical criticism on the *Fairy Queen*. But my principal argument was that a formal edition of this poem with notes would have been at once impertinent and superfluous, as two publications of Spenser, under that form, are at present expected from the hands of two learned and ingenious critics.[53] Besides, it was never my design to give so complete and perpetual a comment on every part of our author as such an attempt seemed to require. But while some passages are entirely overlooked, or but superficially touched, others will be found to have been discussed more at large and investigated with greater research and accuracy than such an attempt would have permitted.

As to more particular objections, too many, I am sensible, must occur, one of which will probably be that I have been more diligent in remarking the faults than the beauties of Spenser. That I have been deficient in encomiums on particular passages did not proceed from a want of perceiving or acknowledging beauties, but from a persuasion that nothing is more absurd or useless than the panegyrical comments of those who criticize from the imagination rather than from the judgment, who exert their admiration instead of their reason, and discover more of enthusiasm than discernment. And this will most commonly be the case of those critics who profess to point out beauties, because, as they naturally approve themselves to the reader's apprehension by their own force, no reason can often be given why they please. The same cannot always be said of faults, which I have frequently displayed without reserve or palliation.[54]

It was my chief aim to give a clear and comprehensive estimate of the characteristical merits and manner of this admired but neglected poet. For this purpose I have considered the customs and genius of his age; I have searched his contemporary writers, and examined the books on which the peculiarities of his style, taste, and composition are confessedly founded.[55]

I fear I shall be censured for quoting too many pieces of this sort. But experience has frequently and fatally proved that the commentator whose critical inquiries are employed on Spenser,

Jonson, and the rest of our elder poets [56] will in vain give specimens of his classical erudition, unless, at the same time, he brings to his work a mind intimately acquainted with those books which, though now forgotten, were yet in common use and high repute about the time in which his authors respectively wrote, and which they consequently must have read. While these are unknown, many allusions and many imitations will either remain obscure, or lose half their beauty and propriety: "as the figures vanish when the canvas is decayed."

Pope laughs at Theobald for giving us, in his edition of Shakespeare, a sample of

> All such reading *as was never read.*
>
> [*Dunciad* IV, 250]

But these strange and ridiculous books which Theobald quoted were unluckily the very books which Shakespeare himself had studied, the knowledge of which enabled that useful editor to explain so many difficult allusions and obsolete customs in his poet which otherwise could never have been understood. For want of this sort of literature Pope tells us that the *dreadful sagittary* in *Troilus and Cressida* signifies Teucer, so celebrated for his skill in archery. Had he deigned to consult an old history called *The Destruction of Troy,* a book which was the delight of Shakespeare and of his age, he would have found that this formidable archer was no other than an imaginary beast which the Grecian army brought against Troy. If Shakespeare is worth reading, he is worth explaining; and the researches used for so valuable and elegant a purpose merit the thanks of genius and candor, not the satire of prejudice and ignorance. That labor which so essentially contributes to the service of true taste deserves a more honorable repository than "The Temple of Dulness." In the same strain of false satire [57] Pope observes with an air of ridicule that Caxton speaks of the *Aeneid* "as a *history,* as a book *hardly known.*" But the satirist perhaps would have expressed himself with not much more precision or propriety concerning the *Aeneid,* had he been Caxton's contemporary. Certainly, had he wrote English poetry in so unenlightened a period, the world would have lost his refined diction and harmonious versification, the fortunate effects of better times. Caxton, rude and uncouth as he is, co-operated in the noblest cause: he was a very considerable instrument in the grand work of introducing literature into his country. In an illiterate and unpolished age he multiplied books, and consequently readers. The books he printed, besides the grossest barbarisms of style and composition, are chiefly written on subjects of little importance and utility—almost all, except the works of Gower and Chaucer, translations from the French—yet, such as they were, we enjoy their happy consequences at this day. Science, the progressive state of which succeeding generations have improved and completed, dates her original from these artless and imperfect efforts.

Mechanical critics will perhaps be disgusted at the liberties I have taken in introducing so many anecdotes of ancient chivalry. But my subject required frequent proofs of this sort. Nor could I be persuaded that such inquiries were, in other respects, either useless or ridiculous, as they tended at least to illustrate an institution of no frivolous or indifferent nature. Chivalry is commonly looked upon as a barbarous sport or extravagant amusement of the dark ages. It had, however, no small influence on the manners, policies, and constitutions of ancient times, and served many public and important purposes. It was the school of fortitude, honor, and affability. Its exercises, like the Grecian games, habituated the youth to fatigue and enterprise and inspired the noblest sentiments of heroism. It taught gallantry and civility to a savage and ignorant people and humanized the native ferocity of the northern nations. It conduced to refine the manners of the combatants by exciting an emulation in the devices and accoutrements, the splendor and parade, of their tilts and tournaments, while its magnificent festivals, thronged with noble dames and courteous knights, produced the first effort of wit and fancy.[58]

I am still further to hope that, together with other specimens of obsolete literature in general hinted at before, the many references I have made, in particular to romances, the necessary appendage of ancient chivalry, will also plead their pardon. For however monstrous and unnatural these compositions may appear to this age of reason and refinement, they merit more attention than the world is willing to bestow. They preserve many curious historical facts, and throw considerable light on the nature of the feudal system. They are the pictures of ancient usages and customs, and represent the manners, genius, and character of our ancestors. Above all, such are their Terrible Graces of magic and enchantment, so magnificently marvelous are their fictions and fablings, that they contribute, in a wonderful degree, to rouse and invigorate all the powers of imagination, to store the fancy with those sublime and alarming images which true poetry best delights to display.

Lastly, in analyzing the plan and conduct of this poem, I have so far tried it by epic rules as to demonstrate the inconveniencies and incongruities which the poet might have avoided had he been more studious of design and uniformity. It is true that his romantic materials claim great liberties, but no materials exclude order and perspicuity. I have endeavored to account for these defects, partly from the peculiar bent of the poet's genius, which at the same time produced infinite beauties, and partly from the predominant taste of the times in which he wrote.[59]

Let me add that if I have treated some of the Italian poets on certain occasions with too little respect, I did not mean to depreciate their various incidental excellencies. I only suggested that those excellencies, like some of Spenser's, would have appeared to greater advantage had they been more judiciously disposed. I have blamed, indeed, the vicious excess of their fictions; yet I have found no fault in general with their use of magical machinery, notwithstanding I have so far conformed to the reigning maxims of modern criticism as, in the meantime, to recommend classical propriety.[60]

I cannot take my final leave of the reader without the satisfaction of acknowledging that this work has proved a most agreeable task; and I hope this consideration will at least plead my pardon for its length, whatever censure or indulgence the rest of its faults may deserve. The business of criticism is commonly laborious and dry; yet it has here more frequently amused than fatigued my attention in its excursions upon an author who makes such perpetual and powerful appeals to the fancy. Much of the pleasure that Spenser experienced in composing the *Fairy Queen* must, in some measure, be shared by his commentator; and the critic, on this occasion, may speak in the words, and with the rapture, of the poet:

> The waies through which my weary steps I guyde
> In this DELIGHTFUL LAND OF FAERY,
> Are so exceeding spacious and wyde,
> And sprinckled with such sweet variety,
> Of all that pleasant is to ear or eye,
> That I nigh ravisht with rare thoughts delight,
> My TEDIOUS TRAVELL doe forget thereby;
> And when I gin to feele decay of might,
> It strength to me supplies, and cheares my dulled spright.
>
> [VI, *Prol.*, 1]

The History of English Poetry (1774, 1781) [61]

Section XVIII [Chaucer's European Models]

It is not my intention to dedicate a volume to Chaucer, how much soever he may deserve it; nor can it be expected that, in a work of this general nature, I should enter into a critical examination of all Chaucer's pieces. Enough has been said to prove that in elevation and elegance, in harmony and perspicuity of versification, he surpasses his predecessors in an infinite proportion, that his genius was universal and adapted to themes of unbounded variety, that his merit was not less in painting familiar manners with humor and propriety than in moving the passions and in representing the beautiful or the grand objects of nature with grace and sublimity—in a word, that he appeared with all the luster and dignity of a true poet in an age which compelled him to struggle with a barbarous language and a national want of taste, and when to write verses at all was regarded as a singular qualification. It is true indeed that he lived at a time when the French and Italians had made considerable advances and improvements in poetry, and although proofs have already been occasionally given of his imitations from these sources, I shall close my account of him with a distinct and comprehensive view of the nature of the poetry which subsisted in France and Italy when he wrote, pointing out in the meantime how far and in what manner the popular models of those nations contributed to form his taste and influence his genius.

I have already mentioned the troubadours of Provence and have observed that they were fond of moral and allegorical fables. A taste for this sort of composition they partly acquired by reading Boethius and the *Psychomachia* of Prudentius, two favorite classics of the Dark Ages, and partly from the Saracens, their neighbors in Spain, who were great inventors of apologues.[62] The French have a very early metrical romance *De fortune et de félicité,* a translation from Boethius's book *De consolatione,* by Reynault de Louens, a Dominican friar.[63] From this source, among many others of the Provençal poems, came the Tournament of Antichrist above-mentioned, which contains a combat of the Virtues and Vices, the Romaunt of Richard de Lisle in which Modesty fighting with Lust is thrown into the river Seine at Paris, and above all, the *Romaunt of the Rose,* translated by Chaucer and already mentioned at large in its proper place. Visions were a branch of this species of poetry, which admitted the most licentious excursions of fancy in forming personifications and in feigning imaginary beings and ideal habitations. Under these we may rank Chaucer's *House of Fame,* which I have before hinted to have been probably the production of Provence.

But the principal subject of their poems, dictated in great measure by the spirit of chivalry, was love, especially among the troubadours of rank and distinction, whose castles, being crowded with ladies, presented perpetual scenes of the most splendid gallantry. This passion they spiritualized into various metaphysical refinements and filled it with abstracted notions of visionary perfection and felicity. Here, too, they were perhaps influenced by their neighbors, the Saracens, whose philosophy chiefly consisted of fantastic abstractions. It is manifest, however, that nothing can exceed the profound pedantry with which they treated this favorite argument. They defined the essence and characteristics of true love with all the parade of a Scotist in his professorial chair and bewildered their imaginations in speculative questions concerning the most desperate or the most happy situations of a sincere and sentimental heart. But it would be endless and, indeed, ridiculous to describe at length the systematical solemnity with which they clothed this passion. The *Romaunt of the Rose,* which I have just alleged as a proof of their allegorizing turn, is not less an instance of their affectation in writing on this subject, in which the poet, under the agency of allegorical personages, displays the gradual approaches and impediments to fruition and introduces a regular disputation conducted with much formality between Reason and a Lover. Chaucer's *Testament of Love* is also formed on this philosophy of gallantry. It is a lover's parody of Boethius' book *De consolatione* mentioned above. His poem called *La Belle Dame sans Mercy* and his *Assembly of Ladies* are from the same school.[64]

Chaucer's Prioress and Monk, whose lives were devoted to religious reflection and the most serious engagements, and while they are actually traveling on a pilgrimage to visit the shrine of a sainted martyr, openly avow the universal influence of love. They exhibit on their apparel badges entirely inconsistent with their profession but easily accountable for from these principles. The Prioress wears a bracelet on which is inscribed, with a crowned A, *Amor vincit omnia*. The Monk ties his hood with a true-lover's knot. The early poets of Provence, as I before hinted, formed a society called the Court of Love, which gave rise to others in Gascony, Languedoc, Poitou, and Dauphiné; and Picardy, the constant rival of Provence, had a similar institution called *Plaids et gieux sous l'ormel*. These establishments consisted of ladies and gentlemen of the highest rank, exercised and approved in courtesy, who tried with the most consummate ceremony and decided with supreme authority cases in love brought before their tribunal. Martial d'Auvergne, an old French poet, for the diversion and at the request of the Countess of Beaujeu, wrote a poem entitled *Arresta Amorum* [*Arrêts d'amour*], or the *Decrees of Love,* which is a humorous description of the *Plaids* of Picardy. Fontenelle has recited one of their processes which conveys an idea of all the rest.[65] A queen of France was appealed to from an unjust sentence pronounced in the love-pleas where the Countess of Champagne presided. The Queen did not choose to interpose in a matter of so much consequence nor to reverse the decrees of a court whose decision was absolute and final. She answered, "God forbid that I should presume to contradict the sentence of the Countess of Champagne!" This was about the year 1206. Chaucer has a poem called the *Court of Love* which is nothing more than the love-court of Provence.[66] It contains the twenty statutes which that court prescribed to be universally observed under the severest penalties.[67] Not long afterwards, on the same principle, a society was established in Languedoc called the Fraternity of the Penitents of Love. Enthusiasm was here carried to as high a pitch of extravagance as ever it was in religion. It was a contention of ladies and gentlemen who should best sustain the honor of their amorous fanaticism. Their object was to prove the excess of their love by showing with an invincible fortitude and consistency of conduct, with no less obstinacy of opinion, that they could bear extremes of heat and cold. Accordingly the resolute knights and esquires, the dames and damsels, who had the hardiness to embrace this severe institution, dressed themselves during the heat of summer in the thickest mantles lined with the warmest fur. In this they demonstrated, according to the ancient poets, that love works the most wonderful and extraordinary changes. In winter their love again perverted the nature of the seasons; they then clothed themselves in the lightest and thinnest stuffs which could be procured. It was a crime to wear fur on a day of the most piercing cold or to appear with a hood, cloak, gloves, or muff. The flame of love kept them sufficiently warm. Fires all the winter were utterly banished from their houses, and they dressed their apartments with evergreens. In the most intense frost their beds were covered only with a piece of canvas. It must be remembered that in the meantime they passed the greater part of the day abroad in wandering about from castle to castle insomuch that many of these devotees, during so desperate a pilgrimage, perished by the inclemency of the weather and died martyrs to their profession.[68]

The early universality of the French language greatly contributed to facilitate the circulation of the poetry of the troubadours in other countries. The Frankish language was familiar even at Constantinople and in its dependent provinces in the eleventh century and long afterwards. Raymond Montaniero, a historian of Catalonia who wrote about the year 1300, says that the French tongue was as well known in the Morea and at Athens as at Paris. "E parlavan axi belle Francis com dins en Paris." [69] The oldest Italian poetry seems to be founded on that of Provence. The word *sonnet* was adopted from the French into the Italian versification. It occurs in the *Roman de la rose:* "Lais d'amour et sonnets courtois." [70] Boccaccio copied many of his best tales from the troubadours.[71] Several of Dante's fictions are derived from the same fountain. Dante has honored some of them with a seat in his Paradise,[72] and in his tract *De vulgari eloquentia* has mentioned Thibaut, King of Navarre, as a pattern for writing poetry.[73] With regard to Dante's capital work the *Inferno,* Raoul de Houdenc, a Provençal bard about the year 1180, wrote a poem entitled *Le vove ou le songe d'enfer.*[74] Both Boccaccio and Dante studied at Paris, where they much improved their taste by reading the songs of Thibaut, King of Navarre, Gace Brûlé, Châtelain de Couci, and other ancient French fabulists.[75] Petrarch's refined ideas of love are chiefly drawn from those amorous reveries of the Provençals which I have above described, heightened perhaps by the Platonic system and exaggerated by the subtilizing spirit of Italian fancy. Varchi and Pignatelli have written professed treatises on the nature of Petrarch's love. But neither they nor the rest of the Italians, who to this day continue to debate a point of so much consequence, consider how powerfully Petrarch must have been influenced to talk of love in so peculiar a strain by studying the poets of Provence. His *Triumfo di Amore* has much imagery copied from Anselm Fayditt, one of the most celebrated of these bards. He has likewise many imitations from the works of Arnaud Daniel, who is called the most eloquent of the troubadours.[76] Petrarch, in one of his sonnets, represents his mistress Laura sailing on the river Rhone in company with twelve Provençal ladies, who at that time presided over the Court of Love.[77]

Pasquier observes that the Italian poetry arose as the Provençal declined.[78] It is a proof of the decay of invention among the French in the beginning of the fourteenth century that about that period they began to translate into prose their old metrical romances such as the fables of King Arthur, of Charlemagne, of Oddegir the Dane, of Renaud of Montauban, and other illustrious champions whom their early writers had celebrated in rhyme. At length, about the year 1380, in the place of the Provençal a new species of poetry succeeded in France consisting of *chants royaux, ballades, rondeaux,* and *pastorales.* This was distinguished by the appellation of the New Poetry, and Froissart, who has been mentioned above chiefly in the character of a historian, cultivated it with so much success that he has been called its author. The titles of Froissart's poetical pieces alone will serve to illustrate the nature of this New Poetry, but they prove at the same time that the Provençal cast of composition still continued to prevail. They are "The Paradise of Love," "A Panegyric on the Month of May," "The Temple of Honor," "The Flower of the Daisy," "Amorous Lays," "Pastorals," "The Amorous Prison," "Royal Ballads in Honor of our Lady," "The Ditty of the Amorous Spinet," "Virelais," "Rondeaus," and "The Plea of the Rose and Violet." [79] Whoever examines Chaucer's smaller pieces will perceive that they are altogether formed on this plan and often compounded of these ideas. Chaucer himself declares that he wrote

> Many a hymne for your holidaies
> That hightin balades, rondils, virelaies.
>
> [*Legend of Good Women,* Prol. 422]

But above all Chaucer's *Flower and the Leaf*,[80] in which an air of rural description predominates and where the allegory is principally conducted by mysterious allusions to the virtues or beauties of the vegetable world, to flowers and plants, exclusive of its general romantic and allegoric vein, bears a strong resemblance to some of these subjects. The poet is happily placed in a delicious arbor interwoven with eglantine. Imaginary troops of knights and ladies advance; some of the ladies are crowned with flowers and others with chaplets of agnus castus, and these are respectively subject to a "Lady of the Flower" and a "Lady of the Leaf." Some are clothed in green and others in white. Many of the knights are distinguished in much the same manner, but others are crowned with leaves of oak or of other trees. Others carry branches of oak, laurel, hawthorn, and woodbine. Besides this profusion of vernal ornaments, the whole procession glitters with gold, pearls, rubies, and other costly decorations. They are preceded by minstrels clothed in green and crowned with flowers. One of the ladies sings a bargaret, or pastoral, in praise of the daisy.

> A bargaret in praising the daisie,
> For as methought among her notis swete
> She said *si douce est le margaruite*.

This might have been Froissart's song—at least this is one of his subjects. In the meantime a nightingale, seated in a laurel tree whose shade would cover a hundred persons, sings the whole service "longing to May." Some of the knights and ladies do obeisance to the leaf and some to the flower of the daisy. Others are represented as worshiping a bed of flowers. Flora is introduced "of these flouris goddesse." The lady of the leaf invites the lady of the flower to a banquet. Under these symbols is much morality couched. The leaf signifies perseverance and virtue; the flower denotes indolence and pleasure. Among those who are crowned with the leaf are the knights of King Arthur's Round Table and Charlemagne's twelve peers together with the knights of the Order of the Garter now just established by Edward the Third.

But these fancies seem more immediately to have taken their rise from the floral games instituted in France in the year 1324,[81] which filled the French poetry with images of this sort. They were founded by Clementina Isaure, Countess of Toulouse, and annually cele-

brated in the month of May. She published an edict which assembled all the poets of France in artificial arbors dressed with
flowers, and he that produced the best poem was rewarded with a
violet of gold. There were likewise inferior prizes of flowers made
in silver. In the meantime the conquerors were crowned with
natural chaplets of their own respective flowers. During the
ceremony degrees were also conferred. He who had won a prize
three times was created a doctor *en gaye science,* the name of the
poetry of the Provençal troubadours. The instrument of creation
was in verse.[82] This institution, however fantastic, soon became
common through the whole kingdom of France, and these romantic
rewards, distributed with the most impartial attention to merit, at
least infused a useful emulation and in some measure revived the
languishing genius of the French poetry.

The French and Italian poets whom Chaucer imitates abound in
allegorical personages, and it is remarkable that the early poets of
Greece and Rome were fond of these creations. Homer has given us
Strife, Contention, Fear, Terror, Tumult, Desire, Persuasion, and
Benevolence. We have in Hesiod, Darkness, and many others if the
Shield of Hercules be of his hand. Comus occurs in the *Agamemnon*
of Aeschylus, and in the *Prometheus* of the same poet Strength and
Force are two persons of the drama and perform the capital parts.
The fragments of Ennius indicate that his poetry consisted much of
personifications. He says that in one of the Carthaginian wars the
gigantic image of Sorrow appeared in every place, *Omnibus endo
loċis ingens apparet imago Tristitias.* Lucretius has drawn the great
and terrible figure of Superstition, *Quae caput e coeli regionibus
ostendebat.* He also mentions in a beautiful procession of the seasons *Calor Aridus, Hyems,* and *Algus.* He introduces Medicine
"muttering with silent fear" in the midst of the deadly pestilence
at Athens. It seems to have escaped the many critics who have
written on Milton's noble but romantic allegory of Sin and Death
that he took the person of Death from the *Alcestis* of his favorite
tragedian Euripides, where θάνατος is a principal agent in the drama.
As knowledge and learning increase, poetry begins to deal less in
imagination, and these fantastic beings give way to real manners
and living characters.

Section LXI [The Age of Elizabeth]

Enough has been opened of the reign of Queen Elizabeth to afford us an opportunity of forming some general reflections tending to establish a full estimate of the genius of the poetry of that reign and which, by drawing conclusions from what has been said and directing the reader to what he is to expect, will at once be recapitulatory and preparatory. Such a survey perhaps might have stood with more propriety as an introduction to this reign, but it was first necessary to clear the way by many circumstantial details and the regular narration of those particulars which lay the foundation of principles and suggest matter for discursive observation. My sentiments on this subject shall therefore compose the concluding section of the present volume.

The age of Queen Elizabeth is commonly called the golden age of English poetry. It certainly may not improperly be styled the most poetical age of these annals.

Among the great features which strike us in the poetry of this period are the predominancy of fable, of fiction and fancy, and a predilection for interesting adventures and pathetic events. I will endeavor to assign and explain the cause of this characteristic distinction, which may chiefly be referred to the following principles, sometimes blended and sometimes operating singly: the revival and vernacular versions of the classics, the importation and translation of Italian novels, the visionary reveries or refinements of false philosophy, a degree of superstition sufficient for the purposes of poetry, the adoption of the machineries of romance, and the frequency and improvements of allegoric exhibition in the popular spectacles.

When the corruptions and impostures of popery were abolished, the fashion of cultivating the Greek and Roman learning became universal, and the literary character was no longer appropriated to scholars by profession but assumed by the nobility and gentry. The ecclesiastics had found it their interest to keep the languages of antiquity to themselves, and men were eager to know what had been so long injuriously concealed. Truth propagates truth, and the mantle of mystery was removed not only from religion but from literature. The laity, who had now been taught to assert their natural privileges, became impatient of the old monopoly of knowledge and demanded admittance to the usurpations of the clergy. The general curiosity for new discoveries, heightened either by just or imaginary ideas of the treasures contained in the Greek and Roman writers, excited all persons of leisure and fortune to study the classics. The pedantry of the present age was the politeness of the last. An accurate comprehension of the phraseology and peculiarities of the ancient poets, historians, and orators, which yet seldom went farther than a kind of technical erudition, was an indispensable and almost the principal object in the circle of a gentleman's education. Every young lady of fashion was carefully instituted in classical letters, and the daughter of a duchess was taught not only to distill strong waters but to construe Greek. Among the learned females of high distinction Queen Elizabeth herself was the most conspicuous. Roger Ascham, her preceptor, speaks with rapture of her astonishing progress in the Greek nouns and declares with no small degree of triumph that during a long residence at Windsor Castle she was accustomed to read more Greek in a day than "some prebendary of that church did Latin in one week." [83] And although perhaps a princess looking out words in a lexicon and writing down hard phrases from Plutarch's *Lives* may be thought at present a more incompatible and extraordinary character than a canon of Windsor understanding no Greek and but little Latin, yet Elizabeth's passion for these acquisitions was then natural and resulted from the genius and habitudes of her age.

The books of antiquity being thus familiarized to the great, everything was tinctured with ancient history and mythology. The heathen gods, although discountenanced by the Calvinists on a suspicion of their tending to cherish and revive a spirit of idolatry, came into general vogue. When the Queen paraded through a country town almost every pageant was a pantheon. When she paid a visit at the house of any of her nobility, at entering the hall she was saluted by the Penates and conducted to her privy chamber by Mercury. Even the pastry-cooks were expert mythologists. At dinner select transformations of Ovid's *Metamorphoses* were exhibited in confectionery, and the splendid icing of an immense historic plum-cake was embossed with a delicious *basso-relievo* of the destruction of Troy. In the afternoon when she condescended to walk in the garden, the lake was covered with Tritons and Nereids, the pages of the family were converted into wood nymphs who peeped from

every bower, and the footmen gamboled over the lawns in the figure
of satyrs. I speak it without designing to insinuate any unfavorable
suspicions, but it seems difficult to say why Elizabeth's virginity
should have been made the theme of perpetual and excessive
panegyric, nor does it immediately appear that there is less merit
or glory in a married than a maiden queen. Yet the next morning,
after sleeping in a room hung with the tapestry of the voyage of
Aeneas, when her majesty hunted in the park, she was met by
Diana, who, pronouncing our royal prude to be the brightest
paragon of unspotted chastity, invited her to groves free from the
intrusions of Acteon. The truth is, she was so profusely flattered for
this virtue because it was esteemed the characteristical ornament of
the heroines, as fantastic honor was the chief pride of the champions
of the old barbarous romance. It was in conformity to the sentiments of chivalry, which still continued in vogue, that she was
celebrated for chastity; the compliment, however, was paid in a
classical allusion.

Queens must be ridiculous when they would appear as women.
The softer attractions of sex vanish on the throne. Elizabeth sought
all occasions of being extolled for her beauty, of which, indeed, in
the prime of her youth she possessed but a small share, whatever
might have been her pretensions to absolute virginity. Notwithstanding her exaggerated habits of dignity and ceremony and a
certain affectation of imperial severity, she did not perceive this
ambition of being complimented for beauty to be an idle and unpardonable levity totally inconsistent with her high station and
character. As she conquered all nations with her arms, it matters
not what were the triumphs of her eyes. Of what consequence was
the complexion of the mistress of the world? Not less vain of her
person than her politics, this stately coquette, the guardian of
the Protestant faith, the terror of the sea, the mediatrix of the
factions of France, and the scourge of Spain, was infinitely mortified
if an ambassador at the first audience did not tell her she was the
finest woman in Europe. No negotiation succeeded unless she was
addressed as a goddess. Encomiastic harangues drawn from this
topic, even on the supposition of youth and beauty, were surely
superfluous, unsuitable, and unworthy, and were offered and received with an equal impropriety. Yet when she rode through the
streets of the city of Norwich, Cupid, at the command of the mayor
and aldermen, advancing from a group of gods who had left

Olympus to grace the procession, gave her a golden arrow, the most effective weapon of his well-furnished quiver, which under the influence of such irresistible charms was sure to wound the most obdurate heart. "A gift," says honest Holinshed, "which her majesty, now verging to her fiftieth year, received very thankfully." [84] In one of the fulsome interludes at court where she was present, the singing-boys of her chapel presented the story of the three rival goddesses on Mount Ida, to which Her Majesty was ingeniously added as a fourth, and Paris was arraigned in form for adjudging the golden apple to Venus, which was due to the Queen alone.

This inundation of classical pedantry soon infected our poetry. Our writers, already trained in the school of fancy, were suddenly dazzled with these novel imaginations, and the divinities and heroes of pagan antiquity decorated every composition. The perpetual allusions to ancient fable were often introduced without the least regard to propriety. Shakespeare's Mrs. Page, who is not intended in any degree to be a learned or an affected lady, laughing at the cumbersome courtship of her corpulant lover Falstaff, says, "I had rather be a giantess and lie under Mount Pelion." [85] This familiarity with the pagan story was not, however, so much owing to the prevailing study of the original authors as to the numerous English versions of them which were consequently made. The translations of the classics, which now employed every pen, gave a currency and a celebrity to these fancies and had the effect of diffusing them among the people. No sooner were they delivered from the pale of the scholastic languages than they acquired a general notoriety. Ovid's *Metamorphoses,* just translated by Golding [1567], to instance no farther, disclosed a new world of fiction even to the illiterate. As we had now all the ancient fables in English, learned allusions, whether in a poem or a pageant, were no longer obscure and unintelligible to common readers and common spectators. And here we are led to observe that at this restoration of the classics we were first struck only with their fabulous inventions. We did not attend to their regularity of design and justness of sentiment. A rude age beginning to read these writers imitated their extravagances, not their natural beauties. And these, like other novelties, were pursued to a blamable excess.

I have before given a sketch of the introduction of classical stories in the splendid show exhibited at the coronation of Queen

Anne Boleyn. But that is a rare and a premature instance, and the pagan fictions are there complicated with the barbarisms of the Catholic worship and the doctrines of scholastic theology. Classical learning was not then so widely spread, either by study or translation, as to bring these learned spectacles into fashion, to frame them with sufficient skill, and to present them with propriety.

Another capital source of the poetry peculiar to this period consisted in the numerous translations of Italian tales into English. These narratives, not dealing altogether in romantic inventions but in real life and manners and in artful arrangements of fictitious yet probable events, afforded a new gratification to a people which yet retained their ancient relish for tale-telling and became the fashionable amusement of all who professed to read for pleasure. They gave rise to innumerable plays and poems which would not otherwise have existed, and turned the thoughts of our writers to new inventions of the same kind. Before these books became common, affecting situations, the combination of incident, and the pathos of catastrophe were almost unknown. Distress, especially that arising from the conflicts of the tender passion, had not yet been shown in its most interesting forms. It was hence our poets, particularly the dramatic, borrowed ideas of a legitimate plot and the complication of facts necessary to constitute a story either of the comic or tragic species. In proportion as knowledge increased, genius had wanted subjects and materials. These pieces usurped the place of legends and chronicles. And although the old historical songs of the minstrels contained much bold adventure, heroic enterprise, and strong touches of rude delineation, yet they failed in that multiplication and disposition of circumstances and in that description of characters and events approaching nearer to truth and reality which were demanded by a more discerning and curious age. Even the rugged features of the original Gothic romance were softened by this sort of reading, and the Italian pastoral, yet with some mixture of the kind of incidents described in Heliodorus' *Ethiopic History*, now newly translated,[86] was engrafted on the feudal manners in Sidney's *Arcadia*.

But the Reformation had not yet destroyed every delusion, nor disenchanted all the strong holds of superstition. A few dim characters were yet legible in the mouldering creed of tradition. Every goblin of ignorance did not vanish at the first glimmerings of the morning of science. Reason suffered a few demons still to linger, which she chose to retain in her service under the guidance of poetry. Men believed, or were willing to believe, that spirits were yet hovering around who brought with them airs from heaven or blasts from hell, that the ghost was duly released from his prison of torment at the sound of the curfew, and that fairies imprinted mysterious circles on the turf by moonlight. Much of this credulity was even consecrated by the name of science and profound speculation. Prospero had not yet "broken and buried his staff," nor "drowned his book deeper than did ever plummet sound." It was now that the alchemist and the judicial astrologer conducted his occult operations by the potent intercourse of some preternatural being who came obsequious to his call and was bound to accomplish his severest services under certain conditions and for a limited duration of time. It was actually one of the pretended feats of these fantastic philosophers to evoke the Queen of the Fairies in the solitude of a gloomy grove, who, preceded by a sudden rustling of the leaves, appeared in robes of transcendent luster.[87] The Shakespeare of a more instructed and polished age would not have given us a magician darkening the sun at noon, the sabbath of the witches, and the cauldron of incantation.

Undoubtedly most of these notions were credited and entertained in a much higher degree in the preceding periods. But the arts of composition had not then made a sufficient progress, nor would the poets of those periods have managed them with so much address and judgment. We were now arrived at that point when the national credulity, chastened by reason, had produced a sort of civilized superstition and left a set of traditions, fanciful enough for poetic decoration and yet not too violent and chimerical for common sense. Hobbes, although no friend to this doctrine, observes happily, "In a good poem both judgment and fancy are required, but the fancy must be more eminent because they please for the *extravagancy* but ought not to displease by *indiscretion*." [88]

In the meantime the Gothic romance, although somewhat shook by the classical fictions and by the tales of Boccaccio and Bandello, still maintained its ground, and the daring machineries of giants, dragons, and enchanted castles borrowed from the magic storehouse of Boiardo, Ariosto, and Tasso began to be employed by the epic muse. These ornaments have been censured by the bigotry of precise and servile critics as abounding in whimsical absurdities and as unwarrantable deviations from the practice of Homer and

Virgil. The author of *An Inquiry into the Life and Writings of Homer* [89] is willing to allow a fertility of genius and a felicity of expression to Tasso and Ariosto, but at the same time complains that, "quitting life, they betook themselves to aerial beings and utopian characters, and filled their works with charms and visions, the modern supplements of the marvelous and sublime. The best poets copy nature and give it such as they find it. When once they lose sight of this, they write false, be their talents ever so great." But what shall we say of those utopians, the Cyclops and the Lestrigons in the *Odyssey?* The hippogrif of Ariosto may be opposed to the harpies of Virgil. If leaves are turned into ships in the *Orlando,* nymphs are transformed into ships in the *Aeneid.* Cacus is a more unnatural savage than Caliban. Nor am I convinced that the imagery of Ismeno's necromantic forest in the *Jerusalem Delivered,* guarded by walls and battlements of fire, is less marvelous and sublime than the leap of Juno's horses in the *Iliad,* celebrated by Longinus for its singular magnificence and dignity. [90] On the principles of this critic, Voltaire's *Henriad* may be placed at the head of the modern epic. But I forbear to anticipate my opinion of a system which will more properly be considered when I come to speak of Spenser. I must, however, observe here that the Gothic and pagan fictions were now frequently blended and incorporated. The Lady of the Lake floated in the suite of Neptune before Queen Elizabeth at Kenilworth; Ariel assumes the semblance of a sea nymph, and Hecate, by an easy association, conducts the rites of the weird sisters in *Macbeth.*

Allegory had been derived from the religious dramas into our civil spectacles. The masques and pageantries of the age of Elizabeth were not only furnished by the heathen divinities but often by the virtues and vices impersonated, significantly decorated, accurately distinguished by their proper types, and represented by living actors. The ancient symbolical shows of this sort began now to lose their old barbarism and a mixture of religion and to assume a degree of poetical elegance and precision. Nor was it only in the conformation of particular figures that much fancy was shown, but in the contexture of some of the fables or devices presented by groups of ideal personages. These exhibitions quickened creative invention and reflected back on poetry what poetry had given. From their familiarity and public nature they formed a national taste for allegory, and the allegorical poets were now writing to the people. Even romance was turned into this channel. In the *Fairy*

Queen allegory is wrought upon chivalry and the feats and figments of Arthur's Round Table are moralized. The virtues of magnificence and chastity are here personified, but they are imaged with the forms and under the agency of romantic knights and damsels. What was an afterthought in Tasso appears to have been Spenser's premeditated and primary design. In the meantime, we must not confound these moral combatants of the *Fairy Queen* with some of its other embodied abstractions which are purely and professedly allegorical.

It may here be added that only a few critical treatises and but one *Art of Poetry* [91] were now written. Sentiments and images were not absolutely determined by the canons of composition, nor was genius awed by the consciousness of a future and final arraignment at the tribunal of taste. A certain dignity of inattention to niceties is now visible in our writers. Without too closely consulting a criterion of correctness, every man indulged his own capriciousness of invention. The poet's appeal was chiefly to his own voluntary feelings, his own immediate and peculiar mode of conception. And this freedom of thought was often expressed in an undisguised frankness of diction —a circumstance, by the way, that greatly contributed to give the flowing modulation which now marked the measures of our poets and which soon degenerated into the opposite extreme of dissonance and asperity. Selection and discrimination were often overlooked. Shakespeare wandered in pursuit of universal nature. The glancings of his eye are from heaven to earth, from earth to heaven. We behold him breaking the barriers of imaginary method. In the same scene he descends from his meridian of the noblest tragic sublimity, to puns and quibbles, to the meanest merriments of a plebeian farce. In the midst of his dignity, he resembles his own Richard the Second, the "skipping king," who sometimes discarding the state of a monarch, "mingled his royalty with carping fools." [92] He seems not to have seen any impropriety in the most abrupt transitions from dukes to buffoons, from senators to sailors, from counsellors to constables, and from kings to clowns. Like Virgil's majestic oak,

> Quantum vertice ad auras
> aetherias, tantum radice in Tartara tendit.[93]

No satires, properly so called, were written till towards the latter end of the Queen's reign, and then but a few. Pictures drawn at large of the vices of the times did not suit readers who loved to wander in the regions of artificial manners. The Muse, like the people, was too solemn and reserved, too ceremonious and pedantic, to stoop to common life. Satire is the poetry of a nation highly polished.

The importance of the female character was not yet acknowledged, nor were women admitted into the general commerce of society. The effect of that intercourse had not imparted a comic air to poetry, nor softened the severer tone of our versification with the levities of gallantry and the familiarities of compliment, sometimes perhaps operating on serious subjects and imperceptibly spreading themselves in the general habits of style and thought. I do not mean to insinuate that our poetry has suffered from the great change of manners which this assumption of the gentler sex, or rather the improved state of female education, has produced by giving elegance and variety to life, by enlarging the sphere of conversation, and by multiplying the topics and enriching the stores of wit and humor. But I am marking the peculiarities of composition, and my meaning was to suggest that the absence of so important a circumstance from the modes and constitution of ancient life must have influenced the contemporary poetry. Of the state of manners among our ancestors respecting this point, many traces remain. Their style of courtship may be collected from the love dialogues of Hamlet, young Percy, Henry the Fifth, and Master Fenton.[94] Their tragic heroines, their Desdemonas and Ophelias, although of so much consequence in the piece, are degraded to the background. In comedy their ladies are nothing more than "merry wives," plain and cheerful matrons who stand upon the "chariness of their honesty." In the smaller poems, if a lover praises his mistress, she is complimented in strains neither polite nor pathetic, without elegance and without affection; she is described, not in the address of intelligible yet artful panegyric, not in the real colors and with the genuine accomplishments of nature, but as an eccentric ideal being of another system, and as inspiring sentiments equally unmeaning, hyperbolical, and unnatural.

All or most of these circumstances contributed to give a descriptive, a picturesque, and a figurative cast to the poetical language. This effect appears even in the prose compositions of the reign of Elizabeth. In the subsequent age prose became the language of poetry.

In the meantime general knowledge was increasing with a wide diffusion and a hasty rapidity. Books began to be multiplied, and a variety of the most useful and rational topics had been discussed in our own language. But science had not made too great advances. On the whole, we were now arrived at that period, propitious to the operations of original and true poetry, when the coyness of fancy was not always proof against the approaches of reason, when genius was rather directed than governed by judgment, and when taste and learning had so far only disciplined imagination as to suffer its excesses to pass without censure or control for the sake of the beauties to which they were allied.

DAVID HUME ✍

Four Dissertations (1757)

"Of Tragedy"

It seems an unaccountable pleasure which the spectators of a well-written tragedy receive from sorrow, terror, anxiety, and other passions that are in themselves disagreeable and uneasy. The more they are touched and affected, the more are they delighted with the spectacle; and as soon as the uneasy passions cease to operate, the piece is at an end. One scene of full joy and contentment and security is the utmost that any composition of this kind can bear, and it is sure always to be the concluding one. If in the texture of the piece there be interwoven any scenes of satisfaction, they afford only faint gleams of pleasure, which are thrown in by way of variety, and in order to plunge the actors into deeper distress by means of that contrast and disappointment. The whole art of the poet is employed in rousing and supporting the compassion and indignation, the anxiety and resentment, of his audience. They are pleased in proportion as they are afflicted, and never are so happy as when they employ tears, sobs, and cries to give vent to their sorrow and relieve their heart, swollen with the tenderest sympathy and compassion.

The few critics who have had some tincture of philosophy have remarked this singular phenomenon and have endeavored to account for it.

L'Abbé Dubos, in his reflections on poetry and painting,[1] asserts that nothing is in general so disagreeable to the mind as the languid, listless state of indolence into which it falls upon the removal of all passion and occupation. To get rid of this painful situation, it seeks every amusement and pursuit—business, gaming, shows, executions—whatever will rouse the passions and take its attention from itself. No matter what the passion is, let it be disagreeable, afflicting, melancholy, disordered, it is still better than that insipid languor which arises from perfect tranquillity and repose.

It is impossible not to admit this account as being, at least in part, satisfactory. You may observe when there are several tables of gaming that all the company run to those where the deepest play is, even though they find not there the best players. The view, or at least imagination, of high passions arising from great loss or gain affects the spectator by sympathy, gives him some touches of the same passions, and serves him for a momentary entertainment. It makes the time pass the easier with him, and is some relief to that oppression under which men commonly labor when left entirely to their own thoughts and meditations.

We find that common liars always magnify in their narrations all kinds of danger, pain, distress, sickness, deaths, murders, and cruelties; as well as joy, beauty, mirth, and magnificence. It is an absurd secret which they have for pleasing their company, fixing their attention, and attaching them to such marvellous relations, by the passions and emotions which they excite.

There is, however, a difficulty in applying to the present subject in its full extent this solution, however ingenious and satisfactory it may appear. It is certain that the same object of distress which pleases in a tragedy, were it really set before us, would give the most unfeigned uneasiness, though it be then the most effectual cure to languor and indolence. Monsieur Fontenelle seems to have been sensible of this difficulty, and accordingly attempts another solution of the phenomenon, at least makes some addition to the theory above mentioned:

Pleasure and pain, says he, which are two sentiments so different in themselves, differ not so much in their cause. From the instance of tickling it appears that the movement of pleasure pushed a little too far becomes pain, and that the movement of pain a little moderated becomes pleasure. Hence it proceeds that there is such a thing as a sorrow, soft and agreeable; it is a pain weakened and diminished. The heart likes naturally to be moved and affected. Melancholy objects suit it, and even disastrous and sorrowful, provided they are softened by some circumstance. It is certain that on the theater the representation has always the effect of reality; yet it has not altogether that effect.

However we may be hurried away by the spectacle, whatever dominion the senses and imagination may usurp over the reason, there still lurks at the bottom a certain idea of falsehood in the whole of what we see. This idea, though weak and disguised, suffices to diminish the pain which we suffer from the misfortunes of those whom we love and to reduce that affliction to such a pitch as converts it into a pleasure. We weep for the misfortune of a hero to whom we are attached. In the same instant we comfort ourselves by reflecting that it is nothing but a fiction. And it is precisely that mixture of sentiments which composes an agreeable sorrow, and tears that delight us. But as that affliction which is caused by exterior and sensible objects is stronger than the consolation which arises from an internal reflection, they are the effects and symptoms of sorrow that ought to predominate in the composition. (*Réflexions sur la poétique,* xxxvi)

This solution seems just and convincing, but perhaps it wants still some new addition in order to make it answer fully the phenomenon which we here examine. All the passions excited by eloquence are agreeable in the highest degree, as well as those which are moved by painting and the theater. The epilogues of Cicero are, on this account chiefly, the delight of every reader of taste, and it is difficult to read some of them without the deepest sympathy and sorrow. His merit as an orator no doubt depends much on his success in this particular. When he had raised tears in his judges and all his audience, they were then the most highly delighted, and expressed the greatest satisfaction with the pleader. The pathetic description of the butchery made by Verres of the Sicilian captains [2] is a masterpiece of this kind, but I believe none will affirm that the being present at a melancholy scene of that nature would afford any entertainment. Neither is the sorrow here softened by fiction, for the audience were convinced of the reality of every circumstance. What is it, then, which in this case raises a pleasure from the bosom of uneasiness, so to speak, and a pleasure which still retains all the features and outward symptoms of distress and sorrow?

I answer: This extraordinary effect proceeds from that very eloquence with which the melancholy scene is represented. The genius required to paint objects in a lively manner, the art employed in collecting all the pathetic circumstances, the judgment displayed in disposing them—the exercise, I say, of these noble talents, together with the force of expression and beauty of oratorial numbers, diffuse the highest satisfaction on the audience and excite the most delightful movements. By this means the uneasiness of the melancholy passions is not only overpowered and effaced by something stronger of an opposite kind but the whole impulse of those passions is converted into pleasure and swells the delight which the eloquence raises in us. The same force of oratory employed on an uninteresting subject would not please half so much, or rather would appear altogether ridiculous; and the mind, being left in absolute calmness and indifference, would relish none of those beauties of imagination or expression which, if joined to passion, give it such exquisite entertainment. The impulse or vehemence arising from sorrow, compassion, indignation receives a new direction from the sentiments of beauty. The latter, being the predominant motion, seize the whole mind and convert the former into themselves, at least tincture them so strongly as totally to alter their nature. And the soul, being at the same time roused by passion and charmed by eloquence, feels on the whole a strong movement which is altogether delightful.

The same principle takes place in tragedy—with this addition, that tragedy is an imitation; and imitation is always of itself agreeable. This circumstance serves still farther to smooth the motions of passion and convert the whole feeling into one uniform and strong enjoyment. Objects of the greatest terror and distress please in painting, and please more than the most beautiful objects that appear calm and indifferent.[3] The affection, rousing the mind, excites a large stock of spirit and vehemence, which is all transformed into pleasure by the force of the prevailing movement. It is thus the fiction of tragedy softens the passion, by an infusion of a new feeling, not merely by weakening or diminishing the sorrow. You may by degrees weaken a real sorrow till it totally disappears; yet in none of its gradations will it ever give pleasure except, perhaps, by accident, to a man sunk under lethargic indolence whom it rouses from that languid state.

To confirm this theory, it will be sufficient to produce other instances where the subordinate movement is converted into the predominant, and gives force to it, though of a different and even sometimes though of a contrary nature.

Novelty naturally rouses the mind and attracts our attention, and the movements which it causes are always converted into any passion belonging to the object, and join their force to it. Whether an event excite joy or sorrow, pride or shame, anger or good will, it is sure to produce a stronger affection when new or unusual. And though novelty of itself be agreeable, it fortifies the painful as well as agreeable passions.

Had you any intention to move a person extremely by the narration of any event, the best method of increasing its effect would be artfully to delay informing him of it, and first to excite his curiosity and impatience before you let him into the secret. This is the artifice practiced by Iago in the famous scene of Shakespeare, and every spectator is sensible that Othello's jealousy acquires additional force from his preceding impatience and that the subordinate passion is here readily transformed into the predominant one.

Difficulties increase passions of every kind, and by rousing our attention and exciting our active powers, they produce an emotion which nourishes the prevailing affection.

Parents commonly love that child most whose sickly, infirm frame of body has occasioned them the greatest pains, trouble, and anxiety in rearing him. The agreeable sentiment of affection here acquires force from sentiments of uneasiness.

Nothing endears so much a friend as sorrow for his death. The pleasure of his company has not so powerful an influence.

Jealousy is a painful passion; yet without some share of it, the agreeable affection of love has difficulty to subsist in its full force and violence. Absence is also a great source of complaint among lovers, and gives them the greatest uneasiness, yet nothing is more favorable to their mutual passion than short intervals of that kind. And if long intervals often prove fatal, it is only because through time men are accustomed to them, and they cease to give uneasiness. Jealousy and absence in love compose the *dolce peccante* of the Italians, which they suppose so essential to all pleasure.

There is a fine observation of the elder Pliny, which illustrates the principle here insisted on.

It is very remarkable, says he, that the last works of celebrated artists, which they left imperfect, are always the most prized, such as the *Iris* of Aristides, the *Tyndarides* of Nicomachus, the *Medea* of Timomachus, and the *Venus* of Apelles. These are valued even above their finished productions. The broken lineaments of the piece, and the half-formed idea of the painter, are carefully studied; and our very grief for that curious hand, which had been stopped by death, is an additional increase to our pleasure. [*Nat. hist.* xxxv. 40]

These instances (and many more might be collected) are sufficient to afford us some insight into the analogy of nature, and to show us that the pleasure which poets, orators, and musicians give us by exciting grief, sorrow, indignation, compassion, is not so extraordinary or paradoxical as it may at first sight appear. The force of imagination, the energy of expression, the power of numbers, the charms of imitation—all these are naturally, of themselves, delightful to the mind. And when the object presented lays also hold of some affection, the pleasure still rises upon us by the conversion of this subordinate movement into that which is predominant. The passion, though perhaps naturally, and when excited by the simple appearance of a real object, it may be painful, yet is so smoothed and softened and mollified when raised by the finer arts that it affords the highest entertainment.

To confirm this reasoning, we may observe that if the movements of the imagination be not predominant above those of the passion, a contrary effect follows, and the former, being now subordinate, is converted into the latter, and still farther increases the pain and affliction of the sufferer.

Who could ever think of it as a good expedient for comforting an afflicted parent to exaggerate, with all the force of elocution, the irreparable loss which he has met with by the death of a favorite child? The more power of imagination and expression you here employ, the more you increase his despair and affliction.

The shame, confusion, and terror of Verres, no doubt, rose in proportion to the noble eloquence and vehemence of Cicero; so also did his pain and uneasiness. These former passions were too strong for the pleasure arising from the beauties of elocution, and operated, though from the same principle, yet in a contrary manner, to the sympathy, compassion, and indignation of the audience.

Lord Clarendon, when he approaches towards the catastrophe of the royal party, supposes that his narration must then become infinitely disagreeable; and he hurries over the king's death without giving us one circumstance of it.[4] He considers it as too horrid a scene to be contemplated with any satisfaction, or even without the utmost pain and aversion. He himself, as well as the readers of that age, were too deeply concerned in the events, and felt a pain from subjects which a historian and a reader of another age would regard as the most pathetic and most interesting, and by consequence, the most agreeable.

An action represented in tragedy may be too bloody and atrocious. It may excite such movements of horror as will not soften into pleasure, and the greatest energy of expression bestowed on descriptions of that nature serves only to augment our uneasiness. Such is that action represented in the *Ambitious Stepmother,*[5] where a venerable old man, raised to the height of fury and despair, rushes against a pillar, and striking his head upon it, besmears it all over with mingled brains and gore. The English theater abounds too much with such shocking images.

Even the common sentiments of compassion require to be softened by some agreeable affection in order to give a thorough satisfaction to the audience. The mere suffering of plaintive virtue under the triumphant tyranny and oppression of vice forms a disagreeable spectacle, and is carefully avoided by all masters of the drama. In order to dismiss the audience with entire satisfaction and contentment, the virtue must either convert itself into a noble, courageous despair, or the vice receive its proper punishment.

Most painters appear in this light to have been very unhappy in their subjects. As they wrought much for churches and convents, they have chiefly represented such horrible subjects as crucifixions and martyrdoms, where nothing appears but tortures, wounds, executions, and passive suffering, without any action or affection. When they turned their pencil from this ghastly mythology, they had commonly recourse to Ovid, whose fictions, though passionate and agreeable, are scarcely natural or probable enough for painting.

The same inversion of that principle which is here insisted on displays itself in common life, as in the effects of oratory and poetry. Raise so the subordinate passion that it becomes the predominant, it swallows up that affection which it before nourished and increased. Too much jealousy extinguishes love. Too much difficulty renders us indifferent. Too much sickness and infirmity disgusts a selfish and unkind parent.

What so disagreeable as the dismal, gloomy, disastrous stories with which melancholy people entertain their companions? The uneasy passion being there raised alone, unaccompanied with any spirit, genius, or eloquence, conveys a pure uneasiness, and is attended with nothing that can soften it into pleasure or satisfaction.

"Of the Standard of Taste" [6]

The great variety of taste, as well as of opinion, which prevails in the world is too obvious not to have fallen under everyone's observation. Men of the most confined knowledge are able to remark a difference of taste in the narrow circle of their acquaintance, even where the persons have been educated under the same government and have early imbibed the same prejudices. But those who can enlarge their view to contemplate distant nations and remote ages are still more surprised at the great inconsistence and contrariety. We are apt to call barbarous whatever departs widely from our own taste and apprehension, but soon find the epithet of reproach retorted on us. And the highest arrogance and self-conceit is at last startled on observing an equal assurance on all sides, and scruples amidst such a contest of sentiment to pronounce positively in its own favor.

As this variety of taste is obvious to the most careless inquirer, so will it be found, on examination, to be still greater in reality than in appearance. The sentiments of men often differ with regard to beauty and deformity of all kinds, even while their general discourse is the same. There are certain terms in every language which import blame, and others praise; and all men who use the same tongue must agree in their application of them. Every voice is united in applauding elegance, propriety, simplicity, spirit in writing; and in blaming fustian, affectation, coldness, and a false brilliancy. But when critics come to particulars, this seeming unanimity vanishes, and it is found that they had affixed a very different meaning to their expressions. In all matters of opinion and science, the case is opposite. The difference among men is there oftener found to lie in generals than in particulars, and to be less in reality than in appearance. An explanation of the terms commonly ends the controversy, and the disputants are surprised to find that they had been quarreling, while at bottom they agreed in their judgment.

Those who found morality on sentiment more than on reason are inclined to comprehend ethics under the former observation, and to maintain that in all questions which regard conduct and manners the difference among men is really greater than at first sight it appears. It is indeed obvious that writers of all nations and all ages concur in applauding justice, humanity, magnanimity, prudence, veracity; and in blaming the opposite qualities. Even poets and other authors whose compositions are chiefly calculated to please the imagination are yet found, from Homer down to Fénelon, to inculcate the same moral precepts, and to bestow their applause and blame on the same virtues and vices. This great unanimity is usually ascribed to the influence of plain reason, which in all these cases maintains similar sentiments in all men and prevents those controversies to which the abstract sciences are so much exposed. So far as the unanimity is real, this account may be admitted as satisfactory. But we must also allow that some part of the seeming harmony in morals may be accounted for from the very nature of language. The word *Virtue,* with its equivalent in every tongue, implies praise; as that of *vice* does blame. And no one, without the most obvious and grossest impropriety, could affix reproach to a term which in general acceptation is understood in a good sense, or bestow applause where the idiom requires disapprobation. Homer's general precepts, where he delivers any such, will never be controverted; but it is obvious that when he draws particular pictures of manners and represents heroism in Achilles and prudence in Ulysses, he intermixes a much greater degree of ferocity in the former and of cunning and fraud in the latter than Fénelon would admit of. The sage Ulysses in the Greek poet seems to delight in lies and fictions and often employs them without any necessity or even advantage. But his more scrupulous son, in the French epic writer, exposes himself to the most imminent perils rather than depart from the most exact line of truth and veracity.

The admirers and followers of the *Alcoran* insist on the excellent moral precepts interspersed throughout that wild and absurd performance. But it is to be supposed that the Arabic words which correspond to the English *equity, justice, temperance, meekness, charity,* were such as, from the constant use of that tongue, must always be taken in a good sense; and it would have argued the greatest ignorance, not of morals, but of language, to have mentioned them with any epithets besides those of applause and approbation. But would we know whether the pretended prophet had really attained a just sentiment of morals? Let us attend to his narration, and we shall soon find that he bestows praise on such instances of treachery, inhumanity, cruelty, revenge, bigotry as are utterly incompatible with civilized society. No steady rule of right seems there to be attended to, and every action is blamed or praised so far only as it is beneficial or hurtful to the true believers.

The merit of delivering true general precepts in ethics is indeed very small. Whoever recommends any moral virtues really does no more than is implied in the terms themselves. That people who invented the word *charity* and used it in a good sense inculcated more clearly and much more efficaciously the precept "be charitable" than any pretended legislator or prophet who should insert such a maxim in his writings. Of all expressions, those which together with their other meaning imply a degree either of blame or approbation are the least liable to be perverted or mistaken.

It is natural for us to seek a "standard of taste," a rule by which the various sentiments of men may be reconciled, at least a decision afforded, confirming one sentiment and condemning another.

There is a species of philosophy which cuts off all hopes of success in such an attempt and represents the impossibility of ever attaining any standard of taste. The difference, it is said, is very wide between judgment and sentiment. All sentiment is right, because sentiment has a reference to nothing beyond itself, and is always real wherever a man is conscious of it. But all determinations of the understanding are not right, because they have a reference to something beyond themselves, to wit, real matter of fact, and are not always conformable to that standard. Among a thousand different opinions which different men may entertain of the same subject, there is one, and but one, that is just and true; and the only difficulty is to fix and ascertain it. On the contrary, a thousand different sentiments excited by the same object are all right, because no sentiment represents what is really in the object. It only marks a certain conformity or relation between the object and the organs or faculties of the mind; and if that conformity did not really exist, the sentiment could never possibly have being. Beauty is no quality in things themselves. It exists merely in the mind which contemplates them, and each mind perceives a different beauty. One person may even perceive deformity where another is sensible of beauty, and every individual ought to acquiesce in his own sentiment without pretending to regulate those of others. To seek the real beauty or real deformity is as fruitless an inquiry as to pretend to ascertain the real sweet or real bitter. According to the disposition of the organs, the same object may be both sweet and bitter, and the proverb has justly determined it to be fruitless to dispute concerning tastes. It is very natural, and even quite necessary, to extend this axiom to mental as well as bodily taste, and thus common sense, which is so often at variance with philosophy, especially with the sceptical kind, is found, in one instance at least, to agree in pronouncing the same decision.

But though this axiom by passing into a proverb seems to have attained the sanction of common sense, there is certainly a species of common sense which opposes it, at least serves to modify and restrain it. Whoever would assert an equality of genius and elegance between Ogilby and Milton, or Bunyan and Addison, would be thought to defend no less an extravagance than if he had maintained a molehill to be as high as Teneriffe, or a pond as extensive as the ocean. Though there may be found persons who give the preference to the former authors, no one pays attention to such a taste, and we pronounce, without scruple, the sentiment of these pretended critics to be absurd and ridiculous. The principle of the natural equality of tastes is then totally forgot, and while we admit it on some occasions, where the objects seem near an equality, it appears an extravagant paradox, or rather a palpable absurdity, where objects so disporportioned are compared together.

It is evident that none of the rules of composition are fixed by reasonings *a priori,* or can be esteemed abstract conclusions of the understanding, from comparing those habitudes and relations of ideas which are eternal and immutable. Their foundation is the same with that of all the practical sciences, experience; nor are they anything but general observations concerning what has been universally found to please in all countries and in all ages. Many of the beauties of poetry, and even of eloquence, are founded on falsehood and fiction, on hyperboles, metaphors, and an abuse or perversion of terms from their natural meaning. To check the sallies of the imagination and to reduce every expression to geometrical truth and exactness would be the most contrary to the laws of criticism, because it would produce a work which by universal experience has been found the most insipid and disagreeable. But though poetry can never submit to exact truth, it must be confined by rules of art, discovered to the author either by genius or observation. If some negligent or irregular writers have pleased, they have not pleased by their transgressions of rule or order, but in spite of these transgressions. They have possessed other beauties, which were conformable to just criticism, and the force of these beauties has been able to overpower censure, and give the mind a satisfaction superior to the disgust arising from the blemishes. Ariosto pleases, but not by his monstrous and improbable fictions, by his bizarre mixture of the serious and comic styles, by the want of coherence in his stories, or by the continual interruptions of his narration. He charms by the force and clearness of his expression, by the readiness and variety of his inventions, and by his natural pictures of the passions, especially those of the gay and amorous kind. And however his faults may diminish our satisfaction, they are not able entirely to destroy it. Did our pleasure really arise from those parts of his poem which we denominate faults, this would be no objection to criticism in general. It would only be an objection to those particular rules of criticism which would establish such circumstances to be faults and would represent them as universally blameable. If they are found to please, they cannot be faults, let the pleasure which they produce be ever so unexpected and unaccountable.

But though all the general rules of art are founded only on experience and on the observation of the common sentiments of human nature, we must not imagine that on every occasion the feelings of men will be conformable to these rules. Those finer emotions of the mind are of a very tender and delicate nature, and require the concurrence of many favorable circumstances to make them play with facility and exactness according to their general and established principles. The least exterior hindrance to such small springs or the least internal disorder disturbs their motion and confounds the operation of the whole machine. When we would make an experiment of this nature and would try the force of any beauty or deformity, we must choose with care a proper time and place and bring the fancy to a suitable situation and disposition. A perfect serenity of mind, a recollection of thought, a due attention to the object, if any of these circumstances be wanting, our experiment will be fallacious, and we shall be unable to judge of the catholic and universal beauty. The relation which nature has placed between the form and the sentiment will at least be more obscure, and it will require greater accuracy to trace and discern it. We shall be able to ascertain its influence not so much from the operation of each particular beauty as from the durable admiration which attends those works that have survived all the caprices of mode and fashion, all the mistakes of ignorance and envy.

The same Homer who pleased at Athens and Rome two thousand years ago is still admired at Paris and at London. All the changes of climate, government, religion, and language have not been able to obscure his glory. Authority or prejudice may give a temporary vogue to a bad poet or orator, but his reputation will never be durable or general. When his compositions are examined by posterity or by foreigners, the enchantment is dissipated, and his faults appear in their true colors. On the contrary, a real genius, the longer his works endure, and the more wide they are spread, the more sincere is the admiration which he meets with. Envy and jealousy have too much place in a narrow circle, and even familiar acquaintance with his person may diminish the applause due to his performances. But when these obstructions are removed, the beauties which are naturally fitted to excite agreeable sentiments immediately display their energy; and while the world endures, they maintain their authority over the minds of men.

It appears, then, that amidst all the variety and caprice of taste there are certain general principles of approbation or blame whose influence a careful eye may trace in all operations of the mind. Some particular forms or qualities from the original structure of the internal fabric are calculated to please, and others to displease, and if they fail of their effect in any particular instance, it is from some apparent defect or imperfection in the organ. A man in a fever would not insist on his palate as able to decide concerning flavors; nor would one affected with the jaundice pretend to give a verdict with regard to colors. In each creature there is a sound and a defective state, and the former alone can be supposed to afford us a true standard of taste and sentiment. If in the sound state of the organ there be an entire or a considerable uniformity of sentiment among men, we may thence derive an idea of the perfect beauty, in like manner as the appearance of objects in daylight to the eye of a man in health is denominated their true and real color, even while color is allowed to be merely a phantasm of the senses.

Many and frequent are the defects in the internal organs which prevent or weaken the influence of those general principles on which depends our sentiment of beauty or deformity. Though some objects by the structure of the mind be naturally calculated to give pleasure, it is not to be expected that in every individual the pleasure will be equally felt. Particular incidents and situations occur which either throw a false light on the objects or hinder the true from conveying to the imagination the proper sentiment and perception.

One obvious cause why many feel not the proper sentiment of beauty is the want of that delicacy of imagination which is requisite to convey a sensibility of those finer emotions.[7] This delicacy everyone pretends to. Everyone talks of it, and would reduce every kind of taste or sentiment to its standard. But as our intention in this essay is to mingle some light of the understanding with the feelings of sentiment, it will be proper to give a more accurate definition of delicacy than has hitherto been attempted. And not to draw our philosophy from too profound a source, we shall have recourse to a noted story in *Don Quixote*.

It is with good reason, says Sancho to the squire with the great nose, that I pretend to have a judgment in wine: this is a quality hereditary in our family. Two of my kinsmen were once called to give their opinion of a hogshead which was supposed to be excellent, being old and of a good vintage. One of them tastes it, considers it, and after mature reflection pronounces the wine to be good, were it not for a small taste of leather which he perceived in it. The other, after using the same precautions, gives also his verdict in favor of the wine, but with the reserve of a taste of iron which he could easily distinguish. You cannot imagine how much they were both ridiculed for their judgment. But who laughed in the end? On emptying the hogshead, there was found at the bottom an old key with a leathern thong tied to it.

The great resemblance between mental and bodily taste will easily teach us to apply this story. Though it be certain that beauty and deformity, more than sweet and bitter, are not qualities in objects, but belong entirely to the sentiment, internal or external, it must be allowed that there are certain qualities in objects which are fitted by nature to produce those particular feelings. Now as these qualities may be found in a small degree, or may be mixed and confounded with each other, it often happens that the taste is not affected with such minute qualities, or is not able to distinguish all the particular flavors amidst the disorder in which they are presented. Where the organs are so fine as to allow nothing to escape them, and at the same time so exact as to perceive every ingredient in the composition, this we call delicacy of taste, whether we employ these terms in the literal or metaphorical sense. Here then the general rules of beauty are of use, being drawn from established models and from the observation of what pleases or displeases when presented singly and in a high degree. And if the same qualities, in a continued composition, and in a smaller degree, affect not the organs with a sensible delight or uneasiness, we exclude the person from all pretensions to this delicacy. To produce these general rules or avowed patterns of composition is like finding the key with the leathern thong, which justified the verdict of Sancho's kinsmen and confounded those pretended judges who had condemned them. Though the hogshead had never been emptied, the taste of the one was still equally delicate, and that of the other equally dull and languid. But it would have been more difficult to have proved the superiority of the former, to the conviction of every bystander. In like manner, though the beauties of writing had never been methodized or reduced to general principles, though no excellent models had ever been acknowledged, the different degrees of taste would still have subsisted, and the judgment of one man been preferable to that of another; but it would not have been so easy to silence the bad critic, who might always insist upon his particular sentiment and refuse to submit to his antagonist. But when we show him an avowed principle of art, when we illustrate this principle by examples whose operation, from his own particular taste, he acknowledges to be conformable to the principle, when we prove that the same principle may be applied to the present case, where he did not perceive or feel its influence, he must conclude, upon the whole, that the fault lies in himself, and that he wants the delicacy which is requisite to make him sensible of every beauty and every blemish, in any composition or discourse.

It is acknowledged to be the perfection of every sense or faculty to perceive with exactness its most minute objects and allow nothing to escape its notice and observation. The smaller the objects are which become sensible to the eye, the finer is that organ, and the more elaborate its make and composition. A good palate is not tried by strong flavors, but by a mixture of small ingredients, where we are still sensible of each part, notwithstanding its minuteness and its confusion with the rest. In like manner, a quick and acute perception of beauty and deformity must be the perfection of our mental taste, nor can a man be satisfied with himself while he suspects that any excellence or blemish in a discourse has passed him unobserved. In this case, the perfection of the man and the perfection of the sense or feeling are found to be united. A very delicate palate on many occasions may be a great inconvenience both to a man himself and to his friends, but a delicate taste of wit or beauty must always be a desirable quality, because it is the source of all the finest and most innocent enjoyments of which human nature is susceptible. In this decision the sentiments of all mankind are agreed. Wherever you can ascertain a delicacy of taste, it is sure to meet with approbation, and the best way of ascertaining it is to appeal to those models and principles which have been established by the uniform consent and experience of nations and ages.

But though there be naturally a wide difference in point of delicacy between one person and another, nothing tends further to increase and improve this talent than practice in a particular art, and the frequent survey or contemplation of a particular species of beauty. When objects of any kind are first presented to the eye or imagination, the sentiment which attends them is obscure and confused, and the mind is, in a great measure, incapable of pronouncing concerning their merits or defects. The taste cannot perceive the several excellencies of the performance, much less distinguish the particular character of each excellency and ascertain its quality and degree. If it pronounce the whole in general to be beautiful or deformed, it is the utmost that can be expected, and even this judgment a person so unpracticed will be apt to deliver with great hesitation and reserve. But allow him to acquire experience in those objects, his feeling becomes more exact and nice. He not only perceives the beauties and defects of each part but marks the distinguishing species of each quality and assigns it suitable praise or blame. A clear and distinct sentiment attends him through the whole survey of the objects, and he discerns that very degree and kind of approbation or displeasure which each part is naturally fitted to produce. The mist dissipates which seemed formerly to hang over the object. The organ acquires greater perfection in its operations and can pronounce, without danger of mistake, concerning the merits of every performance. In a word, the same address and dexterity which practice gives to the execution of any work is also acquired by the same means, in the judging of it.

So advantageous is practice to the discernment of beauty that before we can give judgment on any work of importance it will even be requisite that that very individual performance be more than once perused by us and be surveyed in different lights with attention and deliberation. There is a flutter or hurry of thought which attends the first perusal of any piece and which confounds the genuine sentiment of beauty. The relation of the parts is not discerned. The true characters of style are little distinguished. The several perfections and defects seem wrapped up in a species of confusion, and present themselves indistinctly to the imagination. Not to mention that there is a species of beauty which, as it is florid and superficial, pleases at first, but being found incompatible with a just expression either of reason or passion, soon palls upon the taste and is then rejected with disdain, at least rated at a much lower value.

It is impossible to continue in the practice of contemplating any order of beauty without being frequently obliged to form comparisons between the several species and degrees of excellence, and estimating their proportion to each other. A man who has had no opportunity of comparing the different kinds of beauty is indeed totally unqualified to pronounce an opinion with regard to any object presented to him. By comparison alone we fix the epithets of praise or blame and learn how to assign the due degree of each. The coarsest daubing contains a certain luster of colors and exactness of imitation, which are so far beauties, and would affect the mind of a peasant or Indian with the highest admiration. The most vulgar ballads are not entirely destitute of harmony or nature, and none but a person familiarized to superior beauties would pronounce their numbers harsh, or narration uninteresting. A great inferiority of beauty gives pain to a person conversant in the highest excellence of the kind, and is for that reason pronounced a deformity, as the most finished object with which we are acquainted is naturally supposed to have reached the pinnacle of perfection and to be entitled to the highest applause. One accustomed to see and examine and weigh the several performances admired in different ages and nations can alone rate the merits of a work exhibited to his view and assign its proper rank among the productions of genius.

But to enable a critic the more fully to execute this undertaking, he must preserve his mind free from all prejudice and allow nothing to enter into his consideration but the very object which is submitted to his examination. We may observe that every work of art, in order to produce its due effect on the mind, must be surveyed in a certain point of view, and cannot be fully relished by persons whose situation, real or imaginary, is not conformable to that which is required by the performance. An orator addresses himself to a particular audience, and must have a regard to their particular genius, interests, opinions, passions, and prejudices; otherwise he hopes in vain to govern their resolutions and inflame their affections. Should they even have entertained some prepossessions against him, however unreasonable, he must not overlook this disadvantage but, before he enters upon the subject, must endeavor to conciliate their affection and acquire their good graces. A critic of a different age or nation who should peruse this discourse must have all these circumstances in his eye and must place himself in the same situation as the audience, in order to form a true judgment of the oration. In like manner, when any work is addressed to the public, though I should have a friendship or enmity with the author, I must depart from this situation, and considering myself as a man in general, forget, if possible, my individual being and my peculiar circumstances. A person influenced by prejudice complies not with this condition, but obstinately maintains his natural position without placing himself in that point of view which the performance supposes. If the work be addressed to persons of a different age or nation, he makes no allowance for their peculiar views and prejudices, but full of the manners of his own age and country, rashly condemns what seemed admirable in the eyes of those for whom alone the discourse was calculated. If the work be executed for the public, he never sufficiently enlarges his comprehension or forgets his interest as a friend or enemy, as a rival or commentator. By this means, his sentiments are perverted; nor have the same beauties and blemishes the same influence upon him as if he had imposed a proper violence on his imagination and had forgotten himself for a moment. So far his taste evidently departs from the true standard, and of consequence loses all credit and authority.

It is well known that in all questions submitted to the understanding, prejudice is destructive of sound judgment and perverts all operations of the intellectual faculties. It is no less contrary to good taste, nor has it less influence to corrupt our sentiment of beauty. It belongs to good sense to check its influence in both cases, and in this respect, as well as in many others, reason, if not an essential part of taste, is at least requisite to the operations of this latter faculty. In all the nobler productions of genius there is a mutual relation and correspondence of parts, nor can either the beauties or blemishes be perceived by him whose thought is not capacious enough to comprehend all those parts and compare them with each other in order to perceive the consistence and uniformity of the whole. Every work of art has also a certain end or purpose for which it is calculated, and is to be deemed more or less perfect as it is more or less fitted to attain this end. The object of eloquence is to persuade, of history to instruct, of poetry to please by means of the passions and the imagination. These ends we must carry constantly in our view when we peruse any performance, and we must be able to judge how far the means employed are adapted to their respective purposes. Besides, every kind of composition, even the most poetical, is nothing but a chain of propositions and reasonings—not always, indeed, the justest and most exact, but still plausible and specious, however disguised by the coloring of the imagination. The persons introduced in tragedy and epic poetry must be represented as reasoning and thinking and concluding and acting suitably to their character and circumstances; and without judgment, as well as taste and invention, a poet can never hope to succeed in so delicate an undertaking. Not to mention that the same excellence of faculties which contributes to the improvement of reason, the same clearness of conception, the same exactness of distinction, the same vivacity of apprehension, are essential to the operations of true taste, and are its infallible concomitants. It seldom or never happens that a man of sense who has experience in any art cannot judge of its beauty; and it is no less rare to meet with a man who has a just taste without a sound understanding.

Thus, though the principles of taste be universal, and nearly, if not entirely, the same in all men, yet few are qualified to give judgment on any work of art, or establish their own sentiment as the standard of beauty. The organs of internal sensation are seldom so perfect as to allow the general principles their full play, and produce a feeling correspondent to those principles. They either labor under some defect, or are vitiated by some disorder, and by that means excite a sentiment which may be pronounced erroneous. When the critic has no delicacy, he judges without any distinction, and is only affected by the grosser and more palpable qualities of the object; the finer touches pass unnoticed and disregarded. Where he is not aided by practice, his verdict is attended with confusion and hesitation. Where no comparison has been employed, the most frivolous beauties, such as rather merit the name of defects, are the object of his admiration. Where he lies under the influence of prejudice, all his natural sentiments are perverted. Where good sense is wanting, he is not qualified to discern the beauties of design and reasoning, which are the highest and most excellent. Under some or other of these imperfections, the generality of men labor, and hence a true judge in the finer arts is observed, even during the most polished ages, to be so rare a character. Strong sense, united to delicate sentiment, improved by practice, perfected by comparison, and cleared of all prejudice, can alone entitle critics to this valuable character; and the joint verdict of such, wherever they are to be found, is the true standard of taste and beauty.

But where are such critics to be found? By what marks are they to be known? How distinguish them from pretenders? These questions are embarrassing, and seem to throw us back into the same uncertainty from which, during the course of this essay, we have endeavored to extricate ourselves.

But if we consider the matter aright, these are questions of fact, not of sentiment. Whether any particular person be endowed with good sense and a delicate imagination, free from prejudice, may often be the subject of dispute, and be liable to great discussion and inquiry; but that such a character is valuable and estimable will be agreed in by all mankind. Where these doubts occur, men can do no more than in other disputable questions which are submitted to the understanding: They must produce the best arguments that their invention suggests to them; they must acknowledge a true and decisive standard to exist somewhere, to wit, real existence and matter of fact; and they must have indulgence to such as differ from them in their appeals to this standard. It is sufficient for our present purpose if we have proved that the taste of all individuals is not upon an equal footing and that some men in general, however difficult to be particularly pitched upon, will be acknowledged by universal sentiment to have a preference above others.

But in reality the difficulty of finding, even in particulars, the standard of taste is not so great as it is represented. Though in speculation we may readily avow a certain criterion in science and deny it in sentiment, the matter is found in practice to be much more hard to ascertain in the former case than in the latter. Theories of abstract philosophy, systems of profound theology, have prevailed during one age. In a successive period these have been universally exploded; their absurdity has been detected; other theories and systems have supplied their place, which again gave place to their successors. And nothing has been experienced more liable to the revolutions of chance and fashion than these pretended decisions of science. The case is not the same with the beauties of eloquence and poetry. Just expressions of passion and nature are sure, after a little time, to gain public applause, which they maintain for ever. Aristotle and Plato and Epicurus and Descartes may successively yield to each other, but Terence and Virgil maintain a universal, undisputed empire over the minds of men. The abstract philosophy of Cicero has lost its credit; the vehemence of his oratory is still the object of our admiration.

Though men of delicate taste be rare, they are easily to be distinguished in society by the soundness of their understanding and the superiority of their faculties above the rest of mankind. The ascendant which they acquire gives a prevalence to that lively approbation with which they receive any productions of genius, and renders it generally predominant. Many men when left to themselves have but a faint and dubious perception of beauty who yet are capable of relishing any fine stroke which is pointed out to them. Every convert to the admiration of the real poet or orator is the cause of some new conversion. And though prejudices may prevail for a time, they never unite in celebrating any rival to the true genius, but yield at last to the force of nature and just sentiment. Thus, though a civilized nation may easily be mistaken in the choice of their admired philosopher, they never have been found long to err in their affection for a favorite epic or tragic author.

But notwithstanding all our endeavors to fix a standard of taste and reconcile the discordant apprehensions of men, there still remain two sources of variation which are not sufficient indeed to confound all the boundaries of beauty and deformity, but will often serve to produce a difference in the degrees of our approbation or blame. The one is the different humors of particular men, the other, the particular manners and opinions of our age and country. The general principles of taste are uniform in human nature; where men vary in their judgments, some defect or perversion in the faculties may commonly be remarked, proceeding either from prejudice, from want of practice, or want of delicacy, and there is just reason for approving one taste and condemning another. But where there is such a diversity in the internal frame or external situation as is entirely blameless on both sides, and leaves no room to give one the preference above the other, in that case a certain degree of diversity in judgment is unavoidable, and we seek in vain for a standard by which we can reconcile the contrary sentiments.

A young man whose passions are warm will be more sensibly touched with amorous and tender images than a man more advanced in years who takes pleasure in wise, philosophical reflections concerning the conduct of life and moderation of the passions. At twenty Ovid may be the favorite author, Horace at forty, and perhaps Tacitus at fifty. Vainly would we, in such cases, endeavor to enter into the sentiments of others, and divest ourselves of those propensities which are natural to us. We choose our favorite author as we do our friend, from a conformity of humor and disposition. Mirth or passion, sentiment or reflection, whichever of these most predominates in our temper, it gives us a peculiar sympathy with the writer who resembles us.

One person is more pleased with the sublime; another with the tender; a third with raillery. One has a strong sensibility to blemishes, and is extremely studious of correctness; another has a more lively feeling of beauties, and pardons twenty absurdities and defects for one elevated or pathetic stroke. The ear of this man is entirely turned towards conciseness and energy; that man is delighted with a copious, rich, and harmonious expression. Simplicity is affected by one; ornament by another. Comedy, tragedy, satire, odes, have each its partisans, who prefer that particular species of writing to all others. It is plainly an error in a critic to confine his approbation to one species or style of writing and condemn all the rest. But it is almost impossible not to feel a predilection for that which suits our particular turn and disposition. Such preferences are innocent and unavoidable and can never reasonably be the object of dispute, because there is no standard by which they can be decided.

For a like reason we are more pleased, in the course of our reading, with pictures and characters that resemble objects which are found in our own age or country than with those which describe a

different set of customs. It is not without some effort that we reconcile ourselves to the simplicity of ancient manners and behold
princesses carrying water from the spring, and kings and heroes
dressing their own victuals. We may allow in general that the representation of such manners is no fault in the author nor deformity
in the piece; but we are not so sensibly touched with them. For this
reason, comedy is not easily transferred from one age or nation to
another. A Frenchman or Englishman is not pleased with the
Andria of Terence, or *Clitia* of Machiavelli, where the fine lady
upon whom all the play turns never once appears to the spectators,
but is always kept behind the scenes, suitably to the reserved humor
of the ancient Greeks and modern Italians. A man of learning and
reflection can make allowance for these peculiarities of manners,
but a common audience can never divest themselves so far of their
usual ideas and sentiments as to relish pictures which nowise resemble them.

But here there occurs a reflection which may, perhaps, be useful
in examining the celebrated controversy concerning ancient and
modern learning, where we often find the one side excusing any
seeming absurdity in the ancients from the manners of the age, and
the other refusing to admit this excuse, or at least admitting it only
as an apology for the author, not for the performance. In my opinion, the proper boundaries in this subject have seldom been fixed
between the contending parties. Where any innocent peculiarities
of manners are represented, such as those above mentioned, they
ought certainly to be admitted, and a man who is shocked with
them gives an evident proof of false delicacy and refinement. The
poet's "monument more durable than brass" must fall to the ground
like common brick or clay, were men to make no allowance for the
continual revolutions of manners and customs, and would admit of
nothing but what was suitable to the prevailing fashion. Must we
throw aside the pictures of our ancestors because of their ruffs and
farthingales? But where the ideas of morality and decency alter
from one age to another, and where vicious manners are described
without being marked with the proper characters of blame and
disapprobation, this must be allowed to disfigure the poem, and to
be a real deformity. I cannot, nor is it proper I should, enter into
such sentiments; and however I may excuse the poet on account of
the manners of his age, I never can relish the composition. The want
of humanity and of decency, so conspicuous in the characters drawn

by several of the ancient poets, even sometimes by Homer and the Greek tragedians, diminishes considerably the merit of their noble performances and gives modern authors an advantage over them. We are not interested in the fortunes and sentiments of such rough heroes; we are displeased to find the limits of vice and virtue so much confounded; and whatever indulgence we may give to the writer on account of his prejudices, we cannot prevail on ourselves to enter into his sentiments, or bear an affection to characters which we plainly discover to be blamable.

The case is not the same with moral principles as with speculative opinions of any kind. These are in continual flux and revolution. The son embraces a different system from the father. Nay, there scarcely is any man who can boast of great constancy and uniformity in this particular. Whatever speculative errors may be found in the polite writings of any age or country, they detract but little from the value of those compositions. There needs but a certain turn of thought or imagination to make us enter into all the opinions which then prevailed and relish the sentiments or conclusions derived from them. But a very violent effort is requisite to change our judgment of manners and excite sentiments of approbation or blame, love or hatred, different from those to which the mind from long custom has been familiarized. And where a man is confident of the rectitude of that moral standard by which he judges, he is justly jealous of it, and will not pervert the sentiments of his heart for a moment in complaisance to any writer whatsoever.

Of all speculative errors those which regard religion are the most excusable in compositions of genius; nor is it ever permitted to judge of the civility or wisdom of any people, or even of single persons, by the grossness or refinement of their theological principles. The same good sense that directs men in the ordinary occurrences of life is not hearkened to in religious matters, which are supposed to be placed altogether above the cognizance of human reason. On this account, all the absurdities of the pagan system of theology must be overlooked by every critic who would pretend to form a just notion of ancient poetry; and our posterity, in their turn, must have the same indulgence to their forefathers. No religious principles can ever be imputed as a fault to any poet while they remain merely principles and take not such strong possession of his heart as to lay him under the imputation of bigotry or superstition. Where that happens, they confound the sentiments of morality and alter the natural boundaries of vice and virtue. They are therefore eternal blemishes according to the principle above mentioned; nor are the prejudices and false opinions of the age sufficient to justify them.

It is essential to the Roman Catholic religion to inspire a violent hatred of every other worship and to represent all pagans, Mohammedans, and heretics as the objects of divine wrath and vengeance. Such sentiments, though they are in reality very blamable, are considered as virtues by the zealots of that communion and are represented in their tragedies and epic poems as a kind of divine heroism. This bigotry has disfigured two very fine tragedies of the French theater, *Polyeucte* and *Athalie,* where an intemperate zeal for particular modes of worship is set off with all the pomp imaginable, and forms the predominant character of the heroes. "What is this," says the sublime Joad to Josabet, finding her in discourse with Mathan, the priest of Baal, "Does the daughter of David speak to this traitor? Are you not afraid lest the earth should open and pour forth flames to devour you both? Or, lest these holy walls should fall and crush you together? What is his purpose? Why comes that enemy of God hither to poison the air which we breathe with his horrid presence?" Such sentiments are received with great applause on the theater of Paris; but at London the spectators would be full as much pleased to hear Achilles tell Agamemnon that he was a dog in his forehead and a deer in his heart, or Jupiter threaten Juno with a sound drubbing if she will not be quiet.

Religious principles are also a blemish in any polite composition when they rise up to superstition and intrude themselves into every sentiment, however remote from any connection with religion. It is no excuse for the poet that the customs of his country had burdened life with so many religious ceremonies and observances that no part of it was exempt from that yoke. It must forever be ridiculous in Petrarch to compare his mistress, Laura, to Jesus Christ. Nor is it less ridiculous in that agreeable libertine, Boccaccio, very seriously to give thanks to God Almighty and the ladies, for their assistance in defending him against his enemies.

SIR JOSHUA REYNOLDS ✦

The Idler (1759)

No. 76, September 29, 1759
[False Criticisms of Painting]

SIR—I was much pleased with your ridicule of those shallow critics whose judgment, though often right as far as it goes, yet reaches only to inferior beauties, and who, unable to comprehend the whole, judge only by parts, and from thence determine the merit of extensive works. But there is another kind of critic still worse, who judges by narrow rules, and those too often false, and which, though they should be true and founded on nature, will lead him but a very little way towards the just estimation of the sublime beauties in works of genius; for whatever part of an art can be executed or criticized by rules, that part is no longer the work of genius, which implies excellence out of the reach of rules. For my own part, I profess myself an Idler, and love to give my judgment, such as it is, from my immediate perceptions, without much fatigue of thinking; and I am of opinion that if a man has not those perceptions right, it will be vain for him to endeavor to supply their place by rules, which may enable him to talk more learnedly, but not to distinguish more acutely. Another reason which has lessened my affection for the study of criticism is that critics, so far as I have observed, debar themselves from receiving any pleasure from the polite arts, at the same time that they profess to love and admire them; for these rules, being always uppermost, give them such a propensity to criticize that instead of giving up the reins of their imagination into their author's hands, their frigid minds are employed in examining whether the performance be according to the rules of art.

To those who are resolved to be critics in spite of nature, and at the same time have no great disposition to much reading and study, I would recommend to assume the character of connoisseur, which may be purchased at a much cheaper rate than that of a critic in poetry. The remembrance of a few names of painters, with their general characters, and a few rules of the Academy, which they may pick up among the painters, will go a great way towards making a very notable connoisseur.

With a gentleman of this cast I visited last week the cartoons at Hampton Court. He was just returned from Italy, a connoisseur, of course, and of course his mouth full of nothing but the grace of Raphael, the purity of Domenichino, the learning of Poussin, the air of Guido, the greatness of taste of the Caracci,[1] and the sublimity and grand contorno of Michelangelo; with all the rest of the cant of criticism, which he emitted with that volubility which generally those orators have who annex no ideas to their words.

As we were passing through the rooms, in our way to the gallery, I made him observe a whole length of Charles the First, by Van Dyke, as a perfect representation of the character as well as the figure of the man. He agreed it was very fine, but it wanted spirit and contrast, and had not the flowing line,[2] without which a figure could not possibly be graceful. When we entered the gallery, I thought I could perceive him recollecting his rules by which he was to criticize Raphael. I shall pass over his observation of the boats being too little, and other criticisms of that kind, till we arrived at "St. Paul Preaching." "This," says he, "is esteemed the most excellent of all the cartoons. What nobleness, what dignity there is in that figure of St. Paul! And yet what an addition to that nobleness could Raphael have given, had the art of contrast been known in his time; but above all, the flowing line, which constitutes grace and beauty! You would not then have seen an upright figure standing equally on both legs, and both hands stretched forward in the same direction, and his drapery, to all appearance, without the least art of disposition." The following picture is the "Charge to Peter." "Here," says he, "are twelve upright figures; what a pity it is that Raphael was not acquainted with the pyramidal principle! He would then have contrived the figures in the middle to have been on higher ground, or the figures at the extremities stooping or lying, which would not only have formed the group into the shape of a pyramid, but likewise contrasted the standing figures. Indeed," added he, "I have often lamented that so great a genius as Raphael had not lived in this enlightened age, since the art has been reduced to principles, and had his education in one of the modern Academies; what glorious works might we then have expected from his divine pencil!"

I shall trouble you no longer with my friend's observations, which, I suppose, you are now able to continue by yourself. It is curious to observe that at the same time that great admiration is pretended for a name of fixed reputation, objections are raised against those very qualities by which that great name was acquired.

These critics are continually lamenting that Raphael had not the coloring and harmony of Rubens, or the light and shadow of Rembrandt, without considering how much the gay harmony of the former and affectation of the latter would take from the dignity of Raphael; and yet Rubens had great harmony, and Rembrandt understood light and shadow; but what may be an excellence in a lower class of painting becomes a blemish in a higher; as the quick, sprightly turn, which is the life and beauty of epigrammatic compositions, would but ill suit with the majesty of heroic poetry.

To conclude, I would not be thought to infer from anything that has been said that rules are absolutely unnecessary, but to censure scrupulosity, a servile attention to minute exactness, which is sometimes inconsistent with higher excellence and is lost in the blaze of expanded genius.

I do not know whether you will think painting a general subject. By inserting this letter perhaps you will incur the censure a man would deserve whose business being to entertain a whole room should turn his back on the company and talk to a particular person.

I am, Sir, etc.

No. 79, October 20, 1759
[The Grand Style of Painting]

SIR—Your acceptance of a former letter on painting gives me encouragement to offer a few more sketches on the same subject.

Amongst the painters and the writers on painting there is one maxim universally admitted and continually inculcated. "Imitate nature" is the invariable rule, but I know none who have explained in what manner this rule is to be understood; the consequence of which is that everyone takes it in the most obvious sense—that objects are represented naturally when they have such relief that they seem real. It may appear strange, perhaps, to hear this sense of the rule disputed, but it must be considered that if the excellency of a painter consisted only in this kind of imitation, painting must lose its rank and be no longer considered as a liberal art and sister to poetry, this imitation being merely mechanical, in which the slowest intellect is always sure to succeed best; for the painter of genius cannot stoop to drudgery, in which the understanding has no part; and what pretence has the art to claim kindred with poetry but by its power over the imagination? To this power the painter of genius directs his aim; in this sense he studies nature, and often arrives at his end, even by being unnatural, in the confined sense of the word.

The grand style of painting requires this minute attention to be carefully avoided, and must be kept as separate from it as the style of poetry from that of history. Poetical ornaments destroy that air of truth and plainness which ought to characterize history, but the very being of poetry consists in departing from this plain narration and adopting every ornament that will warm the imagination. To desire to see the excellencies of each style united, to mingle the Dutch with the Italian School, is to join contrarieties which cannot subsist together, and which destroy the efficacy of each other. The Italian attends only to the invariable, the great and general ideas which are fixed and inherent in universal nature; the Dutch, on the contrary, to literal truth and a minute exactness in the detail, as I may say, of nature, modified by accident. The attention to these petty peculiarities is the very cause of this naturalness so much admired in the Dutch pictures, which, if we suppose it to be a beauty, is certainly of a lower order, that ought to give place to a beauty of a superior kind, since one cannot be obtained but by departing from the other.

If my opinion were asked concerning the works of Michelangelo, whether they would receive any advantage from possessing this mechanical merit, I should not scruple to say they would lose, in a great measure, the effect which they now have on every mind susceptible of great and noble ideas. His works may be said to be all genius and soul; and why should they be loaded with heavy matter, which can only counteract his purpose by retarding the progress of the imagination?

If this opinion should be thought one of the wild extravagancies of enthusiasm, I shall only say that those who censure it are not conversant in the works of the great masters. It is very difficult to determine the exact degree of enthusiasm that the arts of painting and poetry may admit. There may perhaps be too great an indulgence, as well as too great a restraint of imagination; and if the one produces incoherent monsters, the other produces what is full as bad, lifeless insipidity. An intimate knowledge of the passions and good sense, but not common sense, must at last determine its limits. It has been thought, and I believe with reason, that Michelangelo sometimes transgressed those limits, and I think I have seen figures by him of which it was very difficult to determine whether they were in the highest degree sublime or extremely ridiculous. Such faults may be said to be the ebullition of genius, but at least he had this merit, that he never was insipid; and whatever passion his works may excite, they will always escape contempt.

What I have had under consideration is the sublimest style, particularly that of Michelangelo, the Homer of painting. Other kinds may admit of this naturalness, which of the lowest kind is the chief merit, but in painting, as in poetry, the highest style has the least of common nature.

One may safely recommend a little more enthusiasm to the modern painters; too much is certainly not the vice of the present age. The Italians seem to have been continually declining in this respect from the time of Michelangelo to that of Carlo Maratti,[3] and from thence to the very bathos of insipidity to which they are now sunk; so that there is no need of remarking that where I mentioned the Italian painters in opposition to the Dutch, I mean not the moderns, but the heads of the old Roman and Bolognian Schools; nor did I mean to include in my idea of an Italian painter the Venetian School, which may be said to be the Dutch part of the Italian genius. I have only to add a word of advice to the painters— that however excellent they may be in painting naturally, they would not flatter themselves very much upon it; and to the connoisseurs, that when they see a cat or a fiddle painted so finely that, as the phrase is, "it looks as if you could take it up," they would not for that reason immediately compare the painter to Raphael and Michelangelo.

No. 82, November 10, 1759
[The True Idea of Beauty]

SIR—Discoursing in my last letter on the different practice of the Italian and Dutch painters, I observed that "the Italian painter attends only to the invariable, the great, and general ideas, which are fixed and inherent in universal nature."

I was led into the subject of this letter by endeavoring to fix the original cause of this conduct of the Italian masters. If it can be proved that by this choice they selected the most beautiful part of the creation, it will show how much their principles are founded on reason, and at the same time discover the origin of our ideas of beauty.

I suppose it will be easily granted that no man can judge whether any animal be beautiful in its kind or deformed who has seen only one of that species; this is as conclusive in regard to the human figure; so that if a man born blind were to recover his sight, and the most beautiful woman were brought before him, he could not determine whether she was handsome or not; nor if the most beautiful and most deformed were produced, could he any better determine to which he should give the preference, having seen only those two. To distinguish beauty, then, implies the having seen many individuals of that species. If it is asked, how is more skill acquired by the observation of greater numbers? I answer that in consequence of having seen many the power is acquired, even without seeking after it, of distinguishing between accidental blemishes and excrescences which are continually varying the surface of Nature's works, and the invariable general form which Nature most frequently produces and always seems to intend in her productions.

Thus amongst the blades of grass or leaves of the same tree, though no two can be found exactly alike, the general form is invariable. A naturalist, before he chose one as a sample, would examine many, since if he took the first that occurred, it might have by accident or otherwise such a form as that it would scarce be known to belong to that species; he selects, as the painter does, the most beautiful, that is, the most general form of nature.

Every species of the animal as well as the vegetable creation may be said to have a fixed or determinate form, towards which nature is continually inclining, like various lines terminating in the center; or it may be compared to pendulums vibrating in different directions over one central point, and as they all cross the center, though only one passes through any other point, so it will be found that perfect beauty is oftener produced by nature than deformity —I do not mean than deformity in general, but than any one kind of deformity. To instance in a particular part of a feature: The line that forms a ridge of the nose is beautiful when it is straight; this, then, is the central form, which is oftener found than either concave, convex, or any other irregular form that shall be proposed. As we are then more accustomed to beauty than deformity, we may conclude that to be the reason why we approve and admire it, as we approve and admire customs and fashions of dress for no other reason than that we are used to them; so that though habit and custom cannot be said to be the cause of beauty, it is certainly the cause of our liking it; and I have no doubt but that if we were more used to deformity than beauty, deformity would then lose the idea now annexed to it, and take that of beauty—as if the whole world should agree that *yes* and *no* should change their meaning: *yes* would then deny, and *no* would affirm.

Whoever undertakes to proceed further in this argument and endeavors to fix a general criterion of beauty respecting different species, or to show why one species is more beautiful than another, it will be required from him first to prove that one species is really more beautiful than another. That we prefer one to the other, and with very good reason, will be readily granted; but it does not follow from thence that we think it a more beautiful form; for we have no criterion of form by which to determine our judgment. He who says a swan is more beautiful than a dove means little more than that he has more pleasure in seeing a swan than a dove, either from the stateliness of its motions or its being a more rare bird; and he who gives the preference to the dove does it from some association of ideas of innocence which he always annexes to the dove; but if he pretends to defend the preference he gives to one or the other by endeavoring to prove that this more beautiful form proceeds from a particular gradation of magnitude, undulation of a curve, or direction of a line, or whatever other conceit of his imagination he shall fix on as a criterion of form, he will be continually contradicting himself, and find at last that the great mother of nature will not be subjected to such narrow rules. Among the various reasons why we prefer one part of her works to another, the most general, I believe, is habit and custom; custom makes, in a certain sense, white black, and black white; it is custom alone determines our preference of the color of the Europeans to the Ethiopians, and they, for the same reason, prefer their own color to ours.[4] I suppose nobody will doubt, if one of their painters were to paint the Goddess of Beauty, but that he would represent her black, with thick lips, flat nose, and woolly hair; and, it seems to me, he would act very unnaturally if he did not, for by what criterion will anyone dispute the propriety of his idea? We indeed say that the form and color of the European is preferable to that of the Ethiopian; but I know of no other reason we have for it but that we are more accustomed to it. It is absurd to say that beauty is possessed of attractive powers which irresistibly seize the corresponding mind with love and admiration, since that argument is equally conclusive in favor of the white and the black philosophers.

The black and white nations must, in respect of beauty, be considered as of different kinds, at least a different species of the same kind; from one of which to the other, as I observed, no inference can be drawn.

Novelty is said to be one of the causes of beauty. That novelty is a very sufficient reason why we should admire is not denied, but because it is uncommon, is it therefore beautiful? The beauty that is produced by color, as when we prefer one bird to another, though of the same form, on account of its color, has nothing to do with the argument, which reaches only to form. I have here considered the word *beauty* as being properly applied to form alone. There is a necessity of fixing this confined sense, for there can be no argument if the sense of the word is extended to everything that is approved. A rose may as well be said to be beautiful because it has a fine smell, as a bird because of its color. When we apply the word *beauty*, we do not mean always by it a more beautiful form, but something valuable on account of its rarity, usefulness, color, or any other property. A horse is said to be a beautiful animal, but had a horse as few good qualities as a tortoise, I do not imagine that he would then be deemed beautiful.

A fitness to the end proposed is said to be another cause of beauty, but supposing we were proper judges of what form is the most proper in an animal to constitute strength or swiftness, we always determine concerning its beauty before we exert our understanding to judge of its fitness.

From what has been said it may be inferred that the works of nature, if we compare one species with another, are all equally beautiful, and that preference is given from custom or some association of ideas; and that, in creatures of the same species, beauty is the medium or center of all its various forms.

To conclude, then, by way of corollary: If it has been proved that the painter, by attending to the invariable and general ideas of nature, produces beauty, he must, by regarding minute particularities and accidental discriminations, deviate from the universal rule, and pollute his canvas with deformity.[5]

HENRY HOME, LORD KAMES ✍

Elements of Criticism (1762)

Volume I, chapter ii, part 1, section 7, "Emotions Caused by Fiction"

The attentive reader will observe that hitherto no fiction hath been assigned as the cause of any passion or emotion; whether it be a being, action, or quality that moveth us, it is supposed to be really existing. This observation shows that we have not yet completed our task, because passions, as all the world know, are moved by fiction as well as by truth. In judging beforehand of man, so remarkably addicted to truth and reality, one should little dream that fiction can have any effect upon him; but man's intellectual faculties are not sufficiently perfect to dive far even into his own nature. I shall take occasion afterward to show that the power of fiction to generate passion is an admirable contrivance, subservient to excellent purposes; in the meantime, we must try to unfold the means that give fiction such influence over the mind.

That the objects of our external senses really exist in the way and manner we perceive is a branch of intuitive knowledge. When I see a man walking, a tree growing, or cattle grazing, I cannot doubt but that these objects are really what they appear to be. If I be a spectator of any transaction or event, I have a conviction of the real existence of the persons engaged, of their words, and of their actions. Nature determines us to rely on the veracity of our senses, for otherwise they could not in any degree answer their end, that of laying open things existing and passing around us.

By the power of memory, a thing formerly seen may be recalled to the mind with different degrees of accuracy. We commonly are satisfied with a slight recollection of the capital circumstances; and in such recollection the thing is not figured as in our view nor any image formed. We retain the consciousness of our present situation and barely remember that formerly we saw that thing. But with respect to an interesting object or event that made a strong impression, I am not satisfied with a cursory review, but must dwell upon every circumstance. I am imperceptibly converted into a spectator and perceive every particular passing in my presence, as when I was in reality a spectator. For example, I saw yesterday a beautiful woman in tears for the loss of an only child and was greatly moved with her distress. Not satisfied with a slight recollection or bare remembrance, I ponder upon the melancholy scene; conceiving myself to be in the place where I was an eyewitness, every circumstance appears to me as at first; I think I see the woman in tears and hear her moans. Hence it may be justly said that in a complete idea of memory there is no past nor future; a thing recalled to the mind with the accuracy I have been describing is perceived as in our view, and consequently as existing at present. Past time makes part of an incomplete idea only. I remember or reflect that some years ago I was at Oxford and saw the first stone laid of the Radcliffe Library; and I remember that at a still greater distance of time I heard a debate in the House of Commons about a standing army.

Lamentable is the imperfection of language almost in every particular that falls not under external sense. I am talking of a matter exceedingly clear in the perception; and yet I find no small difficulty to express it clearly in words, for it is not accurate to talk of incidents long past as passing in our sight, nor of hearing at present what we really heard yesterday or at a more distant time. And yet the want of proper words to describe ideal presence, and to distinguish it from real presence, makes this inaccuracy unavoidable. When I recall anything to my mind in a manner so distinct as to form an idea or image of it as present, I have not words to describe that act but that I perceive the thing as a spectator and as existing in my presence; which means not that I am really a spectator, but only that I conceive myself to be a spectator and have a perception of the object similar to what a real spectator hath.

As many rules of criticism depend on ideal presence, the reader, it is hoped, will take some pains to form an exact notion of it, as distinguished on the one hand from real presence, and on the other from a superficial or reflective remembrance. In contradistinction to real presence, ideal presence may properly be termed a waking dream, because, like a dream, it vanisheth the moment we reflect upon our present situation. Real presence, on the contrary, vouched by eyesight, commands our belief not only during the direct perception, but in reflecting afterward on the object. To distinguish ideal presence from reflective remembrance, I give the following illustration: When I think of an event as past, without forming any image, it is barely reflecting or remembering that I was an eyewitness; but when I recall the event so distinctly as to form a complete image of it, I perceive it as passing in my presence; and this perception is an act of intuition, into which reflection enters not more than into an act of sight.

Though ideal presence is thus distinguished from real presence on the one side, and from reflective remembrance on the other, it is however variable without any precise limits, rising sometimes toward the former and often sinking toward the latter. In a vigorous exertion of memory, ideal presence is extremely distinct. Thus, when a man entirely occupied with some event that made a deep impression forgets himself, he perceives everything as passing before him and hath a consciousness of presence similar to that of a spectator, with no difference but that in the former the perception of presence is less firm and clear than in the latter. But such vigorous exertion of memory is rare. Ideal presence is oftener faint, and the image so obscure as not to differ widely from reflective remembrance.

Hitherto of an idea of memory. I proceed to consider the idea of a thing I never saw, raised in me by speech, by writing, or by painting. That idea, with respect to the present subject, is of the same nature with an idea of memory, being either complete or incomplete. A lively and accurate description of an important event raises in me ideas no less distinct than if I had been originally an eyewitness: I am insensibly transformed into a spectator and have an impression that every incident is passing in my presence. On the other hand, a slight or superficial narrative produceth but a faint and incomplete idea, of which ideal presence makes no part. Past time is a circumstance that enters into this idea, as it doth into an incomplete idea of memory. I believe that Scipio existed about 2000 years ago and that he overcame Hannibal in the famous battle of Zama. When I reflect so slightly upon that memorable event, I consider it as long past. But let it be spread out in a lively and beautiful description, I am insensibly transformed into a spectator: I perceive these two heroes in act to engage; I perceive them brandishing their swords and cheering their troops; and in that manner I attend them through the battle, every incident of which appears to be passing in my sight.

I have had occasion to observe that ideas both of memory and of speech produce emotions of the same kind with what are produced by an immediate view of the object, only fainter in proportion as an idea is fainter than an original perception. The insight we have now got unfolds that mystery: Ideal presence supplies the want of real presence, and in idea we perceive persons acting and suffering precisely as in an original survey. If our sympathy be engaged by the latter, it must also in some degree be engaged by the former, especially if the distinctness of ideal presence approach to that of real presence. Hence the pleasure of a reverie, where a man, forgetting himself, is totally occupied with the ideas passing in his mind, the objects of which he conceives to be really existing in his presence. The power of language to raise emotions depends entirely on the raising such lively and distinct images as are here described; the reader's passions are never sensibly moved till he be thrown into a kind of reverie, in which state, forgetting that he is reading, he conceives every incident as passing in his presence precisely as if he were an eyewitness. A general or reflective remembrance cannot warm us into any emotion. It may be agreeable in some slight degree, but its ideas are too faint and obscure to raise anything like an emotion; and were they ever so lively, they pass with too much precipitation to have that effect. Our emotions are never instantaneous; even such as come the soonest to their height have different periods of birth and increment; and to give opportunity for these different periods, it is necessary that the cause of every emotion be present to the mind a due time; for an emotion is not carried to its height but by reiterated impressions. We know that to be the case of emotions arising from objects of sight, a quick succession, even of the most beautiful objects, scarce making any impression; and if this hold in the succession of original perceptions, how much more in the succession of ideas?

Though all this while I have been only describing what passeth in the mind of everyone and what everyone must be conscious of, it was necessary to enlarge upon the subject because, however clear in the internal conception, it is far from being so when described in words. Ideal presence, though of general importance, hath scarce ever been touched by any writer; and however difficult the explication, it could not be avoided in accounting for the effects produced by fiction. Upon that point, the reader, I guess, has prevented me. It already must have occurred to him that if, in reading, ideal presence be the means by which our passions are moved, it makes no difference whether the subject be a fable or a true history. When ideal presence is complete, we perceive every object as in our sight, and the mind, totally occupied with an interesting event, finds no leisure for reflection. This reasoning is confirmed by constant and universal experience. Let us take under consideration the meeting of Hector and Andromache in the Sixth Book of the *Iliad,* or some of the passionate scenes in *King Lear.* These pictures of human life, when we are sufficiently engaged, give an impression of reality not less distinct than that given by Tacitus describing the death of Otho. We never once reflect whether the story be true or feigned; reflection comes afterward, when we have the scene no longer before our eyes. This reasoning will appear in a still clearer light by opposing ideal presence to ideas raised by a cursory narrative, which ideas, being faint, obscure, and imperfect, leave a vacuity in the mind, which solicits reflection. And accordingly, a curt narrative of feigned incidents is never relished; any slight pleasure it affords is more than counterbalanced by the disgust it inspires for want of truth.

To support the foregoing theory, I add what I reckon a decisive argument, which is that even genuine history has no command over our passions but by ideal presence only, and consequently that in this respect it stands upon the same footing with fable. To me it appears clear that in neither can our sympathy hold firm against reflection, for if the reflection that a story is a pure fiction prevent our sympathy, so will equally the reflection that the persons described are no longer existing. What effect, for example, can the belief of the rape of Lucretia have to raise our sympathy, when she died above two thousand years ago and hath at present no painful feeling of the injury done her? The effect of history in point of instruction depends in some measure upon its veracity. But history cannot reach the heart while we indulge any reflection upon the facts. Such reflection, if it engage our belief, never fails at the same time to poison our pleasure by convincing us that our sympathy for those who are dead and gone is absurd. And if reflection be laid aside, history stands upon the same footing with fable; what effect either may have to raise our sympathy depends on the vivacity of the ideas they raise, and with respect to that circumstance fable is generally more successful than history.

Of all the means for making an impression of ideal presence, theatrical representation is the most powerful. That words independent of action have the same power in a less degree everyone of sensibility must have felt: a good tragedy will extort tears in private, though not so forcibly as upon the stage. That power belongs also to painting: a good historical picture makes a deeper impression than words can, though not equal to that of theatrical action. Painting seems to possess a middle place between reading and acting: in making an impression of ideal presence, it is not less superior to the former than inferior to the latter.

It must not, however, be thought that our passions can be raised by painting to such a height as by words. A picture is confined to a single instant of time and cannot take in a succession of incidents. Its impression indeed is the deepest that can be made instantaneously, but seldom is a passion raised to any height in an instant, or by a single impression. It was observed above that our passions, those especially of the sympathetic kind, require a succession of impressions, and for that reason reading and acting have greatly the advantage by reiterating impressions without end.

Upon the whole, it is by means of ideal presence that our passions are excited; and till words produce that charm, they avail nothing. Even real events entitled to our belief must be conceived present and passing in our sight before they can move us. And this theory serves to explain several phenomena otherwise unaccountable. A misfortune happening to a stranger makes a less impression than happening to a man we know, even where we are no way interested in him: our acquaintance with this man, however slight, aids the conception of his suffering in our presence. For the same reason, we are little moved by any distant event because we have more difficulty to conceive it present than an event that happened in our neighborhood.

Everyone is sensible that describing a past event as present has

a fine effect in language—for what other reason than that it aids
the conception of ideal presence? Take the following example:

> And now with shouts the shocking armies clos'd,
> To lances lances, shields to shields oppos'd;
> Host against host the shadowy legions drew,
> The sounding darts, an iron tempest, flew;
> Victors and vanquish'd join promiscuous cries,
> Triumphing shouts and dying groans arise,
> With streaming blood the slipp'ry field is dy'd,
> And slaughter'd heroes swell the dreadful tide.
>
> [Pope's *Iliad*, IV, 508]

In this passage we may observe how the writer, inflamed with the
subject, insensibly advances from the past time to the present, led
to that form of narration by conceiving every circumstance as
passing in his own sight, which at the same time has a fine effect
upon the reader by presenting things to him as a spectator. But
change from the past to the present requires some preparation and
is not sweet where there is no stop in the sense. Witness the following passage:

> Thy fate was next, O Phaestus! doom'd to feel
> The great Idomeneus' protended steel;
> Whom Borus sent (his son and only joy)
> From fruitful Tarnè to the fields of Troy.
> The Cretan jav'lin reach'd him from afar,
> And pierc'd his shoulder as he mounts his car.
>
> [*Ibid.*, V, 57]

It is still worse to fall back to the past in the same period, for that
is an anticlimax in description:

> Through breaking ranks his furious course he bends,
> And at the goddess his broad lance extends;
> Through her bright veil the daring weapon drove,
> Th' ambrosial veil, which all the graces wove:
> Her snowy hand the razing steel profan'd,
> And the transparent skin with crimson stain'd. [*Ibid.*, V, 415]

Again, describing the shield of Jupiter:

> Here all the terrors of grim War appear,
> Here rages Force, here tremble Flight and Fear,
> Here storm'd Contention, and here Fury frown'd,
> And the dire orb portentous Gorgon crown'd. [*Ibid.*, V, 914]

Nor is it pleasant to be carried backward and forward alternately in a rapid succession:

> Then dy'd Scamandrius, expert in the chase,
> In woods and wilds to wound the savage race;
> Diana taught him all her sylvan arts,
> To bend the bow and aim unerring darts:
> But vainly here Diana's arts he tries,
> The fatal lance arrests him as he flies;
> From Menelaus' arm the weapon sent,
> Through his broad back and heaving bosom went.
> Down sinks the warrior with a thund'ring sound,
> His brazen armour rings against the ground. [*Ibid.*, V, 65]

It is wonderful to observe upon what slight foundations nature erects some of her most solid and magnificent works. In appearance at least, what can be more slight than ideal presence? And yet from it is derived that extensive influence which language hath over the heart, an influence which, more than any other means, strengthens the bond of society, and attracts individuals from their private system to perform acts of generosity and benevolence. Matters of fact, it is true, and truth in general, may be inculcated without taking advantage of ideal presence; but without it, the finest speaker or writer would in vain attempt to move any passion. Our sympathy would be confined to objects that are really present, and language would lose entirely its signal power of making us sympathize with beings removed at the greatest distance of time as well as of place. Nor is the influence of language by means of ideal presence confined to the heart; it reacheth also the understanding and contributes to belief. For when events are related in a lively manner, and every circumstance appears as passing before us, we suffer not patiently the truth of the facts to be questioned. A historian accordingly who hath a genius for narration seldom fails to engage our belief. The same facts related in a manner cold and indistinct are not suffered to pass without examination: a thing ill described is like an object seen at a distance or through a mist—we doubt whether it be a reality or a fiction. Cicero says that to relate the manner in which an event passed not only enlivens the story, but makes it appear more credible.[1] For that reason a poet who can warm and animate his reader may employ bolder fictions than ought to be ventured by an inferior genius; the reader, once thoroughly engaged is susceptible of the strongest impressions:

Veraque constituunt, quae belle tangere possunt
auris, et lepido quae sunt fucata sonore.[2]

A masterly painting has the same effect. Le Brun is no small support
to Quintus Curtius,[3] and among the vulgar in Italy the belief of
scripture-history is perhaps founded as much upon the authority
of Raphael, Michelangelo, and other celebrated painters, as upon
that of the sacred writers.[4]

The foregoing theory must have fatigued the reader with much
dry reasoning, but his labor will not be fruitless, because from that
theory are derived many useful rules in criticism which shall be
mentioned in their proper places. One specimen shall be our
present entertainment. Events that surprise by being unexpected,
and yet are natural, enliven greatly an epic poem; but in such a
poem, if it pretend to copy human manners and actions, no improbable incident ought to be admitted; that is, no incident contrary to the order and course of nature. A chain of imagined
incidents linked together according to the order of nature, finds
easy admittance into the mind; and a lively narrative of such
incidents occasions complete images, or in other words ideal
presence. But our judgment revolts against an improbable incident;
and if we once begin to doubt of its reality, farewell relish and
concern—an unhappy effect; for it will require more than an
ordinary effort to restore the waking dream and to make the reader
conceive even the more probable incidents as passing in his presence.

I never was an admirer of machinery in an epic poem, and I
now find my taste justified by reason—the foregoing argument
concluding still more strongly against imaginary beings than against
improbable facts. Fictions of that nature may amuse by their
novelty and singularity, but they never move the sympathetic passions, because they cannot impose on the mind any perception of
reality. I appeal to the discerning reader, whether that observation
be not applicable to the machinery of Tasso and of Voltaire. Such
machinery is not only in itself cold and uninteresting, but gives an
air of fiction to the whole composition. A burlesque poem, such as
the *Lutrin* or the *Dispensary*,[5] may employ machinery with success,
for these poems, though they assume the air of history, give entertainment chiefly by their pleasant and ludicrous pictures, to which
machinery contributes. It is not the aim of such a poem to raise
our sympathy, and for that reason a strict imitation of nature is not

required. A poem professedly ludicrous may employ machinery to great advantage, and the more extravagant the better.

Having assigned the means by which fiction commands our passions, what only remains for accomplishing our present task is to assign the final cause. I have already mentioned that fiction, by means of language, has the command of our sympathy for the good of others. By the same means, our sympathy may also be raised for our own good. In the fourth section of the present chapter it is observed that examples both of virtue and of vice raise virtuous emotions which, becoming stronger by exercise, tend to make us virtuous by habit as well as by principle. I now further observe that examples confined to real events are not so frequent as without other means to produce a habit of virtue; if they be, they are not recorded by historians. It therefore shows great wisdom to form us in such a manner as to be susceptible of the same improvement from fable that we receive from genuine history. By that contrivance, examples to improve us in virtue may be multiplied without end. No other sort of discipline contributes more to make virtue habitual, and no other sort is so agreeable in the application. I add another final cause with thorough satisfaction because it shows that the author of our nature is not less kindly provident for the happiness of his creatures than for the regularity of their conduct. The power that fiction hath over the mind affords an endless variety of refined amusements, always at hand to employ a vacant hour. Such amusements are a fine resource in solitude and by cheering and sweetening the mind contribute mightily to social happiness.

HUGH BLAIR ✎

From *A Critical Dissertation on the Poems of Ossian, the Son of Fingal* (1763)

Among the monuments remaining of the ancient state of nations, few are more valuable than their poems or songs. History, when it treats of remote and dark ages, is seldom very instructive. The beginnings of society, in every country, are involved in fabulous confusion; and though they were not, they would furnish few events worth recording. But in every period of society human manners are a curious spectacle, and the most natural pictures of ancient manners are exhibited in the ancient poems of nations. These present to us, what is much more valuable than the history of such transactions as a rude age can afford, the history of human imagination and passion. They make us acquainted with the notions and feelings of our fellow creatures in the most artless ages, discovering what objects they admired and what pleasures they pursued before those refinements of society had taken place which enlarge, indeed, and diversify the transactions, but disguise the manners of mankind.

Besides this merit which ancient poems have with philosophical observers of human nature, they have another with persons of taste. They promise some of the highest beauties of poetical writing. Irregular and unpolished we may expect the productions of uncultivated ages to be, but abounding, at the same time, with that enthusiasm, that vehemence and fire, which are the soul of poetry. For many circumstances of those times which we call barbarous are favorable to the poetical spirit. That state in which human nature shoots wild and free, though unfit for other improvements, certainly encourages the high exertions of fancy and passion.

In the infancy of societies men live scattered and dispersed in the midst of solitary rural scenes, where the beauties of nature are their chief entertainment. They meet with many objects to them new and strange; their wonder and surprise are frequently excited, and by the sudden changes of fortune occurring in their unsettled state of life, their passions are raised to the utmost. Their passions have nothing to restrain them, their imagination has nothing to check it. They display themselves to one another without disguise and converse and act in the uncovered simplicity of nature. As their feelings are strong, so their language, of itself, assumes a poetical turn. Prone to exaggerate, they describe everything in the strongest colors, which, of course, renders their speech picturesque and figurative. Figurative language owes its rise chiefly to two causes: to the want of proper names for objects, and to the influence of imagination and passion over the form of expression. Both these causes concur in the infancy of society. Figures are commonly considered as artificial modes of speech devised by orators and poets after the world had advanced to a refined state. The contrary of this is the truth. Men never have used so many figures of style as in those rude ages, when, besides the power of a warm imagination to suggest lively images, the want of proper and precise terms for the ideas they would express obliged them to have recourse to circumlocution, metaphor, comparison, and all those substituted forms of expression which give a poetical air to language. An American chief at this day harangues at the head of his tribe in a more bold metaphorical style than a modern European would adventure to use in an epic poem.

In the progress of society the genius and manners of men undergo a change more favorable to accuracy than to sprightliness and sublimity. As the world advances, the understanding gains ground upon the imagination; the understanding is more exercised; the imagination, less. Fewer objects occur that are new or surprising. Men apply themselves to trace the causes of things; they correct and refine one another; they subdue or disguise their passions; they form their exterior manners upon one uniform standard of politeness and civility. Human nature is pruned according to method and rule. Language advances from sterility to copiousness, and at the same time, from fervor and enthusiasm to correctness and precision.

Style becomes more chaste but less animated. The progress of the world in this respect resembles the progress of age in man. The powers of imagination are most vigorous and predominant in youth; those of the understanding ripen more slowly and often attain not their maturity till the imagination begin to flag. Hence poetry, which is the child of imagination, is frequently most glowing and animated in the first ages of society. As the ideas of our youth are remembered with a peculiar pleasure on account of their liveliness and vivacity, so the most ancient poems have often proved the greatest favorites of nations.

Poetry has been said to be more ancient than prose, and however paradoxical such an assertion may seem, yet in a qualified sense it is true. Men certainly never conversed with one another in regular numbers, but even their ordinary language would in ancient times, for the reasons before assigned, approach to a poetical style, and the first compositions transmitted to posterity, beyond doubt, were in a literal sense poems—that is, compositions in which imagination had the chief hand, formed into some kind of numbers, and pronounced with a musical modulation or tone. Music or song has been found coeval with society among the most barbarous nations. The only subjects which could prompt men in their first rude state to utter their thoughts in compositions of any length were such as naturally assumed the tone of poetry: praises of their gods or of their ancestors, commemorations of their own warlike exploits, or lamentations over their misfortunes. And before writing was invented, no other compositions except songs or poems could take such hold of the imagination and memory as to be preserved by oral tradition and handed down from one race to another.

Hence we may expect to find poems among the antiquities of all nations. It is probable too that an extensive search would discover a certain degree of resemblance among all the most ancient poetical productions, from whatever country they have proceeded. In a similar state of manners, similar objects and passions operating upon the imaginations of men will stamp their productions with the same general character. Some diversity will, no doubt, be occasioned by climate and genius. But mankind never bear such resembling features as they do in the beginnings of society. Its subsequent revolutions give rise to the principal distinctions among nations and divert into channels widely separated that current of human genius and manners which descends originally from one

spring. What we have been long accustomed to call the oriental
vein of poetry, because some of the earliest poetical productions
have come to us from the East, is probably no more oriental than
occidental; it is characteristical of an age rather than a country,
and belongs, in some measure, to all nations at a certain period.
Of this the works of Ossian seem to furnish a remarkable proof.

.   .   .   .   .

[Blair gives a translation of the song of Lodbrog from Wormius.]

When we open the works of Ossian . . . we find the fire and the
enthusiasm of the most early times, combined with an amazing
degree of regularity and art. We find tenderness, and even delicacy
of sentiment, greatly predominant over fierceness and barbarity.
Our hearts are melted with the softest feelings, and at the same time
elevated with the highest ideas of magnanimity, generosity, and true
heroism. When we turn from the poetry of Lodbrog to that of
Ossian, it is like passing from a savage desert into a fertile and
cultivated country. How is this to be accounted for? Or by what
means to be reconciled with the remote antiquity attributed to
these poems? This is a curious point, and requires to be illustrated.

That the ancient Scots were of Celtic original is past all doubt.
Their conformity with the Celtic nations in language, manners,
and religion proves it to a full demonstration. The Celtae, a great
and mighty people, altogether distinct from the Goths and Teu-
tones, once extended their dominion over all the west of Europe,
but seem to have had their most full and complete establishment
in Gaul. Wherever the Celtae or Gauls are mentioned by ancient
writers, we seldom fail to hear of their Druids and their bards, the
institution of which two orders was the capital distinction of their
manners and policy. The Druids were their philosophers and
priests, the bards, their poets and recorders of heroic actions. And
both these orders of men seem to have subsisted among them as
chief members of the state from time immemorial. We must not
therefore imagine the Celtae to have been altogether a gross and
rude nation. They possessed from very remote ages a formed system
of discipline and manners which appears to have had a deep and
lasting influence. Ammianus Marcellinus [1] gives them this express
testimony, that there flourished among them the study of the most
laudable arts, introduced by the bards, whose office it was to sing

in heroic verse the gallant actions of illustrious men, and by the Druids, who lived together in colleges or societies, after the Pythagorean manner, and philosophizing upon the highest subjects, asserted the immortality of the human soul. Though Julius Caesar in his account of Gaul does not expressly mention the bards, yet it is plain that under the title of Druids he comprehends that whole college or order of which the bards, who, it is probable, were the disciples of the Druids, undoubtedly made a part.[2] It deserves remark that according to his account the Druidical institution first took rise in Britain and passed from thence into Gaul, so that they who aspired to be thorough masters of that learning were wont to resort to Britain. He adds, too, that such as were to be initiated among the Druids were obliged to commit to their memory a great number of verses, insomuch that some employed twenty years in this course of education, and that they did not think it lawful to record these poems in writing, but sacredly handed them down by tradition from race to race.

So strong was the attachment of the Celtic nations to their poetry and their bards that amidst all the changes of their government and manners, even long after the order of the Druids was extinct and the national religion altered, the bards continued to flourish, not as a set of strolling songsters, like the Greek Ἀοιδοί, or rhapsodists, in Homer's time, but as an order of men highly respected in the state and supported by a public establishment. We find them, according to the testimonies of Strabo and Diodorus, before the age of Augustus Caesar,[3] and we find them remaining under the same name and exercising the same functions as of old in Ireland and in the north of Scotland almost down to our own times. It is well known that in both these countries, every *regulus,* or chief, had his own bard, who was considered as an officer of rank in his court and had lands assigned him, which descended to his family. Of the honor in which the bards were held many instances occur in Ossian's poems. On all important occasions they were the ambassadors between contending chiefs, and their persons were held sacred. "Cairbar feared to stretch his sword to the bards, though his soul was dark. . . . 'Loose the bards,' said his brother Cathmor, 'they are the sons of other times. Their voice shall be heard in other ages, when the kings of Temora have failed.'"

From all this, the Celtic tribes clearly appear to have been addicted in so high a degree to poetry and to have made it so much their study from the earliest times as may remove our wonder at meeting with a vein of higher poetical refinement among them than was at first sight to have been expected among nations whom we are accustomed to call barbarous. *Barbarity,* I must observe, is a very equivocal term; it admits of many different forms and degrees, and though in all of them it exclude polished manners, it is, however, not inconsistent with generous sentiments and tender affections. What degrees of friendship, love, and heroism may possibly be found to prevail in a rude state of society no one can say. Astonishing instances of them we know from history have sometimes appeared, and a few characters distinguished by those high qualities might lay a foundation for a set of manners being introduced into the songs of the bards more refined, it is probable, and exalted, according to the usual poetical licence, than the real manners of the country. In particular, with respect to heroism, the great employment of the Celtic bards was to delineate the characters and sing the praises of heroes. So Lucan:

> Vos quoque, qui fortes animas belloque peremptas,
> laudibus in longum vates dimittitis aevum
> plurima securi fudistis carmina, Bardi.[4]

Now when we consider a college or order of men who, cultivating poetry throughout a long series of ages, had their imaginations continually employed on the ideas of heroism, who had all the poems and panegyrics which were composed by their predecessors handed down to them with care, who rivaled and endeavored to outstrip those who had gone before them, each in the celebration of his particular hero, is it not natural to think that at length the character of a hero would appear in their songs with the highest luster, and be adorned with qualities truly noble? Some of the qualities indeed which distinguish a Fingal, moderation, humanity, and clemency, would not probably be the first ideas of heroism occurring to a barbarous people, but no sooner had such ideas begun to dawn on the minds of poets than, as the human mind easily opens to the native representations of human perfection, they would be seized and embraced; they would enter into their panegyrics; they would afford materials for succeeding bards to work upon and improve; they would contribute not a little to exalt the public manners. For such songs as these, familiar to the Celtic warriors from their childhood, and throughout their whole life, both in war and in peace, their principal entertainment, must have had a very considerable influence in propagating among them real manners nearly approaching to the poetical, and in forming even such a hero as Fingal. Especially when we consider that among their limited objects of ambition, among the few advantages which in a savage state man could obtain over man, the chief was fame and that immortality which they expected to receive from their virtues and exploits in the songs of bards.

Having made these remarks on the Celtic poetry and bards in general, I shall next consider the particular advantages which Ossian possessed. He appears clearly to have lived in a period which enjoyed all the benefit I just now mentioned of traditionary poetry. The exploits of Trathal, Trenmor, and the other ancestors of Fingal are spoken of as familiarly known. Ancient bards are frequently alluded to. In one remarkable passage, Ossian describes himself as living in a sort of classical age, enlightened by the memorials of former times conveyed in the songs of bards, and points at a period of darkness and ignorance which lay beyond the reach of tradition. "His words," says he, "came only by halves to our ears; they were dark as the tales of other times, before the light of the song arose." Ossian himself appears to have been endowed by nature with an exquisite sensibility of heart, prone to that tender melancholy which is so often an attendant on great genius, and susceptible equally of strong and of soft emotions. He was not only a professed bard, educated with care, as we may easily believe, to all the poetical art then known, and connected, as he shows us himself, in intimate friendship with the other contemporary bards, but a warrior also, and the son of the most renowned hero and prince of his age. This formed a conjunction of circumstances uncommonly favorable towards exalting the imagination of a poet. He relates expeditions in which he had been engaged; he sings of battles in which he had fought and overcome; he had beheld the most illustrious scenes which that age could exhibit, both of heroism in war and magnificence in peace. For however rude the magnificence of those times may seem to us, we must remember that all ideas of magnificence are comparative, and that the age of Fingal was an era of distinguished splendor in that part of the world. Fingal reigned over a considerable territory; he was enriched with the spoils of the Roman province; he was ennobled by his victories and great actions; and was in all respects a personage of much higher dignity than any of the chieftains or heads of clans who lived in the same country after a more extensive monarchy was established.

The manners of Ossian's age, so far as we can gather them from his writings, were abundantly favorable to a poetical genius. The two dispiriting vices, to which Longinus imputes the decline of poetry, covetousness and effeminacy, were as yet unknown.[5] The cares of men were few. They lived a roving indolent life; hunting and war, their principal employments; and their chief amusements, the music of bards and the feast of shells. The great object pursued by heroic spirits was "to receive their fame," that is, to become worthy of being celebrated in the songs of bards, and "to have their name on the four gray stones." To die unlamented by a bard was deemed so great a misfortune as even to disturb their ghosts in another state. After death they expected to follow employments of the same nature with those which had amused them on earth: to fly with their friends on clouds, to pursue airy deer, and to listen to their praise in the mouths of bards. In such times as these, in a country where poetry had been so long cultivated and so highly honored, is it any wonder that among the race and succession of bards, one Homer should arise—a man who, endowed with a natural happy genius, favored by peculiar advantages of birth and condition, and meeting in the course of his life with a variety of incidents proper to fire his imagination and to touch his heart, should attain a degree of eminence in poetry worthy to draw the admiration of more refined ages?

The compositions of Ossian are so strongly marked with characters of antiquity that although there were no external proof to support that antiquity, hardly any reader of judgment and taste could hesitate in referring them to a very remote era. There are four great stages through which men successively pass in the progress of society. The first and earliest is the life of hunters; pasturage succeeds to this, as the ideas of property begin to take root; next, agriculture; and lastly, commerce. Throughout Ossian's poems we plainly find ourselves in the first of these periods of society, during which hunting was the chief employment of men and the principal method of their procuring subsistence. Pasturage was not indeed wholly unknown, for we hear of dividing the herd in the case of a divorce; but the allusions to herds and to cattle are not many; and of agriculture, we find no traces. No cities appear to have been built in the territories of Fingal. No art is mentioned except that of working in iron. Everything presents to us the most simple and unimproved manners. At their feasts, the heroes prepared their own repast; they sat round the light of the burning oak; the wind lifted their locks and whistled through their open halls. Whatever was beyond the necessaries of life was known to them only as the spoil of the Roman province: "the gold of the stranger, the lights of the stranger, the steeds of the stranger, the children of the rein."

This representation of Ossian's times must strike us the more as genuine and authentic when it is compared with a poem of later date which Mr. Macpherson has preserved in one of his notes. It is that wherein five bards are represented as passing the evening in the house of a chief, and each of them separately giving his description of the night. The night scenery is beautiful, and the author has plainly imitated the style and manner of Ossian, but he has allowed some images to appear which betray a later period of society. For we meet with windows clapping, the herds of goats and cows seeking shelter, the shepherd wandering, corn on the plain, and the wakeful hind rebuilding the shocks of corn which had been overturned by the tempest. Whereas in Ossian's works, from beginning to end, all is consistent; no modern allusion drops from him; but everywhere the same face of rude nature appears: a country wholly uncultivated, thinly inhabited, and recently peopled. The grass of the rock, the flower of the heath, the thistle with its beard, are the chief ornaments of his landscapes. "The desert," says Fingal, "is enough to me, with all its woods and deer."

The circle of ideas and transactions is no wider than suits such an age, nor any greater diversity introduced into characters than the events of that period would naturally display. Valor and bodily strength are the admired qualities. Contentions arise, as is usual among savage nations, from the slightest causes. To be affronted at a tournament or to be omitted in the invitation to a feast kindles a war. Women are often carried away by force, and the whole tribe, as in the Homeric times, rise to avenge the wrong. The heroes show refinement of sentiment indeed on several occasions, but none of manners. They speak of their past actions with freedom, boast of their exploits, and sing their own praise. In their battles, it is evident that drums, trumpets, or bagpipes, were not known or used. They had no expedient for giving the military alarms but striking a shield or raising a loud cry, and hence the loud and terrible voice of Fingal is often mentioned, as a necessary qualification of a great general; like the βοὴν ἀγαθὸς Μενέλαος of Homer. Of military discipline or skill, they appear to have been entirely destitute. Their armies seem not to have been numerous; their battles were disorderly, and terminated, for the most part, by a personal combat or wrestling of the two chiefs, after which, "The bard sung the song of peace, and the battle ceased along the field."

The manner of composition bears all the marks of the greatest antiquity. No artful transitions nor full and extended connection of parts such as we find among the poets of later times, when order and regularity of composition were more studied and known; but a style always rapid and vehement; in narration concise, even to abruptness, and leaving several circumstances to be supplied by the reader's imagination. The language has all that figurative cast which, as I before showed, partly a glowing and undisciplined imagination, partly the sterility of language and the want of proper terms, have always introduced into the early speech of nations; and in several respects, it carries a remarkable resmblance to the style of the Old Testament. It deserves particular notice, as one of the most genuine and decisive characters of antiquity, that very few general terms or abstract ideas are to be met with in the whole collection of Ossian's works. The ideas of men at first were all particular. They had not words to express general conceptions. These were the consequence of more profound reflection and longer acquaintance with the arts of thought and of speech. Ossian, accordingly, almost never expresses himself in the abstract. His ideas extended little farther than to the objects he saw around him. A public, a community, the universe, were conceptions beyond his sphere. Even a mountain, a sea, or a lake which he has occasion to mention, though only in a simile, are for the most part particularized; it is the hill of Cromla, the storm of the sea of Malmor, or the reeds of the lake of Lego—a mode of expression which, whilst it is characteristical of ancient ages, is at the same time highly favorable to descriptive poetry. For the same reasons personification is a poetical figure not very common with Ossian. Inanimate objects, such as winds, trees, flowers, he sometimes personifies with great beauty. But the personifications which are so familiar to later poets of Fame, Time, Terror, Virtue, and the rest of that class, were unknown to our Celtic bard. These were modes of conception too abstract for his age.

All these are marks so undoubted, and some of them, too, so nice and delicate, of the most early times, as put the high antiquity of these poems out of question. Especially when we consider that if there had been any imposture in this case, it must have been contrived and executed in the Highlands of Scotland two or three centuries ago, as up to this period, both by manuscripts and by the testimony of a multitude of living witnesses concerning the uncontrovertible tradition of these poems, they can clearly be traced. Now this is a period when that country enjoyed no advantages for a composition of this kind which it may not be supposed to have enjoyed in as great, if not in a greater, degree a thousand years before. To suppose that two or three hundred years ago, when we well know the Highlands to have been in a state of gross ignorance and barbarity, there should have arisen in that country a poet of such exquisite genius and of such deep knowledge of mankind and of history as to divest himself of the ideas and manners of his own age, and to give us a just and natural picture of a state of society ancienter by a thousand years—one who could support this counterfeited antiquity through such a large collection of poems without the least inconsistency, and who, possessed of all this genius and art, had at the same time the self-denial of concealing himself and of ascribing his own works to an antiquated bard, without the imposture being detected, is a supposition which transcends all bounds of credibility.

There are, besides, two other circumstances to be attended to, still of greater weight, if possible, against this hypothesis. One is the total absence of religious ideas from this work, for which the translator has, in his preface, given a very probable account on the footing of its being the work of Ossian. The Druidical superstition was in the days of Ossian on the point of its final extinction, and for particular reasons, odious to the family of Fingal; whilst the Christian faith was not yet established. But had it been the work of one to whom the ideas of Christianity were familiar from his infancy, and who had superadded to them also the bigoted superstition of a dark age and country, it is impossible but in some passage or other the traces of them would have appeared. The other circumstance is the entire silence which reigns with respect to all the great clans or families which are now established in the Highlands. The origin of these several clans is known to be very ancient, and it is as well known that there is no passion by which a native Highlander is more distinguished than by attachment to his clan and jealousy for its honor. That a Highland bard, in forging a work relating to the antiquities of his country, should have inserted no circumstance which pointed out the rise of his own clan, which ascertained its antiquity, or increased its glory, is of all suppositions that can be formed the most improbable; and the silence on this head amounts to a demonstration that the author lived before any of the present great clans were formed or known.

Assuming it then, as we well may, for certain that the poems now under consideration are genuine venerable monuments of very remote antiquity, I proceed to make some remarks upon their general spirit and strain. The two great characteristics of Ossian's poetry are tenderness and sublimity. It breathes nothing of the gay and cheerful kind; an air of solemnity and seriousness is diffused over the whole. Ossian is perhaps the only poet who never relaxes or lets himself down into the light and amusing strain, which I readily admit to be no small disadvantage to him with the bulk of readers. He moves perpetually in the high region of the grand and the pathetic. One keynote is struck at the beginning and supported to the end, nor is any ornament introduced but what is perfectly concordant with the general tone or melody. The events recorded are all serious and grave, the scenery throughout, wild and romantic. The extended heath by the sea shore, the mountain shaded with mist, the torrent rushing through a solitary valley, the scattered oaks, and the tombs of warriors overgrown with moss, all produce a solemn attention in the mind and prepare it for great and extraordinary events. We find not in Ossian an imagination that sports itself and dresses out gay trifles to please the fancy. His poetry, more perhaps than that of any other writer, deserves to be styled "the poetry of the heart." It is a heart penetrated with noble sentiments and with sublime and tender passions, a heart that glows and kindles the fancy, a heart that is full, and pours itself forth. Ossian did not write, like modern poets, to please readers and critics. He sung from the love of poetry and song. His delight was to think of the heroes among whom he had flourished, to recall the affecting incidents of his life, to dwell upon his past wars and loves and friendships till, as he expresses it himself, "the light of his soul arose; the days of other years rose before him"; and under this true poetic inspiration, giving vent to his genius, no wonder we should so often hear, and acknowledge in his strains, the powerful and ever-pleasing voice of nature.

> Arte, natura potentior omni. . . .
> Est deus in nobis, agitante calescimus illo.

RICHARD HURD ✍

A Dissertation on the Idea
of Universal Poetry (1766)

When we speak of poetry as an art, we mean such a way or method of treating a subject as is found most pleasing and delightful to us. In all other kinds of literary composition, pleasure is subordinate to use; in poetry only, pleasure is the end, to which use itself (however it be, for certain reasons, always pretended) must submit.

This idea of the end of poetry is no novel one, but indeed the very same which our great philosopher entertained of it, who gives it as the essential note of this part of learning "that it submits the shows of things to the desires of the mind, whereas reason doth buckle and bow the mind unto the nature of things." For to gratify the desires of the mind is to please. Pleasure, then, in the idea of Lord Bacon, is the ultimate and appropriate end of poetry, for the sake of which it accommodates itself to the desires of the mind, and doth not (as other kinds of writing, which are under the control of reason) "buckle and bow the mind to the nature of things." [1]

But they who like a principle the better for seeing it in Greek may take it in the words of an old philosopher, Eratosthenes, who affirmed ποιητὴν πάντα στοχάζεσθαι ψυχαγωγίας ὀυ διδασκαλίας, of which words the definition given above is the translation.

This notion of the end of poetry, if kept steadily in view, will unfold to us all the mysteries of the poetic art. There needs but to evolve the philosopher's idea, and to apply it, as occasion serves. The art of poetry will be universally the art of pleasing, and all its rules but so many means which experience finds most conducive to that end:

Sic animis natum inventumque poema juvandis.[2]

Aristotle has delivered and explained these rules so far as they respect one species of poetry, the dramatic, or more properly speaking, the tragic. And when such a writer as he shall do as much by the other species, then, and not till then, a complete art of poetry will be formed.

I have not the presumption to think myself in any degree equal to this arduous task, but from the idea of this art, as given above, an ordinary writer may undertake to deduce some general conclusions concerning universal poetry which seem preparatory to those nicer disquisitions concerning its several sorts or species.

I. It follows from that idea that it should neglect no advantage that fairly offers itself of appearing in such a dress or mode of language as is most taking and agreeable to us. We may expect then, in the language or style of poetry, a choice of such words as are most sonorous and expressive, and such an arrangement of them as throws the discourse out of the ordinary and common phrase of conversation. Novelty and variety are certain sources of pleasure; a construction of words which is not vulgar is therefore more suited to the ends of poetry than one which we are every day accustomed to in familiar discourse. Some manners of placing them are, also, more agreeable to the ear than others. Poetry, then, is studious of these, as it would by all means not manifestly absurd give pleasure. And hence a certain musical cadence, or what we call rhythm, will be affected by the poet.

But of all the means of adorning and enlivening a discourse by words, which are infinite, and perpetually grow upon us as our knowledge of the tongue in which we write and our skill in adapting it to the ends of poetry increases, there is none that pleases more than figurative expression.

By figurative expression I would be understood to mean here that which respects the pictures or images of things. And this sort of figurative expression is universally pleasing to us because it tends to impress on the mind the most distinct and vivid conceptions; and truth of representation being of less account in this way of composition than the liveliness of it, poetry, as such, will delight in tropes and figures, and those the most strongly and forcibly expressed. And though the application of figures will admit of great variety according to the nature of the subject, and the management of them must be suited to the taste and apprehension of the people to whom they are addressed, yet in some way or other they will find a place in all

works of poetry; and they who object to the use of them only show
that they are not capable of being pleased by this sort of composition,
or do, in effect, interdict the thing itself.

The ancients looked for so much of this force and spirit of expression in whatever they dignified with the name of *poem* that Horace
tells us it was made a question by some whether comedy were rightly
referred to this class, because it differed only in point of measure
from mere prose.

> Idcirco quidam comoedia necne poema
> esset quaesivere, quod acer spiritus ac vis
> nec verbis nec rebus inest, nisi quod pede certo
> differt sermoni, sermo merus.[3]

But they might have spared their doubt, or at least have resolved
it, if they had considered that comedy adopts as much of this "force
and spirit of words" as is consistent with the nature and degree of
that pleasure which it pretends to give. For the name of poem will
belong to every composition whose primary end is to please, provided
it be so constructed as to afford all the pleasure which its kind or sort
will permit.

II. From the idea of the end of poetry, it follows that not only
figurative and tropical terms will be employed in it, as these, by the
images they convey, and by the air of novelty which such indirect
ways of speaking carry with them, are found most delightful to us,
but also that fiction, in the largest sense of the word, is essential to
poetry. For its purpose is not to delineate truth simply, but to present
it in the most taking forms; not to reflect the real face of things, but to
illustrate and adorn it; not to represent the fairest objects only, but to
represent them in the fairest lights, and to heighten all their beauties
up to the possibility of their natures; nay, to outstrip nature, and to
address itself to our wildest fancy, rather than to our judgment and
cooler sense.

> Οὔτ’ ἐπιδερκτὰ τάδ’ ἀνδράσιν, οὔτ’ ἐπακουστά
> οὔτε νόῳ περίληπτα,

as sings one of the profession,[4] who seems to have understood his
privileges very well.

For there is something in the mind of man, sublime and elevated,
which prompts it to overlook all obvious and familiar appearances,
and to feign to itself other and more extraordinary—such as cor-

respond to the extent of its own powers, and fill out all the faculties and capacities of our souls. This restless and aspiring disposition poetry, first and principally, would indulge and flatter, and thence takes its name of *divine,* as if some power above human conspired to lift the mind to these exalted conceptions.

Hence it comes to pass that it deals in apostrophes and invocations; that it impersonates the virtues and vices; peoples all creation with new and living forms; calls up infernal spectres to terrify, or brings down celestial natures to astonish, the imagination; assembles, combines, or connects its ideas at pleasure; in short, prefers not only the agreeable and the graceful but, as occasion calls upon her, the vast, the incredible, I had almost said, the impossible, to the obvious truth and nature of things. For all this is but a feeble expression of that magic virtue of poetry which our Shakespeare has so forcibly described in those well-known lines:

> The poet's eye, in a fine frenzy rolling,
> Doth glance from heaven to earth, from earth to heaven;
> And, as imagination bodies forth
> The forms of things unknown, the poet's pen
> Turns them to shapes, and gives to airy nothing
> A local habitation and a name.

When the received system of manners or religion in any country happens to be so constituted as to suit itself in some degree to this extravagant turn of the human mind, we may expect that poetry will seize it with avidity, will dilate upon it with pleasure, and take a pride to erect its specious wonders on so proper and convenient a ground. Whence it cannot seem strange that, of all the forms in which poetry has appeared, that of pagan fable and Gothic romance should, in their turns, be found the most alluring to the true poet. For in defect of these advantages he will ever adventure, in some sort, to supply their place with others of his own invention; that is, he will mould every system, and convert every subject, into the most amazing and miraculous form.

And this is that I would say at present of these two requisites of universal poetry (namely, that licence of expression which we call the style of poetry and that licence of representation which we call fiction): The style is, as it were, the body of poetry; fiction is its soul. Having thus taken the privilege of a poet to create a Muse, we have only now to give her a voice, or more properly to tune it, and then she will be in a condition, as one of her favorites speaks, "to ravish all the gods." For

III. It follows from the same idea of the end which poetry would accomplish that not only rhythm but numbers, properly so called, is essential to it. For, this art undertaking to gratify all those desires and expectations of pleasure that can be reasonably entertained by us, and there being a capacity in language, the instrument it works by, of pleasing us very highly, not only by the sense and imagery it conveys but by the structure of words and still more by the harmonious arrangement of them in metrical sounds or numbers, and lastly there being no reason in the nature of the thing itself why these pleasures should not be united, it follows that poetry will not be that which it professes to be, that is, will not accomplish its own purpose, unless it delight the ear with numbers, or, in other words, unless it be clothed in verse.

The reader, I dare say, has hitherto gone along with me in this deduction; but here, I suspect, we shall separate. Yet he will startle the less at this conclusion if he reflect on the origin and first application of poetry among all nations.

It is everywhere of the most early growth, preceding every other sort of composition; and being destined for the ear, that is, to be either sung, or at least recited, it adapts itself, even in its first rude essays, to that sense of measure and proportion in sounds which is so natural to us. The hearer's attention is the sooner gained by this means, his entertainment quickened, and his admiration of the performer's art excited. Men are ambitious of pleasing, and ingenious in refining upon what they observe will please. So that musical cadences and harmonious sounds which nature dictated are farther softened and improved by art, till poetry become as ravishing to the ear as the images it presents are to the imagination. In process of time, what was at first the extemporaneous production of genius or passion, under the conduct of a natural ear, becomes the labor of the closet, and is conducted by artificial rules, yet still with a secret reference to the sense of hearing and to that acceptation which melodious sounds meet with in the recital of expressive words.

Even the prose writer (when the art is enough advanced to produce prose), having been accustomed to have his ear consulted and gratified by the poet, catches insensibly the same harmonious affection, tunes his sentences and periods to some agreement with song, and transfers into his coolest narrative, or gravest instruction, something of that music with which his ear vibrates from poetic impressions.

In short, he leaves measured and determinate numbers, that is, meter, to the poet, who is to please up to the height of his faculties and the nature of his work; and only reserves to himself, whose purpose of giving pleasure is subordinate to another end, the looser musical measure, or what we call rhythmical prose.

The reason appears from this deduction why all poetry aspires to please by melodious numbers. To some species it is thought more essential than to others because those species continue to be sung, that is, are more immediately addressed to the ear, and because they continue to be sung in concert with musical instruments, by which the ear is still more indulged. It happened in ancient Greece that even tragedy retained this accompaniment of musical instruments through all its stages, and even in its most improved state. Whence Aristotle includes music, properly so called, as well as rhythm and meter, in his idea of the tragic poem. He did this because he found the drama of his country *omnibus numeris absolutum,* I mean in possession of all the advantages which could result from the union of rhythmical, metrical, and musical sounds. Modern tragedy has relinquished part of these; yet still, if it be true that this poem be more pleasing by the addition of the musical art, and there be nothing in the nature of the composition which forbids the use of it, I know not why Aristotle's idea should not be adopted, and his precept become a standing law of the tragic stage. For this, as every other poem, being calculated and designed properly and ultimately to please, whatever contributes to produce that end most perfectly, all circumstances taken into the account, must be thought of the nature or essence of the kind.

But without carrying matters so far, let us confine our attention to meter, or what we call verse. This must be essential to every work bearing the name of poem, not because we are only accustomed to call works written in verse poems, but because a work which professes to please us by every possible and proper method and yet does not give us this pleasure which it is in its power, and is no way improper for it, to give must so far fall short of fulfilling its own engagements to us; that is, it has not all those qualities which we have a right to expect in a work of literary art of which pleasure is the ultimate end.

To explain myself by an obvious instance. History undertakes

to instruct us in the transactions of past times. If it answer this purpose, it does all that is of its nature, and if it find means to please us
besides by the harmony of its style and vivacity of its narration, all
this is to be accounted as pure gain; if it instructed only, by the
truth of its reports and the perspicuity of its method, it would fully
attain its end. Poetry, on the other hand, undertakes to please. If
it employ all its powers to this purpose, it effects all that is of its
nature; if it serve besides to inform or instruct us by the truths it
conveys and by the precepts or examples it inculcates, this service
may rather be accepted than required by us; if it pleased only by
its ingenious fictions and harmonious structure, it would discharge
its office and answer its end.

In this sense the famous saying of Eratosthenes, quoted above,
that the poet's aim is to please, not to instruct, is to be understood;
nor does it appear what reason Strabo could have to take offence
at it, however it might be misapplied, as he tells us it was, by that
writer. For, though the poets no doubt (and especially *the poet,*
whose honor the great geographer would assert, in his criticism on
Eratosthenes) frequently instruct us by a true and faithful representation of things, yet even this instructive air is only assumed for the
sake of pleasing, which, as the human mind is constituted, they
could not so well do if they did not instruct at all, that is, if truth
were wholly neglected by them. So that pleasure is still the ultimate
end and scope of the poet's art, and instruction itself is, in his hands,
only one of the means by which he would effect it.[5]

I am the larger on this head to show that it is not a mere verbal
dispute, as it is commonly thought, whether poems should be
written in verse or no. Men may include or not include the idea of
meter in their complex idea of what they call a poem. What I contend for is that meter, as an instrument of pleasing, is essential to
every work of poetic art, and would therefore enter into such idea if
men judged of poetry according to its confessed nature and end.

Whence it may seem a little strange that my Lord Bacon should
speak of poesy as a "part of learning in measure of words *for the
most part* restrained," when his own notion, as we have seen above,
was that the essence of poetry consisted in "submitting the shows
of things to the desires of the mind." For these "shows of things"
could only be exhibited to the mind through the medium of words,
and it is just as natural for the mind to desire that these words

should be harmonious as that the images conveyed in them should be illustrious, there being a capacity in the mind of being delighted through its organ the ear, as well as through its power or faculty of imagination. And the wonder is the greater because the great philosopher himself was aware of the agreement and consort which poetry hath with music, as well as with man's nature and pleasure, that is, with the pleasure which naturally results from gratifying the imagination. So that to be consistent with himself he should, methinks, have said that "poesy was a part of learning in measure of words *always* restrained"; such poesy as, through the idleness or negligence of writers, is not so restrained not agreeing to his own idea of this part of learning.[6]

These reflections will afford a proper solution of that question which has been agitated by the critics, whether a work of fiction and imagination (such as that of the Archbishop of Cambray,[7] for instance), conducted in other respects according to the rules of the epic poem, but written in prose, may deserve the name of poem or not. For though it be frivolous indeed to dispute about names, yet from what has been said it appears that if meter be not incongruous to the nature of an epic composition and it afford a pleasure which is not to be found in mere prose, meter is for that reason essential to this mode of writing; which is only saying in other words that an epic composition, to give all the pleasure which it is capable of giving, must be written in verse.

But secondly, this conclusion, I think, extends farther than to such works as aspire to the name of epic. For instance, what are we to think of those novels or romances, as they are called, that is, fables constructed on some private and familiar subject, which have been so current of late through all Europe? As they propose pleasure for their end, and prosecute it, besides, in the way of fiction, though without metrical numbers, and generally, indeed, in harsh and rugged prose, one easily sees what their pretensions are, and under what idea they are ambitious to be received. Yet, as they are wholly destitute of measured sounds (to say nothing of their other numberless defects), they can at most be considered but as hasty, imperfect, and abortive poems, whether spawned from the dramatic or narrative species it may be hard to say.

> Unfinish'd things, one knows not what to call,
> Their generation's so equivocal. [Pope, *E.C.*, 43]

However, such as they are, these novelties have been generally well received: some for the real merit of their execution, others for their amusing subjects, all of them for the gratification they afford, or promise at least, to a vitiated, palled, and sickly imagination— that last disease of learned minds, and sure prognostic of expiring letters. But whatever may be the temporary success of these things (for they vanish as fast as they are produced, and are produced as soon as they are conceived), good sense will acknowledge no work of art but such as is composed according to the laws of its kind. These kinds, as arbitrary things as we account them (for I neither forget nor dispute what our best philosophy teaches concerning kinds and sorts), have yet so far their foundation in nature and the reason of things that it will not be allowed us to multiply or vary them at pleasure. We may, indeed, mix and confound them if we will (for there is a sort of literary luxury which would engross all pleasures at once, even such as are contradictory to each other), or in our rage for incessant gratification we may take up with half-formed pleasures, such as come first to hand and may be administered by anybody; but true taste requires chaste, severe, and simple pleasures, and true genius will only be concerned in administering such.

Lastly, on the same principle on which we have decided on these questions concerning the absolute merits of poems in prose in all languages, we may also determine another which has been put concerning the comparative merits of rhymed and what is called blank verse, in our own and the other modern languages.

Critics and antiquaries have been solicitous to find out who were the inventors of rhyme, which some fetch from the monks, some from the Goths, and others from the Arabians; whereas the truth seems to be that rhyme, or the consonance of final syllables occurring at stated intervals, is the dictate of nature, or, as we may say, an appeal to the ear, in all languages, and in some degree pleasing in all. The difference is that in some languages these consonances are apt of themselves to occur so often that they rather nauseate than please, and so, instead of being affected, are studiously avoided by good writers; while in others, as in all the modern ones, where these consonances are less frequent, and where the quantity of syllables is not so distinctly marked as of itself to afford an harmonious measure and musical variety, there it is of necessity that poets have had recourse to rhyme or to some other expedient of the like nature such as the alliteration, for instance, which is only another way of delighting the ear by iterated sound, and may be defined "the consonance of initial letters" as rhyme is "the consonance of final syllables." All this, I say, is of necessity, because what we call verses in such languages will be otherwise untuneful and will not strike the ear with that vivacity which is requisite to put a sensible difference between poetic numbers and measured prose.

In short, no method of gratifying the ear by measured sound which experience has found pleasing is to be neglected by the poet; and although from the different structure and genius of languages these methods will be different, the studious application of such methods as each particular language allows becomes a necessary part of his office. He will only cultivate those methods most which tend to produce in a given language the most harmonious structure or measure of which it is capable.

Hence it comes to pass that the poetry of some modern languages cannot so much as subsist without rhyme; in others, it is only embellished by it. Of the former sort is the French, which therefore adopts, and with good reason, rhymed verse, not in tragedy only, but in comedy. And though foreigners who have a language differently constructed are apt to treat this observance of rhyme as an idle affectation, yet it is but just to allow that the French themselves are the most competent judges of the natural defect of their own tongue, and the likeliest to perceive by what management such defect is best remedied or concealed.

In the latter class of languages, whose poetry is only embellished by the use of rhyme, we may reckon the Italian and the English, which, being naturally more tuneful and harmonious than the French, may afford all the melody of sound which is expected in some sorts of poetry by its varied pause and quantity only, while in other sorts, which are more solicitous to please the ear, and where such solicitude, if taken notice of by the reader or hearer, is not resented, it may be proper, or rather it becomes a law of the English and Italian poetry, to adopt rhyme. Thus, our tragedies are usually composed in blank verse, but our epic and lyric compositions are found most pleasing when clothed in rhyme. Milton, I know it will be said, is an exception. But if we set aside some learned persons who have suffered themselves to be too easily prejudiced by their admiration of the Greek and Latin languages and still more perhaps by the prevailing notion of the monkish or Gothic original of rhymed verse, all other readers, if left to themselves, would, I dare say, be more delighted with this poet if, besides his various pause and measured quantity, he had enriched his numbers with rhyme. So that his love of liberty, the ruling passion of his heart, perhaps transported him too far when he chose to follow the example set him by one or two writers of "prime note" (to use his own eulogium) rather than comply with the regular and prevailing practice of his favored Italy, which first and principally, as our best rhymist sings,

> With pauses, cadence, and well-vowell'd words,
> And all the graces a good ear affords,
> Made rhyme an art.[8]

Our comedy, indeed, is generally written in prose, but through the idleness or ill taste of our writers, rather than from any other just cause. For though rhyme be not necessary, or rather would be improper, in the comedy of our language, which can support itself in poetic numbers without the diligence of rhyme, yet some sort of meter is requisite in this humbler species of poem; otherwise it will not contribute all that is within its power and province to please. And the particular meter proper for this species is not far to seek. For it can plainly be no other than a careless and looser iambic, such as our language naturally runs into, even in conversation, and of which we are not without examples in our old and best writers for the comic stage. But it is not wonderful that those critics who take offense at English epic poems in rhyme because the Greek and Latin only observed quantity should require English comedies to be written in prose though the Greek and Latin comedies were composed in verse. For the ill application of examples and the neglect of them may be well enough expected from the same men, since it does not appear that their judgment was employed, or the reason of the thing attended to, in either instance.

And thus much for the idea of universal poetry. It is the art of treating any subject in such a way as is found most delightful to us, that is, in an ornamented and numerous style—in the way of fiction —and in verse. Whatever deserves the name of poem must unite these three properties, only in different degrees of each, according to its nature. For the art of every kind of poetry is only this general art so modified as the nature of each, that is, its more immediate and subordinate end, may respectively require.

We are now, then, at the wellhead of the poetic art; and they

who drink deeply of this spring will be best qualified to perform
the rest. But all heads are not equal to these copious draughts; and
besides, I hear the sober reader admonishing me long since—

Lusisti satis atque bibisti;
tempus abire tibi est, ne potum largius aequo
rideat et pulset lasciva decentius aetas.[9]

SIR WILLIAM JONES ✒

"On the Arts Commonly Called Imitative" (1772)

It is the fate of those maxims which have been thrown out by very eminent writers to be received implicitly by most of their followers and to be repeated a thousand times for no other reason than because they once dropped from the pen of a superior genius. One of these is the assertion of Aristotle that all poetry consists in imitation, which has been so frequently echoed from author to author that it would seem a kind of arrogance to controvert it; for almost all the philosophers and critics who have written upon the subject of poetry, music, and painting, how little soever they may agree in some points, seem of one mind in considering them as arts merely imitative; yet it must be clear to any one who examines what passes in his own mind that he is affected by the finest poems, pieces of music, and pictures upon a principle which, whatever it be, is entirely distinct from imitation. M. le Batteux has attempted to prove that all the fine arts have a relation to this common principle of imitating; [1] but whatever be said of painting, it is probable that poetry and music had a nobler origin; and if the first language of man was not both poetical and musical, it is certain at least that in countries where no kind of imitation seems to be much admired there are poets and musicians both by nature and by art—as in some Mohammedan nations, where sculpture and painting are forbidden by the laws, where dramatic poetry of every sort is wholly unknown, yet where the pleasing arts of expressing the passions in verse and of enforcing that expression by melody are cultivated to a degree of enthusiasm. It shall be my endeavor in this paper to prove that though poetry and music have, certainly, a power of imitating the manners of men and several objects in nature, yet that their greatest effect is not produced by imitation, but by a very different principle, which must be sought for in the deepest recesses of the human mind.

To state the question properly we must have a clear notion of what we mean by poetry and music, but we cannot give a precise definition of them till we have made a few previous remarks on their origin, their relation to each other, and their difference.

It seems probable then that poetry was originally no more than a strong and animated expression of the human passions, of joy and grief, love and hate, admiration and anger, sometimes pure and unmixed, sometimes variously modified and combined, for if we observe the voice and accents of a person affected by any of the violent passions, we shall perceive something in them very nearly approaching to cadence and measure, which is remarkably the case in the language of a vehement orator whose talent is chiefly conversant about praise or censure, and we may collect from several passages in Tully that the fine speakers of old Greece and Rome had a sort of rhythm in their sentences, less regular, but not less melodious, than that of the poets.

If this idea be just, one would suppose that the most ancient sort of poetry consisted in praising the deity; for if we conceive a being, created with all his faculties and senses, endued with speech and reason, to open his eyes in a most delightful plain, to view for the first time the serenity of the sky, the splendor of the sun, the verdure of the fields and woods, the glowing colors of the flowers, we can hardly believe it possible that he should refrain from bursting into an ecstasy of joy and pouring his praises to the creator of those wonders and the author of his happiness. This kind of poetry is used in all nations, but as it is the sublimest of all when it is applied to its true object, so it has often been perverted to impious purposes by pagans and idolaters; everyone knows that the dramatic poetry of the Europeans took its rise from the same spring and was no more at first than a song in praise of Bacchus, so that the only species of poetical composition (if we except the epic) which can in any sense be called imitative was deduced from a natural emotion of the mind in which imitation could not be at all concerned.

The next source of poetry was probably love, or the mutual inclination which naturally subsists between the sexes and is founded upon personal beauty; hence arose the most agreeable odes and love songs, which we admire in the works of the ancient lyric poets, not filled, like our sonnets and madrigals, with the insipid babble of darts and Cupids, but simple, tender, natural, and consisting of such unaffected endearments, and mild complaints,

> Teneri sdegni, e placide e tranquille
> Repulse, e cari vezzi, e liete paci,[2]

as we may suppose to have passed between the first lovers in a state of innocence before the refinements of society and the restraints which they introduced had made the passion of love so fierce and impetuous as it is said to have been in Dido, and certainly was in Sappho, if we may take her own word for it.[3]

The grief which the first inhabitants of the earth must have felt at the death of their dearest friends and relations gave rise to another species of poetry which originally, perhaps, consisted of short dirges, and was afterwards lengthened into elegies.

As soon as vice began to prevail in the world, it was natural for the wise and virtuous to express their detestation of it in the strongest manner, and to show their resentment against the corrupters of mankind; hence moral poetry was derived, which, at first, we find, was severe and passionate, but was gradually melted down into cool precepts of morality or exhortations to virtue. We may reasonably conjecture that epic poetry had the same origin, and that the examples of heroes and kings were introduced to illustrate some moral truth by showing the loveliness and advantages of virtue or the many misfortunes that flow from vice.

Where there is vice, which is detestable in itself, there must be hate, since the strongest antipathy in nature, as Mr. Pope asserted in his writings and proved by his whole life, subsists between the good and the bad. Now this passion was the source of that poetry which we call *satire,* very improperly and corruptly, since the satire of the Romans was no more than a moral piece which they entitled *satura* or *satyra,*[4] intimating that the poem, like a dish of fruit and corn offered to Ceres, contained a variety and plenty of fancies and figures; whereas the true invectives of the ancients were called *jambi,* of which we have several examples in Catullus, and in the *Epodes* of Horace, who imitated the very measures and manner of Archilochus.

These are the principal sources of poetry, and of music also, as it shall be my endeavor to show; but it is first necessary to say a few words on the nature of sound, a very copious subject, which would require a long dissertation to be accurately discussed. Without entering into a discourse on the vibrations of chords or the undulations of the air, it will be sufficient for our purpose to observe that there is a great difference between a common sound and a musical sound, which consists chiefly in this, that the former is simple and entire in itself like a point, while the latter is always accompanied with other sounds, without ceasing to be one—like a circle, which is an entire figure, though it is generated by a multitude of points flowing at equal distances round a common center. These accessory sounds, which are caused by the aliquots of a sonorous body vibrating at once, are called harmonics, and the whole system of modern harmony depends upon them, though it were easy to prove that the system is unnatural and only made tolerable to the ear by habit; for whenever we strike the perfect accord on a harpsichord or an organ, the harmonics of the third and fifth have also their own harmonics, which are dissonant from the principal note.[5]

Now let us conceive that some vehement passion is expressed in strong words exactly measured, and pronounced in a common voice, in just cadence, and with proper accents—such an expression of the passion will be genuine poetry; and the famous ode of Sappho is allowed to be so in the strictest sense. But if the same ode with all its natural accents were expressed in a musical voice (that is, in sounds accompanied with their harmonics), if it were sung in due time and measure, in a simple and pleasing tune that added force to the words without stifling them, it would then be pure and original music, not merely soothing to the ear, but affecting to the heart, not an imitation of nature, but the voice of nature herself. But there is another point in which music must resemble poetry or it will lose a considerable part of its effect: we all must have observed that a speaker agitated with passion, or an actor, who is, indeed, strictly an imitator, are perpetually changing the tone and pitch of their voice as the sense of their words varies; it may be worth while to examine how this variation is expressed in music. Everybody knows that the musical scale consists of seven notes, above which we find a succession of similar sounds repeated in the same order, and above that, other successions, as far as they can be continued by the human voice, or distinguished by the human ear. Now each of these seven sounds has no more meaning when it is heard separately than a single letter of the alphabet would have; and it is only by their succession and their relation to one principal sound that they take any rank in the scale or differ from each other, except as they are graver or more acute. But in the regular scale each interval assumes a proper character, and every note stands related to the first or principal one by various proportions.[6] Now a series of sounds relating to one leading note is called a *mode,* or a *tone,* and, as there are twelve [7] semitones in the scale, each of which may be made in its turn the leader of a mode, it follows that there are twelve modes; and each of them has a peculiar character, arising from the position of the modal note, and from some minute difference in the ratios, as of 81 to 80, or a comma; for there are some intervals which cannot easily be rendered on our instruments yet have a surprising effect in modulation, or in the transitions from one mode to another.

The modes of the ancients are said to have had a wonderful effect over the mind; and Plato, who permits the Dorian in his imaginary republic on account of its calmness and gravity, excludes the Lydian because of its languid, tender, and effeminate character—not that any series of mere sounds has a power of raising or soothing the passions, but each of these modes was appropriated to a particular kind of poetry and a particular instrument; and the chief of them, as the Dorian, Phrygian, Lydian, Ionian, Eolian, Locrian, belonged originally to the nations from which they took their names; thus the Phrygian mode, which was ardent and impetuous, was usually accompanied with trumpets, and the Mixolydian, which, if we believe Aristoxenus, was invented by Sappho, was probably confined to the pathetic and tragic style. That these modes had a relation to poetry, as well as to music, appears from a fragment of Lasus in which he says, "I sing of Ceres, and her daughter Meliboea, the consort of Pluto, in the Eolian mode, full of gravity." And Pindar calls one of his odes an Eolian song. If the Greeks surpassed us in the strength of their modulations, we have an advantage over them in our minor scale, which supplies us with twelve new modes, where the two semitones are removed from their natural position between the third and fourth, the seventh and eighth notes, and placed between the second and third, the fifth and sixth; this change of the semitones, by giving a minor third to the modal note, softens the general expression of the mode, and adapts it admirably to subjects of grief and affliction. The minor mode of D is tender, that of C, with three flats, plaintive, and that of F, with four, pathetic and mournful to the highest degree, for which reason it was chosen by the excellent Pergolesi in his *Stabat Mater*. Now these twenty-four modes, artfully interwoven, and changed as often as the sentiment changes, may, it is evident, express all the variations in the voice of a speaker, and give an additional beauty to the accents of a poet. Consistently with the foregoing principles, we may define "original and native poetry" to be "the language of the violent passions, expressed in exact measure, with strong accents and significant words"; and true music to be no more than "poetry, delivered in a succession of harmonious sounds, so disposed as to please the ear." It is in this view only that we must consider the music of the ancient Greeks, or attempt to account for its amazing effects, which we find related by the gravest historians and philosophers; it was wholly passionate or descriptive, and so closely united to poetry that it never obstructed, but always increased its influence; whereas our boasted harmony, with all its fine accords and numerous parts, paints nothing, expresses nothing, says nothing to the heart, and consequently can only give more or less pleasure to one of our senses; and no reasonable man will seriously prefer a transitory pleasure which must soon end in satiety, or even in disgust, to a delight of the soul arising from sympathy and founded on the natural passions, always lively, always interesting, always transporting. The old divisions of music into celestial and earthly, divine and human, active and contemplative, intellective and oratorial, were founded rather upon metaphors and chimerical analogies, than upon any real distinctions in nature; but the want of making a distinction between the music of mere sounds and the music of the passions has been the perpetual source of confusion and contradictions both among the ancients and the moderns. Nothing can be more opposite in many points than the systems of Rameau and Tartini,[8] one of whom asserts that melody springs from harmony, and the other deduces harmony from melody; and both are in the right, if the first speaks only of that music which took its rise from the "multiplicity of sounds heard at once in the sonorous body," and the second, of that which rose from "the accents and inflexions of the human voice, animated by the passions." To decide, as Rousseau says, whether of these two schools ought to have the preference, we need only ask a plain question: Was the voice made for the instruments, or the instruments for the voice?[9]

In defining what true poetry ought to be according to our principles, we have described what it really was among the Hebrews, the

Greeks and Romans, the Arabs and Persians. The lamentation of David and his sacred odes or psalms, the song of Solomon, the prophecies of Isaiah, Jeremiah, and the other inspired writers, are truly and strictly poetical; but what did David or Solomon imitate in their divine poems? A man who is really joyful or afflicted cannot be said to imitate joy or affliction. The lyric verses of Alcaeus, Alcman, and Ibycus, the hymns of Callimachus, the elegy of Moschus on the death of Bion, are all beautiful pieces of poetry; yet Alcaeus was no imitator of love, Callimachus was no imitator of religious awe and admiration, Moschus was no imitator of grief at the loss of an amiable friend. Aristotle himself wrote a very poetical elegy on the death of a man whom he had loved; but it would be difficult to say what he imitated in it:

O virtue, who proposest many labors to the human race, and art still the alluring object of our life, for thy charms, O beautiful goddess, it was always an envied happiness in Greece even to die, and to suffer the most painful, the most afflicting evils—such are the immortal fruits which thou raisest in our minds: fruits more precious than gold, more sweet than the love of parents, and soft repose. For thee Hercules the son of Jove and the twins of Leda sustained many labors, and by their illustrious actions sought thy favor; for love of thee, Achilles and Ajax descended to the mansion of Pluto; and through a zeal for thy charms, the prince of Atarne also was deprived of the sun's light. Therefore shall the muses, daughters of memory, render him immortal for his glorious deeds, whenever they sing the god of hospitality, and the honors due to a lasting friendship.[10]

In the preceding collection of poems there are some Eastern fables, some odes, a panegyric, and an elegy; yet it does not appear to me that there is the least imitation in either of them. Petrarch was, certainly, too deeply affected with real grief, and the Persian poet was too sincere a lover, to imitate the passions of others. As to the rest, a fable in verse is no more an imitation than a fable in prose; and if every poetical narrative which describes the manners and relates the adventures of men be called imitative, every romance, and even every history, must be called so likewise, since many poems are only romances, or parts of history, told in a regular measure.

What has been said of poetry may with equal force be applied to music, which is poetry dressed to advantage; and even to painting, many sorts of which are poems to the eye, as all poems, merely descriptive, are pictures to the ear. And this way of considering them will set the refinements of modern artists in their true light, for the passions, which were given by nature, never spoke in an unnatural form, and no man truly affected with love or grief ever expressed the one in an acrostic, or the other in a fugue. These remains, therefore, of the false taste which prevailed in the Dark Ages should be banished from this, which is enlightened with a just one.

It is true that some kinds of painting are strictly imitative, as that which is solely intended to represent the human figure and countenance; but it will be found that those pictures have always the greatest effect which represent some passion, as the martyrdom of St. Agnes by Domenichino, and the various representations of the Crucifixion by the finest masters of Italy; and there can be no doubt but that the famous sacrifice of Iphigenia by Timanthes was affecting to the highest degree, which proves, not that painting cannot be said to imitate, but that its most powerful influence over the mind arises, like that of the other arts, from sympathy.

It is asserted also that descriptive poetry and descriptive music, as they are called, are strict imitations; but, not to insist that mere description is the meanest part of both arts, if indeed it belongs to them at all, it is clear that words and sounds have no kind of resemblance to visible objects; and what is an imitation but a resemblance of some other thing? Besides, no unprejudiced hearer will say that he finds the smallest traces of imitation in the numerous fugues, counterfugues, and divisions which rather disgrace than adorn the modern music. Even sounds themselves are imperfectly imitated by harmony, and if we sometimes hear the murmuring of a brook or the chirping of birds in a concert, we are generally apprised beforehand of the passages where we may expect them. Some eminent musicians, indeed, have been absurd enough to think of imitating laughter and other noises, but if they had succeeded, they could not have made amends for their want of taste in attempting it; for such ridiculous imitations must necessarily destroy the spirit and dignity of the finest poems, which they ought to illustrate by a graceful and natural melody. It seems to me that as those parts of poetry, music, and painting which relate to the passions affect by sympathy, so those which are merely descriptive act by a kind of substitution, that is, by raising in our minds affections or sentiments analogous to those which arise in us when the respective objects in nature are presented to our senses. Let us suppose that a poet, a musician, and a painter are striving to give their friend or patron a pleasure similar to that which he feels at the sight of a beautiful prospect. The first will form an agreeable assemblage of lively images which he will express in smooth and elegant verses of a sprightly measure; he will describe the most delightful objects, and will add to the graces of his description a certain delicacy of sentiment, and a spirit of cheerfulness. The musician who undertakes to set the words of the poet will select some mode which, on his violin, has the character of mirth and gaiety, as the Eolian, or E flat, which he will change as the sentiment is varied. He will express the words in a simple and agreeable melody which will not disguise, but embellish them, without aiming at any fugue or figured harmony. He will use the bass to mark the modulation more strongly, especially in the changes, and he will place the tenor generally in union with the bass, to prevent too great a distance between the parts. In the symphony he will, above all things, avoid a double melody and will apply his variations only to some accessory ideas, which the principal part, that is, the voice, could not easily express. He will not make a number of useless repetitions, because the passions only repeat the same expressions and dwell upon the same sentiments, while description can only represent a single object by a single sentence. The painter will describe all visible objects more exactly than his rivals, but he will fall short of the other artists in a very material circumstance: namely, that his pencil, which may, indeed, express a simple passion, cannot paint a thought or draw the shades of sentiment. He will, however, finish his landscape with grace and elegance; his colors will be rich and glowing; his perspective striking; and his figures will be disposed with an agreeable variety, but not with confusion. Above all, he will diffuse over his whole piece such a spirit of liveliness and festivity that the beholder shall be seized with a kind of rapturous delight, and, for a moment, mistake art for nature.

Thus will each artist gain his end, not by imitating the works of nature, but by assuming her power and causing the same effect upon the imagination which her charms produce to the senses. This must be the chief object of a poet, a musician, and a painter who know that great effects are not produced by minute details, but by the general spirit of the whole piece, and that a gaudy composition may strike the mind for a short time, but that the beauties of simplicity are both more delightful and more permanent.

As the passions are differently modified in different men, and as even the various objects in nature affect our minds in various degrees, it is obvious that there must be a great diversity in the pleasure which we receive from the fine arts, whether that pleasure arises from sympathy or substitution, and that it were a wild notion in artists to think of pleasing every reader, hearer, or beholder, since every man has a particular set of objects and a particular inclination which direct him in the choice of his pleasures and induce him to consider the productions, both of nature and of art, as more or less elegant in proportion as they give him a greater or smaller degree of delight. This does not at all contradict the opinion of many able writers that there is one uniform standard of taste, since the passions and, consequently, sympathy are generally the same in all men till they are weakened by age, infirmity, or other causes.

If the arguments used in this essay have any weight, it will appear that the finest parts of poetry, music, and painting are expressive of the passions, and operate on our minds by sympathy; that the inferior parts of them are descriptive of natural objects, and affect us chiefly by substitution; that the expressions of love, pity, desire, and the tender passions, as well as the descriptions of objects that delight the senses, produce in the arts what we call the beautiful; but that hate, anger, fear, and the terrible passions, as well as objects which are unpleasing to the senses, are productive of the sublime when they are aptly expressed or described.

These subjects might be pursued to infinity; but if they were amply discussed, it would be necessary to write a series of dissertations, instead of an essay.

ALEXANDER GERARD ✒

An Essay on Genius (1774)

Part I, Section iii, "How Genius Arises from the Imagination"

When memory presents ideas, it annexes to them a conviction that the ideas themselves, or the objects from which they are copied, were formerly perceived; and it exhibits the ideas in the same form and order in which the things themselves appeared. In time remembrance fails, ideas are perceived without being referred to any prior sensations of their originals, the order of the parts is forgotten. But even then, ideas do not lie in the mind without any connection or dependence. Imagination can connect them by new relations. It knits them together by other ties than what connected the real things from which they are derived, and often bestows a union upon ideas whose archetypes had no relation. In this operation it is far from being capricious or irregular, but for the most part observes general and established rules. There are certain qualities which either really belong, or at least are supposed to belong, to all the ideas that are associated by the imagination. These qualities must be considered as, by the constitution of our nature, rendering ideas fit to be associated. It is impossible to give a reason why these qualities unite ideas; it is not necessary at present to explain particularly what they are. Experience informs us that the influence of association is very great. By means of it multitudes of ideas originally distinct and unconnected rise always in company, so that one of them cannot make its appearance without introducing all the rest. On this account, human thought is perfectly restless. It requires no labor to run from one idea to others. We have so great a propensity to do it that no resolution has force enough to restrain us from it, nor will the strongest efforts be able to confine us long to the contemplation of a single idea. We are incessantly looking round to every side without intending it; we employ ourselves about many objects, almost at the same instant.[1] Nay, association is often so strong that it bestows a sort of cohesion on several separate ideas, and makes them start up in numberless combinations, many of them different from every form which the senses have perceived, and thus produces a new creation. In this operation of the imagination, its associating power, we shall, on a careful examination, discover the origin of genius.

Association being an operation of fancy common to all men, some of its effects are universal. In every individual it displays itself in many instances. Not to mention such cases as are totally unconnected with our present subject, scarce any person is so stupid as not to have sometime in his life produced a bright flash of imagination, though surrounded, it may be, with a wide extent of darkness. But such transient blazes do not necessarily imply real genius. It is something more permanent and uniform. It requires a peculiar vigor of association. In order to produce it, the imagination must be comprehensive, regular, and active.

Genius implies such *comprehensiveness* of imagination as enables a man on every occasion to call in the conceptions that are necessary for executing the designs or completing the works in which he engages. This takes place when the associating principles are strong and fit for acting in an extensive sphere. If they be weak, they will call in memory to their aid. Unable to guide our steps in an unknown country, they keep in the roads to which we have been accustomed, and are directed in suggesting ideas by the connections which we remember. Every production of a man who labors under this debility of mind bears evident marks of barrenness, a quality more opposite to true genius than any other. Nothing appears in it uncommon or new; everything is trite and unoriginal. Or, if he attempts to quit the beaten path and start new game, he can find out but a few ideas; he is exhausted by a short excursion and must either make a stop or return to the tracks of memory. Industry, endeavoring in this manner to supply the want of a copious imagination by accurate remembrance or diligent observation, will produce instead of a philosopher a devoted follower or a dull laborious commentator; instead of a poet, a servile imitator or a painful translator. But when the associating principles are vigorous, imagination, conscious as it were of its own strength, sallies forth, without needing support or asking assistance, into regions hitherto unexplored, and penetrates into their remotest corners, unfatigued with the length of the way. In a man of genius, the power of association is so great that when any idea is present to his mind, it immediately leads him to the conception of those that are connected with it. No sooner almost is a design formed, or the hint of a subject started, than all the ideas which are requisite for completing it rush into his view as if they were conjured up by the force of magic. His daring imagination traverses all nature and collects materials fit for his purpose from all the most distant corners of the universe and presents them at the very instant when they become useful or necessary. In consequence of this, he takes in a comprehensive view of every subject to which his genius is adapted.

Thus, when the associating principles are strong and have an extensive influence, they naturally form, in proportion to the degree of their strength, that boundless fertility, that inexhaustible copiousness of invention, which is not only one necessary ingredient in true genius but the first and most essential constituent of it. The smallest production will in some measure discover in what extent this power is possessed. A work of real genius always proclaims in the clearest manner that immense quantities of materials have been collected by fancy and subjected to the author's choice. There is no particular, perhaps, in the works of Homer that has been more universally remarked and admired than the prodigious compass of imagination which they show. His penetration has gained him access to all the magazines of ideas and enabled him to draw materials from every part of nature and from the whole circle of human arts. Knowledge of them was prerequisite, but could have been of no service after it was obtained, without the liveliest fancy, suggesting them readily and applying them on suitable occasions. A comprehensive imagination gave Newton so great command over the natural and the intellectual world that in his philosophical inquiries he misses no experiment which is necessary for promoting his investigation, and in his mathematical researches discovers every idea which can be a proper medium for inferring his conclusion, and includes in his problems almost every case that can occur.

This extensive compass of thought enables a man to derive from his own treasure what they who want it are indebted for to the works of others. He who possesseth a fertile imagination is under no necessity of arrogating to himself the discoveries of others or of adorning his own productions with the beauties which he has pilfered from them. He will not decline to use, on proper occasions, the inventions of his predecessors, either in science or in the arts; but in using them, he will display his own genius. He will at least preserve the full spirit of the original, not contented with merely transmitting its form; the propriety with which the imitation or the theory is introduced and the force with which it is applied will show that it was not merely copied from memory but appositely suggested by a vigorous imagination; and frequently he will give farther proof of genius by improving on the borrowed hint by adding new beauties or delivering a known truth with greater elegance and justness.

Genius implies *regularity*, as well as comprehensiveness of imagination. Regularity arises in a great measure from such a turn of imagination as enables the associating principles not only to introduce proper ideas but also to connect the design of the whole with every idea that is introduced. When the design is steadily kept in view and the mind so formed as to be strongly affected by that associating quality by which the design is related to the means of executing it, the imagination can scarce fail of being regular and correct. Any conception that is present will introduce most readily those ideas which are related to the main design as well as to itself, though there should be a thousand others bearing the same relation to itself but unconnected with the general subject. These latter have only one tie, but the former have a double relation and will therefore rush into the thoughts with double violence. They will occur and be observed, while the rest never come into view, or if they make their appearance, are rejected so quickly that we instantly forget our ever having thought of them. No sooner does the imagination, in a moment of wandering, suggest any idea not conducive to the design than the conception of this design breaks in of its own accord, and like an antagonist muscle, counteracting the other association, draws us off to the view of a more proper idea.

In this manner an attachment to the design naturally produces that regularity of imagination, that capacity of avoiding foreign, useless, and superfluous conceptions at the same time that none necessary or proper are passed by, which is always most perfect in the greatest geniuses and constitutes no inconsiderable part of their excellence. As acuteness of smell carries a dog along the path of the game for which he searches and secures him against the danger of quitting it upon another scent; so this happy structure of imagination leads the man of genius into those tracks where the proper ideas lurk, and not only enables him to discover them but, by a kind of instinctive infallibility, prevents him from turning aside to wander in improper roads or to spend his time in the contemplation of unapposite ideas. As the bee extracts from such flowers as can supply them the juices which are proper to be converted into honey, without losing its labor in sipping those juices which would be pernicious, or in examining those vegetables which are useless, so true genius discovers at once the ideas which are conducive to its purpose, without at all thinking of such as are unnecessary or would obstruct it. The extent of Homer's imagination is not more remarkable than its regularity. Poets of inferior genius would have comprehended a history of the Trojan war in one of his poems, and all the events of the life of Ulysses in the other; but his correct imagination admits no detail inconsistent with the unity of the fable,[2] no shining episode that can be deemed unconnected with the subject, nor a single image unsuitable to the nature of his work. In the writings of Newton we scarce find any observation that is superfluous, any experiment whose force is fully implied in any other, any question or problem which has not something peculiar.

Neither fertility nor regularity of imagination will form a good genius if the one be disjoined from the other. If fertility be wanting, the correctest imagination will be confined within narrow bounds and will be very slow in its operations; there can be no penetration or copious invention. If regularity be absent, an exuberant invention will lose itself in a wilderness of its own creation. There is a false fertility which arises from a disordered and irregular fancy. As the same idea bears some relation to an infinite number of other ideas, the associating principles may lead us, after a very few steps, to such ideas as are connected with the last that was present, yet have no connection either with the former ones or with the main design. A man, therefore, who follows any association, however trivial or devious, that hits his fancy, may show a great deal of imagination without displaying any real genius. The imagination produces abundance of glaring, brilliant thoughts; but not being conducive to any fixed design, nor organized into one whole, they can be regarded only as an abortion of fancy, not as the legitimate progeny of genius. A multitude of ideas collected by such an imagination form a confused chaos in which inconsistent conceptions are often mixed, conceptions so unsuitable and disproportioned that they can no more be combined into one regular work than a number of wheels taken from different watches can be united into one machine. Were it necessary to produce instances of a fruitful imagination unproductive of true genius, we might find enough among those pretenders to poetry who can, through many lines, run from one shining image to another, and finish many harmonious periods, without any sentiment or design—or among those pretenders to science, who can devise a hundred experiments, coinciding in all their material circumstances, without a view to any conclusion, and without advancing useful knowledge a single step. Such imagination is like a tree so overcharged with fruit that no part of it can come to full maturity.

But even when a false luxuriance of fancy does not extinguish true genius, it very much diminishes its force and beauty. Sometimes it overloads every subject with a superfluity of illustration or of ornament which either wearies by introducing prolixity or dazzles too much to give entire satisfaction. A painter who indulges this exuberance of fancy will multiply figures which increase the composition of his work without adding to its expression, which embarrass the spectator without having any share in the action, and which seem to be introduced only that they may awkwardly fill up an empty space upon the canvas. Marino, says a French critic,[3] if he mentions a nightingale or a rose, says everything on the subject that he can imagine; far from rejecting any idea that occurs to him, he goes in search of such as cannot naturally occur; he always lavishes on his subject everything that can be thought or said. Sometimes luxuriance of imagination produces an irregular conduct in works of genius, carrying the author every now and then out of sight of his design, into digressions which have a very slender connection with it. This is remarkably exemplified in Ariosto. He possesses great readiness and quickness of genius; his inventions are surprisingly various; but that vivacity and agility of fancy from which he derives these virtues has betrayed him into continual disorder and incoherence, and unnatural interruptions of his story. The *Fairy Queen* discovers inexhaustible richness of invention, but is chargeable with the like irregularity. It would be possible to bring instances of both these kinds of vicious redundance from the writings of a very great philosopher; we might point out many passages in *The Essay on Human Understanding* in which Mr. Locke has indulged both a tedious diffuseness in the illustration of his subject and unseasonable digressions from it.

A man is sometimes so entirely under the power of accidental associations that he seems scarce to have proposed any end, but to have designed to begin with one idea, to go from that to any other which it happened by any means to suggest, and so from this to others, yielding up the mind to follow passively whatever associations chance to affect it. This is in an eminent degree the case of Montaigne in many of his essays. He says justly of himself, "What are these essays of mine but grotesques and monstrous pieces of patchwork, put together without any certain figure, or any order, connection, or proportion, but what is accidental?" (I, 27). This style of composition, carried to the utmost degree of incoherence, has been lately introduced. Novelty, along with a great degree of wit, humor, and fine feelings, procured the first attempt considerable success; and this success has raised a multitude of insipid imitators. It is only uncommon merit in the parts that can gain indulgence to such writings; the total want of design is an essential defect, and shows a capital imperfection in the genius of the writer, an irregularity of imagination.

There is in the human mind a strong propensity to make excursions, which may naturally be expected to exert itself most in those who have the greatest quickness and compass of imagination. If it be indulged without reserve, it will produce incoherent medleys, fantastical rhapsodies, or unmeaning reveries. Often, however, the byroads of association, as we may term them, lead to rich and unexpected regions, give occasion to noble sallies of imagination, and proclaim an uncommon force of genius, able to penetrate through unfrequented ways to lofty or beautiful conceptions. This is the character of Pindar's genius, the boldness of which more than compensates for its irregularity. The truest genius is in hazard of sometimes running into superfluities, and will find occasion to prune the luxuriance and rectify the disorder of its first conceptions. But this faculty can never be reckoned perfect till it has acquired a capacity of avoiding them in most cases. It must supply a large stock, and at the same time manage it with economy. While it produces all that is necessary, it must evite all that is superfluous.[4]

Thus to render genius complete, fertility and regularity of the imagination must be united. Their union forms that boundless penetration which characterizes true genius. By their union they will be both improved. The one will give us an ample choice; the other will prevent our choice from being perplexed with needless multiplicity. An extensive imagination, impressed with a strong association of the design and regulated by it, will draw out from the whole compass of nature the suitable ideas without attending to any other. In studying the works of a great genius, we can scarce avoid supposing that all possible conceptions have been explicitly exposed to his view and subjected to his choice. The apposite materials are collected in as great abundance and presented with as great propriety as if this had been the case, and yet perhaps no other ideas have occurred to him but those which he has used. They, and they alone, have been presented with entire propriety by the regularity of a comprehensive imagination retaining sight of the design through all the steps of its progress. This effect, which results from the union of these two virtues, is conspicuous in the great poet and in the great philosopher whom we have already mentioned as eminently possessing both. It may be observed by contrasting a single description of Shakespeare or Thomson with the labored delineations of a poetaster who would supply the want of genuine fancy by the industry of observation. In the former, all the striking features of the object, and none else, are strongly marked; in the latter, every circumstance seems to be taken notice of with the minuteness of a natural historian; but after all, those features are omitted which are fittest for making an impression on the fancy. Compare Euclid with his commentators; the opposition that may be remarked between them will set the character of real genius in a strong light. The train of Euclid's propositions is simple yet complete; his laborious expositors appear to have intended to amass all possible propositions, however trifling or unnecessary. One can scarce read a paragraph in Butler's *Analogy* or a chapter in Montesquieu's *Spirit of Laws* without being struck with the notion that the whole course of Providence was directly in the view of the one, and the whole history of mankind in the view of the other—with so great appearance of readiness do they observe even the remotest and least obvious circumstances which can anywise affect their argument. In studying a work of true genius, when we attend to the multitude and variety of the materials, we wonder how the author could have found them all; and when we reflect how proper and apposite every part is, we are apt to think that it must have occurred to almost any person. Such is the effect of copiousness and regularity of imagination, united and harmoniously exerted.

Genius implies likewise *activity* of imagination. Whenever a fine imagination possesses healthful vigor, it will be continually starting hints and pouring in conceptions upon the mind. As soon as any of them appears, fancy, with the utmost alertness, places them in every light and enables us to pursue them through all their consequences, that we may be able to determine whether they will promote the design which we have in eye. This activity of imagination, by which it darts with the quickness of lightning through all possible views of the ideas which are presented, arises from the same perfection of the associating principles which produces the other qualities of genius. These principles are so vigorous that they will not allow the mind to be unemployed for a moment, and at the same time constantly suggest the design of the work as the point to which all this employment tends. A false agility of imagination produces mere useless musing or endless reveries, and hurries a man over large fields without any settled aim; but true genius pursues a fixed direction and employs its activity in continually starting such conceptions as not only arise from the present idea but also terminate in the general subject. And though a thousand arrangements of the conceptions which it starts should fail of answering the intention, it is indefatigable in trying new arrangements till it can happily accomplish one that answers it. Whenever an image or a sentiment occurs to the poet or the orator, imagination sets it in every possible light, enables him to conceive its genuine effect, and thus puts it in his power to judge whether it ought to be rejected or retained. A philosopher no sooner thinks of an experiment or an argument than imagination, by representing it in every attitude, enables him to determine what will be its force and whether it will be to his purpose. In this manner the restless activity of imagination quickly constructs a sort of model by which we may form some idea of the work before we proceed to execute it.

This activity of imagination is of great importance to genius. Genius may indeed, in some degree, exist without it; imagination may be comprehensive when it is exerted, and correct, and yet not active. But without activity, genius will never exert itself except when excited and pushed forward by some external cause; activity of fancy is like an internal stimulus, which will not allow genius to lie idle or dormant, but makes it operate spontaneously and with constancy. Without it, invention would at best be very slow. Even after materials were suggested, their propriety could not be judged of till actual trial were made of their positions and effects, at a great expense of time and labor; and as such trial would be extremely tedious and difficult, we would either take up with the first view or position that occurred, or relinquish all attempts, discouraged by the prospect of that fatigue which must attend the improvement of our plan. But when fancy is expeditious in exhibiting every possible arrangement of our conceptions, it quickly puts it in our power to perceive all their consequences and relations to our subject, and enables us easily to make a choice and soon to finish our invention.

Thus the force of the imagination, or the vigor of the associating principles, produces genius, so far as it regards the collection, and even the choice, of fit materials for the discovery that is proposed.

But invention is not completed by merely depositing a sufficient quantity of proper materials in any order, as in a magazine or store-house. In every case, some degree of regular disposition is implied in the very motion of invention and comes within the province of genius.[5] It is not sufficient for a builder to collect stones, timber, and whatever else is necessary for the edifice, except they be also properly disposed and united in the fabric; so in the arts and sciences, a huge collection of conceptions which bear some relation to one another and to the main subject will form only a confused heap if they be not, by a proper disposition, united into one regular work.[6] A piece of painting cannot be said to be designed, though all the figures were conceived in their due proportions, till the artist has also formed a distinct idea of the economy of the whole. If the order of the notes in a musical composition were altered, it would destroy the harmony, which was the sole object of invention. As an animal body will become monstrous, though it has all its essential members, if one of them be transferred to the place of another; so a poem will become perfectly disagreeable and fantastical by the transposition of its parts. A dislocation destroys the vigor of any member of the body and unfits it for its proper function; and an oration will lose its whole effect if arguments, instead of being distinctly urged, are blended together without articulation. In science too, a multitude of ideas, if they be not arranged in such a manner that their connection may be perceived, instead of leading us to discover a conclusion, will only involve us in perplexity, as an army thrown into disorder can make no advantage of its numbers, but on the contrary, obstructs its own motions. In every case, disposition is so intimately connected with invention, and even interwoven with it, that it is impossible to separate them even in idea. If therefore imagination contribute nothing to the disposition of the materials, it will follow that genius must, in a considerable degree, derive its origin from some other power of the mind. But it will appear upon inquiry that imagination contributes very much to the disposition of every work.

When a person starts the first hint of a new invention and begins to meditate a work either in art or science, his notion of the whole is generally but imperfect and confused. When a number of apposite conceptions are collected, various views of their connections open to him and perplex his choice. But by degrees the prospect clears. As related ideas are apt to be associated, so by the very same constitution of our nature those that are most nearly related will be most strongly and intimately associated together. The operations of genius in forming its designs are of a more perfect kind than the operations of art or industry in executing them. A statuary conceives all the parts of his work at once, though when he comes to execute it, he can form only one member at a time and must during this interval leave all the rest a shapeless block. An architect contrives a whole palace in an instant, but when he comes to build it, he must first provide materials and then rear the different parts of the edifice only in succession. But to collect the materials and to order and apply them are not to genius distinct and successive works. This faculty bears a greater resemblance to *nature* in its operations than to the less perfect energies of *art*. When a vegetable draws in moisture from the earth, nature, by the same action by which it draws it in, and at the same time, converts it to the nourishment of the plant; it at once circulates through its vessels, and is assimilated to its several parts. In like manner, genius arranges its ideas by the same operation, and almost at the same time, that it collects them. The same force of association which makes us perceive the connection of all the ideas with the subject leads us soon to perceive also the various degrees of that connection. By means of it, these ideas, like a well-disciplined army, fall of their own accord into rank and order, and divide themselves into different classes according to their different relations. The most strongly related unite of course in the same member, and all the members are set in that position which association leads us to assign to them as the most natural. If the principles of association should not at first lead readily to any disposition, or should lead to one which is disapproved on examination, they continue to exert themselves, labor in searching for some other method, project new ones, throw out the unapposite ideas which perplex the mind and impede its operations, and thus by their continued efforts and unremitted activity conduct us at length to a regular form in which reason can find scarce any idea that is misplaced.

Thus imagination is no unskillful architect; it collects and chooses the materials; and though they may at first lie in a rude and undigested chaos, it in a great measure, by its own force, by means of its associating power, after repeated attempts and transpositions, designs a regular and well-proportioned edifice.

A weakness of this methodizing power may arise either from a want of activity in the imagination or from our having a slight association of the design. The former prevents our turning our conceptions readily into different forms and thereby leads us to take up with the first that offers, however incorrect. The latter prevents our being affected by the different connections of the parts, which arise from their having different respects and subordinations to the general design. From whatever cause this weakness proceeds, it is a great imperfection in genius. It renders it slow in forming its productions, as the confusion of the materials occasions difficulty in applying them to use; it also renders them less valuable when they are formed, as they retain, in some measure, the appearance of disorder, intricacy, and disagreeable perplexity. Aristotle considers the irregularity of disposition in Euripides as a capital imperfection, for which nothing almost but his singular power of interesting and affecting could have made atonement.[7] In every art the disposition of the subject into a consistent plan is indeed one of the most important offices of invention; nor is it a less momentous article in discoveries which respect the sciences. It is not more absolutely necessary in an algebraical investigation to ascertain the several quantities by distinct symbols than to dispose these symbols and the equations which are composed of them in a regular and convenient order.

Enthusiasm has been generally considered as a very common, if not an inseparable, attendant of genius. Poets have been looked upon as inspired, both by themselves and others. No man can be an accomplished orator who is not possessed of such sensibility of heart as to be actuated at pleasure by the passions which he would excite in others. Even the speculative philosopher and the cool mathematician have often displayed a very high degree of ardor in the exertion of their genius. The explication which has been given of the nature of genius will not only enable us to account for this but incline us also to reckon it impossible that ever a high degree of genius should be unaccompanied with something of that elevation and warmth of imagination which we term enthusiasm.[8] Genius turns our thoughts habitually to such subjects as are adapted to it; habitual application to any subject enables us to form strong and lively conceptions of everything relating to it; a strong conception naturally invigorates and elevates the imagination in contemplating it; and while this frame continues, all the actions of the mind will be strong and vehement. Such is the disposition with which a man of genius turns his view to any subject; as soon as he begins to think how it may be completed, he eyes it as a rich treasure, with delight and conscious pride; he triumphs in the prospect of forming "he knows not what excelling things," and pursues all the associations which it presents with incredible eagerness and spirit. When an ingenious track of thinking presents itself, though but casually, to true genius, occupied it may be with something else, imagination darts alongst it with great rapidity, and by this rapidity its ardor is more inflamed. The velocity of its motion sets it on fire, like a chariot wheel which is kindled by the quickness of its revolution. As a sprightly courser continually mends his pace, so genius, in proportion as it proceeds in its subject, acquires new force and spirit, which urges it on so vehemently that it cannot be restrained from prosecuting it. Difficulties in the execution only excite its vigor, rouse its keenness, and draw out its utmost efforts to surmount them. Its motions become still more impetuous, till the mind is enraptured with the subject and exalted into an ecstasy. In this manner the fire of genius, like a divine impulse, raises the mind above itself, and by the natural influence of imagination actuates it as if it were supernaturally inspired. The ardor which thus springs from the exertion of genius has sometimes risen to a degree of fervor perfectly astonishing. Archimedes,[9] Protogenes,[10] and Parmigiano [11] are said to have been so totally entranced, the two latter in painting, and the former in the less enthusiastic investigation of mathematical truth, as not to be diverted from their works by all the terrors of hostile armies taking by storm the places where they were employed. It is reported of Marino that he was so intent on revising some stanzas of his *Adonis* that he suffered one of his legs to be burnt for a considerable time before he was sensible of it.[12] We may remark farther that as a kind of enthusiastic ardor naturally arises from the exertion of genius, so this ardor greatly assists and improves the operations of genius. By elevating and enlivening the fancy, it gives vigor and activity to its associating power, enables it to proceed with alacrity in searching out the necessary ideas, and at the same time, by engrossing us wholly in the present subject, preserves us from attending to foreign ideas which would confound our thought and retard our progress.[13]

We have now explained how genius arises from the perfection and vigor of the *imagination*. However capricious and unaccountable this faculty may be often reckoned, yet it is subject to established laws and is capable not only of such extent as qualifies it for collecting ideas from all the parts of nature but also of such regularity and correctness as is in a great measure sufficient for avoiding all improper ideas, for selecting such as are subordinate to the design, and for disposing them into a consistent plan or a distinct method. It is the first author of all inventions, and has greater influence in carrying them to perfection than we are ready to suspect. It forms what we properly call genius in every art and in every science. It is always necessary, indeed, that judgment attend it in its operations and assist it in discovering truth or beauty. In what ways it does so we shall next inquire.

Part II, Section iii, "Of the Influence of the Passions on Association"

The other principle in human nature which has an influence on the association of ideas, which either promotes the introduction of such as are linked together by some of the associating qualities or introduces ideas unconnected with each other merely by means of their relation to itself, is a present passion.

A passion in strict propriety means only such an emotion as is produced by some one particular cause and directed to some one determinate object. There are several emotions, as remorse, self-approbation, and the like, which may perhaps be reckoned sensations rather than passions, but our present design does not render it necessary to attend to that distinction. A passion is something different from an habitual temper or turn of mind; the latter may in some instances have derived its origin from the frequent returns or the long continuance of a particular passion; but once formed, it sub-

sists without the operation of any particular cause and without being
fixed on any precise object, and produces a permanent propensity
to any sentiments or passions which are congruous to it. But a passion and an habitual temper have so many things in common that
we may without any inconvenience include both in the cause of
association which we are now examining. It will be sufficient to
distinguish them in particular instances (when such shall happen
to occur) in which their influence on the introduction of ideas is
different, or in which they run counter to one another.

In general, that the train of ideas suggested to the mind has a
very great dependence on the passions is obvious. Mention some
actions of a person whom we love, our love will suggest such circumstances as tend to make us approve these actions. Mention the
very same actions to another who entertains resentment against the
person who did them, and his imagination will immediately clothe
them with such circumstances as destroy their merit or render them
blameable. Let us barely think of any person. If we love him, we
readily recollect and dwell upon the fair and worthy parts of his
character; if we hate him, his wrong or suspicious actions crowd into
our thoughts. The joyful heart runs easily into a gay and pleasant
train of thinking, but does not naturally recollect anything that is
gloomy, and instantly rejects it if it be suggested by peculiar causes.
The observation holds of every emotion, passion, and disposition.

It will be proper, however, to attempt a fuller explication of the
manner in which the passions influence the association of ideas. To
understand this is of great importance in a theory of the varieties of
genius, for to give a just representation of the passions is one of the
greatest efforts of genius, and it can be accomplished only by following those paths into which the passions naturally direct the
thoughts. But the influence of the passions on the succession of our
ideas, though thus important, relates only to one species of genius,
genius for the *arts*. It would therefore be improper to enter on a full
discussion of it at present when we are tracing out the *general*
sources of the varieties of genius. In the observations which we are
now to make on this subject, some examples will be necessary both
for illustrating and for confirming our principles. It may perhaps
be thought most proper to draw these from our own experience in
real life. But to be able to select examples from real life and to set
them in a striking light would require no small degree of one of the
highest and rarest kinds of poetical genius. It will therefore be both

the safest and the best way to take our examples from such representations of the passions in poetry as are confessedly natural, and will approve themselves natural to the taste of the reader. Such examples have as great authority as instances which a person himself observes in ordinary life. Shakespeare alone will almost supply us with as many as are necessary.

In taking a general view of the influence of the passions on association, it will be necessary first to point out the manner in which they affect the *nature* of the ideas selected and introduced.

There are some ideas intimately connected with a passion—as the object of the passion, its cause, what is fit for supporting it, or what gratifies it. Every passion has a strong tendency to suggest such ideas, to force them into our view, to make us prone to conceive them. We naturally continue fixed in attention to such ideas, or recur often to the contemplation of them. A passion leads us to them, solely by its own force, without any assistance from a present perception connected with them. When a person is under the influence of any passion, the difficulty is not to recollect the objects closely connected with it, but to prevent their haunting him continually. An angry man, for example, can scarce avoid thinking of the person who has offended him, and of the injury which he has done him, recollecting everything he can dishonorable to that person, remembering with pleasure the misfortunes which have happened to him, even imagining distresses into which he may fall, and in a word dwelling on the conception of everything immediately relating to his anger. Angelo's description of his own disposition when he was under the power of love, is perfectly natural;

> When I would pray and think, I think and pray
> To several subjects. Heaven hath my empty words,
> Whilst my intention, hearing not my tongue,
> Anchors on Isabel. Heaven in my mouth,
> As if I did but only chew its name,
> And in my heart the strong and swelling evil
> Of my conception. [*Measure for Measure*, II, iv]

Different ideas are in different ways closely connected with the same passion; the passion tends to introduce all these. On this account it often happens that the mind does not rest on any one of them, but conceives them all by turns. Every passion often occasions an abruptness of thought; this is one cause of that abruptness: Different ideas being connected with the passion, in different respects, but with almost equal closeness, the passion introduces them all, or several of them at least, in alternate succession. Sebastian overwhelmed with fear and grief by the prospect of immediate shipwreck, exclaims,

> Mercy on us!
> We split, we split! Farewell, my wife and children!
> Farewell, brother! We split, we split, we split!
>
> [*Tempest,* I, i]

His passion leads him to think of himself, its most immediate object; but without suffering him to rest a moment on this, it hurries him on to a conception of the cause of his passion, the splitting of the ship; it allows him to make but a very short stop here; it causes his family and friends, objects which were likewise nearly related to his grief, to crowd into his view; and from these, it forces him back to the thought of the immediate cause of his passion, and makes his mind to dwell upon it. It suffers him not to think of anything that has not an intimate relation to itself, and it makes his imagination to vibrate between those which have such relation. Isabel, being informed that her brother had been put to death by Angelo's command, her resentment immediately suggests some means of revenging his death; but without suffering her to rest on these means or to take any notice of the impossibility of her employing them (even though it is mentioned to her), resentment brings into her thoughts in an instant her brother, herself, the wickedness of mankind, and the baseness of Angelo, all objects naturally connected with her passion:

> *Isab.*   Oh, I will to him and pluck out his eyes!
> *Duke.*   You shall not be admitted to his sight.
> *Isab.*   Unhappy Claudio! Wretched Isabel!
> Injurious world! Most damned Angelo!
>
> [*Measure for Measure,* IV, iii]

If a passion can thus introduce ideas suitable to it, merely by its own force, it will much more introduce them when there happens to be a perception present to the mind to which they bear any of the associating relations. Either the passion alone or that relation alone would have been sufficient for the effect; when both therefore operate together, they are like mechanical forces acting in the same direction which produce a double effect or produce the same effect with half the difficulty. When any passion prevails in the soul, ideas strictly connected with that passion are in a continual readiness to rush into the thoughts on every the slightest occasion. Hence it is commonly observed that the most distant hint is sufficient to direct the imagination to an object which is congruous to the present disposition of the mind. We have a very natural and strong representation of this in Lear's grief and indignation on account of the unkindness of his daughters. When he sees Edgar's dismal situation, he says, "Didst thou give all to thy daughters? And art thou come to this?" On hearing his raving, the same thought again rushes into Lear's mind,

> What! have his daughters brought him to this pass?
> Couldst thou save nothing? Would'st thou give 'em all?

The fool's interruption could not divert the thought; he goes on,

> Now all the plagues that in the pendulous air
> Hang fated o'er men's faults light on thy daughters!

"He hath no daughters, sir," says Kent; but still the object before him keeps the same idea riveted in his imagination:

> Death, traitor! Nothing could have subdu'd nature
> To such a lowness but his unkind daughters.
> Is it the fashion that discarded fathers
> Should have thus little mercy on their flesh?
> Judicious punishment! 'twas this flesh begot
> Those pelican daughters. [*King Lear*, III, iv]

There are ordinarily many occasions which have a powerful tendency to suggest to a person possessed by a passion objects altogether unrelated to that passion; the mind is always disposed to reject these, and in consequence of this, it pursues one of two courses. Sometimes it takes a handle from the objects that occur, whatever they be, to recollect something suitable to the present passion; it imagines those objects related to this passion, though their analogy to it be very remote, as in the example just now given—nay, though they have not even a shadow of connection with it. Harpagon going out of his garden in quest of the officers of justice, after he had missed his casket of money, and seeing the people in the street, is naturally made to say:

What a crowd's here got together! I can cast my eyes on nobody who gives me not suspicion; everything seems my thief. Heh! what are they talking of there? Of him that robbed me? What noise is that above?

Is it my thief that's there? For heaven's sake, if you know tidings of my thief, I beseech you tell me. Is he not hid there amongst you? They all stare at me, and fall a-laughing. You'll see that they are certainly concerned in this robbery committed upon me. Here, quick, commissaries, archers, provosts, judges, racks, gibbets, and executioners.[14]

This happens when the passion is violent, and when the tendency of the present objects to suggest ideas unsuitable to it is not very strong. But when the passion is not so violent, or when it is an habitual disposition that prevails in the soul, and when at the same time the present objects have a strong tendency to lead the thoughts to ideas unrelated to that passion or disposition, the mind takes a different course: It goes backward and forward between the ideas suggested by the passion and the ideas suggested by the present objects; there is a constant struggle between these, and a quick and frequent variation of thought. This is another cause of abruptness and unconnectedness in the sentiments of a person under the power of any passion; his mind vibrates between conceptions suitable to his passion and dissimilar conceptions arising from different circumstances in his situation. Molière has represented this strongly in Harpagon; however he is engaged, his avarice makes the thought of the money which he had hid in his garden to intermix itself with his present employment.

Those objects which are closely connected with any passion are likewise connected by some of the associating qualities with other objects, which therefore they have a natural tendency to suggest. Now as it appears from what has been said that every passion exerts itself in confining our thoughts to the objects immediately connected with it, it would seem to follow that a passion must hinder these from suggesting any other objects, however nearly related to themselves, and thus to put a stop to all succession of ideas. It has plainly a tendency to this; and the tendency takes effect in some degree. A passion never fails to confine our attention very much to the ideas which are most immediately related to itself. But such is the constitution of the human mind that it cannot confine its attention altogether to one unvaried object for any considerable time. The passions, being opposed by this law of our constitution, cannot keep the mind long fixed on one view of the object which it has first suggested. Yet it endeavors to do so; and the first effect of the endeavor is that the mind, averse from quitting that object, turns it to every side and views it in various lights. In the following example, this effect appears very strinkingly with respect to the passion of love:

Ros. Orlando?

Cel. Orlando.

Ros. Alas the day! what shall I do with my doublet and hose? What did he when thou saw'st him? What said he? How look'd he? Wherein went he? What makes he here? Did he ask for me? Where remains he? How parted he with thee? And when shalt thou see him again? Answer me in one word.

Cel. You must borrow me Garagantua's mouth first; 'tis a word too great for any mouth of this age's size. To say ay and no to these particulars is more than to answer in a catechism.

Ros. But doth he know that I am in this forest and in man's apparel? Looks he as freshly as he did the day he wrestled?

Cel. It is as easy to count atomies as to resolve the propositions of a lover. [*As You Like It,* III, ii]

We have already discovered two sources of the abruptness of thought occasioned by passion, and we may now perceive another source of it. Different views of the same object are very unlike; a passion brings these different views before the mind in a rapid succession and in an irregular group.

In this way the passion prevents a change of object for some time. But the different views of the same object are not inexhaustible. The passion, therefore, yielding to the impulse of our constitution, allows the present object to suggest ideas related to it. Hence it arises that under the influence of any passion we conceive not only the objects which are intimately related to it but also such others as are strongly connected with these by any of the associating qualities. The former objects would suggest these latter if we were not under the influence of any passion; these, therefore, will occur more readily than any others when, notwithstanding the influence of the passion, we must have some ideas on which to employ our thoughts. Besides, an idea connected with objects closely related to a passion may by its presence gratify the passion or support it or fall in with it in other ways; and in this case such an idea is often suggested even when the mind is under no necessity of being relieved from a conception which has long occupied it. The Countess of Rousillon parting with her son Bertram, who is going to the army, the grief

which this produces, suggests to them both an event related by resemblance, and in some measure also by causation, to the occasion
of that grief: the loss of her husband and his father:

Countess. In delivering up my son from me, I bury a second husband.
Bertr.   And I in going, madam, weep o'er my father's death anew.
[*All's Well That Ends Well*, I, i]

The mother does not say, "The delivering up of my son reminds me
of my burying my husband"; she expresses it much more strongly;
the son speaks in a manner equally forcible; the imagination of both
converts the present event into the similar event suggested by it.
This figure is felt by every person to be perfectly natural and proper;
and its being so shows that when an object strictly connected with a
passion introduces another object associated with itself, the passion
impells the mind to conceive this other object very strongly and to
bestow upon it as intimate a relation to the passion as possible.

But though a passion does not hinder an object from suggesting
others, it has a great influence on the nature of the ideas suggested.
An object which has been brought into view immediately by a
passion may be related by one or other of the associating qualities
to a great multitude of ideas of very different kinds, but it will not
in this case introduce any of these indiscriminately; the passion which
brought itself into view will direct it to introduce such of these only
as are suitable to that passion. The perception present to the mind,
considered simply in itself, has an equal fitness to bring into view
any one of a hundred ideas; but itself was introduced by a passion
which still continues to exert its power and indisposes the mind
for thinking on anything unsuitable to it, and which thus diverts the
associating force of the present perception from the direction it
might have otherwise taken, and leads the imagination to select and
take notice of only such ideas as are suitable to the passion as well as
to the present perception, overlooking many others which are equally
connected with the latter. The associating forces of these two have
some similitude to compound powers in mechanics, which by their
joint action produce motion in a direction different from that in
which either acts, and lying between the separate directions of the
two. Or to set the matter in a different light, those ideas which are
not only associated with the present perception but also suitable to
the passion that introduced it are dragged into the mind by a double
force, whereas the present perception alone tends to draw in other

ideas associated with it, and the passion opposes their entrance, often with superior strength. The latter cannot, therefore, fail to be neglected; the former must be introduced in preference to them. Thus, though a passion allows an object immediately connected with it to introduce ideas, yet it always moulds those which are introduced into its own likeness, or into a form agreeable to itself, and it suffers none to enter which are not susceptible of this form. When Alonzo's companions are endeavoring to alleviate his grief for the supposed loss of his son by diverting his thoughts to his daughter's marriage with the King of Tunis, in their return from which they now suffered shipwreck, he answers them:

> You cram these words into mine ears against
> The stomach of my sense. Would I had never
> Married my daughter there; for, coming thence,
> My son is lost; and, in my rate, she too,
> Who is so far from Italy removed
> I ne'er again shall see her. O thou mine heir
> Of Naples and of Milan! what strange fish
> Hath made his meal on thee? [*Tempest*, II, i]

This example illustrates and confirms almost every observation we have had occasion to make concerning the influence of the passions upon association. His grief keeps his attention fixed on the loss of his son, an object immediately connected with it as being its cause, and that in spite of every thought by which his companions endeavored to divert it. This object suggests an idea related to it by causation, his daughter's marriage at Tunis, the event which occasioned that loss. This event carries his thoughts back again to the death of his son, which, when thus again presented to his imagination, suggests a second time his daughter's marriage by means of its resemblance to it in one particular, that her distance deprived him of all intercourse with her, as much as if she too had been dead. But sorrow for his son allows him not to rest long upon this thought, suitable as it is to his passion, or to pursue any others which this might have introduced; it maks his imagination instantly to recur to the loss of his son, to view it in every light, to conceive many circumstances relating to him, his being his heir, his being entitled to large dominions, his being devoured by fishes. This example is thus a new illustration of the principles formerly explained, that a passion tends to fix the view on objects intimately connected with it, or to make it often recur to them, not only on the slightest hint, but even without any occasion, and that these objects suggest ideas related to them. It is likewise a direct illustration of the principle now under consideration, and for the sake of which we have cited it. It is a striking instance of the power of a passion to enable a perception connected with it to introduce, not indiscriminately any ideas related to itself, but only such as are at the same time suitable to the nature of the passion. No ideas are conceived but such as are perfectly suitable to Alonzo's sorrow. Claribel's marriage was in itself fully as fit for suggesting ideas of the mirth or pomp which attended it, or of the circumstances which rendered it desirable and moved Alonzo to urge it, as for suggesting ideas of its disagreeable circumstances and consequences. It had actually suggested ideas of the former kind to the rest of the company, but Alonzo's sorrow hinders them from occurring to him and forces into his view such thoughts as are unpleasant and excite regret.

Further, a passion has an influence on the *number* as well as on the nature of the ideas introduced. It tends so strongly to keep the attention fixed on the objects strictly connected with it that is suffers not these to suggest a long train of ideas successively related to each other. It generally allows us to go only one step or two beyond them; after we have been led by means of them to conceive one idea, we go not forward to the view of others associated with that; still the passion makes the object nearly allied to it to dwell upon the thought; we recur to the contemplation of this object, and it suggests a new idea, related to itself but not to that idea which it had introduced formerly. In other cases, after the imagination has once received an impulse, it readily goes on from one perception through a number of others, till it arrive at a great distance from that with which it began, and it would be difficult to stop its career, to bring it back to the object from which it set out, or to make it enter into a different track. But when the mind is occupied by a passion, the difficulty lies wholly on the other side: The passion directs the view to things closely connected with it so powerfully and so constantly that the imagination is drawn backward to repeated conceptions of them; when our natural propensity to vary the object of our thought indisposes us for dwelling longer on them alone, they yet retain their hold of us so far that we enter easily into another track pointed out by them; we cannot without a painful effort, often we cannot at all, proceed so long in one path as to leave them far behind us; all the ideas introduced after a few removes are but slightly connected with the object which the passion disposes us to rest upon, and that passion checks all propensity to go through or attend to many ideas but slightly connected. The imagination resembles a person attached to home who cannot without reluctance undertake a long journey, but can with pleasure make short excursions, returning home from each and thence setting out anew. Opposite forces in mechanics tend to destroy one another. This is analogous to the case before us. The objects strictly connected with a passion are naturally fit for introducing ideas related to themselves; the passion acts in a contrary direction and endeavors to keep the mind from running off to these; there is a perpetual struggle between the two. The passion having kept the attention fixed for some time on an object intimately connected with it, its force begins to flag; that object is conceived in a lively and vigorous manner by reason of its relation to the passion, and therefore very powerfully draws in ideas associated with it. But the conception of all the succeeding objects drawn by it is still weaker and weaker. On this account their power of introducing ideas becomes continually less and less, so that after a few steps they give us a very inconsiderable propensity to go forward. The passion exerts a force superior to theirs; it therefore prevails, it prevents farther association, it brings back the attention to some object closely connected with it, it invigorates the conception of that object so as to enable it to suggest a new idea; but it hinders us from going to a greater distance than before. Here we discover a new cause of that abruptness of thought which a passion occasions. It arises partly, we have seen, from the mind's dividing its attention between several objects all closely and almost equally connected with the passion, partly from the rapidity with which the mind takes in dissimilar views of any one of these objects, and partly from the struggle between objects suggested by the passion and objects suggested by other means; but it also arises partly from the constant vibration of the thought between the objects immediately connected with the passion and the ideas which they tend to introduce. The mind leaves any of these ideas as soon as it has conceived it; it lays hold of an object more closely connected with the passion; it runs from it to an idea suggested by it, but wholly unrelated to the former. This alone must produce a great want of connection, and many breaks, in the expression of sentiments resulting from a passion. These principles now laid down are sufficiently illustrated by the last example which we cited. Alonzo's grief made the loss of his son to suggest the distance of his daughter and the consequence of that distance, the improbability of his ever seeing her, but without allowing him to pursue that thought, hurries him back to the loss of his son and sets him a thinking on new circumstances connected with it. The marriage of his daughter, the loss of his son, the loss of his daughter, her distance, the little chance for his seeing her again, the loss of his son, his being heir to extensive territories, his being devoured by fishes, all succeed one another in his thoughts with great abruptness and rapidity.

There is a fault very common in dramatic poetry: Persons are made to express their passions, not as if they were really actuated by them, but as if they were spectators of them in others; the poet gives, not a natural *representation* of the passion, but a labored *description* of it. The observations just now made lead us to a discovery of the source of this fault. An object which is in a prticular instance strictly connected with a passion and forced into the mind by it may be considered, not only in this particular point of view but also simply in itself, as a present perception. Its influence on association is very different, according as it stands in one of these situations or the other. When it is in the mind simply as a present perception, it tends to suggest any ideas whatever that are connected with it by any of the associating qualities and to cause the mind [to] run from one of these through a long train of ideas successively introducing one another. But when it is brought into the mind by a passion to which it is intimately related, it receives a tincture from that passion, it is wholly under the direction of that passion, it exerts its power of association only in such ways and so far as the passion permits, it introduces such ideas alone as are suitable to the passion, and it introduces no long trains of ideas, but suffers the mind to return quickly to the conception of itself or of some other object as intimately related to the passion. For example, a person may think of the distress of another without feeling pity; in this case the thought of that distress may lead him to conceive any of the actions of the person who suffers it, any other persons who have had a concern in these actions or a connection with the actor, any particulars of the conduct or fortunes of these persons—and may thus open a boundless field of thought. But when the distress excites pity, this passion extinguishes all propensity to such excursions, it fixes our view on the distress by which it is produced. This distress may suggest, by means of resemblance, other instances of distress in other persons; it may suggest, by means of contrariety, such circumstances of former prosperity as aggravate the present distress; it may lead us to think of the cause of it or to trace out its consequences; in a word, it may introduce any ideas strictly connected with it and congruous to the passion of pity; but it has no tendency to suggest any others or to lead the imagination into a remote or extensive wandering. Did it attempt this, and did the mind follow it without reserve, it must quickly come to some ideas repugnant to the passion and fit for producing an opposite disposition; but this cannot naturally or easily happen to a person under the power of any passion. A passion leaves no inclination for going through a long train of ideas, and if the mind should run off to any distance or to unsuitable ideas, the passion would immediately check it and recall the attention to ideas congruous to itself as well as related to the object immediately suggested by it. Now an indifferent poet, having conceived some of the objects strictly connected with a passion, considers that object only in general and abstractly as a present perception; he therefore allows himself to run into such a train of thought as that object present to the mind would dictate if it were unconnected with any passion; he goes on coolly imagining such ideas as it suggests by means of any of the principles of association; and he makes the person possessed by the passion to express all these ideas. He feels not the passion, he has not force of genius or sensibility of heart sufficient for conceiving how it would affect a person who felt it, or for entering into the sentiments which it would produce in him. The sentiments which he makes him utter might all be very proper in a description, a discourse, or a meditation occasioned by the view of such an object; but they are not natural to a person in whom that object produces a suitable passion. In order to conceive sentiments natural to him, the poet ought to have confined himself to the consideration of the object in this one point of view, as strictly connected with a passion and suggested by it; he ought to indulge only such a train of thought as it would lead to in these circumstances, or such a train as the passion with which it is presently connected would introduce into the mind of a person under the power of that passion.

This is indeed so difficult that the best poets cannot always perfectly attain it. Shakespeare makes the Duchess of Gloucester, in parting with John of Gaunt, to express her grief in this manner:

Yet one word more—grief boundeth where it falls,
Not with the empty hollowness, but weight.
I take my leave before I have begun,
For sorrow ends not when it seemeth done.
Commend me to thy brother, Edmund York.
Lo, this is all—nay, yet depart not so;
Though this be all, do not so quickly go;
I shall remember more. Bid him—ah, what?—
With all good speed at Plashy visit me.
Alack, and what shall good old York there see
But empty lodgings and unfurnish'd walls,
Unpeopled offices, untrodden stones?
And what hear there for welcome but my groans?
Therefore commend me; let him not come there
To seek out sorrow that dwells every where.
Desolate, desolate, will I from hence and die;
The last leave of thee takes my weeping eye.
                                    [*Richard II*, I, ii]

The latter part of the speech is a natural expression of grief, and of violent grief; the first four lines are a description, not an expression of it, and therefore unsuitable to the duchess' state of mind; the reflection which they contain is just, but too cool for the temper of the speaker.

It follows from the observations which have been made that a passion tends to hinder the mind from running into the conception of such ideas as have no connection with that passion. Since a passion fixes the view on objects immediately connected with it, since it continually draws the mind back to the conception of these objects even from ideas suggested by themselves, since it prevents their introducing many ideas naturally connected with them, the necessary consequence is that it will much more exclude ideas which have no relation either to these objects or to the passion and will render a very strong effort requisite for bringing them into view. A direct proof of this arises from the difficulty which we experience in diverting any passion which has taken firm possession of the soul by application to such subjects as have a tendency to banish it; the strongest resolution and the intensest endeavors are often insufficient for bringing the mind to fix on these subjects. Nay, so great is the force of the passion that when other subjects are most powerfully urged upon us, when we have the strongest calls to give application to them, yet we cannot enter into them with spirit; the passion mixes with all our thoughts, and continually disturbs the course of them.

It often happens that two different passions, or that a present passion and an habitual disposition, occupy the mind together. Each of these having a tendency to fix the mind on objects strictly connected with itself or to direct it to such ideas as these objects suggest, the mind turns quickly from thoughts introduced by the one passion to those which are introduced by the other, and runs constantly backward and forward between them without resting a moment on either. In this case, the thoughts must have an uncommon degree of abruptness. Each of the passions singly would have occasioned abruptness in the ways already taken notice of, but to this is superadded the unconnectedness which arises from the view being successively directed to objects associated with different passions. Shakespeare affords us a striking instance of this when he represents Shylock agitated by avarice, by grief for the loss of his daughter, and by rage at her having married a Christian and stolen his money, and in consequence of that agitation exclaiming:

> My daughter! O my ducats! O my daughter!
> Fled with a Christian? Oh my Christian ducats!
> Justice! the law! my ducats, and my daughter!
> A sealed bag, two sealed bags of ducats,
> Of double ducats, stol'n from me by my daughter!
> And jewels! two stones, rich and precious stones,
> Stol'n by my daughter! Justice! find the girl!
> She hath the stones upon her, and the ducats!
>
> [*Merchant of Venice,* II, viii]

It was evinced that *habit* not only promotes the introduction of such ideas as it has rendered familiar but also gives the mind, in some cases, a propensity to associate ideas by one relation rather than by others. It does not appear that the passions give an absolute preference to any one relation. An object immediately connected with a passion suggests indiscriminately ideas connected with itself by any of the associating qualities. Some of these qualities may, however, be considered as in some sense more suitable to the passions than others, and that in two respects: a passion introduces ideas connected with its immediate objects by some of the associating qualities more commonly and frequently than such as are connected with them by other associating qualities; and some of the associating qualities lead the mind to a greater distance from the objects strictly connected with the passion than others of them. Ideas introduced by some associating qualities have a less perfect relation to the passion than ideas introduced by others; the former ideas are rarely suggested by a passion, the latter often; the qualities which give ideas introduced by them but an imperfect relation scarce ever lead the mind more than one step beyond the objects strictly connected with the passion; the others may lead it several steps, introducing a series of ideas successively associated with one another.

Resemblance is a quality of the former kind. There are many ways in which ideas may resemble an object intimately connected with a passion that will not lead that object to suggest these ideas. The resemblance must be of a peculiar kind, must be such as fits an idea to affect the passion in the same way with the object which suggests it, else the passion will check its operation. When the resemblance is thus peculiar, the association is indeed very strong; there are few ideas which occur more readily, either to a person suffering any distress, or to a spectator moved with pity for his suffering, than the idea of a similar distress. But other sorts of resemblance have no such effect; hence it is universally allowed that similitudes are in general unsuitable to the language of passion, and that even metaphors ought to be admitted into it with great reserve. In this respect what Shakespeare puts into the mouth of the Queen when she sees her husband King Richard a prisoner is faulty and unnatural:

> But soft, but see, or rather do not see,
> My fair rose wither. Yet look up, behold,
> That you in pity may dissolve to dew,
> And wash him fresh again with true-love tears.
> Ah! thou, the model where old Troy did stand,
> Thou map of honour, thou king Richard's tomb,
> And not king Richard; thou most beauteous inn,
> Why should hard-favour'd grief be lodg'd in thee,
> When triumph is become an alehouse guest?
> [*Richard II*, V, i]

Besides, resemblance leads the mind only one step; an idea suggested by means of its resemblance to any of the objects strictly connected with a passion seldom suggests another idea resembling itself. A passion occupies the mind too much to leave it leisure or inclination for hunting after similitudes. One resembling idea is often suitable to the passion and fit to influence it; but by conceiving another idea resembling that, much more by going through several ideas each of which is suggested by its resemblance to the preceding, we must come to such as are no ways related to the passion, as are wholly unfit for influencing it, and as bear no likeness to any of the objects closely connected with it. But the nature of passion permits us not to indulge ourselves in the conception of such ideas. Richard, giving vent to his grief in prison, might naturally say, on hearing time broke in music:

> And here have I the daintiness of ear
> To check time broke in a disorder'd string;
> But, for the concord of my state and time,
> Had not an ear to hear my true time broke.
> I wasted time, and now doth time waste me.

But he could scarce naturally add:

> For now hath time made me his numb'ring clock:
> My thoughts are minutes; and with sighs they jar
> Their watches on unto mine eyes, the outward watch,
> Whereto my finger, like a dial's point,
> Is pointing still, in cleansing them from tears.
>
> [*Richard II*, V, v]

Objects strictly connected with a passion often suggest *contrary* objects, but they suggest only such as are contrary in some particular ways which render them fit for influencing the present passion; objects in all other ways contrary, the passion leads the mind to reject.

Lady. Madam, we'll tell tales.
Queen. Of sorrow or of joy?
Lady. Of either, Madam.
Queen. Of neither, girl;
For if of joy, being altogether wanting,
It doth remember me the more of sorrow;
Or if of grief, etc. [*Ibid.*, III, iv]

Contrariety seldom leads the mind more than one step from the object immediately suggested by the passion. A short contrast may very much enliven our conception of that object; it thus naturally falls in with the passion. But a series of contrasts would produce a very different effect; a multitude of antitheses in writing of any sort show an imagination disposed to seek amusement, not a mind intensely engaged by its subject.

Objects strictly connected with a passion often suggest likewise the ideas of other objects associated with them by vicinity. Indeed

contiguous objects are frequently connected together by other relations, and in that case a passion leads us strongly to conceive them.
But vicinity alone is sufficient for producing this effect. A view of
the contiguous objects renders our conception of a thing determinate
and lively, and thus, when that thing is intimately related to a passion, tends to invigorate and support the passion. A passion makes
us prone to this and naturally assists vicinity in introducing such
ideas as can promote it. But vicinity never introduces a long train
of ideas. It would be unnatural for a person actuated by any passion
to run along a multitude of objects contiguous to one another either
in place or in time, for this would tend to divert the passion by variety.

Coexistence and the relation of *cause and effect* are the principles
of association which the passions employ most frequently, and which
suggest the longest trains of ideas. These give ideas the most perfect
relation to a passion, and almost every idea introduced by means of
these principles really influences the passion. Coexistence suggests
the qualities, the circumstances, the accessories, and the concomitants
of those objects which are closely connected with the passion; and
the more of these we have in our view, the stronger and livelier is
our conception of those objects. All the objects almost which the
relation of cause and effect can suggest contribute either more immediately or more remotely to the production of the passion itself,
and therefore are strongly connected with it. Accordingly, in most of
the examples which have been produced, the ideas suggested by
objects strictly connected with the passions are such as are suggested
by means of these two principles of association.

It is a natural inference from the observations which have been
already made that the passions, far from disposing us to follow order
in the train of our ideas, render us incapable of preserving order.
The inference is so obvious that it is not necessary to spend time in
confirming it. Abruptness, incoherence, fluctuation of thought are
the consequences of passion; and these are the reverse of order. But
it is worth while to observe that a passion even inverts the natural
order of our ideas. As the imagination passes from one idea to another connected with it, so a passion once excited does not confine
itself to its first object, but readily extends itself to other objects
connected with that; love or hatred to any person seldom fails to
produce some degree of love or hatred to such as are connected with
him. It has been shown by philosophers that the imagination passes

most readily from a less considerable to a more considerable object, but that a passion, on the contrary, passes with greatest ease from the more to the less considerable object; [15] and what we would now observe is that a passion prevailing in the mind causes the imagination to proceed in this latter direction. Indeed if it did not, the passion itself could not be extended to the inferior and subordinate objects, for it cannot be directed to them till we have formed ideas of them. When the mind is cool, and not under the influence of any passion, the idea of a son or of a servant suggests the idea of the father or the master more naturally and more certainly than the idea of the father or the master would suggest that of the son or the servant. On the contrary, love, hatred, resentment towards a father or a master very readily extend themselves to the son or the servant, though we might feel the same passions towards these latter without conceiving any degree of them towards the former. At the same time the passion towards the superior gives the imagination an irresistible propensity to run into the conception of the inferior or dependent; eager to extend itself, it forces upon us the idea without which it could not be extended.

JAMES BEATTIE ✐

Essays on Poetry and Music,
as They Affect the Mind (1776)

Chapter VII, "Of Sympathy"

As a great part of the pleasure we derive from poetry depends on our sympathetic feelings, the philosophy of sympathy ought always to form a part of the science of criticism. On this subject, therefore, I beg leave to subjoin a few brief remarks that may possibly throw light on some of the foregoing, as well as subsequent, reasonings.

When we consider the condition of another person, especially if it seem to be pleasureable or painful, we are apt to fancy ourselves in the same condition and to feel in some degree the pain or pleasure that we think we should feel if we were really in that condition. Hence the good of others becomes in some measure our good, and their evil our evil, the obvious effect of which is to bind men more closely together in society and prompt them to promote the good and relieve the distresses of one another. Sympathy with distress is called compassion or pity; sympathy with happiness has no particular name, but when expressed in words to the happy person, is termed congratulation.

We sympathize, in some degree, even with things inanimate. To lose a staff we have long worn, to see in ruins a house in which we have long lived, may affect us with a momentary concern, though in point of value the loss be nothing. With the dead we sympathize, and even with those circumstances of their condition whereof we know that they are utterly insensible, such as their being shut up in a cold and solitary grave, excluded from the light of the sun and from all the pleasures of life, and liable in a few years to be forgotten forever. Towards the brute creation our sympathy is, and ought to be, strong, they being percipient creatures like ourselves. A merciful man is merciful to his beast, and that person would be deemed melancholy or hard-hearted who should see the frisking lamb, or hear the cheerful song of the lark, or observe the transport of the dog when he finds the master he had lost, without any participation of their joy. There are few passages of descriptive poetry into which we enter with a more hearty fellow feeling than where Virgil and Lucretius paint so admirably, the one the sorrow of a steer for the loss of his fellow, the other the affliction of a cow deprived of her calf.[1] But our sympathy exerts itself most powerfully towards our fellow men, and other circumstances being equal, is stronger or weaker according as they are more or less nearly connected with us and their condition more or less similar to our own.

We often sympathize with one another when the person principally concerned has little sense of either good or evil. We blush for another's ill breeding, even when we know that he himself is not aware of it. We pity a madman, though we believe him to be happy in his frenzy. We tremble for a mason standing on a high scaffold, though we know that custom has made it quite familiar to him. It gives us pain to see another on the brink of a precipice, though we be secure ourselves, and have no doubt of his circumspection. In these cases it would seem that our sympathy is raised not so much by our reflecting on what others really feel as by a lively conception of what they would feel if their nature were exactly such as ours, or of what we ourselves should feel if we were in their condition with the same sentiments we have at present.[2]

Many of our passions may be communicated and strengthened by sympathy. If we go into a cheerful company, we become cheerful; if into a mournful one, we become sad. The presence of a multitude engaged in devotion tends to make us devout. Cowards have behaved valiantly when all their companions were valiant, and the timidity of a few has struck a panic into a whole army. We are not, however, much inclined to sympathize with violent anger, jealousy, envy, malevolence, and other sanguinary or unnatural passions; we rather take part against them, and sympathize with those persons who are in danger from them, because we can more easily enter into their distress and suppose ourselves in their condition. But indignation at vice, particularly at ingratitude, cruelty, treachery, and the like, when we are well acquainted with the case, awakens in us a most intense fellow feeling, and the satisfaction we are conscious of when such crimes are adequately punished, though somewhat stern and gloomy, is, however, sincere and by no means dishonorable or detrimental to our moral nature nor at all inconsistent with that pity which the sufferings of the criminal extort from us when we are made to conceive them in a lively manner.

Of sympathy all men are not equally susceptible. They who have a lively imagination, keen feelings, and what we call a tender heart are most subject to it. Habits of attention, the study of the works of nature and of the best performances in art, experience of adversity, the love of virtue and of mankind tend greatly to cherish it; and those passions whereof self is the object, as pride, self-conceit, the love of money, sensuality, envy, vanity, have a tendency no less powerful to destroy it. Nothing renders a man more amiable or more useful than a disposition to rejoice with them that rejoice and to weep with those that weep, to enter heartily, not officiously, into the concerns of his fellow creatures, to comply with the innocent humor of his company, more attentive to them than to himself, and to avoid every occasion of giving pain or offence. And nothing but downright immorality is more disagreeable than that person is who affects bluntness of manner and would be thought at all times to speak all that he thinks, whether people take it well or ill, or than those pedants are, of whatever profession (for we have them of all professions), who, without minding others or entering into their views of things, are continually obtruding themselves upon the conversation, and their own concerns and the sentiments and language peculiar to their own trades and fraternities. This behavior, though under the name of plain-dealing it may arrogate a superiority to artificial rules, is generally the effect of pride, ignorance, or stupidity, or rather of all the three in conjunction. A modest man who sympathetically attends to the condition and sentiments of others will of his own accord make those allowances in their favor which he wishes to be made in his own, and will think it as much his duty to promote their happiness as he thinks it theirs to promote his. And such a man is well principled in equity, as well as in good breeding; and though, from an imperfect knowledge of forms, or from his having had but few opportunities to put them in practice, his manner may not be so graceful or so easy as could be wished, he will never give offence to any person of penetration and good nature.

With feelings which we do not approve or have not experienced we are not apt to sympathize. The distress of the miser when his hoard is stolen, of the fop when he soils his fine jubilee clothes, of the vaunting coxcomb when his lies are detected, of the unnatural parent when his daughter escapes with a deserving lover, is more likely to move laughter than compassion. At Sparta, every father had the privilege of correcting any child, he who had experience of paternal tenderness being supposed incapable of wounding a parent's sensibility by unjust or rigorous chastisement. When the Cardinal of Milan would expostulate with the Lady Constance upon her violent sorrow for the loss of her child, she answers, but without deigning to address her answer to one who she knew could be no competent judge of her case, "He speaks to me who never had a son." [3] The Greeks and Romans were as eminent for public spirit and for parental affection as we, but for a reason elsewhere assigned,[4] knew little of that romantic love between unmarried persons which modern manners and novels have a tendency to inspire. Accordingly, the distress in their tragedies often arose from patriotism and from the conjugal and filial charities, but not from the romantic passion whereof we now speak. But there are few English tragedies, and still fewer French, wherein some love affair is not connected with the plot. This always raises our sympathy, but would not have been so interesting to the Greeks or Romans, because they were not much acquainted with the refinements of this passion.

Sympathy, as the means of conveying certain feelings from one breast to another, might be made a powerful instrument of moral discipline if poets and other writers of fable were careful to call forth our sensibility towards those emotions only that favor virtue and invigorate the human mind. Fictions that breathe the spirit of patriotism or valor, that make us sympathize with the parental, conjugal, or filial charities, that recommend misfortune to our pity or expose crimes to our abhorrence, may certainly be useful in a moral view by cherishing passions that, while they improve the heart, can hardly be indulged to excess. But those dreadful tales that only give anguish to the reader can never do any good. They fatigue, enervate, and overwhelm the soul, and when the calamities they describe are made to fall upon the innocent, our moral principles are in some danger of a temporary depravation from the perusal, whatever resemblance the fable may be supposed to bear to the events of real life. Some late authors of fiction seem to have thought it incumbent upon them not only to touch the heart but to tear it in pieces. They heap "misfortune on misfortune, grief on grief," without end, and without mercy, which discomposes the reader too much to give him either pleasure or improvement, and is contrary to the practice of the wiser ancients, whose most pathetic scenes were generally short.

It is said that at the first representation of *The Furies* of Aeschylus the horror of the spectacle was so great that several women miscarried, which was indeed pathos with a vengeance. But though the truth of that story should be questioned, it admits of no doubt that objects of grief and horror too much enlarged on by the poet or novelist may do more harm than good, and give more pain than pleasure to the mind of the reader. Surely this must be contrary to the essential rules of art, whether we consider poetry as intended to please that it may instruct, or to instruct that it may the more effectually please. And supposing the real evils of life to be as various and important as is commonly believed, we must be thought to consult our own interest very absurdly if we seek to torment ourselves with imaginary misfortune. Horace insinuates that the ancient satyric drama (a sort of burlesque tragicomedy) was contrived for the entertainment of the more disorderly part of the audience; [5] and our critics assure us that the modern farce is addressed to the upper gallery, where, it is supposed, there is no great relish for the sublime graces of the tragic muse. Yet I believe these little pieces, if consistent with decency, will be found neither unpleasant nor unprofitable, even to the most learned spectator. A man, especially if advanced in years, would not choose to go home with that gloom upon his mind which an affecting tragedy is intended to diffuse, and if the play has conveyed any sound instruction, there is no risk of its being dissipated by a little innocent mirth.

Upon the same principle I confess that I am not offended with those comic scenes wherewith our great dramatic poet has occasionally thought proper to diversify his tragedies. Such a licence will at least be allowed to be more pardonable in him than it would be in other tragic poets. They must make their way to the heart as an army does to a strong fortification, by slow and regular approaches, because they cannot, like Shakespeare, take it at once, and by storm. In their pieces, therefore, a mixture of comedy might have as bad an effect as if besiegers were to retire from the outworks they had gained and leave the enemy at leisure to fortify them a second time. But

Shakespeare penetrates the heart by a single effort and can make us as sad in the present scene as if we had not been merry in the former. With such powers as he possessed in the pathetic, if he had made his tragedies uniformly mournful or terrible from beginning to end, no person of sensibility would have been able to support the representation. As to the probability of these mixed compositions, it admits of no doubt. Nature everywhere presents a similar mixture of tragedy and comedy, of joy and sorrow, of laughter and solemnity, in the common affairs of life. The servants of a court know little of what passes among princes and statesmen, and may therefore, like the porter in *Macbeth*, be very jocular when their superiors are in deep distress. The death of a favorite child is a great affliction to parents and friends, but the man who digs the grave may, like Goodman Delver in *Hamlet*, be very cheerful while he is going about his work. A conspiracy may be dangerous, but the constable who apprehends the traitors may, like *Dogberry*, be a ludicrous character, and his very absurdities may be instrumental in bringing the plot to light, as well as in delaying or hastening forward the discovery. I grant that compositions like those I would now apologize for cannot properly be called either tragedies or comedies, but the name is of no consequence; let them be called *plays*. And if in them nature is imitated in such a way as to give pleasure and instruction, they are as well entitled to the denomination of *dramatic poems* as anything in Sophocles, Racine, or Voltaire. But to return:

Love is another "tyrant of the throbbing breast," of whom they who wish to see the stage transformed into a school of virtue complain that his influence in the modern drama is too despotical. Love, kept within due bounds, is no doubt, as the song says, "a gentle and a generous passion," but no other passion has so strong a tendency to transgress the due bounds; and the frequent contemplation of its various ardors and agonies, as exhibited in plays and novels, can scarce fail to enervate the mind and to raise emotions and sympathies unfriendly to innocence. And certain it is that fables in which there is neither love nor gallantry may be made highly interesting even to the fancy and affections of a modern reader. This appears, not only from the writings of Shakespeare, and other great authors, but from the *Pilgrim's Progress* of Bunyan, and the history of *Robinson Crusoe*, than which last there is not perhaps in any language a more interesting narrative or a tale better contrived for communicating to the reader a lively idea of the importance of the mechanic arts, of the sweets of social life, and of the dignity of independence.

Dissertations Moral and Critical
(1783)

From "On Fable and Romance"

. . . . .

The origin of the old romance, which after this long historical deduction we are now arrived at, has been already accounted for. It was one of the consequences of chivalry. The first writers in this way exhibited a species of fable different from all that had hitherto appeared. They undertook to describe the adventures of those heroes who professed knight-errantry. The world was then ignorant and credulous, and passionately fond of wonderful adventures and deeds of valor. They believed in giants, dwarfs, dragons, enchanted castles, and every imaginable species of necromancy. These form the materials of the old romance. The knight-errant was described as courteous, religious, valiant, adventurous, and temperate. Some enchanters befriended, and others opposed him. To do his mistress honor and prove himself worthy of her, he was made encounter the warrior, hew down the giant, cut the dragon in pieces, break the spell of the necromancer, demolish the enchanted castle, fly through the air on wooden or winged horses, or with some magician for his guide to descend unhurt through the opening earth, and traverse the caves in the bottom of the ocean. He detected and punished the false knight, overthrew or converted the infidel, restored the exiled monarch to his dominions, and the captive damsel to her parents; he fought at the tournament, feasted in the hall, and bore a part in the warlike procession; or when the enchanter who befriended his enemy prevailed, he did penance in the desert or groaned in the dungeon, or perhaps, in the shape of a horse or hart, grazed in the valley till some other valiant knight broke the spell and restored to him his form, his arms, and his freedom. At last, after innumerable toils, disasters, and victories, he married his mistress and became a great lord, a prince, or perhaps an emperor.

It will appear from this account that nature, probability, and even possibility were not much attended to in those compositions. Yet with them all Europe was intoxicated; and in every nation that had pretensions to a literary character multitudes of them were written, some in verse, and others in prose. To give a list is unnecessary and would be tedious. *Amadis de Gaul* was one of the first, and is, in the opinion of Cervantes, one of the best. Several others are mentioned and characterized by that excellent author in his account of the purgation of Don Quixote's library.

While the taste continued for everything that was incredible and monstrous, we may suppose that true learning and the natural simplicity of the classics would not be held in general estimation. Accordingly, though the knowledge of Greek and Latin was now advancing apace in the western world, Homer, Virgil, Cicero, and all the most elegant authors were much neglected. The first accounts that circulated among us concerning the siege of Troy seem to have been taken, not from Homer, but from Dares Phrygius and Dictys Cretensis, two writers in prose, who have given a fabulous and marvellous history of it; and as late as the age of George Buchanan, our modern Latin poets, Vida excepted, were, if I mistake not, more ambitious to imitate Claudian than Virgil in their hexameters. Ovid, too, was a favorite author, partly on account of the astonishing fables of the *Metamorphoses,* and partly, no doubt, for the sake of his love verses, so well adapted to the gallantry of this period.

The passion for romance was attended with other bad consequences. Men of warlike genius and warm fancy, charmed to infatuation with the supposed achievements of knights errant, were tempted to appear in that character, though the profession was now considered as a nuisance, and proscribed by law in some parts of Europe. This folly seems to have been most prevalent in Spain; which may be thus accounted for. The first romances were written in the language of that kingdom. The Spaniards were then, as they are now, a valiant and enterprising people. And they had long been enslaved by the Moors from Africa, whom, after a seven hundred years war (according to the historians), and after fighting three thousand and seven hundred battles, they at last drove out of Spain. This produced many wonderful adventures, made them fierce, romantic, and haughty, and confirmed their attachment to their own religion, and their abhorrence of that of their enemies.

But the final extirpation of chivalry and all its chimeras was now approaching. What laws and force could not accomplish was brought about by the humor and satire of one writer. This was the illustrious Miguel de Cervantes Saavedra. He was born at Madrid in the year one thousand five hundred and forty-nine. He seems to have had every advantage of education, and to have been a master in polite learning. But in other respects fortune was not very indulgent. He served many years in the armies of Spain, in no higher station than that of a private soldier. In that capacity he fought at the battle of Lepanto, under Don John of Austria, and had the misfortune, or as he rather thought, the honor, to lose his left hand. Being now disqualified for military service, he commenced author, and wrote many dramatic pieces, which were acted with applause on the Spanish theater, and acquired him both money and reputation. But want of economy and unbounded generosity dissipated the former, and he was actually confined in prison for debt when he composed the first part of *The History of Don Quixote,* a work which everybody admires for its humor, but which ought also to be considered as a most useful performance, that brought about a great revolution in the manners and literature of Europe by banishing the wild dreams of chivalry and reviving a taste for the simplicity of nature. In this view, the publication of *Don Quixote* forms an important era in the history of mankind.

Don Quixote is represented as a man whom it is impossible not to esteem for his cultivated understanding and the goodness of his heart, but who, by poring night and day upon the old romances, had impaired his reason to such a degree as to mistake them for history, and form the design of going through the world in the character, and with the accoutrements, of a knight-errant. His distempered fancy takes the most common occurrences for adventures similar to those he had read in his books of chivalry. And thus the extravagance of those books being placed, as it were, in the same group with the appearances of nature and the real business of life, the hideous disproportion of the former becomes so glaring by the contrast that the most inattentive observer cannot fail to be struck with it. The person, the pretensions, and the exploits of the errant knight are held up to view in a thousand ridiculous attitudes. In a word, the humor and satire are irresistible, and their effects were instantaneous.

This work no sooner appeared than chivalry vanished, as snow melts before the sun. Mankind awoke as from a dream. They laughed at themselves for having been so long imposed on by absurdity, and wondered they had not made the discovery sooner. It astonished them to find that nature and good sense could yield a more exquisite entertainment than they had ever derived from the most sublime frenzies of chivalry. For, that this was indeed the case, that Don Quixote was more read and more relished than any other romance had ever been, we may infer from the sudden and powerful effects it produced on the sentiments of mankind, as well as from the declaration of the author himself, who tells us that upwards of twelve thousand copies of the first part were sold before the second could be got ready for the press—an amazing rapidity of sale at a time when the readers and purchasers of books were but an inconsiderable number compared to what they are in our days. "The very children," says he, "handle it; boys read it; men understand, and old people applaud, the performance. It is no sooner laid down by one than another takes it up, some struggling, and some entreating, for a sight of it. In fine," continues he, "this history is the most delightful and the least prejudicial entertainment that ever was seen; for in the whole book there is not the least shadow of a dishonorable word, nor one thought unworthy of a good catholic." [6]

Don Quixote occasioned the death of the old romance and gave birth to the new. Fiction henceforth divested herself of her gigantic size, tremendous aspect, and frantic demeanor, and descending to the level of common life, conversed with man as his equal and as a polite and cheerful companion. Not that every subsequent romance writer adopted the plan or the manner of Cervantes, but it was from him they learned to avoid extravagance and to imitate nature. And now probability was as much studied as it had been formerly neglected.

But before I proceed to the new romance, on which I shall be very brief, it is proper just to mention a species of romantic narrative which cannot be called either old or new, but is a strange mixture of both. Of this kind are the *Grand Cyrus, Clelia,* and *Cleopatra,* each consisting of ten or a dozen large volumes, and pretending to have a foundation in ancient history.[7] In them, all facts and characters, real and fabulous, and all systems of policy and manners, the

Greek, the Roman, the feudal, and the modern, are jumbled together and confounded, as if a painter should represent Julius Caesar drinking tea with Queen Elizabeth, Jupiter, and Dulcinea del Toboso, and having on his head the laurel wreath of ancient Rome, a suit of Gothic armor on his shoulders, laced ruffles at his wrist, a pipe of tobacco in his mouth, and a pistol and tomahawk stuck in his belt. But I should go beyond my depth if I were to criticize any of those enormous compositions. For, to confess the truth, I never had patience to read one half of one of the volumes, nor met with a person who could give me any other account of them than that they are intolerably tedious and unspeakably absurd.

The new romance may be divided into the serious and the comic, and each of these kinds may be variously subdivided.

I. 1. Of serious romances, some follow the historical arrangement, and instead of beginning, like Homer and Virgil, in the middle of the subject, give a continued narrative of the life of some one person, from his birth to his establishment in the world, or till his adventures may be supposed to have come to an end. Of this sort is *Robinson Crusoe*. The account commonly given of that well-known work is as follows.

Alexander Selkirk, a Scotch mariner, happened, by some accident which I forget, to be left in the uninhabited island of Juan Fernandes in the South Seas. Here he continued four years alone, without any other means of supporting life than by running down goats and killing such other animals as he could come at. To defend himself from danger during the night, he built a house of stones rudely put together, which a gentleman who had been in it (for it was extant when Anson arrived there) described to me as so very small that one person could with difficulty crawl in and stretch himself at length. Selkirk was delivered by an English vessel, and returned home. A late French writer says he had become so fond of the savage state that he was unwilling to quit it. But that is not true. The French writer either confounds the real story of Selkirk with a fabulous account of one Philip Quarl, written after *Robinson Crusoe*, of which it is a paltry imitation,[8] or wilfully misrepresents the fact in order to justify, as far as he is able, an idle conceit, which, since the time of Rousseau, has been in fashion amongst infidel and affected theorists on the continent, that savage life is most natural to us, and that the more a man resembles a brute in his mind, body, and behavior, the happier he becomes, and the more perfect. Selkirk was advised to get his story put in writing and published. Being illiterate himself, he told everything he could remember to Daniel Defoe, a professed author of considerable note, who, instead of doing justice to the poor man, is said to have applied these materials to his own use by making them the groundwork of *Robinson Crusoe,* which he soon after published, and which, being very popular, brought him a good deal of money.

Some have thought that a love tale is necessary to make a romance interesting. But *Robinson Crusoe,* though there is nothing of love in it, is one of the most interesting narratives that ever was written (at least in all that part which relates to the desert island), being founded on a passion still more prevalent than love, the desire of self-preservation, and therefore likely to engage the curiosity of every class of readers, both old and young, both learned and unlearned.

I am willing to believe that Defoe shared the profits of this publication with the poor seaman, for there is an air of humanity in it which one would not expect from an author who is an arrant cheat. In the preface to his second volume, he speaks feelingly enough of the harm done him by those who had abridged the first in order to reduce the price. "The injury," says he, "which these men do to the proprietors of works is a practice all honest men abhor; and they believe they may challenge them to show the difference between that and robbing on the highway, or breaking open a house. If they cannot show any difference in the crime, they will find it hard to show why there should be any difference in the punishment." Is it to be imagined that any man of common prudence would talk in this way if he were conscious that he himself might be proved guilty of that very dishonesty which he so severely condemns?

Be this however as it may, for I have no authority to affirm anything on either side, *Robinson Crusoe* must be allowed, by the most rigid moralist, to be one of those novels which one may read not only with pleasure but also with profit. It breathes throughout a spirit of piety and benevolence; it sets in a very striking light, as I have elsewhere observed, the importance of the mechanic arts, which they who know not what it is to be without them are so apt to undervalue; it fixes in the mind a lively idea of the horrors of solitude and, consequently, of the sweets of social life, and of the blessings we derive from conversation and mutual aid; and it shows how, by laboring with one's own hands, one may secure independence and open for oneself many sources of health and amusement. I agree, therefore, with Rousseau, that this is one of the best books that can be put in the hands of children.[9] The style is plain, but not elegant, nor perfectly grammatical; and the second part of the story is tiresome.

2. A second species of the modern serious romance is that which follows the poetical arrangement, and in order to shorten the time of the action, begins in the middle of the story. Such, partly, are *Sir Charles Grandison* and *Clarissa Harlowe,* by Mr. Richardson. That author has adopted a plan of narrative of a peculiar kind: the persons who bear a part in the action are themselves the relaters of it. This is done by means of letters, or epistles, wherein the story is continued from time to time, and the passions freely expressed as they arise from every change of fortune, and while the persons concerned are supposed to be ignorant of the events that are to follow. And thus the several agents are introduced in their turns, speaking or, which is the same thing in this case, writing suitably to their respective feelings and characters; so that the fable is partly epic and partly dramatic. There are some advantages in this form of narrative. It prevents all anticipation of the catastrophe and keeps the reader in the same suspense in which the persons themselves are supposed to be, and it pleases further by the varieties of style suited to the different tempers and sentiments of those who write the letters. But it has also its inconveniencies. For unless the fable be short and simple, this mode of narration can hardly fail to run out into an extravagant length and to be encumbered with repetitions. And indeed, Richardson himself, with all his powers of invention, is apt to be tedious, and to fall into a minuteness of detail which is often unnecessary. His pathetic scenes, too, are overcharged and so long continued as to wear out the spirits of the reader. Nor can it be denied that he has given too much prudery to his favorite women and something of pedantry or finicalness to his favorite men. Clementina was, no doubt, intended as a pattern of female excellence, but though she may claim veneration as a saint, it is impossible to love her as a woman. And Grandison, though both a good and a great character, is in everything so perfect as in many things to discourage imitation, and so distant and so formal as to forbid all familiarity and, of course, all cordial attachment. Alworthy is as good a man as he, but his virtue is purely human, and having a little of our own weakness in it, and assuming no airs of superiority, invites our acquaintance and engages our love.

For all this, however, Richardson is an author of uncommon merit.

His characters are well drawn and distinctly marked, and he delineates the operation of the passions with a picturesque accuracy which discovers great knowledge of human nature. His moral sentiments are profound and judicious; in wit and humor he is not wanting; his dialogue is sometimes formal; but many of his conversation pieces are executed with elegance and vivacity. For the good tendency of his writings he deserves still higher praise, for he was a man of unaffected piety, and had the improvement of his fellow creatures very much at heart.

Yet, like most other novel-writers, he represents some of his wicked characters as more agreeable than was necessary to his plan, which may make the example dangerous. I do not think that an author of fable, in either prose or verse, should make his bad characters completely bad; for in the first place, that would not be natural, as the worst of men have generally some good in them; and, secondly, that would hurt his design, by making the tale less captivating, as the history of a person so very worthless as to have not one good quality would give disgust or horror, instead of pleasure. But, on the other hand, when a character like Richardson's Lovelace, whom the reader ought to abominate for his crimes, is adorned with youth, beauty, eloquence, wit, and every other intellectual and bodily accomplishment, it is to be feared that thoughtless young men may be tempted to imitate, even while they disapprove, him. Nor is it a sufficient apology to say that he is punished in the end. The reader knows that the story is a fiction; but he knows too that such talents and qualities, if they were to appear in real life, would be irresistibly engaging, and he may even fancy that a character so highly ornamented must have been a favorite of the author. Is there not, then, reason to apprehend that some readers will be more inclined to admire the gay profligate than to fear his punishment? Achilles in Homer and Macbeth in Shakespeare are not without great and good qualities to raise our admiration and make us take concern in what befalls them. But no person is in any danger of being perverted by their example, their criminal conduct being described and directed in such a manner, by the art of the poet, as to show that it is hateful in itself and necessarily productive of misery, both to themselves and to mankind.

I may add that the punishment of Lovelace is a death, not of infamy, according to our notions, but rather of honor—which surely he did not deserve—and that the immediate cause of it is not his wickedness, but some inferiority to his antagonist in the use of the small sword. With a little more skill in that exercise, he might, for anything that appears in the story, have triumphed over Clarissa's avenger, as he had done over herself, and over the censure of the world. Had his crime been represented as the necessary cause of a series of mortifications, leading him gradually down to infamy, ruin, and despair, or producing by probable means an exemplary repentance, the fable would have been more useful in a moral view, and perhaps more interesting. And for the execution of such a plan the genius of Richardson seems to me to have been extremely well formed. These remarks are offered, with a view rather to explain my own ideas of fable than to detract from an author who was an honor to his country and of whose talents and virtues I am a sincere admirer.

His epistolary manner has been imitated by many novel-writers, particularly by Rousseau in his *New Eloisa,* a work not more remarkable for its eloquence, which is truly great, than for its glaring and manifold inconsistencies. For it is full of nature and extravagance, of sound philosophy and wild theory, of useful instruction and dangerous doctrine.

II. 1. The second kind of the new romance is the comic, which, like the first, may with respect to the arrangement of events be subdivided into the historical and the poetical.

Of the historical form are the novels of Marivaux, and *Gil Blas,* by M. le Sage.[10] These authors abound in wit and humor and give natural descriptions of present manners in a simple and very agreeable style. And their works may be read without danger, being for the most part of a moral tendency. Only Le Sage appears to have had a partiality for cheats and sharpers, for these are people whom he introduces often; nor does he always paint them in the odious colors that properly belong to all such pests of society. Even his hero Gil Blas he has made too much a rogue, which, as he is the relater of his own story, has this disagreeable effect, that it conveys to us, all the while we read him, an idea that we are in bad company and deriving entertainment from the conversation of a man whom we cannot esteem.

Smollet follows the same historical arrangement in *Roderick Random* and *Peregrine Pickle,* two performances of which I am sorry to say that I can hardly allow them any other praise than that they are humorous and entertaining. He excels, however, in drawing the characters of seamen, with whom in his younger days he had the best opportunities of being acquainted. He seems to have collected a vast number of merry stories, and he tells them with much vivacity and energy of expression. But his style often approaches to bombast, and many of his humorous pictures are exaggerated beyond all bounds of probability. And it does not appear that he knew how to contrive a regular fable by making his events mutually dependent and all co-operating to one and the same final purpose. On the morality of these novels I cannot compliment him at all. He is often inexcusably licentious. Profligates, bullies, and misanthropes are among his favorite characters. A duel he seems to have thought one of the highest efforts of human virtue, and playing dextrously at billiards, a very genteel accomplishment. Two of his pieces, however, deserve to be mentioned with more respect. *Count Fathom,* though an improbable tale, is pleasing and upon the whole not immoral, though in some passages very indelicate. And *Sir Launcelot Greaves,* though still more improbable, has great merit, and is truly original in the execution, notwithstanding that the hint is borrowed from *Don Quixote.*

2. The second species of the new comic romance is that which in the arrangement of events follows the poetical order, and which may properly enough be called the epic comedy, or rather the comic epic poem: epic, because it is narrative; and comic, because it is employed on the business of common life and takes its persons from the middle and lower ranks of mankind.

This form of the comic romance has been brought to perfection in England by Henry Fielding, who seems to have possessed more wit and humor, and more knowledge of mankind, than any other person of modern times, Shakespeare excepted, and whose great natural abilities were refined by a classical taste which he had acquired by studying the best authors of antiquity, though it cannot be denied that he appears on some occasions to have been rather too ostentatious, both of his learning and of his wit.

Some have said that *Joseph Andrews* is the best performance of Fielding. But its chief merit is parson Adams, who is indeed a character of masterly invention and, next to Don Quixote, the most ludicrous personage that ever appeared in romance. This work, though full of exquisite humor, is blamable in many respects. Several passages offend by their indelicacy. And it is not easy to imagine what could induce the author to add to the other faults of his hero's father, Wilson, the infamy of lying and cowardice, and then to dismiss him, by very improbable means, to a life of virtuous tranquility, and endeavor to render him upon the whole a respectable character. Some youthful irregularities, rather hinted at than described, owing more to imprudence and unlucky accident than to confirmed habits of sensuality, and followed by inconvenience, perplexity, and remorse, their natural consequences, may, in a comic tale, be assigned even to a favorite personage and, by proper management, form a very instructive part of the narration; but crimes that bring dishonor or that betray a hard heart or an injurious disposition should never be fixed on a character whom the poet or novel-writer means to recommend to our esteem. On this principle, Fielding might be vindicated in regard to all the censurable conduct of Tom Jones, provided he had been less particular in describing it; and by the same rule Smollet's system of youthful profligacy, as exemplified in some of his libertines, is altogether without excuse.

Tom Jones and *Amelia* are Fielding's best performances, and the most perfect, perhaps, of their kind in the world. The fable of the latter is entirely poetical and of the true epic species, beginning in the middle of the action, or rather as near the end as possible, and introducing the previous occurrences in the form of a narrative episode. Of the former, the introductory part follows the historical arrangement, but the fable becomes strictly poetical as soon as the great action of the piece commences, that is, if I mistake not, immediately after the sickness of Alworthy, for from that period the incidents proceed in an uninterrupted series to the final event, which happens about two months after.

Since the days of Homer the world has not seen a more artful epic fable. The characters and adventures are wonderfully diversified, yet the circumstances are all so natural, and rise so easily from one another, and cooperate with so much regularity in bringing on, even while they seem to retard, the catastrophe, that the curiosity of the reader is kept always awake, and instead of flagging, grows more and more impatient as the story advances, till at last it becomes downright anxiety. And when we get to the end, and look back on the whole contrivance, we are amazed to find that of so many incidents there should be so few superfluous, that in such variety of fiction there should be so great probability, and that so complex a tale should be so perspicuously conducted, and with perfect unity of design. These remarks may be applied either to *Tom Jones* or to

Amelia, but they are made with a view to the former chiefly, which might give scope to a great deal of criticism if I were not in haste to conclude the subject. Since the time of Fielding, who died in the year one thousand seven hundred and fifty-four, the comic romance, as far as I am acquainted with it, seems to have been declining apace, from simplicity and nature into improbability and affectation.

Let not the usefulness of romance writing be estimated by the length of my discourse upon it. Romances are a dangerous recreation. A few, no doubt, of the best may be friendly to good taste and good morals, but far the greater part are unskilfully written, and tend to corrupt the heart and stimulate the passions. A habit of reading them breeds a dislike to history and all the substantial parts of knowledge, withdraws the attention from nature and truth, and fills the mind with extravagant thoughts and too often with criminal propensities. I would therefore caution my young reader against them; or, if he must, for the sake of amusement, and that he may have something to say on the subject, indulge himself in this way now and then, let it be sparingly, and seldom.

GEORGE CAMPBELL ✍

Introduction to *The Philosophy of Rhetoric* (1776)

All art is founded in science, and the science is of little value which does not serve as a foundation to some beneficial art. On the most sublime of all sciences, theology and ethics, is built the most important of all arts, the art of living. The abstract mathematical sciences serve as a groundwork to the arts of the land measurer and the accountant, and in conjunction with natural philosophy, including geography and astronomy, to those of the architect, the navigator, the dialist, and many others. Of what consequence anatomy is to surgery, and that part of physiology which teaches the laws of gravitation and of motion is to the artificer, is a matter too obvious to need illustration. The general remark might, if necessary, be exemplified throughout the whole circle of arts, both useful and elegant. Valuable knowledge therefore always leads to some practical skill, and is perfected in it. On the other hand, the practical skill loses much of its beauty and extensive utility which does not originate in knowledge. There is by consequence a natural relation between the sciences and the arts like that which subsists between the parent and the offspring.

I acknowledge indeed that these are sometimes unnaturally separated and that by the mere influence of example on the one hand, and imitation on the other, some progress may be made in an art without the knowledge of the principles from which it sprang. By the help of a few rules which men are taught to use mechanically, a good practical arithmetician may be formed who neither knows the reasons on which the rules he works by were first established, nor ever thinks it of any moment to inquire into them. In like manner, do we not frequently meet with expert artisans who are ignorant of the six mechanical powers which, though in the exercise of their profession they daily employ, they do not understand the principles whereby, in any instance, the result of their application is ascertained? The propagation of the arts may therefore be compared more justly to that variety which takes place in the vegetable kindgom than to the uniformity which obtains universally in the animal world, for as to the anomalous race of zoophytes, I do not comprehend them in the number. It is not always necessary that the plant spring from the seed; a slip from another plant will often answer the purpose. There is, however, a very considerable difference in the expectations that may justly be raised from the different methods followed in the acquisition of the art. Improvements, unless in extraordinary instances of genius and sagacity, are not to be expected from those who have acquired all their dexterity from imitation and habit. One who has had an education no better than that of an ordinary mechanic may prove an excellent manual operator, but it is only in the well-instructed mechanician that you would expect to find a good machinist. The analogy to vegetation above suggested holds here also. The offset is commonly no more than a mere copy of the parent plant. It is from the seed only you can expect, with the aid of proper culture, to produce new varieties, and even to make improvements on the species. "Expert men," says Lord Bacon, "can execute and judge of particulars, one by one; but the general counsels, and the plots and marshalling of affairs, come best from those that are learned."

Indeed, in almost every art, even as used by mere practitioners, there are certain rules, as hath been already hinted, which must carefully be followed, and which serve the artist instead of principles. An acquaintance with these is one step, and but one step towards science. Thus in the common books of arithmetic, intended solely for practice, the rules laid down for the ordinary operations, as for numeration, or numerical notation, addition, subtraction, multiplication, division, and a few others, which are sufficient for all the purposes of the accountant, serve instead of principles—and, to a superficial observer, may be thought to supersede the study of anything further. But their utility reaches a very little way, compared with that which results from the knowledge of the foundations of the art, and of what has been, not unfitly, styled "arithmetic universal." It may be justly said that, without some portion of this knowledge, the practical rules had never been invented. Besides, if by these, the particular questions which come exactly within the description of the rule may be solved, by the other, such general rules themselves as serve for the solution of endless particulars may be discovered.

The case, I own, is somewhat different with those arts which are entirely founded on experiment and observation and are not derived, like pure mathematics, from abstract and universal axioms. But even in these, when we rise from the individual to the species, from the species to the genus, and thence to the most extensive orders and classes, we arrive, though in a different way, at the knowledge of general truths which, in a certain sense, are also scientific and answer a similar purpose. Our acquaintance with nature and its laws is so much extended that we shall be enabled, in numberless cases, not only to apply to the most profitable purposes the knowledge we have thus acquired, but to determine beforehand, with sufficient certainty, the success of every new application. In this progress we are like people who from a low and narrow bottom, where the view is confined to a few acres, gradually ascend a lofty peak or promontory. The prospect is perpetually enlarging as we mount, and when we reach the summit, the boundless horizon, comprehending all the variety of sea and land, hill and valley, town and country, arable and desert, lies under the eye at once.

Those who in medicine have scarcely risen to the discernment of any general principles and have no other directory but the experiences gained in the first and lowest stage, or as it were at the foot of the mountain, are commonly distinguished by the name of empirics. Something similar may be said to obtain in the other liberal arts, for in all of them more enlargement of mind is necessary than is required for the exercise of those called mechanical. The character directly opposite to the empiric is the visionary, for it is not in theology only that there are visionaries. Of the two extremes I acknowledge that the latter is the worse. The first founds upon facts, but the facts are few, and commonly in his reasonings, through his imperfect knowledge of the subject, misapplied. The second often argues very consequentially from principles which, having no foundation in nature, may justly be denominated the illegitimate issue of his own imagination. He in this resembles the man of science, that he acts systematically (for there are false as well as true theorists) and is influenced by certain general propositions, real or imaginary. But the difference lies here: that in the one they are real, in the other imaginary. The system of the one is reared on the firm basis of experience; the theory of the other is no better than a castle in the air. I mention characters only in the extreme, because in this manner they are best discriminated. In real life, however, any two of these, sometimes all the three, in various proportions, may be found blended in the same person.

The arts are frequently divided into the useful, and the polite, fine, or elegant; for these words are, in this application, used synonymously. This division is not coincident with that into the mechanical and the liberal. Physic, navigation, and the art of war, though properly liberal arts, fall entirely under the denomination of the useful, whereas painting and sculpture, though requiring a good deal of manual labor, and in that respect more nearly related to the mechanical, belong to the class denominated elegant. The first division arises purely from the consideration of the end to be attained, the second from the consideration of the means to be employed. In respect of the end, an art is either useful or elegant; in respect of the means, it is either mechanical or liberal. The true foundation of the former distribution is that certain arts are manifestly and ultimately calculated for profit or use, whilst others, on the contrary, seem to terminate in pleasing. The one supplies a real want; the other only gratifies some mental taste. Yet in strictness, in the execution of the useful arts there is often scope for elegance, and the arts called elegant are by no means destitute of use. The principal difference is that use is the direct and avowed purpose of the former, whereas it is more latently and indirectly effected by the latter. Under this class are commonly included not only the arts of the painter and the statuary but those also of the muscian and the poet. Eloquence and architecture, by which last term is always understood more than building merely for accommodation, are to be considered as of a mixed nature, wherein utility and beauty have almost equal influence.

The elegant arts, as well as the useful, are founded in experience, but from the difference of their nature there arises a considerable difference both in their origin and in their growth. Necessity, the mother of invention, drives men, in the earliest state of society, to the study and cultivation of the useful arts; it is always leisure and abundance which lead men to seek gratifications no way conducive to the preservation either of the individual or of the species. The elegant arts, therefore, are doubtless to be considered as the younger sisters. The progress of the former towards perfection is, however, much slower than that of the latter. Indeed, with regard to the first, it is impossible to say as to several arts what is the perfection of the art, since we are incapable of conceiving how far the united discernment and industry of men, properly applied, may yet carry them. For some centuries backwards, the men of every age have made great and unexpected improvements on the labors of their predecessors. And it is very probable that the subsequent age will produce discoveries and acquisitions which we of this age are as little capable of foreseeing as those who preceded us in the last century were capable of conjecturing the progress that would be made in the present. The case is not entirely similar in the fine arts. These, though later in their appearing, are more rapid in their advancement. There may, indeed, be in these a degree of perfection beyond what we have experienced, but we have some conception of the very utmost to which it can proceed. For instance, where resemblance is the object, as in a picture or a statue, a perfect conformity to its archetype is a thing at least conceivable. In like manner, the utmost pleasure of which the imagination is susceptible by a poetical narrative or exhibition is a thing, in my judgment, not inconceivable. We Britons, for example, do by immense degrees excel the ancient Greeks in the arts of navigation and shipbuilding; and how much farther we may still excel them in these by means of discoveries and improvements yet to be made it would be the greatest presumption in any man to say. But as it requires not a prophetic spirit to discover, it implies no presumption to affirm that we shall never excel them so far in poetry and eloquence, if ever in these respects we come to equal them. The same thing might probably be affirmed in regard to painting, sculpture, and music, if we had here as ample a fund of materials for forming a comparison.

But let it be observed that the remarks now made regard only the advancement of the arts themselves, for though the useful are of slower growth than the other, and their utmost perfection cannot always be so easily ascertained, yet the acquisition of any one of them by a learner, in the perfection which it has reached at the time, is a much easier matter than the acquisition of any of the elegant arts —besides that the latter require much more of a certain happy combination in the original frame of spirit, commonly called genius, than is necessary in the other.

Let it be observed further that as the gratification of taste is the immediate object of the fine arts, their effect is in a manner instantaneous, and the quality of any new production in these is immediately judged by everybody, for all have in them some rudiments of taste, though in some they are improved by a good, in others corrupted by a bad education, and in others almost suppressed by a total want of education. In the useful arts, on the contrary, as more time and experience are requisite for discovering the means by which our accommodation is effected, so it generally requires examination, time, and trial, that we may be satisfied of the fitness of the work for the end proposed. In these we are not near so apt to consider ourselves as judges, unless we be either artists, or accustomed to employ and examine the works of artists in that particular profession.

I mentioned some arts that have their fundamental principles in the abstract sciences of geometry and arithmetic, and some in the doctrine of gravitation and motion. There are others, as the medical and surgical arts, which require a still broader foundation of science in anatomy, the animal economy, natural history, diseases, and remedies. Those arts which, like poetry, are purely to be ranked among the elegant as their end is attained by an accommodation to some internal taste, so the springs by which alone they can be regulated must be sought for in the nature of the human mind, and more especially in the principles of the imagination. It is also in the human mind that we must investigate the source of some of the useful arts: logic, whose end is the discovery of truth, is founded in the doctrine of the understanding, and ethics (under which may be comprehended economics, politics, and jurisprudence) are founded in that of the will.

This was the idea of Lord Verulam, perhaps the most comprehensive genius in philosophy that has appeared in modern times. But these are not the only arts which have their foundation in the science of human nature. Grammar too, in its general principles, has a close connection with the understanding and the theory of the association of ideas.

But there is no art whatever that hath so close a connection with all the faculties and powers of the mind as eloquence, or the art of speaking, in the extensive sense in which I employ the term. For, in the first place, that it ought to be ranked among the polite or fine arts is manifest from this, that in all its exertions, with little or no exception (as will appear afterwards), it requires the aid of the imagination. Thereby it not only pleases but by pleasing commands attention, rouses the passions, and often at last subdues the most stubborn resolution. It is also a useful art. This is certainly the case if the power of speech be a useful faculty, as it professedly teaches us how to employ that faculty with the greatest probability of success. Further, if the logical art and the ethical be useful, eloquence is useful, as it instructs us how these arts must be applied for the conviction and the persuasion of others. It is indeed the grand art of communication not of ideas only, but of sentiments, passions, dispositions, and purposes. Nay, without this, the greatest talents, even wisdom itself, lose much of their luster, and still more of their usefulness. "The wise in heart," saith Solomon, "shall be called prudent, but the sweetness of the lips increaseth learning" (Proverbs 16:21). By the former a man's own conduct may be well regulated, but the latter is absolutely necessary for diffusing valuable knowledge and enforcing right rules of action upon others.

Poetry indeed is properly no other than a particular mode or form of certain branches of oratory. But of this more afterwards. Suffice it only to remark at present that the direct end of the former, whether to delight the fancy as in epic, or to move the passions as in tragedy, is avowedly in part the aim, and sometimes the immediate and proposed aim, of the orator. The same medium—language—is made use of; the same general rules of composition in narration, description, argumentation, are observed; and the same tropes and figures, either for beautifying or for invigorating the diction, are employed by both. In regard to versification, it is more to be considered as an appendage than as a constituent of poetry. In this lies what may be called the more mechanical part of the poet's work, being at most but a sort of garnishing, and by far too unessential to give a designation to the kind. This particularity in form, to adopt an expression of the naturalist, constitutes only a variety, and not a different species.

Now though a considerable proficiency in the practice of the oratorical art may be easily and almost naturally attained by one in whom clearness of apprehension is happily united with sensibility of taste, fertility of imagination, and a certain readiness in language, a more thorough investigation of the latent energies, if I may thus express myself, whereby the instruments employed by eloquence produce their effect upon the hearers will serve considerably both to improve the taste and to enrich the fancy. By the former effect we learn to amend and avoid faults in composing and speaking, against which the best natural but uncultivated parts give no security; and by the latter, the proper mediums are suggested whereby the necessary aids of topics, arguments, illustrations, and motives may be procured. Besides, this study, properly conducted, leads directly to an acquaintance with ourselves; it not only traces the operations of the intellect and imagination but discloses the lurking springs of action in the heart. In this view it is perhaps the surest and the shortest, as well as the pleasantest, way of arriving at the science of the human mind. It is a humble attempt to lead the mind of the studious inquirer into this tract that the following sheets are now submitted to the examination of the public.

When we consider the manner in which the rhetorical art hath arisen and been treated in the schools, we must be sensible that in this, as in the imitative arts, the first handle has been given to criticism by actual performances in the art. The principles of our nature will, without the aid of any previous and formal instruction, sufficiently account for the first attempts. As speakers existed before grammarians, and reasoners before logicians, so doubtless there were orators before there were rhetoricians, and poets before critics. The first impulse towards the attainment of every art is from nature. The earliest assistance and direction that can be obtained in the rhetorical art, by which men operate on the minds of others, arises from the consciousness a man has of what operates on his own mind, aided by the sympathetic feelings and by that practical experience of mankind which individuals, even in the rudest state of society, are capable of acquiring. The next step is to observe and discriminate, by proper appellations, the different attempts, whether modes of arguing or forms of speech, that have been employed for the purposes of explaining, convincing, pleasing, moving, and persuading. Here we have the beginnings of the critical science. The third step is to compare with diligence the various effects, favorable or unfavorable, of those attempts, carefully taking into consideration every attendant circumstance by which the success appears to have been influenced and by which one may be enabled to discover to what particular purpose each attempt is adapted and in what circumstances only to be used. The fourth and last is to canvass those principles in our nature to which the various attempts are adapted and by which, in any instance, their success or want of success may be accounted for.

By the first step the critic is supplied with materials. By the second, the materials are distributed and classed; the forms of argument, the tropes and figures of speech, with their divisions and subdivisions, are explained. By the third, the rules of composition are discovered, or the method of combining and disposing the several materials so as that they may be perfectly adapted to the end in view. By the fourth, we arrive at that knowledge of human nature which, beside its other advantages, adds both weight and evidence to all precedent discoveries and rules.

The second of the steps above-mentioned, which, by the way, is the first of the rhetorical art, for all that precedes is properly supplied by nature, appeared to the author of *Hudibras* the utmost pitch that had even to his time been attained:

> For all a rhetorician's rules
> Teach nothing but to name his tools. [I, i]

In this, however, the matter hath been exaggerated by the satirist. Considerable progress had been made by the ancient Greeks and Romans in devising the proper rules of composition not only in the two sorts of poesy, epic, and dramatic, but also in the three sorts of orations which were in most frequent use among them, the deliberative, the judiciary, and the demonstrative. And I must acknowledge that, as far as I have been able to discover, there has been little or no improvement in this respect made by the moderns. The observations and rules transmitted to us from these distinguished names in the learned world, Aristotle, Cicero, and Quintilian, have been for the most part only translated by later critics, or put into a modish dress and new arrangement. And as to the fourth and last step, it may be said to bring us into a new country, of which, though there have been some successful incursions occasionally made upon its frontiers, we are not yet in full possession.

The performance which, of all those I happen to be acquainted with, seems to have advanced farthest in this way is the *Elements of Criticism*. But the subject of the learned and ingenious author of that work is rather too multifarious to admit so narrow a scrutiny as would be necessary for a perfect knowledge of the several parts. Everything that is an object of taste, sculpture, painting, music, architecture, and gardening, as well as poetry and eloquence, come within his plan. On the other hand, though his subject be more multiform, it is in respect of its connection with the mind less extensive than that here proposed. All those particular arts are examined only on that side wherein there is found a pretty considerable coincidence with one another; namely, as objects of taste which, by exciting sentiments of grandeur, beauty, novelty, and the like, are calculated to delight the imagination. In this view, eloquence comes no farther under consideration than as a fine art, and adapted, like the others above mentioned, to please the fancy and to move the passions. But to treat it also as a useful art, and closely connected with the understanding and the will, would have led to a discussion foreign to his purpose.

I am aware that from the deduction given above it may be urged that the fact as here represented seems to subvert the principle formerly laid down, and that as practice in the art has given the first scope for criticism, the former cannot justly be considered as deriving light and direction from the latter; that, on the contrary, the latter ought to be regarded as merely affording a sort of intellectual entertainment to speculative men. It may be said that this science, however entertaining, as it must derive all its light and information from the actual examples in the art, can never in return be subservient to the art, from which alone it has received whatever it has to bestow. This objection, however specious, will not bear a near examination. For let it be observed that though in all the arts the first rough draughts or imperfect attempts that are made precede everything that can be termed criticism, they do not precede everything that can be termed knowledge, which every human creature that is not an idiot is every day from his birth acquiring by experience and observation. This knowledge must of necessity precede even those rudest and earliest essays; and if in the imperfect and indigested state in which knowledge must always be found in the mind that is rather self-taught than totally untaught, it deserves not to be dignified with the title of science, neither does the first awkward attempt in practice merit to be honored with the name of art. As is the one, such is the other. It is enough for my purpose that something must be known before anything in this way, with a view to an end, can be undertaken to be done.

At the same time it is acknowledged that as man is much more an active than a contemplative being, and as generally there is some view to action, expecially in uncultivated minds, in all their observations and inquiries, it cannot be doubted that in composition the first attempts would be in the art and that afterwards from the comparison of different attempts with one another, and the consideration of the success with which they had been severally attended, would arise gradually the rules of criticism. Nor can it, on the other hand, be pleaded with any appearance of truth that observations derived from the productions of an art can be of no service for the improvement of that art, and consequently of no benefit to future artists. On the contrary, it is thus that every art, liberal or mechanical, elegant or useful, except those founded in pure mathematics, advances toward perfection. From observing similar but different attempts and experiments, and from comparing their effects, general remarks are made which serve as so many rules for directing future practice; and from comparing such general remarks together, others still more general are deduced. A few individual instances serve as a foundation to those observations which, when once sufficiently established, extend their influence to instances innumerable. It is in this way that, on experiments comparatively few, all the physiological sciences have been reared; it is in this way that those comprehensive truths were first discovered which have had such an unlimited influence on the most important arts and given man so vast a dominion over the elements, and even the most refractory powers of nature. It is evident, therefore, that the artist and the critic are reciprocally subservient, and the particular province of each is greatly improved by the assistance of the other.

RICHARD CUMBERLAND ✑

The Observer (1785)

No. 76   [*Samson Agonistes*]

In my foregoing paper, when I remarked that Jonson in his comedy of *The Fox* was a close copier of the ancients, it occurred to me to say something upon the celebrated drama of the *Samson Agonistes,* which, though less beholden to the Greek poets in its dialogue than the comedy above mentioned, is in all other particulars as complete an imitation of the ancient tragedy as the distance of times and the difference of languages will admit of.

It is professedly built according to "ancient rule and example," and the author, by taking Aristotle's definition of tragedy for his motto, fairly challenges the critic to examine and compare it by that test. His close adherence to the model of the Greek tragedy is in nothing more conspicuous than in the simplicity of his diction; in this particular he has curbed his fancy with so tight a hand that, knowing as we do the fertile vein of his genius, we cannot but lament the fidelity of his imitation, for there is a harshness in the meter of his Chorus which to a certain degree seems to border upon pedantry and affectation. He premises that the measure is indeed of all sorts, but I must take leave to observe that in some places it is no measure at all, or such, at least, as the ear will not patiently endure nor which any recitation can make harmonious. By casting out of his composition the strophe and antistrophe, those stanzas which the Greeks appropriated to singing, or in one word, by making his chorus monostrophic, he has robbed it of that lyric beauty which he was capable of bestowing in the highest perfection, and why he should stop short in this particular when he had otherwise gone so far in imitation is not easy to guess. For surely it would have been quite as natural to suppose those stanzas, had he written any, might be sung as that all the other parts as the drama now stands, with a Chorus of such irregular measure, might be recited or given in representation.

Now it is well known to every man conversant in the Greek theater how the Chorus, which in fact is the parent of the drama, came in process of improvement to be woven into the fable, and from being at first the whole, grew in time to be only a part. The fable being simple and the characters few, the striking part of the spectacle rested upon the singing and dancing of the interlude, if I may so call it, and to these the people were too long accustomed and too warmly attached to allow of any reform for their exclusion. The tragic poet therefore never got rid of his Chorus, though the writers of the Middle Comedy contrived to dismiss theirs, and probably their fable being of a more lively character, their scenes were better able to stand without the support of music and spectacle than the mournful fable and more languid recitation of the tragedians. That the tragic authors labored against the Chorus will appear from their efforts to expel Bacchus and his satyrs from the stage, in which they were long time opposed by the audience, and at last, by certain ingenius expedients which were a kind of compromise with the public, effected their point. This, in part, was brought about by the introduction of a fuller scene and a more active fable, but the Chorus, with its accompaniments, kept its place, and the poet, who seldom ventured upon introducing more than three speakers in the scene at the same time, qualified the sterility of his business by giving to the Chorus a share of the dialogue, who, at the same time that they furnished the stage with numbers, were not counted amongst the speaking characters, according to the rigor of the usage above mentioned. A man must be an enthusiast for antiquity who can find charms in the dialogue part of a Greek Chorus and reconcile himself to their unnatural and chilling interruptions of the action and pathos of the scene. I am fully persuaded they came there upon motives of expediency only and kept their post upon the plea of long possession and the attractions of spectacle and music. In short, nature was sacrificed to the display of art, and the heart gave up its feelings that the ear and eye might be gratified.

When Milton therefore takes the Chorus into his dialogue, excluding from his drama the lyric strophe and antistrophe, he rejects what I conceive to be its only recommendation, and which an elegant contemporary,[1] in his imitations of the Greek tragedy, is more properly attentive to. At the same time, it cannot be denied that Milton's Chorus subscribes more to the dialogues and harmonizes better with the business of the scene than that of any Greek tragedy we can now refer to.

I would now proceed to a review of the performance itself, if it were not a discussion which the author of the *Rambler* has very ably prevented me in. Respect, however, to an authority so high in criticism must not prevent me from observing that when he says, "This is the tragedy which ignorance has admired and bigotry applauded," [2] he makes it meritorious in any future critic to attempt at following him over the ground he has trod, for the purpose of discovering what those blemishes are which he has found out by superior sagacity and which others have so palpably overlooked as to merit the disgraceful character of ignorance and bigotry.

The principal, and in effect the only, objection which he states is "that the poem wants a middle, since nothing passes between the first act and the last that either hastens or delays the death of Samson." This demands examination. The death of Samson I need not describe; it is a sudden momentary event. What can hasten or delay it but the will of the person who, by an exertion of miraculous strength, was to bury himself under the ruins of a structure in which his enemies were assembled? To determine that will depends upon the impulse of his own spirit or, it may be, upon the inspiration of Heaven. If there are any incidents in the body of the drama which lead to this determination and indicate an impulse either natural or preternatural, such must be called leading incidents, and those leading incidents will constitute a middle, or in more diffusive terms, the middle business of the drama. Manoah, in his interview with Samson, which the author of the *Rambler* denominates the second act of the tragedy, tells him,

> This day the *Philistines* a popular Feast
> Here celebrate in *Gaza;* and proclaim
> Great Pomp, and Sacrifice, and Praises loud
> To *Dagon,* as their God. [434]

Here is information of a meeting of his enemies to celebrate their idolatrous triumphs, an incident of just provocation to the servant of the living God, an opportunity perhaps for vengeance, either human or divine. If it passes without notice from Samson, it is not to be styled an incident; if, on the contrary, he remarks upon it, it must be one—but Samson replies,

> *Dagon* must stoop, and shall ere long receive
> Such a discomfit, as shall quite despoil him
> Of all these boasted Trophies won on me,
> And with confusion blank his Worshippers. [468]

Who will say the expectation is not here prepared for some catastrophe, we know not what, but awful it must be, for it is Samson which denounces the downfall of the idol; it is God who inspires the denunciation. The crisis is important, for it is that which shall decide whether God or Dagon is to triumph; it is in the strongest sense of the expression *dignus vindice nodus,* and therefore we may boldly pronounce *Deus intersit!*

That this interpretation meets the sense of the author is clear from the remark of Manoah, who is made to say that he receives these words as a prophecy. Prophetic they are and were meant to be by the poet, who, in this use of his sacred prophecy, imitates the heathen oracles on which several of their dramatic plots are constructed, as might be shown by obvious examples. The interview with Manoah, then, is conducive to the catastrophe, and the drama is not in this scene devoid of incident.

Dalila next appears, and if whatever tends to raise our interest in the leading character of the tragedy cannot rightly be called episodical, the introduction of this person ought not to be accounted such, for who but this person is the cause and origin of all the pathos and distress of the story? The dialogue of this scene is moral, affecting, and sublime; it is also strictly characteristic.

The next scene exhibits the tremendous giant Harapha, and the contrast thereby produced is amongst the beauties of the poem, and may of itself be termed an important incident. That it leads to the catastrophe I think will not be disputed, and if it is asked in what manner, the Chorus will supply us with an answer.

> He will directly to the Lords, I fear,
> And with malitious counsel stir them up
> Some way or other yet further to afflict thee. [1250]

Here is another prediction connected with the plot and verified by its catastrophe, for Samson is commanded to come to the festival and entertain the revelers with some feats of strength. These commands he resists, but obeys an impulse of his mind by going afterward and thereby fulfills the prophetic declaration he had made to his father in the second act. What incident can show more management and address in the poet than this of Samson's refusing the summons of the idolaters and obeying the visitation of God's Spirit?

And now I may confidently appeal to the judicious reader whether the *Samson Agonistes* is so void of incident between the opening and conclusion as fairly to be pronounced "to want a middle." Simple it is from first to last, simple perhaps to a degree of coldness in some of its parts, but to say that nothing passes between the first act and the last which hastens or delays the death of Samson is not correct, because the very incidents are to be found which conduce to the catastrophe and but for which it could not have come to pass.

The author of the *Rambler* professes to examine the *Samson Agonistes* according to the rule laid down by Aristotle for the disposition and perfection of a tragedy, and this rule, he informs us, is that it should have a "beginning, a middle, and an end." And is this the mighty purpose for which the authority of Aristotle is appealed to? If it be thus the author of the *Rambler* has read the *Poetics*, and this be the best rule he can collect from that treatise, I am afraid he will find it too short a measure for the poet he is examining or the critic he is quoting. Aristotle had said that "not every whole hath amplitude enough for the construction of a tragic fable; now by a whole (adds he in the way of illustration), I mean that which hath beginning, middle, and end." This and no more is what he says upon beginning, middle, and end, and this, which the author of the *Rambler* conceives to be a rule for tragedy, turns out to be merely an explanation of the word *whole*, which is only one term amongst many employed by the critic in his professed and complete definition of tragedy. I should add that Aristotle gives a further explanation of the terms *beginning, middle,* and *end,* which the author of the *Rambler* hath turned into English, but in so doing, he hath inexcusably turned them out of their original sense as well as language, as any curious critic may be convinced of who compares them with Aristotle's words in the eighth chapter of the *Poetics*.

Of the poetic diction of the *Samson Agonistes* I have already spoken in general; to particularize passages of striking beauty would draw me into too great length. At the same time, not to pass over so pleasing a part of my undertaking in absolute silence, I will give the following reply of Samson to the Chorus:

> Wherever fountain or fresh current flow'd
> Against the Eastern ray, translucent, pure,
> With touch ethereal of Heav'ns fiery rod
> I drank, from the clear milky juice allaying
> Thirst, and refresht; nor envied them the grape
> Whose heads that turbulent liquor fills with fumes. [547]

Of the character I may say in a few words that Samson possesses all the terrific majesty of Prometheus chained, the mysterious distress of Oedipus, and the pitiable wretchedness of Philoctetes. His properties, like those of the first, are something above human; his misfortunes, like those of the second, are derivable from the displeasure of Heaven, and involved in oracles; his condition, like that of the last, is the most abject which human nature can be reduced to from a state of dignity and splendor.

Of the catastrophe there remains only to remark that it is of unparalleled majesty and terror.

No. 77   [*The Fair Penitent,* I]

Dr. Samuel Johnson, in his life of Rowe, pronounces of *The Fair Penitent* that it is one of the most pleasing tragedies on the stage, where it still keeps its turns of appearing and probably will long keep them, for that there is scarcely any work of any poet at once so interesting by the fable and so delightful by the language. The story, he observes, is domestic and therefore easily received by the imagination and assimilated to common life; the diction is exquisitely harmonious and soft or sprightly, as occasion requires. Few people, I believe, will think this character of *The Fair Penitent* too lavish on the score of commendation; the high degree of public favor in which this tragedy has long stood has ever attracted the best audiences to it and engaged the talents of the best performers in its display. As there is no drama more frequently exhibited or more generally read, I propose to give it a fair and impartial examination, jointly with the more unknown and less popular tragedy from which it is derived.

The Fair Penitent is in fable and character so closely copied from *The Fatal Dowry* that it is impossible not to take that tragedy along with it; and it is matter of some surprise to me that Rowe should have made no acknowledgement of his imitation either in his dedication or prologue, or anywhere else that I am apprised of.

This tragedy of *The Fatal Dowry* was the joint production of Massinger and Nathaniel Field. It takes a wider compass of fable than *The Fair Penitent,* by which means it presents a very affecting scene at the opening which discovers young Charalois attended by his friend Romont, waiting with a petition in his hand to be presented to the judges when they shall meet, praying the release of his dead father's body, which had been seized by his creditors and detained in their hands for debts he had incurred in the public service as field marshal of the armies of Burgundy. Massinger, to whose share this part of the tragedy devolved, has managed this pathetic introduction with consummate skill and great expression of nature. A noble youth in the last state of worldly distress, reduced to the humiliating yet pious office of soliciting an unfeeling and unfriendly judge to allow him to pay the solemn rites of burial to the remains of an illustrious father, who had fought his country's battles with glory and had sacrificed life and fortune in defense of an ungrateful state, impresses the spectator's mind with pity and respect, which are felt through every passage of the play. One thing in particular strikes me at the opening of the scene, which is the long silence that the poet has artfully imposed upon his principal character (Charalois) who stands in mute sorrow with his petition in his hand whilst his friend Romont and his advocate Charmi urge him to present himself to the judges and solicit them in person. The judges now make their entrance; they stop upon the stage; they offer him the fairest opportunity for tendering his petition and soliciting his suit. Charalois remains fixed and speechless; Romont, who is all eagerness in his cause, presses him again and again:

> Now, put on your spirits.
>
> .   .   .   .   .
>
> Now, sir, lose not this offered means; their looks,
> Fixed on you with a pitying earnestness,
> Invite you to demand their furtherance
> To your good purpose. [I, i]

The judges point him out to each other; they lament the misfortunes of his noble house; they observe:

> *Roch.*   It is young Charalois,
> Son to the marshal, from whom he inherits
> His fame and virtues only.
>   *Rom.* Ha! they name you.
>   *Du Croy.* His father died in prison two days since.
>   *Roch.* Yes, to the shame of this ungrateful state;
> That such a master in the art of war,
> So noble, and so highly meriting
> From this forgetful country, should, for want
> Of means to satisfy his creditors
> The sums he took up for the general good,
> Meet with an end so infamous.
>   *Rom.* Dare you ever
> Hope for like opportunity?

It is in vain; the opportunity passes off, and Charalois opens not his mouth nor even silently tenders his petition.

I have, upon a former occasion, both generally and particularly observed upon the effects of dramatic silence; the stage cannot afford a more beautiful and touching instance than this before us. To say it is not inferior to the silence of Hamlet upon his first appearance would be saying too little in its favor. I have no doubt but Massinger had this very case in his thoughts, and I honor him no less for the imitating than I should have done for striking out a silence so naturally and so delicately preserved. What could Charalois have uttered to give him that interest in the hearts of his spectators which their own conclusions during his affecting silence have already impressed? No sooner are the judges gone than the ardent Romont again breaks forth:

> This obstinate spleen,
> You think, becomes your sorrow, and sorts well
> With your black suits.

This is Hamlet himself, his inky cloak and customary suits of solemn black. The character of Charalois is thus fixed before he speaks; the poet's art has given the prejudice that is to bear him in our affection through all the succeeding events of the fable, and a striking contrast is established between the undiscerning fiery zeal of Romont and Charalois's fine sensibility and highborn dignity of soul.

A more methodical and regular dramatist would have stopped here, satisfied that the impression already made was fully sufficient for all the purposes of his plot, but Massinger, according to the busy spirit of the stage for which he wrote, is not alarmed by a throng of incidents, and proceeds to open the court and discuss the pleadings on the stage. The advocate Charmi, in a set harangue, moves the judges for dispensing with the rigor of the law in favor of creditors and for rescuing the marshal's corpse out of their clutches; he is browbeaten and silenced by the presiding judge, old Novall. The plea is then taken up by the impetuous Romont and urged with so much personal insolence that he is arrested on the spot, put in charge of the officers of the court, and taken to prison. This is a very striking mode of introducing the set oration of Charalois. A son, recounting the military achievements of a newly deceased father and imploring mercy from his creditors and the law towards his unburied remains, now claims the attention of the court, who had been hitherto unmoved by the feeble formality of a hired pleader and the turbulent passion of an enraged soldier. Charalois's argument takes a middle course between both, the pious feelings of a son tempered by the modest manners of a gentleman. The creditors however are implacable, the judge is hostile, and the law must take its course.

> *1st Cred.* It is the city's doctrine:
> We stand bound to maintain it.
>   *Charal.* Be constant in it;
> And since you are as merciless in your natures,
> As base and mercenary in your means
> By which you get your wealth, I will not urge
> The court to take away one scruple from
> The right of their laws, or wish one good thought
> In you, to mend their dispositions with.
> I know there is no music to your ears
> So pleasing as the groans of men in prison;
> And that the tears of widows, and the cries
> Of famished orphans, are the feasts that take you;
> That to be in your danger, with more care
> Should be avoided than infectious air,
> The loathed embraces of diseasèd women,
> A flatterer's poison, or the loss of honour.—
> Yet, rather than my father's reverend dust
> Shall want a place in that fair monument
> In which our noble ancestors lie entombed,
> Before the court I offer up myself
> A prisoner for it. Load me with those irons

That have worn out his life; in my best strength
I'll run to the encounter of cold, hunger,
And choose my dwelling where no sun dares enter,
So he may be released. [I, ii]

There was yet another incident which the poet's passion for business and spectacle induced him to avail himself of, viz., the funeral of the Marshal. This he displays on the stage with a train of captains and soldiers following the body of their general. Charalois and Romont, under the custody of their jailors, appear as chief mourners, and a party of creditors are concerned in the group.

After this solemnity is dispatched, the poet proceeds to develop the amiable generosity of old Rochfort, who, being touched with the gallant spirit of Romont and still more penetrated with the filial piety of young Charalois, delivers them both from imprisonment and distress by discharging the debts of the Marshal and dismissing the creditors. This also passes before the eyes of the spectators. Before Charalois has given full expression to his gratitude for this extraordinary benefaction, Rochfort follows it with a further act of bounty, which he introduces in the style of a request:

> *Roch.* Call in my daughter. Still I have a suit to you,
> Would you requite me.
>
> .   .   .   .   .
>
> This is my only child. [II, ii]

Beaumelle, Rochfort's daughter, is presented to Charalois; the scene is hurried on with a precipitation almost without example. Charalois asks the lady,

> Fair Beaumelle, can you love me?
> *Beaumel.* Yes, my lord.
> *Charal.* You need not question me if I can you;
> You are the fairest virgin in Dijon,
> And Rochfort is your father.

The match is agreed upon as soon as proposed, and Rochfort hastens away to prepare the celebration.

In this cluster of incidents, I must not fail to remark that the poet introduces young Novall upon the scene in the very moment when the short dialogue above quoted was passing. This Noval had before been exhibited as a suitor to Beaumelle, and his vain, frivolous character had been displayed in a very ridiculous and contemptible light; he is now again introduced to be a witness of his own disappointment, and his only observation upon it is, "What's this change?" Upon the exit of the father, however, he addresses himself to the lady, and her reply gives the alarming hint that makes discovery of the fatal turn which the plot is now about to take, for when Novall, turning aside to Beaumelle, by one word, "Mistress!" conveys the reproach of inconstancy, she replies,

> O, servant!—Virtue strengthen me!
> Thy presence blows round my affection's vane:—
> You will undo me, if you speak again.

Young Novall is left on the scene with certain followers and dependants, which hang upon his fortune, one of which, Pontalier by name, a man under deep obligations to him, yet of an honest nature, advises him to an honorable renunciation of all further hopes or attempts to avail himself of the affections of Beaumelle:

> Though you have saved my life,
> Rescued me often from my wants, I must not
> Wink at your follies: that will ruin you.
> You know my blunt way, and my love to truth—
> Forsake the pursuit of this lady's honour,
> Now you do see her made another man's.

This honorable advice is rejected with contempt. Novall, in whose mean bosom there does not seem a trace of virtue, avows a determined perseverance; and the poet, having in this hasty manner completed these unauspicious nuptials, closes the second act of his tragedy.

No. 78   [*The Fair Penitent*, II]

We have now expended two entire acts of *The Fatal Dowry* in advancing to that period in the fable at which the tragedy of *The Fair Penitent* opens. If the author of this tragedy thought it necessary to contract Massinger's plot and found one upon it of a more regular construction, I know not how he could do this any otherwise than by taking up the story at the point where we have now left it and throwing the antecedent matter into narration; and though these two prefatory acts are full of very affecting incidents, yet the pathos which properly appertains to the plot and conduces to the catastrophe of the tragedy does not in strictness take place before the event of the marriage. No critic will say that the pleadings before the judges, the interference of the creditors, the distresses of Charalois, or the funeral of the Marshal are necessary parts of the drama; at the same time no reader will deny (and neither could Rowe himself overlook) the effect of these incidents. He could not fail to forsee that he was to sacrifice very much of the interest of his fable when he was to throw that upon narration which his original had given in spectacle; and the loss was more enhanced by falling upon the hero of the drama. For who that compares Charalois, at the end of the second act of Massinger, with Rowe's Altamont at the opening scene of *The Fair Penitent,* can doubt which character has most interest with the spectators? We have seen the former in all the most amiable offices which filial piety could perform, enduring insults from his inveterate oppressors and voluntarily surrendering himself to a prison to ransom the dead body of his father from unrelenting creditors. Altamont presents himself before us in his wedding suit, in the splendor of fortune and at the summit of happiness; he greets us with a burst of exultation.

> Let this auspicious day be ever sacred,
> No mourning, no misfortunes happen on it;
> Let it be markt for triumphs and rejoycings;
> Let happy lovers ever make it holy,
> Chuse it to bless their hopes, and crown their wishes
> This happy day that gives me my Calista. [I, i]

The rest of the scene is employed by him and Horatio alternately in recounting the benefits conferred upon them by the generous Sciolto; and the very same incident of the seizure of his father's corpse by the creditors, and his redemption of it, is recited by Horatio.

> When his hard creditors,
> Urg'd and assisted by Lothario's father,
> (Foe to thy house, and rival of their greatness)
> By sentence of the cruel law, forbid
> His Venerable corps to rest in earth,
> Thou gav'st thy self a ransom for his bones;
> With piety uncommon, didst give up
> Thy hopeful youth to slaves who ne'er knew mercy.

It is not however within the reach of this, or any other description, to place Altamont in that interesting and amiable light as circumstances have already placed Charalois; the happy and exulting bridegroom may be an object of our congratulation, but the virtuous and suffering Charalois engages our pity, love and admiration. If Rowe would have his audience credit Altamont for that filial piety which marks the character he copied from, it was a small oversight to put the following expression into his mouth:

> Oh great Sciolto! Oh my more than father!

A closer attention to character would have reminded him that it was possible for Altamont to express his gratitude to Sciolto without setting him above a father to whose memory he had paid such devotion.

From this contraction of his plot, by the defalcation of so many pathetic incidents, it became impossible for the author of *The Fair Penitent* to make his Altamont the hero of his tragedy, and the leading part is taken from him by Horatio, and even by Lothario, throughout the drama. There are several other reasons which concur to sink Altamont upon the comparison with Charalois, the chief of which arises from the captivating colors in which Rowe has painted his libertine. On the contrary, Massinger gives a contemptible picture of his young Novall; he makes him not only vicious, but ridiculous; in foppery and impertinence he is the counterpart of Shakespeare's Osric; vainglorious, purse-proud, and overbearing amongst his dependents; a spiritless poltroon in his interview with Romont. "Lothario" (as Johnson observes) "with gaiety which cannot be hated and bravery which cannot be despised, retains too much of the spectator's kindness." His high spirit, brilliant qualities, and fine person are so described as to put us in danger of false impressions in his favor and to set the passions in opposition to the moral of the piece. I suspect that the gallantry of Lothario makes more advocates for Calista than she ought to have. There is another consideration which operates against Altamont, and it is an indelicacy in his character which the poet should have provided against. He marries Calista with the full persuasion of her being averse to the match; in his first meeting with Sciolto he says,

> Oh! could I hope there was one thought of Altamont,
> One kind remembrance in Calista's breast.

. . . . . .

I found her cold
As a dead lover's statue on his tomb;
A rising storm of passion shook her breast,
Her eyes a piteous show'r of tears let fall,
And then she sigh'd as if her heart were breaking.
With all the tend'rest eloquence of love
I beg'd to be a sharer in her grief;
But she, with looks averse, and eyes that froze me,
Sadly reply'd, her sorrows were her own,
Nor in a father's pow'r to dispose of.

I am aware that Sciolto attempts to parry these facts by an interpretation too gross and unbecoming for a father's character and only fit for the lips of a Lothario; but yet it is not in nature to suppose that Altamont could mistake such symptoms, and it fixes a meanness upon him which prevails against his character throughout the play. Nothing of this sort could be discovered by Massinger's bridegroom, for the ceremony was agreed upon and performed at the very first interview of the parties; Beaumelle gave a full and unreserved assent, and though her character suffers on the score of hypocrisy on that account, yet Charalois is saved by it. Less hypocrisy appears in Calista, but hers is the deeper guilt because she was already dishonored by Lothario, and Beaumelle's coquetry with Novall had not yet reached the length of criminality. Add to this that Altamont appears in the contemptible light of a suitor whom Calista had apprised of her aversion and to whom she had done a deliberate act of dishonor, though his person and character must have been long known to her. The case is far otherwise between Charalois and Beaumelle who never met before, and every care is taken by the poet to save his hero from such a deliberate injury as might convey contempt; with this view the marriage is precipitated; nothing is allowed to pass that might open the character of Charalois to Beaumelle. She is hurried into an assignation with Novall immediately upon her marriage; every artifice of seduction is employed by her confidante Bellaperte and Aymer the parasite of Novall to make this meeting criminal; she falls the victim of passion, and when detection brings her to a sense of her guilt, she makes this penitent and pathetic appeal to Charalois:

Oh my fate!
That never would consent that I should see
How worthy you were both of love and duty,

Before I lost you; and my misery made
The glass in which I now behold your virtue!
With justice, therefore, you may cut me off,
And from your memory wash the remembrance
That e'er I was; like to some vicious purpose,
Which, in your better judgment, you repent of,
And study to forget.

.   .   .   .   .

             Yet you shall find,
Tho' I was bold enough to be a strumpet,
I dare not yet live one. Let those fam'd matrons,
That are canoniz'd worthy of our sex,
Transcend me in their sanctity of life;
I yet will equal them in dying nobly,
Ambitious of no honour after life,
But that, when I am dead, you will forgive me. [IV, iv]

Compare this with the conduct of Calista, and then decide which frail fair one has the better title to the appellation of a penitent, and which drama conveys the better moral by its catastrophe.

There is indeed a grossness in the older poet which his more modern imitator has refined, but he has only sweetened the poison, not removed its venom; nay, by how much more palatable he has made it, so much more pernicious it is become in his tempting sparkling cup than in the coarse deterring dose of Massinger.

Rowe has no doubt greatly outstepped his original in the striking character of Lothario, who leaves Novall as far behind him as Charalois does Altamont. It is admitted then that Calista has as good a plea as any wanton could wish to urge for her criminality with Lothario, and the poet has not spared the ear of modesty in his exaggerated description of the guilty scene: every luxurious image that his inflamed imagination could crowd into the glowing rhapsody is there to be found, and the whole is recited in numbers so flowing and harmonious that they not only arrest the passions but the memory also, and, perhaps, have been and still can be as generally repeated as any passage in English poetry. Massinger, with less elegance, but not with less regard to decency, suffers the guilty act to pass within the course of his drama; the greater refinement of manners in Rowe's day did not allow of this, and he anticipated the incident; but when he revived the recollection of it by such a studied description, he plainly showed that it was not from moral principle

that he omitted it. And if he has presented his heroine to the spectators with more immediate delicacy during the compass of the play,
he has at the same time given her greater depravity of mind; her
manners may be more refined, but her principle is fouler than
Beaumelle's. Calista, who yielded to the gallant gay Lothario, "hot
with the Tuscan grape," might perhaps have disdained a lover who
addressed her in the holiday language which Novall uses to Beaumelle.

> Best day to Nature's curiosity,
> Star of Dijon, the lustre of all France!
> Perpetual spring dwell on thy rosy cheeks,
> Whose breath is perfume to our continent!
> See! Flora trimmed in her varieties.
>
> .   .   .   .   .
>
> No autumn, nor no age ever approach
> This heavenly piece; which Nature having wrought,
> She lost her needle, and did then despair
> Ever to work so lively and so fair! [II, ii]

The letter of Calista (which brings about the discovery by the poor
expedient of Lothario's dropping it and Horatio's finding it) has
not even the merit of being characteristically wicked, and is both
in its matter and mode below tragedy. It is Lothario's cruelty has
determined her to yield a perfect obedience to her father and give
her hand to Altamont, in spite of her weakness for the false Lothario.
If the lady had given her "perfect obedience" its true denomination, she had called it a most dishonorable compliance; and if we
may take Lothario's word (who seems full correct enough in describing facts and particulars), she had not much cause to complain of
his being false; for he tells Rossano:

> I lik'd her, wou'd have marry'd her
> But that it pleas'd her father to refuse me,
> To make this honourable fool her husband. [I, i]

It appears by this that Lothario had not been *false* to her in the
article of marriage, though he might have been *cruel* to her on the
score of passion, which indeed is confessed on his part with as much
cold indifference as the most barefaced avowal could express. But
to return to the letter. She proceeds to tell him "that she could
almost wish she had that heart, and that honour to bestow with it,
which he has robbed her of." But lest this half wish should startle
him, she adds "But oh! I fear, could I retrieve them, I should again

be undone by the too faithless, yet too lovely Lothario." This must be owned as full a reason as she could give why she should only "almost wish" for her lost honor when she would make such a use of it if she had it again at her disposal. And yet the very next paragraph throws everything into contradiction, for she tells him this is the last weakness of her pen, and tomorrow shall be the last in which she will indulge her eyes. If she could keep to that resolution, I must think the recovery of her innocence would have been worth a whole wish and many a wish; unless we are to suppose she was so devoted to guilt that she could take delight in reflecting upon it. This is a state of depravity which human nature hardly ever attains and seems peculiar to Calista. She now grows very humble, and concludes in a style well suited to her humility, "Lucilla shall conduct you, if you are kind enough to let me see you; it shall be the last trouble you shall meet from—The lost Calista."

It was very ill done of Horatio's curiosity to read this letter, and I must ever regret that he has so unhandsomely exposed a lady's private correspondence to the world.

No. 79   [*The Fair Penitent*, III]

Though the part which Horatio takes in the business of the drama is exactly that which falls to the share of Romont in the *Fatal Dowry*, yet their characters are of a very different cast; for as Rowe had bestowed the fire and impetuosity of Romont upon his Lothario, it was a very judicious opposition to contrast it with the cool deliberate courage of the sententious Horatio, the friend and brother-in-law of Altamont.

When Horatio has read Calista's letter, which Lothario had dropped (an accident which more frequently happens to gentlemen in comedies than in tragedies) he falls into a very long meditation and closes it with putting this question to himself:

> What if I give this paper to her father?
> It follows that his justice dooms her dead,
> And breaks his heart with sorrow; hard return
> For all the good his hand has heap'd on us:
> Hold, let me take a moment's thought. [I, i]

At this moment he is interrupted in his reflections by the presence of Lavinia, whose tender solicitude fills up the remaining part of the dialogue and concludes the act without any decisive resolution on the part of Horatio, an incident well contrived and introduced with much dramatic skill and effect. Though pressed by his wife to disclose the cause of his uneasiness, he does not impart to her the fatal discovery he has made; this also is well in character. Upon his next entrance he has withdrawn himself from the company and, being alone, resumes his meditation.

> What if, while all are here intent on revelling,
> I privately went forth, and sought Lothario?
> This letter may be forg'd; perhaps the wantonness
> Of his vain youth, to stain a lady's fame;
> Perhaps his malice, to disturb my friend.
> Oh no! my heart forebodes it must be true.
> Methought ev'n now I mark'd the starts of guilt
> That shook her soul; tho' damn'd dissimulation
> Skreen'd her dark thoughts, and set to publick view
> A specious face of innocence and beauty. [II, i]

This soliloquy is succeeded by the much-admired and striking scene between him and Lothario; rigid criticism might wish to abridge some of the sententious declamatory speeches of Horatio and shorten the dialogue to quicken the effect; but the moral sentiment and harmonious versification are much too charming to be treated as intruders, and the author has also struck upon a natural expedient for prolonging the dialogue without any violence to probability by the interposition of Rossano, who acts as a mediator between the hostile parties. This interposition is further necessary to prevent a decisive rencounter for which the fable is not ripe; neither would it be proper for Horatio to anticipate that revenge which is reserved for Altamont. The altercation therefore closes with a challenge from Lothario.

> West of the town a mile, among the rocks,
> Two hours e'er noon tomorrow I expect thee,
> Thy single hand to mind. [II, ii]

The place of meeting is not well ascertained, and the time is too long deferred for strict probability; there are, however, certain things in all dramas which must not be too rigidly insisted upon, and provided no extraordinary violence is done to reason and common sense, the candid critic ought to let them pass. This I take to be a case in point, and though Horatio's cool courage and ready presence of mind are not just the qualities to reconcile us to such an oversight, yet I see no reason to be severe upon the incident, which is followed by his immediate recollection:

> Two hours e'er noon tomorrow! Hah, e'er that
> He sees Calista! oh unthinking fool—
> What if I urg'd her with the crime and danger?
> If any spark from heav'n remain unquench'd
> Within her breast, my breath perhaps may wake it.
> Cou'd I but prosper there, I wou'd not doubt
> My combat with that loud, vain-glorious boaster.

Whether this be a measure altogether in character with a man of Horatio's good sense and discretion, I must own is matter of doubt with me. I think he appears fully satisfied of her actual criminality; and in that case it would be more natural for him to lay his measures for intercepting Lothario and preventing the assignation than to try his rhetoric in the present crisis upon the agitated mind of Calista. As it has justly occurred to him that he has been overreached by Lothario in the postponement of the duel, the measure I suggest would naturally tend to hasten that rencounter. Now though the business of the drama may require an explanation between Horatio and Calista whereupon to ground an occasion for his interesting quarrel with Altamont, yet I do not see any necessity to make that a premeditated explanation nor to sacrifice character by a measure that is inconsistent with the better judgment of Horatio. The poet, however, has decreed it otherwise, and a deliberate interview with Calista and Horatio accordingly takes place. This, although introduced with a solemn invocation on his part, is very clumsily conducted.

> Teach me, some pow'r, that happy art of speech,
> To dress my purpose up in gracious words,
> Such as may softly steal upon her soul,
> And never waken the tempestuous passions. [III, i]

Who can expect, after this preparation, to hear Horatio thus break his secret to Calista?

> Lothario and Calista!—Thus they join
> Two names, which heav'n decreed shou'd never meet;
> Hence have the talkers of this populous city

> A shameful tale to tell for publick sport,
> Of an unhappy beauty, a false fair one,
> Who plighted to a noble youth her faith,
> When she had giv'n her honour to a wretch.

This I hold to be totally out of nature; first, because it is a palpable departure from his resolution to use "gracious words"; next, because it has a certain tendency to produce rage and not repentance; and thirdly, because it is founded in exaggeration and falsehood; for how is he warranted to say that the story is the public talk and sport of the city? If it were so, what can his interference avail? Why seek this interview?

> Why come to tell her how she might be happy?
> To soothe the secret anguish of her soul?
> To comfort that fair mourner, that forlorn one,
> And teach her steps to know the paths of peace?

No judge of nature will think he takes the means to lead her into the "paths of peace," by hurrying her to the very brink of desperation. I need not enlarge upon this observation and shall therefore only remark that the scene breaks up, as might be expected, with the following proof of her penitence and his success in persuasion.

> Henceforth, thou officious fool,
> Meddle no more, nor dare ev'n on thy life,
> To breathe an accent that may touch my virtue:
> I am my self the guardian of my honour,
> And wo' not bear so insolent a monitor.

Let us now enquire how Romont (the Horatio of Massinger) conducts this incident, a character from whom less discretion is to be expected than from his philosophical successor. Romont himself discovers Beaumelle and Novall engaged in the most wanton familiarities, and with a warmth suitable to his zeal breaks up the amorous conference by driving Novall off the scene with ineffable contempt; he then applies himself to the lady, and with a very natural and manly spirit says,

> I respect you
> Not for yourself, but in remembrance of
> Who is your father, and whose wife you now are. [III, i]

She replies to him with contempt and ridicule; he resumes the same characteristic strain he set out with, and proceeds:

              My intents,
Madam, deserve not this; nor do I stay
To be the whetstone of your wit: preserve it
To spend on such as know how to admire
Such coloured stuff. In me, there now speaks to you
As true a friend and servant to your honour,
And one that will with as much hazard guard it,
As ever man did goodness. But then, lady,
You must endeavour, not alone to be,
But to appear worthy such love and service.

We have just now heard Horatio reproach Calista with the reports
that were circulated against her reputation; let us compare it with
what Romont says upon the same subject:

              But yet be careful!
Detraction's a bold monster, and fears not
To wound the fame of princes, if it find
But any blemish in their lives to work on.
But I'll be plainer with you: had the people
Been learnt to speak but what even now I saw,
Their malice out of that would raise an engine
To overthrow your honour. In my sight,
With yonder painted fool I frighted from you,
You used familiarity beyond
A modest entertainment; you embraced him
With too much ardour for a stranger, and
Met him with kisses neither chaste nor comely.
But learn you to forget him, as I will
Your bounties to him; you will find it safer
Rather to be uncourtly than immodest.

What avails it to attempt drawing a comparison between this conduct and that of Horatio's, where no comparison is to be made? I
leave it to the reader and decline a task at once so unnecessary and
ungrateful.

When Romont finds no impression is to be made upon Beaumelle,
he meets her father and immediately falls into the same reflection
that Horatio had struck upon.

              Her father?—ha!
How if I break this to him? sure it cannot
Meet with an ill construction; his wisdom,
Made powerful by the authority of a father,

Will warrant and give privilege to his counsels.
It shall be so.

If this step needs excuse, the reader will consider that it is a step of prevention. The experiment however fails, and he is rebuffed with some asperity by Rochfort; this draws on a scene between him and Charalois, which, as it is too long to transcribe, so it is throughout too excellent to extract any part from it. I can only express my surprise that the author of *The Fair Penitent,* with this scene before him, could conduct his interview between Altamont and Horatio upon a plan so widely different and so much inferior. I must suppose he thought it a strong incident to make Altamont give a blow to his friend, else he might have seen an interview carried on with infinitely more spirit, both of language and character, between Charalois and Romont in circumstances exactly similar, where no such violence was committed or even meditated. Was it because Pierre had given a blow to Jaffier [3] that Altamont was to repeat the like indignity to Horatio, for a woman of whose aversion he had proofs not to be mistaken? Charalois is a character at least as high and irritable as Altamont, and Romont is out of all comparison more rough and plain-spoken than Horatio. Charalois might be deceived into an opinion of Beaumelle's affection for him; Altamont could not deceive himself into such a notion, and the lady had testified her dislike of him in the strongest terms, accompanied with symptoms which he himself had described as indicating some rooted and concealed affliction. Could any solution be more natural than what Horatio gives? Novall was a rival so contemptible that Charalois could not with any degree of probability consider him as an object of his jealousy; it would have been a degradation of his character had he yielded to such a suspicion. Lothario, on the contrary, was of all men living the most to be apprehended by a husband, let his confidence or vanity be ever so great. Rowe, in his attempt to surprise, has sacrificed nature and the truth of character for stage effect; Massinger, by preserving both nature and character, has conducted his friends through an angry altercation with infinitely more spirit, more pathos and more dramatic effect, and yet dismissed them with the following animated and affecting speech from Charalois to his friend:

> Thou art not my friend,
> Or being so, thou art mad; I must not buy
> Thy friendship at this rate. Had I just cause,

> Thou know'st I durst pursue such injury
> Through fire, air, water, earth, nay, were they all
> Shuffled again to chaos; but there's none.
> Thy skill, Romont, consists in camps, not courts.
> Farewell, uncivil man! let's meet no more:
> Here our long web of friendship I untwist.
> Shall I go whine, walk pale, and lock my wife
> For nothing, from her birth's free liberty,
> That open'd mine to me? yes, if I do,
> The name of cuckold then dog me with scorn.
> I am a Frenchman, no Italian born.

It is plain that Altamont, at least, was an exception to this remark upon Italian husbands. I shall pursue this comparison no further, nor offer any other remark upon the incident of the blow given by Altamont except with regard to Horatio's conduct upon receiving it; he draws his sword, and immediately suspends resentment upon the following motive:

> Yet hold! By heav'n, his father's in his face!
> Spight of my wrongs, my heart runs o'er with tenderness,
> And I cou'd rather die myself than hurt him. [III, i]

We must suppose it was the martial attitude that Altamont had put himself into which brought the resemblance of his father so strongly to the observation of Horatio, otherwise it was a very unnatural moment to recollect it in, when he had just received the deepest insult one man can give to another. It is however worth a remark that this father of Altamont should act on both sides and yet miscarry in his mediation; for it is but a few passages before that Altamont says to Horatio:

> Thou wert my father's friend, he lov'd thee well;
> A kind of venerable mark of him
> Hangs round thee, and protects thee from my vengeance.
> I cannot, dare not, lift my sword against thee.

What this "mark" was is left to conjecture; but it is plain it was as seasonable for Horatio's rescue at this moment as it was for Altamont a few moments after, who had certainly overlooked it when he struck the very friend against whom he could not, dared not, "lift his sword."

When Lavinia's entrance has parted Altamont and Horatio, her husband complains to her of the ingratitude with which he has been treated, and says,

He who was all to me, child! brother! friend!
With barb'rous, bloody malice sought my life.

These are very extraordinary terms for a man like Horatio to use, and seem to convey a charge very unfit for him to make and of a very different nature from the hasty insult he had received; in fact, it appears as if the blow had totally reversed his character, for the resolution he takes in consequence of this personal affront is just such a one as would be only taken by the man who dared not to resent it.

From Genoa, from falsehood and inconstancy,
To some more honest distant clime we'll go,
Nor will I be beholding to my country
For ought but thee, the partner of my flight.

That Horatio's heroism did not consist in the ready forgiveness of injuries is evident from the obstinate sullenness with which he rejects the penitent apologies of Altamont in the further progress of the play; I am at a loss therefore to know what color the poet meant to give his character by disposing him to quit his country with this insult unatoned for and the additional stigma upon him of running away from his appointment with Lothario for the next morning "amongst the rocks." Had he meant to bring him off upon the repugnance he felt of resenting any injury against the son of a father whose image was so visible in his face "that his heart ran o'er with fondness in spite of his wrongs, and he could rather die than hurt him," surely that image would have interceded no less powerfully for him when, penetrated with remorse, he intercedes for pity and forgiveness and even faints at his feet with agony at his unrelenting obduracy. It would be unfair to suppose he was more like his father when he had dealt him an insulting blow than when he was atoning for an injury by the most ample satisfaction and submission.

This is the light in which the conduct of Horatio strikes me; if I am wrong, I owe an atonement to the manes of an elegant poet, which, upon conviction of my error, I will study to pay in the fullest manner I am able.

It now remains only to say a few words upon the catastrophe, in which the author varies from his original by making Calista destroy herself with a dagger put into her hand for that purpose by her father. If I am to moralize upon this proceeding of Sciolto, I know full well the incident cannot bear up against it; a Roman father would stand the discussion better than a Christian one; and I also know that the most natural expedient is unluckily a most undramatic one; yet the poet did not totally overlook it, for he makes Sciolto's first thought turn upon a convent, if I rightly understand the following passage:

> Hence from my sight! thy father cannot bear thee;
> Fly with thy infamy to some dark cell,
> Where on the confines of eternal night,
> Mourning, misfortune, cares and anguish dwell;
> Where ugly shame hides her opprobrious head,
> And death and hell detested rule maintain;
> There howl out the remainder of thy life,
> And wish thy name may be no more remember'd. [IV, i]

Whilst I am transcribing these lines a doubt strikes me that I have misinterpreted them, and yet Calista's answer seems to point to the meaning I had suggested; perhaps, however, they are mere ravings in fine numbers without any determinate idea. Whatever they may be, it is clear they do not go to the length of death. He tells Altamont, as soon as she is departed:

> I wo' not kill her;
> Yet by the ruin she has brought upon us,
> The common infamy that brands us both,
> She sha' not 'scape.

He seems in this moment to have formed the resolution which he afterwards puts into execution; he prompts her to self-murder and arms her for the act. This may save the spectators a sight too shocking to behold, but does it convey less horror to the heart than if he had put her to death with his own hand? A father killing his child for incontinence with the man whom he had not permitted to marry her when he solicited his consent, is an act too monstrous to reflect upon. Is that father less a monster who deliberately and after full reflection puts a dagger into her hand and bids her commit self-murder? I should humbly conceive the latter act a degree in guilt beyond the former, especially when I hear that father coolly demanding of his victim if she has reflected upon what may happen after death:

> Hast thou consider'd what may happen after it?
> How thy account may stand, and what to answer? [V, i]

A parent surely would turn that question upon his own heart before he precipitated his unprepared child to so awful and uncertain an account. Rage and instant revenge may find some plea; sudden passion may transport even a father to lift his hand against his own offspring; but this act of Sciolto has no shelter but in heathen authority.

> 'Tis justly thought, and worthy of that spirit,
> That dwelt in ancient Latian breasts, when Rome
> Was mistress of the world.

Did ever poetry beguile a man into such an allusion? And to what does that piece of information tend, "that Rome was mistress of the world"? If this is human nature, it would almost tempt one to reply in Sciolto's own words,

> I cou'd curse nature.

But it is no more like nature than the following sentiments of Calista are like the sentiments of a penitent or a Christian.

> That I must die! it is my only comfort;
> Death is the privilege of human nature,
> And life without it were not worth our taking.

And again,

> Yet heav'n, who knows our weak, imperfect natures,
> How blind with passions, and how prone to evil,
> Makes not too strict enquiry for offences,
> But is aton'd by penitence and pray'r.
> Cheap recompence! here 'twould not be receiv'd,
> Nothing but blood can make the expiation.

Such is the catastrophe of Rowe's *Fair Penitent,* such is the representation he gives us of human nature, and such the moral of his tragedy.

I shall conclude with an extract or two from the catastrophe of *The Fatal Dowry;* and first, for the "penitence" of Beaumelle, I shall select only the following speech, addressed to her husband:

> I dare not move you
> To hear me speak. I know my fault is far
> Beyond qualification or excuse;
> That 'tis not fit for me to hope, or you
> To think of mercy; only I presume

    To entreat you would be pleased to look upon
    My sorrow for it, and believe these tears
    Are the true children of my grief, and not
    A woman's cunning. [IV, iv]

I need not point out the contrast between this and the quotations
from Calista. It will require a longer extract to bring the conduct of
Rochfort into comparison with that of Sciolto. The reader will observe that Novall's dead body is now on the scene; Charalois, Beaumelle, and Rochfort, her father, are present. The charge of adultery
is urged by Charalois, and appeal is made to the justice of Rochfort
in the case.

    Rochfort. What answer makes the prisoner?
    Beaumelle. I confess
    The fact I'm charg'd with, and yield myself
    Most miserably guilty.
    Rochfort. Heaven take mercy
    Upon your soul, then! It must leave your body.

            .   .   .   .

    Since that the politic law provides that servants,
    To whose care we commit our goods, shall die
    If they abuse our trust, what can you look for,
    To whose charge this most hopeful lord gave up
    All he received from his brave ancestors,
    All he could leave to his posterity?
    His honour, wicked woman! in whose safety
    All his life's joys and comforts were locked up,
    Which thy lust, a thief, hath now stolen from him;
    And therefore—
    Charalois. Stay, just judge:—may not what's lost
    By her one fault (for I am charitable,
    And charge her not with many) be forgotten
    In her fair life hereafter?
    Rochfort. Never, sir.
    The wrong that's done to the chaste married bed,
    Repentant tears can never expiate;
    And be assured, to pardon such a sin,
    Is an offence as great as to commit it.

In consequence of this, the husband strikes her dead before her father's eyes. The act indeed is horrid; even tragedy shrinks from
it, and nature with a father's voice instantly cries out "Is she dead

then?—and you have kill'd her?" Charalois avows it and pleads his
sentence for the deed; the revolting, agonized parent breaks forth
into one of the most pathetic, natural and expressive lamentations
that the English drama can produce.

> But I pronounced it
> As a judge only, and a friend to justice;
> And, zealous in defence of your wronged honour,
> Broke all the ties of nature, and cast off
> The love and soft affection of a father.
> I, in your cause, put on a scarlet robe
> Of red-dyed cruelty; but in return
> You have advanced for me no flag of mercy.
> I looked on you as a wronged husband; but
> You closed your eyes against me as a father.
> O Beaumelle! my daughter!
>   *Charalois.* This is madness.
>   *Rochfort.* Keep from me!—Could not one good
>   thought rise up
> To tell you that she was my age's comfort,
> Begot by a weak man, and born a woman,
> And could not, therefore, but partake of frailty?
> Or wherefore did not thankfulness step forth
> To urge my many merits, which I may
> Object unto you, since you prove ungrateful?
> Flint-hearted Charalois!
>   *Charalois.* Nature does prevail
> Above your virture.

What conclusions can I draw from these comparative examples
which every reader would not anticipate? Is there a man who has
any feeling for real nature, dramatic character, moral sentiment,
tragic pathos, or nervous diction who can hesitate, even for a moment, where to bestow the palm?

HENRY MACKENZIE ✍

The Lounger (1785-1787)

No. 68, May 20, 1786   [Falstaff, I]

That "poet and creator are the same" is equally allowed in criticism as in etymology, and that without the powers of invention and imagination nothing great or highly delightful in poetry can be achieved.

I have often thought that the same thing holds in some measure with regard to the reader as well as the writer of poetry. Without somewhat of a congenial imagination in the former the works of the latter will afford a very inferior degree of pleasure. The mind of him who reads should be able to imagine what the productive fancy of the poet creates and presents to his view, to look on the world of fancy set before him with a native's eye and to hear its language with a native's ear, to acknowledge its manners, to feel its passions, and to trace with somewhat of an instinctive glance those characters with which the poet has peopled it.

If in the perusal of any poet this is required, Shakespeare of all poets seems to claim it the most. Of all poets Shakespeare appears to have possessed a fancy the most prolific, an imagination the most luxuriantly fertile. In this particular he has been frequently compared to Homer, though those who have drawn the parallel have done it, I know not why, with a sort of distrust of their assertion. Did we not look at the Greek with that reverential awe which his antiquity impresses, I think we might venture to affirm that in this respect the other is more than his equal. In invention of incident, in diversity of character, in assemblage of images, we can scarcely indeed conceive Homer to be surpassed, but in the mere creation of fancy, I can discover nothing in the *Iliad* that equals *The Tempest* or the *Macbeth* of Shakespeare. The machinery of Homer is indeed stupendous, but of that machinery the materials were known, or though it should be allowed that he added something to the mythology he found, yet still the language and the manners of his deities are merely the language and the manners of men. Of Shakespeare, the machinery may be said to be produced as well as combined by himself. Some of the beings of whom it is composed neither tradition nor romance afforded him, and of those whom he borrowed thence he invented the language and the manners, language and manners peculiar to themselves, for which he could draw no analogy from mankind. Though formed by fancy, however, his personages are true to nature, and a reader of that pregnant imagination which I have mentioned above can immediately decide on the justness of his conceptions, as he who beholds the masterly expression of certain portraits pronounces with confidence on their likeness though unacquainted with the persons from whom they were drawn.

But it is not only in those untried regions of magic or of witchery that the creative power of Shakespeare has exerted itself. By a very singular felicity of invention he has produced in the beaten field of ordinary life characters of such perfect originality that we look on them with no less wonder at his invention than on those preternatural beings which "are not of this earth," and yet they speak a language so purely that of common society that we have but to step abroad into the world to hear every expression of which it is composed. Of this sort is the character of Falstaff.

On the subject of this character I was lately discoursing with a friend who is very much endowed with that critical imagination of which I have suggested the use in the beginning of this paper. The general import of his observations may form neither a useless nor unamusing field for speculation to my readers.

Though the character of Falstaff, said my friend, is of so striking a kind as to engross almost the whole attention of the audience in the representation of the play in which it is first introduced, yet it was probably only a secondary and incidental object with Shakespeare in composing that play. He was writing a series of historical dramas on the most remarkable events of the English history from the time of King John downwards. When he arrived at the reign of Henry IV, the dissipated youth and extravagant pranks of the Prince of Wales could not fail to excite his attention as affording at once a source of moral reflection in the serious department, and a fund of infinite humor in the comic part of the drama. In providing him with associates for his hours of folly and of riot he probably borrowed, as was his custom, from some old play, interlude, or story, the names and incidents which he has used in the first part of *Henry IV*. Oldcastle, we know, was the name of a character in such a play, inserted there, it is probable (in those days of the church's omnipotence in every department of writing), in odium of Sir John Oldcastle, chief of the Lollards, though Shakespeare afterwards, in a Protestant reign, changed it to Falstaff. This leader of the gang which the wanton extravagance of the Prince was to cherish and protect, it was necessary to endow with qualities sufficient to make the young Henry, in his society,

> daff the world aside,
> And bid it pass. (1 *Henry* IV, iv, i)

Shakespeare therefore has endowed him with infinite wit and humor as well as an admirable degree of sagacity and acuteness in observing the characters of men, but has joined those qualities with a grossness of mind which his youthful master could not but see, nor seeing but despise. With talents less conspicuous Falstaff could not have attracted Henry, with profligacy less gross and less contemptible he would have attached him too much. Falstaff's was just "that unyoked humour" of idleness which the Prince could "a while uphold" and then cast off forever. The audience to which this strange compound was to be exhibited were to be in the same predicament with the Prince, to laugh and to admire while they despised; to feel the power of his humor, the attraction of his wit, the justice of his reflections, while their contempt and their hatred attended the lowness of his manners, the grossness of his pleasures, and the unworthiness of his vice.

Falstaff is truly and literally *ex Epicuri grege porcus,* placed here within the pale of this world to fatten at his leisure, neither disturbed by feeling nor restrained by virtue. He is not, however, positively much a villain, though he never starts aside in the pursuit of interest or of pleasure when knavery comes in his way. We feel contempt, therefore, and not indignation, at his crimes, which rather promotes than hinders our enjoying the ridicule of the situation and the admirable wit with which he expresses himself in it. As a man of this world, he is endowed with the most superior degree of good sense and discernment of character; his conceptions, equally acute and just, he delivers with the expression of a clear and vigorous understanding; and we see that he thinks like a wise man, even when he is not at the pains to talk wisely.

Perhaps, indeed, there is no quality more conspicuous throughout the writings of Shakespeare than that of good sense, that intuitive sagacity with which he looks on the manners, the characters, and the pursuits of mankind. The bursts of passion, the strokes of nature, the sublimity of his terrors, and the wonderful creation of his fancy are those excellencies which strike spectators the most and are therefore most commonly enlarged on, but to an attentive peruser of his writings this acute perception and accurate discernment of ordinary character and conduct, that skill, if I may so express it, with which he delineates the plan of common life, will, I think, appear no less striking, and perhaps rather more wonderful, more wonderful because we cannot so easily conceive that power of genius by which it tells us what actually exists, though it has never seen it, than that by which it creates what never existed. This power, when we read the works and consider the situation of Shakespeare, we shall allow him in a most extraordinary degree. The delineation of manners found in the Greek tragedians is excellent and just, but it consists chiefly of those general maxims which the wisdom of the schools might inculcate, which a borrowed experience might teach. That of Shakespeare marks the knowledge of intimacy with mankind. It reaches the elevation of the great and penetrates the obscurity of the low, detects the cunning and overtakes the bold, in short, presents that abstract of life in all its modes, and indeed in every time, which everyone without experience must believe, and everyone with experience must know to be true.

With this sagacity and penetration into the characters and motives of mankind, Shakespeare has invested Falstaff in a remarkable degree; he never utters it, however, out of character, or at a season where it might better be spared. Indeed, his good sense is rather in his thoughts than in his speech, for so we may call those soliloquies in which he generally utters it. He knew what coin was most current with those he dealt with and fashioned his discourse according to the disposition of his hearers; and he sometimes lends himself to the ridicule of his companions when he has a chance of getting any interest on the loan.

But we oftener laugh with than at him, for his humor is infinite and his wit admirable. This quality, however, still partakes in him of that Epicurean grossness which I have remarked to be the ruling characteristic of his disposition. He has neither the vanity of a wit, nor the singularity of a humorist, but indulges both talents like any other natural propensity, without exertion of mind or warmth of enjoyment. A late excellent actor, whose loss the stage will long regret, used to represent the character of Falstaff in a manner different from what had been uniformly adopted from the time of Quin downwards.[1] He exchanged the comic gravity of the old school for those bursts of laughter in which sympathetic audiences have so often accompanied him. From accompanying him it was indeed impossible to refrain, yet, though the execution was masterly, I cannot agree in that idea of the character. He who laughs is a man of feeling in merriment. Falstaff was of a very different constitution. He turned wit, as he says he did "disease, into commodity." "Oh, it is much that a lie with a slight oath and a jest with a sad brow will do with a fellow that never had the ache in his shoulders!" [1 *Henry* IV, I, ii, 48]

No. 69, May 27, 1786 [Falstaff, II]

To a man of pleasure of such a constitution as Falstaff, temper and good humor were necessarily consequent. We find him therefore but once, I think, angry, and then not provoked beyond measure. He conducts himself with equal moderation towards others; his wit lightens, but does not burn; and he is not more inoffensive when the joker, than unoffended when joked upon. "I am not only witty myself, but the cause that wit is in other men." In the evenness of his humor he bears himself thus (to use his own expression), and takes in the points of all assailants without being hurt. The language of contempt, of rebuke, or of conviction neither puts him out of liking with himself or with others. None of his passions rise beyond this control of reason, of self-interest, or of indulgence.

Queen Elizabeth, with a curiosity natural to a woman, desired Shakespeare to exhibit Falstaff as a lover. He obeyed her, and wrote *The Merry Wives of Windsor;* but Falstaff's love is only factor for his interest, and he wishes to make his mistresses his Exchequer, his East and West Indies, to both of which he will trade.

Though I will not go so far as a paradoxical critic[2] has done and ascribe valor to Falstaff, yet if his cowardice is fairly examined, it will be found to be not so much a weakness as a principle. In his very cowardice there is much of the sagacity I have remarked in him; he has the sense of danger, but not the discomposure of fear. His presence of mind saves him from the sword of Douglas where the danger was real, but he shows no sort of dread of the sheriff's visit, when he knew the Prince's company would probably bear him out; when Bardolph runs in frightened and tells that the sheriff, with a most monstrous watch, is at the door, "Out, you rogue!" answers he, "play out the play; I have much to say in behalf of that Falstaff." Falstaff's cowardice is only proportionate to the danger, and so would every wise man's be, did not other feelings make him valiant.

Such feelings it is the very characteristic of Falstaff to want. The dread of disgrace, the sense of honor, and the love of fame he neither feels, nor pretends to feel:

> Like the fat weed
> That roots itself at ease on Lethe's wharf,
>
> [*Hamlet,* I, v, 33]

he is contented to repose on that earthy corner of sensual indulgence in which his fate has placed him, and enjoys the pleasures of the moment without once regarding those finer objects of delight which the children of fancy and of feeling so warmly pursue.

The greatest refinement of morals, as well as of mind, is produced by the culture and exercise of the imagination, which derives, or is taught to derive, its objects of pursuit and its motives of action, not from the senses merely, but from future considerations which fancy anticipates and realizes. Of this, either as the prompter or the restraint of conduct, Falstaff is utterly devoid, yet his imagination is wonderfully quick and creative in the pictures of humor and the associations of wit. But the pregnancy of his wit, according to his own phrase, "is made a tapster"; and his fancy, how vivid soever, still subjects itself to the grossness of those sensual conceptions which are familiar to his mind. We are astonished at that art by which Shakespeare leads the powers of genius, imagination, and wisdom in captivity to this son of earth; it is as if, transported into the enchanted island in *The Tempest,* we saw the rebellion of Caliban successful, and the airy spirits of Prospero ministering to the brutality of his slave.

Hence, perhaps, may be derived great part of that infinite amusement which succeeding audiences have always found from the representation of Falstaff. We have not only the enjoyment of those combinations, and of that contrast to which philosophers have ascribed the pleasure we derive from wit in general, but we have that singular combination and contrast which the gross, the sensual, and the brutish mind of Falstaff exhibits when joined and compared with that admirable power of invention, of wit, and of humor which his conversation perpetually displays.

In the immortal work of Cervantes we find a character with a remarkable mixture of wisdom and absurdity, which in one page excites our highest ridicule and in the next is entitled to our highest respect. Don Quixote, like Falstaff, is endowed with excellent discernment, sagacity, and genius; but his good sense holds fief of his diseased imagination, of his overruling madness for the achievements of knight-errantry, for heroic valor and heroic love. The ridicule in the character of Don Quixote consists in raising low and vulgar incidents, through the medium of his disordered fancy, to a rank of importance, dignity, and solemnity, to which in their nature they are the most opposite that can be imagined. With Falstaff it is nearly the reverse; the ridicule is produced by subjecting wisdom, honor, and other the most grave and dignified principles, to the control of grossness, buffoonery, and folly. It is like the pastime of a family masquerade, where laughter is equally excited by dressing clowns as gentlemen, or gentlemen as clowns. In Falstaff, the heroic attributes of our nature are made to wear the garb of meanness and absurdity. In *Don Quixote,* the common and the servile are clothed in the dresses of the dignified and the majestic, while to heighten the ridicule, Sancho, in the half-deceived simplicity and half discerning shrewdness of his character, is every now and then employed to pull off the mask.

If you would not think me whimsical in the parallel, continued my friend, I should say that Shakespeare has drawn, in one of his immediately subsequent plays, a tragic character very much resembling the comic one of Falstaff, I mean that of Richard III. Both are men of the world, both possess that sagacity and understanding which is fitted for its purposes, both despise those refined feelings, those motives of delicacy, those restraints of virtue which might obstruct the course they have marked out for themselves. The hypocrisy of both costs them nothing, and they never feel that detection of it to themselves which rankles in the conscience of less determined hypocrites. Both use the weaknesses of others as skillful players at a game do the ignorance of their opponents; they enjoy the advantage not only without self-reproach, but with the pride of superiority. Richard indeed aspires to the crown of England because Richard is wicked and ambitious; Falstaff is contented with a thousand pounds of Justice Shallow's because he is only luxurious and dissipated. Richard courts Lady Anne and the Princess Elizabeth for his purposes; Falstaff makes love to Mrs. Ford and Mrs. Page for his. Richard is witty like Falstaff, and talks of his own figure with the same sarcastic indifference. Indeed, so much does Richard in the higher walk of villainy resemble Falstaff in the lower region of roguery and dissipation that it were not difficult to show in the dialogue of the two characters, however dissimilar in situation, many passages and expressions in a style of remarkable resemblance.

Of feeling, and even of passion, both characters are very little susceptible: as Falstaff is the knave and the sensualist, so Richard is the villain of principle. Shakespeare has drawn one of passion in the person of Macbeth. Macbeth produces horror, fear, and sometimes pity; Richard, detestation and abhorrence only. The first he has led amidst the gloom of sublimity, has shown agitated by various and wavering emotions; he is sometimes more sanguinary than Richard because he is not insensible of the weakness or the passion of revenge, whereas the cruelty of Richard is only proportionate to the object of his ambition (as the cowardice of Falstaff is proportionate to the object of his fear); but the bloody and revengeful Macbeth is yet susceptible of compassion and subject to remorse. In contemplating Macbeth, we often regret the perversion of his nature, and even when the justice of Heaven overtakes him, we almost forget our hatred at his enormities in our pity for his misfortunes. Richard, Shakespeare has placed amidst the tangled paths of party and ambition, has represented cunning and fierce from his birth, untouched by the sense of humanity, hardly subject to remorse, and never to contrition; and his fall produces that unmixed and perfect satisfaction which we feel at the death of some savage beast that had desolated the country from instinctive fierceness and natural malignity.

The weird sisters, the gigantic deities of northern mythology, are fit agents to form Macbeth. Richard is the production of those worldly and creeping demons who slide upon the earth, their instruments of mischief to embroil and plague mankind. Falstaff is the work of Circe and her swinish associates, who in some favored hour of revelry and riot moulded this compound of gross debauchery, acute discernment, admirable invention, and nimble wit, and sent him for a consort to England's madcap Prince to stamp currency on idleness and vice and to wave the flag of folly and dissipation over the seats of gravity, of wisdom, and of virtue.

No. 97, December 9, 1786   [Burns]

To the feeling and the susceptible there is something wonderfully pleasing in the contemplation of genius, of that supereminent reach of mind by which some men are distinguished. In the view of highly superior talents, as in that of great and stupendous natural objects, there is a sublimity which fills the soul with wonder and delight, which expands it, as it were, beyond its usual bounds, and which, investing our nature with extraordinary powers and extraordinary honors, interests our curiosity and flatters our pride.

This divinity of genius, however, which admiration is fond to worship, is best arrayed in the darkness of distant and remote periods, and is not easily acknowledged in the present times or in places with which we are perfectly acquainted. Exclusive of all the deductions which envy or jealousy may sometimes be supposed to make, there is a familiarity in the near approach of persons around us not very consistent with the lofty ideas which we wish to form of him who has led captive our imagination in the triumph of his fancy, overpowered our feelings with the tide of passion, or enlightened our reason with the investigation of hidden truths. It may be true that "in the olden time" genius had some advantages which tended to its vigor and its growth, but it is not unlikely that, even in these degenerate days, it rises much oftener than it is observed, that in "the ignorant present time" our posterity may find names which they will dignify, though we neglected, and pay to their memory those honors which their contemporaries had denied them.

There is, however, a natural and indeed a fortunate vanity in trying to redress this wrong which genius is exposed to suffer. In the discovery of talents generally unknown, men are apt to indulge the same fond partiality as in all other discoveries which themselves have made, and hence we have had repeated instances of painters and of poets who have been drawn from obscure situations and held forth to public notice and applause by the extravagant encomiums of their introductors, yet in a short time have sunk again to their former obscurity, whose merit, though perhaps somewhat neglected, did not appear to have been much undervalued by the world, and could not support by its own intrinsic excellence that superior place which the enthusiasm of its patrons would have assigned it.

I know not if I shall be accused of such enthusiasm and partiality when I introduce to the notice of my readers a poet of our own country with whose writings I have lately become acquainted, but if I am not greatly deceived, I think I may safely pronounce him a genius of no ordinary rank. The person to whom I allude is Robert Burns, an Ayrshire plowman, whose poems were some time ago published in a country town in the west of Scotland, with no other ambition, it would seem, than to circulate among the inhabitants of the county where he was born to obtain a little fame from those who had heard of his talents. I hope I shall not be thought to assume too much if I endeavor to place him in a higher point of view, to call for a verdict of his country on the merit of his works, and to claim for him those honors which their excellence appears to deserve.

In mentioning the circumstance of his humble station, I mean not to rest his pretensions solely on that title or to urge the merits of his poetry when considered in relation to the lowness of his birth and the little opportunity of improvement which his education could afford. These particulars, indeed, might excite our wonder at his productions, but his poetry, considered abstractedly and without the apologies arising from his situation, seems to me fully entitled to command our feelings and to obtain our applause. One bar, indeed, his birth and education have opposed to his fame, the language in which most of his poems are written. Even in Scotland, the provincial dialect which Ramsay and he have used is now read with a difficulty which greatly damps the pleasure of the reader; in England it cannot be read at all without such a constant reference to a glossary as nearly to destroy that pleasure.

Some of his productions, however, especially those of the grave style, are almost English. From one of those I shall first present my readers with an extract in which I think they will discover a high tone of feeling, a power and energy of expression particularly and strongly characteristic of the mind and the voice of a poet. It is from his poem entitled "The Vision," in which the genius of his native county, Ayrshire, is thus supposed to address him:

> With future hope, I oft would gaze,
> Fond, on thy little early ways:
> Thy rudely-carroll'd, chiming phrase,
>   In uncouth rhymes;
> Fir'd at the simple, artless lays
>   Of other times.
>
> I saw thee seek the sounding shore,
> Delighted with the dashing roar;
> Or when the North his fleecy store
>   Drove thro' the sky,
> I saw grim Nature's visage hoar
>   Struck thy young eye.
>
> Or when the deep green-mantled earth
> Warm-cherished ev'ry flowret's birth,
> And joy and music pouring forth
>   In every grove;
> I saw thee eye the gen'ral mirth
>   With boundless love.
>
> When ripen'd fields and azure skies
> Call'd forth the reapers' rustling noise,
> I saw thee leave their ev'ning joys,
>   And lonely stalk
> To vent thy bosom's swelling rise
>   In pensive walk.
>
> When youthful Love, warm-blushing, strong,
> Keen-shivering, shot thy nerves along,
> Those accents grateful to thy tongue,
>   Th' adorèd Name,
> I taught thee how to pour in song
>   To soothe thy flame.
>
> I saw thy pulse's maddening play,
> Wild-send thee Pleasure's devious way,
> Misled by Fancy's meteor-ray,
>   By passion driven;
> But yet the light that led astray
>   Was light from Heaven.

Of strains like the above, solemn and sublime, with that rapt and inspired melancholy in which the poet lifts his eye "above this visible diurnal sphere," the poems entitled, "Despondency," the "Lament," "Winter," "A Dirge," and the Invocation to "Ruin," afford no less striking examples. Of the tender and the moral, specimens equally advantageous might be drawn from the elegiac verses entitled "Man was made to mourn," from "The Cotter's Saturday Night," the stanzas "To a Mouse," or those "To a Mountain Daisy, on Turning One down with the Plow in April, 1786." This last poem I shall insert entire, not from its superior merit, but because its length suits the bounds of my paper.

.   .   .   .   .

I have seldom met with an image more truly pastoral than that of the lark in the second stanza. Such strokes as these mark the pencil of the poet, which delineates nature with the precision of intimacy, yet with the delicate coloring of beauty and of taste.

The power of genius is not less admirable in tracing the manners than in painting the passions, or in drawing the scenery of nature. That intuitive glance with which a writer like Shakespeare discerns the characters of men, with which he catches the many-changing hues of life, forms a sort of problem in the science of mind, of which it is easier to see the truth than to assign the cause. Though I am very far from meaning to compare our rustic bard to Shakespeare, yet whoever will read his lighter and more humorous poems, his "Dialogue of the Dogs," his "Dedication to G—— H——, Esq.," his "Epistles to a Young Friend," and "To W. S——n," will perceive with what uncommon penetration and sagacity this heaven-taught plowman, from his humble and unlettered station, has looked upon men and manners.

Against some passages of those last-mentioned poems it has been objected that they breathe a spirit of libertinism and irreligion. But if we consider the ignorance and fanaticism of the lower class of people in the country where these poems were written, a fanaticism of that pernicious sort which sets faith in opposition to good works, the fallacy and danger of which a mind so enlightened as our poet's could not but perceive, we shall not look upon his lighter muse as the enemy of religion (of which in several places he expresses the justest sentiments), though she has sometimes been a little unguarded in her ridicule of hypocrisy.

In this, as in other respects, it must be allowed that there are exceptionable parts of the volume he has given to the public, which caution would have suppressed or correction struck out; but poets are seldom cautious, and our poet had, alas, no friends or companions from whom correction could be obtained. When we reflect on his rank in life, the habits to which he must have been subject, and the society in which he must have mixed, we regret perhaps more than wonder that delicacy should be so often offended in perusing a volume in which there is so much to interest and to please us.

Burns possesses the spirit as well as the fancy of a poet. That honest pride and independence of soul which are sometimes the Muse's only dower break forth on every occasion in his works. It may be, then, I shall wrong his feelings while I indulge my own, in calling the attention of the public to his situation and circumstances. That condition, humble as it was, in which he found content and wooed the Muse might not have been deemed uncomfortable, but grief and misfortunes have reached him there, and one or two of his poems hint what I have learned from some of his countrymen, that he has been obliged to form the resolution of leaving his native land to seek under a West Indian clime that shelter and support which Scotland has denied him. But I trust means may be found to prevent this resolution from taking place, and that I do my country no more than justice when I suppose her ready to stretch out her hand to cherish and retain this native poet whose "wood-notes wild" possess so much excellence. To repair the wrongs of suffering or neglected merit, to call forth genius from the obscurity in which it had pined indignant, and place it where it may profit or delight the world, these are exertions which give to wealth an enviable superiority, to greatness and to patronage, a laudable pride.

THOMAS TWINING ✍

Aristotle's Treatise on Poetry (1789)

Dissertation I, "On Poetry Considered as an Imitative Art"

The word *imitation,* like many others, is used sometimes in a
strict and proper sense and sometimes in a sense more or less extended and improper. Its application to poetry is chiefly of the
latter kind. Its precise meaning, therefore, when applied to poetry
in general is by no means obvious. No one who has seen a picture is
at any loss to understand how painting is imitation. But no man, I
believe, ever heard or read for the first time that poetry is imitation,
without being conscious in some degree of that 'confusion of thought'
which an ingenious writer complains of having felt whenever he has
attempted to explain the imitative nature of music.[1] It is easy to see
whence this confusion arises if we consider the process of the mind
when words thus extended from their proper significations are
presented to it. We are told that "Poetry is an imitative art." In
order to conceive how it is so, we naturally compare it with painting,
sculpture, and such arts as are strictly and clearly imitative. But in
this comparison the difference is so much more obvious and striking
than the resemblance—we see so much more readily in what respects
poetry is *not* properly imitation, than in what respects it *is*—that
the mind at last is left in that sort of perplexity which must always
arise from words thus loosely and analogically applied, when the
analogy is not sufficiently clear and obvious: that is, when of that
mixture of circumstances *like* and *unlike,* which constitutes analogy,
the latter are the most apparent.

In order to understand the following treatise on poetry, in which
imitation is considered as the very essence of the art, it seems nec-

essary to satisfy ourselves, if possible, with respect to two points: I. In what senses the word *imitation* is, or may be, applied to poetry; II. In what senses it was so applied by Aristotle.

I

The only circumstance, I think, common to everything we denominate imitation, whether properly or improperly, is resemblance of some sort or other.

In every imitation strictly and properly so called two conditions seem essential: the resemblance must be immediate, i.e., between the imitation, or imitative work itself, and the object imitated; and it must also be obvious. Thus, in sculpture, figure is represented by similar figure; in painting, color and figure, by similar color and figure; in personal imitation, or mimicry, voice and gesture, by similar voice and gesture. In all these instances the resemblance is obvious—we recognize the object imitated; and it is also *immediate* —it lies in the imitative work or energy itself, or in other words, in the very materials, or "sensible media," [2] by which the imitation is conveyed. All these copies, therefore, are called strictly and intelligibly imitations.

I. The materials of poetic imitation are words. These may be considered in two views: as sounds *merely,* and as sounds *significant,* or arbitrary and conventional signs of ideas. It is evidently in the first view only that words can bear any real resemblance to the things expressed; and accordingly that kind of imitation which consists in the resemblance of words considered as mere sound to the sounds and motions of the objects imitated [3] has usually been assigned as the only instance in which the term *imitative* is, in its strict and proper sense, applicable to poetry.[4] But setting aside all that is the effect of fancy and of accommodated pronunciation in the reader, to which, I fear, many passages repeatedly quoted and admired as the happiest coincidences of sound and sense may be reduced [5]— setting this aside, even in such words and such arrangements of words as are actually in some degree analogous in sound or motion to the thing signified or described, the resemblance is so faint and distant and of so general and vague a nature, that it would never of itself lead us to recognize the object imitated. We discover not the likeness till we know the meaning. The natural relation of the word to the thing signified is pointed out only by its arbitrary or conventional relation.—I do not here mean to deny that such resemblances, however slight and delicate where they really are, and however liable to be discovered by fancy where they are not, are yet a source of real beauties, of beauties actually felt by the reader when they arise, or appear to arise, spontaneously from the poet's feeling, and their effect is not counteracted by the obviousness of cool intention and deliberate artifice. Nor do I mean to object to this application of the word *imitative*. My purpose is merely to show that when we call this kind of resemblance imitation, we do not use the word in its strict sense—that in which it is applied to a picture or a statue. Of the two conditions above mentioned, it wants that which must be regarded as most essential. The resemblance is indeed real as far as it goes, and immediate, but necessarily, from its generality, so imperfect that even when pointed out by the sense it is by no means always obvious, and without that cannot possibly lead to anything like a clear and certain recognition of the particular object imitated. I must observe farther that this kind of imitation, even supposing it much more perfect, is by no means that which would be likely first to occur to anyone in an inquiry concerning the nature of the imitation attributed to poetry, were it not that the circumstance of its real and immediate resemblance has occasioned its being considered, I think not justly, as the strictest sense of the term so applied.

For the most usual and the most important senses, and even, as will perhaps appear, for the strictest sense in which poetry has been, or may be, understood to imitate, we must have recourse to language considered in its most important point of view as composed not of sounds merely but of sounds *significant*.

2. The most general and extensive of these senses is that in which it is applied to description, comprehending not only that poetic landscape-painting which is peculiarly called descriptive poetry, but all such circumstantial and distinct representation as conveys to the mind a strong and clear idea of its object, whether sensible or mental.[6] Poetry, in this view, is naturally considered as more or less imitative in proportion as it is capable of raising an ideal image or picture more or less resembling the reality of things. The more distinct and vivid the ideas are of which this picture is composed and the more closely they correspond to the actual impressions received from nature, the stronger will be the resemblance, and the more perfect the imitation.

Hence it is evident that of all description that of visible objects will be the most imitative, the ideas of such objects being of all others the most distinct and vivid. That such description, therefore, should have been called imitation can be no wonder; and indeed of all the extended or analogical applications of the word this is perhaps the most obvious and natural. There needs no other proof of this than the very language in which we are naturally led to express our admiration of this kind of poetry, and which we perpetually borrow from the arts of strict imitation. We say the poet has *painted* his object; we talk of his *imagery,* of the lively *colors* of his description, and the masterly touches of his *pencil.*[7]

The objects of our other senses fall less within the power of description in proportion as the ideas of those objects are more simple, more fleeting, and less distinct than those of sight. The description of such objects is, therefore, called with less propriety imitation.

Next to visible objects, sounds seem the most capable of descriptive imitation. Such description is, indeed, generally aided by real, though imperfect, resemblance of verbal sound—more, or less, according to the nature of the language and the delicacy of the poet's ear. The following lines of Virgil are, I think, an instance of this:

> Lamentis gemituque et femineo ululatu
> tecta fremunt, resonat magnis plangoribus aether.[8]

But we are not now considering this immediate imitation of sound by sound, but such only as is merely descriptive, and operates, like the description of visible objects, only by the meaning of the words. Now if we are allowed to call description of visible objects imitation when it is such that we seem to see the object, I know of no reason why we may not also consider sounds as imitated when they are so described that we seem to hear them. It would not be difficult to produce from the best poets, and even from prose writers of a strong and poetical imagination, many instances of sound so imitated. Those readers who are both poetical and musical will, I believe, excuse my dwelling a moment upon a subject which has not, as far as I know, been much considered.

Of our own poets I do not recollect any who have presented musical ideas with such feeling, force, and reality of description as Milton and Mr. Mason. When Milton speaks of

> Notes with many a winding bout
> Of linked sweetness long drawn out, [*L'Allegro,* 139]

and of "a soft and solemn-breathing sound" that

> Rose like a steam of rich distill'd Perfumes,
> And stole upon the Air, [*Comus,* 555]

who that has a truly musical ear will refuse to consider such description as in some sort imitative?

In the same spirit both of poetry and of music are these beautiful lines in *Caractacus,* addressed by the Chorus to the Bards:

> Wond'rous men!
> Ye, whose skill'd fingers know how best to lead,
> Through all the maze of sound the wayward step
> Of Harmony, recalling oft, and oft
> Permitting her unbridled course to rush
> Through dissonance to concord, sweetest then
> Ev'n when expected harshest.[9]

It seems scarce possible to convey with greater clearness to the ear of imagination the effect of an artful and well-conducted harmony, of that free and varied range of modulation in which the ear is ever wandering yet never lost, and of that masterly and bold intertexture of discord which leads the sense to pleasure through paths that lie close upon the very verge of pain.

The general and confused effect of complex and aggregated sound may be said to be described when the most striking and characteristic of the single sounds of which it is compounded are selected and enumerated, just as single sounds are described (and they can be described no otherwise) by the selection of their principal qualities or modifications. I cannot produce a finer example of this than the following admirable passage of Dante, in which with a force of representation peculiar to himself in such subjects he describes the mingled terrors of those distant sounds that struck his ear as he entered the gates of his imaginary *Inferno:* "si mise dentro alle segrete cose."

> Quivi sospiri, pianti, ed alti guai
> Risonavan per l'aer senza stelle;
>
> .   .   .   .   .
>
> Diverse lingue, orribili favelle,
> Parole di dolore, accenti d'ira,
> Voci alte fioche, e suon di man con elle.[10]

The reader may be glad to relieve his imagination from the terrible ἐνάργεια of this description by turning his ear to a far different combination of sounds—to the charming description of "the melodies of morn" in the *Minstrel,* or of the melodies of evening in the *Deserted Village:*

> Sweet was the sound, when oft at evening's close,
> Up yonder hill the village murmur rose.
> There as I past with careless steps and slow,
> The mingling notes came soften'd from below;
> The swain responsive as the milk-maid sung,
> The sober herd that low'd to meet their young;
> The noisy geese that gabbled o'er the pool,
> The playful children just let loose from school;
> The watch-dog's voice that bay'd the whisp'ring wind,
> And the loud laugh that spoke the vacant mind.
> These all in soft confusion sought the shade,
> And fill'd each pause the nightingale had made. [113] [11]

But single sounds may also be so described or characterized as to produce a secondary perception of sufficient clearness to deserve the name of imitation. It is thus that we hear the "far-off curfew" of Milton:

> Over some wide-water'd shore
> Swinging slow with sullen roar. [*Il Penseroso,* 75]

And Mr. Mason's "bell of death," that

> pauses now; and now with rising knell
> Flings to the hollow gale its sullen sound. [*Elegy IV*]

I do not know a happier descriptive line in Homer than the following, in his simile of the nightingale:

> Ἥ τε θαμὰ τρωπῶσα χέει πολυηχέα φωνήν.[13]

That which is peculiar in the singing of this bird, the variety, richness, flexibility, and liquid volubility of its notes, cannot well be more strongly characterized, more audibly presented to the mind, than by the πολυηχέα, the χέει, and above all, the θαμὰ τρῶπωσα of this short description.[14] But to return—

I mentioned also description of mental objects: of the emotions, passions, and other internal movements and operations of the mind. Such objects may be described either immediately as they affect the mind, or through their external and sensible effects. Let us take the passion of Dido for an instance:

At regina gravi iamdudum saucia cura
vulnus alit venis, et caeco carpitur igni.[15]

This is immediate description. But when Dido

Incipit effari, mediaque in voce resistit;
nunc eadem labente die convivia quaerit,
Iliacosque iterum demens audire labores
exposcit, pendetque iterum narrantis ab ore.
post ubi digressi, lumenque obscura vicissim
luna premit suadentque cadentia sidera somnos,
Sola domo maeret vacua stratisque relictis
Incubat.[16]

Here, the passion is described, and most exquisitely, by its sensible effects. This, indeed, may be considered as falling under the former kind of descriptive imitation—that of sensible objects. There is this difference, however, between the description of a sensible object and the description of a mental—of any passion, for example—through that of a sensible object: that in the former the description is considered as terminating in the clear and distinct representation of the sensible object, the landscape, the attitude, the sound, etc., whereas in the other the sensible exhibition is only, or chiefly, the means of effecting that which is the principal end of such description—the emotion, of whatever kind, that arises from a strong conception of the passion itself. The image carries us on forcibly to the feeling of its internal cause. When this first effect is once produced, we may, indeed, return from it to the calmer pleasure of contemplating the imagery itself with a painter's eye.

It is undoubtedly this description of passions and emotions by their sensible effects that principally deserves the name of *imitative;* and it is a great and fertile source of some of the highest and most touching beauties of poetry. With respect to immediate descriptions of this kind, they are from their very nature far more weak and indistinct, and do not, perhaps, often possess that degree of forcible representation that amounts to what we call imitative description. But here some distinctions seem necessary. In a strict and philosophical view a single passion or emotion does not admit of description at all. Considered in itself it is a simple internal feeling, and as such can no more be described than a simple idea can be defined. It can be described no otherwise than in its effects, of some kind or other. But the effects of a passion are of two kinds, internal and external.

Now, popularly speaking, by the passion of love, for example, we mean the whole operation of that passion upon the mind—we include all its internal workings; and when it is described in these internal and invisible effects only, we consider it as immediately described, these internal effects being included in our general idea of the passion. Mental objects, then, admit of immediate description only when they are more or less complex; and such description may be considered as more or less imitative in proportion as its impression on the mind approaches more or less closely to the real impression of the passion or emotion itself. Thus, in the passage above referred to as an instance of such immediate description, the mental object described is a complex object—the passion of love, including some of its internal effects: that is, some other passions or feelings which it excites or with which it is accompanied:

> At regina gravi iamdudum saucia cura
> vulnus alit venis, et caeco carpitur igni.
> multa viri virtus animo multusque recursat
> gentis honos: haerent infixi pectore voltus,
> verbaque, nec placidam membris dat cura quietem.[17]

Reduce this passage to the mere mention of the passion itself—the simple feeling or emotion of love, in the precise and strict acceptation of the word, abstractedly from its concomitant effects—it will not even be description, much less imitative description. It will be mere attribution, or predication. It will say only, "Dido was in love."

Thus, again, a complication of different passions admits of forcible and imitative description:

> Aestuat ingens
> uno in corde pudor mixtoque insania luctu
> et furiis agitatus amor et conscia virtus.[18]

Here the mental object described is not any single passion, but the complex passion, if I may call it so, that results from the mixture and fermentation of all the passions attributed to Turnus.

To give one example more: the mind of a reader can hardly, I think, be flung into an imaginary situation more closely resembling the real situation of a mind distressed by the complicated movements of irresolute, fluctuating and anxious deliberation, than it is by these lines of Virgil:

Magno curarum fluctuat aestu;
atque animum nunc huc celerem, nunc dividit illuc,
in partisque rapit varias perque omnia versat.[19]

It may be necessary also, for clearness, to observe that description as applied to mental objects is sometimes used in a more loose and improper sense, and the poet is said to describe in general all the passions or manners which he in any way exhibits, whether in the proper sense of the word *described,* or merely *expressed,* as, for example, in the lines quoted from the opening of the Fourth Book of the *Aeneid,* the passion of Dido is described by the poet. In these:

Quis novus hic nostris successit sedibus hospes,
quem sese ore ferens, quam forti pectore et armis,[20]

it is expressed by herself. But is not this, it may be asked, still imitation? It is; but not descriptive imitation. As expressive of passion it is no farther imitative than as the passion expressed is imaginary, and makes a part of the poet's fiction; otherwise, we must apply the word *imitative* as nobody ever thought of applying it, to all cases in which we are made by sympathy to feel strongly the passion of another expressed by words. The passage is, indeed, also imitative in another view—as *dramatic.* But for an explanation of both these heads of imitation, I must refer to what follows. I shall only add, for fear of mistake, that there is also, in the second of those lines, descriptive imitation, but descriptive of Aeneas only, not of Dido's passion, though it strongly indicates that passion. All I mean to assert is that those lines are not descriptive imitation of a mental object.

So much, then, for the subject of descriptive imitation, which has perhaps detained us too long upon a single point of our general inquiry.

3. The word *imitation* is also, in a more particular but well-known sense, applied to poetry when considered as fiction—to stories, actions, incidents, and characters, as far as they are feigned or invented by the poet in imitation, as we find it commonly and obviously enough expressed, of nature, of real life, of truth, in *general,* as opposed to that individual reality of things which is the province of the historian. Of this imitation the epic and dramatic poems are the principal examples.

That this sense of the term as applied to fiction is entirely distinct from that in which it is applied to description will evidently appear from the following considerations. In descriptive imitation the resemblance is between the ideas raised and the actual impressions, whether external or internal, received from the things themselves. In fictive imitation the resemblance is, strictly speaking, between the ideas raised and other ideas, the ideas raised—the ideas of the poem—being no other than copies, resemblances, or more philosophically, new, though similar, combinations of that general stock of ideas collected from experience, observation, and reading, and reposited in the poet's mind. In description, imitation is opposed to actual *impression,* external or internal: in fiction, it is opposed to *fact.* In their effects, some degree of illusion is implied; but the illusion is not of the same kind in both. Descriptive imitation may be said to produce illusive perception; fictive, illusive belief.

Farther, descriptive imitation may subsist without fictive, and fictive without descriptive. The first of these assertions is too obvious to stand in need of proof. The other may require some explanation. It seems evident that fiction may even subsist in mere narration, without any degree of description properly so called, much more without such description as I have called imitative; that is, without any greater degree of resemblance to the things expressed than that which is implied in all ideas and produced by all language considered merely as intelligible. Let a story be invented and related in the plainest manner possible, in short and general expressions amounting, in the incidents, to mere assertion, and in the account of passions and characters, as far as possible, to mere attribution: this, as fiction, is still imitation, an invented resemblance of real life, or, if you please, of history [21]—though without a single imitative description, a single picture, a single instance of strong and visible coloring throughout the whole.[22] I mean by this only to show the distinct and independent senses in which *imitation* is applied to description and to fiction, by showing how each species of imitation may subsist without the other; but that fictive imitation, though it does not in any degree depend on descriptive for its existence, does in a very great degree depend on it for its beauty is too obvious to be called in question.[23]

The two senses last mentioned of the word *imitative* as applied to description and to fiction are manifestly extended or improper senses, as well as that first mentioned, in which it is applied to language considered as mere sound. In all these imitations, one of the essential conditions of whatever is strictly so denominated is wanting. In sonorous imitation, the resemblance is immediate but not obvious; in the others, it is obvious but not immediate, that is, it lies, not in the words themselves, but in the ideas which they raise as signs; yet as the circumstance of obvious resemblance, which may be regarded as the most striking and distinctive property of imitation, is here found, this extension of the word seems to have more propriety than that in which it is applied to those faint and evanescent resemblances which have, not without reason, been called the echo of sound to sense.[24]

4. There seems to be but one view in which poetry can be considered as imitation in the strict and proper sense of the word. If we look for both immediate and obvious resemblance, we shall find it only in dramatic—or to use a more general term—personative poetry, that is, all poetry in which, whether essentially or occasionally, the poet personates; for here speech is imitated by speech.[25] The difference between this and mere narration or description is obvious. When in common discourse we relate or describe in our own persons, we imitate in no other sense than as we raise ideas which resemble the things related or described. But when we speak as another person, we become mimics, and not only the ideas we convey but the words, the discourse itself, in which we convey them are imitations; they resemble, or are supposed to resemble, those of the person we represent. Now this is the case not only with the tragic and comic poet but also with the epic poet, and even the historian, when either of these quits his own character and writes a speech in the character of another person. He is then an imitator in as strict a sense as the personal mimic. In dramatic and all personative poetry, then, both the conditions of what is properly denominated imitation are fulfilled.

And now the question in what senses the word *imitation* is or may be applied to poetry seems to have received its answer. It appears, I think, that the term ought not to be extended beyond the four different applications which have been mentioned, and that poetry can be justly considered as imitative only by sound, by description, by fiction, or by personation. Whenever the poet speaks in his own person and at the same time does not either feign or make "the sound an echo to the sense" or stay to impress his ideas upon the fancy with some degree of that force and distinctness which we call description, he cannot, in any sense that I am aware of, be said to imitate, unless we extend imitation to all speech—to every mode of expressing our thoughts by words—merely because all words are signs of ideas, and those ideas images of things.[26]

It is scarce necessary to observe that these different species of imitation often run into, and are mixed with, each other. They are, indeed, more properly speaking only so many distinct, abstracted views, in which poetry may be considered as imitating. It is seldom that any of them are to be found separately; and in some of them, others are necessarily implied. Thus, dramatic imitation implies fiction, and sonorous imitation, description; though conversely it is plainly otherwise. Descriptive imitation is manifestly that which is most independent on all the others. The passages in which they are all united are frequent; and those in which all are excluded are, in the best poetry, very rare: for the poet of genius rarely forgets his proper language, and that can scarcely be retained, at least while he relates, without more or less of coloring, of imagery, of that descriptive force which makes us see and hear. A total suspension of all his functions as an imitator is hardly to be found but in the simple proposal of his subject, in his invocation, the expression of his own sentiments, or in those calm beginnings of narration where, now and then, the poet stoops to fact and becomes for a moment little more than a metrical historian.

The full illustration of all this by examples would draw out to greater length a discussion which the reader, I fear, has already thought too long. If he will open the *Aeneid* or any other epic poem and apply these remarks, he may perhaps find it amusing to trace the different kinds of imitation as they successively occur in their various combinations and degrees and to observe the poet varying from page to page, and sometimes even from line to line, the quantity, if I may so speak, of his imitation; sometimes shifting and sometimes, though rarely and for a moment, throwing off altogether his imitative form.

It has been often said that all poetry is imitation.[27] But from the preceding inquiry it appears that if we take poetry in its common acceptation for all metrical composition, the assertion is not true; not, at least, in any sense of the term *imitation* but such as will make it equally true of all speech. If, on the other hand, we depart from that common acceptation of the word *poetry*, the assertion that "all poetry is imitation" seems only an improper and confused way of saying that no composition that is not imitative ought to be called poetry. To examine the truth of this would be to engage in a fresh discussion totally distinct from the object of this dissertation. We have not now been considering what poetry is, or how it should be defined, but only in what sense it is an *imitative art;* or rather, we have been examining the nature and extent of *verbal imitation* in general.[28]

The preceding general inquiry, "in what senses the word *imitation* is, or may be, applied to poetry," brings us with some advantage to the other question proposed, of more immediate concern to the reader of this treatise of Aristotle: "in what senses it was so applied by *him."*

1. It is clearly so applied by him in the sense which from him has, I think, most generally been adopted by modern writers—that of *fiction,* as above explained, whether conveyed in the dramatic or personative form, or by mere narration in the person of the poet himself.[29] This appears from the whole of chapter nine, but especially from the last paragraph, where he expressly says that what constitutes the poet an imitator is the invention of a fable: ποιητὴν μᾶλλον τῶν μύθων εἶναι δεῖ ποιητὴν . . . ὅσῳ ποιητὴς κατὰ τὴν μίμησίν ἐστιν μιμεῖται δὲ τὰς πράξεις.[30] He repeatedly calls the fable, or μύθος, "an imitation of an action"; but this it can be in no other sense than as it is feigned, either entirely, or in part. A history, as far at least as it is strictly history, is not an imitation of an action.

2. It seems equally clear that he considered *dramatic* poetry as peculiarly imitative above every other species. Hence his first rule concerning the epic or narrative imitation, that its fable "should be dramatically constructed, like that of tragedy": τοὺς μύθους, καθαπὲρ ἐν ταῖς τραγῳδίαις, δραματικοὺς: his praise of Homer for "the dramatic spirit of his imitations": ὅτι καὶ μιμήσεις δραματικὰς ἐποίησεν: and above all, the remarkable expression he uses where, having laid it down as a precept that the epic poet "should speak as little as possible in his *own person,"* (αὐτὸν δεῖ τὸν ποιητὴν ἐλάχιστα λέγειν) he gives this reason— οὐ γάρ ἐστι κατὰ ταῦτα μιμητής: "for he is not then the imitator." But he had before expressly allowed the poet to be an imitator even while he retains his own person. I see no other way of removing this apparent inconsistence than by supposing him to speak comparatively and to mean no more than that the poet is not then truly and strictly an imitator; [31] or, in other words, that imitation is applicable in its strict and proper sense only to personative poetry, as above explained—to that poetry in which speech is represented by speech,

and the resemblance, as in painting and sculpture, is immediate. I am not conscious that I am here forcing upon Aristotle a meaning that may not be his. I seem to be only drawing a clear inference from a clear fact. It cannot be denied that in the passages alleged he plainly speaks of personative poetry as that which peculiarly deserves the name of *imitation*. The inference seems obvious—that he speaks of it as peculiarly imitative, in the only sense in which it is so, as being the only species of poetry that is strictly imitative.

I do not find in Aristotle any express application of the term except these two. Of the other two senses in which poetry may be, and by modern writers has been, considered as imitation—resemblance of sound, and description—he says nothing.

With respect, indeed, to the former of these, sonorous imitation, it cannot appear in any degree surprising that he should pass it over in total silence. I have already observed that even in a general inquiry concerning the nature of the imitation attributed to poetry it is by no means that sense of the word which would be likely first to occur; and it would, perhaps, never have occurred at all, if in such inquiries we were not naturally led to compare poetry with painting and other arts strictly imitative and as naturally led by that comparison to admit sonorous imitation as one species from its agreement with those strictly imitative arts in the circumstance of immediate resemblance. But no such general inquiry was the object of Aristotle's work, which is not a treatise on poetic imitation, but on poetry. His subject, therefore, led him to consider, not all that might without impropriety be denominated imitation in poetry, but that imitation only which he regarded as essential to the art, as the source of its greatest beauties and the foundation of its most important rules. With respect, then, to that casual and subordinate kind of imitation which is produced merely by the sound of words, it was not likely even that the idea of it should occur to him. Indeed, it is to be considered as a property of language in general, rather than of poetry; and of speech—of actual pronunciation— rather than of language. Besides that the beauties arising from this source are of too delicate and fugitive a nature to be held by rule. They must be left to the ear of the reader for their effect, and ought to be left to that of the poet for their production.

But neither does Aristotle appear to have included description in his notion of poetic imitation, which, as far as he has explained it, seems to have been simply that of the imitation of human actions, manners, passions, events, etc., in feigned story, and that, principally, when conveyed in a dramatic form. Of description, indeed, important as it is to the beauty of poetry in general, and to that of fiction itself, more particularly in the epic form, he has not said one word throughout his treatise: so far was he from extending poetic imitation, as some have done, to that general sense which comprehends all speech.[32]

But here, to avoid confusion, the sense in which I have used the term *description* must be kept in view. When it is said that Aristotle "did not include description in his notion of imitation," it is not meant that he did not consider the descriptive parts of narrative poetry as in any respect imitative. The subject of a description may be either real or feigned. Almost all the descriptions of the higher poetry, the poetry of invention, are of the latter kind. These Aristotle unquestionably considered as imitation; but it was as fiction, not as description—as falsehood resembling truth, or nature in general, not as verbal expression resembling, by its force and clearness, the visible representations of painting, or the perception of the thing itself. Had he considered description in this sense as imitation, he must necessarily have admitted imitation without fiction.[33] But this seems clearly contrary to the whole tenor of his treatise. The beauty, indeed, of such description was well known to the ancients, and frequent examples of it are to be found in their best writers—their orators and historians, as well as poets—and particularly in Homer.[34] But there is one particular kind of description that may be said to be, in a great measure at least, peculiar to modern times: I mean that which answers to landscape in painting, and of which the subject is prospects, views, rural scenery, etc., considered merely as pictures—as beautiful objects to the eye.[35] As the truth of this observation may not be readily admitted, and as the subject is curious, and has not, that I know of, been discussed, the reader will perhaps pardon me if I suffer it to detain us from our direct path in a digression of some length.

I do not mean to deny that there are some beautiful, though slight, touches of local description to be found in the ancient poets. But it must be confessed, I think, that they scattered these beauties with a sparing hand in comparison with that rich profusion of picturesque ideas which every reader of poetry recollects in Shakespeare, Milton, Spenser, Thomson, and almost all the modern poets of any name. Nor can I say that I am able to point out anything of this sort in the most descriptive of the Greek poets—in Theocritus, or even in Homer—that fairly amounts to such picturesque *landscape description* (if I may call it so), as I mean, and as we find so frequently in the poets just mentioned. In Mr. Pope's *Poetical Index* to his Homer we are referred, indeed, to descriptions of "prospects" and "landscapes of a fine country"; but if we turn to the original, we shall seldom, or never, find these landscapes. They are of Mr. Pope's painting, sometimes suggested by a single epithet, as his:

> grassy Pteleon *deck'd with chearful greens,*
> *The bow'rs of Ceres and the sylvan scenes.*
>
> *[Iliad,* II, 849, 50]

One word only of this description is Homer's property, *grassy,* λεχεποίην.[36] Many other instances may be found, particularly in his catalogue of the ships, which indeed he professes to have endeavored to "make appear as much a *landscape or piece of painting* as possible." (Observations on the Catalogue [at the end of Pope's translation of Book II].) Sometimes he does more than "open the prospect a little," as he expresses it; he creates it. In his perfidious version ("Perfida—sed quamis perfida, cara tamen!") *"lofty* Sesamus *invades the sky";* and the river Parthenius

> roll'd thro' banks of flowers
> Reflects her bord'ring palaces and bowers.

In Homer the mountain and the river are simply named; not a single epithet attends them.[37] In the Index to the *Odyssey* we find, among other descriptions, one of "the landscape about Ithaca." This has a promising appearance. Mr. Pope indeed has done his utmost to make a landscape of this description; yet even his translation, though certainly beautiful, and even picturesque, will hardly, I believe, be thought to come up to what a modern reader would expect from "the landscape about Ithaca." Still less is this title applicable to the original.[38] All that can be said of it without exaggeration is that it is a very pleasing scene, though described, as many things in Homer are described, with that simplicity which leaves a great deal, and may suggest a great deal, to the fancy of the reader. Though it does not answer to the idea given of it in Pope's index, or in the *note* upon the place,[39] yet it must be allowed to furnish at least some good materials for a landscape, such as a grove,[40] water falling from a rock, and a rustic altar. If the description itself is too simple, short, and general to be, properly speaking, picturesque description, yet it is such as wants nothing to become so, but a little more coloring of expression, a little more distinctness and *speciality* of touch. This, and more than this, Mr. Pope has given it; and that his description is, at least, highly picturesque will scarce be disputed. Homer gives us simply "an altar to the nymphs." Pope covers it with "moss" and "embowers it deep in shades," and in his concluding line he goes beyond the description of the place to the description of the *religio loci*—of the effect of the place upon the minds of those who approached it.

> Beneath, *sequester'd* to the nymphs is seen
> A mossy altar, *deep-embower'd in green;*
> Where constant vows by travellers are paid,
> *And holy horrors solemnize the shade.*

The additions of Mr. Pope's pencil are distinguished in the above quotations by *italics*.[41] But to prove the inferiority of the ancients in this species of description by an accurate and comparative examination of all those passages which are commonly produced as examples of it would be a task of considerable length, though I think of no great difficulty. The few instances here given from Homer are intended rather as illustrations of the difference I meant to point out than as proofs of the general fact, which I leave to the recollection and the judgment of the reader. To me, I confess, nothing appears more evident.

And may we not account for this defect in ancient poetry from a similar defect in the sister art of painting? For it appears, I think, from all that has been transmitted to us of the history of that art among the ancients that landscape painting either did not exist, or at least was very little cultivated or regarded among the Greeks.[42] In Pliny's account of Grecian artists we find no landscape painter mentioned, nor anything like a landscape described in his catalogue of their principal works. The first and the only landscapes he mentions are those said to be painted in fresco by one Ludius in the time of Augustus, "qui *primus instituit* amoenissimam parietum picturam;—villas, et porticus, ac topiaria opera—*lucos, nemora, colles,—amnes, littora*—varias ibi obambulantium species, aut navigantium, *terrâque villas adeuntium asellis aut vehiculis,* etc." He likewise painted seaports: "idemque—maritimas urbes pingere *instituit,* blandissimo aspectu." [43] He seems to have been the Claude Lorrain of ancient painting. But that landscape was not, even in Pliny's time, a common and established branch of painting may perhaps be presumed from the single circumstance of its not having acquired a name. In the passage just quoted, Pliny calls it only, periphrastically, "an *agreeable kind* of painting, or subject," "*amoenissiman picturam.*" [44] He is not sparing of technical terms upon other occasions: as *rhyparographus, anthropographus, catagrapha, monocromata, etc.* With respect to the Greeks, at least, this may be allowed to afford somewhat more than a presumption of the fact.

The Greek poets, then, did not describe the scenery of nature in a picturesque manner, because they were not accustomed to see it with a painter's eye. Undoubtedly they were not blind to all the beauties of such scenes, but those beauties were not heightened to them, as they are to us, by comparison with painting—with those models of improved and selected nature which it is the business of the landscape painter to exhibit. They had no Thomsons, because they had no Claudes. Indeed, the influence of painting in this respect, not only on poetry but on the general taste for the visible beauties of rural nature, seems obvious and indisputable. Show the most beautiful prospect to a peasant who never saw a landscape or read a description: I do not say that he will absolutely feel no pleasure from it, but I will venture to say that the pleasure he will feel is very different in kind, and very inferior in degree, compared with that which is felt by a person of a cultivated imagination, accustomed to the representation of such objects either in painting or in picturesque poetry. Such beauty does imitation reflect back upon the object imitated.[45] What may serve to confirm the truth of these remarks is that from the time of Augustus, when, according to Pliny, landscape painting was first cultivated, descriptions of prospects, picturesque imagery, and allusions to that kind of painting seem to have become more common. I do not pretend, however, to have accurately examined this matter. I shall only remind the reader of the acknowledged superiority of Virgil in touches of this kind; of Pliny's description of the view from his villa, mentioned above; and of Aelian's description of the Vale of Tempe, and his allusion to painting in the introduction to it.

To return to description in general: This, as I observed above, Aristotle was so far from including in his notion of imitation that he is even totally silent concerning it; unless he may be thought slightly to allude to it in one passage, where he recommends it to the poet to reserve his highest coloring of language for the inactive, that is, the merely narrative or descriptive parts of his poem.[46] Several obvious circumstances help to account for this silence. Intent on the higher precepts, and on what he regarded as the more essential beauties of the art—the internal construction and contrivance of the fable, the artful dependence and close connection of the incidents, the union of the wonderful and the probable, the natural delineation of character and passion, and whatever tended most effectually to arrest the attention and secure the emotion of the spectator or the reader—intent on these, he seems to have thought the beauties of language and expression a matter of inferior consideration, scarce worthy of his attention. The chapters on diction seem to afford some proof of this. The manner in which he has treated that subject will be found, if I mistake not, to bear strong marks of this comparative negligence and to be, in several respects, not such as the reader from the former parts of the work would naturally expect. To this it should be added that Aristotle's principal object was, evidently, tragedy. Now in tragedy, where the poet himself appears not—where all is action, emotion, imitation—where the succession of incidents is close and rapid, and rarely admits those ἄργα μέρη, those *idle* or *inactive parts,* of which the philosopher speaks—there is, of course, but little occasion and little room for description. It is in the open and extended plan, the varied and digressive narration, of the epic form that the descriptive powers of the poet have full range to display themselves within their proper province.

I have attempted in the preceding discussion to make my way through a subject which I have never seen treated in a way perfectly clear and satisfactory by others, and which I am therefore far from confident that I have treated clearly myself. I can only hope that I have at least left it less embarrassed than I found it.[47] I shall venture, with the same view, to terminate this inquiry by a few remarks on the origin of this doctrine of poetic imitation.

Its history may be sketched in few words. We find it first in Plato alluded to in many parts of his works, but nowhere so clearly and particularly developed as in the Third and Tenth Books of his *Republic.* Aristotle followed, applying and pursuing to its consequences, with the enlarged view of a philosopher and a critic, the principle which his master had considered with the severity of a moral censor and had described as we describe an impostor or a robber: only that, being known, it might be avoided.

From these sources, but principally from the treatise of Aristotle, this doctrine was derived, through the later ancient to the latest modern writers. In general, however, it must be confessed that the way in which the subject has been explained is not such as is calculated to give perfect satisfaction to those fastidious understandings that are not to be contented with anything less than distinct ideas—that, like the sundial in the fable, allow of no medium between knowing clearly and knowing nothing.

> Si je ne vois bien clair, je dis—Je n'en sais rien.[48]

It is one question in what senses and from what original ideas poetry was first called imitation by Plato and Aristotle; and another, what senses may have suggested themselves to modern writers, who finding poetry denominated an imitative art, instead of carefully investigating the original meaning of the expression, have had recourse for its explication to their own ideas, and have, accordingly, extended it to every sense which the widest and most distant analogy would bear.

With respect to the origin of the appellation, the very idea that poetry is imitation may, I think, evidently be traced to the theater as to its natural source; and it may, perhaps, very reasonably be questioned whether, if the drama had never been invented, poetry would ever have been placed in the class of imitative arts.

That Aristotle drew his ideas of poetic imitation chiefly from the drama is evident from what has been already said. His preference, indeed, of dramatic poetry is not only openly declared in his concluding chapter but strongly marked throughout, and by the very plan and texture of his work. The epic—that "greatest work," as Dryden extravagantly calls it, "which the soul of man is capable to perform" [49]—is slightly touched and soon dismissed. Our eye is still kept on tragedy. The form and features of the epic muse are rather described by comparison with those of her sister, than delineated as they are in themselves; and though that preference which is the result of the comparison seems justly given on the whole, yet it must, perhaps, be confessed that the comparison is not completely stated and that the advantages and privileges of the epic are touched with some reserve.[50] It is, indeed, no wonder that he who held imitation to be the essence of poetry should prefer that species which being more strictly imitative was, in his view, more strictly poetry than any other.

With respect to Plato the case is still plainer. In the Third Book of his *Republic,* where he treats the subject most fully and is most

clear and explicit, he is so far from considering "all poetry" as imitation that he expressly distinguishes imitative poetry from "poetry
without imitation." Nor does he leave us in any uncertainty about
his meaning. His imitative poetry is no other than that which I have
called personative, and which the reader will find clearly and precisely described in the passage referred to.[51] Imitation, then, he confines to the drama and the dramatic part of the epic poem; and that
which with Aristotle is the principal, with Plato is the only sense of
imitation applied to poetry. In short, that Plato drew his idea of the
μμησις of poetry from the theater itself and from the personal imitations of represented tragedy is evident from the manner in which
he explains the term and from the general cast and language of all
his illustrations and allusions. "When the poet," he says, "quitting
his narration, makes any speech in the character of another person,
does he not then assimilate, as much as possible, his language to
that of the person introduced as speaking? Certainly. But to assimilate oneself to another person, either in voice or gesture—is
not this to imitate that person?" And in many other passages we find
the same allusion to the imitations, by voice and action, of the actor
and the rhapsodist, and even to ludicrous mimicry of the lowest
kind.[52]

All this will scarce appear strange or surprising if we recollect
the close connection which then subsisted between poetical and
personal imitation. It was by no means with the ancients as it is with
us. Before the multiplication of copies was facilitated by the invention of printing, reading was uncommon. It was not even till long
after that it became in any degree the general practice, as it is now.
Yet poetry, we know, among the Greeks was the common food even
of the vulgar. But they heard it only. The philosopher, the critic,
and the few who collected books when they could be obtained only
by the labor or expense of transcription might, indeed, take a tragedy
or an epic poem into their closets; but to the generality all was
action, representation, and recital. The tragic and even the epic
poet were, in a manner, lost in the actor and the rhapsodist.[53] A
tragedy not intended for the stage would have appeared to the
ancients as great an absurdity as an ode not written for music. With
them there could be no difficulty in conceiving poetry to be an imitative art, when it was scarce known to them but through the visible
medium of arts strictly and literally mimetic.

ERASMUS DARWIN ✒

Interlude I from *The Loves of the Plants* (1789)

Bookseller. Your verses, Mr. Botanist, consist of pure description; I hope there is sense in the notes.

Poet. I am only a flower painter, or occasionally attempt a landscape; and leave the human figure with the subjects of history to abler artists.

B. It is well to know what subjects are within the limits of your pencil; many have failed of success from the want of this self-knowledge. But pray tell me, what is the essential difference between poetry and prose? Is it solely the melody or measure of the language?

P. I think not solely, for some prose has its melody, and even measure. And good verses well spoken in a language unknown to the hearer are not easily to be distinguished from good prose.

B. Is it the sublimity, beauty, or novelty of the sentiments?

P. Not so, for sublime sentiments are often better expressed in prose. Thus when Warwick, in one of the plays of Shakespeare, is left wounded on the field after the loss of the battle, and his friend says to him, "O, could you but fly!" what can be more sublime than his answer, "Why then, I would not fly." No measure of verse, I imagine, could add dignity to this sentiment. And it would be easy to select examples of the beautiful or new from prose writers which, I suppose, no measure of verse could improve.

B. In what then consists the essential difference between poetry and prose?

P. Next to the measure of the language, the principal distinction appears to me to consist in this: that poetry admits of but few words expressive of very abstracted ideas, whereas prose abounds with them. And as our ideas derived from visible objects are more distinct than those derived from the objects of our other senses, the words expressive of these ideas belonging to vision make up the principal part of poetic language. That is, the poet writes principally to the eye; the prose writer uses more abstracted terms. Mr. Pope has written a bad verse in the *Windsor Forest:*

And Kennet swift for silver Eels *renown'd.*

The word *renown'd* does not present the idea of a visible object to the mind, and is thence prosaic. But change this line thus:

And Kennet swift, where silver Graylings *play,*

and it becomes poetry, because the scenery is then brought before the eye.

B. This may be done in prose.

P. And when it is done in a single word, it animates the prose; so it is more agreeable to read in Mr. Gibbon's *History,* "Germany was at this time *overshadowed* with extensive forests" than, "Germany was at this time *full* of extensive forests." But where this mode of expression occurs too frequently, the prose approaches to poetry, and in graver works, where we expect to be instructed rather than amused, it becomes tedious and impertinent. Some parts of Mr. Burke's eloquent orations become intricate and enervated by superfluity of poetic ornament, which quantity of ornament would have been agreeable in a poem, where much ornament is expected.

B. Is then the office of poetry only to amuse?

P. The Muses are young ladies; we expect to see them dressed, though not like some modern beauties, with so much gauze and feather that "the lady herself is the least part of her." There are, however, didactic pieces of poetry which are much admired, as the *Georgics* of Virgil, Mason's *English Garden,* Hayley's *Epistles;* nevertheless science is best delivered in prose, as its mode of reasoning is from stricter analogies than metaphors or similes.

B. Do not personifications and allegories distinguish poetry?

P. These are other arts of bringing objects before the eye, or of expressing sentiments in the language of vision, and are indeed better suited to the pen than the pencil.

B. That is strange, when you have just said they are used to bring their objects before the eye.

P. In poetry the personification or allegoric figure is generally indistinct and therefore does not strike us so forcibly as to make us attend to its improbability, but in painting the figures being all much more distinct, their improbability becomes apparent and seizes our attention to it. Thus the person of concealment is very indistinct and therefore does not compel us to attend to its improbability in the following beautiful lines of Shakespeare:

> She never told her love;
> But let concealment, like a worm i' th' bud,
> Feed on her damask cheek.

But in these lines below the person of Reason obtrudes itself into our company, and becomes disagreeable by its distinctness, and consequent improbability:

> To Reason I flew, and intreated her aid,
> Who paused on my case, and each circumstance weigh'd;
> Then gravely reply'd in return to my prayer,
> That Hebe was fairest of all that were fair.
> That's a truth, reply'd I, I've no need to be taught,
> I came to you, Reason, to find out a fault.
> If that's all, says Reason, return as you came,
> To find fault with Hebe would forfeit my name.

Allegoric figures are on this account in general less manageable in painting and in statuary than in poetry and can seldom be introduced in the two former arts in company with natural figures, as is evident from the ridiculous effect of many of the paintings of Rubens in the Luxemburg gallery, and for this reason: because their improbability becomes more striking when there are the figures of real persons by their side to compare them with.

Mrs. Angelica Kauffmann, well apprised of this circumstance, has introduced no mortal figures amongst her Cupids and her Graces. And the great Roubiliac, in his unrivalled monument of Time and Fame struggling for the trophy of General Wade, has only hung up a medallion of the head of the hero of the piece.[1] There are, however, some allegoric figures which we have so often heard described or seen delineated that we almost forget that they do not exist in common life, and thence view them without astonishment, as the figures of the heathen mythology, of angels, devils, death, and time, and almost believe them to be realities even when they are mixed with representations of the natural forms of man. Whence I conclude that a certain degree of probability is necessary to prevent us from revolting with distaste from unnatural images unless we are otherwise so much interested in the contemplation of them as not to perceive their improbability.

B. Is this reasoning about degrees of probability just? When Sir Joshua Reynolds, who is unequalled both in the theory and practice of his art, and who is a great master of the pen as well as the pencil, has asserted in a discourse delivered to the Royal Academy, December 11, 1786, that "the higher styles of painting, like the higher kinds of the drama, do not aim at anything like deception, or have any expectation that the spectators should think the events there represented are really passing before them." And he then accuses Mr. Fielding of bad judgment when he attempts to compliment Mr. Garrick in one of his novels by introducing an ignorant man mistaking the representation of a scene in *Hamlet* for a reality and thinks because he was an ignorant man he was less liable to make such a mistake.

P. It is a metaphysical question and requires more attention than Sir Joshua has bestowed upon it. You will allow that we are perfectly deceived in our dreams and that even in our waking reveries we are often so much absorbed in the contemplation of what passes in our imagination that for a while we do not attend to the lapse of time or to our own locality and thus suffer a similar kind of deception, as in our dreams. That is, we believe things present before our eyes which are not so.

There are two circumstances which contribute to this complete deception in our dreams. First, because in sleep the organs of sense are closed or inert, and hence the trains of ideas associated in our imaginations are never interrupted or dissevered by the irritations of external objects and cannot, therefore, be contrasted with our sensations. On this account, though we are affected with a variety of passions in our dreams, as anger, love, joy, yet we never experience surprise. For surprise is only produced when any external irritations suddenly obtrude themselves and dissever our passing trains of ideas.

Secondly, because in sleep there is a total suspension of our voluntary power, both over the muscles of our bodies and the ideas of our minds; for we neither walk about nor reason in complete sleep. Hence, as the trains of our ideas are passing in our imaginations in dreams, we cannot compare them with our previous knowledge of things, as we do in our waking hours, for this is a voluntary exertion; and thus we cannot perceive their incongruity.

Thus we are deprived in sleep of the only two means by which we can distinguish the trains of ideas passing in our imaginations from those excited by our sensations, and are led by their vivacity to believe them to belong to the latter. For the vivacity of these trains of ideas passing in the imagination is greatly increased by the causes above mentioned; that is, by their not being disturbed or dissevered either by the appulses of external bodies, as in surprise, or by our voluntary exertions in comparing them with our previous knowledge of things, as in reasoning upon them.

B. Now to apply.

P. When by the art of the painter or poet a train of ideas is suggested to our imaginations which interests us so much by the pain or pleasure it affords that we cease to attend to the irritations of common external objects and cease also to use any voluntary efforts to compare these interesting trains of ideas with our previous knowledge of things, a complete reverie is produced, during which time, however short, if it be but for a moment, the objects themselves appear to exist before us. This, I think, has been called by an ingenious critic "the ideal presence" of such objects. (*Elements of Criticism,* by Lord Kames.) And in respect to the compliment intended by Mr. Fielding to Mr. Garrick, it would seem that an ignorant rustic at the play of *Hamlet* who has some previous belief in the appearance of ghosts would sooner be liable to fall into a reverie and continue in it longer than one who possessed more knowledge of the real nature of things and had a greater facility of exercising his reason.

B. It must require great art in the painter or poet to produce this kind of deception?

P. The matter must be interesting from its sublimity, beauty, or novelty; this is the scientific part; and the art consists in bringing these distinctly before the eye, so as to produce (as above mentioned) the ideal presence of the object, in which the great Shakespeare particularly excels.

B. Then it is not of any consequence whether the representations correspond with nature?

P. Not if they so much interest the reader or spectator as to induce the reverie above described. Nature may be seen in the market place, or at the card table, but we expect something more than this in the playhouse or picture room. The farther the artist recedes from nature, the greater novelty he is likely to produce; if he rises above nature, he produces the sublime; and beauty is probably a selection and new combination of her most agreeable parts. Yourself will be sensible of the truth of this doctrine by recollecting over in your mind the works of three of our celebrated artists. Sir Joshua Reynolds has introduced sublimity even into his portraits; we admire the representation of persons whose reality we should have passed by unnoticed. Mrs. Angelica Kauffmann attracts our eyes with beauty which I suppose nowhere exists; certainly few Grecian faces are seen in this country. And the daring pencil of Fuseli transports us beyond the boundaries of nature and ravishes us with the charm of the most interesting novelty. And Shakespeare, who excels in all these together, so far captivates the spectator as to make him unmindful of every kind of violation of time, place, or existence. As at the first appearance of the ghost of Hamlet, "his ear must be dull as the fat weed which roots itself on Lethe's brink," who can attend to the improbability of the exhibition. So in many scenes of the *Tempest* we perpetually believe the action passing before our eyes and relapse with somewhat of distaste into common life at the intervals of the representation.

B. I suppose a poet of less ability would find such great machinery difficult and cumbersome to manage?

P. Just so; we should be shocked at the apparent improbabilities. As in the gardens of a Sicilian nobleman, described in Mr. Brydone's and in Mr. Swinburne's travels,[2] there are said to be six hundred statues of imaginary monsters, which so disgust the spectators that the state had once a serious design of destroying them; and yet the very improbable monsters in Ovid's *Metamorphoses* have entertained the world for many centuries.

B. The monsters in your *Botanic Garden,* I hope, are of the latter kind?

P. The candid reader must determine.

ARCHIBALD ALISON ✍

Essays on the Nature and Principles of Taste (1790)

Introduction

Taste is in general considered as that faculty of the human mind by which we perceive and enjoy whatever is beautiful or sublime in the works of nature or art.

The perception of these qualities is attended with an emotion of pleasure very distinguishable from every other pleasure of our nature, and which is accordingly distinguished by the name of the *emotion of taste*. The distinction of the objects of taste into the sublime and the beautiful has produced a similar division of this emotion into the *emotion of sublimity* and the *emotion of beauty*.

The qualities that produce these emotions are to be found in almost every class of the objects of human knowledge, and the emotions themselves afford one of the most extensive sources of human delight. They occur to us amid every variety of external scenery and among many diversities of disposition and affection in the mind of man. The most pleasing arts of human invention are altogether directed to their pursuit, and even the necessary arts are exalted into dignity by the genius that can unite beauty with use. From the earliest period of society to its last stage of improvement, they afford an innocent and elegant amusement to private life at the same time that they increase the splendor of national character; and in the progress of nations, as well as of individuals, while they attract attention from the pleasures they bestow, they serve to exalt the human mind from corporeal to intellectual pursuits.

These qualities, however, though so important to human happiness, are not the objects of immediate observation, and in the attempt to investigate them, various circumstances unite to perplex our research. They are often obscured under the number of qualities with which they are accidentally combined. They result often from peculiar combinations of the qualities of objects, or the relation of certain parts of objects to each other. They are still oftener, perhaps, dependent upon the state of our own minds, and vary in their effects with the dispositions in which they happen to be observed. In all cases, while we feel the emotions they excite, we are ignorant of the causes by which they are produced; and when we seek to discover them, we have no other method of discovery than that varied and patient experiment by which, amid these complicated circumstances, we may gradually ascertain the peculiar qualities which, by the constitution of our nature, are permanently connected with the emotions we feel.

In the employment of this mode of investigation there are two great objects of attention and inquiry which seem to include all that is either necessary, or perhaps possible, for us to discover on the subject of taste.

These objects are:

I. To investigate the nature of those qualities that produce the emotions of taste; and,

II. To investigate the nature of that faculty by which these emotions are received.

These investigations, however, are not to be considered only as objects of philosophical curiosity. They have an immediate relation to all the arts that are directed to the production either of the beautiful or the sublime, and they afford the only means by which the principles of these various arts can be ascertained. Without a just and accurate conception of the nature of these qualities, the artist must be unable to determine whether the beauty he creates is temporary or permanent, whether adapted to the accidental prejudices of his age or to the uniform constitution of the human mind; and whatever the science of criticism can afford for the improvement or correction of taste must altogether depend upon the previous knowledge of the nature and laws of this faculty.

To both these inquiries, however, there is a preliminary investigation which seems absolutely necessary and without which every conclusion we form must be either imperfect or vague. In the investigation of causes, the first and most important step is the accurate examination of the effect to be explained. In the science of mind, however, as well as in that of body, there are few effects altogether simple, or in which accidental circumstances are not combined with the proper effect. Unless, therefore, by means of repeated experiments, such accidental circumstances are accurately distinguished from the phenomena that permanently characterize the effect, we are under the necessity of including in the cause the causes also of all the accidental circumstances with which the effect is accompanied.

With the emotions of taste, in almost every instance, many other accidental emotions of pleasure are united: the various simple pleasures that arise from other qualities of the object; the pleasure of agreeable sensation, in the case of material objects; and in all, that pleasure which by the constitution of our nature is annexed to the exercise of our faculties. Unless, therefore, we have previously acquired a distinct and accurate conception of that peculiar effect which is produced on our minds when the emotions of taste are felt and can precisely distinguish it from the effects that are produced by these accidental qualities, we must necessarily include in the causes of such emotions those qualities also which are the causes of the accidental pleasures with which this emotion is accompanied. The variety of systems that philosophers have adopted upon this subject, and the various emotions into which they have resolved the emotion of taste, while they afford a sufficient evidence of the numerous accidental pleasures that accompany these emotions, afford also a strong illustration of the necessity of previously ascertaining the nature of this effect before we attempt to investigate its cause. With regard, therefore, to both these inquiries, the first and most important step is accurately to examine the nature of this emotion itself and its distinction from every other emotion of pleasure; and our capacity of discovering either the nature of the qualities that produce the emotions of taste or the nature of the faculty by which they are received will be exactly proportioned to our accuracy in ascertaining the nature of the emotion itself.

When we look back to the history of these investigations and to the theories which have been so liberally formed upon the subject, there is one fact that must necessarily strike us, viz., that all these theories have uniformly taken for granted the *simplicity* of this emotion; that they have considered it as an emotion too plain and too commonly felt to admit of any analysis; that they have as uniformly, therefore, referred it to some *one* principle or law of the human mind; and that they have therefore concluded that the discovery of that *one* principle was the essential key by which all the pleasures of taste were to be resolved.

While they have assumed this fundamental principle, the various theories of philosophers may, and indeed must, be included in the two following classes of supposition.

I. The first class is that which resolves the emotion of taste directly into an original law of our nature, which supposes a sense, or senses, by which the qualities of beauty and sublimity are perceived and felt as their appropriate objects, and concludes, therefore, that the genuine object of the arts of taste is to discover and to imitate those qualities in every subject which the prescription of nature has thus made essentially either beautiful or sublime.

To this first class of hypotheses belong almost all the theories of music, of architecture, and of sculpture, the theory of Mr. Hogarth, of the Abbé Winkelmann, and perhaps, in its last result, also the theory of Sir Joshua Reynolds. It is the species of hypothesis which is naturally resorted to by all artists and amateurs—by those whose habits of thought lead them to attend more to the causes of their emotions than to the nature of the emotions themselves.

II. The second class of hypotheses arises from the opposite view of the subject. It is that which resists the idea of any new or peculiar sense distinct from the common principles of our nature, which supposes some *one* known and acknowledged principle or affection of mind to be the foundation of all the emotions we receive from the objects of taste, and which resolves, therefore, all the various phenomena into some more general law of our intellectual or moral constitution. Of this kind are the hypotheses of M. Diderot, who attributes all our emotions of this kind to the perception of relation; of Mr. Hume, who resolves them into our sense of utility; of the venerable St. Austin, who, with nobler views, a thousand years ago, resolved them into the pleasure which belongs to the perception of order and design, etc. It is the species of hypothesis most natural to retired and philosophic minds, to those whose habits have led them to attend more to the nature of the emotions they felt than to the causes which produced them.

If the success of these long and varied inquiries has not corresponded to the genius or the industry of the philosophers who have pursued them, a suspicion may arise that there has been something faulty in the principle of their investigation, and that some fundamental assumption has been made which ought first to have been patiently and securely ascertained. It was this suspicion that first led to the following inquiries: It seemed to me that the simplicity of the emotion of taste was a principle much too hastily adopted, and that the consequences which followed from it (under both these classes of hypotheses) were very little reconcilable with the most common experience of human feeling; and from the examination of this preliminary question, I was led gradually to conclusions which seemed not only to me, but to others whose opinion I value far more than my own, of an importance not unworthy of being presented to the public. In doing this, I am conscious that I have entered upon a new and untrodden path; and I feel all my own weakness in pursuing it. Yet I trust my readers will believe that I should not have pursued it so long if I were not convinced that it would finally terminate in views not only important to the arts of taste, but important also to the philosophy of the human mind.

The inquiries which follow naturally divide themselves into the following parts, and are to be prosecuted in the following order:

I. I shall begin with an analysis of the effect which is produced upon the mind when the emotions of beauty or sublimity are felt. I shall endeavor to show that this effect is very different from the determination of a sense; that it is not in fact a simple, but a complex emotion; that it involves in all cases, first, the production of some simple emotion or the exercise of some moral affection, and secondly, the consequent excitement of a peculiar exercise of the imagination; that these concomitant effects are distinguishable and very often distinguished in our experience; and that the peculiar pleasure of the beautiful or the sublime is only felt when these two effects are conjoined, and the complex emotion produced.

The prosecution of the subject will lead to another inquiry of some difficulty and extent, viz., into the origin of the beauty and sublimity of the qualities of matter. To this subordinate inquiry I shall devote a separate essay. I shall endeavor to show that all the phenomena are reducible to the same general principle, and that the qualities of matter are not beautiful or sublime in themselves but as they are, by various means, the signs or expressions of qualities capable of producing emotion.

II. From this examination of the effect I shall proceed, in the second part, to investigate the causes which are productive of it, or, in other words, the sources of the beautiful and the sublime in nature and art.

In the course of this investigation I shall endeavor to show first that there is no single emotion into which these varied effects can be resolved; that on the contrary, every simple emotion, and therefore every object which is capable of producing any simple emotion, *may* be the foundation of the complex emotion of beauty or sublimity. But, in the second place, that this complex emotion of beauty or sublimity is never produced unless, beside the excitement of some simple emotion, the imagination also is excited, and the exercise of the two faculties combined in the general effect. The prosecution of the subject will lead me to the principal object of the inquiry, to show what is that law of mind according to which, in actual life, this exercise or employment of imagination is excited, and what are the means by which, in the different fine arts, the artist is able to awaken this important exercise of imagination, and to exalt objects of simple and common pleasure into objects of beauty or sublimity.

In this part of the subject there are two subordinate inquiries which will necessarily demand attention.

1. The qualities of sublimity and beauty are discovered not only in pleasing or agreeable subjects, but frequently also in objects that are in themselves productive of pain; and some of the noblest productions of the fine arts are founded upon subjects of terror and distress. It will form, therefore, an obvious and important inquiry to ascertain by what means this singular effect is produced in real nature, and by what means it may be produced in the compositions of art.

2. There is a distinction in the effects produced upon our minds by objects of taste, and this distinction, both in the emotions and their causes, has been expressed by the terms of *sublimity* and *beauty*. It will form, therefore, a second object of inquiry to ascertain the nature of this distinction, both with regard to these emotions and to the qualities that produce them.

III. From the preceding inquiries I shall proceed, in the last part, to investigate the nature of that faculty by which these emotions are perceived and felt. I shall endeavor to show that it has no resemblance to a sense; that as, whenever it is employed, two distinct and independent powers of mind are employed, it is not to be considered as a separate and peculiar faculty, and that it is finally to be resolved into more general principles of our constitution. These speculations will probably lead to the important inquiry whether there is any standard by which the perfection or imperfection of our sentiments upon these subjects may be determined; to some explanation of the means by which taste may be corrected or improved; and to some illustration of the purposes which this peculiar constitution of our nature serves in the increase of human happiness and the exaltation of human character.

I feel it incumbent on me, however, to inform my readers that I am to employ in these inquiries a different kind of evidence from what has usually been employed by writers upon these subjects, and that my illustrations will be derived, much less from the compositions of the fine arts, than from the appearances of common nature and the experience of common men. If the fine arts are in reality arts of imitation, their principles are to be sought for in the subject which they imitate; and it is ever to be remembered that "music, architecture, and painting, as well as poetry and oratory are to deduce their laws and rules from the general sense and taste of mankind, and not from the principles of these arts themselves; in other words, that the taste is not to conform to the art, but the art to the taste." [1] In following this mode of illustration, while I am sensible that I render my book less amusing, I trust I may render it more useful. The most effectual method to check the empiricism, either of art or of science, is to multiply as far as possible the number of those who can observe and judge; and whatever may be the conclusions of my readers with regard to my own particular opinions, I shall not have occupied their attention in vain if I can lead them to think and to feel for themselves; to employ the powers which are given them to the ends for which they were given; and upon subjects where all men are entitled to judge, to disregard alike the abstract refinements of the philosopher who speculates in the closet and the technical doctrines of the artist who dictates in the school.

Essay I, "Of the Nature of the Emotions of Sublimity and Beauty"

From Chapter I, "Of the Effect Produced upon the Imagination by Objects of Sublimity and Beauty"

Section I

The emotions of sublimity and beauty are uniformly ascribed, both in popular and in philosophical language, to the imagination. The fine arts are considered as the arts which are addressed to the imagination, and the pleasures they afford are described, by way of distinction, as the pleasures of the imagination. The nature of any person's taste is in common life generally determined by the nature or character of his imagination, and the expression of any deficiency in this power of mind is considered as synonymous with the expression of a similar deficiency in point of taste.

Although, however, this connection is so generally acknowledged, it is not perhaps as generally understood in what it consists, or what is the nature of that effect which is produced upon the imagination by objects of sublimity and beauty. I shall endeavor, therefore, in the first place to state what seems to me that nature of this effect, or in what that exercise of imagination consists which is so generally supposed to take place when these emotions are felt.

When any object, either of sublimity or beauty, is presented to the mind, I believe every man is conscious of a train of thought being immediately awakened in his imagination analogous to the character or expression of the original object. The simple perception of the object, we frequently find, is insufficient to excite these emotions unless it is accompanied with this operation of mind—unless, according to common expression, our imagination is seized and our fancy busied in the pursuit of all those trains of thought which are allied to this character or expression.

Thus, when we feel either the beauty or sublimity of natural scenery—the gay luster of a morning in spring, or the mild radiance of a summer evening, the savage majesty of a wintry storm, or the wild magnificence of a tempestuous ocean—we are conscious of a variety of images in our minds very different from those which the objects themselves can present to the eye. Trains of pleasing or of solemn thought arise spontaneously within our minds; our hearts swell with emotions of which the objects before us seem to afford no adequate cause; and we are never so much satiated with delight as when, in recalling our attention, we are unable to trace either the progress of the connection of those thoughts which have passed with so much rapidity through our imagination.

The effect of the different arts of taste is similar. The landscapes of Claude Lorrain, the music of Handel, the poetry of Milton excite feeble emotions in our minds when our attention is confined to the qualities they present to our senses, or when it is to such qualities of their composition that we turn our regard. It is then only we feel the sublimity or beauty of their productions, when our imaginations are kindled by their power, when we lose ourselves amid the number of images that pass before our minds, and when we waken at last from this play of fancy as from the charm of a romantic dream. The beautiful apostrophe of the Abbé de Lille, upon the subject of gardening,

> N'avez-vous pas souvent, au lieux infrequentés,
> Rencontré tout-à-coup, ces aspects enchantés,
> Qui suspendent vos pas, dont l'image chérie
> Vous jette en une douce et longue rêverie? [2]

is equally applicable to every other composition of taste; and in the production of such trains of thought seems to consist the effect which objects of sublimity and beauty have upon the imagination.

For the truth of this observation itself I must finally appeal to the consciousness of the reader; but there are some very familiar considerations, which it may be useful to suggest, that seem very strongly to show the connection between this exercise of imagination and the existence of the emotions of sublimity or beauty.

Section II

That unless this exercise of imagination is excited, the emotions of beauty or sublimity are unfelt seems capable of illustration from many instances of a very familiar kind.

I

If the mind is in such a state as to prevent this freedom of imagination, the emotion, whether of sublimity or beauty, is unperceived. In so far as the beauties of art or nature affect the external senses, their effect is the same upon every man who is in possession of these senses. But to a man in pain or in grief, whose mind by these means is attentive only to one object or consideration, the same scene or the same form will produce no feeling of admiration which at other times, when his imagination was at liberty, would have produced it in its fullest perfection. Whatever is great or beautiful in the scenery of external nature is almost constantly before us, and not a day passes without presenting us with appearances fitted both to charm and to elevate our minds; yet it is in general with a heedless eye that we regard them, and only in particular moments that we are sensible of their power. There is no man, for instance, who has not felt the beauty of sunset; yet everyone can remember many instances when this most striking scene had no effect at all upon his imagination, and when he has beheld all the magnificence with which nature generally distinguishes the close of day without one sentiment of admiration or delight. There are times, in the same manner, when we can read the *Georgics* or the *Seasons* with perfect indifference and with no more emotion than what we feel from the most uninteresting composition in prose, while in other moments, the first lines we meet with take possession of our imagination and awaken in it such innumerable trains of imagery as almost leave the fancy of the poet behind. In these and similar cases of difference in our feelings from the same objects it will always be found that the difference arises from the state of our imaginations, from our disposition to follow out the train of thought which such objects naturally produce, or our incapacity to do it, from some other idea which has at that time taken possession of our minds and renders us unable to attend to anything else. That state of mind, every man must have felt, is most favorable to the emotions of taste in which the imagination is free and unembarrassed, or in which the attention is so little occupied by any private or particular object of thought as to leave us open to all the impressions which the objects that are before us can produce. It is upon the vacant and the unemployed, accordingly, that the objects of taste make the strongest impression. It is in such hours alone that we turn to the compositions of music or of poetry for amusement. The seasons of care, of grief, or of business have other occupations, and destroy, for the time at least, our sensibility to the beautiful or the sublime in the same proportion that they produce a state of mind unfavorable to the indulgence of imagination.

II

The same thing is observable in criticism. When we sit down to appreciate the value of a poem or of a painting, and attend minutely to the language or composition of the one or to the coloring or design of the other, we feel no longer the delight which they at first produce. Our imagination in this employment is restrained, and instead of yielding to its suggestions, we studiously endeavor to resist them by fixing our attention upon minute and partial circumstances of the composition. How much this operation of mind tends to diminish our sense of its beauty everyone will feel who attends to his own thoughts on such an occasion, or who will recollect how different was his state of mind when he first felt the beauty either of the painting or the poem. It is this, chiefly, which makes it so difficult for young people possessed of imagination to judge of the merits of any poem or fable, and which induces them so often to give their approbation to compositions of little value. It is not that they are incapable of learning in what the merits of such compositions consist, for these principles of judgment are neither numerous nor abstruse; it is not that greater experience produces greater sensibility, for this everything contradicts; but it is because everything in that period of life is able to excite their imaginations and to move their hearts, because they judge of the composition, not by its merits when compared with other works, or by its approach to any abstract or ideal standard, but by its effect in agitating their imaginations and leading them into that fairy land in which the fancy of youth has so much delight to wander. It is their own imagination which has the charm which they attribute to the work that excites it; and the simplest tale or the poorest novel is at that time as capable of awakening it as afterwards the eloquence of Virgil or Rousseau. All this, however, all this flow of imagination, in which youth and men of sensibility are so apt to indulge, and which so often brings them pleasure at the expense of their taste, the labor of criticism destroys. The mind in such an employment, instead of being at liberty to follow whatever trains of imagery the composition before it can excite, is either fettered to the consideration of some of its minute and solitary parts, or pauses, amid the rapidity of its conceptions, to make them the objects of its attention and review. In these operations, accordingly, the emotion, whether of beauty or sublimity, is lost, and if it is wished to be recalled, it can only be done by relaxing this vigor of attention and resigning ourselves again to the natural stream of our thoughts. The mathematician who investigates the demonstrations of the Newtonian philosophy, the painter who studies the design of Raphael, the poet who reasons upon the measure of Milton, all, in such occupations, lose the delight which these several productions can give, and when they are willing to recover their emotion, must withdraw their attention from those minute considerations and leave their fancy to expatiate at will amid all the great or pleasing conceptions which such productions of genius can raise.

III

The effect which is thus produced upon the mind by temporary exertions of attention is also more permanently produced by the difference of original character; and the degree in which the emotions of sublimity or beauty are felt is, in general, proportioned to the prevalence of those relations of thought in the mind upon which this exercise of imagination depends. The principal relation which seems to take place in those trains of thought that are produced by objects of taste is that of resemblance, the relation of all others the most loose and general, and which affords the greatest range of thought for our imagination to pursue. Wherever, accordingly, these emotions are felt, it will be found not only that this is the relation which principally prevails among our ideas but that the emotion itself is proportioned to the degree in which it prevails.

In the effect which is produced upon our minds by the different appearances of natural scenery it is easy to trace this progress of resembling thought and to observe how faithfully the conceptions which arise in our imaginations correspond to the impressions which the characters of these seasons produce. What, for instance, is the impression we feel from the scenery of spring? The soft and gentle green with which the earth is spread, the feeble texture of the plants and flowers, the young of animals just entering into life, and the remains of winter yet lingering among the woods and hills—all conspire to infuse into our minds somewhat of that fearful tenderness with which infancy is usually beheld. With such a sentiment how innumerable are the ideas which present themselves to our imagination! Ideas, it is apparent, by no means confined to the scene before our eyes, or to the possible desolation which may yet await its infant beauty, but which almost involuntarily extend themselves to analogies with the life of man and bring before us all those images of hope or fear which, according to our peculiar situations, have the dominion of our heart! The beauty of autumn is accompanied with a similar exercise of thought: The leaves begin then to drop from the trees; the flowers and shrubs, with which the fields were adorned in the summer months, decay; the woods and groves are silent; the sun himself seems gradually to withdraw his light, or to become enfeebled in his power. Who is there who at this season does not feel his mind impressed with a sentiment of melancholy? Or who is able to resist that current of thought which from such appearances of decay so naturally leads him to the solemn imagination of that inevitable fate which is to bring on alike the decay of life, of empire, and of nature itself? In such cases of emotion every man must have felt that the character of the scene is no sooner impressed upon his mind than various trains of correspondent imagery rise before his imagination; that whatever may be the nature of the impression, the general tone of his thoughts partakes of this nature or character; and that his delight is proportioned to the degree in which this uniformity of character prevails.

The same effect, however, is not produced upon all men. There are many whom the prospect of such appearances in nature excites to no exercise of fancy whatever, who by their original constitution are more disposed to the employment of attention than of imagination, and who in the objects that are presented to them are more apt to observe their individual and distinguishing qualities than those by which they are related to other objects of their knowledge. Upon the minds of such men, the relation of resemblance has little power; the efforts of their imagination, accordingly, are either feeble or slow, and the general character of their understandings is that of steady and precise, rather than that of enlarged and extensive, thought. It is, I believe, consistent with general experience that men of this description are little sensible to the emotions of sublimity or beauty; and they who have attended to the language of such men, when objects of this kind have been presented to them, must have perceived that the emotion they felt was no greater than what they themselves have experienced in those cases where they have exerted a similar degree of attention, or when any other cause has restrained the usual exercise of their imagination. To the qualities which are productive of simple emotion, to the useful, the agreeable, the fitting, or the convenient in objects they have the same sensibility with other men; but of the superior and more complex emotion of beauty they seem to be either altogether unconscious or to share in it only in proportion to the degree in which they can relax this severity of attention and yield to the relation of resembling thought.

It is in the same manner that the progress of life generally takes from men their sensibility to the objects of taste. The season in which these are felt in their fullest degree is in youth, when according to common expression the imagination is warm, or in other words, when it is easily excited to that exertion upon which so much of the emotion of beauty depends. The business of life in the greatest part of mankind, and the habits of more accurate thought which are acquired by the few who reason and reflect tend equally to produce in both a stricter relation in the train of their thoughts and greater attention to the objects of their consideration than can either be expected or can happen in youth. They become by these means not only less easily led to any exercise of imagination, but their associations become at the same time less consistent with the employment of it. The man of business who has passed his life in studying the means of accumulating wealth and the philosopher whose years have been employed in the investigation of causes have both not only acquired a constitution of mind very little fitted for the indulgence of imagination but have acquired also associations of a very different kind from those which take place when imagination is employed. In the first of these characters the prospect of any beautiful scene in nature would induce no other idea than that of its value. In the other it would lead only to speculations upon the causes of the beauty that was ascribed to it. In both it would thus excite ideas which could be the foundation of no exercise of imagination, because they required thought and attention. To a young mind, on the contrary, possessed of any sensibility, how many pleasing ideas would not such a prospect afford? Ideas of peace and innocence, and rural joy, and all the unblemished delights of solitude and contemplation. In such trains of imagery no labor of thought or habits of attention are required; they rise spontaneously in the mind upon the prospect of any object to which they bear the slightest resemblance, and they lead it almost insensibly along in a kind of bewitching reverie through all its store of pleasing or interesting conceptions. To the philosopher or the man of business the emotion of beauty, from such a scene, would be but feebly known; but by the young mind which had such sensibility it would be felt in all its warmth and would produce an emotion of delight which not only would be little comprehended by men of a severer or more thoughtful character but which seems also to be very little dependent upon the object which excites it and to be derived in a great measure from this exercise of mind itself.

In these familiar instances it is obvious how much the emotions of taste are connected with this state or character of imagination and how much those habits or employments of mind which demand attention or which limit it to the consideration of single objects tend to diminish the sensibility of mankind to the emotions of sublimity or beauty.

Section III

There are many other instances equally familiar which are sufficient to show that whatever increases this exercise or employment of imagination increases also the emotion of beauty or sublimity.

I

This is very obviously the effect of all associations. There is no man who has not some interesting associations with particular scenes or airs or books, and who does not feel their beauty or sublimity enhanced to him by such connections. The view of the house where one was born, of the school where one was educated and where the gay years of infancy were passed, is indifferent to no man. They recall so many images of past happiness and past affections, they are connected with so many strong or interesting emotions, and lead altogether to so long a train of feelings and recollections that there is hardly any scene which one ever beholds with so much rapture. There are songs, also, that we have heard in our infancy which, when brought to our remembrance in after years, raise emotions for which we cannot well account, and which, though perhaps very indifferent in themselves, still continue from this association and from the variety of conceptions which they kindle in our minds to be our favorites through life. The scenes which have been distinguished by the residence of any person whose memory we admire produce a similar effect. "Movemur enim, nescio quo pacto, locis ipsis, in quibus eorum, quos diligimus, aut admiramur adsunt vestigia." [3] The scenes themselves may be little beautiful, but the delight with which we recollect the traces of their lives blends itself insensibly with the emotions which the scenery excites, and the admiration which these recollections afford seems to give a kind of sanctity to the place where they dwelt and converts everything into beauty which appears to have been connected with them. There are scenes, undoubtedly, more beautiful than Runnymede, yet to those who recollect the great event which passed there, there is no scene, perhaps, which so strongly seizes upon the imagination; and although the emotions this recollection produces are of a very different kind from those which the mere natural scenery can excite, yet they unite themselves so well with these inferior emotions and spread so venerable a charm over the whole that one can hardly persuade oneself that the scene itself is not entitled to this admiration. The valley of Vaucluse is celebrated for its beauty yet how much of it has been owing to its being the residence of Petrarch!

> Mais ces eaux, ce beau ciel, ce vallon enchanteur,
> Moins que Pétrarque et Laure interessoient mon coeur.
> La voilà dont disois-je, oui, voilà cette rive
> Que Pétrarque charmoit de sa lyre plaintive;
> Ici Pétrarque à Laure exprimant son amour,
> Voyoit naître trop tard, mourir trop tot, le jour.
> Retrouverai-je encore, sur ces rocs solitaires,
> De leurs chiffres unis les tendres caractères?
> Une grotte écartée avoit frappé mes yeux,
> Grotte sombre, dis-moi si tu les vis heureux,
> M'écriois-je! un vieux tronc bordoit-il le rivage?
> Laure avoit reposé sous son antique ombrage;
> Je redmandois Laure à l'echo du vallon,
> Et l'echo n'avoit point oublié ce doux nom,
> Partout mes yeux cherchoient, voyoient, Pétrarque et Laure,
> Et par eux, ces beaux lieux s'embellissoient encore.
>   (*Les Jardins,* III)

The sublime is increased, in the same manner, by whatever tends to increase this exercise of imagination. The field of any celebrated battle becomes sublime from such associations. No man acquainted with English history can behold the field of Agincourt without some emotion of this kind. The additional conceptions which this association produces and which fill the mind of the spectator on the prospect of that memorable field diffuse themselves in some measure over the scene and give it a sublimity which does not naturally belong to it. The majesty of the Alps themselves is increased by the remembrance of Hannibal's march over them, and who is there that could stand on the banks of the Rubicon without feeling his imagination kindle and his heart beat high?

Middleton Dale (says Mr. Whately) is a cleft between rocks, ascending gradually from a romantic village till it emerges, at about two miles distance, on the vast moorlands of the Peak. It is a dismal entrance to a desert; the hills above it are bare, the rocks are of a grey color, their surfaces are rugged, and their shapes savage, frequently terminating in craggy points, sometimes resembling vast unwieldy bulwarks, or rising in heavy buttresses one above another, and here and there a misshapen mass bulging out hangs lowering over its base. No traces of men are to be seen except in a road, which has no effect on such a scene of desolation, and in the limekilns constantly smoking on the side. . . . The soil is disfigured with all the tinges of brown and red, which denote barrenness; in some places it has crumbled away, and strata of loose dark stones only appear; and in others, long lines of dross and rubbish, shovelled out of the mines, have fallen down the steeps. In these mines, the veins of lead on one side of the Dale are observed always to have corresponding veins, in exactly the same direction, on the other; and the rocks, though differing widely in different places, yet always continue in one style for some way together, and seem to have a relation to each other. Both these appearances make it probable that Middleton Dale is a chasm rent in the mountains by some convulsion of nature beyond the memory of man, or perhaps before the island was peopled. The scene, though it does not prove the fact, yet justifies the supposition, and it gives credit to the tales of the country people, who, to aggravate its horrors, always point to a precipice down which they say a young woman of the village threw herself headlong, in despair at the neglect of a man whom she loved; and show a cavern where a skeleton was once discovered, but of what wretch is unknown; his bones were the only memorial left of him. (*Observations upon Modern Gardening*, p. 93)

It is surely unnecessary to remark how much the sublimity of this extraordinary scene is increased by the circumstances of horror which are so finely connected with it.

One of the sublimest objects in natural scenery is an old and deep wood covering the side of a mountain, when seen from below; yet

how much greater sublimity is given to it by Dr. Akenside by the
addition of the solemn images which, in the following lines, are
associated with it!

> Mark the sable woods
> That shade sublime yon mountain's nodding brow.
> With what religious awe the solemn scene
> Commands your steps! as if the reverend form
> Of Minos or of Numa should forsake
> Th'Elysian seats, and down the embowering glade
> Move to your pausing eye.
>
> *(Pleasures of Imagination,* III, 286)

. . . . .

There are associations, also, which arise from particular professions or habits of thought, which serve very well to illustrate the
same observation. No man, in general, is sensible to beauty in those
subjects with regard to which he has not previous ideas. The beauty
of a theory or of a relic of antiquity is unintelligible to a peasant. The
charms of the country are altogether lost upon a citizen who has
passed his life in town. In the same manner, the more that our ideas
are increased, or our conceptions extended upon any subject, the
greater the number of associations we connect with it, the stronger
is the emotion of sublimity or beauty we receive from it.

The pleasure, for instance, which the generality of mankind
receive from any celebrated painting is trifling when compared to
that which a painter feels if he is a man of any common degree of
candor. What is to them only an accurate representation of nature
is to him a beautiful exertion of genius and a perfect display of art.
The difficulties which occur to his mind in the design and execution
of such a performance, and the testimonies of skill, of taste, and of
invention which the accomplishment of it exhibit, excite a variety
of emotions in his breast of which the common spectator is altogether unsusceptible; and the admiration with which he thus contemplates the genius and art of the painter blends itself with the
peculiar emotions which the picture itself can produce and enhances
to him every beauty that it may possess.

The beauty of any scene in nature is seldom so striking to others
as it is to a landscape painter or to those who profess the beautiful
art of laying out grounds. The difficulties both of invention and execution which from their professions are familiar to them render the

profusion with which nature often scatters the most picturesque beauties little less than miraculous. Every little circumstance of form and perspective, and light and shade, which are unnoticed by a common eye are important in theirs, and mingling in their minds the ideas of difficulty and facility in overcoming it, produce altogether an emotion of delight incomparably more animated than any that the generality of mankind usually derive from it.

The delight which most men of education receive from the consideration of antiquity and the beauty that they discover in every object which is connected with ancient times is in a great measure to be ascribed to the same cause. The antiquarian in his cabinet, surrounded by the relics of former ages, seems to himself to be removed to periods that are long since past and indulges in the imagination of living in a world which by a very natural kind of prejudice we are always willing to believe was both wiser and better than the present. All that is venerable or laudable in the history of these times present themselves to his memory. The gallantry, the heroism, the patriotism of antiquity rise again before his view, softened by the obscurity in which they are involved, and rendered more seducing to the imagination by that obscurity itself, which, while it mingles a sentiment of regret amid his pursuits, serves at the same time to stimulate his fancy to fill up, by its own creation, those long intervals of time of which history has preserved no record. The relics he contemplates seem to approach him still nearer to the ages of his regard. The dress, the furniture, the arms of the times are so many assistances to his imagination in guiding or directing its exercise; and offering him a thousand sources of imagery, provide him with an almost inexhaustible field in which his memory and his fancy may expatiate. There are few men who have not felt somewhat, at least, of the delight of such an employment. There is no man in the least acquainted with the history of antiquity who does not love to let his imagination loose on the prospect of its remains, and to whom they are not in some measure sacred from the innumerable images which they bring. Even the peasant, whose knowledge of former times extends but to a few generations, has yet in his village some monument of the deeds or virtues of his forefathers, and cherishes with a fond veneration the memorial of those good old times to which his imagination returns with delight and of which he loves to recount the simple tales that tradition has brought him.

And what is it that constitutes that emotion of sublime delight which every man of common sensibility feels upon the first prospect of Rome? It is not the scene of destruction which is before him. It is not the Tiber, diminished in his imagination to a paltry stream, and stagnating amid the ruins of that magnificence which it once adorned. It is not the triumph of superstition over the wreck of human greatness and its monuments erected upon the very spot where the first honors of humanity have been gained. It is ancient Rome which fills his imagination. It is the country of Caesar and Cicero and Virgil which is before him. It is the mistress of the world which he sees, and who seems to him to rise again from her tomb to give laws to the universe. All that the labors of his youth or the studies of his maturer age have acquired with regard to the history of this great people open at once before his imagination and present him with a field of high and solemn imagery which can never be exhausted. Take from him these associations, conceal from him that it is Rome that he sees, and how different would be his emotion!

II

The effect which is thus produced by associations in increasing the emotions of sublimity or beauty is produced also either in nature or in description by what are generally termed picturesque objects. Instances of such objects are familiar to everyone's observation. An old tower in the middle of a deep wood, a bridge flung across a chasm between rocks, a cottage on a precipice, are common examples. If I am not mistaken, the effect which such objects have on everyone's mind is to suggest an additional train of conceptions, beside what the scene or description itself would have suggested; for it is very obvious that no objects are remarked as picturesque which do not strike the imagination by themselves. They are, in general, such circumstances as coincide but are not necessarily connected with the character of the scene or description, and which, at first affecting the mind with an emotion of surprise, produce afterwards an increased or additional train of imagery. The effect of such objects in increasing the emotions either of beauty or sublimity will probably be obvious from the following instances.

The beauty of sunset in a fine autumnal evening seems almost incapable of addition from any circumstance. The various and radiant coloring of the clouds, the soft light of the sun, that gives so rich a glow to every object on which it falls, the long but mellow shades with which it is contrasted, and the calm and deep repose that seems to steal over universal nature form altogether a scene which serves perhaps better than any other in the world to satiate the imagination with delight. Yet there is no man who does not know how great an addition this fine scene is capable of receiving from the circumstance of the evening bell. In what, however, does the effect of this most picturesque circumstance consist? Is it not in the additional images which are thus suggested to the imagination? Images indeed of melancholy and sadness, but which still are pleasing, and which serve most wonderfully to accord with that solemn and pensive state of mind which is almost irresistibly produced by this fascinating scene.

Nothing can be more beautiful than Dr. Goldsmith's description of evening, in the *Deserted Village:*

> Sweet was the sound, when oft at evening's close
> Up yonder hill the village murmur rose.
> There, as I passed with careless steps and slow,
> The mingling notes came softened from below:
> The swain responsive as the milkmaid sung,
> The sober herd that lowed to meet their young,
> The noisy geese that gabbled o'er the pool,
> The playful children just let loose from school,
> The watch-dog's voice that bayed the whisp'ring wind,
> And the loud laugh that spoke the vacant mind. [113]

Yet how much is the beauty of this description increased by the fine circumstance with which it is closed?

> These all in soft confusion sought the shade,
> And filled each pause the nightingale had made.

There is a beauty of the same kind produced in the *Seasons* by the addition of one of the most picturesque circumstances that was ever imagined by a poet:

> Lead me to the mountain-brow,
> Where sits the shepherd on the grassy turf,
> Inhaling healthful the descending sun.
> Around him feeds his many-bleating flock,
> Of various cadence; and his sportive lambs,
> This way and that convolved in friskful glee,
> Their frolics play. And now the sprightly race
> Invites them forth; when swift, the signal given,
> They start away, and sweep the massy mound
> That runs around the hill—the rampart once
> Of iron war, in ancient barbarous times. (*Spring,* 832)

The scene is undoubtedly beautiful of itself, without the addition of the last circumstance; yet how much more beautiful does it become by the new order of thought which this circumstance awakens in the mind, and which, contrasting the remembrance of ancient warfare and turbulent times with the serenity and repose of the modern scene, agitate the imagination with a variety of indistinct conceptions which otherwise could never have arisen in it!

· · · · ·

All (says Mr. Whately, in describing the Tinian Lawn at Hagley) all here is of an even temper, all mild, placid and serene; in the gayest season of the day, not more than cheerful, in the stillest watch of night, not gloomy. The scene is indeed peculiarly adapted to the tranquillity of the latter, when the moon seems to repose her light on the thick foliage of the grove, and steadily marks the shade of every bough. It is delightful then to saunter here, and see the grass and the gossamer which entwines it glistening with dew, to listen, and hear nothing stir, except perhaps a withered leaf, dropping gently through a tree, and sheltered from the chill, to catch the freshness of the evening air. It is difficult to conceive anything more beautiful than this description, yet how much is its beauty increased by the concluding circumstance? A solitary urn, chosen by Mr. Pope for the spot, and now inscribed to his memory, when seen by a gleam of moonlight through the trees, fixes that thoughtfulness and composure, to which the mind is insensibly led by the rest of this elegant scene. (*Observations on Gardening*, p. 201)

I shall conclude these instances of the effect of picturesque objects in increasing the emotion of beauty, with a passage from the *Iliad* which contains one of the most striking images that I know of in poetry and which I am the more willing to quote as it has not been so much taken notice of as it deserves. It is the appearance of Achilles when Phoenix and Ulysses are sent from the Grecian camp to appease his wrath:

> Thro' the still night they march, and hear the roar
> Of murm'ring billows on the sounding shore.

· · · · ·

> And now, arriv'd, where on the sandy bay
> The Myrmidonian tents and vessels lay,
> Amus'd, at ease, the godlike man they found,
> Pleas'd with the solemn harp's harmonious sound.

· · · · ·

> With this he soothes his angry soul, and sings
> Th'immortal deeds of Heroes and of Kings.
>
> [Pope's *Iliad*, IX, 236]

It was impossible for the poet to have imagined any other occupation so well fitted to the mighty mind of Achilles or so effectual in
interesting the reader in the fate of him whom Dr. Beattie calls,
with truth, the most terrific human personage that poetical imagination has feigned.

The sublime is increased in the same manner by the addition of
picturesque objects. The striking image with which Virgil concludes
the description of the prodigies which attended the death of Caesar
is well known:

> Scilicet et tempus veniet, cum finibus illis
> agricola incurvo terram molitus aratro
> exesa inveniet scabra robigine pila,
> aut gravibus rastris, galeas pulsabit inanes,
> grandiaque effossis mirabitur ossa sepulchris.[4]
>
> .   .   .   .   .

In Thomson's description of winter in the northern regions, though
the description itself is sublime, yet one additional circumstance
adds powerfully to its sublimity:

> Thence, winding eastward to the Tartar's coast,
> She sweeps the howling margin of the main;
> Where, undissolving from the first of time,
> Snows swell on snows, amazing, to the sky;
> And icy mountains, high on mountains piled,
> Seem to the shivering sailor from afar,
> Shapeless and white, an atmosphere of clouds.
>
> .   .   .   .   .
>
> Ocean itself no longer can resist
> The binding fury: but in all its rage
> Of tempest taken by the boundless frost,
> Is many a fathom to the bottom chained,
> And bid to roar no more—a bleak expanse
> Shagged o'er with wavy rocks, cheerless, and void
> Of every life, that from the dreary months
> Flies conscious southward. Miserable they!
> Who, here entangled in the gathering ice,
> Take their last look of the descending sun;
> While, full of death, and fierce with tenfold frost,

> The long, long night incumbent o'er their heads
> Falls horrible! (*Winter*, 902)

. . . . .

I shall conclude these illustrations with a very sublime one from the *Paradise Regained* of Milton, in which I believe the force of the concluding stroke will not be denied.

> Either Tropic now
> 'Gan thunder, and both ends of Heav'n; the Clouds
> From many a horrid rift abortive pour'd
> Fierce rain with lightning mixt.
>   . . . nor slept the winds
> Within thir stony caves, but rush'd abroad
> From the four hinges of the world, and fell
> On the vext Wilderness, whose tallest Pines,
> Though rooted deep as high, and sturdiest Oaks
> Bow'd their Stiff necks, loaden with stormy blasts,
> Or torn up sheer: ill wast thou shrouded then,
> O patient Son of God! [IV, 409]

In these and a thousand other instances that might be produced I believe every man of sensibility will be conscious of a variety of great or pleasing images passing with rapidity in his imagination, beyond what the scene or description immediately before him can of themselves excite. They seem often, indeed, to have but a very distant relation to the object that at first excited them, and the object itself appears only to serve as a hint, to awaken the imagination, and to lead it through every analogous idea that has place in the memory. It is then, indeed, in this powerless state of reverie, when we are carried on by our conceptions, not guiding them, that the deepest emotions of beauty or sublimity are felt, that our hearts swell with feelings which language is too weak to express, and that in the depth of silence and astonishment we pay to the charm that enthralls us the most flattering mark of our applause.

. . . . .

The influence of such additional trains of imagery in increasing the emotions of sublimity or beauty might be illustrated from many other circumstances equally familiar. I am induced to mention only the following, because it is one of the most striking that I know, and because it is probable that most men of education have at least in some degree been conscious of it—the influence, I mean, of an acquaintance with poetry in our earlier years in increasing our sensibility to the beauties of nature.

The generality of mankind live in the world without receiving any kind of delight from the various scenes of beauty which its order displays. The rising and setting of the sun, the varying aspect of the moon, the vicissitude of seasons, the revolution of the planets, and all the stupendous scenery that they produce are to them only common occurrences like the ordinary events of every day. They have been so long familiar that they cease to strike them with any appearance either of magnificence or beauty, and are regarded by them with no other sentiments than as being useful for the purposes of human life. We may all remember a period in our lives when this was the state of our own minds, and it is probable most men will recollect that the time when nature began to appear to them in another view was when they were engaged in the study of classical literature. In most men, at least, the first appearance of poetical imagination is at school, when their imaginations begin to be warmed by the descriptions of ancient poetry and when they have acquired a new sense, as it were, with which they can behold the face of nature.

How different from this period become the sentiments with which the scenery of nature is contemplated by those who have any imagination! The beautiful forms of ancient mythology with which the fancy of poets peopled every element are now ready to appear to their minds upon the prospect of every scene. The descriptions of ancient authors, so long admired and so deserving of admiration, occur to them at every moment, and with them all those enthusiastic ideas of ancient genius and glory which the study of so many years of youth so naturally leads them to form. Or, if the study of modern poetry has succeeded to that of the ancient, a thousand other beautiful associations are acquired which, instead of destroying, serve easily to unite with the former and to afford a new source of delight. The awful forms of Gothic superstition, the wild and romantic imagery which the turbulence of the Middle Ages, the crusades, and the institution of chivalry have spread over every country of Europe, arise to the imagination in every scene, accompanied with all those pleasing recollections of prowess and adventure and courteous manners which distinguished those memorable times. With such images in their minds, it is not common nature that appears to surround them. It is nature embellished and made sacred by the memory of Theocritus and Virgil, and Milton and Tasso; their genius seems still to linger among the scenes which inspired it and to irradiate every object where it dwells; and the creation[s] of their fancy seem the fit inhabitants of that nature, which their descriptions have clothed with beauty.

Nor is it only in providing so many sources of association that the influence of an acquaintance with poetry consists. It is yet still more powerful in giving character to the different appearances of nature, in connecting them with various emotions and affections of our hearts, and in thus providing an almost inexhaustible source either of solemn or of cheerful meditation. What to ordinary men is but common occurrence, or common scenery, to those who have such associations is full of beauty. The seasons of the year, which are marked only by the generality of mankind by the different occupations or amusements they bring, have each of them, to such men, peculiar expressions, and awaken them to an exercise either of pleasing or of awful thought. The seasons of the day, which are regarded only by the common spectator as the call to labor or to rest, are to them characteristic either of cheerfulness or solemnity, and connected with all the various emotions which these characters excite. Even the familiar circumstances of general nature which pass unheeded by a common eye, the cottage, the sheepfold, the curfew, all nave expressions to them, because, in the compositions to which they have been accustomed, these all are associated with peculiar characters or rendered expressive of them, and leading them to the remembrance of such associations, enable them to behold with corresponding dispositions the scenes which are before them and to feel from their prospect the same powerful influence which the eloquence of poetry has ascribed to them.

Associations of this kind, when acquired in early life, are seldom altogether lost; and whatever inconveniences they may sometimes have with regard to the general character, or however much they may be ridiculed by those who do not experience them, they are yet productive, to those who possess them, of a perpetual and innocent delight. Nature herself is their friend; in her most dreadful as well as her most lovely scenes they can discover something either to elevate their imaginations or to move their hearts, and amid every change of scenery or of climate, can still find themselves among the early objects of their admiration or their love.

From Chapter II, "Analysis of This Exercise of Imagination"

Section I

The illustrations in the ,preceding chapter seem to show that whenever the emotions of sublimity or beauty are felt, that exercise of imagination is produced which consists in the indulgence of a train of thought; that when this exercise is prevented, these emotions are unfelt or unperceived; and that whatever tends to increase this exercise of mind, tends in the same proportion to increase these emotions. If these illustrations are just, it seems reasonable to conclude that the effect produced upon the mind by objects of sublimity and beauty consists in the production of this exercise of imagination.

Although, however, this conclusion seems to me both just and consonant to experience, yet it is in itself too general to be considered as a sufficient account of the nature of that operation of mind which takes place in the case of such emotions. There are many trains of ideas of which we are conscious which are unattended with any kind of pleasure. There are other operations of mind in which such trains of thought are necessarily produced without exciting any similar emotion. Even in the common hours of life, every man is conscious of a continued succession of thoughts passing through his mind, suggested either by the presence of external objects, or arising from the established laws of association. Such trains of thought, however, are seldom attended with pleasure, and still seldomer with an emotion corresponding in any degree to the emotions of sublimity or beauty.

There are, in like manner, many cases where objects excite a train of thought in the mind without exciting any emotion of pleasure or delight. The prospect of the house, for instance, where one has formerly lived excites very naturally a train of conceptions in the mind; yet it is by no means true that such an exercise of imagination is necessarily accompanied with pleasure, for these conceptions not only may be but very often are of a kind extremely indifferent and sometimes also simply painful. The mention of an event in history or of a fact in science naturally leads us to the conception of a number of related events or similar facts; yet it is obvious that in such a case the exercise of mind which is produced, if it is accompanied with any pleasure at all, is in most cases accompanied with a pleasure very different from that which attends the emotions of sublimity or beauty.

If therefore some train of thought or some exercise of imagination is necessary for the production of the emotions of taste, it is obvious that this is not every train of thought of which we are capable. To ascertain, therefore, with any precision either the nature or the causes of these emotions, it is previously necessary to investigate the nature of those trains of thought that are produced by objects of sublimity and beauty, and their difference from those ordinary trains which are unaccompanied with such pleasure.

As far as I am able to judge, this difference consists in two things. First, in the nature of the ideas or conceptions which compose such trains, and secondly, in the nature or law of their succession.

I

In our ordinary trains of thought every man must be conscious that the ideas which compose them are very frequently of a kind which excite no emotions either of pleasure or pain. There is an infinite variety of our ideas, as well as of our sensations, that may be termed indifferent, which are perceived without any sentiment either of pain or pleasure, and which pass as it were before the mind without making any farther impression than simply exciting the consciousness of their existence. That such ideas compose a great part, and perhaps the greatest part, of our ordinary trains of thought is apparent from the single consideration that such trains are seldom attended with emotion of any kind.

The trains of thought which are suggested by external objects are very frequently of a similar kind. The greater part of such objects are simply indifferent or at least are regarded as indifferent in our common hours either of occupation or amusement; the conceptions which they produce by the laws of association partake of the nature or character of the object which originally excited them, and the whole train passes through our mind without leaving any farther emotion than perhaps that general emotion of pleasure which accompanies the exercise of our faculties. It is scarcely possible for us to pass an hour of our lives without experiencing some train of thought of this kind, suggested by some of the external objects which happen to surround us. The indifference with which such trains are either pursued or deserted is a sufficient evidence that the ideas of which they are composed are in general of a kind unfitted to produce any emotion, either of pleasure or pain.

In the case of those trains of thought, on the contrary, which are suggested by objects either of sublimity or beauty, I apprehend it will be found that they are in all cases composed of ideas capable of exciting some affection or emotion, and that not only the whole succession is accompanied with that peculiar emotion which we call the emotion of beauty or sublimity but that every individual idea of such a succession is in itself productive of some simple emotion or other. Thus the ideas suggested by the scenery of spring are ideas productive of emotions of cheerfulness, of gladness, and of tenderness. The images suggested by the prospect of ruins are images belonging to pity, to melancholy, and to admiration. The ideas, in the same manner, awakened by the view of the ocean in a storm are ideas of power, of majesty, and of terror. In every case where the emotions of taste are felt, I conceive it will be found that the train of thought which is excited is distinguished by some character of emotion, and that it is by this means distinguished from our common or ordinary successions of thought. To prevent a very tedious and unnecessary circumlocution, such ideas may perhaps, without any impropriety, be termed ideas of emotion; and I shall beg leave therefore to use the expression in this sense.

The first circumstance, then, which seems to distinguish those trains of thought which are produced by objects either of sublimity or beauty is that the ideas or conceptions of which they are composed are ideas of emotion.

II

In our ordinary trains of thought there seldom appears any general principle of connection among the ideas which compose them. Each idea, indeed, is related by an established law of our nature to that which immediately preceded and that which immediately follows it, but in the whole series there is no predominant relation or bond of connection. This want of general connection is so strong that even that most general of all relations, the relation either of pleasure or pain, is frequently violated. Images both of the one kind and the other succeed each other in the course of the train, and when we put an end to it, we are often at a loss to say whether the whole series was pleasant or painful. Of this irregularity, I think every man will be convinced who chooses to attend to it.

In those trains, on the contrary, which are suggested by objects of sublimity or beauty, however slight the connection between individual thoughts may be, I believe it will be found that there is always some general principle of connection which pervades the whole and gives them some certain and definite character. They are either gay or pathetic or melancholy or solemn or awful or elevating, etc., according to the nature of the emotion which is first excited. Thus the prospect of a serene evening in summer produces first an emotion of peacefulness and tranquillity, and then suggests a variety of images corresponding to this primary impression. The sight of a torrent or of a storm, in the same manner, impresses us first with sentiments of awe or solemnity or terror, and then awakens in our minds a series of conceptions allied to this peculiar emotion. Whatever may be the character of the original emotion, the images which succeed seem all to have a relation to this character; and if we trace them back, we shall discover not only a connection between the individual thoughts of the train, but also a general relation among the whole and a conformity to that peculiar emotion which first excited them.

The train of thought, therefore, which takes place in the mind upon the prospect of objects of sublimity and beauty may be considered as consisting in a regular or consistent train of ideas of emotion, and as distinguished from our ordinary trains of thought: first, in respect of the nature of the ideas of which it is composed, by their being ideas productive of emotion; and secondly, in respect of their succession, by their being distinguished by some general principle of connection which subsists through the whole extent of the train.

The truth of the account which I have now given of the nature of that train of thought which attends the emotions of sublimity and beauty must undoubtedly at last be determined by its conformity to general experience and observation. There are some considerations, however, of a very obvious and familiar kind which it may be useful to suggest to the reader for the purpose of affording him a method of investigating with accuracy the truth of this account.

If it is true that the ideas which compose that train of thought which attends the emotions of taste are uniformly ideas of emotion, then it ought in fact to be found that no objects or qualities are experienced to be beautiful or sublime but such as are productive of some simple emotion.

If it is true that such trains of thought are uniformly distinguished by some general principle of connection, then it ought also to be found that no composition of objects or qualities produces such emotions in which this unity of character or of emotion is not preserved.

I shall endeavor, at some length, to illustrate the truth of both these propositions.[5]

.   .   .   .   .

"Conclusion"

I

The illustrations in the first chapter of this essay are intended to show that whenever the emotions of beauty or sublimity are felt, that exercise of imagination is produced which consists in the prosecution of a train of thought.

The illustrations in the second chapter are intended to point out the distinction between such trains and our ordinary trains of thought, and to show that this difference consists, first, in the ideas which compose them being in all cases ideas of emotion; and, secondly, in their possessing a uniform principle of connection through the whole of the train. The effect, therefore, which is produced upon the mind by objects of taste may be considered as consisting in the production of a regular or consistent train of ideas of emotion.

II

The account which I have now given of this effect may perhaps serve to point out an important distinction between the emotions of taste and all our different emotions of simple pleasure. In the case of these last emotions, no additional train of thought is necessary. The pleasurable feeling follows immediately the presence of the object or quality, and has no dependence upon anything for its perfection but the sound state of the sense by which it is received. The emotions of joy, pity, benevolence, gratitude, utility, propriety, novelty, etc. might undoubtedly be felt, although we had no such power of mind as that by which we follow out a train of ideas, and certainly are felt in a thousand cases when this faculty is unemployed.

In the case of the emotions of taste, on the other hand, it seems evident that this exercise of mind is necessary and that unless this train of thought is produced, these emotions are unfelt. Whatever may be the nature of that simple emotion which any object is fitted to excite, whether that of gaiety, tranquillity, melancholy, etc., if it produce not a train of kindred thought in our minds, we are conscious only of that simple emotion. Whenever, on the contrary, this train of thought or this exercise of imagination is produced, we are conscious of an emotion of a higher and more pleasing kind, and which, though it is impossible to describe in language, we yet distinguish by the name of the emotion of taste. If accordingly the author of our nature had denied us this faculty of imagination, it should seem that these emotions could not have been felt and that all our emotions would have been limited to those of simple pleasure.

The emotions of taste may therefore be considered as distinguished from the emotions of simple pleasure by their being dependent upon the exercise of our imagination, and though founded in all cases upon some simple emotion, as yet further requiring the employment of this faculty for their existence.

III

As in every operation of taste there are thus two different faculties employed, viz., some affection or emotion raised, and the imagination excited to a train of thought corresponding to this emotion, the peculiar pleasure which attends and which constitutes the emotions of taste may naturally be considered as composed of the pleasures which separately attend the exercise of these faculties, or in other words, as produced by the union of pleasing emotion with the pleasure which, by the constitution of our nature, is annexed to the exercise of imagination. That both these pleasures are felt in every operation of taste seems to me very agreeable to common experience and observation.

.   .   .   .   .

If it is allowed, then, that there is a pleasure annexed, by the constitution of our nature, to the exercise of imagination, and if the illustrations in the first chapter are just, which are intended to show that when this exercise of mind is not produced the emotions of taste are unfelt, and that when it is increased, these emotions are increased with it, we seem to possess sufficient evidence to conclude that this pleasure exists and forms a part of that peculiar pleasure which we receive from objects of sublimity and beauty.

The pleasure, therefore, which accompanies the emotions of taste may be considered not as a simple, but as a complex pleasure, and as arising not from any separate and peculiar sense, but from the union of the pleasure of simple emotion with that which is annexed, by the constitution of the human mind, to the exercise of imagination.

. . . . . .

Essay II, "Of the Sublimity and Beauty of the Material World"

"Conclusion of This Essay. Of the Final Cause of This Constitution of Our Nature"

The illustrations that have been offered in the course of this essay upon the origin of the sublimity and beauty of some of the principal qualities of matter seem to afford sufficient evidence for the following conclusions:

I. That each of these qualities is, either from nature, from experience, or from accident, the sign of some quality capable of producing emotion or the exercise of some moral affection. And,

II. That when these associations are dissolved, or in other words, when the material qualities cease to be significant of the associated qualities, they cease also to produce the emotions either of sublimity or beauty.

If these conclusions are admitted, it appears necessarily to follow that the beauty and sublimity of such objects is to be ascribed not to the material qualities themselves, but to the qualities they signify; and, of consequence, that the qualities of matter are not to be considered as sublime or beautiful in themselves, but as being the signs or expressions of such qualities as by the constitution of our nature are fitted to produce pleasing or interesting emotion.

The opinion I have now stated coincides in a great degree with a doctrine that appears very early to have distinguished the Platonic school, which is to be traced, perhaps (amid their dark and figurative language), in all the philosophical systems of the East, and which has been maintained in this country by several writers of eminence, by Lord Shaftesbury, Dr. Hutcheson, Dr. Akenside, and Dr. Spence, but which has nowhere so firmly and so philosophically been maintained as by Dr. Reid in his invaluable work *On the Intellectual Powers of Man.* The doctrine to which I allude is that matter is not beautiful in itself but derives its beauty from the expression of mind.

As this doctrine, however, when stated in general terms, has somewhat the air of paradox, I shall beg leave, in a few words, to explain in what sense I understand and adopt it, by enumerating what appear to me the principal classes of this expression, or the principal means by which the qualities of matter become significant to us of those qualities of mind which are destined to affect us with pleasing or interesting emotion.

The qualities of mind which are capable of producing emotion are either its active or its passive qualities; either its powers and capacities, as beneficence, wisdom, fortitude, invention, fancy, etc., or its feelings and affections, as love, joy, hope, gratitude, purity, fidelity, innocence, etc. In the observation or belief of these qualities of mind, we are formed, by the original and moral constitution of our nature, to experience various and powerful emotions.

As it is only, however, through the medium of matter that, in the present condition of our being, the qualities of mind are known to us, the qualities of matter become necessarily expressive to us of all the qualities of mind they signify. They may be the signs, therefore, or expressions of these mental qualities, in the following ways:

I. As the immediate signs of the *powers* or capacities of mind. It is thus that all the works of human art or design are directly significant to us of the wisdom, the invention, the taste, or the benevolence of the artist; and the works of nature of the power, the wisdom, and the beneficence of the divine artist.

II. As the signs of all those *affections*, or dispositions of mind, which we love, or with which we are formed to sympathize. It is thus that the notes and motions of animals are expressive to us of their happiness and joy, that the tones of the human voice are significant of the various emotions by which it is animated, and that all the affections which we either love or admire in the human mind are directly signified to us by the various appearances of the countenance and form.

These may be called the *direct* expressions of mind; and the material qualities which signify such powers or affections produce in us immediately the peculiar emotions which, by the laws of our nature, the mental qualities are fitted to produce. But besides these there are other means by which the qualities of matter may be significant to us of the qualities of mind, *indirectly*, or by means of less universal and less permanent relations.

1. From experience, when peculiar forms or appearances of matter are considered as the *means* or *instruments* by which those feelings or affections of mind are produced with which we sympathize, or in which we are interested. It is thus that the productions of art are in so many various ways significant to us of the conveniences, the pleasures, or the happiness they bestow upon human life, and as the signs of happiness affect us with the emotion this happiness itself is destined to produce. It is thus also that the scenes of nature acquire such an accession of beauty when we consider them as fitted, with such exquisite wisdom, for the habitation of so many classes of sentient being, and when they become thus expressive to us of all the varied happiness they produce and contain and conceal.

2. From analogy or resemblance—from that resemblance which has everywhere been felt between the qualities of matter and of mind and by which the former becomes so powerfully expressive to us of the latter. It is thus that the colors, the sounds, the forms, and above all, perhaps, the motions of inanimate objects are so universally felt as resembling peculiar qualities or affections of mind, and when thus felt, are so productive of the analogous emotion; that the personification of matter is so strongly marked in every period of the history of human thought; and that the poet, while he gives life and animation to everything around him, is not displaying his own invention, but only obeying one of the most powerful laws which regulate the imagination of man.

3. From association (in the proper sense of that term), when by means of education, of fortune, or of accident, material objects are connected with pleasing or interesting qualities of mind, and from this connection become forever afterwards expressive of them. It is thus that colors, forms, etc. derive their temporary beauty from

fashion, that the objects which have been devoted to religion, to patriotism, or to honor affect us with all the emotions of the qualities of which they become significant, that the beauty of natural scenery is so often exalted by the record of the events it has witnessed, and that in every country the scenes which have the deepest effect upon the admiration of the people are those which have become sacred by the memory of ancient virtue or ancient glory.

4. From *individual* association, when certain qualities or appearances of matter are connected with our own private affections or remembrances, and when they give to these material qualities or appearances a character of interest which is solely the result of our own memory and affections.

Of the reality of these expressions I believe no person can doubt; and whoever will attend to the power and extent of their influence will, I think, soon be persuaded that they are sufficient to account for all the beauty or sublimity we discover in the qualities of matter.

The conclusion, therefore, in which I wish to rest is that the beauty and sublimity which is felt in the various appearances of matter are finally to be ascribed to their expression of mind or to their being, either directly or indirectly, the signs of those qualities of mind which are fitted by the constitution of our nature to affect us with pleasing or interesting emotion.

WILLIAM GILPIN ✒

Three Essays (1792)

"On Picturesque Beauty"

Disputes about beauty might perhaps be involved in less confusion if a distinction were established, which certainly exists, between such objects as are beautiful and such as are picturesque—between those which please the eye in their natural state and those which please from some quality capable of being illustrated by painting.

Ideas of beauty vary with objects and with the eye of the spectator. The stonemason sees beauties in a well-jointed wall which escape the architect, who surveys the building under a different idea. And thus the painter, who compares his object with the rules of his art, sees it in a different light from the man of general taste, who surveys it only as simply beautiful.

As this difference therefore between the beautiful and the picturesque appears really to exist, and must depend on some peculiar construction of the object, it may be worth while to examine what that peculiar construction is. We inquire not into the general sources of beauty, either in nature or in representation. This would lead into a nice and scientific discussion, in which it is not our purpose to engage. The question simply is, "What is that quality in objects which particularly marks them as picturesque?"

In examining the real object, we shall find one source of beauty arises from that species of elegance which we call *smoothness,* or *neatness,* for the terms are nearly synonymous. The higher the marble is polished, the brighter the silver is rubbed, and the more the mahogany shines, the more each is considered as an object of beauty, as if the eye delighted in gliding smoothly over a surface.

In the class of larger objects the same idea prevails. In a pile of building we wish to see neatness in every part added to the elegance of the architecture. And if we examine a piece of improved pleasure ground, everything rough and slovenly offends.

Mr. Burke, enumerating the properties of beauty, considers smoothness as one of the most essential.

A very considerable part of the effect of beauty, says he, is owing to this quality—indeed the most considerable—for take any beautiful object and give it a broken and rugged surface, and however well formed it may be in other respects, it pleases no longer. Whereas, let it want ever so many of the other constituents, if it want not this, it becomes more pleasing than almost all the others without it.[1]

How far Mr. Burke may be right in making smoothness the most considerable source of beauty I rather doubt.[2] A considerable one it certainly is.

Thus then, we suppose, the matter stands with regard to beautiful objects in general. But in picturesque representation it seems somewhat odd, yet perhaps we shall find it equally true, that the reverse of this is the case, and that the ideas of neat and smooth, instead of being picturesque, in reality strip the object in which they reside of all pretensions to picturesque beauty. Nay, farther, we do not scruple to assert that roughness forms the most essential point of difference between the beautiful and the picturesque, as it seems to be that particular quality which makes objects chiefly pleasing in painting. I use the general term *roughness*, but properly speaking roughness relates only to the surfaces of bodies; when we speak of their delineation, we use the word *ruggedness*. Both ideas, however, equally enter into the picturesque, and both are observable in the smaller as well as in the larger parts of nature— in the outline and bark of a tree, as in the rude summit and craggy sides of a mountain.

Let us then examine our theory by an appeal to experience, and try how far these qualities enter into the idea of picturesque beauty, and how far they mark that difference among objects which is the ground of our inquiry.

A piece of Palladian architecture may be elegant in the last degree. The proportion of its parts, the propriety of its ornaments, and the symmetry of the whole may be highly pleasing. But if we introduce it in a picture, it immediately becomes a formal object and ceases to please. Should we wish to give it picturesque beauty, we must use the mallet instead of the chisel, we must beat down one half of it, deface the other, and throw the mutilated members around in heaps. In short, from a smooth building we must turn it into a rough ruin. No painter who had the choice of the two objects would hesitate which to choose.

Again, why does an elegant piece of garden ground make no figure on canvas? The shape is pleasing, the combination of the objects harmonious, and the winding of the walk in the very line of beauty. All this is true; but the smoothness of the whole, though right, and as it should be in nature, offends in picture. Turn the lawn into a piece of broken ground, plant rugged oaks instead of flowering shrubs, break the edges of the walk, give it the rudeness of a road, mark it with wheel tracks, and scatter around a few stones and brushwood—in a word, instead of making the whole smooth, make it rough—and you make it also picturesque. All the other ingredients of beauty it already possessed.

You sit for your picture. The master, at your desire, paints your head combed smooth and powdered from the barber's hand. This may give it a more striking likeness, as it is more the resemblance of the real object. But is it therefore a more pleasing picture? I fear not. Leave Reynolds to himself, and he will make it picturesque by throwing the hair dishevelled about your shoulders. Virgil would have done the same. It was his usual practice in all his portraits. In his figure of Ascanius, we have the *fusos crines;* and in his portrait of Venus, which is highly finished in every part, the artist has given her hair *diffundere ventis.*[3] Modern poets, also, who have any ideas of natural beauty do the same. I introduce Milton to represent them all. In his picture of Eve he tells us that [she]

> to her slender waist
> Her unadorned golden tresses wore
> Dishevelled, and in wanton ringlets waved.

That lovely face of youth smiling with all its sweet dimpling charms, how attractive is it in life! How beautiful in representation! It is one of those objects that please, as many do, both in nature and on canvas. But would you see the human face in its highest form of picturesque beauty, examine that patriarchal head. What is it which gives that dignity of character, that force of expression, those lines of wisdom and experience, that energetic meaning so far beyond the rosy hue, or even the bewitching smile, of youth? What is it but the forehead furrowed with wrinkles, the prominent cheek bone catching the light, the muscles of the cheek strongly marked and losing themselves in the shaggy beard, and above all, the austere brow projecting over the eye—the feature which particularly struck Homer in his idea of Jupiter,[4] and which he had probably seen finely represented in some statue—in a word, what is it but the rough touches of age?

As an object of the mixed kind, partaking both of the beautiful and the picturesque, we admire the human figure also. The lines and surface of a beautiful human form are so infinitely varied; the lights and shades which it receives, are so exquisitely tender in some parts, and yet so round, and bold in others; its proportions are so just, and its limbs so fitted to receive all the beauties of grace and contrast, that even the face, in which the charms of intelligence and sensibility reside, is almost lost in the comparison. But although the human form in a quiescent state is thus beautiful, yet the more its smooth surface is ruffled, if I may so speak, the more picturesque it appears. When it is agitated by passion and its muscles swollen by strong exertion, the whole frame is shown to the most advantage. But when we speak of muscles swollen by exertion, we mean only natural exertions, not an affected display of anatomy in which the muscles, though justly placed, may still be overcharged.

It is true we are better pleased with the usual representations we meet with of the human form in a quiescent state than in an agitated one, but this is merely owing to our seldom seeing it naturally represented in strong action. Even among the best masters we see little knowledge of anatomy. One will inflate the muscles violently to produce some trifling effect; another will scarce swell them in the production of a labored one. The eye soon learns to see a defect, though unable to amend it. But when the anatomy is perfectly just, the human body will always be more picturesque in action than at rest. The great difficulty, indeed, of representing strong muscular motion seems to have struck the ancient masters of sculpture, for it is certainly much harder to model from a figure in strong, momentary action, which must, as it were, be shot flying, than from one sitting or standing, which the artist may copy at leisure. Amidst the variety of statues transmitted from their hands, we have only three or four in very spirited action.[5] Yet when we see an effect of this kind well executed, our admiration is greatly increased. Who does not admire the Laocoön more than the Antinous?

Animal life, as well as human, is in general beautiful both in nature and on canvas. We admire the pampered horse as a real object—the elegance of his form, the stateliness of his tread, the spirit of all his motions, and the glossiness of his coat. We admire him also in representation. But as an object of picturesque beauty, we admire more the worn-out cart horse, the cow, the goat, or the ass, whose harder lines and rougher coats exhibit more the graces of the pencil. For the truth of this we may examine Berghem's pictures; we may examine the smart touch of Rosa of Tivoli. The lion with his rough mane, the bristly boar, and the ruffled plumage of the eagle [6] are all objects of this kind. Smooth coated animals could not produce so picturesque an effect.

But when the painter thus prefers the cart-horse, the cow, or the ass to other objects more beautiful in themselves, he does not certainly recommend his art to those whose love of beauty makes them anxiously seek by what means its fleeting forms may be fixed.

Suggestions of this kind are ungrateful. The art of painting allows you all you wish. You desire to have a beautiful object painted —your horse, for instance, led out of the stable in all his pampered beauty. The art of painting is ready to accommodate you. You have the beautiful form you admire in nature exactly transferred to canvas. Be then satisfied. The art of painting has given you what you wanted. It is no injury to the beauty of your Arabian if the painter think he could have given the graces of his art more forcibly to your cart horse.

But does it not depreciate his art if he give up a beautiful form for one less beautiful merely because he can give it the graces of his art more forcibly—because its sharp lines afford him a greater facility of execution? Is the smart touch of a pencil the grand desideratum of painting? Does he discover nothing in picturesque objects but qualities which admit of being rendered with spirit?

I should not vindicate him if he did. At the same time, a free execution is so very fascinating a part of painting that we need not wonder if the artist lay a great stress upon it.—It is not, however, entirely owing, as some imagine, to the difficulty of mastering an elegant line that he prefers a rough one. In part, indeed, this may be the case, for if an elegant line be not delicately hit off, it is the most insipid of all lines, whereas in the description of a rough object, an error in delineation is not easily seen. However this is not the whole of the matter. A free, bold touch is in itself pleasing.[7] In elegant figures indeed there must be a delicate outline—at least a line true to nature. Yet the surfaces even of such figures may be touched with freedom, and in the appendages of the composition there must be a mixture of rougher objects, or there will be a want of contrast. In landscape universally the rougher objects are admired, which give the freest scope to execution. If the pencil be timid or hesitating, little beauty results. The execution then only is pleasing when the hand, firm and yet decisive, freely touches the characteristic parts of each object.

If, indeed, either in literary or in picturesque composition you endeavor to draw the reader or the spectator from the subject to the mode of executing it, your affectation disgusts.[8] At the same time, if some care and pains be not bestowed on the execution, your slovenliness disgusts as much. Though perhaps the artist has more to say than the man of letters for paying attention to his execution. A truth is a truth, whether delivered in the language of a philosopher or of a peasant, and the intellect receives it as such. But the artist, who deals in lines, surfaces, and colors, which are an immediate address to the eye, conceives the *very truth itself* concerned in his *mode* of representing it. Guido's angel and the angel on a sign-post are very different beings, but the whole of the difference consists in an artful application of lines, surfaces, and colors.

It is not however merely for the sake of his execution that the artist values a rough object. He finds it in many other respects accommodated to his art. In the first place, his composition requires it. If the history painter threw all his draperies smooth over his figures, his groups and combinations would be very awkward. And in landscape painting smooth objects would produce no composition at all. In a mountain scene what composition could arise from the corner of a smooth knoll coming forward on one side, intersected by a smooth knoll on the other, with a smooth plain perhaps in the middle, and a smooth mountain in the distance? The very idea is disgusting. Picturesque composition consists in uniting in one whole a variety of parts, and these parts can only be obtained from rough objects. If the smooth mountains, and plains were broken by different objects, the composition would be good, if we suppose the great lines of it were so before.

Variety, too, is equally necessary in his composition; so is contrast. Both these he finds in rough objects, and neither of them in smooth. Variety, indeed, in some degree he may find in the outline of a smooth object, but by no means enough to satisfy the eye without including the surface also.

From rough objects also he seeks the effect of light and shade, which they are as well disposed to produce as they are the beauty of composition. One uniform light or one uniform shade produces no effect. It is the various surfaces of objects, sometimes turning to the light in one way, and sometimes in another, that give the painter his choice of opportunities in massing and graduating both his lights and shades. The richness also of the light depends on the breaks and little recesses which it finds on the surfaces of bodies. What the painter calls richness on a surface is only a variety of little parts, on which the light shining shows all its small inequalities and roughness, or in the painter's language, enriches it. The beauty also of catching lights arises from the roughness of objects. What the painter calls a catching light is a strong touch of light on some prominent part of a surface, while the rest is in shadow. A smooth surface hath no such prominences.

In coloring also, rough objects give the painter another advantage. Smooth bodies are commonly as uniform in their color as they are in their surface. In glossy objects, though smooth, the coloring may sometimes vary. In general, however, it is otherwise —in the objects of landscape, particularly. The smooth side of a hill is generally of one uniform color, while the fractured rock presents its grey surface adorned with patches of greensward running down its guttered sides, and the broken ground is everywhere varied with an ochery tint, a grey gravel, or a leaden colored clay, so that, in fact, the rich colors of the ground arise generally from its broken surface.

From such reasoning, then, we infer that it is not merely for the sake of his execution that the painter prefers rough objects to smooth. The very essence of his art requires it.

As picturesque beauty therefore so greatly depends on rough objects, are we to exclude every idea of smoothness from mixing with it? Are we struck with no pleasing image when the lake is spread upon the canvas the *marmoreum aequor,* pure, limpid, smooth as the polished mirror?

We acknowledge it to be picturesque, but we must at the same time recollect that in fact the smoothness of the lake is more in reality than in appearance. Were it spread upon the canvas in one simple hue, it would certainly be a dull, fatiguing object. But to the eye it appears broken by shades of various kinds, or by reflections from all the rough objects in its neighborhood.

It is thus, too, in other glossy bodies. Though the horse, in a rough state as we have just observed, or worn down with labor, is more adapted to the pencil than when his sides shine with brushing and high feeding, yet in this latter state also he is certainly a picturesque object. But it is not his smooth and shining coat that makes him so. It is the apparent interruption of that smoothness by a variety of shades and colors which produces the effect. Such a play of muscles appears everywhere, through the fineness of his skin, gently swelling and sinking into each other—he is all over so *lubricus aspici,* the reflections of light are so continually shifting upon him and playing into each other, that the eye never considers the smoothness of the surface, but is amused with gliding up and down among those endless transitions, which in some degree supply the room of roughness.

It is thus too in the plumage of birds. Nothing can be softer, nothing smoother to the touch, and yet it is certainly picturesque. But it is not the smoothness of the surface which produces the effect—it is not this we admire. It is the breaking of the colors; it is the bright green, or purple, changing perhaps into a rich azure, or velvet black; from thence taking a semi-tint; and so on through all the varieties of color. Or if the colors be not changeable, it is the harmony of them which we admire in these elegant little touches of nature's pencil. The smoothness of the surface is only the ground of the colors. In itself we admire it no more than we do the smoothness of the canvas which receives the colors of the picture. Even the plumage of the swan, which to the inaccurate observer appears only of one simple hue, is in fact varied with a thousand soft shadows and brilliant touches, at once discoverable to the picturesque eye.

Thus, too, a piece of polished marble may be picturesque, but it is only when the polish brings out beautiful veins which in appearance break the surface by a variety of lines and colors. Let the marble be perfectly white, and the effect vanishes. Thus, also, a mirror may have picturesque beauty, but it is only from its reflections. In an unreflecting state it is insipid.

In statuary we sometimes see an inferior artist give his marble a gloss, thinking to atone for his bad workmanship by his excellent polish. The effect shows in how small a degree smoothness enters into the idea of the picturesque. When the light plays on the shining coat of a pampered horse, it plays among the lines and muscles of nature, and is therefore founded in truth. But the polish of marble flesh is unnatural.[9] The lights therefore are false, and smoothness being here one of the chief qualities to admire, we are disgusted, and say it makes bad worse.

After all, we mean not to assert that even a simple smooth surface is in no situation picturesque. In contrast it certainly may be; nay, in contrast it is often necessary. The beauty of an old head is greatly improved by the smoothness of the bald pate, and the rougher parts of the rock must necessarily be set off with the smoother. But the point lies here: To make an object in a peculiar manner picturesque, there must be a proportion of roughness, so much, at least, as to make an opposition, which in an object simply beautiful is unnecessary.

Some quibbling opponent may throw out that wherever there is smoothness, there must also be roughness. The smoothest plain consists of many rougher parts, and the roughest rock of many smoother; and there is such a variety of degrees in both that it is hard to say where you have the precise ideas of rough and smooth.

To this it is enough that the province of the picturesque eye is to survey nature, not to anatomize matter. It throws its glances around in the broadcast style. It comprehends an extensive tract at each sweep. It examines parts, but never descends to particles.

Having thus from a variety of examples endeavored to show that roughness, either real or apparent, forms an essential difference between the beautiful and the picturesque, it may be expected that we should point out the reason of this difference. It is obvious enough why the painter prefers rough objects to smooth; but it is not so obvious why the quality of roughness should make an essential difference between objects of beauty and objects suited to artificial representation.

To this question we might answer that the picturesque eye abhors art and delights solely in nature, and that as art abounds with regularity (which is only another name for smoothness), and the images of nature with irregularity (which is only another name for roughness), we have here a solution of our question.

But is this solution satisfactory? I fear not. Though art often abounds with regularity, it does not follow that all art must necessarily do so. The picturesque eye, it is true, finds its chief object in nature, but it delights also in the images of art if they are marked with the characteristics which it requires. A painter's nature is whatever he imitates, whether the object be what is commonly called natural or artificial. Is there a greater ornament of landscape than the ruins of a castle? What painter rejects it because it is artificial? What beautiful effects does Vandervelde produce from shipping? In the hands of such a master it furnishes almost as beautiful forms as any in the whole circle of picturesque objects. And what could the history painter do without his draperies to combine, contrast, and harmonize his figures? Unclothed, they could never be grouped. How could he tell his story without arms, religious utensils, and the rich furniture of banquets? Many of these contribute greatly to embellish his pictures with pleasing shapes.

Shall we then seek the solution of our question in the great foundation of picturesque beauty? In the happy union of simplicity and variety to which the rough ideas essentially contribute? An extended plain is a simple object. It is the continuation of only one uniform idea. But the mere simplicity of a plain produces no beauty. Break the surface of it, as you did your pleasure ground; add trees, rocks, and declivities; that is, give it roughness, and you give it also variety. Thus by enriching the parts of a united whole with roughness, you obtain the combined idea of simplicity and variety; from whence results the picturesque. Is this a satisfactory answer to our question?

By no means. Simplicity and variety are sources of the beautiful, as well as of the picturesque. Why does the architect break the front of his pile with ornaments? Is it not to add variety to simplicity? Even the very blacksmith acknowledges this principle by forming ringlets and bulbous circles on his tongs and pokers. In nature it is the same; and your plain will just as much be improved in reality by breaking it, as upon canvas. In a garden scene the idea is different. There every object is of the neat and elegant kind. What is otherwise is inharmonious, and roughness would be disorder.

Shall we then change our ground and seek an answer to our question in the nature of the art of painting? As it is an art strictly imitative, those objects will of course appear most advantageously to the picturesque eye which are the most easily imitated. The stronger the features are, the stronger will be the effect of imitation; and as rough objects have the strongest features, they will consequently, when represented, appear to most advantage. Is this answer more satisfactory?

Very little, in truth. Every painter knows that a smooth object may be as easily and as well imitated as a rough one.

Shall we then take an opposite ground and say just the reverse (as men pressed with difficulties will say anything) that painting is not an art strictly imitative, but rather deceptive—that by an assemblage of colors, and a peculiar art in spreading them, the painter gives a semblance of nature at a proper distance, which at hand is quite another thing—that those objects which we call picturesque are only such as are more adapted to this art—and that as this art is most concealed in rough touches, rough objects are of course the most picturesque. Have we now attained a satisfactory account of the matter?

Just as much so as before. Many painters of note did not use the rough style of painting, and yet their pictures are as admirable as the pictures of those who did; nor are rough objects less picturesque on their canvas than on the canvas of others. That is, they paint rough objects smoothly.

Thus foiled, should we, in the true spirit of inquiry, persist, or honestly give up the cause and own we cannot search out the source of this difference? I am afraid this is the truth; whatever airs of dogmatizing we may assume, inquiries into principles rarely end in satisfaction. Could we even gain satisfaction in our present question, new doubts would arise. The very first principles of our art would be questioned. Difficulties would start up *vestibulum ante ipsum.* We should be asked, "What is beauty?" "What is taste?" Let us step aside a moment and listen to the debates of the learned on these heads. They will at least show us that however we may wish to fix principles, our inquiries are seldom satisfactory.

One philosopher will tell us that taste is only the improvement of our own ideas. Every man has naturally his proportion of taste. The seeds of it are *innate.* All depends on cultivation.

Another philosopher following the analogy of nature, observes that as all men's faces are different, we may well suppose their minds to be so likewise. He rejects the idea therefore of innate taste, and in the room of this makes *utility* the standard both of taste and beauty.

A third philosopher thinks the idea of utility as absurd as the last did that of innate taste. "What," cries he, "can I not admire the beauty of a resplendent sunset till I have investigated the utility of that peculiar radiance in the atmosphere?" He then wishes we had a little less philosophy among us, and a little more common sense. *Common sense* is despised like other common things, but in his opinion, if we made common sense the criterion in matters of art, as well as science, we should be nearer the truth.

A fourth philosopher apprehends common sense to be our standard only in the ordinary affairs of life. The bounty of nature has furnished us with various other senses suited to the objects, among which we converse; and with regard to matters of taste, it has supplied us with what, he doubts not, we all feel within ourselves *a sense of beauty.*

Pooh! says another learned inquirer, what is a sense of beauty? Sense is a vague idea, and so is beauty; and it is impossible that anything determined can result from terms so inaccurate. But if we lay aside a sense of beauty and adopt *proportion,* we shall all be right. Proportion is the great principle of taste and beauty. We admit it both in lines, and colors, and indeed refer all our ideas of the elegant kind to its standard.

True, says an admirer of the antique, but this proportion must have a rule, or we gain nothing; and a *rule* of proportion there certainly is, but we may inquire after it in vain. The secret is lost. The ancients had it. They well knew the principles of beauty and had that unerring rule which in all things adjusted their taste. We see it even in their slightest vases. In their works, proportion, though varied through a thousand lines, is still the same; and if we could only discover their principles of proportion, we should have the arcanum of this science and might settle all our disputes about taste with great ease.

Thus, in our inquiries into first principles we go on without end and without satisfaction. The human understanding is unequal to the search. In philosophy we inquire for them in vain—in physics, in metaphysics, in morals. Even in the polite arts, where the subject, one should imagine, is less recondite, the inquiry, we find, is equally vague. We are puzzled and bewildered, but not informed; all is uncertainty, a strife of words, the old contest,

> Empedocles, an Stertinium deliret acumen?
> [Horace *Epist.* I. xii. 20]

In a word, if a cause be sufficiently understood, it may suggest useful discoveries. But if it be not so (and where is our certainty in these disquisitions) it will unquestionably mislead.

As the subject of the foregoing essay is rather new, and I doubted whether sufficiently founded in truth, I was desirous, before I printed it, that it should receive the imprimatur of Sir Joshua Reynolds. I begged him, therefore, to look it over, and received the following answer.

London,
April 19, 1791

DEAR SIR,

Though I read now but little, yet I have read with great attention the essay which you was so good to put into my hands, on the difference between the beautiful and the picturesque; and I may truly say I have received from it much pleasure and improvement.

Without opposing any of your sentiments, it has suggested an idea that may be worth consideration—whether the epithet *picturesque* is not applicable to the excellences of the inferior schools, rather than to the higher. The works of Michael Angelo, Raphael, etc. appear to me to have nothing of it; whereas Reubens and the Venetian painters may almost be said to have nothing else.

Perhaps *picturesque* is somewhat synonymous to the word *taste,* which we should think improperly applied to Homer or Milton, but very well to Pope or Prior. I suspect that the application of these words are to excellences of an inferior order, and which are incompatible with the grand style.

You are certainly right in saying that variety of tints and forms is picturesque, but it must be remembered, on the other hand, that the reverse of this (uniformity of color and a long continuation of lines) produces grandeur.

I had an intention of pointing out the passages that particularly struck me, but I was afraid to use my eyes so much.

The essay has lain upon my table, and I think no day has passed without my looking at it, reading a little at a time. Whatever objections presented themselves at first view [10] were done away on a closer inspection, and I am not quite sure but that is the case in regard to the observation which I have ventured to make on the word *picturesque.*

I am, etc.
JOSHUA REYNOLDS

To the revd. Mr. Gilpin,
Vicar's-hill

The answer

May 2d, 1791

DEAR SIR,

I am much obliged to you for looking over my essay at a time when the complaint in your eyes must have made an intrusion of this kind troublesome. But as the subject was rather novel, I wished much for your sanction; and you have given it me in as flattering a manner as I could wish.

With regard to the term *picturesque,* I have always myself used it merely to denote "such objects as are proper subjects for painting," so that, according to my definition, one of the cartoons and a flower piece are equally picturesque.

I think, however, I understand your idea of extending the term to what may be called "taste in painting"—or the art of fascinating the eye by splendid coloring and artificial combinations, which the inferior schools valued, and the dignity of the higher perhaps despised. But I have seen so little of the higher schools that I should be very ill able to carry the subject farther by illustrating a disquisition of this kind. Except the cartoons, I never saw a picture of Raphael's that answered my idea; and of the original works of Michael Angelo I have little conception.

But though I am unable, through ignorance, to appreciate fully the grandeur of the Roman school, I have at least the pleasure to find I have always held as a principle your idea of the production of greatness by uniformity of color and a long continuation of line, and when I speak of variety, I certainly do not mean to confound its effects with those of grandeur.

I am, etc.

WILLIAM GILPIN

To Sir Joshua Reynolds,
Leicester Square

From "On Picturesque Travel"

.   .   .   .   .

That we may examine picturesque objects with more ease, it may be useful to class them into the sublime and the beautiful, though, in fact, this distinction is rather inaccurate. Sublimity alone cannot make an object picturesque. However grand the mountain or the rock may be, it has no claim to this epithet unless its form, its color, or its accompaniments have some degree of beauty. Nothing can be more sublime than the ocean, but wholly unaccompanied, it has little of the picturesque. When we talk, therefore, of a sublime object, we always understand that it is also beautiful, and we call it sublime or beautiful only, as the ideas of sublimity or of simple beauty prevail.

The curious and fantastic forms of nature are by no means the favorite objects of the lovers of landscape. There may be beauty in a curious object, and so far it may be picturesque; but we cannot admire it merely for the sake of its curiosity. The *lusus naturae* is the naturalist's province, not the painter's. The spiry pinnacles of the mountain and the castle-like arrangement of the rock give no peculiar pleasure to the picturesque eye. It is fond of the simplicity of nature, and sees most beauty in her most usual forms. The Giant's causeway in Ireland may strike it as a novelty, but the lake of Killarney attracts its attention. It would range with supreme delight among the sweet vales of Switzerland, but would view only with a transient glance the Glaciers of Savoy. Scenes of this kind, as unusual, may please once, but the great works of nature in her simplest and purest style open inexhausted springs of amusement.

But it is not only the form and the composition of the objects of landscape which the picturesque eye examines; it connects them with the atmosphere, and seeks for all those various effects which are produced from that vast and wonderful storehouse of nature. Nor is there in travelling a greater pleasure than when a scene of grandeur bursts unexpectedly upon the eye, accompanied with some accidental circumstance of the atmosphere which harmonizes with it and gives it double value.

Besides the inanimate face of nature, its living forms fall under the picturesque eye in the course of travel and are often objects of great attention. The anatomical study of figures is not attended to; we regard them merely as the ornament of scenes. In the human figure we contemplate neither exactness of form nor expression any farther than it is shown in action; we merely consider general shapes, dresses, groups, and occupations, which we often find casually in greater variety and beauty than any selection can procure.

In the same manner animals are the objects of our attention, whether we find them in the park, the forest, or the field. Here too we consider little more than their general forms, actions, and combinations. Nor is the picturesque eye so fastidious as to despise even less considerable objects. A flight of birds has often a pleasing effect. In short, every form of life and being may have its use as a picturesque object till it become too small for attention.

But the picturesque eye is not merely restricted to nature. It ranges through the limits of art. The picture, the statue, and the garden are all the objects of its attention. In the embellished pleasure ground, particularly, though all is neat and elegant—far too neat and elegant for the use of the pencil—yet, if it be well laid out, it exhibits the lines and principles of landscape, and is well worth the study of the picturesque traveller. Nothing is wanting but what his imagination can supply—a change from smooth to rough.

But among all the objects of art, the picturesque eye is perhaps most inquisitive after the elegant relics of ancient architecture: the ruined tower, the Gothic arch, the remains of castles, and abbeys. These are the richest legacies of art. They are consecrated by time, and almost deserve the veneration we pay to the works of nature itself.

Thus universal are the objects of picturesque travel. We pursue beauty in every shape, through nature, through art, and all its various arrangements in form and color, admiring it in the grandest objects, and not rejecting it in the humblest.

.   .   .   .   .

It may perhaps be objected to the pleasurable circumstances which are thus said to attend picturesque travel that we meet as many disgusting, as pleasing objects; and the man of taste, therefore, will be as often offended as amused.

But this is not the case. There are few parts of nature which do not yield a picturesque eye some amusement.

> Believe the Muse,
> She does not know that unauspicious spot,
> Where beauty is thus niggard of her store.
> Believe the Muse, through this terrestrial waste
> The seeds of grace are sown, profusely sown,
> Even where we least may hope.

It is true, when some large tract of barren country interrupts our expectation, wound up in quest of any particular scene of grandeur or beauty, we are apt to be a little peevish, and to express our discontent in hasty exaggerated phrase. But when there is no disappointment in the case, even scenes the most barren of beauty will furnish amusement.

Perhaps no part of England comes more under this description than that tract of barren country through which the great military road passes from Newcastle to Carlisle. It is a waste, with little interruption, through a space of forty miles. But even here we have always something to amuse the eye. The interchangeable patches of heath and greensward make an agreeable variety. Often, too, on these vast tracts of intersecting grounds we see beautiful lights, softening off along the sides of hills, and often we see them adorned with cattle, flocks of sheep, heathcocks, grouse, plover, and flights of other wild fowl. A group of cattle standing in the shade on the edge of a dark hill and relieved by a lighter distance beyond them will often make a complete picture without any other accompaniment. In many other situations also we find them wonderfully pleasing and capable of making pictures amidst all the deficiencies of landscape. Even a winding road itself is an object of beauty, while the richness of the heath on each side, with the little hillocks and crumbling earth, give many an excellent lesson for a foreground. When we have no opportunity of examining the grand scenery of nature, we have everywhere at least the means of observing with what a multiplicity of parts, and yet with what general simplicity, she covers every surface.

But if we let the imagination loose, even scenes like these administer great amusement. The imagination can plant hills, can form rivers and lakes and valleys, can build castles and abbeys, and if it find no other amusement, can dilate itself in vast ideas of space.

But although the picturesque traveller is seldom disappointed with pure nature, however rude, yet we cannot deny but he is often offended with the productions of art. He is disgusted with the formal separations of property—with houses, and towns, the haunts of men, which have much oftener a bad effect in landscape than a good one. He is frequently disgusted also when art aims more at beauty than she ought. How flat and insipid is often the garden scene; how puerile and absurd! The banks of the river, how smooth and parallel! The lawn and its boundaries, how unlike nature! Even in the capital collections of pictures, how seldom does he find design, composition, expression, character, or harmony either in light or coloring! And how often does he drag through saloons and rooms of state only to hear a catalogue of the names of masters!

The more refined our taste grows from the study of nature, the more insipid are the works of art. Few of its efforts please. The idea of the great original is so strong that the copy must be pure if it do not disgust. But the varieties of nature's charts are such that, study them as we can, new varieties will always arise; and let our taste be ever so refined, her works, on which it is formed, at least when we consider them as objects, must always go beyond it and furnish fresh sources both of pleasure and amusement.

WALTER WHITER ✒

A Specimen of a Commentary
on Shakespeare (1794)

From I, "Notes on *As You Like It*"

·   ·   ·   ·   ·

> Helen's cheek, but not her heart,
>   Cleopatra's majesty,
> Atalanta's better part,
>   Sad Lucretia's modesty.
> [As You Like It, III, ii, 135]

There is no passage in Shakespeare which has more embarrassed his commentators than this celebrated line which enumerates among the perfections of a beauty "the better part of Atalanta." Dr. Johnson observes that the better part of Atalanta "seems to have been her heels"; yet he is inclined to think that our poet, though no despicable mythologist, has mistaken some other character for that of Atalanta. Dr. Farmer is of opinion that her better part is her wit, that is, the swiftness of her mind; and Mr. Malone observes that a passage in Marston's *Insatiate Countess* might lead us to suppose that the better part of Atalanta was her lips. Mr. Tollet remarks that perhaps the poet means her beauty and graceful elegance of shape, which he would prefer to her swiftness; but he afterwards asks whether Atalanta's better part may not mean her virtue or virgin chastity.[1]

The explication of Mr. Tollet is the only one which affords any suitable sense to this disputed expression; yet I am persuaded that the genuine spirit of the image is yet perfectly unknown. The reader of taste who is ardent in the study of our poet will, I hope, be con-

siderably gratified when I shall have placed before him the whole
passage with a new vein of illustration; nor will he, I trust, be of
opinion that I have been too labored or minute in the discussion of
a principle which refers not only to the present instance but may be
frequently applied with singular success in the elucidation of Shakespeare. It is well known and acknowledged that our old poets derived
many of their allusions and descriptions from pictures and representations in tapestry,[2] which were then equally familiar to themselves
and to their readers. We must not therefore be astonished if their
imagery should sometimes be deficient in that abstraction of sentiment which we have been so accustomed to admire in the delineations of other poets, nor is it difficult to imagine that their colorings
would be often marked by some peculiar allusions which can now
only be understood by conceiving that the works of the artist were
still present to the mind of the poet and that the operations of the
fancy were controlled by the impressions of the eye. This observation, which is rigorously applicable to our ancient bards—Chaucer,
Gower, and Lydgate—may be extended likewise with considerable
truth to the poets of succeeding times, and will afford the intelligent
critic a very important principle in illustrating the writers of the
sixteenth century. It has been remarked by our commentators that
Shakespeare has himself borrowed many of his images from prints,[3]
statues,[4] paintings,[5] and exhibitions in tapestry; and we may observe
that some allusions of this sort are to be found in the play before
us, and especially in those places which describe the beauties of
Rosalind.[6] There was, however, another reason why this peculiar
vein of allusion should naturally abound in dramatic compositions,
as the stage was not only covered with arras or tapestry hangings,
but when that arras was faded or decayed, they were accustomed to
adorn it (according to the expression of Jonson) with "fresh pictures." I have not the smallest doubt but that this practice suggested
to Shakespeare the idea in *Hamlet* of presenting before the Queen
the portraits of her two husbands:

> Look here upon this picture, and on this,
> The counterfeit presentment of two brothers.

It is evident, as the commentators have remarked, from the following words, "a station like the herald Mercury," that these pictures which are now produced on the stage as miniatures were meant
as full lengths, being part of the furniture of the Queen's closet, and

that the introduction of these miniatures is a modern innovation. Mr. Malone is of opinion that when tragedies were acted, the stage was hung with black, and I am inclined to think in general that the stage was often furnished with those pictures which were somewhat suitable to the genius of the performance. Let me venture likewise to conjecture that possibly the subject of these pictures and the representations on these hangings might be of such a nature as to supply the place of that dumb show which Mr. Warton [7] is surprised to find discontinued in the plays of Shakespeare, and for the absence of which he professes himself unable to account. Let us now examine whether the present passage may not be illustrated by a principle which has been allowed universally to operate on our ancient poets and which has been proved in various instances to have acted on the imagination of Shakespeare. I have always been firmly persuaded that the imagery which our poet has selected to discriminate the more prominent perfections of Helen, Cleopatra, Atalanta, and Lucretia was not derived from the abstract consideration of their general qualities, but was caught from those peculiar traits of beauty and character which are impressed on the mind of him who contemplates their portraits. It is well known that these celebrated heroines of romance were in the days of our poet the favorite subjects of popular representation and were alike visible in the coarse hangings of the poor and the magnificent arras of the rich. In the portraits of Helen, whether they were produced by the skillful artist or his ruder imitator, though her face would certainly be delineated as eminently beautiful, yet she appears not to have been adorned with any of those charms which are allied to modesty; and we accordingly find that she was generally depicted with a loose and insidious countenance which but too manifestly betrayed the inward wantonness and perfidy of her heart. The following quotation from *Don Quixote* is singularly in point, as it will serve to show us how universally the same expressions of faithless beauty were considered as characteristic of the portraits of Helen.

He was lodged in a low chamber, to which certain old worn curtains of painted serge served in lieu of tapestry hangings, as commonly they use in country villages. In one of the pieces might be seen painted by a bungling and unskillful hand the rape of Helen at what time her fond, hardy guest stole her from Menelaus. In another was the history of Dido [8] and Aeneas; she on a high turret with a sheet making sign unto her fugitive guest, who on the sea carried in a ship was running away from her. Don Quixote observed in these two stories that Helen seemed not to be discontented with her rape, for so much as she leered and smiled under hand. Whereas beauteous Dido seemed to trickle down tears from her eyes as big as walnuts.[9]

With respect to the majesty of Cleopatra, it may be observed that this notion is not derived from classical authority, but from the more popular storehouse of legend and romance, for though indeed many instances of her majestic appearance and conduct might be collected from the former source, yet I think that we should not from thence be led to speak familiarly of that quality as the most prominent and distinguished part of her character. When our poet had afterwards occasion in his *Antony and Cleopatra* to delineate her portrait at full length from a classical original, we do not find that the idea of her majesty is particularly inculcated. I infer therefore that the familiarity of this image was impressed both on the poet and his reader from pictures and representations in tapestry, which were the lively and faithful mirrors of popular romances. Atalanta, we know, was considered likewise by our ancient poets as a celebrated beauty, and we may be assured therefore that her portraits were everywhere to be found.[10] From the passage in Pliny quoted by Mr. Tollet, we learn that there were two pictures at Lanuvium placed by each other of Helen and Atalanta which were both painted by the same artist and represented as eminently beautiful, though the charms of the latter were distinguished from those of the former by the appearance of a virgin modesty. Whether among the painters of after ages it was customary thus to contrast the dissimilar beauties of Helen and Atalanta I cannot determine. We know, however, that such contrasts are familiar to the artists of every period, and the quotation which I have above produced from *Don Quixote* may show us that in the most rude and imperfect pieces it was not unusual to imitate the refinements of more exquisite performances. Since the story of Atalanta represents that heroine as possessed of singular beauty, zealous to preserve her virginity even with the death of her lovers, and accomplishing her purposes by extraordinary swiftness in running, we may be assured that the skill of the artist would be employed in displaying the most perfect expressions of virgin purity and in delineating the fine proportions and elegant symmetry of her person. "Lucretia" (we know) "was the grand example of conjugal fidelity throughout the Gothic ages"; and it is this spirit of unshaken chastity which is here celebrated under the title of modesty. The epithet *sad* is but ill calculated to represent the abstract notion of conjugal virtue, and we may be assured therefore that it was forced upon the mind of our poet from a very different impression. I am aware, how-ever, that *sad* may signify in certain cases (as Dr. Johnson supposes it in the present) *grave* or *solemn,* yet even in this sense the idea of something gloomy or unengaging is, I believe, generally understood, and it is certain that the epithet cannot with any propriety be ap-plied to the abstract notion of that species of beauty in which the charms of nature are rendered still more attractive by the cheerful though composed graces of a genuine modesty. I am persuaded that the meaning of *sad* in this passage is *sorrowful* or *lamenting* and that it was impressed on the imagination of our bard by the melancholy appearance which Lucretia commonly bore in her portraits and representations.[11] Sir Philip Sidney in his *Defense of Poesy* talks of "the constant though lamenting look of Lucretia," as she is ex-hibited in paintings; and in our author's *Rape of Lucrece* the epithet *sad* frequently occurs in the same sense, and is often applied to Lucretia herself in the several mournful occasions of her affecting story. In the following lines, which are taken from the above poem, we find the sadness of her countenance combined with the graces of her modesty:

> Her pity-pleading eyes are sadly fixed
> In the remorseless wrinkles of his face.
> Her modest eloquence with sighs is mixed,
> Which to her oratory adds more grace. [561]

Let us suppose, therefore, that the portraits of these celebrated beauties—Helen, Cleopatra, Atalanta, and Lucretia—were delin-eated as I have above described, that in the days of Shakespeare they continued to be the favorite subjects of popular representation, and that consequently they were familiarly impressed on the mind of the poet and on the memory of his audience. Let us now investigate what the bard, or the lover, under the influence of this impression would select as the better parts of these celebrated heroines, which he might wish to be transferred to his own mistress as the perfect model of female excellence. In contemplating the portrait of Helen, he is attracted only by those charms which are at once the most dis-tinguished, and at the same time are the least employed in expressing the feelings of the heart. He wishes therefore for that rich bloom of beauty which glowed upon her cheek, but he rejects those lineaments of her countenance which betrayed the loose inconstancy of her mind, the insidious smile and the wanton brilliancy of her eye. Impressed with the effect, he passes instantly to the cause. He is enamored with the better part of the beauty of Helen, but he is shocked at the depravity of that heart, which was too manifestly exhibited by the worse. To convince the intelligent reader that *cheek* is not applied to beauty [12] in general, but that it is here used in its appropriate and original sense, we shall produce a very curious passage from one of our author's sonnets, by which it will appear that the portraits of Helen were distinguished by the consummate beauty which was displayed upon her cheek.

> Describe Adonis, and the counterfeit (i.e., picture)
> Is poorly imitated after you.
> On Helen's cheek all art of beauty set,
> And you in Grecian tires are painted new. [Sonnet 53]

In viewing the portrait of Cleopatra, we should all naturally agree in admiring the stately air and majestic appearance of her person, though in the bare contemplation of her character we should not have equally concurred in speaking familiarly of her majesty as the most eminent and distinguished of her qualities. In surveying the portrait of Atalanta and in reflecting on the character which it displayed, the lover would not find it difficult to select the better part both of her mind and of her form, which he might wish to be transfused into the composition of his mistress. He would not be desirous of that perfection in her person which contributed nothing to the gratification of his passion, and he would reject that principle of her soul which was adverse to the object of his wishes. He would be enamored with the fine proportions and elegant symmetry of her limbs, though his passion would find but little reason to be delighted with the quality of swiftness with which that symmetry was connected. He would be captivated with the blushing charms of unsullied virginity, but he would abhor that unfeeling coldness which resisted the impulse of love, and that unnatural cruelty which rejoiced in the murder of her lovers. The poet lastly wishes for the modesty of the sad Lucretia, that firm and deep-rooted principle of female chastity which is so visibly depicted in the sadness of her countenance lamenting for its involuntary loss, and which has rendered her through all ages the pride and pattern of conjugal fidelity.

Such then are the wishes of the lover in the formation of his mistress, that the ripe and brilliant beauties of Helen should be united to the elegant symmetry and virgin graces of Atalanta, and that this union of charms should be still dignified and ennobled by the majestic mien of Cleopatra and the matron modesty of Lucretia.

Finally, it is extremely observable and will indeed considerably confirm the diligent reader of our poet in the truth of this new interpretation that allusions to pictures, or at least terms which are on all hands acknowledged to be derived from painting, are found to accompany the passage which is the subject of our present commentary.

> But upon the fairest boughs,
>   Or at every sentence end,
> Will I Rosalinda write,
>   Teaching all that read to know
> The quintessence of every sprite
>   Heaven would in little [13] show.
> Therefore Heaven Nature charged
>   That one body should be filled
> With all graces wide-enlarged.
>   Nature presently distilled
> Helen's cheek, but not her heart,
>   Cleopatra's majesty,
> Atalanta's better part,
>   Sad Lucretia's modesty.
> Thus Rosalind of many parts
>   By heavenly synod was devised,
> Of many faces, eyes, and hearts,
>   To have the touches [14] dearest prized. [III, ii, 125]

I will conclude this note by observing likewise what our commentators appear not to have considered, that our poet, in forming this model of female excellence, has not shown himself forgetful of that description which he had before given us of Rosalind. She is represented as more than common tall, and on that account best qualified to assume the dress and appearance of a man.

> Were it not better,
> Because that I am more than common tall,
> That I did suit me all points like a man?
> A gallant curtal-ax upon my thigh,
> A boar spear in my hand. [I, iii, 110]

The poet [15] therefore might very properly invest her with the majestic air of Cleopatra, and that figure which was so well adapted to become the curtle ax and the boar spear would naturally suggest to his recollection the manly though elegant appearance of Atalanta attired for the exercise of the course, or furnished with the dress and implements of the chase. We may observe that in our ancient poets the huntress and the swift-footed Atalanta seem to have been confounded. As I consider the subject of this note to be intimately connected with a theory which I propose afterwards to unfold, I have not hesitated to be thus minute and circumstantial in the explanation of this passage, that the reader might be at once possessed with a general [16] notion of a species of indirect allusion which occurs perpetually in our ancient poets, and which, when duly understood, will afford us a new and uniform light in discovering the peculiar spirit of their descriptions and the associating principle of their imagery. In the present instance it will not, I trust, be objected that I have imposed a meaning on the passage which is too ample both for the words which convey it and the occasion which I have imagined to suggest it. The reader of taste will not fail to remember that the vigorous language of the poet will express concisely what he at once conceives richly, while the humble critic must be contented to illustrate by a long, a labored, and a feeble commentary.

.   .   .   .   .

From II, "An Attempt to Explain and Illustrate Various Passages of Shakespeare, on a New Principle of Criticism, Derived from Mr. Locke's Doctrine of the Association of Ideas"

The association of ideas is a fruitful and popular theme in the writings of metaphysicians, and they have supplied us with innumerable examples which prove at once the extent and the activity of its influence. They have taught us that our modes of reasoning, our habits of life, and even the motions of our body are affected by its energy, and that it operates on the faculties by a kind of fascinating control which we sometimes cannot discover and which generally we are unable to counteract. The consideration, however, of this doctrine, curious and extensive as it may appear, has commonly been confined to the admirers of metaphysical researches; nor has the theory, I believe, ever been systematically discussed as a point of taste or as a subject of criticism. We have seen the question totally exhausted as it refers to the general powers of the understanding and the habitual exercise of the reasoning faculty; but we may justly be astonished that the effects of this principle should never have been investigated as it operates on the writer in the ardor of invention by imposing on his mind some remote and peculiar vein of language or of imagery. If, in the ordinary exertions of the understanding, the force of such an association has been found so powerful and extensive, it may surely be concluded that its influence would predominate with absolute authority over the vigorous workings of a wild and fertile imagination. In the pages of the poet, therefore, may we expect to be supplied with the most curious and abundant materials for the discussion of this principle, and in none can we hope to find such frequent and singular examples of its effect as may probably be discovered by the diligent reader in the writings of Shakespeare.

By the associating principle I do not mean (as it appears to be understood by some metaphysicians) that faculty of the understanding by which on all occasions the chain of our ideas is generated and preserved; nor, as referred to the genius of the poet, do I mean that active power which passes rapidly through a variety of successive images, which discovers with so wonderful an acuteness their relations and dependencies, and which combines them with such exquisite effect in all the pleasing forms of fiction and invention. In this indefinite and unlimited sense, the association of ideas, when applied to the general operations of the mind, expresses little less than the whole arrangement of the reasoning principle, and as referred to the workings of imagination must signify all the embellishments of eloquence and all the graces of poetry.

In the theory of Mr. Locke, by the term *association* is not understood the combination of ideas naturally connected with each other, for these, as he observes, "it is the office and the excellency of our reason to form and preserve in that union and correspondence which is founded on their peculiar beings." On the contrary, it is understood to express the combination of those ideas which have no natural alliance or relation to each other, but which have been united ·only by chance or by custom. Now it is observable that no task can be imposed on the understanding of greater difficulty than to separate ideas thus accidentally combined, as the mind is commonly passive in admitting their original formation and often totally unconscious of the force and principle of their union.

In the application of this theory to the subject of the present inquiry, the definition of the term association might remain unaltered, though, as it may well be imagined, there will not appear to be the smallest resemblance between the illustrations which have been usually produced to describe its effect in the one case and those various instances which I now propose to lay before the reader as new and curious examples of its existence in the other. Though I am strongly impressed likewise with the truth of the well-known maxim that "to define is dangerous," and fully sensible that it is almost impossible to describe with precision at one view every case to which the question may be extended; yet, I am still desirous of attempting a plain and concise definition of the general principle in its peculiar application to the object of my inquiry. I define, therefore, the power of this association over the genius of the poet, to consist in supplying him with words and with ideas which have been suggested to the mind by a principle of union unperceived by himself and independent of the subject to which they are applied. From this definition it follows, first, that as these words and sentiments were prompted by a cause which is concealed from the poet, so they contain no intentional allusion to the source from whence they are derived; and secondly, that as they were forced on the recollection of the writer by some accidental concurrence not necessarily dependent on the sense or spirit of the subject, so they have no necessary resemblance in this secondary application to that train of ideas in which they originally existed. We might thus perhaps arrange in a more ample yet inadequate manner the principal objects of the general definition, though the examples only will enable us to understand the force and propriety of the arrangement.

1. It will often happen that a certain word, expression, sentiment, circumstance, or metaphor will lead the writer to the use of that appropriate language by which they are each of them distinguished,

even on occasions where the metaphor is no longer continued, where there is no allusion intended to the circumstance, nor is there any sense conveyed under this language which bears a peculiar reference to the words or sentiments that excited it. It is merely accidental that the imagery in whose service the language thus suggested is employed has any affinity to the subject from which it is borrowed. Now, as it is the business of the critic to discover and establish the original language of the author and to reject what is sometimes called the improved text of an ingenious commentator, we shall instantly perceive that from this principle may probably be derived a very important canon for the confirmation of disputed readings, which have perhaps been too hastily condemned as quaint, remote, or unintelligible. If the discerning critic should discover that the train of thought which had just occupied the attention of the writer would naturally conduct him to the use of this controverted expression, we should certainly have little difficulty in admitting the reading to be genuine, even though it had before appeared to us under a questionable shape from the singular mode in which it was applied. On an art not capable of demonstration, surely no principle can be engrafted more sure and infallible than that which is derived from some acknowledged powers in the understanding, roused and controlled as they are by an active and a regular influence.

2. Certain terms containing an equivocal meaning, or sounds suggesting such a meaning, will often serve to introduce other words and expressions of a similar nature. This similarity is formed by having in some cases a coincidence in sense or an affinity arising from sound, though the signification in which they are really applied has never any reference and often no similitude to that which caused their association.

3. The remembrance of a similar phraseology, of a known metaphor, or of a circumstance, not apparent in the text, will often lead the writer into language or imagery derived from these sources; though the application may be sometimes totally different from the meaning and spirit of the original.

4. An impression on the mind of the writer, arising from something which is frequently presented to his senses, or which passes within the sphere of his ordinary observation, will supply him with the union of words and sentiments which are not necessarily con-

nected with each other and which are combined only from the powerful influence of external impressions on the faculties of the understanding.

These objects may be general and therefore equally apparent to the observers of every period, but the more curious examples of this nature will be derived from those impressions which are peculiar to the country, the age, and the situation of the writer. Here, likewise, we are still to understand that as these combinations were not formed by the invention, but forced on the fancy of the poet, he is totally unconscious of the effect and principle of their union. This then is a portion of criticism to which the diligence of commentators has never, I believe, been systematically applied. They have exhausted the abundance of their knowledge in discovering the direct, though sometimes perhaps obscure, allusions which the poet has intentionally made to the customs of his own age, and to the various vices, follies, passions, and prejudices which are the pointed objects of his satire or his praise. But the commentators have not marked those indirect and tacit references which are produced by the writer with no intentional allusion, or rather, they have not unfolded those trains of thought, alike pregnant with the materials peculiar to his age, which often prompt the combinations of the poet in the wildest exertions of his fancy, and which conduct him, unconscious of the effect, to the various peculiarities of his imagery or his language. To illustrate passages which are dictated by a train of thoughts abounding with these materials, the critic must exert the same knowledge in the phraseology and customs belonging to the age of his author which he employed in the explanation of direct and intentional allusions, as they alike contain the forgotten circumstances of a remote period and differ only in the mode by which these circumstances are presented. As the poet indeed rises in genius, as he advances to the rank of that select and exalted band "who are not for an age, but for all time," it is certain that his attention will be proportionally abstracted from the fleeting topics of his own period and the minute concerns of his peculiar situation; he will perhaps studiously avoid all occasions of satire on the characters of his age and all direct allusions to the occurrences before him. His pictures of nature and of life will be drawn from broad and general views of our condition, from scenes to which the eye of every age is witness, and from those passions and affections of men which have been perpetually found to amuse or agitate our being. Still, however, the secret energy of local influence will continue to operate on his mind: his modes of conception will be still affected by the ideas which were most familiar to the habits of his life. In the fictions, the thoughts, and the language of the poet, you may ever mark the deep and unequivocal traces of the age in which he lived, of the employments in which he was engaged, and of the various objects which excited his passions or arrested his attention. Nothing, therefore, is wanting but the sagacity and diligence of the critic to discover and illustrate the examples in which these effects may be evidently traced; and the reader will immediately acknowledge that the principles of this theory are capable of affording a conviction which the art of criticism cannot of itself be expected to produce. To the ordinary resources of the critic we have applied an additional confirmation, derived from the most indubitable principle in the doctrine of metaphysics.

As the writers of one period may be distinguished from those of another by direct references to the customs of the age in which they lived, so they may more certainly be discriminated by a minute investigation of these indirect and involuntary allusions. And here we shall easily understand that this part of our theory may be applied with singular success to decide on a very important question which has been often agitated in the republic of letters. What subject has more embarrassed the critics than to determine on the merits of a cause in which it is affirmed on the one side that a certain composition was to be referred to an author of a distant period, and contended on the other that it is nothing but the production of a modern forger who has endeavored to imitate the language and to adopt the customs of the age in which his imaginary writer was supposed to have existed? When the various modes by which questions of this kind have been usually tried are found to be inadequate, we may confidently resort to the present theory as a sure and infallible touchstone. If the traces of modern phraseology should be apparent in the composition, this may certainly have proceeded from the indiscrete forgery of a modern author, but it may likewise be ascribed to the ignorance, the rashness, or the negligence of a modern transcriber. If the style of such a composition should be thought to possess the excellencies of a more advanced and cultivated period, it is certain that he who imitates the writings of a former age may incautiously adorn his performance with the graces of the present; yet we must likewise remember that the exertions of an original genius are not bounded within the limits of his own age, and that the knowledge of succeeding generations has sometimes taught us only to understand and admire the progress of a single being who has himself begun and ended the career, who at once conceived and consummated his art. It was reserved for the knowledge of the present age to discover that Shakespeare has enriched and ennobled our poetry with new forms of language, rhythm, fiction, and imagery which we know that he first invented and believe that he has finally completed. If again there should appear in this disputed composition direct and pointed allusions to the customs and manners of a certain age, these indeed might very justly be attributed to an author of that period; but we must still be mindful that they might likewise have fallen within the knowledge of a recent forger, and therefore may be equally considered as the production of a modern writer. We see, therefore, that with the present resources of criticism, the arguments on a disputed question of this nature may be equally balanced and that the judgment may rest suspended in doubt and uncertainty. Our conviction, however, would be immediate and invincible if we should discover in this questionable composition the manners and circumstances of a distant age, not indeed directly and immediately delineated by the intention of the writer, but apparent only in the style of his descriptions and in the coloring of his sentiments, his thoughts, or his language. For what can exceed the evidence arising from a principle which shall conduct us even to the very mind of the writer and discover to us the causes and effects of its internal operation, unknown even to himself; which shall exhibit to us the train of his ideas impregnated with the objects peculiar to his age; and which shall enable us, when we again review the composition itself, to mark the deep and distinct traces of the same ideas, though under a new modification, with all the kindred peculiarities of the original impression. As this subtle species of metaphysical forgery has never yet been attempted or conceived,[17] we should pronounce with the most perfect confidence that the writings which are thus marked with the impressions of a distant age were certainly not the productions of modern invention.

Though I do not think that the effects of these ideal forms, which are appropriate to every age, will ever be successfully represented by the most consummate master in the art of imitation, yet I cannot but imagine that they might be investigated and described with sufficient accuracy for the purposes of criticism by the sagacity of an intelligent inquirer. From a minute study of the genius of a certain age, its language and its progress in the arts of civil society, from a knowledge of the more general objects and occurrences of domestic and public life, its pursuits, pleasures, and opinions, from an accurate inquiry into the character and situation of the author himself, a judicious critic might perhaps conjecture with considerable probability what would be the effect which these impressions, continually working on the mind, would necessarily produce on the composition of the writer. Among the various circumstances which might be selected on this occasion, there are two particulars eminently distinguishing the present time from the age of Shakespeare and the periods preceding which must operate with singular effect on the genius of the poet as they are connected with the great resources of his art, with the colorings of description and the variety of invention: I mean the universal custom in those days of covering the walls of their chambers with arras or tapestry hangings which represented the celebrated stories of ancient or modern times, and the frequent exhibition of masques, pageants, and processions.[18] In these wild and motley spectacles, the illustrious personages of history, romance, and mythology; the tales and fictions of every period, whether they were of Grecian, Gothic, Roman, Saracen, or Christian origin; the creatures of the imagination and the living characters of the world were all blended and confounded by the licentious fancy or the ignorance of the inventor. The reader will instantly perceive that these must influence with considerable energy the imagination of the poet, as the former will impart to his descriptions certain traits of a precise and definite coloring which are adventitious and accidental rather than general and characteristic, which belong rather to the impressions of the eye than to those abstract and universal conceptions that are formed by the contemplation of the mind. The latter will enrich the stores of his fancy with wild and original combinations, with a splendid train of lively and various imagery, and above all with the most ample materials for allegorical fictions and personified agencies. To these objects, striking and familiar as they would be to the eye of an observer, we may not perhaps frequently discover direct and immediate allusions in the writings of a bard whose powers enabled him to range over the various scenery of universal poetry: he would find little reason to be gratified with the coarse or inadequate representations of the tapestry, and he would be often shocked at the motley absurdity of the pageant; still, however, they would engrave upon his mind a deep and lasting impression, of which the effects may be perpetually traced by the observing critic when the poet himself is totally unconscious of this predominating influence. Of the effects produced by the former I have given a general view in my remarks on the better part of Atalanta; and I have taken occasion in the following pages to introduce certain observations on the power of the latter.

I shall now proceed to the examples themselves, which are intended to illustrate or confirm the theory of this associating principle. I have only to request the reader that they may not be hastily perused, but diligently studied; as the traces of so subtle an influence will often be invisible to the hasty glance of a superficial observer, though they will be apparent to a more careful view in distinct and unequivocal characters. I must again suggest to the reader that he will be frequently induced to wonder or to smile at the minute and even ridiculous combinations which have been thus imposed on the mind of the poet and which are able to deceive and control the most acute and powerful understanding. I have been desirous from various motives to confine within these narrow limits the present dissertation, which might easily have been extended to a more ample form and connected with other branches of critical inquiry; and I have only to add that if the ensuing pages should not convey to the reader all the conviction which they might be expected to afford, he has only to object that the author has been unfortunate in the proofs, not unfounded in the principles. It is universally acknowledged that such an influence exists, nor can it be doubted that it must thus operate on the composition of the poet. I may therefore at least assume the merit of opening a new path to the researches of the critic and of supplying a future theme of investigation to a more sagacious or a more diligent inquirer.

The first example which I shall produce is the very passage which originally led me to the present inquiry. In *Timon of Athens,* when Timon has retired into the woods, Apemantus thus upbraids him with the contrast of his past and present condition:

> What, think'st
> That the bleak air, thy boisterous chamberlain,
> Will put thy shirt on warm? Will these moist trees,
> That have outlived the eagle, page thy heels
> And skip when thou point'st out? [IV, iii, 221]

Sir Thomas Hanmer for *moist* reads very elegantly, says Dr. Johnson, *moss'd*. Mr. Steevens confirms the emendation by examples; and Mr. Malone believes it to be the true reading. I agree with our commentators that *moss'd* is a more elegant epithet and at the same time better calculated to express the antiquity of trees that have outlived the eagle. It is certain however that *moist* is not altogether destitute of force and propriety; as in many parts of old and rotten trees a kind of moist exudation is often to be seen, though perhaps other parts may be dry and withered by age. If, therefore, I can show with extreme probability, from some acknowledged principle in the mind, why this peculiar word might be suggested to our poet, it surely ought to be considered as a valuable touchstone in the art of criticism, of which it is certainly the business to discover and ascertain what the author really *has* written, and not what he *ought* to have done. The reader then is to be informed that *warm* and *moist* were the appropriate terms in the days of Shakespeare for what we should now call an *air'd* and a *damp* shirt. So John Florio (*Second Fruits*, 1591) in a dialogue between the master Torquato and his servant Ruspa.

T. Dispatch and give me a *shirt?*
R. Here is one with ruffes.
T. Thou dolte, seest thou not how moist it is?
R. Pardon me, good sir, I was not aware of it.
T. Go into the kitchen and warm it.

Can the reader doubt (though he may perhaps smile at the association) that the image of the chamberlain putting the shirt on warm impressed the opposite word *moist* on the imagination of the poet? Though he was himself unconscious how he came by it, and certainly never would have applied it as an epithet to trees if it had not been fixed on his mind by a kind of fascinating power which concealed from him not only the origin but the effect likewise of so strange an association.

. . . . . .

It will readily be understood and acknowledged that this propensity in the mind to associate subjects so remote in their meaning and so heterogeneous in their nature must of necessity sometimes deceive the ardor of the writer into whimsical or ridiculous combinations. As the reader, however, is not blinded by this fascinating principle, which while it creates the association conceals likewise

its effect, he is instantly impressed with the quaintness or the absurdity of the imagery and is inclined to charge the writer with the intention of a foolish quibble or an impertinent allusion. I shall now
therefore produce some passages of Shakespeare which have fallen
under suspicions of this nature and which I think may be completely
defended by the application of the present theory. Our bard has so
many grievous and undoubted quibbles of his own to answer for
that it is surely unreasonable, as Mr. Steevens has somewhere observed, to censure him for those which exist only in the imagination of others.

> He had a fever when he was in Spain,
> And when the fit was on him, I did mark
> How he did shake. 'Tis true this God did shake.
> His coward lips did from their color fly.
>
> [*Julius Caesar*, I, ii, 119]

"A plain man," says Warburton, "would have said 'the color fled
from his lips,' and not his 'lips from their color.' But the false expression was for the sake of as false a piece of wit: a poor quibble,
alluding to a coward flying from his colors." The critic has discovered the association, which had escaped the author, who indeed
intended no quibble but was himself entangled by the similitude
of *color* and *colors*. This introduced to him the appropriate terms
of *coward* and *fly,* and thus, under the influence of such an embarrassment it was scarcely possible to express the sentiment in a form
less equivocal than the present. Let me add likewise another circumstance which might operate in suggesting this military metaphor—that the cowardice of a soldier is the subject of the narrative.

.   .   .   .   .

> Come, thick night,
> And pall thee in the dunnest smoke of Hell,
> That my keen knife see not the wound it makes,
> Nor Heaven peep through the blanket of the dark
> To cry "Hold, hold!" [*Macbeth*, I, v, 51]

"A *pall*," says Mr. Steevens, "is a robe of state. So in Milton's 'Penseroso,'

> Sometime let gorgeous Tragedy,
> In scepter'd pall come sweeping by.

Dr. Warburton seems to mean the covering which is thrown over the dead."—"The word *knife*," says Mr. Malone, "has been objected to as being connected with the most sordid offices and therefore unsuitable to the great occasion on which it is employed. But, however mean it may sound to our ears, it was formerly a word of sufficient dignity, and is constantly used by Shakespeare and his contemporaries as synonymous to *dagger*." Mr. Malone is certainly right, and the instances which he has produced are perfectly satisfactory. Amongst the rest there is one from *A Warning for Fair Women* (1599) where Tragedy enters with a whip in one hand, "in the other a knife." *Blanket,* Mr. Malone observes, was certainly the poet's word, and "perhaps was suggested to him by the coarse woolen curtain of his own theater, through which probably, while the house was yet but half lighted, he had himself often peeped." Let not the reader smile at this specimen of conjectural criticism, nor imagine that it ought to be regarded only as a quaint and whimsical conceit. Nothing is more certain than that all the images in this celebrated passage are borrowed from the stage. Let Mr. Malone again review his own note and that of Mr. Steevens, and he will be gratified in discovering how everything coincides to favor this hypothesis. He will observe that the peculiar and appropriate dress of Tragedy personified is a pall with a knife. The curiosity of Mr. Malone will perhaps be still more gratified when he recollects what he has before observed himself in his *Account of the English Stage* from *Heywood's Apology for Actors,* "that the covering or internal roof of the stage was anciently termed *the heavens.* . . . It was probably painted of a sky-blue color, or perhaps pieces of drapery tinged with blue were suspended across the stage to represent the heavens" (*History of the Stage,* p. 90). The curious reader who for the first time is informed that this extraordinary term was the known and familiar name for the visible roof of the stage will certainly have much cause to wonder that so peculiar a circumstance should not have opened to the critics an ample vein of illustration which might successfully be applied to our ancient dramatic writers, and especially to Shakespeare, whose mind, we may well conceive, must be perpetually occupied with every object that had reference to the theater. With respect to the passage before us, I imagine that the whole of this image was suggested to our poet from the appearance of the stage as it was furnished at those times when tragedies were represented:

it was then hung with black, as Mr. Malone conjectures in his *Theatrical Memoirs* (p. 89), though, as he supposes in another place (note to *Rape of Lucrece*, l. 766), "this hanging was no more than one piece of black baize placed at the back of the stage, in the room of the tapestry, which was the common decoration when comedies were acted." I am persuaded, however, that on the same occasions the *heavens,* or the roof of the stage, underwent likewise some gloomy transformation. The effect intended to be produced by such a change consisted, I imagine, in conveying to the audience the idea of a dark and gloomy night in which every luminary was hidden from the view. This might perhaps be represented by hanging the roof of the theater, or the *heavens,* with black: that is, in other words, by covering with black those decorations about the roof which were designed to imitate the appearance of the heavens. I am led to conclude this circumstance by the application of my present theory, which, I hope, is now so understood and acknowledged by the reader that I may safely assume it is a principle to confirm and illustrate a conjecture which is itself neither remote nor improbable. Among the passages which Mr. Malone has produced to prove that the stage was hung with black when tragedies were acted, the two following will convince us likewise that the roof of the theater, under the title of "Heavens," if not distinguished by a direct allusion, is at least latently involved in the image of the poet:

> The stage of heaven is hung with solemn black,
> A time best fitting to act Tragedies.
> > [Marston's *Insatiate Countess,* 1613]

> Hung be the heavens with black, yield day to night.
> > [*1 Henry VI,* I, i, 1]

The passage which Mr. Malone has produced from the *Rape of Lucrece* deserves our notice:

> Black stage for tragedies and murders fell.

The reader will be surprised to find from the context that the black stage for tragedies is the dismal night of Lucretia's calamity, which the poet has furnished with the horrid subjects and personages of tragic representation, Death and Treason—the conspirator and the ravisher.

> O comfort-killing Night, image of Hell!
> Dim register and notary of shame!

> Black stage for tragedies and murders fell!
> Vast sin-concealing chaos; nurse of blame!
> Blind muffled bawd! Dark harbor for defame!
> Grim cave of death! Whispering conspirator
> With close-tongued Treason and the ravisher!

The imagery in the passage of *Macbeth* which is the subject of our commentary has a wonderful coincidence with the sentiment in the lines before us. In the former we may observe not only that the terms which are probably taken from the stage—the pall and knife of Tragedy, the heavens, the peeping through the blanket of the dark—agree with the direct allusion to the theater in the latter passage, "Black stage for tragedies and murders fell," but we find likewise "Thick Night and the dunnest smoke of Hell" coinciding with "comfort-killing Night, image of Hell."

In the two next stanzas the same subject is continued, and the beginning of the third, which Mr. Malone produces as parallel to the passage in *Macbeth,* runs thus:

> Were Tarquin Night, as he is but Night's child,
> The silver-shining Queen he would distain.
> Her twinkling handmaids too, by him defiled,
> Through Night's black bosom should not peep again.

To these instances let the reader add the following curious and decisive passage from *Macbeth* that describes the horrors of the night in which Duncan was murdered:

> *Ross.*   Ah, good Father,
> Thou seest the heavens, as troubled with man's act,
> Threatens his bloody stage. [II, iv, 4] [19]

In these passages we find that the obscurity of the heavens and the gloom of night are connected with the stage and with the terms belonging to it.

It is impossible, surely, for the reader to believe that chance only could have operated in producing this union of images which have no natural affinity or relation to each other. We certainly should not expect to discover in a modern dramatic writer a combination of this sort so frequently repeated, though we are well aware that in the subjects themselves, abstractly considered, the same principle of association must have invariably existed. We are led therefore to investigate by what peculiar circumstance the ancient theater was distinguished from the present which could operate in producing a combination of so singular a nature. From our critics we are able to learn nothing on this subject but that when tragedies were acted one piece of black baize was substituted for the ordinary tapestry at the back of the stage. Such Mr. Malone believes to be the only alteration which took place on these occasions, though there is certainly nothing in so simple a change by which the mind of the poet could be conducted to this train of imagery. If, however, my hypothesis should be granted, that at the acting of tragedies the heavens of the theater were hung with black and converted into the representation of a gloomy night, the association between the stage and the obscurity of the heavens becomes highly natural and almost inevitable. In short, we must certainly acknowledge that if such a circumstance had really existed, we might have expected to find in some ancient dramatic writer precisely the same vein of language and sentiments which we have just seen exhibited in the preceding passages.

I cannot forbear adding some celebrated lines which I think may receive a new light from this theatrical application of the word *heavens*. I do not determine whether our poet intends a direct allusion to it, though I have not the smallest doubt but that he was indebted for his conception to this intermediate idea. The Chorus in *Henry V* begins the play thus:

> O for a Muse of fire, that would ascend
> The brightest heaven of invention.

Dr. Johnson observes that this alludes to the aspiring "nature of fire, which by its levity, at the separation of the chaos, took the highest seat of all the elements"; and Dr. Warburton remarks likewise that it is derived from "the notion of the peripatetic system, which imagines several heavens one above another, the last and highest of which was one of fire." With all this Shakespeare was, I believe, perfectly acquainted; I am persuaded, however, that the image of ascending to the highest of these succeeding heavens was suggested to the poet by the little scene of his own performances—by that obscure and humble heaven within which were bounded the loftiest flights of his muse and the brightest efforts of his invention.

If this opinion should be already received as somewhat probable, without a perfect remembrance of the context, what will be the force of our conviction when we shall learn that the succeeding lines are employed in describing the meanness of his own theater and the flat, unraised spirit of his dramatic muse?

> O for a Muse of fire, that would ascend
> The brightest heaven of invention,
> A kingdom for a stage, princes to act
> And monarchs to behold the swelling scene!
> Then should the warlike Harry, like himself,
> Assume the port of Mars, and at his heels,
> Leashed in like hounds, should famine, sword, and fire,
> Crouch for employment. But pardon, gentles all,
> The flat unraised spirit that hath dar'd
> On this unworthy scaffold to bring forth
> So great an object. Can this cockpit hold
> The vasty fields of France? Or may we cram
> Within this wooden O the very casques
> That did affright the air at Agincourt?
>
> .   .   .   .   .
>
> Suppose within the girdle of these walls
> Are now confin'd two mighty monarchies.

As I am well aware that my illustrations of this passage may appear to the cautious reader as a remote or perhaps unfounded refinement on the more obvious and popular sense of the words, I shall remove all his doubts on this occasion by the following lines from Hall's *Satires,* 1597:

> One higher pitch'd doth set his soaring thought
> On crowned kings that Fortune hath low brought:
> Or some upreared high aspiring swain
> As it might be the Turkish Tamberlaine,[20]
> Then weeneth he his base drink-drowned spright,
> Rapt to the threefold loft of heauens hight,
> When he conceiues vpon his fained stage.
> The stalking steps of his great personage,
> Graced with huffcap termes and thundring threats
> That his poore hearers hayre quite vpright sets.
> Such soone, as some braue-minded hungry youth,
> Sees fitly frame to his wide-strained mouth,
> He vaunts his voyce upon a hyred stage,
> With high-set steps, and princely carriage:
> There if he can with termes Italianate,

> Big-sounding sentences, and words of state,
> Faire patch me vp his pure Iambik verse,
> He rauishes the gazing Scaffolders.
> (See Mr. Malone's *Account of the English Stage,* p. 116)

When we have carefully reviewed the several passages which are brought forward in the above discussion, we shall certainly be compelled to acknowledge that they are all employed either obscurely or directly on the same objects of theatrical representation.

The reader will have some cause to respect the principles of our theory if it should lead us, by a train of synthetical reasoning, to discover a fact which relates to our ancient theaters, and which, as far as my information extends on the subject, is perfectly unknown to the antiquaries and critics of the present age. I had been often somewhat astonished to observe in various passages where the fancy of the poet was manifestly impressed with the objects of the theater that the obscurity of the heavens was not represented merely as an ordinary darkness of nature, but was combined likewise with the gloom of hell and associated with a peculiar train of ideas and imagery which had no necessary connection with the spirit and purpose of the narrative. In the original passage of *Macbeth* we find "the dunnest smoke of Hell," and in that from the *Rape of Lucrece,* "Comfort-killing Night, image of Hell." The whole context belonging to this latter quotation is extremely curious and well worthy of the careful consideration of the reader, especially when it shall be compared with the passages which I propose afterwards to communicate.

> Oh comfort-killing *Night,* image of *Hell!*
> Dim register and notary of shame!
> *Black stage for tragedies* and murders fell!
> Vast sin-concealing chaos; nurse of blame!
> Blind muffled bawd! Dark harbor for defame!
> *Grim cave of death!* Whispering conspirator
> With close-tongued Treason and the ravisher!
>
> *O hateful, vaporous and foggy Night!*
> Since thou art guilty of my cureless crime,
> *Muster thy mists to meet the eastern light,*
> Make war against proportioned course of time,
> Or if thou wilt permit the sun to climb
> His wonted height, yet ere he go to bed,
> Knit poisonous clouds about his golden head.

With rotten damps ravish the morning air;
Let their exhal'd unwholesome breaths make sick
The life of purity, the supreme fair,
Ere he arrive his weary noontide prick;
And let thy *misty vapors* march so thick
That in their *smoky ranks his smothered light*
May set at noon and make perpetual *night.*

Were Tarquin Night, as he is but *Night's child,*
The silver-shining Queen he would distain.
Her *twinkling handmaids* too, by him defil'd,
Through Night's black bosom should not peep again.
So should I have co-partners in my pain—
And fellowship in woe doth woe assuage,
As palmers chat makes short their pilgrimage.

O Night, thou *furnace of foul-reeking smoke,*
Let not the jealous Day behold that face
Which underneath thy black all-hiding cloak
Immodestly lies martyred with disgrace!
Keep still possession of thy gloomy place,
That all the faults which in thy reign are made
May likewise be *sepulchr'd* in thy shade! [764–805]

  Ross.   Ah, good Father,
Thou seest the *heavens,* as troubled with man's *act,*
Threatens his *bloody stage.* By the clock 'tis day,
And yet dark *night strangles* the traveling *lamp.*
Is't night's predominance, or the day's shame,
That darkness doth the *face* of earth *entomb*
When *living light* should *kiss* it? [Macbeth, II, iv, 4]

The reader will not fail to observe that the quotation from the *Rape of Lucrece* contains a peculiarity of sentiment and language which may be traced to a wonderful degree of resemblance in the latter passage produced from *Macbeth.* They not only commence with a similarity already pointed out, with a darkness which is associated with the horrors of the stage, but we may observe likewise that in the former of these quotations the "morning air" is "ravished" by the damps of darkness—that "the life of purity," existing in the essence of light, the supreme beauty of nature, sickens at the "unwholesome breath" and is "smothered" by the baleful exhalations of the night. In the latter passage the "lamp of day" is "strangled" by the night, and the "face" of nature is buried in darkness "when living light should kiss it." Let us not fail likewise to observe that in both passages darkness is the sepulcher and the tomb of nature.

Though I am unable to discover from what source a portion of the preceding imagery is derived, yet nothing can be more manifest than that the same association exerted in both cases its direct or latent influence on the fancy of the poet. The next passage which I shall produce has already in part been presented to the reader, and the inference which is to be drawn from it on either occasion only gains our conviction by comparing it with other passages in which similar trains of thought apparently exist.

> And now loud-howling wolves arouse the jades
> That drag the *tragic* melancholy *night,*
> Who with their drowsy, slow, and flagging wings
> Clip dead men's graves, and from their *misty jaws*
> Breathe foul *contagious darkness in the air.*
>
> [2 *Henry VI,* IV, i, 3]

To the line in the original passage from *Macbeth,* "Nor Heaven peep through the *blanket* of the dark," Mr. Steevens produces, as a parallel sentiment, the following verse from Drayton's *Polyolbion:* "Thick vapors that like *rugs* still hang the troubled air." Now if my hypothesis should be true, that the above quotations are either directly or obscurely employed about the same objects, and if the line from the *Polyolbion* be indeed a parallel passage to that of *Macbeth,* it will follow that the mind of Drayton was likewise occupied by a similar train of ideas which I have imagined to exist in all the preceding examples. Before I had consulted the context belonging to the line from Drayton, I had convinced myself that a similarity of this sort, either in language or sentiment, would be found to exist; yet I cannot but own that my expectations of such a coincidence were exceeded by the fact when I discovered that the Peake of Derbyshire was the subject of Drayton's narrative, in which was the dark *cave*—"the image of Hell," with all the *fogs,* the *mists,* and the *damps,* which we have just seen so fully displayed in the preceding passages, and which are there connected with the subject of theatrical exhibition.

> Ye dark and hollow *caves,* the portraiture of *Hell,*
> Where *fogs and misty damps* continually do dwell;
> O ye, my lovely joys, my darlings, in whose eyes

Horror assumes her seat, from whose abiding flies
Thick vapors, that like rugs still hang the troubled air;
Ye of your mother Peake the only hope and care.

[Polyolbion, Song 26]

In the two succeeding quotations *Hell* and *Night* are again united:

Never sees horrid *night,* the child of *Hell.*

[Henry V, IV, i, 288]

The sea, with such a storm as his bare head
In *hell*-black *night* endur'd, would have buoy'd up,
And quench'd the stelled fires. [*Lear*, III, vii, 58]

Let the reader remark that Mr. Steevens has quoted the line from *Henry V* as a parallel passage to that in the *Rape of Lucrece,* "Were Tarquin Night, as he is but Night's child"; and let me add that I have often been indebted to the sagacity of our commentators in the discovery of similar passages, though they have not been aware of the nature or extent of the similarity. This circumstance will certainly afford additional conviction for the truth of any deduction which I may form by a comparison of these passages with each other, as it will show that they were not all cautiously selected by myself to support the refinements of a favorite hypothesis, but that they really contain within themselves the most unquestionable characteristics of a common origin, since they present even to the hasty glance of the general commentator such distinct and striking features of resemblance.

My purest thoughts work in a pitchy vale,
Which are as different as heaven and hell;
One peers for day, the other gapes for night.
That *yawning beldam with her jetty skin,*
'Tis she I hug as mine effeminate bride,
For such complexions best appease my pride.

[First Part of Jeronimo, Old Plays, III, 67]

Cres. Night hath been too brief.
Tro. Beshrew the witch! With venomous wights she stays
As tediously as *Hell,* but flies the grasps of love
With wings more momentary-swift than thought.

[Troilus and Cressida, IV, ii, 11]

Light the fair grandchild to the glorious sun,
Opening the casements of the rosy morn,
Makes the abashed heavens soon to shun

The ugly darkness it embraced before;
And at his first appearance puts to flight
The utmost relics of the *hell*-born night.

[*Lingua, Old Plays,* V, 179]

He told me that his horrid tragedy
Was acted over every night in Hell.

. . . . .

I'll trace th'infernal theatre and view
Those squalid actors, and the tragic pomp
Of hell and night. [*The Antiquary, Old Plays,* X, 102]

The reader, when he has attentively considered the preceding passages, will not, I trust, hesitate to pronounce that they all receive their peculiar coloring from the same train of ideas, and ought all to be referred to one common origin, though perhaps they are related to each other in various degrees of resemblance and affinity. This metaphor may serve still farther to illustrate our meaning; for as among different persons of the same family a resemblance (which perhaps might on the first view appear but faint and imperfect, or might even have altogether escaped our notice) often strikes us with peculiar force when it is compared with the original features of the common parent, so the resemblance, and thereby the affinity, of sentiments will be seen and ascertained by a comparison with some common standard where those different traits of thought and language are united by which the character and complexion of each are individually distinguished. Thus the similarity which appears between the sentiments of Shakespeare and Drayton in the *"blanket* of the dark" and the *"rugs* of the troubled air" will acquire the evidence of affinity or of a common origin when they are contrasted with the passage in the *Rape of Lucrece,* which not only contains the resemblance common to both but possesses likewise other features which are peculiar to each. On the whole, we may remind the reader of a maxim which will direct him in discovering the examples of this associating principle, that things which are related to the same are related to each other; so we may observe likewise that different passages which are found separately to bear an affinity to the same must be conceived as ultimately derived from some common train of ideas, though perhaps in the comparison with each other they will not always afford the most striking marks of resemblance, as they may present us with different objects of which that train is composed. With respect to the quotations which I have above produced, their affinity with each other is of such a nature that by connecting as it were link by link the corresponding passages they will at last appear to form one complete chain and continued series of ideas.

We have in some of these passages a *tomb,* a *cave,* a *furnace* reeking with smoke, and the *vapors* ascending either from the jaws of a cavern or of a monster smothering the light of heaven. We have moreover that which led me to the following discovery: a *night* sometimes associated with *hell,* and sometimes with the objects of the theater. The fact, then, which the application of my theory has enabled me to discover respecting our ancient theaters is that as a part of the roof was denominated the *heavens,* so a portion likewise of the lower part of the stage was distinguished by the name of *hell.* Of this fact I am perfectly persuaded, though I cannot expect my reader to be so convinced of the truth and extent of my present theory as to admit at once a deduction which is derived from such obscure and subtle operations of the mind and which must finally depend for its confirmation on the testimony of historical authority.

I should not therefore have ventured to incur the charge of hypothetical refinement by disclosing my own conviction of such a fact had I not been able to produce one example in which there is a direct allusion to this remarkable circumstance of the name, and other passages, to prove likewise that imitations of hell-mouth were frequently attempted on the stage by the rude contrivance and licentious fancy of our ancestors. I shall produce my passages (as they occur) respecting the simple mechanism of our ancient theaters, and shall afterwards direct the attention of the reader to the peculiar purpose for which they were intended.

You shall then have three ladies walk to gather flowers, and then we must believe the stage to be a garden. By and by we hear news of shipwreck in the same place, and then we are to blame if we accept it not for a rock. Upon the back of that comes out a *hideous monster with fire and smoke,* and then the miserable beholders are bound to take it for a *cave;* while in the meantime two armies fly in, represented with four swords and bucklers, and then what hard heart will not receive it for a pitched field? (Sidney, *Defense of Poesy*)

The mechanism of our ancient theaters seldom went beyond a tomb, a painted chair, a sinking caldron or a trap door. (Malone's *History of the Stage,* p. 72)

"Undoubtedly our poet's company were furnished with some wooden fabric sufficiently resembling a tomb, for which they must have had occasion in several plays" (*Idem,* 74). Mr. Malone doubts whether the tomb in *Romeo and Juliet* was anything but the ordinary trap door of the stage, by which Romeo descended to a vault beneath it: "Why I descend into this bed of death."

The little children were never so afraid of hell-mouth in the old plays painted with great gang teeth, staring eyes, and a foul bottle nose, as the poor devils are scared with the hell-mouth of a priest. (*Declaration of Popish Impostures,* 1603. See Capell's *School,* p. 2)

> First Hell-mouth with a nether chap.
> A tomb with a covering.

(List of properties in a mystery, 1563. See Malone's *History,* p. 19)

> Item, 1 rock, 1 cage, 1 tomb, 1 Hell-mouth
> Item, 1 tomb of Guido, 1 tomb of Dido.

(Inventory of properties for my Lord Admiral's Men, 1598. See Malone's *History,* p. 302)

Here then we discover the origin of that imagery which on the first view appeared of so remote and singular a nature. We now see that the ordinary properties, or the little mechanical appendages of our ancient stage were a *tomb,* a *caldron,* a *cavern,* and the mouth of *hell.* We no longer, therefore, are to wonder that the *night,* which is the "image of *hell,*" should be combined with the "black *stage* for *tragedies* and murders fell"; that the same night should be the "grim *cave* of death," "the *furnace* of foul reeking smoke"; and that the crimes, of which it is conscious, should be *"sepulcher'd* in its shade." If we shall moreover suppose (what indeed we can scarcely imagine not to have taken place) that the mechanism extended to supplying the *mouth of hell* with a representation of smoke and vapors issuing from its jaws, the coincidence will be complete. We shall then have all the *mists, smoke,* and contagious exhalations which we have just seen so pointedly exhibited in the preceding passages. That a contrivance of this sort sometimes took place we find from the "hideous monster with *fire* and *smoke*" described by Sir Philip Sidney. On the whole, if we had concluded a priori that such theatrical apparatus would operate on the mind of the poet and produce in certain subjects a vein of imagery impregnated with scenical materials, we surely never could have expected to find a single passage so completely abounding with such imagery as we have really seen existing in that singular example which the *Rape of Lucrece* has afforded us. We must acknowledge likewise that the other quotations concur to the same purpose, and might be considered as the most fortunate instances to illustrate such a hypothesis. It remains for me now to produce the very passage in which there is as direct an allusion to the *hell* of the lower part of the stage as there is to the *heavens* belonging to the roof.

> The fortune of a *stage* (like fortune's self)
> Amazeth greatest judgments; and none knows
> The hidden causes of those strange effects,
> That rise from this *Hell,* or fall from this *Heaven.*
> (Prologue to *All Fools,* by Chapman, 1605. *Old Plays,* IV, 116)

I shall not detain the reader by any unnecessary comment on this very curious passage, as I consider it absolutely decisive in determining the question. With respect to the whole combination of imagery which I have unfolded in the above discussion, we shall receive additional conviction of its existence and effect when we observe the powerful impressions which concurred to produce it. Let us consider the striking change of the theater into *black,* the extraordinary terms of *heaven* and *hell* belonging to the stage, the *obscuring* of these theatrical *heavens* or the representation of a gloomy *Night* in order to bring forward the personages and the crimes of *tragic exhibition,* and finally, the general connection existing in an age of superstition between the crimes of tragedy and the punishments of *hell,* added to the artificial union arising not only from the name but from the actual imitation of hell, which, we may observe, could never be introduced as an object of terror unless when tragic crimes were the subject of the performance. Let us consider, I say, all these circumstances, and we shall cease to wonder that in the mind of Shakespeare, ever occupied, as it certainly must be, with the affairs of the theater, so intimate an union should be formed between *hell* and *night;* the *darkened heavens* and the *stage of tragedy.*

> *The tragic pomp of hell and night.*

After we have advanced thus far, we shall readily admit the *tomb,* the *cavern,* and the *furnace* as the natural attendants on this train of imagery. For let it ever be remembered that when the powers of the fancy are once bound by the magic of an association, the mind still hovers about the scene where the charm is deposited.[21]

.   .   .   .   .

In the discussion of a new doctrine which has reference to the more minute and subtle principles of the mind, it is incumbent on the writer to proceed with caution in the explanation of his theory and to unfold the various portions of his subject as the reader himself advances in the necessary knowledge for admitting the force of the example and the spirit of the argument. The consideration of the pageant will afford me an opportunity of producing some additional reflections on various topics which have before occupied my attention, and of extending or confirming my former discussions by a new train of collateral evidence.

We are enabled by the preceding quotations to form some idea of the extraordinary magnificence and extensive machinery which constituted the pageants presented at court and in which royal personages and the chief nobility were not only the spectators but were even frequently the actors. It is impossible for the reader to form an adequate notion of these performances or to conceive their impression on the minds of those to whom they were familiar unless he will himself consult the original narratives which describe their exhibition. When he reflects on the immense sums which were lavished on these occasions and considers that the most celebrated artists and poets of the age were employed in displaying before a voluptuous court the most consummate specimens of their skill, he will readily acknowledge the superior grandeur of these romantic spectacles, nor will he wonder at the apparent labor of the relater in selecting words and ideas to describe the various splendors of so extraordinary a scene. The following quotation from Jonson's *Hymenaei: Or the Solemnities of Masque, and Barriers at a Marriage* will illustrate the general tendency of our argument by showing us that the powers of the writer are sinking under the burden of his own description:

Hitherto extended the first night's solemnity, whose grace in the execution left not where to add to it with wishing—I mean (nor do I court them) in those that sustained the nobler parts. Such was the exquisite performance, as (beside the pomp, splendor, or what we may call appareling of such presentments) that alone (had all else been absent) was of power to surprise with delight, and steal away the spectators from themselves. Nor was there wanting whatsoever might give to the furniture or complement, either in riches, or strangeness of the habits, delicacy of dances, magnificence of the scene, or divine rapture of music. Only the envy was that it lasted not still, or (now it is past) cannot by imagination, much less description, be recovered to a part of that spirit it had in the gliding by.

It appears again from the following passage in the same masque that the poet conceived himself as exerting all the powers of his imagination and invention in the arrangement of these exquisite performances.

Here they danced forth a most neat and curious measure, full of subtility and device, which was so excellently performed as it seemed to take away that spirit from the invention which the invention gave to it, and left it doubtful whether the forms flowed more perfectly from the author's brain or their feet.

We have observed on a former occasion that the imagination of the poet would be deeply impregnated with the wild and visionary forms which were thus frequently passing before his sight, but we may add likewise that his knowledge might receive considerable accessions from the elaborate devices of a learned inventor in Greek and Roman antiquities, in the dogmas and discoveries of philosophers, in the facts of history, and the fables of mythology. The masques of Jonson abound with a profusion of learning, and when we discover in our poet familiar allusions to the opinions and customs of the ancients, we need not always imagine him to have acquired his information by the toil of study or the perusal of books; we have only to suppose him present at these classical exhibitions, and to detail the knowledge which there glided before his eyes. But these spectacles not only supplied the poet with imagery and knowledge; they suggested ideas likewise to the player for the mechanical apparatus of his theater; and we may trace among the properties of our ancient stage a poor and humble imitation of the splendid machinery of the pageant. The following quotation from Mr. Warton will serve to strengthen my opinion, as he confirms the general fact though he does not extend it to the particular circumstances which my hypothesis comprehends:

I have observed in a former work, and it is a topic which will again be considered in its proper place, that the frequent and familiar use of allegoric personifications in the public pageants, I mean the general use of them, greatly contributed to form the school of Spenser. But moreover, from what is here said it seems probable that the pageants, which, being shown on civil occasions, derived great part of their decorations and actors from historical fact, and consequently made profane characters the subject of public exhibition, dictated ideas of a regular drama much sooner than the mysteries, which, being confined to Scripture stories, or rather the legendary miracles of sainted martyrs and the no less ideal personifications of the Christian virtues, were not calculated to make so quick and easy a transition to the representations of real life and rational action. (*History of Poetry,* II, 202)

If such then was the efficacy of the pageant in elevating the fancy of the poet and in supplying the first and most obvious materials for the construction of the drama, how potently must it operate on the genius of Shakespeare, whose mind conceived and embraced at once all the forms of universal poetry while it was at the same time peculiarly occupied in seeking the most impressive subjects of dramatic action, and even perpetually employed in the mechanical arrangements of the stage itself. To the mind of a writer working under impressions of this nature, no train of ideas would be more natural and obvious than to compare the contracted scene of his own performances, the mean devices of his own theater, and the poor player that strutted on the scaffolding of his own stage with those magnificent exhibitions which were presented in palaces, which "stole away the spectators from themselves by the surprising inventions of the machinery," and which were performed not only in the presence of the monarch but oftentimes by the first nobility and princes of the court. When the reader shall have well considered these circumstances and shall likewise recollect (what we have before shown from the masques of Jonson) that a representation of the *sphere of fire* in the *highest heaven* was among the exquisite inventions of such performances, he will at once perceive the full force and spirit of the following passage, which on a former occasion we were enabled only imperfectly to explain; he will discover the source from which the poet probably derived his learning, and will acknowledge that the ideas were suggested from the objects of the stage *when compared with the splendors of the pageant.*

> O for a Muse of *fire,* that would ascend
> The brightest *heaven* of *invention,*
> A kingdom for a stage, *princes* to act,
> And *monarchs* to behold the swelling scene!
> . . . But pardon, gentles all,

> The *flat unraised spirits* that hath dar'd
> On this *unworthy scaffold* to bring forth
> So great an object. Can this cockpit hold
> The vasty fields of France? Or may we cram
> Within this *wooden O* the very casques
> That did affright the air at Agincourt?
> [*Henry V*, Prologue, 1–14]

I cannot forbear adding that in this mode of conceiving the above passage, an objection will be obviated and explained which has been very acutely started by Dr. Johnson. In the idea of princes acting and monarchs beholding, "Shakespeare," says he, "does not seem to set distance enough between the performers and spectators."

That the properties of the ancient theater were borrowed from the masque and the pageant I am perfectly convinced, and instead of considering dramatic exhibitions as an improvement on the mysteries and moralities of a former period, I am disposed to think that they should rather be regarded as feeble efforts to gratify the public with an imitation of those spectacles which were before generally confined within the private walls of the rich and the great. It appears from the preceding quotations and from the various narratives relating to these shows that an imitation of the *heavens* and the *clouds* was a very favorite and almost constant appendage to the machinery of the pageant; and we may conjecture, I think, with great probability, that the name and representation of the heavens on the roof of the stage were derived from this source. I have shown on a former occasion that an imitation of hell-mouth was frequently attempted on the stage, and that the objects which are most allied to this seat of smoke and darkness, the *furnace,* the *caldron,* and the *cavern,* were among the ordinary properties of an ancient playhouse, which were all, I have no doubt, suggested by exquisite devices of the same kind in more complete and furnished spectacles. In an age of superstition the pageant and the theater would certainly abound with the same subjects which the mysteries and moralities afforded, and they would consequently have frequent occasion to exhibit stories which related to the terrors and the punishments of hell. On these occasions the pageant would display all the resources of its machinery and all the wonders of its invention, as, amidst the various materials which folly or fancy or superstition could supply, no subject of exhibition would be more congenial to the nature of these wild performances than the horrors and the torments of hell. We may well conceive that scenery of this kind frequently passing before the eyes would operate with considerable force on the powers of the imagination and would deeply mark with the traces of its effect the descriptions and imagery of the poet. Even the humble imitation of the same objects on the stage would serve to recall the impression, and we may expect to find in the dramatic writers strong and lively testimonies of its existence. From many of the passages which led me to conclude that a portion of the lower part of the stage was denominated by the name of *hell,* I was induced to believe that an imitation of the smoke issuing from the mouth of hell was sometimes exhibited. I will now prove to the reader that such a representation took place in the higher spectacle of the pageant, and the conviction of this fact will add weight to the other part of my hypothesis, as they were both derived from the same passages and from a similar principle of criticism. I will produce in this place an additional body of quotations illustrative of my former topic and therefore connected with the present, and I shall request the reader to compare them carefully with the former passages, that he may be fully sensible of their force and similarity. He will perceive that they all contain the same species of imagery, and he will acknowledge that they are derived either remotely or directly from the personifications or devices of scenical exhibition.

NIGHT
1. With *black brows* is drawn by *dragons,* and her abode is the *bed of death.*
2. With a *cloak,* attended by *murder* and *treason.*
3. With a *foul* and *filthy face.*
4. Its *contagious breath smokes* about the sun.

   I. The *ugly* clouds cover the *face* of the morning.

  II. The *contagious* clouds and the *foul* mists *smother* and *strangle* the *beauty* of the sun.

 III. *Mists* arise from a *reeking cave of Death* (or *slaughter*), to infect an object compared to the splendor of the *sun,* in which cave sit *Murder, Rapine,* and *Lust.*

    1. My fairy lord, this must be done with haste,
       For *night's* swift *dragons* cut the clouds full fast,
       And yonder shines Aurora's harbinger,
       At whose approach ghosts, wand'ring here and there,
       Troop home to churchyards. Damned spirits all,
       That in cross-ways and floods have burial,
       Already to their *wormy beds* are gone,

For fear lest day should look their shames upon;
They willfully themselves exile from light,
And must for aye consort with *black-browed night.*
                    [*Midsummer Night's Dream*, III, ii, 378]

2. But when from under this terrestrial ball
   He fires the proud tops of the eastern pines
   And darts his light through every guilty hole,
   Then *murders, treasons,* and detested sins,
   The *cloak of night* being plucked from off their backs,
   Stand bare and naked, trembling at themselves.
                    [*Richard II*, III, ii, 41]

3. And all the while she [*night*] stood upon the ground,
   The wakefull dogs did never cease to bay;
   The messenger of death, the gastly Owle,
   With drearie shriekes did also her bewray;
   And hungry Wolves continually did howle
   At her *abhorred face,* so *filthy* and so *fowle.*
                    [*Fairy Queen*, I, v, 30]

4. But even this *night,* whose black *contagious breath*
   Already *smokes* about the burning crest
   Of the old, feeble, and day-wearied sun.
                    [*King John*, V, iv, 33]

I. Full many a glorious morning have I seen
   Flatter the mountaintops with sovereign eye,

                .   .   .   .   .

   Anon permit the basest clouds to ride
   With *ugly* rack on his celestial *face.* [Sonnet 33]

This is properly quoted by Mr. Malone, as parallel to the succeeding passage:

II. Yet herein will I imitate the sun,
    Who doth permit the base *contagious* clouds
    To *smother* up his *beauty* from the world,
    That, when he please again to be himself,
    Being wanted, he may be more wonder'd at
    By breaking through the *foul* and *ugly mists*
    Of vapors that did seem to *strangle* him. [*1 Henry IV*, I, ii, 190]

III. His former rays did only clear the sky;
     But these his searching beams are cast to pry
     Into those dark and deep concealed vaults,

Where men commit black incest with their faults,
And snore supinely in the stall of sin
Where *Murder, Rapine, Lust* do sit within,
Carousing human blood in iron bowls,
And make their den the *slaughter-house* of souls,
From whose *foul reeking caverns* first arise,
Those damps that so offend all good men's eyes,
And would (if not dispersed) *infect* the crown
And in their vapor her bright metal drown.

(Jonson's "Panegyre on the Happy Entrance of James I into his First High Session of Parliament.")

In the two following quotations from Jonson's masques, *Night* is first, probably, *personified* in a painting; and secondly, she is brought on the stage with her *chariot*.

1. "Here a curtain was drawn, in which the *Night* was painted."

(Works [1692], p. 328)

2. "Here the *Night* rises, and took her *chariot* bespangled with stars." (p. 600)

The following quotations will confirm my hypothesis respecting Hell at the bottom of the stage:

1. "I'll put me on my great carnation nose, and wrap me in a rowsing calf's skin suit, and come like some hobgoblin, or some *devil ascended* from the grisly *pit of Hell,* and like a scarbabe make him take his legs. I'll *play* the *devil,* I warrant ye." (*Wily Beguiled,* 1606)

(I am indebted for this quotation to the editor of the *Old Plays,* II, 34.)

2. Act IV, scene i. Before this act Magaera *riseth* out of *Hell,* with the other furies, Alecto and Tysiphone, dancing an hellish round; which done, she saith:

> Sisters, begone; bequeath the rest to me
> That yet belongs unto this *tragedy.*
> Vengeance and death from forth the deepest *hell,*
> I bring the cursed house where Gismunda dwells.
> (*Tancred and Gismunda, Old Plays,* II, 195)

3. "First the music of oboes began to play, during which there came *from under the stage, as though out of hell,* three furies, Alecto, Megera, and Ctisiphone, clad in black garments." (Explanation of the dumb show before the fourth act of *Gorboduc*)

4. "In the *Necromancer*, by Shelton, the last scene is closed with a view of hell and a dance between the devil and necromancer. The dance ended, the devil trips up the necromancer's heels and disappears in fire and smoke." (Warton's *History of English Poetry*, II, 363)

5. "In the mystery of Mary Magdalen, one of the stage directions is *Here enters the prince of the devils in a stage, with hell underneath the stage.*" (Warton, *ibid.*)

6. "In the heat of their dance, on the sudden was heard a sound of loud music, as if many instruments had made one blast, and with which not only the hags themselves, but the *hell* into which they ran, quite vanished." (Jonson's *Masque of Queens*, p. 351)

7. "His majesty then being set, and the whole company in full expectation, the part of the scene which first presented itself was an *ugly Hell, which flaming beneath smoked to the top of the roof.*" (Jonson's *Masque of Queens*, p. 345)

I consider the last quotation as altogether decisive on the material parts of my hypothesis. It establishes the conjecture respecting the imitation of smoke from the mouth of hell and accounts for all that abundance of imagery which describes the mists, the smoke, the vapors, and the reeking of the furnace or the cavern.

On the whole of this discussion, the reader will, I trust, be of opinion that my hypothesis, formed and supported [22] as it is by such a mode of illustration, may at least claim the distinction of novelty; that the body of coinciding evidence produced on this occasion is altogether irresistible; and that the doctrine of association, when applied to criticism, is still exercised in examining the most subtle objects of metaphysical inquiry, while it escapes in a considerable degree the tedious obscurity of those investigations. In the reasoning of metaphysicians, the operations of the mind are discussed in general and abstracted terms, and we too often search for existing facts to which they may be referred and from which they are derived. We "bend our eye on vacancy" and sink under the languor of study, alike destitute of objects and ideas. The critic who should pursue the researches which we have opened to his view at once forms and elucidates his inquiry by the evidence of examples; and though his own arrangement of the argument should be somewhat deficient in spirit and perspicuity, the mind of the reader will be yet enlivened by the effusions of the poet, who suggests the principles of the theory and supplies the materials of the discussion.

ALEXANDER KNOX ✒

The Flapper (1796)

No. 30, May 14, 1796 [Cowper, I]

Amidst the sportive varieties of the fashionable world and the more awful vicissitudes of the political, it is matter of consolation to perceive that the radical characters of human nature still remain the same—that common sense, though like the great luminary in the heavens, occasionally obscured by passing clouds, is by no means extinguished—and that the real majority of society taste and feel and relish and prefer pretty nearly as they did in less questionable times.

Amongst many other obvious marks of undeclining humanity there is one which I always think of with peculiar pleasure. I mean the reception which the poems of the excellent Cowper have met with from all classes of readers. His two volumes, which were first published about fourteen years ago, have passed already through at least seven editions; and while love for the man mingles in every instance with admiration of the poet, even republicanism itself seems to relax from its wonted sternness at the mention of that well-known act of munificence by which his present Majesty has done equal honor to Mr. Cowper and to himself.[1]

To point out the reasons why poetry pleases, to analyze its characters, and to show that its laws are founded on the nature of things— these form the appropriate task of the professor of polite literature. But common experience is sufficient to prove that the gratification arising from poetry is not limited to the knowledge of its principles; and if we observe attentively, we shall probably find that even amongst common readers the degree of the pleasure bears a near proportion to the merit of the performance.[2] At least it will appear that where poetry is really excellent, it never fails more or less to interest the human mind, except in cases of absolute insensibility.

At the same time it must be allowed that some species of poetic composition may be much better calculated than others to obtain general acceptance. For instance, it can hardly be supposed that the *Paradise Lost* of Milton, transcendent as it is, should be as popular as the *Seasons* of Thomson. In the former, the grandeur of the subject, the loftiness of the conceptions, the profusion both of classical and scientific learning, together with that transposition of language, it might almost be said that Latinized English, which obtains throughout the whole of the poem, keep the unlettered reader at an awful distance and preclude that degree of familiarity which is essential to enjoyment. Thomson, on the contrary, though elegant, is accessible. Though he thinks with the wise, he speaks a language intelligible even to the vulgar; he describes for the most part what the village swain has contemplated in common with the philosopher; and he expresses feelings which every well-formed mind has experienced, though it may not always be able to clothe them in suitable language; he paints with justness of design and in the most glowing colors from originals generally known and generally interesting; and because all can judge of the likeness, all derive pleasure from the performance.

To similar causes we may attribute the popularity of Cowper. He too, perhaps in as high a degree as any man who ever lived, is the poet of nature; led by his excursive muse through many a mazy path, he returns to the scenes which nature herself has formed with ever new delight; from these he takes the darling subjects of his poetic pencil; and though in his hands they seem to display new beauties and appear more interesting, they lose nothing of their familiarity. His descriptions strike every mind which is endued with the common powers of discernment; his thoughts meet something in unison with themselves in every heart that is human.

I believe I need not scruple to assert that in the power of giving universal gratification Cowper very much exceeds even Thomson himself. Thomson undoubtedly describes what every man may see, and what indeed almost every man has seen at one time or other; [3] but Cowper describes what every man *must* see; he takes his materials from the everyday walks of life; he seizes on those little domestic circumstances which perhaps no poet before him ever thought of making use of, and he forms from them pictures which astonish no less than they please. We wonder at the interest we now for the first

time take in what we have so often seen without any pleasurable
sensation, and we wonder still more that such an effect should be so
easily produced; we observe no labor, no search for ornament, but on
the contrary, an execution as artless as the conception is vigorous. In
this, perhaps, also Cowper has a material advantage over Thomson;
the latter leaves no circumstance unexpressed, no grace neglected,
no aid of coloring omitted—all is beautiful, but all is elaborate.
Cowper, on the contrary, looks out for nothing; he takes just so much
as has made an impression on his own mind, and which will of course
produce the effect on the mind of his reader, and having completed
his design with a few masterly strokes, he hurries on to some new
subject. The descriptions of Thomson are like the most highly
finished paintings of the Flemish school; those of Cowper are little
more than sketches, but they are the sketches of a Raphael.

Let it not be thought that I wish to depreciate by an invidious
comparison the admirable author of the *Seasons*. His pure gold
could not be tarnished by the breath of malevolence, nor has it anything to apprehend from the assay of candid criticism. But the excellence of Cowper has no need of being illustrated by contrast—to
know him is to admire him. In particular, it is impossible to look
into his invaluable *Task* (the work in which he has given the most
unbounded license to his fancy) without being charmed even to
transport at the wildly beautiful varieties of vivid description and
glowing thought, of images the gravest and the gayest, the most
humorous and the most pathetic, the most obvious in substance, and
in manner the most novel, which, following each other in rapid
succession, would almost bespeak a magic creation like that of the
airy phantoms in the cave of Prospero.

The limits which I have assigned myself would almost forbid my
indulging in quotation, were it not necessary to support by a few
instances what might otherwise appear to those who are but slightly
acquainted with Cowper's poetry a fanciful panegyric. I transcribe
the following description of the coming in of the post in a winter
afternoon, not because it is the most beautiful I could find, but because it is the first passage which happens to occur, and being the
exordium of a book, its meaning is independent of anything preceding.

> Hark! 'tis the twanging horn o'er yonder bridge,
> That with its wearisome but needful length
> Bestrides the wintry flood, in which the moon

> Sees her unwrinkled face reflected bright;
> He comes, the herald of a noisy world,
> With spatter'd boots, strapp'd waist and frozen locks;
> News from all nations lumb'ring at his back.
> True to his charge, the close pack'd load behind,
> Yet careless what he brings, his one concern
> Is to conduct it to the destin'd inn:
> And having dropp'd th' expected bag, pass on.
> He whistles as he goes, light-hearted wretch,
> Cold and yet cheerful: messenger of grief
> Perhaps to thousands, and of joy to some;
> To him indiff'rent whether grief or joy.
> Houses in ashes, and the fall of stocks,
> Births, deaths, and marriages, epistles wet
> With tears, that trickled down the writer's cheeks
> Fast as the periods from his fluent quill,
> Or charg'd with am'rous sighs of absent swains,
> Or nymphs responsive, equally affect
> His horse and him, unconscious of them all. [*The Task,* IV, i]

The lovely domestic picture which follows almost immediately and which introduces a most whimsical yet most literally just description of a newspaper, is too long to be wholly transcribed and yet too beautiful to be entirely omitted. I will transcribe a part, in the hope that it may excite a wish to read the remainder.

> Now stir the fire, and close the shutters fast,
> Let fall the curtains, wheel the sofa round,
> And while the bubbling and loud-hissing urn
> Throws up a steamy column, and the cups
> That cheer but not inebriate, wait on each,
> So let us welcome peaceful ev'ning in.
> Not such his ev'ning, who with shining face
> Sweats in the crowded theatre, and squeez'd
> And bor'd with elbow-points through both his sides,
> Out-scolds the ranting actor on the stage:
> Nor his, who patient stands till his feet throb,
> And his head thumps, to feed upon the breath
> Of patriots bursting with heroic rage,
> Or placemen, all tranquillity and smiles.
> This folio of four pages, happy work!
> Which not ev'n critics criticise; that holds
> Inquisitive attention, while I read,
> Fast bound in chains of silence, which the fair

> Though eloquent themselves, yet fear to break;
> What is it but a map of busy life,
> Its fluctuations, and its vast concerns?
> Here runs the mountainous and craggy ridge
> That tempts ambition, etc.
>
> .   .   .   .   .
>
> Here rills of oily eloquence in soft
> Meanders lubricate the course they take.
>
> .   .   .   .   .
>
> Cat'racts of declamation thunder here;
> There forests of no meaning spread the page.
>
> .   .   .   .   .
>
> The rest appears a wilderness of strange
> But gay confusion; roses for the cheeks,
> And lilies for the brows of faded age,
> Teeth for the toothless, ringlets for the bald,
> Heav'n, earth and ocean, plunder'd of their sweets,
> Nectareous essences, Olympian dews,
> Sermons, and city feasts, and fav'rite airs,
>
> .   .   .   .   .
>
> And Katterfelto, with his hair on end
> At his own wonders, wond'ring for his bread. (IV, 36)

The discerning reader will easily perceive that simplicity is a prevailing character in the poetry of Cowper, and that his thoughts appear to retain on paper the very order and shape which they assumed at first in his mind. One consequence of this certainly is that his verses are unequal and that many of his lines, if they stood alone, or were fraught with less noble matter, could not be considered as more than prose which had fallen by accident into a metrical form. In such cases Cowper seems never once to have thought of stopping to correct or improve. He was too powerfully attracted by the objects that lay before him; perhaps also he considered the occasional occurrence of verses comparatively flat as advantageous on the whole, and that the remark of Horace,

> Operi longo fas est obrepere somnum,[4]

implied a precept as well as a permission.

Another consequence of Cowper's writing precisely as he thought is a total dereliction of all method. This might seem at first sight to be the very thing which he intended; but on a closer view he appears frequently to have formed some previous plan from which the fervidness of his mind carries him away, and he wanders on through a wilderness indeed, but like that of Eden "a wilderness of sweets," over which the fancy of his reader delights to follow him. He describes this versatile turn in his own happy manner, in a passage with which for the present I shall conclude, requesting only the permission of my readers to resume this subject (which I acknowledge to be a favorite one) at some future opportunity.

After describing in a vein of poignant humor "the world's time as time in masquerade,"

> His pinions fledg'd
> With motley plumes, [IV, 214]

tinctured black and red with card spots, furnished with a dicebox in lieu of an hourglass, and a billiard mace as a substitute for his scythe; and having touched on the modern education of young misses, who at the age,

>   their mothers wore
> The back-string and the bib, assume the dress
> Of womanhood, sit pupils in the school
> Of card-devoted time, and night by night,
> Plac'd at some vacant corner of the board,
> Learn ev'ry trick. [IV, 226]

He proceeds,

> But truce with censure. Roving as I rove,
> Where shall I find an end, or how proceed?
> As he that travels far oft turns aside
> To view some rugged rock or mould'ring tower,
> Which seen, delights him not; then, coming home,
> Describes and prints it, that the world may know
> How far he went for what was nothing worth;
> So I, with brush in hand and pallet spread,
> With colours mix'd for a far different use,
> Paint cards and dolls, and ev'ry idle thing
> That fancy finds in her excursive flights. [IV, 231]

No. 34, May 28, 1796   [Cowper, II]

Aux régions à lui même inconnues,
Où voleront ses gracieux écrits,
A ce tableau de ses moeurs ingénues,
Tous ses lecteurs deviennent ses amis.—GRESSET [5]

His the high honour that, in climes unknown,
Where'er his wand'ring volume may extend,
Where'er that picture of his mind is shewn,
In every reader he shall find a friend.
                              —Altered from HAYLEY

In the remarks which I gave lately on the poetry of Cowper I observed that in his descriptions he avoids all unnecessary minuteness of detail and confines himself to those striking features which are most likely to make a forcible impression on the mind. Though in this particular he seems merely to have followed the instinctive bent of his genius, he has perhaps attained one of the most desirable ends of poetic skill and labor. A poet who describes justly and beautifully will necessarily give pleasure, even though he should say all that can be said and anticipate every conceivable idea. But he will afford a much more exalted delight when he impregnates the mind with the seeds of new conceptions, and instead of thinking exclusively for his reader, inspires him with a power of thinking for himself. It is in this instance, amongst others, that the father of Grecian poetry has outdone all the world—and may I be permitted to add that it is in this particular too that his most celebrated translator seems chiefly to have failed. The ancient bard, in the energy of his soul, darts forth the pregnant thought and leaves it to fructify where it falls. Pope, on the contrary, forestalls the process of nature, expands the precious germ with an elegant but officious care, and reduces his reader to the sterile pleasure of inactive contemplation.

Having mentioned this subject, it may not be amiss to give an instance. Homer, in describing the eloquence of Ulysses, says simply that it was like the falling flakes of the winter snows, leaving it to his reader to discover for himself that it must of course be "soft," "copious," "pure," and "penetrating." Pope, artful rather than ardent, and perhaps judging it more prudent to give an inferior pleasure to the many than a more refined gratification to the intelligent few,

displays at once and in open view the rich contents of his master's
teeming idea.

> But when he speaks what elocution flows!
> Soft as the fleeces of descending snows.
> His copious accents fall with easy art,
> Melting they fall, and sink into the heart.
>
> [*Iliad,* III, 283]

That this is uncommonly beautiful I readily acknowledge, but it
is a beauty as unlike that of the original as can possibly be conceived.

But it is Cowper with whom I am concerned. I shall therefore exemplify my observations respecting him by adducing what the passage I have just quoted naturally suggests, his description of a
shower of snow.

> Fast falls a fleecy show'r: the downy flakes
> Descending, and with never-ceasing lapse,
> Softly alighting upon all below,
> Assimilate all objects. Earth receives
> Gladly the thick'ning mantle. [*The Task,* IV, 326]

The copious brevity of this passage, as well as its exquisite justness and simplicity, must be evident to every reader. I cannot, however, omit the opportunity of comparing it with a beautiful but
much more labored picture of the same object given by the amiable
poet already mentioned in his charming poem on *Winter.*

> Through the hushed air the whitening shower descends,
> At first thin-wavering; 'till at last the flakes
> Fall broad, and wide, and fast, dimming the day
> With a continual flow. The cherished fields
> Put on their winter-robe of purest white.
> 'Tis brightness all.
>
> .   .   .   .   .
>
> Earth's universal face, deep-hid and chill
> Is one wild dazzling waste that buries wide
> The works of man. [229]

But although Cowper shuns minuteness of description, he very
frequently, as has been already observed, describes minute or trivial
matters—and it is certain that on these a master of the imitative arts
can display his excellence no less than on the most dignified subjects.
For example, there is nothing very remarkable or striking in a lighted

candle—we see it without a thought—but a lighted candle may be
so painted as to excite both pleasure and surprise and perhaps to
arrest the attention of a common observer more powerfully than the
best executed landscape or history piece. In like manner it would
hardly be imagined that there could be anything very interesting in
the appearance of a boor going from his cottage at peep of day to hew
timber in a neighboring wood. And yet from this familiar circumstance Cowper has formed a poetic sketch which it is scarcely possible
to read without being delighted and which has furnished an eminent
artist with a subject for a very beautiful print that I dare say few of
my readers are unacquainted with. I am sure I shall be excused for
transcribing the passage to which I refer.

> Forth goes the woodman, leaving unconcern'd
> The cheerful haunts of man; to wield the axe
> And drive the wedge, in yonder forest drear,
> From morn to eve his solitary task.
> Shaggy, and lean, and shrewd, with pointed ears
> And tail cropp'd short, half lurcher and half cur
> His dog attends him. Close behind his heel
> Now creeps he slow; and now, with many a frisk
> Wide-scamp'ring, snatches up the drifted snow
> With iv'ry teeth, or ploughs it with his snout;
> Then shakes his powder'd coat and barks for joy.
> Heedless of all his pranks, the sturdy churl
> Moves right toward the mark; nor stops for aught,
> But now and then with pressure of his thumb
> T' adjust the fragrant charge of a short tube
> That fumes beneath his nose: the trailing cloud
> Streams far behind him, scenting all the air.
>
> [*The Task,* V, 41]

Descriptions of this kind, in which nature and simplicity are the
prevailing characters, have a kind of mysterious power of captivating
the human mind. The degree of the pleasure they afford is greater
than can be rationally accounted for. It must be ultimately resolved
into the wise and gracious appointment of our Creator, who by the
original laws of our nature has fitted us for deriving the purest and
most perfect gratification from those scenes and objects of which we
are least liable to be deprived by casualty, and which, instead of
exposing us (like the far greater number of those enjoyments which
we have formed for ourselves) to guilt and turbulence, are the means
as well as the preservatives of innocence and tranquillity. I cannot,

therefore, help considering it as one of the happiest exercises of genius thus to restore the mind to its safe and natural habits and to awaken by sweet strains of the poetic lyre those capacities of guiltless delight which, though still existing in the soul, are too frequently benumbed by the opiates of luxury.

It is thus that the poet becomes a benefactor of human kind and a minister of Heaven, and it is in this point of view that the descriptive powers of Cowper appear to me to be invaluable. By the happiest choice of subjects and the most lively representation of them he perpetually allures the wandering fancy to the sources of harmless satisfaction, and even his most trifling pictures are so many new proofs that to a well-formed and uncorrupted mind the means of innocent amusement are inexhaustible. Instances of this kind occur so frequently, particularly in the *Task,* that it would be impossible to enumerate them. He who has read this poem, need not, I am sure, be reminded of the progress of seats from the joint-stool to the sofa, the Thresher, the Waggoner, or even the still lighter subjects of cutting fodder for cattle from a stack, or the lengthened shadows of a bright winter morning. The last, in particular, is so striking an instance of that very talent of which I am speaking that I cannot deny myself the pleasure of inserting the passage.

> 'Tis morning; and the sun with ruddy orb
> Ascending, fires th' horizon; while the clouds
> That crowd away before the driving wind,
> More ardent as the disk emerges more,
> Resemble most some city in a blaze
> Seen through the leafless wood. His slanting ray
> Slides ineffectual down the snowy vale,
> And tinging all with his own rosy hue,
> From ev'ry herb and ev'ry spiry blade
> Stretches a length of shadow o'er the field.
> Mine, spindling into longitude immense,
> In spite of gravity, and sage remark
> That I myself am but a fleeting shade,
> Provokes me to a smile. With eye askance
> I view the muscular, proportion'd limb,
> Transform'd to a lean shank. The shapeless pair,
> As they design'd to mock me, at my side
> Take step for step; and as I near approach
> The cottage, walk along the plaster'd wall,
> Prepost'rous sight! the legs without the man. [V, 1]

There is scarcely anything which more contributes to make Cowper's poetry popular than the power which he possesses of enlivening his descriptions with strokes of the most genuine humor, and it frequently heightens the effect that we find this where we least expect it. In this particular, Cowper seems to bear a near resemblance to the celebrated Hogarth; and though the pen of the poet may be thought to possess less poignancy than the pencil of the painter, the difference appears to have arisen rather from want of inclination than of power. What Cowper could have done in this way, had he chosen to indulge in it, he has shown in an instance which also furnishes the most striking proof of that very congeniality with Hogarth which I have mentioned—I mean his admirable representation of the well-known female figure in that painter's *Winter Morning*. If Hogarth had wished to see a poetic expansion of his own idea, Cowper would doubtless have been the man of his choice. There is not a thought intimated in the original which Cowper does not appear to have imbibed in all its native warmth. By the aid of his muse he places the full figure before us and enables us to view it in all directions, while the more limited powers of the sister art could only present to us a single surface. It is necessary to keep this in mind and to recollect that Hogarth's is the original work, lest he should sink on a comparison. When Fielding seems to convey a complete idea of his Mrs. Bridget Alworthy, he refers to Hogarth's figure, but without attempting a transcript. What Fielding seems to have shrunk from, Cowper, with Fielding's caution in his view, undertakes and executes. The reader will find this entertaining passage (which my limits will not permit me to transcribe) in a poem entitled *Truth* in Cowper's first volume.

At present I shall add but one remark more. It is observed by Horace in his *Art of Poetry* that apt words spontaneously follow just conceptions:

Verbaque provisam rem non invita sequentur.[6]

Perhaps never was this more perfectly exemplified than in Cowper. His verse might no doubt frequently admit of improvement —his expressions scarcely ever. His fancy, softly ductile and strongly tenacious, receives and keeps the vivid impress of each object, and the cast from so fair a mould must of course present every feature and lineament with the ease of nature and the accuracy of truth. I would beg leave to recommend this observation in particular to the examination of my critical readers, and I dare to believe many of them will join me in the opinion that in choice of expression (if choice it can be called where there is no mark of forethought) Cowper yields to no poet in the English language.

No. 38, June 11, 1796 [Cowper, III]

Non satis est pulchra esse poemata dulcia sunto —HORACE [7]

The subject of Cowper's poetry having grown upon me beyond my expectation, I find myself reduced to the necessity of leaving my design abruptly incomplete or of extending it to a third paper. A confidence in the indulgence of my readers has determined me in favor of the latter.

It is obvious that poetry owes its very existence to that natural exercise of the human mind which is usually termed the association of ideas. Of this, in a greater or less degree, we are all sensible. We look at an object—that brings another to our mind, and that another, and so on in succession. We see, for example, a distant city; we are led to think of its inhabitants, to form conjectures about their occupations and pursuits, their pleasures and their pains. We turn our view to the country, and our fancy immediately begins to range amongst the probabilities of rustic life. A poet chiefly differs from a common man in the superior liveliness and justness with which he exercises this faculty. The greater his ability in forming these ideal pictures—in conceiving them with strength, with nearness to nature and fact, and with discriminative selection—and in expressing what he himself feels so as to make others participate in his feelings, the more, undoubtedly, does he possess of the radical qualities of a poet.

But in order to give full delight it is not enough that the powers of his mind merely should be employed. His heart must be engaged, else the pleasure which he either feels himself or causes others to feel must be comparatively dull and vapid. That poet will please both most extensively and most lastingly whose affections are as vivid as his fancy is fertile; and who, while in every scene through which his imagination strays he finds matter for humane and tender thought not discernible by vulgar minds, has only need to give vent to the genuine feelings of his own breast in order to excite congenial sensations in the breasts of his readers.

This, then, I conceive is after all the supreme attraction in the poetry of Cowper; on every occasion he writes not merely from his fancy but from his heart, and a heart, it is evident, as widely expansive and as tenderly sympathetic as ever animated a human bosom. He loves to recollect at all times that he is a man, and his ambition as a poet is to be the bard of humanity. With the sublimity of Milton or the changeful excellence of Shakespeare he aims at no rivalry. The style of his plain and artless verse may be fairly postponed to the "majestic march" [8] of Dryden and will be thought by many to bear no comparison with the melodious flow of Pope. But above them all, he claims this distinguished honor—that his muse is but the minister of his benevolence—that under his culture Parnassus itself teems with a new growth, since on every stem he has engrafted the scions of charity.

Nor does the affectionate sensibility of Cowper enter into his compositions merely as an ingredient. It appears rather as the invigorating principle of his poetry, the strong pinion on which his genius rises to its height. Longinus demands certain moral qualities for his poet, without which he supposes the character cannot be complete. In Cowper we have a direct proof, such as it is painful to consider has too seldom been afforded, that the sentiment of that ancient critic was exquisitely just. Had Cowper been less kind, less fraternally disposed to his fellow mortals, it is plain he must have been less successful in selecting, less powerful in executing his designs. If he fixes on images irresistibly interesting, his philanthropy no less than his ingenuity has directed his choice. The passages which might be adduced in support of this position are so numerous and of such equal excellence, especially in that delightful poem to which the reader may observe I have chiefly directed my view, I mean the *Task*, that I dare not quote any single instance. It is however impossible not to mention the descriptions of the crazed wanderer on the common, the prisoner in the bastile, and the cottage scene in a winter evening [I, 534; V, 397; IV, 375].

But the melting warmth of Cowper's heart does not transfuse itself merely into scenes which are in themselves pathetic. The interest he feels in everything human induces him to regard the most common objects as they may be connected with man and to describe them not so much by their own proper characteristics as by their accidental relations to human pains or pleasures. Thus in mentioning

> The savage rock
> That hides the sea-mew in his hollow clefts
> Above the reach of man, [I, 519]

he animates what would otherwise be a piece of still life with the transports of the returning seaman on approaching the long-wished-for shore.

> His hoary head
> Conspicuous many a league, the mariner
> Bound homeward, and in hope already there,
> Greets with three cheers exulting. [I, 520]

And when he speaks of the music of the village bells, what he dwells upon with delight is the effect which such sounds are apt to have on the imagination.

> There is in souls a sympathy with sounds;
> And, as the mind is pitch'd, the ear is pleas'd
> With melting airs, or martial, brisk or grave:
> Some chord in unison with what we hear
> Is touch'd within us, and the heart replies.
> How soft the music of those village bells,
> Falling at intervals upon the ear
> In cadence sweet, now dying all away,
> Now pealing loud again, and louder still,
> Clear and sonorous, as the gale comes on!
> With easy force it opens all the cells
> Where mem'ry slept. Wherever I have heard
> A kindred melody, the scene recurs
> And with it all its pleasures and its pains.
> Such comprehensive views the spirit takes,
> That in a few short moments I retrace
> (As in a map the voyager his course)
> The windings of my way through many years [VI, 1]

And through this way it is so pleasant to travel back with Cowper that I cannot refrain from adding part of the just and tender reflections which the retrospect suggests, and which indeed do no more than express in the happiest manner those feelings which every worthy heart in similar circumstances has experienced.

How readily we wish time spent revok'd,
That we might try the ground again, where once
(Through inexperience, as we now perceive)
We miss'd that happiness we might have found!
Some friend is gone, perhaps his son's best friend!
A father, whose authority in show
When most severe and must'ring all its force,
Was but the graver countenance of love;
Whose favour,·like the clouds of spring, might low'r,
And utter now and then an awful voice,
But had a blessing in its darkest frown,
Threat'ning at once and nourishing the plant.
We loved, but not enough, the gentle hand
That rear'd us. At a thoughtless age, allur'd
By ev'ry gilded folly, we renounced
His shelt'ring side, and wilfully forewent
That converse which we now in vain regret. [VI, 25]

Sentiments such as these, so conceived and so expressed, will, I apprehend, endear the poetry of Cowper so long as the tender charities which knit society together shall be felt in the world. The effect of this ingenuity of the heart (if I may use such a term) can never fail. It is independent of varying customs or evanescent prejudices and acts upon the inborn feelings of human nature as the magnet on the steel. Where this is wanting, the most powerful talents in other respects have not supplied the deficiency. Of this Dryden is a remarkable instance. "The power," saith Johnson, "that predominated in his intellectual operations was rather strong reason than quick sensibility; with the simple and elemental passions as they spring separate in the mind he seems not much acquainted, and seldom describes them." [9] We see accordingly that Dryden, admirable as he is, is applauded without being loved. He is always in the library, but seldom or never in the closet. On the other hand, Goldsmith is a universal favorite. There are not perhaps in the whole English language two poems which have been more repeatedly read than the *Traveller* and *Deserted Village*. And why? Is it because Goldsmith excels in the sublimer qualities of a poet, in grandeur of conception and in energy of expression? No. It is simply because he is pathetic—because his affections keep pace with his fancy. And yet may we not assert that while the affections of Goldsmith glide like a gentle rivulet, not languid certainly, but seldom vigorous, those of Cowper gush forth like the profluent stream, and in their clear though rapid course frequently rise even above the banks of poetic regularity?

Amongst the advantages which Cowper has possessed from his moral dispositions I cannot overlook those which he has enjoyed from his piety. In him humanity has been sublimed by religion, and his imagination as well as his language evidently appears to be heightened by his deep acquaintance with the Holy Scriptures. That poetry may be infinitely indebted to these stores of unsummed excellence is demonstrated in the instance of the *Paradise Lost*. That, which is "not the greatest of heroic poems only because it is not the first," never could have been written if its wonderful author had not loved as well as studied the Bible. That this was actually the case, and that even after long and thorough knowledge he used to recur to it with fresh avidity, "smit," as he says, "with the love of sacred song," we know from the record of his own immortal verse. Much as he delighted in the sages of the heathen world, and to

> Wander where the Muses. haunt,
> Clear spring, or shady Grove, or Sunny Hill, [III, 27]

still his supreme recreation lay in the sacred volume.

> But chief
> Thee *Sion* and the flow'ry Brooks beneath
> That wash thy hallow'd feet, and warbling flow,
> Nightly I visit. [III, 29]

And that Cowper has been no less devoted to the same happy exercise, were we even ignorant of his habits, we should discover from those ever-occurring figures of divine rhetoric which declare at once by their peculiar character the single source from which they could be derived.

Of the various instances which might be adduced on this head I shall confine myself to a few passages in the description of the earthquake which, some years since, desolated so large a part of the island of Sicily:

> Alas, for Sicily! rude fragments now
> Lie scatter'd where the shapely column stood.
> Her palaces are dust. In all her streets
> The voice of singing and the sprightly chord
> Are silent. Revelry and dance and show,
> Suffer a syncope and solemn pause;
> While God performs upon the trembling stage

Of his own works his dreadful part alone.
How does the earth receive him?

. . . . .

Pours she not all her choicest fruits abroad?

. . . . .

She quakes at his approach. . . .
The hills move lightly, and the mountains smoke,
For he has touch'd them. From th' extremest point
Of elevation down into th' abyss,
His wrath is busy and his frown is felt.

. . . . .

What solid was, by transformation strange
Grows fluid; and the fixt and rooted earth,
Tormented into billows, heaves and swells,
Or with vortiginous and hideous whirl
Sucks down its prey insatiable.
. . . The sylvan scene
Migrates uplifted. . . .
Ocean has caught the frenzy, and upwrought

. . . . .

Not by a mighty wind, but by that voice
Which winds and waves obey, invades the shore
Resistless. Never such a sudden flood
Upridg'd so high, and sent on such a charge
Possess'd an inland scene. Where now the throng
That press'd the beach and hasty to depart,
Look'd to the sea for safety? They are gone,
Gone with the refluent wave into the deep
A prince with half his people! [II, 25]

I cannot help subjoining a passage in the prophet Jeremiah which
Cowper seems clearly to have had in view and which appears to me
to combine in a very remarkable degree the highest sublimity of
matter with the most perfect simplicity of language.

I beheld the earth, and lo! it was without form and void; and the
heavens, and they had no light—I beheld the mountains, and lo! they
trembled; and all the hills moved lightly—I beheld, and lo! the fruitful
place was a wilderness, and all the cities thereof were broken down, at
the presence of the Lord and by his fierce anger. [4: 23–26]

After enlarging so much on the beauties of Cowper it may be
expected that I should take some notice of his blemishes. I scarcely

lament that by the narrowness of my limits I am obliged on this particular to be very brief. I have already hinted at the frequent occurrence of passages in which nothing of poetry is to be found but the form of the line. In this instance I conceive Cowper to have sacrificed the dignity of his verse to his earnestness to do good, as on every such occasion he pursues, perhaps beyond those bounds which his general plan prescribed, some subject so merely moral as not to be susceptible of poetic imagery; and let it be remembered that the merely theological parts of *Paradise Lost* have subjected even Milton to somewhat of a similar charge. A severe critic might also accuse Cowper of dwelling in a few instances on subjects scarcely worthy of his pen, and I own I myself could wish that his love for gardening had permitted him to be less exact in describing the apparatus for a hotbed. I fear too that his piety (a matter of infinitely more importance than all the rest) may be less attractive from being marked by some peculiarity of opinion and perhaps tinged by that morbid melancholy under which Mr. Cowper is known to have long struggled. But still it is sincere, it is ardent, it is venerable, and on the whole his praise is (and what more valuable can there be) that what Johnson has said of Watts may be said with no less justice of Cowper. "He is one of those few poets with whom youth and ignorance may be safely pleased, and happy will that reader be whose mind is disposed by his verses to copy his benevolence to man, and his reverence to God." [10]

NOTES

Abbreviations

For works frequently referred to the following abbreviations have been used:

Bailey *Lucretius on the Nature of Things.* Tr. by Cyril Bailey. Oxford, 1910.

Bennett *Horace, The Odes and Epodes.* Tr. by C. E. Bennett. The Loeb Classical Library. New York, 1914.

Butler Quintilian, *The Institutio Oratoria.* Tr. by H. E. Butler. The Loeb Classical Library. New York, 1921–2.

Duff *Lucan. The Civil War, Books I–X.* Tr. by J. D. Duff. The Loeb Classical Library. New York, 1928.

DNB *The Dictionary of National Biography.* Ed. by Sir Leslie Stephen and Sir Sidney Lee. London, 1885–1900.

Elledge
and Schier *The Continental Model: Selected French Critical Essays of the Seventeenth Century.* Ed. by Scott Elledge and Donald Schier. Minneapolis, 1960.

Fairclough Horace, *Satires, Epistles, and Ars Poetica.* Tr. by H. Rushton Fairclough. The Loeb Classical Library. New York, 1926.
Virgil. Tr. by H. Rushton Fairclough. The Loeb Classical Library. New York, 1912.

Heseltine *Petronius.* Tr. by Michael Heseltine. The Loeb Classical Library. New York, 1913.

Hooker *The Critical Works of John Dennis.* Ed. by Edward Niles Hooker. Baltimore, 1939–43.

Ker John Dryden, *Essays.* Ed. by W. P. Ker. Oxford, 1900.

Murray Homer, *The Odyssey.* Tr. by A. T. Murray. The Loeb Classical Library. New York, 1919.
Homer, *The Iliad.* Tr. by A. T. Murray. The Loeb Classical Library. New York, 1924–5.

Nixon *Plautus.* Tr. by Paul Nixon. The Loeb Classical Library. New York, 1916.

Ramsay *Juvenal and Persius.* Tr. by G. G. Ramsay. The Loeb Classical Library. New York, 1918.

Roberts *Longinus on the Sublime.* Tr. by W. Rhys Roberts. Cambridge, 1907.

Robertson	Anthony Ashley Cooper, Third Earl of Shaftesbury, *Characteristics.* Ed. by J. M. Robertson. London, 1900.
Sandys	*The Odes of Pindar.* Tr. by Sir John Sandys. The Loeb Classical Library. New York, 1912.
Sargeaunt	*Terence.* Tr. by John Sargeaunt. The Loeb Classical Library. New York, 1912.
Spingarn	*Critical Essays of the Seventeenth Century.* Ed. by Joel E. Spingarn. New York, 1908–9.
Zimansky	*The Critical Works of Thomas Rymer.* Ed. by Curt A. Zimansky. New Haven, 1956.

The following abbreviations have been used for periodicals:

ELH	*English Literary History.*
JEGP	*Journal of English and Germanic Philology.*
MLN	*Modern Language Notes.*
MLS	*Modern Language Studies.*
MP	*Modern Philology.*
N&Q	*Notes and Queries.*
PMLA	*Publications of the Modern Language Association.*
PQ	*Philological Quarterly.*
RES	*Review of English Studies.*
SP	*Studies in Philology.*

Notes preceded by an asterisk (*) are those of the author, not the editor.

SAMUEL JOHNSON

Dr. Johnson's fame as a literary critic probably rests most heavily upon *The Lives of the Poets,* written during the last years of his life, but he would have been the central figure of eighteenth-century criticism even if he had written only the essays reprinted in the present collection. Indeed, he would still be one of the most interesting critics of the century had he written nothing but those minor pieces excluded from this collection, as for example, his reviews for the *Gentleman's Magazine,* his *Miscellaneous Observations on Macbeth* (1745), his *Plan of an English Dictionary* (1747), *Rambler* essays 2, 60, 102, 154, and 176, *Adventurer* essays 58, 85, 92, 95, 115, 137, and 138, *Idler* essays 3, 34, 36, 44, 59, 63, 65, 66, 68–70, 85, 90, and 91, Chapter X of *Rasselas* (1759), and the notes and "General Observations" in his edition of Shakespeare (1765). G. B. Hill's edition of the *Lives* (Oxford, 1905) has been indispensable to serious students of Johnson; a comprehensive edition of the rest of Johnson's criticism will be very welcome. A useful compilation of Johnson's statements, written and oral, about literary theory as well as about particular writers and works is J. E. Brown's *The Critical Opinions of Samuel Johnson* (Princeton, 1926).

The most important general studies of Johnson's criticism are W. B. C.

Watkins, *Johnson and English Poetry before 1660* (Princeton, 1936); J. H. Hagstrum, *Samuel Johnson's Literary Criticism* (Minneapolis, 1952); W. R. Keast, "The Theoretical Foundations of Johnson's Criticism," in *Critics and Criticism: Ancient and Modern*, ed. by R. S. Crane (Chicago, 1952); René Wellek, *A History of Modern Criticism: 1750–1950* (New Haven, 1955), I, 79–104; W. K. Wimsatt and Cleanth Brooks, *Literary Criticism* (New York, 1957), pp. 313–336. Studies of particular works are mentioned in the notes below.

For some of the following explanatory notes I am indebted to W. R. Keast, B. H. Bronson, and probably others.

1. The *Rambler* came out regularly on Tuesdays and Fridays, from March 20, 1750, to March 17, 1752. Each issue consisted of one essay, printed on three half-sheets; it cost 2d.; it was published by Edward Cave, who paid Johnson two guineas for each essay. Its circulation was small, less than 500, but in the collected form it became very popular. The first four volumes appeared in 1751, the complete set (208 papers, six volumes) in 1752. It reached a tenth edition by 1784 (see W. P. Courtney, *Bibliography of Johnson* [Oxford, 1915]). Johnson wrote all but five or six of the 208 essays. The present text follows that prepared by W. R. Keast for his forthcoming edition of Johnson's criticism; it is based on the first edition (1750–1752) and is corrected by the editions of 1752 and 1756. For a study of Johnson's style in the *Rambler*, see W. K. Wimsatt, *The Prose Style of Johnson* (New Haven, 1941) and *Philosophic Words: A Study of Style and Meaning in the* Rambler *and* Dictionary *of Samuel Johnson* (New Haven, 1948), chaps. iii and iv.

2. *Rambler* 4 concerns a subject pervasive in Johnson's criticism, the pre-eminence, above all other considerations, of the influence of art on morality. Unlike the writers of romances (Johnson says), modern novelists must present a realistic portrayal of life, but since novels are read by the "young, ignorant, and idle," novelists should remember that their works "serve as lectures on conduct and introductions to life," and they should, therefore, exercise their prerogative of selection in such a way as to avoid giving bad examples, or at least to avoid giving their portraits of vice those attractive features which might mislead the unwary. Novels should show that "virtue is the highest proof of understanding" and that vice is the "natural consequence" of ignorance and error.

3. In the first edition the mottoes were not translated; Johnson supplied translations for the second. See Ellen Douglass Leyburn, "The Translations of the Mottoes and Quotations in the *Rambler*," *RES*, XVI (1940), 169–172; and Arthur Sherbo, in *N & Q*, CXCVII (1952), 278–279.

4. J. C. Scaliger, *Poetices*, V, iv.

5. *Epist.* II. i. 170.

6. See Pliny XXXV. xxxvi. 12.

7. Juvenal *Satires* xiv.

8. Johnson's essays on pastoral poetry are important not so much for what he says about pastorals as for what he says about the nature of poetry and the methods of criticism. The history of criticism of pastoral poetry is given in

full in James Congleton, *Theories of Pastoral Poetry in England, 1684–1798* (Gainesville, 1952). Johnson's criticism of "Lycidas" in his *Life of Milton* should, of course, be referred to; and his essay in *Adventurer* 92, where he modifies his praise of Virgil as a pastoral poet.

I. Pastoral poetry, Johnson says, has always been popular because its subject suggests "peace, leisure, and innocence," things that all men are willing to imagine in the midst of their absence. Young people like pastorals because they are acquainted with the images, and old people like to be reminded of their youth, when such images of nature were fresh. In spite of the popularity of the form, however, few modern poets succeed in writing good pastorals. One cause of their failure is that though the variety of nature is unlimited, the "general effects of nature are uniform and incapable of variety." "Poetry cannot dwell upon the minuter distinctions by which one species differs from another without departing from that simplicity of grandeur which fills the imagination; nor dissect the latent qualities of things, without losing its general power of gratifying every mind by recalling its conceptions." A second cause of failure is that poets, ignorant of rural life, write "literary" imitations. A third is that rural life is by definition uncomplicated, and therefore free of the complexities of human nature and human relationships that give other writers their material. Even the efforts to vary the form by changing the time and place (e.g., from ancient Greece to modern England) are not likely to produce effective variety, for the poetry "has to do rather with the passions of men, which are uniform, than their customs, which are changeable."

II. Critics have theorized about pastoral poetry without looking closely at the classical pastoral poems, and they "have advanced principles . . . having no foundation in the nature of things." Virgil should be a good guide in this matter because (a) he was innately a good critic, (b) he was born in an enlightened age, and (c) he took his greatest predecessor in pastoral poetry, Theocritus, for a model. Virgil did not say that pastoral poems must be set in the golden age. The modern notion that they should be is based on a pedantic argument that (a) pastoral poems are dialogues between shepherds, (b) the dialogue should be elevated, (c) shepherds are illiterate, and (d) to raise the shepherds or lower the sentiments would violate decorum. Most of the thousand precepts and inconsistencies derive from this primary error. If poets would accept the Virgilian conception of pastoral poems as "representations of an action or passion by its effects upon a country life," they would see that "persons of all ranks" may be the speakers, since "persons of all ranks inhabit the country," and that all ideas "owing their original to rural objects" are equally suitable. But that is not to say that a poet can simply begin a dialogue between shepherds by a brief reference to the countryside, or to sheep, and then devote the rest of the poem to a discussion of corruption in the church or to the death of a great man whom one of the speakers calls a shepherd. The subject ought to be "at least not inconsistent with a country life or less likely to interest those who have retired into places of solitude and quiet than the more busy part of mankind."

9. *Paradise Lost*, IV, 724; V, 153.

10. This important thesis Johnson repeats many times; three other much-

quoted expressions of it occur in *Rasselas* X, *Idler* 59, and the Preface to Shakespeare (p. 648). For discussions of it, see Wimsatt, *The Prose Style of Samuel Johnson*, pp. 93–96; Scott Elledge, "The Background and Development in English Criticism of the Theories of Generality and Particularity," *PMLA*, LXII (1947), 147–182; W. R. Keast's review of that article in *PQ*, XXVII (1948), 130–132; M. H. Abrams, *The Mirror and the Lamp* (New York, 1953), pp. 38–40; and Arthur Sherbo, *Samuel Johnson, Editor of Shakespeare* (Urbana, 1956), pp. 53–56.

11. Jacopo Sannazaro (1458–1530).

12. Dionysius Periegetes (3rd or 4th century A.D.), who wrote *De situ orbis*.

13. Compare Johnson's criticisms of Virgil's pastorals in the *Adventurer* 92.

14. See *Eclog.* iii. 40; and Pope's "Spring," l. 39:

> And what is that, which binds the radiant sky,
> Where twelve fair signs in beauteous order lie?

15. *Shepherd's Calendar*, "September."

16. "Autumn," l. 89. Johnson here slightly misquotes the earlier version of the first couplet, which Pope revised to read:

> I know thee, Love, on foreign mountains bred,
> Wolves gave thee suck, and savage tigers fed.

The last line should read:

> Got by fierce whirlwinds, and in thunders born!

17. See *Carminum minorum corpusculum* XX (LII).

18. Paul Fussell, Jr., *Theory of Prosody in Eighteenth-Century England* (New London, 1954), should be consulted for full background to, and discussion of, Johnson's notions about prosody. The origin of the error that English verse is measured in number of syllables, not in number of accents or feet, is demonstrated in A. Dwight Culler, "Edward Bysshe and the Poet's Handbook," *PMLA*, LXIII (1948), 858–885. See also the essay by Samuel Say in the present collection. Johnson included a section on prosody, in the "Grammar" prefixed to his *Dictionary*.

Of Johnson's five weekly papers on Milton's versification (86, 88, 90, 92, and 94), the first three are introduced by an apology and a justification. Johnson considered the art of verse as a means of *adding* to the beauty of poetry, a way of joining "music with reason," of acting "at once upon the senses and the passions." Hence, though important, it was not primary. And he several times reminds his reader of the critic's difficulty in steering safely between a study too detailed to interest the general reader and one too general to be useful. The first paper is on meter, the second on vowel and consonant sounds and Milton's elisions, the third on the location of the caesura, and the fourth and fifth on "accommodation of sound to sense."

No. 86. Milton's variation of the meter was not always successful, and a poet "lacking Milton's invention and knowledge," and needing "to allure his audience" should not allow more than one irregular foot in any one line. On the whole, trochees and iambs should not be mixed; our ear is sufficient authority for the rule.

No. 88. Knowledge of the classical languages and love of Italian misled Milton in his efforts to make English verse less harsh; his elision of vowels, "however graceful it may seem to other nations, may be very unsuitable to the genius of the English tongue," for English has already lost some of its vowels (the silent "e" at the end of monosyllables), and elision serves only to make "our harsh cadences harsher."

No. 90. In respect to placing the caesura, Milton must be allowed to have done "all that our language would admit." The difficulties are greater in the English ten-syllable line than in the classical fifteen-syllable line, which "allowed greater variety of pauses." A comparison of Milton's versification with that of other English writers of heroic poetry, Johnson concludes, "will show that he excelled as much in the lower as the higher parts of his art and that his skill in harmony was not less than his invention or his learning."

No. 92. The fourth paper is a long introduction to a consideration of examples of Miltonic diction in which the sound of the word suggests its meaning. Although, Johnson says, it seems likely that Virgil aimed to achieve many of the sound-sense effects in the *Aeneid,* surely many of the like beauties which critics think they see in Homer are either not there or are there by chance. And in Pope's much-praised lines in the *Essay on Criticism,* Johnson finds the sound-sense parallels simply not there. This essay is interesting for its introduction, in which Johnson defines the function of criticism. It is "to establish principles, to improve opinion into knowledge, and to distinguish those means of pleasing which depend upon known causes and rational deduction from the nameless and inexplicable elegancies which appeal wholly to the fancy. . . . Criticism reduces those regions of literature under the dominion of science which have hitherto known only the anarchy of ignorance, the caprices of fancy, and the tyranny of prescription." The notion that words, phrases, and sentences by their sound often suggest their meanings is an example of a caprice of fancy.

No. 94. But it would be "too daring to declare that all the celebrated adaptations of harmony are chimerical." And certainly the musician Milton, conscious of the possible conformities of sound to meaning, produced some good examples of the device. But he also described harmonious angels in unharmonious verse, and in other places wrote lines in which the sound counteracted the meaning.

Johnson's conclusions are that in general critics who talk about this subject are more fanciful than scientific, that though the sound of Milton's verse sometimes echoes the sense, in many places it works against the sense, and that Milton, knowing he had more important matters to consider, did not exert himself to achieve such effects.

19. Lucretius *De rerum nat.* iv. 1.

20. In his *Spectator* papers on *Paradise Lost* Addison did not consider Milton's versification.

21. See *Spectator* 253.

22. "A Translation out of *Virgil*" (*Georg.* ii. 458 ff.) in *Essays, in Verse and Prose.*

23. "To Mr. H. Lawes, on his Airs."

24. *Institutio* i. Proem. 4–5.

25. Dedication of the *Aeneid* (Ker, II, 226): "It is possible, I confess, though it rarely happens, that a verse of monosyllables may sound harmoniously."

26. Horace *Serm.* I. iv. 62: "Even when he is dismembered you would find the limbs of a poet" (Fairclough).

27. Johnson, misquoting, wrote *Drawn.*

28. See *Pensées,* ed. by Léon Brunschvicg (Paris, 1904), I, 42.

29. Here Johnson quotes lines 365–386 from Book III of Vida's *Art of Poetry* (1527). See Pitt's translation (which Johnson added to later editions) in A. S. Cook, *Art of Poetry* (Boston, 1892), pp. 141–142.

30. See Addison, in *Spectator* 253.

31. The judgments of critics are unreliable for various reasons. First, of course, they deal with beauty, or beauties, where demonstration or proof is impossible. And since it is impossible to please a man against his will, prejudice is stronger in the judgment of writing than it is in the judgment of more scientific subjects. Second, critics often simply do not know all they need to know. Third, they are moved by "interest"; in spite of their best motives, they protect what is their own, just as they are prejudiced in favor of the works of their own nation.

It is a very common notion among critics that they ought not to find fault. But, Johnson says, though a certain tenderness is due the living, a critic ought not to hesitate to point out the faults in the work of a man whom death has taken beyond the reach of the critic's harm. For the "faults of a writer of achieved excellence are more dangerous because the influence of his example is more extensive."

32. Adrien Baillet (1649–1760), *Jugements des savants sur les principaux ouvrages des auteurs* (1685–1686).

33. *Ludus de morte Claudii* xii.

34. Gerard Langbaine (1656–1692), *An Account of the English Dramatic Poets* (1691); Oluf Borch (1626–1690), *Dissertationes academicae de poetis* (1683); René Rapin (1621–1687), *Réflexions sur la poétique d'Aristote et sur les ouvrages des poëtes anciens et modernes* (1674).

35. See *Spectator* 40.

36. *Ibid.* 291.

37. See Locke's *Essay on Human Understanding,* III, iv, 11.

38. This essay begins with an answer to a complaint that university students "content themselves with secondary knowledge." Since most men are not geniuses and will never "build new systems" of their own, they must be content to be "collectors of fortuitous knowledge," "intelligent hearers in the schools of art," "able to comprehend what others discover and to remember what others teach."

In literature, however, unlike science, one might suppose that imagination could carry writers in an infinite variety of directions, since though the "roads of science are narrow," the regions of fiction are filled with thousands of undiscovered places. But the truth is that poets have always been much less venturesome than one might suppose. Johnson's example is Virgil's following of Homer, and the dangers of such following are illustrated by Virgil's imitation of the meeting of Ulysses and Ajax in the lower world. Virgil erred in making Dido (a woman) answer Aeneas with silence, as inarticulate Ajax answered his enemy Ulysses. If Virgil could be so tempted, is it surprising that lesser men (university students) should parrot the opinions of their elders?

Johnson concludes with a criticism of the fashion of imitating Spenser—not his fictions and sentiments, but his diction and his stanza. The multiplication of rhyme (necessary in Italian) he considers unpleasant in English, and the introduction of archaic words without the elimination of modern words, unreasonable.

39. See *Odyssey* xi. 563. Longinus (ix. 2) said, "The silence of Ajax in the Underworld is great and more sublime than words" (Rhys Roberts). Addison had written a *Tatler* (No. 133, Feb. 14, 1710) on Dido's silence, as had someone else in the *Old Maid* (No. 8, Jan. 3, 1751).

40. See *Aeneid* vi. 469.

41. *Discoveries*, in *Works*, ed. by C. H. Herford and P. and E. M. Simpson (Oxford, 1947), VIII, 618.

42. In his note entitled "The Verse" prefixed to *Paradise Lost*.

43. *Troilus and Cressida*, II, ii, 173:

> Unlike young men, whom Aristotle thought
> Unfit to hear moral philosophy.

Dennis had pointed out this anachronism in his *Essay on the Genius and Writings of Shakespeare* (1712).

44. All definition is "hazardous," but works of art are especially difficult to define because they are the product of the imagination, which has always resisted definition and "burst the enclosures of regularity." It is impossible, therefore, to name the "essence" or list the "constituents" of any species of writing. "Every new genius produces some innovation . . . which subverts the rules which the practice of foregoing authors had established."

Comedy has been particularly hard to define; most critics have erred by trying to define the form according to the means used to achieve the effect, whereas they might have done better to define according to the effects of the form on the mind of the audience. For example, comedy is a drama that "excites mirth." If critics had made such definitions, they might have prevented some poets from such absurdities as the confounding of tragic with comic sentiments.

Johnson objects not to introducing comic scenes in tragedies, but to allowing dignified characters in solemn situations to utter comic speeches, appropriate to such characters only in "hours of ease and the intermission of danger." He gives examples from two of Dryden's plays and concludes that "there is scarce any tragedy of the last century which has not debased its most important incidents . . . with buffoonery and meanness." The bombast of contemporary tragedies may be a worse fault, but if they will not move us to terror and pity they at least do not make us laugh at the wrong time.

45. Three studies of Johnson's notions about the imagination are Irving Babbitt, *On Being Creative* (Boston, 1932), pp. 80–96; R. D. Havens, "Johnson's Distrust of the Imagination," *ELH*, X (1943), 243–255; W. B. C. Watkins, *Perilous Balance* (Princeton, 1939), pp. 92–98.

46. *Ars poet.* 93.

47. *Don Sebastian* and *Aureng-Zebe* were written by Dryden.

48. The two consecutive essays on *Samson Agonistes* treat mainly the faults of the poem; Johnson, feeling that "critical integrity" required that he speak of its beauties, devotes the last two pages of the second essay to a random sample of excellent passages. In the first essay Johnson considers the plot; in the second, sentiments, diction, and versification. Both essays are introduced by justifications for finding faults in Milton: blind worship does not do Milton honor; honest criticism will not detract from his glory; any writer "whose genius can embellish impropriety and whose authority can make error venerable" is a "proper object of inquisition."

The summary of the plot shows that though the play has a beginning and an end, "it must be allowed to want a middle," for none of the episodes tend "to introduce anything that follows it." The visit of Dalilah, for example, has "no effect but that of raising the character of Samson."

No. 140. The sentiments of a play may be judged proper if they are appropriate to (a) the character or circumstance, (b) to the "rules of the composition," and (c) to "the nature of things." Johnson objects to references to Chalybean steel, to the Alps, and to Circe and the Sirens as violations of "local or chronological" propriety. He especially objects to the introduction of the fable of the phoenix as if it were history. The numerous epigrammatical expressions and conceits in *Samson Agonistes* are inappropriate in a tragedy. Language and versification are only briefly mentioned: Johnson objects to two mixed metaphors and to the irregularity of the meter in the speeches of the Chorus. For a rejoinder to Johnson's criticism of *Samson Agonistes*, see Richard Cumberland's essay in the present collection.

49. "Father Bouhours replied: 'Great men are the proper objects of criticism, lest the faults they commit against rule should serve as a rule to inferior writers'" (Voltaire, *The Temple of Taste* [London, 1734], p. 34).

50. *Essays*, XIX, "of Empire": "For it is the solecism of power to think to command the end, and yet not to endure the means."

51. Christopher Marlowe, *Tamburlaine the Great*, pt. II, II, iv, 81.

52. Keast notes that this is a reference to Johnson's own *Irene*, I, ii, 57.

53. This and the following essay (158) are essentially concerned with the function of criticism; Johnson makes his point by examining, in the first, the rules for drama, and in the second, the rules for lyric poetry. Critics, those "who presume to superintend the taste or morals of mankind," must always distinguish between what is reasonable and grounded in nature and what is arbitrary or fanciful and based on precedent, which may be accidental. Criticism "has not yet attained the certainty and stability of science," but by constant re-examinaton of critical doctrine we may hope to keep clear the distinction between the scientific (or reasonable) parts of criticism, and those aspects which perhaps can never come under the rules of logical demonstration.

Because rules have generally been deduced by examination of works of art, they are really only "accidental prescriptions" based on precedent, not laws of nature, and are therefore not useful to succeeding artists, whose originality may simply produce new precedents from which later critics may alter their rules. Unfortunately the word of the critic has often intimidated the artist, and "blind reverence" has tyrannized over genius. It is not that all rules are vain, however; some are "fundamental and indispensable," "dictated by reason and necessity," and "supported by their conformity to the laws of nature." That in a play "the chief action should be single" and that tragedy must have a hero are examples of such rules.

But the rules requiring five acts, limiting the action to "a certain number of hours," and forbidding the mixing of tragedy and comedy are all unnatural and arbitrary. Another example of ill-founded "law," but one tending in the other direction, is the critical dogma that lyric poetry should be unrestrained by the laws of logical discourse. Such a law makes a virtue out of the accident that very early poetry was lyrical, and was written in an unphilosophic age when audiences were untrained in logical discourse. Poets then found "attention more successfully excited by sudden sallies and unexpected exclamations than by the more artful and placid beauties of methodical deduction." But their neglect of logical connections was not a virtue, for "to proceed from one truth to another and connect distant propositions by regular consequences is the great prerogative of man."

A second error of critics is simply misreading the texts, both of poetry and of earlier criticism. Johnson gives as an example Addison's comment on the first lines of *Paradise Lost,* in which he shows Addison's misunderstanding of a passage in the *Ars poetica* and his faulty judgment of Homer's proems.

54. Presumably Montaigne.

55. *Spectator* 303.

56. The *Idler* is the name of the column written by Johnson for the *Universal Chronicle: Or Weekly Gazette,* which appeared from April 8, 1758, to Dec. 29, 1759, and which was continued until April 5, 1760, as the *Universal Chronicle and Westminster Journal.* The first collected edition of the essays appeared in 1761; a seventh edition was published in 1807. Johnson wrote all but twelve of the 104 essays. The text follows that of Keast, which is based on that of the 1761 edition.

57. Minim's select writers were certainly Addison and Pope, in whose works most of the clichés occur, but Minim may also have taken with him Warton's new *Essay on Pope,* and probably the *Rambler.* Since Johnson's fun depends upon the triteness of Minim's remarks, it is not hard to multiply "sources" for them—from Horace, Dryden, Dennis, *et al.* The following selection from the notes of G. B. Hill (*Select Essays of Dr. Johnson* [London, 1889], II, 208–216) should sufficiently labor the point:

Business of art to copy nature: Pope, *E. C.,* 68. Perfect writer not to be expected: *ibid.,* 253. Genius decays as judgment increases: *ibid.,* 56. Art of blotting, Pope, *Imitations of Horace, Epist.* II. i. 280. Every piece should be kept nine years: Pope, *Prologue to the Satires,* 39. Shakespeare wanted that correctness which learning would have given him: Pope, *Dunciad,* II, 223. Jonson did not sufficiently cast his eye on nature: Johnson, *Prologue at the Opening of Drury Lane Theatre.* Blamed Spenser, and could not bear Sidney: Pope, *Imitations of Horace, Epist.* II, i, 97. Denham and Waller first reformers of English numbers: Dryden, Preface to Fables (Ker, II, 259). Nothing wanting to complete a poet: Pope, *E. C.*, 361. Dryden's poverty: Pope, *Prologue to the Satires*, 247. Otway's general negligence: Pope, *Imitations of Horace, Epist. II, i*, 278. Making a conspirator a hero: *Spectator* 39. The versification of Rowe: J. Warton, *Essay on Pope*, ed. 1762, I, 271. *Cato* a poem rather than a play: *ibid.*, I, 259. Addison master of grave humor: *ibid.*, 269. Pope a versifier: *ibid., passim*. Lamented the neglect of *Phaedra and Hippolytus: Spectator* 18. We live in a country which produces more originals than all the rest of the world together: Temple, *Of Poetry*.

58. By Edmund Smith, 1707.

59. By John Brown, 1754.

60. By Robert Dodsley, 1758.

61. Johnson might have italicized the commonplaces in this paragraph: *noble simplicity, false delicacy, true sublime, barbarity of rhyme* (see Preface to *Paradise Lost*), *the shackles of rhyme*.

62. Johnson slightly misquotes both passages from *Paradise Lost*.

63. "The discriminating character of ease consists principally in the diction." Easy poetry does not contain "harsh or daring figures," words used in unusual meaning, self-regarding artifice, unnecessary epithets, "curious repetition of the same word," or inversions of natural word order. Nor should poets think that ease may be achieved by introducing colloquialisms. Easy poetry may be sublime; it may be witty. Cowley of all English poets had the greatest gift for this kind of poetry. Since Dryden poets have "departed from simplicity and ease." See Pope's two essays on easy writing, *Guardians* 12 and 15.

64. *Ars poet.* 240.

65. Pope, "On the Countess of Burlington Cutting Paper."

66. "The Waiting Maid."

67. Johnson's interest in editing Shakespeare may be said to have started with his *Miscellaneous Observations on the Tragedy of Macbeth . . . To which is affixed Proposals for a new Edition of Shakespeare, with a Specimen* (1745). But it was not until after 1756, when he published new Proposals, that he began to work on the task which took him nine years to complete. The Preface was written probably during a short period in the summer of 1765, a month or so before the edition appeared. During the twenty years between the first Proposals and the finished work, Johnson wrote several things closely related to the subject of the Preface: the Prologue for the opening of Drury Lane Theatre (1747), the Dedication to Mrs. Charlotte Lennox' *Shakespeare Illustrated* (1753–1754), and various essays in the *Rambler, Adventurer*, and *Idler*.

The notes and the General Observations are, of course, an important part of Johnson's criticism, and as Arthur Sherbo points out in *Samuel Johnson, Editor of Shakespeare* (Urbana, 1956), they have been unjustly overshadowed by the Preface. Selections from the notes may be found in Walter Raleigh, *Johnson on Shakespeare* (Oxford, 5th impr., 1925), and in Mona Wilson, *Johnson, Prose and Poetry* (Cambridge, Mass., 1951). All the notes have been reprinted by the Augustan Reprint Society: *Notes to Shakespeare*, ed. by Arthur Sherbo (Los Angeles, 1956, 1957, 1958). But since 1903, when David Nichol Smith reprinted it in his *Eighteenth Century Essays on Shakespeare*,

the Preface has come more and more to be valued as Johnson's best essay
in criticism. As a study of Johnson's predecessors will show (or as even my
notes will show), Johnson's ideas were here not very original. His genius
for "general" wisdom, for comprehensive views and comprehensive expression,
is what made the essay a classic.

In addition to the two essential works of Smith and Sherbo, cited above,
on which most of my notes depend, the following works are useful studies of
the Preface: Karl Young, "Samuel Johnson on Shakespeare, One Aspect," in
University of Wisconsin Studies in Language and Literature, XVIII (Madison,
1923), 147–227; David Nichol Smith, *Shakespeare in the Eighteenth Century*
(Oxford, 1928); R. W. Babcock, *The Genesis of Shakespeare Idolatry, 1766–
1799* (Chapel Hill, 1931).

My text is taken from that established by W. R. Keast for his forthcoming
edition of Johnson's criticism. It is based on the first edition and corrected
from the editions of 1765b, 1768, 1773, and 1778.

In the Preface, Johnson treats five main subjects: (a) Shakespeare's virtues,
(b) his faults, (c) the sources of his knowledge, (d) the work of previous editors,
and (e) his own editorial principles.

Since the value of literary works cannot be measured absolutely, Johnson
thinks a critic must be satisfied to explain why the ages have judged a poem
or a poet as they have. Since that judgment is the result of a continuing
process of comparison, we may discuss Shakespeare's greatness by examining
the ways in which he is superior to other writers. All these ways may be sub-
sumed under one superiority: that more than any other writer he gave us
"just representations of general nature"—*just,* in that they are not "irregular
combinations of fanciful invention"; *general,* in that their characters are not
"modified by the customs of particular places," but are the "genuine progeny
of common humanity"; and "of *nature,*" in that they give us "manners"
and "life." Shakespeare's plots and his sentiments are similarly just, general,
and natural: the plots allow all the common passions as motives—not just
love, as do the plots of most other plays; and the dialogue seems to have
been "gleaned . . . out of common conversation and common occurrences."
Two other examples of his "adherence to general nature" are the distinctive-
ness of each of his characters and the absence in his plays of heroic heroes;
that is, all his men act as men act in real life (in supernatural situations, they
act as men *would* act), and their dialogue is always "level with life."

Even the mixture of comedy and tragedy, for which Shakespeare has been
censured, is really proof not only of his superiority to unnatural or unreasonable theory, but also of his aim to be true to life, or general nature. Because his plays are not strictly comedies or tragedies, but "exhibitions of the
real state of sublunar life," they are unlike ancient drama: in them good
and evil, joy and sorrow, are juxtaposed, and the action of a fool may influence the fate of a noble person, just as a tragic action may immediately
precede or follow episodes of common life. No matter what the precedent
or the theory may rule, Shakespeare successfully appeals his case from the
court of criticism to that of nature, for it cannot be denied that his "mixed"
drama not only pleases and instructs, but also "approaches nearer" than either
tragedy or comedy to the "appearance of life."

The definitions of tragedy and comedy in his day were superficial and almost meaningless, as a study of the classification of the plays in the Folio will show. Unrestrained by fear of audience or critic, Shakespeare followed his inclination to comedy, which he wrote more easily and more successfully than tragedy, and his excellence in it may, again, be attributed to his representation of general (universal) passions, not adventitious peculiarities, and to his skill in dialogue, where he used the essence of a permanent idiom, "found among those who speak to be understood," a level of diction "above grossness and below refinement."

The second part of the essay is a census of Shakespeare's faults. That Shakespeare did not write like a man who really cared about the moral purpose of his plays is a serious matter because "it is always a writer's duty to make the world better." His plots are loose; he commits chronological and geographical inconsistencies; the repartee is often indelicate; scenes of tragedy are often labored and the speeches tumid and tedious; in an effort to give dignity to long narrative speeches he made them pompous; his "set speeches are . . . cold and weak"; some passages are simply not clear; "a quibble was to him the fatal Cleopatra for which he lost the world and was content to lose it."

Among Shakespeare's faults, however, the one most commonly agreed upon is his failure to observe the rules for the unity of time and place; but this is, in fact, not a fault at all. These rules were based on the fallacy that audiences are deceived by a play: "it is false that any representation is mistaken for reality, that any dramatic fable in its materiality was ever credible, or, for a single moment, credited." Therefore, if we may imagine that we are in Alexandria in the first scene, in the second we can imagine that we are in Rome. Shifts in place and time do not offend our reason, for our reason is never deceived by the play: the spectators are "always in their senses." A playwright who can write a good play and still preserve the unities deserves our applause for his ingenuity, but we demand no more than that he produce the "greatest graces" of a play; "to copy nature and to instruct."

Those not convinced by this rational defense of Shakespeare's irregularity ought to be moved by considering the unavoidable effect of the taste of Shakespeare's age upon his works. His age was young, unlearned, and unable to judge as later ages could. It had been reared on romantic tales, and "the mind which has feasted on the luxuries of fiction has no taste for the insipidities of truth." Because his audience was not highly literate, he chose his plots from stories they knew well and could easily follow. Because their attention was not easily held, he crowded his plot with incident. No writer except Homer was so successful in arousing "unquenchable curiosity" about the outcome. And because they were more used to being pleased by what they saw than by what they heard, Shakespeare indulged in "show and bustle."

Part Three, a discussion of Shakespeare's learning, is introduced by an answer to Voltaire's question: How could a nation that had seen Addison's *Cato* endure "our author's extravagancies"? Addison, Johnson says, "speaks the language of poets; Shakespeare, of men." Addison's play may have the beauties of a perfect formal garden, but who would not exchange them for a great forest, in spite of its underbrush?

In respect to form, matter, and style Johnson thinks Shakespeare learned more from experience than from his reading. It seems clear that Shakespeare read only the classics which he found in translation, and though he may have read much in English we are not persuaded that his wisdom came from books. His excellence proceeds from "a vigilance of observation and accuracy of distinction which books and precepts cannot confer." Besides, there *were* no books on tragedy or comedy, or on psychology. Nor did he owe his learning to having been born to the vantage point of a comfortable social and economic station.

The last part of the essay concerns the editing of the plays, a criticism of previous work, and a statement of Johnson's principles. The "depravations" that "obscure" the plays, all the apparently corrupt places in the text, are the result of Shakespeare's own carelessness of his "future fame." He did not bother to supervise their publication before he died. His "ungrammatical, perplexed, and obscure" style, the fact that the plays were often transcribed by players who did not understand the lines, and the mutilations suffered in a script in the course of a production—all are to blame for the multitude of errors which have challenged editors ever since: Rowe, many of whose silent emendations were accepted by later editors without acknowledgment; Pope, who was "unable to suppress his contempt of 'the dull duty of an editor,'" a necessary and honorable duty for which Pope was not temperamentally suited; Theobald, "weak and ignorant . . . mean and faithless . . . petulant and ostentatious"; Hanmer, who "never writes without careful inquiry and diligent consideration"; and Warburton, whose "predominant error . . . is acquiescence in his first thoughts—that precipitation which is produced by consciousness of quick discernment and that confidence which presumes to do by surveying the surface what labor only can perform by penetrating the bottom." A review of the work of these men, of the proud and ill-natured sentences pronounced by each on the errors of his predecessors, should humble future editors. None of these critics failed to make some improvements; to all of them Johnson is indebted; and all the debts Johnson was aware of he acknowledged.

In his own editorial procedures, he says, he was guided by three principles: (a) In his illustrative notes he tried to avoid giving too much or too little. Some of the allusions may never be explained, and no one man can explain as many as will be explained over a period of time by a series of commentators. (b) In the judicial notes in which an editor points out the beauties and faults of an author, "chance and caprice" governed him, his aim being "to show so much as may enable the candidate of criticism to discover the rest." Though his judgments were his own, he did not strive to "deviate from current opinion." (c) Emendations can be made only by collation of the existing texts (a "safe and easy" task) and by conjecture ("a perilous and difficult" task that must not be avoided). In his emendations he was guided by the principle that the editor must first try to make sense out of the oldest reading without emending, and that that "reading is right which requires many words to prove it wrong." He has tried to restore every corrupt passage and has admitted all his failures.

The mind of a reader is "refrigerated" by constant reference to notes, and only those no longer pleased by the novelty of the plays should consult commentators. Johnson concludes the Preface by quoting Dryden's famous praise of Shakespeare and by expressing the wish that his edition will be judged only by "the skillful and the learned."

68. Warburton had opened his Preface to his edition of Shakespeare (1747) with a similar remark; see I, vii (Sherbo).

69. See George Sewell, "An Essay on the . . . Stage," in Pope's edition of Shakespeare (1725–1728) X, 2 (Sherbo).

70. See Aristotle *Metaphysics* i. 5 (Bronson).

71. See Horace *Epist.* II. i. 39, and Pope, *Epistle to Augustus,* 55–56 (Smith).

72. See Cicero *Epistolae ad familiares* xvi. 8 (Bronson).

73. Hierocles Alexandrinus. See *Commentarius in aurea carmina,* etc., ed. by Peter Needham (1709), p. 462 (Smith).

74. See J. Warton, *Essay on Pope* (1756), below, p. 744; Trapp, *Lectures on Poetry* (1742), p. 270; *Remarks on . . . Hamlet* (1736), 1864 ed., p. 4; Dennis, *The Advancement and Reformation of Modern Poetry* (1701—Hooker, I, 203) (Sherbo).

75. In his note to a similar remark in Dennis' *Essay on Shakespeare,* Hooker shows how commonplace the notion was (II, 424–425).

76. In the Preface to his edition of Shakespeare, above, p. 279.

77. Addison said the same thing in *Spectator* 419, see above, p. 70; and he was remembering Dryden's remarks on Caliban in the Preface to *Troilus and Cressida* (1769—Ker, I, 219–220) (Sherbo).

78. See Dennis, *Essay on Shakespeare* (Hooker, II, 5); Rymer, *A Short View of Tragedy* (1692—Zimansky, p. 165); Voltaire, *Du théâtre anglais* (1761), in *Oeuvres complètes* (1785), XLVII, 290. Several passages in the Preface reflect Johnson's lively memory of Voltaire's criticism of Shakespeare, which appeared in *Du théâtre anglais,* under the pseudonym of "Jérome Carré" (Paris, 1761). A translation of his *Lettres sur les Anglais* (1734) appeared in London in 1738, and again in 1741. In Letter XVIII, Voltaire said Shakespeare was "natural and sublime, but had not so much as a single spark of good taste, or knew one rule of the drama"; he praised Addison's *Cato,* and said that thanks to its influence English drama had become more regular and more dull. In the *Dictionnaire philosophique* (under "Du théâtre anglais") Voltaire replied to Johnson's remarks.

79. See John Upton, *Critical Observations on Shakespeare* (2nd ed., 1748), p. 93 (Sherbo).

80. Voltaire, in *Lettres sur les Anglais,* Letter XVIII, had objected to the gravediggers in *Hamlet* and the shoemakers and cobblers in *Julius Caesar.* See also *Remarks on Hamlet* (1736), 1864 ed., pp. 18–19.

81. "Johnson forgets the *Cyclops* of Euripides" (Smith).

82. See Upton, *op. cit.,* pp. 94–98 (Sherbo).

83. John Heming and Henry Condell, who edited the first folio edition (1623).

84. See Pope, Preface to *Shakespeare,* above, p. 281.

85. The reference is to Voltaire's *Du théâtre anglais* and to Chapter VII of *A Short View* (Zimansky, pp. 136–137).

86. *A Short View* (Zimansky, p. 169).

87. On the division of critical opinion about Shakespeare's superiority in comedy, see Hooker, II, 432–433.

88. In the Life of Addison (*Lives*, I, 452), Johnson said: "Whatever pleasure there may be in seeing crimes punished and virtue rewarded, yet, since wickedness often prospers in real life, the poet is certainly at liberty to give it prosperity on the stage. For if poetry is an imitation of reality, how are its laws broken by exhibiting the world in its true form? The stage may sometimes gratify our wishes; but if it be truly the 'mirror of life,' it ought to show us sometimes what we are to expect."

In the General Observation on *King Lear,* however, he said, "Since all reasonable beings naturally love justice, I cannot easily be persuaded that the observation of justice makes a play worse."

89. See Dennis, *Essay on Shakespeare* (Hooker, II, 6), who blamed Shakespeare's neglect of poetical justice on his ignorance of the "Poetical Art."

90. See Dryden, "Defense of the Epilogue" (1672—Ker, I, 165); Rymer, *A Short View, passim;* and Dennis, *Essay on Shakespeare, passim.*

91. See Rymer (Zimansky, p. 164) and Dryden, Preface to *Troilus and Cressida* (Ker, I, 203) (Sherbo).

92. In Preface to *Shakespeare,* above, p. 285.

93. See Addison, *Spectators* 39 and 285 (Sherbo).

94. See Dryden, "Defense of the Epilogue" (1672—Ker, I, 172) (Sherbo).

95. For the background and development of the question of the unities, see Ker, I, xxxix–xlix; Hooker, II, 455–456; Smith, *18th Century Essays,* p. 322; T. M. Raysor, "The Downfall of the Unities," *MLN,* XLII (1927), 1–9; Sherbo, *op. cit.,* pp. 57–58. Three of the most interesting forerunners of this attack are in the present collection; see Farquhar, p. 96; *Remarks on Hamlet,* p. 449; and *Rambler* 156, p. 632.

96. "Corneille published his *Discours dramatiques,* the second [third] of which dealt with the three unities, in 1660; but he had observed the unities since the publication of the *Sentiments de l'Académie sur le Cid* (1638)" (Smith).

97. Lucan *Pharsalia* iii. 138 (Bronson): "The course of time has not wrought such confusion that the laws would not rather be trampled on by Caesar than saved by Metellus" (Duff).

98. William Lily (1468–1522), Thomas Linacre (1460?–1524), Sir Thomas More (1478–1535), Reginald Pole (1500–1558), Sir John Cheke (1514–1557), Stephen Gardiner (1483?–1555), Sir Thomas Smith (1513–1577), John Clerk (d. 1541), Walter Haddon (1516–1572), and Roger Ascham (1515–1568).

99. See Peter Whalley, *An Inquiry into the Learning of Shakespeare* (1748), p. 17; Pope, above, p. 280 (Sherbo).

100. As Thomas Warton had suggested in his *Observations on the Fairy Queen* (1754), 2nd ed., 1762, I, 27–28 (Sherbo).

101. *Palmerin d'Oliva* and *Guy of Warwick* were popular, dreadfully exaggerated romances, scorned by the well educated.

102. "The *Tale of Gamelyn,* no longer regarded as Chaucer's work, was the

ancestor of Thomas Lodge's *Rosalynde* (1590), which in turn supplied Shake-speare with a plot" (Bronson).

103. Colley Cibber (1671–1757), actor and poet laureate (Smith).

104. "Johnson refers to the ballad of *King Lear and His Daughters*. But the ballad is of later date than the play" (Smith).

105. Sir Thomas North's translation of Plutarch first appeared in 1579. Dennis had remarked on Shakespeare's dependence on a translation; see Hooker, II, 9 (Sherbo).

106. In addition to the places cited above, see also *Le Siècle de Louis XIV*, chap. xxxiv (Smith).

107. See also Theobald's comparison of Shakespeare and Addison, *op. cit.*, I, xxv–xxvii, and Young's discussion of *Cato* in *Conjectures on Original Composition* (1759), in *English Critical Essays*, ed. by E. D. Jones (Oxford, 1922), pp. 352 ff. (Smith).

108. See *Spectator* 160 (Sherbo).

Addison had suggested in *Spectator* 414 that the rudeness of continental gardens was preferable to the "neatness and elegancy" of English gardens. To conclude his comparison of Addison and Shakespeare, Voltaire (*Letters*, XVIII), had said, "The shining monsters of Shakespeare give infinitely more delight than the judicious images of the moderns. Hitherto the poetical genius of the English resembles a tufted tree planted by the hand of nature, that throws out a thousand branches at random, and spreads unequally, but with great vigor. It dies if you attempt to force its nature, and to lop and dress it in the same manner as the trees of the garden of Marli."

109. In "To the Memory of Mr. William Shakespeare." Dr. Johnson, mis-quoting, said, "no Greek."

110. See Whalley, *op. cit.*, pp. 55 ff.; Theobald, *op. cit.*, p. xxix (Sherbo). For a survey of the controversy about Shakespeare's learning, see Smith, *18th Century Essays*, pp. xxi–xxvii; also, of course, T. W. Baldwin, *William Shake-speare's Small Latine and Lesse Greeke* (Urbana, 1944).

111. Zachary Grey, *Critical, Historical, and Explanatory Notes on Shake-speare* (1754), II, 53; *Richard III*, I, i, 143; Terence, *Andria* i. 171 (Smith).

112. See Dennis, *Essay on Shakespeare* (Hooker, II, 14) (Sherbo).

113. In his Preface, above, p. 283.

114. See Dryden, "Original and Progress of Satire" (1693—Ker, II, 17): "Shakespeare, who created the stage among us." And Upton, *op. cit.*, p. 98; etc. (Sherbo).

115. *Life of Shakespeare*, prefixed to Pope's ed., p. xxxiii (Bronson). As re-printed in Smith: "Perhaps we are not to look for his beginnings, like those of other authors, among their least perfect writings; art had so little, and nature so large a share in what he did, that, for aught I know, the performances of his youth, as they were the most vigorous, and had the most fire and strength of imagination in them, were the best."

116. See Pope's Preface, above, p. 279 (Sherbo).

117. That is, the contest initiated by Hobbes.

118. See Birch's *Life of Robert Boyle* (1744), pp. 18, 19 (Smith).

119. *Troilus and Cressida*, III, iii, 224.

120. The comparison with Homer was a commonplace, as Sherbo's note indicates.

121. *Essay on Shakespeare* (Hooker, II, 4).

122. Upton, *op. cit.,* pp. 294–365 (Smith).

123. *Othello,* III, iii, 265.

124. See Warburton, *op. cit.,* p. vii; Pope, above, p. 285; Upton, *op. cit.,* p. 177; Theobald, *op. cit.,* pp. xxxvii–xxxix (Sherbo).

125. As Warburton had said; p. viii (Smith).

126. Warburton.

127. The first by Thomas Edwards; the second by Benjamin Heath.

128. *Coriolanus,* IV, iv, 5:

> Lest that thy wives with spits and boys with stones
> In puny battle slay me.

129. *2 Henry VI,* IV, i, 106.

130. "This passage is said to have been aimed especially at Garrick. At least Garrick took offense at it. . . . See Wooll's *Biographical Memoirs of Joseph Warton* (1806), p. 313. Cf. *The London Magazine,* October, 1765, p. 538" (Smith). See Boswell, *Life,* I, 468.

131. See Upton, *op. cit.,* p. 133 (Sherbo).

132. Pierre-Daniel Huet wrote *De interpretatione* (1661), as well as his *Traité de l'origine des romans* (1670) and many other scholarly works.

133. "Temple of Fame," 37.

134. "Giovanni Antonio Andrea (1417–c. 1480), . . . librarian and secretary to Pope Sixtus IV, and editor of Herodotus, Livy, Lucan, Ovid, Quintilian, etc." (Smith).

135. Richard Bentley (1662–1742), the great classical scholar.

136. Claude de Saumaise (1588–1658), a classical scholar, was a student at Leyden of the great Joseph Scaliger (1540–1609), the founder of modern methods of editing classical texts.

137. "Our conjectures make fools of us, putting us to shame, when later ye hit upon better MSS" (Bronson).

138. Justus Lipsius (1547–1606), a Flemish scholar, who edited Tacitus and the tragedies of Seneca.

139. "As formerly we toiled over corruptions, so now we struggle with corrections" (Bronson).

140. *An Essay of Dramatic Poetry* (1668—Ker, I, 79–80). Virgil, *Eclog.* i. 25: "As cypresses oft do among the bending osiers" (Fairclough).

ROBERT LOWTH

Robert Lowth (1710–1787) was the fifth to hold the Oxford chair of poetry; he was appointed to it in 1741, succeeding Joseph Spence. The thirty-four lectures which later appeared as *De sacra poesi Hebraeorum praelectiones academenica Oxonii habitae,* etc., were delivered during the nine years of his tenure. After he had resigned the chair and become rector of Woodhay in

Hampshire, he prepared the lectures for publication. A year after they appeared, Oxford awarded him an honorary degree.

Lowth was distinguished not only as a scholar but as a clergyman. He was a member of the Royal Society, and six years after he had been made Bishop of London, the king offered him the archbishopric of Canterbury, which he declined.

A second edition of the *Praelectiones* was published in 1763, and a third in 1766. After that the book was edited by J. D. Michaelis, and in this form it went through numerous editions before it was translated into English by G. Gregory in 1787. This translation was reprinted several times during the following half-century. The present text is taken from the edition of 1847.

For discussions of Lowth's place in the history of criticism, see Samuel H. Monk, *The Sublime: A Study of Critical Theories in Eighteenth-Century England* (New York, 1935), pp. 77–83, and René Wellek, *The Rise of English Literary History* (Chapel Hill, 1941), *passim*.

Of the thirty-four lectures on Hebrew poetry the first seventeen consist of discussions of matters of style: the various kinds of imagery, allegory, and sublimity to be found in the Old Testament. The remaining seventeen lectures are on the kinds of poetry in the Old Testament: prophetic, elegiac, didactic, lyric, and dramatic.

Lecture XIV is the first of four lectures on sublimity. Lowth begins by giving Longinus' definition of the sublime as a quality in writing that overpowers the mind and excites passion. It is a quality of the thought as well as of the expression. Though sublimity of thought and sublimity of expression usually occur simultaneously, they may be considered separately. This lecture considers sublimity in expression.

In all languages prose differs from poetry in several common ways: prose expresses the reason; poetry, the passions. The language of poetry is impetuous, vivid, and energetic. Poetic descriptions may be inexact. Sublimity in poetry reveals itself in splendid imagery and in other extraordinary forms of expression that represent the state of the soul. Such expressions are the work of nature, not of art.

In Hebrew, poetry is easily distinguished from prose by inspection of the word order. Hebrew prose is very simple, clear, and logical; first comes the verb, then the subject, then the other words in a conventional order. The Book of Job furnishes a good example of the difference between prose and poetry. Its proem is written in historical prose, in great contrast with the poetry of Job's first dramatic speech. The elliptical statements, the crowded and abrupt sentences, the bold expressions, the redundancy—indeed, the disregard of normal syntax—are all characteristic of the sublimity of expression in Job.

Lecture XXXIII, one of five lectures on dramatic poetry and one of three on Job, is interesting because it deals with one of the central concerns of the whole book: how to consider Hebrew literature by classical criteria. Here the problem is genre. Lowth concludes that one may call Job a drama only if one means by drama a poem consisting of dialogue. In an Aristotelian sense it is not a drama because, in effect, it has no plot, no beginning, middle and end.

JOSEPH WARTON

Though Joseph Warton (1722–1800) was a schoolmaster throughout most of his life, he began his career as a mildly revolutionary poet. At the age of 22, in 1744, the year of Pope's death, he published a satire in which he placed Pope among the philosophers, not among the poets, in the Elysian Fields. Two years later he published a book of verse called *Odes on Various Subjects,* to which he prefixed the following manifesto:

The public has been so much accustomed of late to didactic poetry alone, and essays on moral subjects, that any work where the imagination is much indulged will perhaps not be relished or regarded. The author, therefore, of these pieces is in some pain lest certain austere critics should think them too fanciful or descriptive. But as he is convinced that the fashion of moralizing in verse has been carried too far, and as he looks upon invention and imagination to be the chief faculties of a poet, so he will be happy if the following odes may be looked upon as an attempt to bring back poetry into its right channel.

In 1753 he published *The Works of Virgil,* with notes, translations, and miscellaneous observations, dissertations, and essays. For this edition Warton wrote all the notes, the verse translations of the *Eclogues* and *Georgics,* and three essays: "A Dissertation upon Pastoral Poetry" (half of which consisted of the full text of Johnson's *Rambler* 37 on the same subject), "Reflections on Didactic Poetry," and "A Dissertation on the Nature and Conduct of the *Aeneid.*" Shortly thereafter Johnson, on behalf of the editor John Hawkesworth, asked Warton to contribute essays on "criticism and literature" to the *Adventurer.* During the sixteen months of its existence, Warton contributed twenty-four papers.

In 1755 he went as second master to Winchester College; from 1766 to 1793 he was headmaster. His *Essay on the Writings and Genius of Pope,* Vol. I, appeared anonymously in 1756; Vol. II (with the title altered to *An Essay on the Genius and Writings of Pope*) was not published until 1782. In 1797 he published his edition of Pope's *Works* in nine volumes, and when he died in 1800 he had completed the manuscript for two volumes of an edition of Dryden.

The chief works on Joseph Warton are John Wooll, *Biographical Memoirs of the Late Rev. Joseph Warton, D.D.* (London, 1806); an essay by Nathan Drake, in *Essays Biographical, Critical, and Historical,* etc. (London, 1810), II, 112–151; Sir Edmund Gosse, *Two Pioneers of Romanticism, Joseph and Thomas Warton,* Warton Lecture on English Poetry VI (London, 1919); Eric Partridge, *The Three Wartons: A Choice of Their Verse, Edited with a Note and a Select Bibliography* (London, 1927); Hoyt Trowbridge, "Joseph Warton on the Imagination," *MP,* XXXV (1937), 73–87. Works specifically on the *Essay on Pope* are listed below.

Abridgments of Warton's two *Adventurer* papers on the *Tempest* and his three on *King Lear* are in David Nichol Smith's *Shakespeare Criticism* (Oxford, 1916). These five essays, Smith says, "have the historical interest of being the first pieces of Shakespeare criticism to form a series in a periodical. In this respect they correspond to Addison's papers on Milton in *The Spectator.*" And in the Introduction to his *Eighteenth Century Essays on Shakespeare* Smith says they signal the "coming change in critical methods" in that Warton concentrates his attention on the characters. On the whole, they and the essays on the *Odyssey* and *Paradise Lost,* here reprinted, are the best things Warton wrote for the *Adventurer.* The *Adventurer* was a somewhat more popular periodical than the *Rambler,* and in its collected form it went to at least eight editions in forty years.

Johnson's influence on Warton may be reflected in the *Adventurer* papers, for in the *Rambler* Johnson had several times said that it was the duty of criticism to re-examine fearlessly the bases of the reputations of great poets. In the essay on the *Odyssey* (the third and last paper in the series, No. 83, on the plot, is here omitted) Warton argues that to a modern taste the *Odyssey* is not inferior to the *Iliad;* in the essay on Milton, he points out various anachronisms, inconsistencies, and improprieties in *Paradise Lost.*

My text of the *Adventurer* essays is based on the fourth edition (1762). Warton's few revisions were all stylistic.

1. See Le Bossu, *Traité du poème épique,* I, x.
2. Horace *Epist.* I. i. 23: "So slow and thankless flow for me the hours" (Fairclough).
3. *Discourses* iii. 11.
4. *Lettre sur les occupations de l'Académie française,* V, "Projet de poétique." *Clélie* and *Cléopâtre* are romances by Mlle de Scudéry and La Calprenède.
5. See *Republic* iii (S. 397).
6. *Zayde, A Spanish History or Romance, Originally written in French. By Monsieur Segray. Done into English by P. Porter* (1678). Actually it was written by Marie Madeleine, Comtesse de Lafayette, with the help of Jean Regnauld de Segrais.
7. Horace *Ars poet.* 145.
8. Milton, *Comus,* 479.
9. *On the Sublime* ix. 8.
10. Paraphrase of *Paradise Lost,* IV, 237 ff.
11. *The Faithful Shepherdess,* III, i, 460.
12. *On the Sublime* xxxvi. 2.
13. Vol. I of the *Essay* appeared anonymously in 1756. It was promptly reviewed by Johnson in the *Literary Magazine* (April–May, 1756). He complimented the work by giving it serious attention, though he pointed out small inconsistencies in it and on the whole was somewhat patronizing. He concluded by saying: "He must be much acquainted with literary history, both of remote and late times, who does not find, in this essay, many things which he did not know before; and if there be any too learned to be instructed in facts or opinions, he may yet properly read this book as a just specimen of literary moderation."

Apparently Warton completed the manuscript of Vol. II by 1759, and at that time Dodsley printed the first two hundred pages. But for reasons not known the printing of the rest and the publication of the second volume were delayed until 1782. Meanwhile Vol. I had gone through three editions and one Dublin piracy. The complete two-volume work of 1782, with the new title (*Genius and Writings* in place of *Writings and Genius*) consisted therefore of the fourth edition of Vol. I and the first edition of Vol. II, the latter of which, however, consisted of 200 pages printed thirteen years earlier and 280 pages revised as late as 1782. This edition was revised and completely reset later in the same year. The second issue of the fourth edition (1782) is, therefore, the most authentic, and the present text is based on it. I have not included all of Warton's notes.

For details, see W. D. MacClintock, *Joseph Warton's Essay on Pope* (Chapel Hill, 1933); J. Kinsley, "The Publication of Warton's *Essay on Pope*," *MLR*, XLIV (1949), 91–93; G. B. Schick, "Delay in the Publication of the Second Volume of Joseph Warton's *Essay on Pope*," *N & Q*, CC (1955), 67–69.

As my notes will show, in later editions Warton made significant changes in his original classification of the poets. Hoyt Trowbridge has shown that the changes follow the suggestions made by a reviewer in the *Monthly Review*, XIV, 528–554, and XV, 52–78. See "Joseph Warton's Classification of English Poets," in *MLN*, LI (1936), 515–518. See also Paul F. Leedy, "Genres Criticism and the Significance of Warton's *Essay on Pope*," in *JEGP*, XLV (1946), 140–146, and W. J. Bate's review of it in *PQ*, XXVI (1947), 143–144.

The *Essay* is over five times as long as the present abridgment, which, though large enough to be a good epitome of the work, fails to do full justice to Warton's scholarship, since it omits most of Warton's historical criticism. Warton not only was remarkably well read in the modern and contemporary French critics (he refers to fifteen or more in the present abridgment), but he was at home in many of the historical fields his brother labored in. Many of his critical excursions consist in tracing the development of a form or in comparing one example (from Pope or another) with an analogue. The abridgment further distorts Warton's method by failing to show how systematically he went through each of Pope's works. In making the abridgment I aimed less at showing Warton's criticism of Pope than at showing Warton's dominant critical notions. Of these, the following is a summary:

a) The highest kind of poetry, "true," "pure," or "genuine" poetry, is sublime and pathetic. Its greatness does not depend on rhyme or meter, or on correctness. It is original, not imitative; it contains new images; it always precedes the formation of rules (critics learn from it; they do not influence it). It contains strokes of nature worth a hundred well-phrased moral observations. It requires of the poet powers of imagination so rare that only a few true poets have appeared in history; and of the reader, similarly, it requires an imagination so rare as to limit the size of its public and to make poetry of a lower order a surer way to extensive reputation.

b) Next in worth to sublime poetry comes moral, ethical, didactic, or satiric poetry. This, the poetry of reason, is not to be despised because of its inferiority to sublime poetry, for it has always been of value to the generality of men. Horace's *Odes* and *Satires* were more cited in Latin literature than the *Aeneid* and the *Georgics*.

c) The third order of poetry is descriptive—description of men and manners (familiar life) and description of things. When modern manners afford no fit subject of poetry, poets describe things. Descriptive poetry has its value, which is chiefly its ability to make men and things vivid to the reader. The vividness is achieved by the "judicious addition of circumstances and adjuncts"; by such means poetry may be a "more lively imitation of nature than prose." Milton's early poems are good examples of such vivid detail. Thomson looked at the things he painted. Nature cannot be described from the vantage point of the Strand—nor in "hereditary images." Pastoral poets should represent not the golden age, but what they see and feel around them. "Minute and particular enumeration of circumstances judiciously selected is what chiefly discriminates poetry from history and renders the former . . . a more close and faithful representation of nature than the latter." "The use, the force, and the excellence of language certainly consists in raising clear, complete, and circumstantial images and in turning readers into spectators."

d) The second and third kinds of poetry are often mixed. One of the virtues of descriptive poetry is that it may contain instruction, moral and other; such instruction is best when it is obliquely stated; therefore "pathetic reflections" in descriptive poems are better than moral observations.

e) Just as the concrete particular enhances descriptive poetry, so does the use of historical fact make stories more vivid. "Nature is more powerful than fancy; . . . we can always feel more than we can imagine; . . . the most artful fiction can give way to truth." For example, see the *Inferno*, with its many true stories, a poem which is perhaps "in point of originality and sublimity" next to the *Iliad*. It is unfortunate that British playwrights do not make use of the annals of England as sources for their plays. "*Domestica facta* are more interesting [than Greek and Roman stories] as well as more useful."

f) Aristotle is the best of critics. The formulation of rules always follows, never precedes, periods of great poetic achievement; no great poetry was written after Aristotle in Greece, after Horace in Italy, after Boileau in France. Some rules nature and necessity dictate, such as the rules of unity of time and place; but many are absurd, such as the rule that tragedy should consist of five acts.

g) The *Essay* is full of miscellaneous critical dicta. Of the relationship between poetry and the society in which it is produced, Warton says that though the sciences require an atmosphere of freedom the fine arts seem to thrive in periods of strong national political power and of luxury. He thinks modern playwrights err in assuming that love is "the only passion capable of producing any great calamities of human life"; and this error is related to the fact that, whereas Greek tragedies evoke terror, English and French tragedies evoke only pity. In philosophy and the literature of manners the French are equaled by the English, for example, Bacon, Hobbes, Hume, Prior, Richardson (*Clarissa*), and Fielding (*Tom Jones*). In respect to diction he praises "the use of common and familiar words and objects judiciously managed." Of gardening, he thinks Milton's description of Eden responsible for the change of taste from formal to informal gardens. Similarly he thinks Thomson's *Seasons* "very instrumental in diffusing a general taste for the beauties of nature and land-scape."

14. Warton had two reasons for dedicating his book to Edward Young: one was that Warton admired Young's poems because they were true works of the imagination and exemplified the kind of poetry Warton thought was superior to mere poetry of wit; the other was that he wished to honor the most distinguished living alumnus of Winchester College. In 1753 Warton had asked Young to write a letter in his behalf, a request which Young felt he could not fulfill. See Wooll, *op. cit.*, p. 218.

15. This sentence was not in the first edition (1756). Dryden, in "The Original and Progress of Satire" (Ker, II, 102), said, "If we are not so great wits as Donne, yet certainly we are better poets."

16. Horace *Serm.* I. iv. 46: "The fire and force of inspiration" (Fairclough).

17. In Young's *Love of Fame, the Universal Passion. In Seven Character-istical Satires* (1725, 1726, 1728).

18. Horace *Serm.* I. iv. 54: "It is not enough to write out a line of simple words" (Fairclough).

19. *Serm.* I. iv. 40: "For you would not call it enough to round off a verse" (Fairclough).

20. See *Serm.* I. iv. 56 ff.; also Sidney's *Defense of Poesy*, ed. by A. S. Cook (Boston, 1890), p. 47, and Plato *Republic* x (S. 601).

21. Pope's *Moral Essays*, I, 1.

22. 1756: "very sublime or very pathetic."

23. *Instit.* X. i. 78: "Nothing irrelevant or far-fetched. None the less I would compare him to a clear spring rather than to a mighty river" (Butler).

24. 1756: "ashamed or afraid."

25. *Discours à sa réception à l'Académie française, prononcée le lundi 9 mai 1746 (Oeuvres* [ed. 1784], XLVII, 12).

26. 1756: "Spenser, Shakespeare, Milton, and then, at proper intervals, Otway and Lee."

27. 1756: "talents for moral and ethical poesy."

28. 1756: "Dryden, Donne, Denham, Cowley, Congreve."

29. 1756 omits "though not the higher scenes of poetry."

30. 1756: "Prior, Waller, Parnell, Swift, Fenton."

31. 1756 omits this sentence.

32. For background to Warton's criticism of the *Pastorals*, see Pope's *Guardian* essay, p. 251; Hughes, "Remarks on the *Shepherd's Calendar*," p. 304; *Ramblers* 36 and 37, p. 575; and my notes to them.

33. René Rapin, *Idylliums of Theocritus with Rapin's Discourse of Pastorals* (1684); Bernard le Bovier de Fontenelle, *Poésies pastorales . . . avec un traité sur la nature de l'églogue* (1688—Elledge and Schier, pp. 339-357).

34. 1756: "one of his juvenile pieces."

35. 1756: "pity being a stronger sensation than complacency."

36. 1756: "a noble English poet."

37. See Dominique Bouhours, *La Manière de bien penser dans les ouvrages d'esprit* (1687) and *Les Entretiens d'Ariste et d'Eugène* (1671—Elledge and Schier, p. 210).

38. At this point in the first edition were the following lines:

To this purpose I may add a passage in an "Ode to Fancy" [Note: Dodsley's *Miscell.* Pag. 80. Ver. 3] which I have heard commended for a singular stroke of a pathetic nature. After passing through various scenes the poet leads us,

> "To some abbey's mouldering towers,
> Where to avoid cold wintry showers,
> The naked beggar shivering lies,
> While whistling tempests round her rise,
> And trembles, least the tottering wall
> Should on her sleeping infants fall."

The object of fear indicated in the two last lines, is, I believe, new and unborrowed, and interests us in the scene described.

*39. By the epithet *graves* Virgil insinuates after his manner the difficulty and laboriousness of the work.

40. *Georgics* iii. 526: "And yet no Massic gifts of Bacchus, no feasts, oft renewed, did harm to him and his. They feed on leaves and simple grass; their cups are clear springs and rivers racing in their course, and no care breaks their healthful slumbers" (Fairclough).

*41. In this light also his poem on the "Ruins of Rome" deserves a perusal. Dodsley's *Miscellany*, I, 78. His "Fleece," which I had the pleasure of reading in manuscript with Dr. Akenside, is written in a pure and classical taste and with many happy imitations of Virgil.

*42. See also verses written "At a Solemn Music," "The Passion," and "At a Vacation Exercise in the College," in all which are to be found many strokes of the sublime.

43. Warton underestimated Milton's popularity. See George Sherburn, "The Early Popularity of Milton's Minor Poems," *MP*, XVII (1919–1920).

*44. This conceit, with the rest, however, is more excusable if we recollect how great a reader, especially at this time, Milton was of the Italian poets. It is certain that Milton in the beginning of the ode had the third sonnet of Petrarch strong in his fancy.

> Era 'l giorno, ch' al sol si scoloraro
> Per la pieta del suo fattore i rai;
> Quand', etc.

*45. A summer evening, for instance, after a shower, has been frequently described, but never, that I can recollect, so justly as in the following lines, whose greatest beauty is that hinted above, a simple enumeration of the appearances of nature and of what is actually to be seen at such a time. They are not unworthy the correct and pure Tibullus. They were written by the late Mr. Robert Bedingfield, author of "The Education of Achilles," a poem in Dodsley's *Miscellanies*.

> Vespere sub verno, tandem actis imbribus, aether
>   Guttatim sparsis rorat apertus aquis.
> Aureus abrupto curvamine desuper arcus
>   Fulget, et ancipiti lumine tingit agros.
> Continuo sensus pertentat frigoris aura
>   Vivida, et insinuans mulcet amaenus odor.

Pallentes sparsim accrescunt per pascua fungi,
    Laetius et torti graminis herba viret.
Plurimus annose decussus ab arbore limax
    In putri lentum tramite sulcat iter.
Splendidus accendit per dumos lampida vermis.
    Roscida dum tremula semita luce micat.

These are the particular circumstances that usually succeed a shower at that season, and yet these are new and untouched by any other writer. The *Carmina Quadragesimalia*, vol. II (Oxford, 1748), from whence this is transcribed (p. 14), contain many copies of exquisite descriptive poetry in a genuine classical style. See particularly "The Rivers," p. 4; "The Morning," p. 12; "The House of Care," from Spenser, p. 16; "The Mahometan Paradise," p. 32; "The Trees of Different Soils," p. 63; "The Bird's Nest," p. 82; "Geneva," p. 89; "Virgil's Tomb," p. 97; "The Indian," p. 118; "The House of Discord," p. 133; "Columbus First Discovering the Land of the West Indies," p. 125; etc.

46. No. 156. In the first edition Warton here added two paragraphs from *Rambler* 158, beginning, "Criticism, though dignified from the earliest ages . . ."

*47. *Essai sur la Poésie Epique, Les Oeuvres* [Paris, 1828, XIII, 434–435].

48. *Spectator* 267.

49. In Book XXI.

50. For a discussion of them, see M. T. Herrick, *The Poetics of Aristotle in England* (New Haven, 1930), 92 ff.

51. Beginning at line 158.

52. 1756: "The vulgar notion that Horace wrote his 'Epistle to the Pisos' without method has been lately confuted, as we hinted before. It is equally false that the epistle contains a complete art of poetry." Warton referred to Hurd's Introduction to his edition of the *Art of Poetry* (1751), where both points are made.

53. *Epist.* II. i. 224: "When we complain that men lose sight of our labors, and of our poems so finely spun . . ." (Fairclough).

*54. *Advice to an Author,* II, i. [See above, p. 186.]

55. See Longinus xliv. 1, and *Spectator* 287.

*56. See [Thomas Blackwell] *An Inquiry into the Life and Writings of Homer* [1736], sec. V, p. 67.

*57. It is remarkable Boileau declared he had never read Vida, to whom, indeed, he is much superior. Patru, whom he always consulted on his works, dissuaded him from undertaking this subject because he thought the French language incapable of delivering precepts of this sort with becoming elegance and grace.

*58. *Oeuvres* (Paris, 1752), III, 376.

59. *Rambler* 152.

60. See *The Correspondence of Alexander Pope,* ed. by George Sherburn (Oxford, 1956), I, 18, 20, 21.

61. *Athalie,* by Racine; *La Henriade,* by Voltaire.

62. 1756: "and to be original and new, do not become distorted and unnatural in their thoughts and diction."

*63. Aulus Gellius, *Noctes Atticae* VII. v.

*64. The First.

*65. *Carm.* II. xiii.

66. Thomas Southerne's tragedy *Oroonoko* (1696) was founded on Aphra Behn's historical novel *Oroonoko* (1688), "founded on events witnessed by the authoress."

*67. It was thought not improper to distinguish the more moving passages by italics. Sir Joshua Reynolds, whose mind is stored with great and exalted ideas, has lately shown, by a picture on this subject, how qualified he is to preside at a Royal Academy, and that he has talents that ought not to be confined to portrait painting.

*68. Mr. [Jonathan] Richardson was the first that gave an English translation in blank verse of this passage of Dante in his book entitled *A Discourse on the Dignity of the Science of a Connoisseur [Two Discourses]* (1719), p. 30. [This was the earliest translation of Dante into English. "The same passage was turned into blank verse by Gray. . . . It inspired a picture by Sir Joshua Reynolds, exhibited in 1773" (René Wellek, *The Rise of English Literary History* [Chapel Hill, 1941], p. 129).]

69. *Inferno,* XXXIII.

*70. Milton was particularly fond of this writer. The following passage is curious, and has not been taken notice of by the late writers of his life; "Ego certe istis utrisque linguis non extremis tantummodo labris madidus; sed siquis alius, quantum per annos licuit, poculis majoribus prolutus, possum tamen nonnunquam ad illum Dantem, et Petrarcham, aliosque vestros complusculos, libenter et cupide comessatum ire. Nec me tam ipsae Athenae Atticae cum illo suo pellucido Ilisso, nec illa vetus Roma sua Tiberis ripa retinere valuerunt, quin saepe Arnum vestrum, et Faesulanos illos Colles invisere amem." Milton. *Epistol.* Epist. viii. B. Bommathaeo Florentino. Michelangelo, from a similarity of genius, was fond of Dante. Both were great masters in the terrible. Michelangelo made a bas-relief on this subject which I have seen.

*71. "L'amour furieux, criminel, malheureux, suivi de remords, arrache de nobles larmes. Point de milieu: il faut, ou que l'amour domine en tiran, ou qu'il ne paroisse pas." *Oeuvres de Voltaire* [Paris, 1828, V, 445]. I have just been told that Chateaubrun also very lately made poor Philoctetes in love in his *Desert Island.*

72. Monimia is a character in Otway's *Orphan* (1680).

*73. The introduction of female actresses on the modern stage, together with that importance which the ladies in these latter ages have justly gained in comparison to what the ancients allowed them, are the two great reasons, among others, of the prevalence of these tender tales. The ladies of Athens had not interest or abilities enough to damn a piece of Sophocles or Euripides.

74. *Spectators* 183, 159, 56, 164.

*75. In some of the eastern stories lately published in the *Adventurer* much invention is displayed, and this too by an author that I have never heard has written any considerable verses. See, particularly, the story of Amurath, No. 20, of Nouraddin and Amana, No. 73, and of Carazan, No. 132, by Mr. Hawkesworth.

76. Thomas Burnet (1635–1715), *The Sacred Theory of the Earth* (1684).

77. Warton's note refers to *Spectators* 106–132, 329, 335.

78. See Congreve's *Love for Love*.

*79. There are, however, some images in Rowe strongly painted, such, particularly, as the following, which is worthy of Spenser; speaking of the Tower:

> Methinks suspicion and distrust dwell here,
> Staring with meagre forms thro' grated windows.
> [*Lady Jane Grey*, II, ii.]

*80. He has translated Lucan with force and spirit. It is undoubtedly one of the best translations in the English language and seems not to be sufficiently valued.

81. In *Tamerlane*.

82. 1756: "It is absolute pedantry."

*83. Milton has left in a manuscript thirty-three subjects for tragedies, all taken from the English annals, which manuscript the curious reader may see printed in Newton's edition of Milton, III, 331; and in Birch's *Life of Milton*, prefixed to his edition of Milton's prose works, p. 51; and in Peck's *Memoirs and the Life and Writings of Milton*, p. 90.

84. 1756: "all the Achilleses or Brutus's."

85. "Distance increases respect."

*86. Read with this passage Mr. Gray's account of his journey to the Grande Chartreuse. [*Correspondence of Thomas Gray*, ed. by P. Toynbee and L. Whibley (Oxford, 1935), I, 121–129.]

87. See Shaftesbury, "Soliloquy: or Advice to an Author" (above, p. 180).

88. Girolamo Fracastoro's *Syphilis* (1530) is an allegorical account of the origin of the disease. Marco Vida (1480–1566) wrote these two Latin poems in imitation of Virgil's *Georgics*. The *Ambra* is one of the four extant Latin verse declamations of Politian (1454–1494); it is on Homer. Luigi Alamanni (1495–1556) wrote his *Coltivazione* on agriculture. René Rapin's *Hortorum* (1665) appeared in English in 1672. John Philips' *Cyder* (1708), William Somerville's *Chace* (1735), Mark Akenside's *Pleasures of Imagination* (1744), John Armstrong's *Art of Preserving Health* (1744), and John Dyer's *Fleece* (1757) were contemporary didactic poems. Louis Racine (1692–1763) was the son of Jean. Isaac Browne's Latin poem was *De Animi Immortalitate* (1754). Benedetto Stay (1714–1801) and Ruggiero Giuseppe Boscowich (1711–1787) were Sicilians who wrote on scientific subjects in Latin verse. Gray's "The Alliance of Education and Government" was published in Mason's edition of the *Poems* (1775). Mason's *English Garden* appeared in 1772.

89. Thomas Catesby Paget, Lord Paget, had published *An Essay on Human Life* in 1734. John Desaguliers, fellow of the Royal Society, was a popular lecturer on scientific subjects.

90. See *Pope's Correspondence* (Sherburn, III, 438).

91. Neoplatonists of the fourth and sixth centuries respectively.

92. *Iliad* xiii. 12: "high on the topmost peak of wooded Samothrace, for from thence all Ida was plain to see; and plain to see were the city of Priam and the ships of the Achaians" (Murray).

93. Sophocles *Trachiniae* 905: "And when she touched any household thing

that she had been wont to use, poor lady, in the past, her tears would flow" (R. C. Jebb, *Sophocles* [London, 1883]).

94. *De rerum nat.* iv. 1137: "Because she has thrown out some idle word and left its sense in doubt . . . or because he thinks she casts her eyes around too freely, and looks upon some other, or sees in her face some trace of laughter." i. 89: "She saw her sorrowing sire stand at the altar's side, and near him the attendants hiding their knives." iii. 154: "[We see] sweat and pallor break out over all the body, and the tongue is crippled and the voice is choked, the eyes grow misty, the ears ring, the limbs give way beneath us" (Bailey).

*95. Mr. Walpole, *Anecdotes of Painting* [Strawberry Hill, 1762–1771], IV, 108.

*96. Though he always thought highly of Addison's *Letter from Italy* [Note: See Spence, *Anecdotes* (1820), p. 316], yet he said the poet had spoken in terms too general of the finest buildings and paintings, and without much discrimination of taste.

*97. "Who had both taste and zeal for the present style," says Mr. Walpole, p. 134.

*98. Our author was so delighted with Graevius that he drew up a little Latin treatise on the chief buildings of Rome collected from this antiquarian. [Note: *Ibid.*, p. 204.] Mr. Gray had also an exquisite taste in architecture, joined to the knowledge of an accurate antiquarian. See the introduction to [James] Bentham's *History of Ely Cathedral* [1771], supposed to be drawn up by Gray, or under his eye.

*99. To see all the beauties that a place was susceptible of was to possess, as Mr. Pitt expressed it, "the prophetic eye of taste."

*100. [Spence, *Anecdotes*], pp. 11–12.

101. See above, p. 504, n. 106.

*102. I cannot forbear adding in this place the following anecdote from Pope to Mr. Spence, which I give in his own words: "Lord Peterborough, after a visit to Fénelon, Archbishop of Cambray, said to me, 'Fénelon is a man that was cast in a particular mold, that was never made use of for anybody else. He's a delicious creature! But I was forced to get from him as soon as I possibly could, or else he would have made me pious.' "

103. Pope, *Imitations of Horace, Sat.* ii. 1.

104. But see Addison, *Spectator* 414.

*105. How astonishing that his spirit could not be diminished or crushed by poverty, danger, blindness, disgrace, solitude, and old age!

*106. It is only within a few years that the picturesque scenes of our own country, our lakes, mountains, cascades, caverns, and castles, have been visited and described.

THOMAS WARTON

In 1756, at the age of twenty-eight, Thomas Warton (1728–1790) was elected professor of poetry at Oxford. Though his appointment came two years after he had published his *Observations on the* Fairy Queen, he had, like his father (who had also held the Oxford professorship) and his brother Joseph, first made his reputation as a poet. His first poems were published when he was seventeen or eighteen, and his collected *Poems* went to a fourth edition before he died. The Warton Lecture on English Poetry, delivered annually since 1910 before the British Academy, was, however, named to commemorate his work as a scholar and historian of literature, and the works now read with most interest are his *Observations*, his *History of English Poetry, from the Close of the Eleventh to the Commencement of the Eighteenth Century* (4 vols.; London, 1774–1781), and his edition of *Milton's Poems upon Several Occasions* (1785), the Preface to which is reprinted in E. D. Jones, *English Critical Essays* (Oxford, 1922). Of these works *Milton's Poems* has been least superseded by later work and has, therefore, the most lasting value; but the *Observations* and the *History* produced the greatest effects, the first in helping to alter the taste of the eighteenth century, the latter in instituting the kind of historical criticism which became so well developed in the following century.

The best works on Thomas Warton are the following: W. P. Ker, "Thomas Warton," Warton Lecture on English Poetry I, *Proceedings of the British Academy 1910–11* (London, 1911; also in *Collected Essays* [London, 1925], I, 92–108); David Nichol Smith, "Warton's History of English Poetry," Warton Lecture, *Proceedings of the British Academy,* vol. XV (London, 1929); Clarissa Rinaker, *Thomas Warton* (Urbana, 1916); Odell Shepard's long review of Rinaker, in *JEGP,* XVI (1917), 153 ff.; R. D. Havens, "Thomas Warton and the Eighteenth-Century Dilemma," *SP,* XXV (1928), 36 ff.; M. G. Robinson and Leah Dennis, eds., *The Correspondence of Thomas Percy and Thomas Warton* (Baton Rouge, 1951). The most essential book for an understanding of the significance of Warton's work is, of course, René Wellek, *The Rise of English Literary History* (Chapel Hill, 1941).

The *Observations on the* Faerie Queene (1754—Warton spelled it *Fairy Queen* in the second edition) consists of over 300 octavo pages; what is here reprinted is somewhat more than one-tenth of the book. The titles of the chapters are: "Of the Plan and Conduct of the *Fairy Queen*"; "Of Spenser's Imitations from Old Romances"; "Of Spenser's Use and Abuse of Ancient History and Mythology"; "Of Spenser's Stanza, Versification, and Language"; "Of Spenser's Imitations from Chaucer"; "Of Spenser's Imitations from Ariosto"; "Of Spenser's Inaccuracies"; "Of Spenser's Imitations of Himself"; "Mr. Upton's Opinion Concerning Several Passages in Spencer Examined"; "Of Spenser's Allegorical Character"; "Miscellaneous Remarks."

On July 16, 1754, Johnson wrote Warton about the recently published *Observations:* "You have shown to all who shall hereafter attempt the study of our ancient authors the way to success: by directing them to the perusal of the books which those authors had read. Of this method Hughes, and men much greater than Hughes, seem never to have thought. The reason why the authors which are yet read of the sixteenth century are so little understood is that they are read alone; and no help is borrowed from those who lived with them, or before them" (Boswell's *Life* [Oxford, 1933], I, 179).

The second edition (1762), from which the present text is taken, represents an extensive revision. I have not tried to furnish a collation of the editions, but I have given a few variant readings which seem to indicate something more than stylistic revision. The significance of the changes has perhaps been exaggerated by those who think that Hurd's *Letters on Chivalry and Romance,* which appeared in May, 1762, substantially modified Warton's critical position. The truth is that though certain of Warton's changes seem to be traceable to Hurd, Warton had for some time been assuming several of the essentials of Hurd's thesis. My notes will suggest what may have been Warton's last-minute changes before the book went to press. I have omitted some of Warton's footnotes.

Like Dryden and Hughes before him, Warton says that Ariosto's influence on Spenser accounts for the lack of unity in the *Fairy Queen.* The literary taste in Elizabethan England was dominated by Italian writers and critics, who in spite of the rediscovery of the classics in the Renaissance preferred the "romantic manners of the Provençal bards" to the "more legitimate taste" of antiquity. His analysis of the structure of the poem leads to the already well-accepted conclusion that the presence of Arthur in each of the Books is not enough to unify the poem, and that the unity of each of the Books works against the unity of the whole. Nevertheless, he says, a comparison of the *Fairy Queen* and *Orlando Furioso* shows how much more regular Spenser was than Ariosto.

But, Warton says, modern readers must not judge either poem by precepts which neither poet regarded. Since "the chief sources of delight" in his age were "the various and the marvelous," Spenser's aim was to supply bold and striking images and romantic flights of imagination that would move the heart no matter how they might offend the judgment. And, he concludes, we are glad to give up the classical beauties of structure in return for all those graces beyond the reach of art, in which we feel the effects of Spenser's "creative imagination." "If the critic is not satisfied, yet the reader is transported."

In the chapter on Spenser's allegory Warton makes four points. (a) If readers made themselves acquainted with the manners of the age in which the poet lived, they would better understand the poetry and would not make the error of judging the poetry of one age by the taste of another. Three facts about Spenser's age are commonly neglected: (1) that "encounters of chivalry subsisted in our author's age"; (2) that "romances were then most eagerly and universally studied"; and (3) that much of the literary taste for allegory was formed by the popularity of public shows, in which the virtues and vices were commonly personified.

(b) Spenser's allegory is different from Ariosto's in that in *Orlando Furioso* "moral doctrine is adumbrated under actions of men," whereas under the allegory of Spenser there is frequently no meaning. Spenser thought of his allegories as masks, in which unsubstantial, abstract, ideal things are simply personified. His allegories are frequently merely descriptions—not imitations of actions.

(c) Without intending to be, Spenser was sacrilegious in his allegories because he "mingled divine mystery with human allegory." It is one thing to deal with religious teachings by allegorical representations of Faith, Despair, etc., but it is another to mingle the imagery of the Book of Revelation with that of human life.

(d) The last section is a brief historical survey of English literature from Chaucer to the Restoration, in which Warton shows that before Spenser English literature consisted largely of allegories and visions and that after Spenser tastes changed in such a way as to make allegory unpalatable. Beginning at about the accession of James I, the images of poetry became metaphysical as a result of "the predominant studies of the times." And soon poets began to be more attentive "to words than to things." "The nicer beauties of happy expression were preferred to the daring strokes of great conception." In the *Fairy Queen,* therefore, allegory "received its ultimate consummation."

The Postscript (considerably longer in 1762 than in 1754; see notes below) makes six points. (a) Warton preferred to write his observations as essays, not as notes attached to particular passages, because in this way he could "exhibit a course of systematical criticism" and could have room to show the results of his "research"; and he has made few observations on the "beauties" of the poem because such observations usually show more "admiration" than "reason." (b) He has quoted extensively from literature contemporary with the *Fairy Queen* because recent criticism of English poets has shown the error of neglecting the contemporary books the poets read. (c) His many "anecdotes of ancient chivalry" he justifies by suggesting that the virtues of chivalry are worth knowing in themselves. (d) Similarly, the many romances he discusses have a value in themselves, as a source of information on the history of manners and as a storehouse of "sublime and alarming images, which true poetry best delights to display." (e) He has used the "epic rules" as criteria in judging the unity of the poem, because, no matter what the virtues of Spenser's materials, the poem would be better if it were a unit. (This is a rejoinder to Hurd's claim that even the rules of unity are irrelevant to criticism of the *Fairy Queen.*) (f) He did not mean to condemn Italian poetry, though he did condemn "the vicious excess of their fictions." (This is also directed at Hurd.)

1. Thomas Rymer was the first critic to relate early English poetry to the "Provençal bards." See *A Short View of Tragedy* (1692—Zimansky, pp. 120 ff.).

*2. *Comparazione di T. Tasso con Omero e Virgilio, insieme con la difesa dell' Ariosto paragonato ad Omero.* [Paolo Beni (1552–1625), *Comparatione di Homero, Virgilio, e Torquato, et a chi di loro si debba la palma nell' heroico poema* (Padua, 1607).]

*3. *L'Italia Liberata di Goti,* 1524. It is in blank verse, which the author would have introduced instead of the terza rima of Dante, or the ottava of Boccace.

4. 1754: "In the midst of this bad taste, Spenser . . ."

5. 1754: "It may indeed be urged, as an instance of Spenser's weak and undiscerning judgment, that he chose to follow Ariosto rather than Tasso, the plan and conduct of whose poem was much more regular and legitimate than that of his rival."

6. "A Discourse Concerning the Original and Progress of Satire" (1693—Ker, II, 28).

7. *Aeneid* vi. 727.

*8. "Remarks on the *Fairy Queen.*" Hughes's ed. of Spenser, Vol. I.

*9. Letter to Sir W. Raleigh. [Here in 1754 Warton quoted from the letter.]

10. Horace *Ars poet.* 8: "So that neither head nor foot can be assigned to a single shape" (Fairclough).

11. 1754 omits "Ariosto has his admirers, and most deservedly." It reads simply: "The very idea of celebrating the madness of a hero carries with it somewhat extravagant and absurd." The toning down of the criticism of Ariosto may have been the consequence of the ill-tempered attack of William Huggins, translator of Ariosto, in *The Observer Observed* (1756).

12. 1754: "The author . . ."

13. 1754: "episode, an expedient not more inartificial than that which the first painters were obliged to make use of, in order to assist their want of skill, who having drawn the figure of a man, a bird, or a quadruped, found it necessary to write underneath the name of the kind to which the thing represented belonged."

14. *Réflexions critiques sur la poésie et sur la peinture* [1719], I, xxxiv.

15.   Of dames, of knights, of arms, of love's delight,
        Of courtesies, of high attempts, I sing (Harrington).

*16. Montesquieu has partly characterized Spenser in the judgment he has passed upon the English poets, which is not true with regard to all of them. "Leurs poètes auroient plus souvent cette rudesse originale de l'invention, qu'une certaine délicatesse que donne le goût: on y trouveroit quelque chose qui approcheroit plus de la force de M. Ange, que de la grâce du Raphael." *L'Esprit des lois,* XIX, xxvii. The French critics are too apt to form their general notions of English poetry from our fondness for Shakespeare.

17. This paragraph was not in 1754.

*18. Hume's *History of England under the House of Tudor* [*The History of England,* Vol. IV] (1759), II, 739.

*19. Before the *Shepherd's Calendar.* The gallantries of civilized chivalry, in particular, were never carried to a higher pitch than in the Queen's court, of which, says our author, describing the manners of that court:

        Ne any there doth braue or valiant seeme,
        Unlesse that some gay Mistresse badge he beares.
                Colin Clout's Come Home Again

[This note and the preceding paragraph were not in 1754.]

*20. Spenser himself wrote a set of pageants, which were descriptions of these feigned representations.

Cervantes, whose aim was to expose the abuses of imagination, seems to have left us a burlesque on pageantries, which he probably considered as an appendage of romance, partaking, in great measure, of the same chimerical spirit. This ridicule was perfectly consistent with the general plan and purpose of his comic history. See the masque at Chamacho's wedding, where Cupid, Interest, Poetry, and Liberality are the personages. A castle is represented called the "Castle of Discretion," which Cupid attacks with his arrows; but Interest throws a purse at it, when it immediately falls to pieces, etc. *Don*

Quixote, II, iii. But under due regulation, and proper contrivance, they were a beautiful and useful spectacle.

*21. *Chronicle* [London, 1587], III, 1297.

*22. Exhibited before the Queen at Westminster, *ibid.*, pp. 1317 ff.

*23. It is observed by Plutarch that "allegory is that in which one thing is related and another understood." Thus Ariosto relates the adventures of Orlando, Rogero, Bradamante, etc., by which is understood the conquest of the passions, the importance of virtue, and other moral doctrines; on which account we may call the *Orlando* a moral poem; but can we call the *Fairy Queen,* upon the whole, a moral poem? Is it not equally a historical or political poem? For though it be, according to its author's words, an "allegory or dark conceit," yet that which is couched or understood under this allegory is the history and intrigues of Queen Elizabeth's courtiers, which however are introduced with a moral design.

*24. It is not improbable that Milton in "Il Penseroso," took his thought of hearing music from the earth, produced by some spirit or genius:

> And as I wake, sweet music breath,
> Above, about, or underneath . . .

from some machinery of Inigo Jones, in his masques. Hollingshed mentions something like this in a very curious "demise" presented before Queen Elizabeth; speaking of the music of some fictitious nymphs, he adds, "Which sure had been a noble hearing, and the more melodious for the variety thereof, because it should come secretly and strangely out of the earth." *Ubi supr.,* p. 1297. It may perhaps be readily admitted that Milton drew the whole from what had been represented in a masque. This particular artifice, however, was not uncommon in an age which aimed to please by surprise. Sandys tells us, "In the garden of the Tuilleries, at Paris, by an artificial device under ground invented for music, I have known an echo repeat a verse, etc."—Sandys's *Ovid* (Oxon., 1632), Book III, p. 103. [This note was not in 1754.]

*25. Thus also, in the *Ruins of Time,* he calls his noble allegoric representations of Empire, Pleasure, Strength, etc. "tragic pageants."

> Before mine eyes strange sights presented were
> Like tragic pageants seeming to appear.

26. Footnote in 1754: "This consisted of dumb actors, who by their dress and action prepared the spectators for the matter and substance of each ensuing act respectively, as also of much hieroglyphical scenery calculated for the same purpose. See *Gordobucke* [sic], a tragedy, written by T. Sackville, 1561, lately reprinted by Mr. Spence; *Jocasta,* a tragedy, written by G. Gascoyne and F. Kinwelmarshe, and acted at Gray's Inn, 1566; and the introduction to III, vii, of Shakespeare's *Hamlet.*"

27. *Oculis subjecta fidelibus* (*Ars poet.* 182).

*28. *Polymetis,* X, 4.

*29. Abbé Dubos, *Réflexions,* I, xxiv.

*30. By the triple crown he plainly glances at popery.

31. This and the preceding sentence were not in 1754. Wharton's note here

in 1762 says, "This subject may probably be one day considered more at large in a regular history."

*32. That laborious antiquary Thomas Hearne first printed this author, at Oxford, 1724.

33. Adam Davy's "Five Dreams about Edward II" [ed. by F. J. Furnivall, publications of the Early English Text Society, LXIX (London, 1878), 11].

*34. The book on which it is founded, viz., Boccace *De casibus virorum illustrium*, is a plain historical narrative.

35. *The Daunce of Machabree.*

*36. These were the only historians, and their pieces were sung, as I before observed. In the statutes of a college at Oxford, founded about 1386, it is prescribed that the scholars, on festival days, for their common entertainment in the hall, shall sing Chronica *Regum Angliae—Coll. Nov. Stat. Rubric,* xviii.

37. John Hardyng, *English Chronicle in Meter from the First Beginning of England unto the Reign of Edward the Fourth* (1543).

*38. [*The Pastime of Pleasure: Or the History of Graunde Amoure and la Bel Pucel* (1509).] In a note after the contents it is said to be written an. 21. Hen. VII, or 1505. "Such is the state of poetry," says Wood, "that this book, which in the time of Henry VII and VIII was taken into the hands of all ingenious men, is now thought but worthy of a ballad-monger's stall." *Athenae Oxoniensis,* ed. 2 [London, 1721], I, 6, col. 2. It is in Mus. Ashmol. Oxon. Cod. *impress.* A. Wood. He also wrote the *Temple of Glass,* Wynk. de Worde, 1500, 4to., and other pieces.

*39. Wood, *op. cit.,* and [John] Bale, *Scriptorum [Illustrium Majoris Brytanniae Catalogus a Japheto per 3618 Annos, usque ad annum hunc Domini 1557* (Basel, 1559)], VIII, 58.

*40. [By Alexander Barclay.] Finished 1508.

41. This sentence was not in 1754.

*42. Wood informs us that Skelton for his satirical abuses of the Dominican monks incurred the severe censure of Richard Nykke, Bishop of Norwich, and that he was, moreover, "guilty of certain crimes, *as most poets are.*" *Op. cit.,* I, 23.

*43. Every person is introduced speaking. Richard II is thus introduced in a particular situation: "Suppose you see the corpse of this prince, all to be mangled with blewe wounds, lying pale and wan, all naked, upon the stones, in St. Paules Church, the people standing round about him, and making his complaynt, in manner following, etc. . . ." Lydgate's *Fall of Princes* gave rise to the *Mirror of Magistrates.* In the year 1550, R. Baldwine [Warton refers to William Baldwin] was requested to continue Lydgate's series of the great unfortunate, but he chose rather to confine himself entirely to our English story, and began with Robert Tresilian, 1388, and ended with Lord Hastings, 1483. In this work he was assisted by others, and particularly by Thomas Sackville, who wrote the life of the Duke of Buckingham, together with this Induction, intending at the same time to write all those remarkable lives which occurred from the Conquest to Tresilian, with whom Baldwine originally begun, and to have printed his additional part, together with all that Baldwine and his friends had already performed, in one volume, and to have prefixed this Induction as a general preface to the whole. But this was never executed. Afterwards another collection appeared under the same title, by W. Higgins, 1587. The last edition of the whole, without additions, was published by Richard Niccols, 1610. Drayton's "Legends" were written on this plan, and are therefore added in Niccols's edition.

Mr. Walpole, in his entertaining account of *Royal and Noble Authors* [*A Catalogue of the . . .* , Strawberry Hill, 1758] remarks that this set of poems gave rise to the fashion of historical plays, particularly to Shakespeare's (Vol. I, p. 166). But the custom of acting histories seems to have been very old on our stage. Stowe seems to make them a distinct species of drama, but perhaps improperly. "Of late days, instead of those stageplays [at Skinner's Well, 1391 and 1409, Warton adds], have been used comedies, tragedies, interludes, and *histories,* both *true* and *feigned." Survey of London,* ed. 1618, p. 144.

*44. Bishop Hall ridicules the *Mirror of Magistrates* in the following passage of his satires.

> Another whose more heavie-hearted saint
> Delights in nought but notes of ruefull plaint
> Urgeth his melting muse with solemn tears,
> Rhyme of some *drearie fates of luckless peers.*
> Then *brings he up* some branded *whining ghost,*
> To tell how *old misfortunes* have him tost. (I, 5)

*45. [1754 reads: "a species of composition in which the perplexed subtilities of metaphysical disquisition strongly prevailed, and which perhaps took its rise from the taste and influence of that pacific prince and profound scholastic James I." Warton's note in 1762 reads:] Mason's *Musaeus.* But the spirit of chivalry, of which Prince Henry was remarkably fond, together with shows and pageantries, still continued yet in a less degree. Hence G. Wither introduces Britannia thus lamenting the death of Prince Henry:

> Alas, who now shall grace my Turnaments,
> Or honour me with deeds of Chivalrie?
> What shall become of all my Merriments,
> My Ceremonies, Showes of Heraldrie,
> And other Rites?
> —Elegy 31, *Prince Henry's Obsequies* (London, 1617 [1612?]), p. 368.

*46. See [Sir John] Davies on the Immortality of the Soul [*Nosce Teipsum* (1599)]; [Sir Fulke Greville] Lord Brooke's *Treatise of Human Learning;* Donne's works, etc.

47. This paragraph is not in 1754.

*48. Printed in the year 1633. The principal fault of this poem is that the author has discovered too much of the anatomist. *The Purple Island* is the Isle of Man, whose parts and construction the poet has described in an allegorical manner, viz., the bones are the foundation of it, the veins its brooks, etc. Afterwards the intellectual faculties are represented as persons. But he principally shines where he personifies the passions and evil concupiscencies of the heart, who attack the good qualities of the heart alike personified, which under the conduct of their leader Intellect, rout the former. In this poem there is too somewhat of a metaphysical turn. As the whole is supposed to be sung by two shepherds, the poet has found an opportunity of adorning the beginnings and endings of his cantos with some very pleasing pastoral touches. This poem seems to bear some resemblance to the *Psychomachia* of Prudentius.

49. This sentence is not in 1754.

*50. Thus when Voltaire read his *Henriade* to Malezieu, that learned man assured him his work would not be tasted; for, says he, "Les François n'ont pas la tête épique" [*Essai sur la poésie épique*]. In other words, "The French have no idea of solemn and sublime poetry; of fiction and fable; the satires of Boileau will be preferred to the best epic poem."

*51. [1754 reads: "The simplicity and true sublime of the *Paradise Lost* was by these triflers either totally disregarded or else mistaken for insipidity and bombast." Warton's note in 1762 reads:] Even Dryden, blinded by the beauties of versification only, seems not to have had a just idea of Milton's greatness. It is odd that in praising Milton he should insist on these circumstances. "No man has so copiously translated Homer's Grecisms and the Latin elegancies of Virgil." By what follows it appears that he had no notion of Milton's simplicity. "He runs into a flat thought sometimes for a hundred lines together, but it is when he is got into a track of Scripture." He afterwards strangely misrepresents Milton's reason for writing in blank verse. "Neither will I justify Milton for his writing in blank verse; for whatever causes he alleges for the abolishing of rhyme (which I have not now the leisure to examine), his own particular reason is plainly this, that rhyme was not his talent." Whether rhyme was Milton's talent or not I shall not inquire, but shall infer from this reason assigned by Dryden that had Dryden composed the *Paradise Lost*, he would have written it in rhyme, and that consequently, with Burnet, he judged the want of it an imperfection in Milton's poem. See dedication to Dryden's *Juvenal* [Ker, II, 29]. [Bishop Gilbert Burnet's *History of His Own Time* (1753), I, 228.]

*52. *Réflexions*, I, xxv.

53. The editions of John Upton and of Ralph Church both appeared in 1758.

54. 1754 added: "it being my chief aim, together with that of particular illustration, to give an impartial estimate of the merit of this original genius."

55. This sentence marks the beginning of a long passage introduced into the second edition. The passage ends with the beginning of the last paragraph of the Postscript.

The first point made in the added passage, the importance of reading a poet's contemporary writers, Warton had made in 1754 in Section XI: "In criticizing upon Milton, Jonson, Spenser, and some other of our elder poets, not only a competent knowledge of all ancient classical learning is requisite but also an acquaintance with those books which, though now forgotten and lost, were yet in repute about the time in which each author respectively wrote, and which it is most likely he had read."

56. Warton probably refers to John Jortin's *Remarks on Spenser's Poems and on Milton's* Paradise Lost (1734), Peter Whalley's edition of Jonson (1756), and Patrick Hume's annotations on *Paradise Lost* (1695). Whalley,

John Upton, and Zachary Grey were chief among those who had annotated Shakespeare with parallel passages from the classics and whose error was demonstrated by Richard Farmer's *Essay on the Learning of Shakespeare* (1767).

*57. *Dunciad,* I, 149 (note).

58. This paragraph was not in the first edition. It may have been added because of what Hurd had said in his *Letters on Chivalry and Romance* about six months earlier, but its probable source was a work which Warton may have called to Hurd's attention: Sainte-Palaye's *Mémoires sur l'ancienne chevalerie* (Paris, 1759–1781). "The greater part of this work was originally printed in the *Mémoires de littérature, tirés des registres de l'Académie Royale des Inscriptions et Belles-Lettres.* The 'Mémoire concernant la lecture des anciens romans de chevalerie' appeared in 1751 (XVII, 757–799) and the five 'Mémoires sur l'ancienne chevalerie,' in 1753 (XX, 595–847)" (Robinson and Dennis, *op. cit.,* p. 49).

59. This and the preceding paragraphs are good evidence to support the claim made by the reviewers of the second edition that Warton had been reading Hurd's *Letters.*

60. This too seems to reflect the influence of Hurd and is in line with some of the revisions noted above in which Warton toned down his criticism of the Italian poets.

61. Warton seems to have conceived the idea for his *History of English Poetry* while he was writing his *Observations* (see note 31, above). Three years after the second edition of the *Observations* had appeared, he believed himself to be well on toward finishing Vol. I, which was not, however, published until 1774. The work occupied him off and on for about the last thirty years of his life. A revised edition of Vol. I appeared in 1775; Vol. II was published in 1778 and Vol. III in 1781; when he died, eighty-eight pages of Vol. IV had been printed (edited and reprinted by Rodney M. Baine, Augustan Reprint Society, Pub. 39, Los Angeles, 1953).

Warton rejected the plans, proposed by Pope and Gray, for a history of English poetry in which the poets would have been arranged by schools, in favor of a chronological order which would allow him more freedom. He considered his task to be not so much that of a critic as that of a historian, and his Preface is an interesting statement of the values of cultural history. He thought a history of poetry "especially productive of entertainment and utility" because (a) poetry is "an art whose object is human society"; (b) "it has the peculiar merit, in its operations on that object, of faithfully recording the features of the times and of preserving the most picturesque and expressive representations of manners; and, [(c) since] the first moments of composition in every nation are those of the poet, it possesses the additional advantage of transmitting to posterity genuine delineations of life in its simplest stages." It should be observed, however, that Warton was constantly reversing the process to make the historical facts illuminate the poetry.

The *History* begins after the Norman conquest and ends with the Elizabethan period (Warton was not competent in Old English, nor were his readers). By liberal quotation and paraphrase Warton described the chief works of the poets he discussed, as well as many of their sources. He indulged in many digressions into history of manners, religion, politics, philosophy, and even invention, as his table of contents for Section IV will illustrate: "Examination and specimens of the metrical romance of Richard the First. Greek fire. Military machines used in the Crusades. Musical instruments of the Saracen armies. Ignorance of geography in the Dark Ages." In addition to his three dissertations, "Of the Origin of Romantic Fiction in Europe," "On the Introduction of Learning into England," and "On the *Gesta Romanorum*," he included two long digressions on the history of drama, a subject he had planned to exclude, and a long chapter on the authenticity of the Rowley poems.

Of such a work it is impossible to give a fair impression by means of two short chapters. The two here reprinted were chosen because in their form as summaries they best show the effect of Warton's scholarship (he uses the word *research*) upon his study of literature. Sections XXXVII and XXXVIII, on Surrey and Wyatt, are also good examples of Warton at his best. Lamb and Hazlitt thought them influential in re-establishing the sonnet.

A few of Warton's notes have been omitted. In editing his notes I have relied almost entirely upon Rinaker's list of Warton's sources (*op. cit.*, pp. 179–232); Rinaker (*op. cit.*) and Wellek (*op. cit.*) are indispensable to a study of the *History*, but Richard Price's hundred-page Preface to the 1824 edition should not be neglected.

62. Warton had developed this notion at some length in his dissertation "Of the Origin of Romantic Fiction in Europe," prefixed to Vol. I of the *History*.

*63. [*Mémoires de littérature, tirés des registres de l'Académie Royale des Inscriptions et Belles-Lettres* (Paris, 1717–   ),] XVIII, 741.

64. *La Belle Dame Sans Merci* has been ascribed to Sir Richard Ros; Tyrwhitt rejected the *Assembly of Ladies* from the Chaucer canon.

*65. *Histoire du théâtre français*, in *Oeuvres* (Paris, 1742), III, 15.

66. This also was accepted as Chaucer's work by both Urry and Tyrwhitt.

*67. [Jacques-François Sade, *Mémoires pour la*] *Vie de François Petrarque* [Amsterdam, 1764–1767], II, 60, n. xix.

*68. [Joseph] Vaisette and Claude de Vic, *Histoire Générale de Languedoc* [*par deux religieux Bénédictins de la Congregation de S. Maur* (Paris 1730–1745)], IV, 184 ff.

69. Ramon Muntaner, *Chronica de Jaune primer rey de Aragon* (Valencia, 1558).

*70. Line 720.

*71. See *Mémoires de littérature*, II, 731; [Claude] Fauchet, *Recueil de l'origine de la langue et poésie françoise*, etc. (Paris, 1581), pp. 106 and 160; [Pierre-Daniel] Huet, *Traité de l'origine des romans*, p. 136 [Elledge and Schier, p. 198]; [Joannes Albertus] Fabricus, *Bibliotheca Graeca* [Hamburg, 1705–1707], X, 339; [Guillaume] Massieu, *Histoire de la poésie françoise* [1739], p. 137; [Giovanni Mario] Crescimbeni, *L'Istoria della volgar poesia* [Venice, 1730–1731], I, v, 332.

*72. Compare Crescimbeni, *Volg. Poes.*, I, xiv, p. 162.

*73. *Inferno* XXII.

*74. Fauchet, *Rec.,* p. 96.

*75. *Ibid.,* pp. 47 and 116. And Huet, *Rom.* pp. 121 and 108.

*76. [Pierre-François Godard de] Beauchamps, *Recherches [sur les théâtres de France* (Paris, 1735)],* p. 5.

*77. Sonnet clxxxviii.

*78. [Etienne] Pasquier, *Les Recherches de la France* [Paris, 1643], VII, v, 609, 611.

79. *Ibid.,* p. 612. He calls such pieces *mignardises.*

80. The author of this poem has not been identified.

*81. *Mem. Lit.,* VII, 422.

*82. *Ibid.,* X, 567.

*83. *Schoolmaster,* ed. 1589, p. 19.

84. *Chronicle* [1587], III, 1297.

*85. *Merry W.,* II, i.

86. By Thomas Underdowne in 1587.

87. William Lilly, *Mr. Lilly's History of His Life and Times* (1715), London, 1721, pp. 102–103.

*88. *Leviathan,* I, viii.

89. Thomas Blackwell (1735), p. 69.

*90. *Iliad* v. 770. Longinus ix.

91. George Puttenham, *The Art of English Poesy* (1589).

*92. *1 Hen. IV,* III, ii.

93. *Georg.* ii, 291: "Strikes its roots down towards the nether pit as far as it lifts its top to the airs of heaven" (Fairclough).

94. In *Merry Wives of Windsor.*

DAVID HUME

"Of Tragedy" and "Of the Standard of Taste" first appeared in *Four Dissertations* in 1757. The first had been written several years earlier; the second was written in 1757 to take the place of one of the essays Hume decided at the last moment not to publish. The essays were reprinted several times during Hume's life; the present text follows that of the posthumous but authoritative 1777 edition of *Essays and Treatises on Several Subjects.*

For a study of Hume as critic, see Teddy Brunius, *David Hume on Criticism* (Stockholm, 1952), and the following reviews of this work: Elder Olson, in *PQ,* XXXII (1953), 272–273; Ralph Cohen in *RES,* n.s. V (1954), 197–200; and Martin Kallich in *MLN,* LXIX (1954), 130–132.

Hume begins "Of Tragedy" by asking an old question: Why does the audience enjoy witnessing, and even experiencing, the painful passions that are represented in a tragedy? Dubos' answer to the question, he thinks, is partly right: men would rather be excited even by painful passions than not be excited at all—tragedy is an escape from boredom. But this answer still does not explain why dramatic representations of painful actions should be more pleasant than the sight of similar actions in real life. Another explanation, offered by Fontenelle, is that pain and pleasure are separated by a very narrow margin, and that pain which has been weakened or diminished becomes pleasant. In tragedy, it is the knowledge that the action is not real that brings about this weakening or diminishing and thereby turns pain into pleasure. This second theory, Hume objects, does not account for all the facts either. Those who heard Cicero's description of "the butchery made by Verres of the Sicilian captains" enjoyed the speech though they knew the story to be true; and one may diminish a real sorrow until it disappears, yet at no point will it seem pleasant. Hume's theory is that the feelings of sorrow, anxiety, terror, and indignation which the action or story of a play evokes in the audience are "converted," "overpowered," or at least "tinctured" by the infusion of other feelings of an opposite nature—by the pleasure of the act of recognition, common to all imitation, and by the pleasure produced by the display of the writer's genius, by the rhythm and harmony of his language, by the very eloquence of the presentation. Or, to put it another way, the dominant feelings of pleasure evoked by the art of the play are made more intense by the addition of the power of the feelings of pity and fear. The art converts the melancholy passions; the melancholy passions give force to the feelings of admiration and delight. Hume supports his argument by examples from everyday life. A parent's love for his child is increased by his anxiety over its illness; a lover's passion is increased by his jealousy; the dominant passion of love "converts" the power of anxiety and jealousy.

1. Jean-Baptiste Dubos (1670–1742); his *Réflexions critiques sur la poésie et la peinture* (1719) was translated into English in 1748 by Thomas Nugent.

2. *In C. Verrem* II. v. 118.

*3. Painters make no scruple of representing distress and sorrow as well as any other passion, but they seem not to dwell so much on these melancholy affections as the poets, who, though they copy every motion of the human breast, yet pass quickly over the agreeable sentiments. A painter represents only one instant; and if that be passionate enough, it is sure to affect and delight the spectator. But nothing can furnish to the poet a variety of scenes and incidents and sentiments except distress, terror, or anxiety. Complete joy and satisfaction is attended with security, and leaves no farther room for action.

4. *The History of the Rebellion and Civil Wars in England Begun in the Year 1641* (1702–1704), Bk. XI, near the end.

5. Written by Nicholas Rowe (1700).

6. In this essay, Hume says that in matters of taste men differ even more widely than is apparent at first glance, because, just as in ethics men agree that justice is a virtue but disagree about the justice of certain acts, so in criticism men agree that propriety and simplicity are virtues but disagree about the propriety or simplicity of certain works of art. According to one "species of philosophy" a standard of taste is impossible because taste is a matter not of judgment or opinion but of sentiment, and since sentiments do not exist in the objects prompting them, but in the person entertaining them, all sentiments are real and therefore right—unlike opinions, which have to do with matters of fact which exist outside the observer, which therefore

can be observed and verified. Beauty, like sweetness or bitterness, is not a quality belonging to the object itself, but only a mark of a relationship between the object and the organ of sense.

Still common sense tells us that Ogilby is not so good as Milton, or Bunyan so good as Addison, and we do not in fact accept the principle of the equality of taste. Now, the principles of art ("composition") are simply "observations concerning what has been universally found to please in all countries and all ages." These principles cannot be mechanically applied, to be sure, for some highly irregular artists are still pleasing; but they please in spite of their violations of the principles. And when they are applied by a critic, he must remember that no single experience of a work of art is the same as the generalized experience on which the principles are founded. To make a just judgment a critic must observe the work at the right time, in the right place, and in the right state of mind.

His failure to make a just judgment may be due to one or more of several causes. First, his own organs of perception may be imperfect: things taste different to a sick man. Second, he may lack the sensitivity ("delicacy") "necessary to convey a sensibility of those finer emotions." Such delicacy of taste was enjoyed by the two winetasters in *Don Quixote* who, tasting the same cask of wine, agreed that the wine was good but disagreed in that one said it had a faint flavor of leather and the other a faint flavor of iron. That their taste was superior to that of the common people who ridiculed them for their disagreement was proved when the cask was emptied and an old key on a leather thong was discovered at the bottom. Elements in a work of art are like the elements in wine: they are many and mixed, and a good critic must have a sensitive taste to discover them all. The more delicate the taste the better the critic. The men in *Don Quixote* were more fortunate than critics, for in art the principles or elements cannot be produced in evidence as easily as was the key. A third cause of wrong judgment may be a lack of practice or a failure to look several times at the object. Fourth, the critic may have tried to judge without comparing the work with other works. Fifth, he may have failed to suppress his prejudices; a critic must forget himself. Sixth, he may not have considered the purpose or end of the work and thus have failed to judge the means in respect to that end. Finally, he may not have exercised his reason in judging the logic of the action or the speeches. Most men labor under "some or other of their imperfections."

Though it is not easy to say how to identify a superior critic, still some men will be generally admitted to have superior abilities as critics. Actually, certainty is more nearly approached in art than it is in science or philosophy. Over the centuries philosophical theories have come and gone, but men have not changed their opinions about what are the great works of art. Civilized nations have been often misled in their admiration of philosophies, but they have seldom been misled in their admiration for an epic or a tragedy.

Two other sources of disagreement in matters of taste, unlike those mentioned earlier, are not the fault of the critic. One is the variation in humors in men. Young men's tastes are not the same as old men's tastes (we like Ovid at twenty, Horace at forty, and Tacitus at fifty). Some by nature prefer the sublime; others, the tender; others, raillery. Some react more strongly to faults; others neglect faults in their admiration for beauties. The other source of variety is man's predilection for things of his own country.

In the quarrel between the Ancients and the Moderns one distinction has been neglected. In judging works of the past, though we must allow for differences in manners, we should not make a similar allowance in morality; what is atrocious must always detract from the worth of any poem. But in respect to differences of opinion in speculative matters—particularly in religion—errors are not important. It is never proper "to judge of the civility or wisdom of any people, or even of single persons, by the grossness or refinement of their theological principles." But that is not to excuse fanaticism, which confounds morality and "alters the natural boundaries of vice and virtue." Bigotry has disfigured *Polyeucte* and *Athalie*. And religious principles are also a blemish when they intrude into every sentiment.

7. See Hume's essay "Of the Delicacy of Taste."

SIR JOSHUA REYNOLDS

Sir Joshua Reynolds' (1723–1792) chief contribution to criticism was his *Discourses,* a series of fifteen letcures on art, delivered at the Royal Academy from 1769 to 1790. Some of his most important ideas (particularly those in Discourses III, IV, VI, XI, and XIII) were, however, first expressed by Reynolds in 1759 in three anonymous letters to the *Idler,* written at Samuel Johnson's urgent request. Presumably Johnson needed three essays, as well as the money he received for them, and Reynolds, who is said to have stayed up all night to finish them, did his friend a generous favor at the same time that he began his own literary career. The letters were reprinted as one article in the *London Chronicle* in May, 1761. This information as well as some of the following notes comes from Frederick W. Hilles' *The Literary Career of Sir Joshua Reynolds* (Cambridge, 1936), pp. 15–22. For discussions of Reynolds' criticism see also Hoyt Trowbridge, "Platonism and Sir Joshua Reynolds," *ES,* XXI (1939), 1–7; and Walter J. Hipple, Jr., "General and Particular in the Discourses of Sir Joshua Reynolds," *Journal of Aesthetics and Art Criticism,* XI (1953), 231–247. The *Discourses* have been edited, with introduction and notes, by Robert R. Wark (San Marino, 1959).

The first letter ridicules the "connoisseur" who knows all the clichés about painters and the art of painting but who is so worried about what to say about a work of art that he does not enjoy it. Genius cannot be judged by rules, and a good critic trusts his "immediate perceptions" in judging the "higher excellency" of great art.

In the second letter Reynolds discusses the meaning of "imitation of nature," as that phrase is used to define art, and denies that it means producing a realistic likeness, which requires not art but simply mechanical skill. Painters in the grand style avoid the "minute attention" to details which characterizes the Dutch school; instead they follow the great Italian masters, Raphael and Michelangelo, who in their efforts to move the imagination of men may be allowed to produce the "unnatural." They paint only the "great and general ideas which are fixed and inherent in universal nature." It is pointless to wish that Michelangelo had added to the grandeur of his painting the natural detail that the Dutch are famous for. Such detail would only impede the flight of the imagination in works that "may be said to be all genius and soul." In the present age we do not suffer so much from the excesses of "enthusiasm" as we do from a lack of it.

The central argument of the third letter is that our ideas of beauty are based on custom and habit, not on universal principles of beauty. It does not make sense to try to prove that a swan is more beautiful than a dove by referring to such criteria as the "undulation of a curve" or the "direction of a line," for the "great mother of nature" will not be subjected to such narrow rules. Similarly we should admit that Europeans think Europeans more beautiful than Ethiopians simply because Europeans are accustomed to Europeans. Nor will such "universal principles" as novelty or utility serve any better, for in fact we decide on the beauty of a thing before we think. When we say one species is more beautiful than another, we are only expressing a preference. We would do better to reserve the word *beauty* for comparisons of two objects of the same species. In such comparisons we shall find that the more beautiful is the one that more closely approximates a general, or ideal, norm for the species. Hence the Italians, in avoiding the particular, come closer to the beautiful than do the Dutch.

1. Il Domenichino (Domenico Zampieri—1581–1641) and Guido Reni (1575–1642) were leaders of the Eclectic school of painting, founded at Bologna by the Caracci family, which included Lodovico (1555–1619), Annibale (1560–1609), and Agostino (1557–1602). Nicolas Poussin (1597–1665) was a French classical painter who did most of his work at Rome.

2. The "flowing line" and the "pyramidal principle," referred to later on in the paragraph, are probably glances at Hogarth's theory that these two things were essential to beautiful paintings. See *The Analysis of Beauty* (1753).

3. An eclectic painter (1625–1713) of the late Roman baroque style.

4. Adam Smith, in *The Theory of Moral Sentiments* (1759), V, i, makes a similar observation about the folly of assuming that the whiteness of Europeans accounts for their superior beauty.

5. Boswell (*Life*, I, 330) says that Johnson wrote the last six words of this sentence. The idea of the sentence had been developed in Chapter X of Johnson's *Rasselas*.

LORD KAMES

Henry Home, Lord Kames (1696–1782), a judge in Edinburgh for thirty years, was a prolific writer on many subjects: law, legal history, British history, ethics, and religion. *Elements of Criticism,* published when he was sixty-six, became the most widely read of his works. It ran to eight editions in Scotland within forty-five years, and by the middle of the nineteenth century at least

six editions or versions of it had appeared in America. Two German translations of it were published within ten years of its first appearance.

The book is the result of an effort to write a systematic and complete work on what is now called aesthetics, and it is important because Kames was "one of the first to incorporate into critical theory the results of the aesthetic and psychological speculation of the empiricists." In Chapter III he said that his aim was to "show that the fine arts are a subject of reasoning as well as of taste," and he described his method as follows: "It has been observed that things are the causes of emotions, by means of their properties and attributes. This furnisheth a hint for distribution. Instead of a painful and tedious examination of the several passions and emotions, I propose to confine my inquiries to such attributes, relations, and circumstances as in the fine arts are chiefly employed to raise agreeable emotions. Attributes of single objects, as the most simple, will take the lead; to be followed with particulars that depend on the relations of objects, and are not to be found in any one object singly considered." The titles of the chapters give some notion of the book's form: "Grandeur and Sublimity," "Novelty," "Risible Objects," "Resemblance and Contrast," "Uniformity and Variety," "Congruity and Propriety," "Dignity and Grace," "Rididicule," "Wit," "Custom and Habit," "External Signs of Emotions and Passions," "Beauty of Language," "Comparisons," "Figures," "Narration and Description," "Epic and Dramatic Compositions," "The Three Unities," "Gardening and Architecture," "Standard of Taste." No excerpt can do justice to the work nor suggest its scope. The section here reprinted (from the revised edition of 1785) does not, for example, suggest Kames's characteristics as a practical critic. David Nichol Smith (*Eighteenth Century Essays on Shakespeare,* p. xxxiii) noted Kames's ability as a critic of Shakespeare, the historical significance of Kames's distinction between the dramatic presentation of passion and the description of passion, and his praise of Shakespeare's avoidance of abstract and general terms. I. A. Richards' interesting discussion of Kames, in *The Philosophy of Rhetoric* (New York, 1936), concerns Kames's theory of metaphor.

The chief works on Kames's criticism are Gordon McKenzie, "Lord Kames and the Mechanist Tradition," in *Essays and Studies* (University of California Publications in English, XIV; 1943), pp. 93–121; Helen Whitcomb Randall, *The Critical Theory of Lord Kames (Smith College Studies in Modern Languages,* XXII; Northampton, 1944); and Walter John Hipple, Jr., *The Beautiful, the Sublime, and the Picturesque in Eighteenth-Century British Aesthetic Theory* (Carbondale, 1957), pp. 99–121.

Kames's point in the short section here reprinted is that fiction is just as good as fact for the purposes of raising emotion in readers because in either case it is the vividness of the "ideal presence" which produces sympathy. "Ideal presence" is Kames's term for the "waking dream," the presence of things or events before the mind's eye, produced either by the memory of the things or events or by the creation of them by words or discourse. It is different from "real presence" in being somewhat less vivid than the "presence" produced by viewing the actual thing or event, and from "reflective remembrance" by being more vivid and particular than a vague, general recollection of something. Though historical paintings may produce very strong ideal presences, words are the most effective means to vividness and hence to strong feeling, or sympathy. Of all forms of literature, the theater is most effective in this respect. Whatever the form, however, "the power of language to raise emotions depends entirely on the raising [of] . . . lively and distinct images."

Reflection is a hindrance to ideal presence, for to be reminded that what we are hearing or "seeing" in a fable weakens its vividness. This is the reason for the rule of criticism concerning probability; it is also an explanation of the ill effects of machinery in epic poetry. The final cause for ideal presence is that by being moved, we are persuaded to act virtuously and to do those things which bind men together and make society possible.

*1. *De oratore* II. 81.

2. Lucretius *De rerum nat.* i. 643: "For fools laud and love all things more which they can descry hidden beneath twisted sayings, and they set up for true what can tickle the ear with a pretty sound and is tricked out with a smart ring" (Bailey).

3. Quintus Curtius, a Latin historian, wrote a history of the life of Alexander the Great; Charles Le Brun (1619–1690) was commissioned by Louis XIV at Fontainebleau to paint a series of subjects based on the life of Alexander the Great.

*4. At quae Polyclito defuerunt, Phidiae atque Alcameni dantur. Phidias tamen diis quam hominibus efficiendis melior artifex creditur, in ebore vero longe citra aemulum, vel si nihil nisi Minervam Athenis, aut Olympium in Elide Jovem fecisset, cujus pulchritudo adjecisse aliquid etiam receptae religioni videtur; adeo majestas operis deum aequavit. ["But the qualities lacking in Polyclitus are allowed to have been possessed by Phidias and Alcamenes. On the other hand, Phidias is regarded as more gifted in his representation of gods than of men, and indeed for chryselephantine statues he is without a peer, as he would in truth be even if he had produced nothing in this material beyond his Minerva at Athens and his Jupiter at Olympia in Elis, whose beauty is such that it is said to have added something even to the awe with which the god was already regarded: so perfectly did the majesty of the work give the impression of godhead" (Butler).] Quintilian *Instit.* XII. x. 8, 9.

5. *Le Lutrin* (1674) is by Boileau, *The Dispensary* (1699) by Samuel Garth.

HUGH BLAIR

The fame of Hugh Blair (1718–1800), Scottish minister and for over twenty years professor of rhetoric at Edinburgh, is chiefly due to his *Lectures on Rhetoric and Belles Lettres* (1783), which went through scores of editions, was translated into French, Italian, and Spanish, and was used as a textbook in American schools for over a hundred years, although his *Sermons* were nearly as long lived, going to a twenty-fourth edition within seventy-five years, in England alone. But what first made him famous was his support of James

Macpherson, a fellow Scot who claimed to have discovered the works of an ancient Gaelic poet named Ossian. When, in 1759, Blair first saw what Macpherson claimed were translations of fragments of the poems of Ossian, he was so impressed that he gave copies of the translations to a friend who sent them to Horace Walpole, who in turn circulated them in London, where in 1760 they became the talk of the town. In his *London Journal* (London, 1951, p. 102) under the date of Nov. 4, 1762, Boswell wrote that he had heard David Hume say that *Fingal,* the epic poem supposed to be the work of Ossian, was "not heard at present. The English [he continued] were exceedingly fond of it at first, but hearing that it was Scotch, they became jealous and silent. Dr. Blair's *Dissertation* will awaken attention to it. It is a fine piece of criticism; but it were to be wished that he had kept it a little lower than Homer. For it might be a very excellent poem and yet fall short of the *Iliad.*" The note is interesting because it explains in part why Blair was so taken in (pride in Scotland and a hope, shared by many in Edinburgh, of equaling England in belles-lettres); it also explains why Hume stood by his friend Blair in spite of misgivings. Two years later (1764) Hume wrote a very convincing essay showing why, judged on external evidence alone, the poem ("a tiresome, insipid performance," he called it) was a fraud. But he did not publish the essay, presumably out of friendship for the professor, who had already had to endure the unfortunate remark of Dr. Johnson, who, ignorant of Blair's *Dissertation,* was asked in Blair's presence whether he thought any man today could have written such poems as those of Ossian. Dr. Johnson replied, "Yes, Sir, many men, many women, and many children." But most people were not so skeptical as Hume and Johnson, and the *Dissertation,* which was printed with most of the later editions of Ossian, brought Blair world-wide fame. At least, both German and French writers were taken by Blair's "romantic" taste and his exposition of what was already a commonplace notion in England—that the best poetry was written in uncultivated societies.

The present excerpt (taken from the first edition, 1763) consists of the first quarter of the essay. The remainder of the essay is a piece of practical criticism modeled on Addison's criticism of *Paradise Lost.* Blair points out the beauties of the poem under the heads of subject, characters, sentiments, imagery, etc. In the introduction Blair first discusses the virtues of ancient poetry. Ancient poetry not only tells us how men thought and felt before the "refinements of society disguised the manners of mankind," it also pleases men of taste. For no modern poetry is likely to equal it in "enthusiasm, vehemence, and fire," which are the soul of poetry. The reasons for its superiority are that in primitive cultures everything is new and able to inspire surprise; "sudden changes of fortune" easily raise men's passions; men are not restrained by convention but express themselves naturally; and language, lacking many general terms, is necessarily highly figurative. As civilization progresses, style becomes more accurate but less lively.

Turning to the poetry of Ossian, Blair sketches the history of the Druidic bards, and describes their training and their place in society. From this sketch it is easy to see why Ossian's poetry should reflect less *barbarity* than such poetry as that of Lodbrog: the bards made a study of poetry, and were probably in their refinement somewhat ahead of their audience. Indeed, the poetry probably helped to refine the manners of the people by showing examples of great friendship, love, and heroism.

Ossian's particular advantages were that he lived late enough in ancient times to have known the earlier poetry and to have become steeped in the traditions of heroes of earlier times. He was not only well educated in the school for bards, he was himself the son of a famous hero and had been in many battles.

The rest of the introduction consists of proof of the antiquity of Ossian's poems: They reflect the life of a hunting society, which is the first stage in the evolution of a society; no cities are mentioned; no modern allusions raise inconsistencies; the manners are rude, and military art seems undeveloped; the poems lack the marks of conscious artistry; Ossian does not use general terms or express abstract ideas—both signs of a more mature society than that of antiquity, where both thought and expression dealt only in particulars. Two other signs of ancientness are the lack of religious ideas and of references to any of the great clans or families of modern Scotland. It is impossible to believe that any modern Scot, wishing to forge such a poem, could have resisted the temptation to bring glory to his own clan.

1. xv. 9.
2. *De bell. Gall.* vi. 13–14.
3. Strabo iv; Diodorus Siculus v.
4. *De bell. civ.* i. 447: "The bards also, who by the praises of their verse transmit to distant ages the fame of heroes slain in battle, poured forth at ease their lays in abundance" (Duff).
5. *On the Sublime* xliv.

RICHARD HURD

Richard Hurd (1720–1808), for twenty-seven years Bishop of Worcester, is best known to students of literary criticism as the author of *Letters on Chivalry and Romance* (1762), in which Hurd argued that critics of a work of art should study the age in which it was written, that the history of the medieval period provides good material for poetry, and that "Gothic" poetry may be just as good as classical poetry. These ideas, with their emphasis upon the historical method, were not new (see Thomas Warton's *Observations on the Fairy Queen* and my notes, above), but Hurd's *Letters* became a *locus classicus* in the history of romanticism. They were edited by E. J. Morley (London, 1911), who did not, however, make any scholarly contribution to the understanding of them. Two recent studies are more useful: Audley L. Smith, "Richard Hurd's Letters on Chivalry and Romance," in *ELH*, VI (1939), 58–81; and Edwine Montague, "Bishop Hurd's Association with Thomas Warton," in *Stanford Studies in Language and Literature* (Stanford, 1941), 233–256. These essays served as a point of departure for Hoyt Trowbridge, who suggested that the *Letters* did not mark a sudden change in Hurd's critical

theory from an earlier nonclassicism, but were consistent with his earlier assumptions as well as with what Trowbridge called Hurd's most important critical work, *A Dissertation on the Idea of Universal Poetry*. See "Bishop Hurd: A Reinterpretation," in *PMLA*, LVIII (1943), 450–465.

Hurd's first criticism appeared in his edition of Horace's *Ars poetica* (1749), which he followed with an edition of Horace's *Epistola ad Augustum*, to which he appended "A Discourse concerning Poetical Imitation" (1751). When these two editions were republished as one work in two volumes in 1753, Hurd added an essay "On the Provinces of the Drama." A third essay appeared in Cambridge, in 1757, *A Letter to Mr. Mason, on the Marks of Imitation*. These are workmanlike essays, in which the pervasive neoclassical tastes are justified by quotations from Aristotle and Longinus. Certainly the *Letters on Chivalry and Romance* are of a different kind and order, but Trowbridge and M. H. Abrams (*The Mirror and the Lamp* [New York, 1953], p. 18) are right in their emphasis upon Hurd's last essay, the *Idea of Universal Poetry*, which appeared anonymously in 1766. The present text of the essay is taken from Vol. II of *The Works of Richard Hurd* (London, 1811).

The thesis of Hurd's essay is that, since the chief aim of poetry is to please, all the effective sources of the pleasure produced by discourse should be exploited in poetry: the diction should be delightful, ornamented, out of the ordinary; its truth should be presented in its most appealing form, which may exceed nature and be fiction; this fiction may take the form of such unnatural expressions as apostrophes, invocations, personifications, unnatural creatures ("it is no wonder that pagan myth and Gothic romance were the most alluring to the true poet"). Poetry that is not in rhymed verse is imperfect. In fact, there is no reason why modern tragedy should not use music, as did tragedy in Aristotle's time. Modern romances and novels in prose are simply imperfect poems. In spite of Milton's well-known contempt of rhyme, the truth is that most people of sound taste would enjoy *Paradise Lost* even more if it were rhymed, for rhyme is not an invention of a barbaric age—it is a natural source of natural pleasure. Hurd explains why the form of, and taste for, rhyme varies from country to country.

1. Bacon, *Advancement of Learning*, II, iv, 2.

2. Horace *Ars poet*. 377: "So a poem, whose birth and creation are for the soul's delight . . ." (Fairclough).

3. *Serm.* I. iv. 45: "Hence some have questioned whether comedy is or is not poetry; for neither in diction nor in matter has it the fire and force of inspiration, and save that it differs from prose-talk in its regular beat, it is mere prose" (Fairclough).

*4. Empedocles. Plutarch, Vol. I, p. 15, par. 1624.

*5. See Strabo I. ii. 3.

*6. *Advancement of Learning*, II, iv, 1.

7. François de Salignac de la Mothe Fénelon (1651–1715), *Télémaque* (1699).

8. Dryden, "To the Earl of Roscommon, on His Excellent Essay on Translated Verse," ll. 17–19.

9. Horace *Epist*. II. ii. 214: "You have played enough and drunk enough.

'Tis time to quit the past, lest, when you have drunk too freely, youth mock and jostle you, playing the wanton with better grace" (Fairclough).

SIR WILLIAM JONES

Sir William Jones (1746–1794) was one of the most brilliant scholars of his time. He is said to have been fluent in thirteen languages and to have known twenty-eight others. His chief field of study was Oriental languages and literatures. He was "the first English scholar to master Sanskrit" and he is credited with the important discovery of the significance of Sanskrit in the history of European languages. But he also mastered law, wrote a famous essay *On the Law of Bailments,* and was for ten years judge of the high court at Calcutta. He was always interested in politics and was outspoken in his opposition to the American war and to the slave trade. He was learned in music and botany. He was a member of the Royal Society and Johnson's Literary Club, and a close friend of Burke and Gibbon. His first published work (1770), a translation into French of a Persian life of Nadir Shah, was followed in the same year by a *Traité sur la Poésie Orientale.* In 1771 he published his *Grammar of the Persian Language.* "On the Arts Commonly Called Imitative" is one of two essays appended to his *Poems, Consisting Chiefly of Translations from the Asiatic Languages* (1772), published anonymously at the age of twenty-six, four years after he had graduated from Oxford, where he was a fellow of University College. Most of his important work in Oriental studies appeared during the last ten years of his life. His poems were reprinted several times during the early nineteenth century, and his poem *Cassia, or the Game at Chess* was frequently reprinted in *An* EASY *Introduction to the Game of Chess.* These biographical data are from the article in the *DNB,* which was written mainly from *The Memoirs of the Life, Writings, and Correspondence of Sir William Jones* (London, 1804), by Lord Teignmouth, Jones's friend, whose misguided partiality produced an imperfect biography.

A. J. Arberry has thrown "New Light on Sir William Jones," in the *Bulletin of the School of Oriental and African Studies, University of London,* Vol. XI, pt. 4, pp. 673–685. In the same volume is an essay by V. de Sola Pinto, "Sir William Jones and English Literature." Another essay on Jones the poet is R. M. Hewitt, "Harmonius Jones," in *Essays and Studies by Members of the English Association,* Vol. XXVIII (Oxford, 1943).

Jones's thesis in the present essay is that though poetry and music may imitate manners of men and objects of nature its distinguishing function is the expression of passion. The earliest poetry was probably simple praise of the deity; after that the expression of love of human beings for one another, then of grief for the loss of friends and relations, then of hatred of vice and love of virtue (moral poetry). These impulses to passionate expression were also the principal sources of music. "Pure and original music" was not "music of mere sounds" but "poetry dressed to advantage."

Such poetry and music are not an imitation of nature but the "voice of nature herself." It would be difficult to say what Aristotle himself, the originator of the imitative fallacy, was imitating when he wrote "a very poetical elegy on the death of a man."

At the end of a long digression on the technical nature of harmony, in which he discusses the causes and effects of the variations in mood in music, Jones says, "The old divisions of music into celestial and earthly, divine and human, active and contemplative, intellective and oratorial, were founded rather upon metaphors, and chimerical analogies, than upon any real distinctions in nature." Of the two true kinds of music, he thinks no reasonable man will prefer the music of mere sounds to the music which gives "a delight of the soul arising from sympathy and founded on the natural passions."

Even in painting, much of which is "strictly imitative," the most effective works are those that express passion and move their viewers by sympathy. In all three arts, it is "not by imitating the works of nature but by assuming her power and causing the same effect upon the imagination which her charms produce to the senses," that the artist "gains his end."

The essay is distinguished by (a) Jones's Longinian distinction between the artistic act which is imitative and that which is natural, or nature acting in the artist; (b) his primary concern with what we call lyric poetry; (c) his references to "sympathy" as a means of communication; and (d) his insistence upon passion as the subject of poetry.

The present text follows that of the first edition of *Poems* (1772).

1. In *Les Beaux-Arts réduits à un même principe* (1746).

*2. Two lines of Tasso.

*3. See the ode of Sappho quoted by Longinus, and translated by Boileau.

*4. Some Latin words were spelled either with an *u* or a *y*, as Sulla or Sylla.

*5. Suppose C, E, G, are struck together: then E gives g sharp, b, and G, b, d, which g Sharp, b, d, are dissonant from C, the first being its superfluous fifth, and the two last its seventh and second; and, to complete the harmony, as it is called, g sharp and g natural are heard together, than which nothing can be more absurd; these horrid dissonances are, indeed, almost overpowered by the natural harmonics of the principal chord, but that does not prove them agreeable. Since nature has given us a delightful harmony of her own, why should we destroy it by the additions of art? It is like painting a face naturally beautiful.

*6. The proportions of the intervals are these: 2d. maj. 8 to 9. 2d. min. 15 to 16. 3d. maj. 4 to 5. 3d. min. 5 to 6. 4th. 3 to 4. 5th. 2 to 3. 6th. maj. 3 to 5. 6th. min. 5 to 8. 7th. maj. 8 to 15. 7th. min. 5 to 9. These proportions are determined by the length of the strings, but, when they are taken from the vibrations of them, the ratios are inverted, as 2d. maj. 9 to 8, 2d. min. 16 to 15, etc.; that is, while one string vibrates nine times, its second major makes eight vibrations, and so forth. It happens that the intervals which have the simplest ratios are generally the most agreeable; but that simplicity must not be thought to occasion our pleasure, as it is not possible that the ear should determine those proportions.

*7. There are no more than six full notes in a scale of eight sounds, or an octave, because the intervals between C D, D E, F G, G A, A B, are equal, and the intervals between E F, B C, are also equal, but are almost half as small as the others; and C D E $= 2$ n $+$ E F $= \frac{1}{2}$ n $+$ F G A B $= 3$ n $+$ B C $= \frac{1}{2}$ n $= 6$ n. But though the interval E F be usually called a semitone, yet it is more properly a *limma,* and differs from a semitone by a comma, or $^{81}\!/_{80}$; and that it is less than a semitone was asserted by Pythagoras, and thus demonstrated by Euclid of Alexandria, in his treatise *On the division of the Monochord:* if the diatessaron C F contain two full tones and a semitone, then the diapason C c (which comprises two diatessarons, and a whole tone) will be equal to six tones. But the diapason is less than six tones; therefore C F is less than two, and a semitone; for if $\frac{9}{8}$, the ratio of a tone, be six times compounded, it will be a fraction greater than that, which is equal to $\frac{2}{1}$, or the ratio of the diapason; therefore, the diapason is less than six tones. Ptolemy has proved the same truth more at large in the tenth and eleventh chapters of his first book of *Harmonics,* where he refutes the assertions of the Aristoxenians, and exposes their errors with great clearness.

8. Jean Philippe Rameau (1683–1764) and Giuseppe Tartini (1692–1770).

9. *Lettre sur la musique française* (1753).

10. Diog. Laert. v, vii (Teubner ed., *Fragmenta,* Leipzig, 1886, p. 422).

ALEXANDER GERARD

Alexander Gerard (1728–1795), Scottish preacher and professor of philosophy at Marischal College, Aberdeen, won a prize in 1756 offered by the Philosophical Society of Edinburgh for his *Essay on Taste,* published in 1759 "with three dissertations on the same subject by De Voltaire, D'Alembert, De Montesquieu." This work, important in the history of associationist aesthetics, is analyzed and discussed in: Marjorie Greene, "Gerard's *Essay on Taste," MP,* XLI (1943), 45–58; Gordon McKenzie, *Critical Responsiveness* (University of California Publications in English, Vol. XX; Berkeley, 1949); and Walter John Hipple, Jr., *The Beautiful, the Sublime, and the Picturesque* (Carbondale, 1957).

In 1760 Gerard was appointed professor of divinity at Marischal, and in 1771 he resigned that post to accept the chair of divinity at King's College. During the last half of his life he published five or six works on theological subjects, but only one on aesthetics, *An Essay on Genius.* Though not so frequently referred to by students of the subject and period as the *Essay on Taste,* it is a considerably more interesting work.

The comprehensiveness of Gerard's treatment is suggested by the Table of Contents. Part I, "Of the Nature of Genius," consists of five sections: "Of the Province and Criterion of Genius," "To What Faculty of the Mind Genius Properly Belongs," "How Genius Arises from the Imagination," "Of the Influence of Judgment upon Genius," and "Of the Dependence of Genius on Other Intellectual Powers." Part II, "Of the General Sources of the Varieties of Genius," consists of ten sections: "Of the Sources of the Varieties of Genius in the Imagination; Particularly of the Qualities of Ideas which Produce Association," "Of the Influence of Habit in Association," "Of the Influence of the Passions in Associations," four sections on the "Associating Principles," and "Of Flexibility of Imagination," "Of the Varieties of Memory, and Their Influence on Genius," and "Of Varieties of Judgment, and Their Influence on Genius." Part III consists of seven sections comparing genius for science with genius for the arts.

The two sections here reprinted, consisting of about one-sixth of the whole *Essay,* show Gerard as theorist and as literary critic and reveal his application of associationist theory to aesthetics, his emphasis on imagination (invention), and his interest in the effect of passion on verbal expression.

Though all men, he says, have some imagination—the faculty by which ideas are associated—only men of genius have the "comprehensiveness of imagination" that enables them to "call in the conceptions that are necessary for executing their designs." Lesser men must rely on the pedestrian faculty of memory, by means of which they may become commentators or translators— not philosophers or poets. Homer and Newton are Gerard's examples; here and elsewhere both artists and "scientists" are referred to. A second mark of genius is "regularity of imagination," by which "a false luxuriance of fancy" is avoided. Pindar, Marino, Ariosto, and Spenser lacked this quality of imagination, as did Locke and Montaigne. But Shakespeare and Euclid were more fortunate. "Activity of imagination" is the third mark of genius.

Gerard's dependence on classical rhetoric becomes clear in the second part of this Section, where he argues for the equal importance of *disposition* and *invention* (or imagination), but his originality is revealed in his use of organic and mechanical analogies in his discussion of the creative process. "When a vegetable draws in moisture from the earth, nature by the same action by which it draws it in, and at the same time, converts it to the nourishment of the plant. . . . In like manner genius arranges its ideas by the same operation, and almost at the same time, that it collects them." The "methodizing power" is therefore part of the power of the imagination in a genius; it is independent of judgment. Disposition is a function of invention.

The Section is concluded by a discussion of "enthusiasm."

Section iii of Part II, "Of the Influence of the Passions on Association," with its analyses of passages from Shakespeare, shows Gerard at his best. He makes an interesting and detailed demonstration of the truth of the eighteenth-century cliché that Shakespeare's characters *represent* rather than *describe* passions, at the same time that he shows how the tyranny of a "present passion" controls the process of association.

*1. Natura humani ingenii ita est agilis et velox, sic in omnem partem, ut ita dixerim, spectat, ut ne possit quidem aliquid agere, tantum unum, in plura vero, non eodem die modo, sed eodem temporis momento vim suam impendat. —Quint. *Instit.* I. xx.

*2. This is remarked particularly by Aristotle, as one of Homer's chief and distinguishing virtues. *Poetics,* viii.

*3. Cavalier Marin ne s'est jamais veu une imagination plus fertile ne moins reglée que la sienne. S'il parle d'un rossignol ou d'un rose, il en dit tout ce qu'on en peut imaginer; bien loin de rejeter ce qui se presente, il va chercher ce qui ne se presente pas, il épuise toujours son sujet.—BOUHOURS, *Les Entretiens d'Ariste et d'Eugène,* IV.

*4. This is well expressed by Quintilian: speaking of rhetorical commonplaces, he observes that they will be hurtful, rather than beneficial; "Nisi et animi quaedam ingenita natura, et studio exercitata velocitas, recta nos ad ea quae conveniunt causae, serant."—*Instit.* V. x.

*5. Collocare autem, etsi est commune, tamen ad inveniendum refertur.—CIC. *partit. Orat.*

*6. *Sed ut opera extruentibus satis non est, saxa atque materiam, et caetera aedificanti utilia congerere, nisi disponendis iis collocandisque artificum manus adhibeatur: sic in dicendo quamlibet abundans rerum copia, cumulum tantum habeat atque congestum, nisi illas eadem dispositio in ordinem digestas, atque inter se commissas devinxerit. Nec immerito secunda quinque partium posita est, cum sine ea prior nihil valeat. Neque enim, quanquam fusis omnibus membris statua sit, nisi collocetur. Et siquam in corporibus nostris aliorumve animalium partem permutes et transferas, licet habeat eadem omnia, prodigium sit tamen. Et artus etiam leviter loco moti, perdunt quo viguerunt usum: et turbati exercitus sibiipsi sunt impedimento. Nec mihi videntur errare, qui ipsam rerum naturam stare ordine putant; quo confuso, peritura sunt omnia. —QUINT. *Instit.* VII. i.

*7. *Poetics,* xiii.

*8. Aristotle, who will not be suspected to be too great a favorer of enthusiasm, seems to assert that it alone can dispose men to search for new inventions in philosophy. Διὰ γὰρ τὸ ΘΑΥΜΑΖΕΙΝ οἱ ἄνθρωποι χαὶ νῦν, καὶ τὸ πρῶτον ἤρξαντο φιλοσοφεῖν.—*Metaphysics,* I. 2.

*9. Quem ardorem studii censetis fuisse in Archimede, qui, dum in pulvere quaedam describit attentius, ne patriam quidem captam esse senserit?—CIC. *De fin.* v.

*10. Erat Protogenes in suburbano hortulo suo, hoc est Demetrii castris. Neque interpellatus praeliis, inchoata opera intermisit omnino.

*11. Graham's account of painters.

*12. *Éloges des Sçavans,* II.

*13. Les peintres et les poètes ne peuvent inventer de sang froid. On fait bien qu'ils entrent en un espèce d'enthousiasme, lorsqu'ils produisent leurs idées, etc.—*Réflec. crit. sur la poés. et sur la peint.,* II, 2.

*14. Molière, *L'Avare,* IV, vii.

*15. *Treatise of Human Nature,* II, ii, 2.

JAMES BEATTIE

James Beattie (1735–1803) was a member of the philosophical club, founded in Aberdeen in 1750, of which Blackwell, Gerard, and Campbell were members. He was professor of moral philosophy and logic at Marischal College. When the *Essays on Poetry and Music* appeared, he had already achieved some fame for his poetry: *Original Poems and Translations* (1760), *Judgment of Paris* (1765), and especially *The Minstrel* (1771–1774). *Essays on Poetry and Music* appeared first as an appendix to *An Essay on the Nature and Immutability of Truth* (1776). It was published separately in 1778 and 1779. The present text follows that of the 1778 edition.

"Of Sympathy" is the last chapter in Part I of the *Essays*. Most of the chapter consists of a fairly commonplace discussion of the nature of sympathy, a discussion which Beattie justifies on the ground that since much of our pleasure in poetry "depends on our sympathetic feelings," the "philosophy of sympathy" should be a part of critical theory. The more remarkable part of the essay is the conclusion, in which he says that poets ought to "call forth our sensibility towards those emotions only that favor virtue and invigorate the human mind." Tales of horror never do us any good, but some modern authors seem to think that they must not only touch the heart but "tear it in pieces." And with so many evils in real life, why should the poet give us more?

Comedy, so far from spoiling tragedy, probably enhances it. Who wants all gloom? And "if the play has conveyed any sound instruction, there is no risk of its being dissipated by a little innocent mirth."

The comic scenes in Shakespeare's tragedies not only relieve the audience of what would be otherwise the unsupportable terror of the principal action; they also make the tragedy more true to life by reminding us that the setting for all kinds of painful events is usually filled with commonplace people and action, and such representations are pleasant.

On the subject of "sympathy" in critical theory, see W. J. Bate, "The Sympathetic Imagination in Eighteenth-Century English Criticism," *ELH*, XII (1945), 144–164, or his *From Classic to Romantic* (Cambridge, Mass., 1946). Also W. J. Ong, "Psyche and the Geometers: Aspects of the Associationist Critical Theory," *MP*, XLVIII (1951), 16–27.

Beattie's essay "On Fable and Romance" appeared in *Dissertations Moral and Critical* (1783) and has never been reprinted. Only the last quarter of the essay is here reprinted; in the central part of the essay Beattie traces the rise of the medieval romance. Interest in England in the subject of the relationship of medieval history to medieval romances may be dated from the publication in 1672 of an anonymous translation of Huet's *Traité de l'origine des romans,* which was later (1715) translated by Stephen Lewis. Most eighteenth-century writing on the subject was inaccurate speculation and is of antiquarian interest only. See William Warburton's "Supplement to the Translator's Preface," in Charles Jarvis' translation of *Don Quixote* (1742), a short criticism of Huet which Warburton reprinted as a note to *Love's Labour's Lost* I, i, in his edition of Shakespeare; and Thomas Tyrwhitt's scathing criticism of Warburton's thesis, in *Supplement to the Edition of Shakespeare's Plays* (1780), I, 373. Both are reprinted in Malone's Shakespeare. See also the first chapter of William Robertson, *History of the Reign of Charles V* (1769), Hurd's *Letters on Chivalry and Romance* (1762), and Thomas Warton's *History of English Poetry* (1774–1781). Clara Reeve's *The Progress of Romance* came out a year after Beattie's essay, and John Moore's *A View of the Commencement and Progress of Romance* was published in 1797.

Beattie's essay begins with a few pages devoted to fables and Oriental tales. From Aesop to La Fontaine and Gay, he says, fables have been a means of moral instruction. In style and purpose they were quite different from such Eastern tales as those in the *One Thousand and One Nights,* which were invented only to help luxurious men kill time and in which there is nothing that "elevates the mind or touches the heart." Modern tales told in the Eastern manner, like those of Addison, Johnson, and Hawkesworth, do, however, have a "moral tendency."

The outline of the body of the essay follows Beattie's classification of modern prose fables: (I) allegorical and (II) poetic. The allegorical fable he subdivides into (1) historical allegory (e.g., Arbuthnot's *History of John Bull,* a political satire) and (2) moral satire (e.g., *Pilgrim's Progress, Gulliver's Travels, Tale of a Tub*). In prose fables of the second main kind, the poetic, "we attend only to the events that are before us"; there is no reference in them to real events. Beattie calls them poetic because, though prose and verse are opposite, "prose and poetry may be consistent." *Tom Jones* and *Telemachus* are epic or narrative poems in prose. After a long excursion into the social history of the Middle Ages, Beattie shows, in a summary, how the romance was one of the consequences of chivalry. The passage here reprinted begins with this summary.

Europe became intoxicated with these "unnatural, improbable, and impossible" tales of chivalry; Homer, Virgil, and Cicero were neglected; Ovid became the most popular classical poet. But *Don Quixote* killed the medieval romance. "In a word, the humor and satire are irresistible, and their effects were instantaneous."

Of the serious romances Beattie distinguishes two kinds: those following a historical arrangement (e.g., *Robinson Crusoe*) and those following a poetical arrangement, which is to say those that begin in the middle of the action (e.g., *Clarissa*). Beattie's critique of Richardson includes a complaint that Richardson's wicked characters are "too agreeable." The comic romance is similarly divided. *Gil Blas* and the novels of Smollet follow a "historical order"; Fielding's follow a "poetical." After strong praise for Fielding, Beattie closes the essay with the warning that romances are a dangerous recreation. If young people feel they must read them, "let it be sparingly, and seldom."

*1. *Georg.* iii. 519; *De rerum nat.* ii. 355.
*2. See [Adam] Smith's *Theory of Moral Sentiments,* I.
*3. *King John,* III, iv, 91.
*4. See Beattie's *Essay on Laughter,* IV.
*5. *Ars poet.* 221.
6. *Don Quixote,* II, iii.
7. *The Grand Cyrus* (1649–1653) and *Clelia* (1656–1660), by Madeleine de Scudéry, and *Cleopatra* (1647–1656), by Gauthier de Costes de La Calprenède, were widely read in England in translation during the seventeenth century.
8. *The Adventures of Philip Quarll* (1727) was attributed to Edward Dorrington.
9. In *Emile, Robinson Crusoe* is the only book allowed the child when he is fifteen.
10. Translations of *Le Paysan parvenu* and *La Vie de Marianne* first appeared in London in 1735 and 1736; of *Histoire de Gil Blas,* in 1716.

GEORGE CAMPBELL

George Campbell (1719–1796) was a member of the philosophical society in Aberdeen that included Reid, Beattie, Gerard, and Blackwell. He was a well-known preacher in Aberdeen and published collections of his sermons and some theological works. He became principal of Marischal College in 1759, and in 1776 he published *The Philosophy of Rhetoric*, which reached its twelfth London edition in 1850. Its popularity as a textbook in America kept it constantly in print for more than a century. It is a two-volume, encyclopedic work distinguished by Campbell's dual aim of studying both the mind of the audience and the work of art. Its purpose, as outlined in his Preface, is "to exhibit . . . a tolerable sketch of the human mind, and aided by the lights which the poet and the orator so amply furnish, to disclose its secret movements, tracing its principal channels of perception and action, as near as possible, to their source; and on the other hand, from the science of human nature to ascertain, with greater precision, the radical principles of that art whose object it is by the use of language to operate on the soul of the hearer in the way of informing, convincing, pleasing, moving, or persuading."

Campbell opens his Introduction by defining the difference between arts and sciences. The art of surgery consists in the practice of surgery; the science of surgery consists in a knowledge of anatomy. Art is the doing; science is the knowing. An art may be practiced without a knowledge of its science, by natural gift, by experience, by imitation, or by following rules; but the knowing artist is distinguished from the natural artist by the fact that his art is founded upon an understanding of the principles upon which the rules rest, or upon an understanding of the causes of the effects achieved by intuitive skill. In general, progress in an art depends upon mastery of its science.

The classification of the arts as useful or elegant is based on *ends;* the classification of the arts as liberal or mechanical, on *means.* Navigation is a useful, liberal art; painting is an elegant, mechanical art. The history of the useful arts begins earlier than that of the fine arts, since men must have first invented means to satisfy "real" needs; progress in the useful arts has been slow; their future development may be almost infinite. The fine arts came later, developed very rapidly, and may already have approached a perfection beyond which they cannot go.

The science upon which the useful arts of logic, ethics, grammar, and rhetoric are based is the science of the human mind. Rhetoric, of course, is both a fine art (its aim is to please) and a useful art (it is a means of communication, and it moves men to action). Poetics is a special form of rhetoric, not a separate kind. The history of the science of rhetoric proceeded in four steps: first, men "naturally" became aware of the art—they noticed that by speeches men influenced the minds of other men; second, they discriminated between different kinds of speeches—speeches to explain, convince, please, move, and persuade (this was the first step in "criticism"); third, they compared the various levels of success achieved by the various means; and, fourth, they sought the principles in human nature by which the various successes could be accounted for. In this last step lies one of the important uses of the science of rhetoric, for by seeking the causes in human nature men learn about themselves. His book, Campbell says, is a study of the science of rhetoric, unlike Kames's *Elements of Criticism,* which is a study of the art of rhetoric.

Campbell admits that strictly speaking the science rests on the art, not vice versa—the critics always follow the artist and cannot work except from what has already been written. But, on the other hand, it cannot be argued that art will not be improved by study of the science.

RICHARD CUMBERLAND

Richard Cumberland (1732–1811), a grandson of the famous scholar Richard Bentley, was given some of his grandfather's books and papers while he was at Trinity College, Cambridge. His study of this legacy may have inspired his interest in Greek comedy, about which he wrote years later a series of critical essays published in the *Observer.* When he was about thirty, he began to write plays for a living, and for the next forty years he spent most of his time writing; his works include over fifty plays, two novels, a translation of Aristophanes' Clouds, essays in religious controversy, odes, and other poems. The papers which make up the *Observer* were written at Tunbridge Wells and published, not as a periodical, but as collected essays. The first edition of Vol. I, containing forty essays, appeared in 1785. Vols. I, II, and III appeared in 1786, and a "second edition" of these three volumes, in 1787. In 1788 Vol. IV appeared, and in 1790, Vol. V. The work went through twelve editions in seventy years. The present text was taken from the fifth edition, 1798. Cumberland's criticism is described in S. T. Williams, *Richard Cumberland: His Life and Dramatic Works* (New Haven, 1917).

Cumberland's essay on *Samson Agonistes* is mainly a reply to Dr. Johnson's objection that the play has no middle. The reply consists of two parts, the first being a demonstration that all the episodes contain incidents which lead to the "determination" of Samson's will to do the deed which is the catastrophe of the play; and the second, presenting the argument that Johnson misinterpreted Aristotle, who spoke of beginning, middle, and end only in order to explain the word *whole* as he used it in the statement that "not every whole hath amplitude enough for the construction of a tragic fable."

The essay on Rowe's *The Fair Penitent* (1703) takes off from Johnson's praise of the play and consists of a comparison of it with *The Fatal Dowry* (1632), by Philip Massinger and Nathaniel Field, on which play Rowe's was based. The detailed comparison leads Cumberland to the conclusion that anyone with a "feeling for real nature, dramatic character, moral sentiment, tragic pathos, or nervous diction" will prefer the earlier play.

1. William Mason, whose *Elfrida* (1752) was prefaced by an essay on the use of the chorus.

2. *Rambler,* No. 139, July 16, 1751.

3. In Otway's *Venice Preserved.*

HENRY MACKENZIE

Henry Mackenzie (1745–1831) of Edinburgh, friend of the great Scotsmen from Hume to Scott, published his first novel, *The Man of Feeling,* anonymously, in 1771. Two other novels followed during the next ten years. Mackenzie also wrote plays, only one of which was successfully produced. He persuaded his literary club to sponsor a periodical like Addison's *Spectator.* The paper, called the *Mirror,* appeared weekly from Jan. 23, 1779, to May 27, 1780. Five years later the club published the *Lounger,* a periodical very much like the *Mirror,* that appeared weekly from Feb. 5, 1785, to Jan. 6, 1787. It was popular in both London and Edinburgh, the collected editions running to at least eighteen during the next hundred years. Of the 101 numbers of the *Lounger,* Mackenzie wrote over half. Some of his contributions were sentimental tales, some, informal essays on manners and morals in the style of the *Spectator.* Among his essays in literary criticism were one on the novel, one on tragedy, and one on comedy. In the earlier *Mirror* Mackenzie had devoted two numbers to an essay on *Hamlet,* "the first romantic criticism of Shakespeare" (Harold Thompson, *A Scottish Man of Feeling, Some Account of Henry Mackenzie,* etc. [London, 1931], p. 207).

The thesis of Mackenzie's essay on Falstaff is that our pleasure in the character consists not only in the usual incongruities that are the substance of Falstaff's wit but also in the grand incongruity of Falstaff's character, in which are combined a "gross, sensual, brutish mind" and the "admirable power of invention, wit, and humor." Falstaff is a fine example of Shakespeare's supreme genius because in creating the character Shakespeare did something even harder than making preternatural beings seem true to life—he drew an original character from the materials of ordinary life. He gave to Falstaff his own "sagacity" and power to "penetrate into the characters and motives of mankind," but he put these powers of imagination not in a "man of feeling" but in a man who never allowed his passions to rule his reason or his self-interest. Though it may not be right to consider Falstaff as brave, he was never any more cowardly than common sense required. He may be seen as a kind of comic counterpart to Richard III, another man who acted not out of passion but of cool interest and who had no dread of disgrace or sense of honor or love of fame. "Circe and her swinish associates . . . molded this compound of gross debauchery, acute discernment, admirable invention, and nimble wit."

The essay on Burns here reprinted, the poet's first important critical notice, was written a few days before or after Burns and Mackenzie met in Edinburgh. The review was reprinted by the *Scots Magazine* and the *Edinburgh Magazine* and was "read in every corner of Britain" (Thompson, *op. cit.,* p. 225).

Mackenzie's praise of Burns calls attention to the poet's skill in "painting the passions," in describing scenes from nature, and in tracing the manners of men—the last with a skill reminiscent of Shakespeare. In the first kind of poetry, Burns displays with power and energy "a high tone of feeling." In his descriptive poetry he "delineates nature with the precision of intimacy, yet with . . . taste." In his dramatic pieces Burns has been accused of irreligion, but in fact all the poet has done is to ridicule fanaticism. Mackenzie ends his essay with the news of Burns's financial distress and his plans to emigrate, and with a plea for patronage which will rescue this "genius."

1. John Henderson (1746–1785).
2. Maurice Morgann's *Essay on the Dramatic Character of Sir John Falstaff* was published in 1777.

THOMAS TWINING

Apparently not much is known about Thomas Twining (1735–1804) beyond the information given in the *DNB*, the chief source of which is *Recreations and Studies of a Country Clergyman of the Eighteenth Century, Being Selections from the Correspondence of Thomas Twining, edited by his grand-nephew, Richard* (1882–1883). He was the son of a tea merchant; he was a fellow of Sidney Sussex at Cambridge; he became rector of St. Mary's in Colchester. His greatest interests were literature and music, and two of his best friends were Samuel Parr, the great Latin scholar, and Charles Burney, to whom he once wrote, about his work on the edition of the *Poetics*, that much of his effort was going into philological problems, and into "proving passages to be unintelligible. But what then? When people fancy they understand what they do not, it is doing some good to show them that they do not." Except for two sermons, his only published work was *Aristotle's Treatise on Poetry, Translated: With . . . Two Dissertations, on Poetical and Musical Imitation* (1789), which for a century was the standard English version of the *Poetics*. The present text, of the first dissertation, is taken from the second edition (1812). A few of Twining's long footnotes have been deleted, and a few abridged.

As the footnotes show, Twining's aim in the first dissertation was to clear up the confusion about the meaning of poetry as imitation which had grown out of the writings of Hurd, Harris, Beattie, Kames, and others. The first part of the dissertation discusses the ways in which poetry may properly be called imitation; the second, the sense in which Aristotle used the word with respect to poetry. Discussions of poetry as imitation are not satisfactory, Twining says, when they are based on analogies between poetry and the other arts, because they use *imitation* in an extended and improper sense. The ways in which poetry, painting, and sculpture "imitate" are much more different from than similar to each other. What is common to the uses of the word *imitation* as applied to these arts is the notion of resemblance. The proper sense of the word demands, however, that the resemblance should be both *immediate* and *obvious*.

In the first of the four kinds of imitation in poetry, the imitation of sounds, the resemblance is immediate but not obvious, for in spite of all that has been said on the subject, we cannot recognize any object simply by the sound of its name. Although the slight resemblances between the sounds and the sense may be a source of real beauty, we still "discover not the likeness till we know the meaning." The second kind of imitation, description, is obvious but not immediate, for it depends on sounds significant, which require an intermediate step between the medium of imitation and the imitation itself. The "most general and extensive of the senses" in which *imitation* is applied to poetry is the sense in which it is applied to descriptions, of which Twining discusses three kinds: descriptions of visible objects (the most imitative), descriptions of sounds (not immediate imitation), and description of mental actions, "of the emotions, passions, and other internal movements and operations of the mind." These last may be described either in respect to the way they affect the mind or in respect to their "external and sensible effects," and because in the second of these two ways the "image carries us on forcibly to the feeling of its internal cause," it is the one that "principally deserves the name of *imitative*."

The third of the four kinds of imitation in poetry is that produced by fiction—plots, episodes, characters—which can be said to be an imitation of nature or life or truth in *general* as opposed to "that individual reality of things which is the province of the historian." The chief examples of this kind are epic and dramatic poems, in which may occur, to be sure, other kinds of imitation, but where the simple narration of action is in itself "an invented resemblance of real life, or . . . of history." "Descriptive imitation" produces "illusive perception"; fictive imitation, "illusive belief." Since the resemblance in the latter is between ideas raised by a narrative and ideas raised by direct observation, fictive imitation, like descriptive, must be said to be obvious but not immediate.

The only truly imitative poetry is the dramatic, for in this fourth kind of poetic imitation the poet creates immediate and obvious resemblances between men in real life and men in his plays.

These four are the only ways in which poetry can be said to imitate. Aristotle did not say that all poetry was imitation—only tragic, comic, and dithyrambic.

In the second part of the dissertation Twining demonstrates that when Aristotle called poetry imitation he was using the word only in the third and fourth sense—poetry as fiction (plot is an imitation of an action), and poetry as drama (dialogue is an imitation of men speaking). Aristotle says nothing about the other two kinds, and indeed, so great is his emphasis on tragedy, it seems likely that he thought that the poet was most truly an imitator when he was writing dialogue, or "personative poetry." That he should not have mentioned the first kind, "sonorous imitation," can be explained by noting that Aristotle was writing about poetry, not imitation. That he neglected descriptive poetry may in part be explained by the fact that in his time there was no landscape painting and that such poetry did not appear until the time of Virgil, when painters were beginning to paint views. "There were no Thomsons because there were no Claudes."

The essay ends with a brief history of the "doctrine of imitation," beginning with Plato's *Republic*. The present confusion in the use of the term *imitation*, Twining concludes, has come from the failure of modern theorists to discover its original meaning. That meaning becomes clear when we consider that both the *Republic* and the *Poetics* were written by men who drew their ideas about poetry chiefly from the drama.

*1. James Beattie, "Essay on Poetry and Music," in *Essays* (Edinburgh, 1778), I, vi, 1.

*2. See James Harris, "Treatise on Music," in *Three Treatises* (London, 1744), ch. i.

*3. See Harris, *op. cit.,* ch. iii.

*4. See Harris; also Henry Home, Lord Kames, *Elements of Criticism* [6th ed., Edinburgh, 1785], II, 1.

*5. See Johnson's *Life of Pope* [Oxford World's Classics, II, 329–331] and the *Rambler,* No. 92; also Kames, *op. cit.,* II, 84–85.

*6. Nothing is more common than this application of the word to description, though the writers who so apply it have not always explained the ground of the application, or pointed out those precise properties of description which entitle it to be considered as imitation. Mr. Addison makes use of *description* as a general term, comprehending all poetic imitation, or imitation by language, as opposed to that of painting, etc. See *Spectator,* No. 416. J. C. Scaliger, though he extended *imitation* to speech in general, did not overlook the circumstances which render description peculiarly imitative. He says, with his usual spirit, speaking of poetic or verbal imitation: "At *imitatio* non uno modo; quando ne *res* quidem. Alia namque est *simplex designatio,* ut, *Aeneas pugnat:* alia *modos* addit et *circumstantias;* verbi gratia—*armatus, in equo, iratus. Jam hic est pugnantis etiam facies,* non solum *actio.* Ita *adjunctae circumstantiae, loci, affectus, occasionis,* etc. *pleniorem* adhuc atque *torosiorem* efficiunt IMITATIONEM" (*Poet.* vii. 2.). We must not, however, confound *imitative description* with such description as is merely an *enumeration of parts.*

*7. See Richard Hurd, "Discourse on Poetical Imitation," in *Q. Horati Flacci, Epistola ad Pisones et Augustum* (1776), III, 10; Beattie, *op. cit.,* p. 97; Joseph Warton, *Essay on the Genius and Writings of Pope* (1756–82), I, 44–45, and II, 223, 227; Kames, *op. cit.,* II, 326. Also Claudius Aelianus, *Hist. Var.* III, i; Lucian, *Eikones.*

8. *Aeneid* iv. 667: "The palace rings with lamentation, with sobbing and women's shrieks, and heaven echoes with loud wails" (Fairclough)

9. From William Mason's play *Caractacus* (1759), 2nd ed., pp. 27–28.

10. *Inferno,* III, 22: "There sighs, laments, and deep wailings were resounding through the starless air. . . . Strange tongues, horrible cries, words of woe, accents of anger, voices high and hoarse and sounds of hands with them . . ." (Norton).

*11. The following stanza of Spenser has been much admired:

> **The** joyous birdes, shrouded in cheareful shade,
> Their notes unto the voice attempred sweet,
> Th' angelical soft trembling voices made
> To th' instruments divine, respondence meet;
> **The silver-sounding instruments did meet**

> With the base murmur of the water's fall;
> The water's fall with difference discreet
> Now soft, now loud, unto the wind did call;
> The gentle warbling wind low answered to all.
>
> [*Fairy Queen*, II, xii, 71]

Dr. Warton says of these lines that they "are of themselves a complete concert of the most delicious music." It is unwillingly that I differ from a person of so much taste. I cannot consider as music, much less as "delicious music," a mixture of incompatible sounds, if I may so call them—of sounds musical with sounds unmusical. The singing of birds cannot possibly be "attempred" to the notes of a human voice. The mixture is, and must be, disagreeable. To a person listening to a concert of voices and instruments, the interruption of singing birds, wind, and waterfalls would be little better than the torment of Hogarth's enraged musician. Farther, the description itself is, like too many of Spenser's, coldly elaborate, and indiscriminately minute. Of the expressions, some are feeble and without effect—as, "*joyous* birds"; some evidently improper—as, "*trembling* voices," and "*cheareful* shade"; for there cannot be a greater fault in a voice than to be tremulous; and *cheareful* is surely an unhappy epithet applied to shade; some cold and labored, and such as betray too plainly the necessities of rhyme; such is, "The water's fall with *difference discreet.*"

*12. The reader who conceives the word *swinging* to be merely descriptive of motion will be far, I think, from feeling the whole force of this passage. They who are accustomed to attend to sounds will, I believe, agree with me that the sound in this case is affected by the motion, and that the swing of a bell is actually heard in its tone, which is different from what it would be if the same bell were struck with the same force, but at rest. The experiment may be easily made with a small hand-bell.

13. *Odyssey* xix. 521: "And with many trilling notes pours forth her rich voice" (Murray).

*14. Not a single beauty of this line is preserved in Mr. Pope's translation. The χέει, "*pours* her voice," is entirely dropped; and the strong and rich expression in θαμὰ τρῶπωσα and πολυηχέα is diluted into "*varied* strains." (Book xix, 607.) For the *particular* ideas of a variety of quick turns and inflexions (θαμὰ τρῶπωσα) and a variety of tones (πολυηχέα) the translator has substituted the *general,* and therefore weak idea of variety in the abstract—of a song or "strains" simply varied. The reader may see this subject—the importance of *particular* and *determinate* ideas to the force and beauty of description—admirably illustrated in the "Discourse on Poetical Imitation" (Hurd, *op. cit.,* III, 15–19).

15. *Aeneid* iv. 1: "But the queen, long since smitten with a grievous love-pang, feeds the wound with her life-blood, and is wasted with fire unseen" (Fairclough).

16. *Ibid.* 76–83: "She essays to speak and stops with the word half-spoken. Now, as day wanes, she seeks that same banquet, again madly craves to hear the sorrows of Ilium and again hangs on the speaker's lips. Then when all have gone their ways, and in turn the dim moon sinks her light, and the setting

stars invite sleep, alone she mourns in the empty hall, and falls on the empty couch he has left" (Fairclough).

17. Lines 3–5 mean: "Oft to her heart rushes back the chief's valour, oft his glorious stock; his looks and words cling fast within her bosom, and the pang withholds calm rest from her limbs" (Fairclough).

18. *Aeneid* xii. 666: "Within that single heart surges mighty shame, and madness mingled with grief, and love stung by fury, and the consciousness of worth" (Fairclough).

19. *Aeneid* viii. 19: "He tosses on a mighty sea of troubles; and now hither, now thither he swiftly throws his mind, casting it in diverse ways and turning it to every shift" (Fairclough).

20. Lines 10, 11: "Who is this stranger guest that hath entered our home? How noble his mien! how brave in heart and feats of arms!" (Fairclough).

*21. "Historiae imitatio ad placitum."—Bacon, *De Augm. Scient.* III, 13.

*22. The *Aeneid,* in this view, is equally imitation in every part where it is not, or is not supposed to be, historically true, even in the simplest and barest narration. In point of fiction, "tres littore cervos prospicit errantes," is as much imitation, though not as poetical, as the fine description of the storm in the same book, or of Dido's conflicting passions, in the Fourth.

*23. Yet even here a distinction obviously suggests itself. A work of fiction may be considered in two views: in the whole, or in its parts: in the general story, the *mythos,* fable, series of events, etc.; or in the detail and circumstances of the story, the account of such places, persons, and things, as the fable necessarily involves. Now, in the first view nothing farther seems requisite to make the fictive imitation good than that the events be in themselves important, interesting, and affecting, and so connected as to appear credible, probable, and natural to the reader, and, by that means, to produce the illusion and give the pleasure that is expected—and this purpose may be answered by mere narration. But in the detail this is not the case. When the poet proceeds to fill up and distend the outline of his general plan by the exhibition of places, characters, or passions, these also, as well as the events, must appear probable and natural; but being more complex objects, they can no otherwise be made to appear so than by some degree of description, and that description will not be good description, that is, will not give the pleasure expected from a work of imagination, unless it be imitative—such as makes us see the place, feel the passion, enter thoroughly into the character described. Here, the *fictive* imitation itself cannot produce its proper effect, and therefore cannot be considered as good, without the assistance of *descriptive.*

*24. Pope's *Essay on Crit.* 365.—Indeed, what Ovid says of the nymph Echo (*Met.* iii. 358) may be applied to this echo of imitative words and construction: Nec *prior ipsa loqui* didicit. The sense of the words must speak first.

*25. The drama, indeed, is said also to imitate action by action; but this is only in actual representation, where the players are the immediate imitators. In the poem itself nothing but words can be immediately copied. Gravina says well, Non è *imitazione poetica* quella, che non è fatta *dalle parole. (Della Trag. sect.* 13).

*26. See James Harris, *Hermes* (1751), p. 329, *et passim*.

*27. This expression is nowhere, that I know of, used by Aristotle. In the beginning of his treatise he asserts only that the epic, tragic, comic, and dithyrambic poems are imitations. Le Bossu, not content with saying that "every sort of poem in general is an imitation," goes so far as even to alter the text of Aristotle in his marginal quotation.

*28. Imitation in every sense of the word that has been mentioned is manifestly independent on meter, though, being more eminently adapted to the nature and end of metrical composition, it has thence been peculiarly denominated poetic imitation and attributed to the poetic art.

*29. Cap. iii.

*30. See James Harris, *Hermes*, p. 139.

*31. So Victorius: "amittit *pené* eo tempore nomen poetae." Castelvetro's solution of this difficulty is the same; and I find his ideas of this matter so coincident with my own that I am induced to transcribe his words: In his comment upon the passage he says, speaking of the dramatic part of epic poetry: "Si domanda qui *solo rassomigliativo*, (i.e. *imitative*) non perché ancora quando il poeta narra senza introducimento di persone à favellare, non rassomigli, ma perché *le parole diritte poste in luogo di parole diritte, figurano, rappresentano, e rassomigliana* MEGLIO *le parole*, che le *parole poste in luogo di* COSE non figurano, non rappresentano, non rassomigliano le *cose*; in guisa che, *in certo modo si puo dire* che il rappresentare *parole con parole* sia rassomigliare; e il rappresentare *cose con parole* non sia rassomigliare, *paragonando l'un rassomigliare con l'altro, non semplicemente*." *Poetica d'Aristotele vulgarizzata e sposta per Lodovico Castelvetro*, etc. (Basel, 1576), p. 554.

*32. Thus J. C. Scaliger, *Poet*. VII, ii. "Denique *imitationem* esse in OMNI SERMONE, *quia verba sunt imagines rerum*." He is followed by Is. Casaubon; *De Rom. Satira*, V, 340. Both these acute critics dispute warmly against Aristotle's principle that the essence of poetry is imitation. And they are undoubtedly so far in the right that if, as they contend, the only proper sense of poetry is that in which it is opposed to prose ("omnem *metro astrictam* orationem et posse et debere *poema* dici." *Cas. ubi sup.*), then there can be no other imitation common to all poetry than that which is common to all speech.

*33. It is obvious that if the imitation attributed to description consists in the clear and distinct image of the object described, every description conveying such an image to the mind must be equally considered as imitative, whether that object be real or imaginary; that is, whether the imitation be of individual or general nature; just as in painting, a portrait or a landscape from nature is as much imitation as a historical figure or an ideal scene of Claude Lorraine, though certainly of an inferior kind. Indeed, that which presents a real, sensible, and precise object of comparison may even be said to be more obviously and properly imitation than that which refers us for its original to a vague and general idea. It may be objected that this will extend imitation to all exact description; and it may be asked whether every such description, of a building or of a machine, for instance, is to be called an imitation? I answer that descriptions may be too exact to be imitative, too detailed and minute to present the whole strongly, as a picture. Technical descriptions are such. They may be said to describe every part without describing the whole. To give a complete idea of all the parts for the mere purpose of information and to give a strong and vivid general idea in order to please the imagination are very different things. It is by selection, not by enumeration, that the latter purpose is to be effected. (See Dr. Beattie's *Essay on Poetry and Music,* I, v, 4.) I believe it will be found on examination that every description, whatever be its purpose or its subject, which does actually convey such a lively and distinct idea of the whole of any object affords some degree of pleasure to the imagination, and is, so far, imitative; but whether it affords such a degree of that pleasure, or whether it be such in other respects as to amount on the whole to what may properly be called poetical imitation is another question. I must again remind the reader that the object of this dissertation is to inquire in what senses the word *imitation* is applied to language in general—not to examine all the requisites of such imitation as deserves the name of poetry. Though it has been said that all poetry is imitation, it has never, I think, been said that all imitation is poetry.

What I said above of the difference between the description of all the parts or circumstances and the description of the whole by the selection of those parts or circumstances which are most striking and characteristic of the thing described may be illustrated by a single description of a machine in Virgil; I mean the description of a plough in his Georgics:

> Continuo in silvis magna vi *flexa domatur*
> in burim, et Curvi *formam accipit ulmus* Aratri.
> Huic a stirpe pedes temo protentus in octo,
> binae aures, duplici aptantur dentalia dorso.
> Caeditur et tilia ante jugo levis, altaque fagus,
> stivaque, quae currus a tergo torqueat imos. [I. 170]

I believe every reader will agree with me that the second line of this description conveys, alone, a clearer *picture* of a plough to the imagination than all that follows, which indeed differs little, if we except the meter, from a mere technical description in a dictionary of arts.

*34. Indeed, the very existence of an appropriated term, *energeia,* to denote the *clearness* and *visibility* of a description, would alone furnish a sufficient proof of this, though every work in which it was exemplified had been lost.

*35. Descriptions of rural objects in the ancient writers are almost always what may be called sensual descriptions. They describe them not as beautiful, but as pleasant; as pleasures, not of the imagination, but of the external senses. Of this kind is the description of a Sicilian scene in the seventh pastoral of Theocritus, from verse 131 to 146.—Refreshing shades, cool fountains, the singing of birds, sweet smells, boughs laden with fruit, the hum of bees, etc.— all this is charming, but it is not a landscape. (See Dr. Warton's *Essay on Pope,* I, 4.) Nor does Virgil paint a landscape, though his reader may paint one for himself, when he exclaims:

> O qui me *gelidis* in vallibus Haemi
> Sistat, et ingenti ramorum *protegat umbra.*

Of the same kind is the famous description, in the *Phaedrus* of Plato, of that spot on the banks of the Ilissus to which Socrates and Phaedrus retire to read and converse together in the heat of a summer's day. The broad shade of a plane tree, refreshing breezes, a spring "to cool their feet," and, "what is best of all," says Socrates, a bed of grass in which they could recline at their ease—these are the materials of the description: not a single allusion to the pleasure of the eye. We learn from a passage that follows this description that the country has no charms for Socrates. His apology is curious. He could "learn nothing from fields and trees." . . . [*Phaedrus* 230 B]

*36. *Iliad* ii. 697.

*37. *Iliad* ii. 853.

*38. *Odyssey* xvii. 204–211.

*39. "It is observable that Homer gives us an exact draught of the country; he sets before us, as in a picture, the city, *etc.*" *Odyssey* xvii, note on v. 224.

*40. Homer's grove is *circular,* a circumstance rather unpicturesque. Mr Pope knew what to suppress, as well as what to add. He softens this into a "*surrounding* grove."

*41. Many such additions and improvements the reader will also find in his translation of Homer's description of the shield in the Eighteenth Book. To give one remarkable specimen: the eleventh compartment of the shield, he tells us in his *Observations on the Shield* at the end of that book, is "an *entire landscape* without human figures, an image of nature solitary and undisturbed, etc." Let us first view this landscape in the original. [*Iliad* xviii. 587] What I said of the simplicity and generality of the description last mentioned, in the *Odyssey,* is exactly applicable to this. Even in his prose translation of these lines Mr. Pope could not perfectly command his fancy. "The divine artist then engraved a large flock of white sheep, *feeding along* a beautiful valley. *Innumerable* folds, *cottages,* and enclosed shelters were SCATTERED *through the* PROSPECT." The expressions I have distinguished are Mr. Pope's; their effect on the visibility and distinctness of the picture I need not point out. The last addition, "scattered through the prospect," is particularly picturesque.—Now, let us turn to his poetic version, and there, indeed, we shall find that finished landscape of which Homer furnished only the simple sketch:

> Next this, *the eye* the art of Vulcan *leads*
> *Deep through* fair *forests,* and *a length of meads;*
> And stalls, and folds, and *scatter'd cots between.*
> And *fleecy* flocks that *whiten all the scene.*

*42. The Abbé Winckelmann, eminent for the accuracy of his researches into everything relative to the subject of ancient arts, gives it as his opinion that the paintings discovered in the ruins of Herculaneum (four only excepted) are not older than the times of the Emperors; and he assigns this reason, among others, that most of them are only *landscapes:* "Paysages, ports, maisons de campagne, chasses, pêches, vues, et que le premier qui travailla dans ce genre fut un certain Ludio qui vivoit du tems d'Auguste." He adds, "Les anciens Grecs ne s'amusoient pas à peindre des objets inanimés, uniquement propres à rejouir agreablement la vue sans occuper l'esprit." (*Hist. de* *l'art chez les anciens*, II, 104.) The remark seems just. Men and manners were the only objects which the Greeks seem to have thought worth regarding, either in painting or poetry.

*43. *Hist. Nat.* XXXV. 10.

*44. It is remarkable also that the younger Pliny, where he describes the view from one of his villas, and compares it to a painted landscape, expresses himself, probably for want of an appropriated term (such as *paysage*, etc.), by a periphrasis: *"formam aliquam ad eximiam pulchritudinem pictam,"* i.e. "a beautiful ideal landscape." *Ep.* V. 6.

*45. "Elegant imitation has strange powers of interesting us in certain views of nature. These we consider but transiently till the poet or painter awake our attention and send us back to life with a new curiosity, which we owe entirely to the copies which they lay before us." Preface to Wood's *Essay on Homer*, p. 13.

*46. Cap. xxxiv.

*47. Some writers by *imitation* understand *fiction* only; others explain it only by the general term *description;* and others, again, give it a greater ex tent, and seem to consider language as imitating whatever it can express. (See above, note 33, and Harris *on Music*, ch. i.) Some speak of it as the imitation of nature in general; others seem to confine it to the imitation of *la belle nature*. By some writers the proposition that "all poetry is imitation" is considered as too plain a point to need any explanation; while others are unable to see why any poetry except the dramatic only should be so denominated. (See Wood's *Essay on Homer*, p. 240, and the note.)

*48. *La montre et le cadran,* in the ingenious and philosophical fables of La Motte, iii, 2.

*49. Preface to his *Aeneid*.

*50. For example, in chapter xxiv he had allowed the greater extent of the epic poem to give it an advantage over tragedy in point of variety and magnificence. But in the comparison between them in his last chapter this important advantage is entirely passed over, and only the disadvantages of the epic extent of plan are mentioned; its variety, the want of which he had before allowed to be a great defect, and even a frequent cause of ill success, in tragedy, is here stated only as a fault—as want of unity.

*51. *Rep.* III. 392 D.

*52. [Twining quotes 395 D.] The reader may also see 396 and 397, in both of which places he alludes even to the lowest and most ridiculous kind of mimicry. The passages are so curious and amusing that the reader will pardon me if I suffer them, in a note, to lead me into a short digression. He speaks in them of imitating or, as we call it, taking off "the neighing of horses, and the bellowing of bulls—the sound of thunder, the roaring of the sea and the winds—the tones of the trumpet, the flute, and all sorts of instruments—the barking of dogs, the bleating of sheep, and the singing of birds—the rattle of a shower of hail, and the rumbling of wheels." The sublime Plato was not always sublime. The expressions here are too strong to be understood merely of the imitations of poetical description; they are applicable only to vocal mimicry. Were there any doubt of this, it might be sufficiently removed

by other passages of ancient authors in which similar feats are recorded. Plutarch, commenting upon Aristotle's distinction between the pleasure we receive from the imitation and that which we receive from the real object, observes that "though the grunting of a hog, the rattle of wheels, the whistling of the wind, and the roaring of the sea, for instance, are sounds in themselves offensive and disagreeable, yet when we hear them well and naturally imitated, they give us pleasure." (*De aud. poet.*, Steph. 31.) And he records the names of two eminent performers in this way, Parmeno and Theodorus, the first of whom possessed the grunt of the hog, and the other the rattle of the wheel, in high perfection. This Theodorus was probably a different person from the tragic actor of the same name whose vocal talents of a higher kind are mentioned by Aristotle in his *Rhetoric* (III. i), and who was eminent for the power of accommodating the tone of his voice to the various characters he represented. "The voice," says the philosopher, "of Theodorus appears always to be that of the very person supposed to speak: not so the voices of other actors." In order fully to understand which praise, it is necessary to recollect that this vocal flexibility in an actor had far greater room to display itself among the ancients than it has with us on account of the exclusion of women from their stage. Hence one of the objections of Plato to the admission of dramatic poetry into his Republic (*Rep.* iii, 395 D), a passage which may also serve to confirm what has been asserted, that Plato, in speaking of poetry as imitation, constantly kept his eye on the personal imitation of the actor or the rhapsodist.—To return to the art of vocal mimicry: the passages above produced show it to have been of very respectable antiquity. But there are two other passages that make it still more venerable: one in the hymn to Apollo attributed to Homer, ll. 162–4,—where the musical imitations of the Delian virgins are described (see Dr. Burney's *Hist. of Music*, I, 372), and another very curious passage in the *Odyssey* iv. 279, by which it appears that the art was practiced even in the Trojan times, and that the beauteous Helen herself, among her other charms, possessed the talent of vocal mimicry in a degree that would, in modern times, have qualified her to make no inconsiderable figure at Bartholomew Fair. She is described as walking round the wooden horse, after its admission within the walls of Troy, calling by name upon each of the Grecian chiefs, and "imitating the voices of their wives." And so well did she take them off, that their husbands were on the point of betraying themselves by answering, or coming out. Anticlus, in particular, would have spoken if Ulysses had not by main force "stopped his mouth with his hand," till Minerva came to their relief, and took Helen away. *Od.* iv. 287, 8.

*53. The rhapsodist was defined to be "the actor of an epic poem." [See] Hesychius . . . [and] . . . Suidas. "Homer's poems," says the ingenious and entertaining author of the *Inquiry into the Life and Writings of Homer*, "were made to be recited or sung to a company, and not read in private or perused in a book, which few were then capable of doing; and I will venture to affirm that whoever reads not Homer in this view loses a great part of the delight he might receive from the poet" (Thomas Blackwell, 2nd ed. [London, 1736], p. 122).

ERASMUS DARWIN

Erasmus Darwin (1731–1802), the grandfather of Charles Darwin, took his A.B. at Cambridge in 1754, studied medicine for two years at Edinburgh, and then began the practice of medicine in Lichfield, where he lived for the next twenty-five years. In 1781, after his first wife had died and he had remarried, he moved to Derby, where he lived for the rest of his life. Darwin was first of all a highly successful physician; James V. Logan, in *The Poetry and Aesthetics of Erasmus Darwin* (Princeton, 1936), says he was the greatest doctor of his day. But Darwin was not only a practicing physician, he was very active in research, and his interest and activity in science were not limited to medicine. In addition to his experiments, observations, and speculations in zoology and botany (in which he anticipated his grandson's theory of evolution), he found time for the study of geology, chemistry, and physics. When he published his *Zoonomia or the Laws of Organic Life* in 1794, he was well prepared to achieve the aim of the work: "to reduce the facts belonging to animal life into classes, orders, genera, and species; and by comparing them with each other, to unravel the theory of diseases." In this analysis Darwin included psychology, and in that subject he followed those eighteenth-century speculations that had tried to account for such matters as taste by a study of the faculties and appetites. James V. Logan has summarized Darwin's theories of aesthetics in the book referred to above.

Before *Zoonomia*, however, Darwin had published, in 1789, *The Loves of the Plants*, a long poem in four cantos. This poem became, in 1791, Part II of *The Botanic Garden*, Part I of which was *The Economy of Vegetation*, another long poem, whose four cantos describe the roles of heat, earth, water, and air in the "economy of vegetation."

The Loves of the Plants is essentially a versified treatise in which plants are described according to the system of Linnaeus, who classified them according to the number and arrangement of the stamens in their flowers. Between the cantos Darwin inserted prose "Interludes," which are dialogues between a bookseller and the poet on questions of art. The third interlude is a discussion of the similarities between poetry and music and includes a brief discussion of the possible relationship between the spectrum and the musical scale, and of the possibility of "luminous music." The second interlude is a brief discussion of the monstrous and the "horrid" in literature and of the reasons why we enjoy "the bitter cup of tragedy."

The chief ideas of Interlude I, here reprinted from the fourth edition of *The Botanic Garden* (1799), are the following: (a) Poetry is distinguished from prose not so much by its meter and rhyme as by its language, which consists primarily of the words which stand for ideas belonging to vision; "poetry admits of but few words expressive of very abstract ideas." (b) Science should be expressed in prose because its analogies must be more strict than the metaphors and similes of poetry. (c) It is the proper function of poetry to deceive the reader, to show him not the nature which he can observe

in everyday life but the things above or beyond nature—art should show us beauty that nowhere exists. And the poet, if he is to deceive successfully, must (a) choose a subject that is "interesting from its sublimity, beauty, or novelty," and (b) bring the ideas "distinctly before the eyes."

1. During her fifteen-year residence in London, Swiss-born Angelica Kauffmann (1741–1807) became famous for her ceiling paintings, the subjects of which were usually allegorical. The monument to General Wade, by Louis François Roubillac (1695–1762), was placed in Westminster Abbey in 1752.

2. Patrick Brydone's *A Tour through Sicily and Malta* (1773) was a popular travel book. Henry Swinburne wrote *Travels in the Two Sicilies* (1783–1785).

ARCHIBALD ALISON

Six editions of *Essays on the Nature and Principles of Taste,* by Archibald Alison (1757–1839), "F. R. S. London and Edinburgh, Prebendary of Sarum, &c. &c. &c.," appeared between 1790 and 1825. Their influence on romantic poets and theorists was considerable. In the Advertisement to the Second Edition (1811), Alison said, "Of the general plan which I have sketched in the Introduction, I lament that so little has been accomplished." What he outlined under I in that introduction was developed in the two essays that make up the work; all that is projected under II and III remained undone: the source of the sublime and the beautiful in nature and art; why in nature and art subjects of terror and distress may produce the pleasant emotions of sublimity and beauty; how the beautiful differs from the sublime; the nature of the faculty by which beauty and the sublime are felt; whether there can be a standard of taste; how taste can be corrected and improved; how "this constitution of our nature" "increases human happiness" and "exalts human character." But one has the feeling that Alison's reason for not completing his project was not so much the "progress of years and the increase of more serious duties" as it was that in the two essays published he had said all he had to say on most of these points.

Since the Introduction and the Conclusions of the essays, all three here reprinted, give the gist of Alison's aesthetics, a further digest is unnecessary. In the edition of 1815, from which the present text is taken, the first essay is 175 pages long. Sections II and III of Chapter II, about 70 pages long, have been omitted. They are developments of the two theses stated at the end of Section I; Section III, on unity, is an interesting attempt to give an aesthetic justification for, or explanation of, the rule of unity in rhetoric and poetic. Alison discusses unity in natural scenes, in landscape painting, in poetic descriptions, and in all forms of poetry. He praises Corneille as "the first tragedian of modern Europe who seems to have been sensible of the necessity of this unity of emotion."

In "The Meaning of Archibald Alison's Essays on Taste" (*PQ*, XXVII [1948], 314–324), Martin Kallich points out that the basis of Alison's theory is laid in the second essay, which develops the thesis that "the qualities of matter are not beautiful or sublime in themselves but as they are, by various means, the signs or expressions of qualities capable of producing emotion." Such a hypothesis, as Kallich says, leads Alison to make "taste entirely dependent on the imagination to the exclusion of judgment and reason."

There are good analyses of the essays in Samuel H. Monk's *The Sublime: A Study of Critical Theories in Eighteenth-Century England* (New York, 1935), pp. 148–153, and in *The Beautiful, the Sublime, and the Picturesque in Eighteenth-Century British Aesthetic Theory* (Carbondale, 1957), pp. 158–181, by Walter John Hipple, Jr., who says that when they appeared, Alison's *Essays* "exhibited an originality, complexity, and logical coherence unmatched in British aesthetics."

*1. Mr. Addison.
2. Jacques Delille (1738–1813), *Les Jardins.*
3. Cicero *De legibus* ii. 4.
4. *Georg.* i. 493: "Yea, and a time shall come when in those lands, as the farmer toils at the soil with crooked plough, he shall find javelins eaten up with rusty mould, or with his heavy hoes shall strike on empty helms, and marvel at the giant bones in the upturned graves" (Fairclough).
5. Here follow Sections II and III. See headnote.

WILLIAM GILPIN

The Reverend William Gilpin (1724–1804), vicar of Boldre and prebendary of Salisbury, taught school for thirty years at Cheam, in Surrey. His summer vacations he spent on sketching tours, and his spare time during the rest of the year, in preparing illustrated accounts of these tours for publication. He also wrote a series of popular biographies of religious reformers, and a widely read *Essay on Prints* (1768). The substantial income from his publications he devoted to good works, notably the founding and endowment of a school for boys and a school for girls in his parish. The popularity of his work is suggested by the fact that during a period of twenty-five years he published seven books on the English countryside, beginning with *Observations on the River Wye* in 1782, and concluding with *Observations on Several Parts of the Counties of Cambridge, Norfolk, Suffolk, and Essex* in 1807. The *Essay on Prints* and several of the *Observations* were translated into German, French, and Dutch.

In these popular works Gilpin "exerted a profound and lasting influence upon the taste not only of England but of Europe," and "made [the word *picturesque*] the key term of the new aesthetic attitude of which he was himself the earliest exponent." Although the subject of his books was the sketching of landscapes, "his central concern was the cultivating of the perceiving taste through the knowledge, and practice, of art" (W. J. Hipple, Jr., *The Beautiful, the Sublime, and the Picturesque in Eighteenth-Century British Aesthetic Theory* [Carbondale, 1957], pp. 192, 308). In addition to Hipple's work, see also Christopher Hussey, *The Picturesque* (London, 1927), and Samuel

Monk, *The Sublime* (New York, 1935). The standard work on Gilpin is William D. Templeman, *The Life and Work of William Gilpin (1724–1804), Master of the Picturesque and Vicar of Boldre* (Illinois Studies in Language and Literature, vol. XXIV, nos. 3 and 4; Urbana, 1939).

The book from which the present selection is taken, *Three Essays: On Picturesque Beauty; On Picturesque Travel; and On Sketching Landscape,* was published in London in 1792; a second edition appeared in 1794; and the three essays were incorporated in *Five Essays,* published posthumously in 1808. The present text is from the second edition.

Gilpin defines the picturesque as that quality which makes certain objects attractive because they are "capable of being illustrated by painting"—in other words, whatever is attractive to a painter is picturesque. The quality is not the same as beauty, a term that may refer to a variety of qualities. *Smoothness* or *neatness* may be sources of beauty, but not of the picturesque, which is often found in roughness or ruggedness. For example, a piece of Palladian architecture to be pleasing in a painting must be a ruin. Similarly an irregular garden is more pleasing to a painter than a formal garden. And even in portraits, Reynolds (as well as such verbal painters as Virgil and Milton) introduces disheveledness, or rugged brows, or shaggy beards. The human form is more picturesque in action or in a state of passion than in quiescence; and in pictures of animals we prefer the worn-out cart horse, the cow, the goat, the bristly boar to the elegant perfection of a pampered horse.

Why this is so is hard to say. Rough objects make possible variety, and hence composition. What composition is there in a landscape consisting simply of smooth knolls intersecting one another? But beyond that the problem remains unsolved. "Whatever airs of dogmatizing we may assume, inquiries into principle rarely end in satisfaction."

At the conclusion of the essay, Gilpin prints a letter from Sir Joshua Reynolds, in which the old man says he has read the essay with interest, and suggests that the term *picturesque* may be synonymous with *taste,* and that it may be "applicable to the excellence of the inferior schools rather than to the higher."

In the second essay, "On Picturesque Travel," Gilpin says a landscape need not be sublime to be picturesque, though much of it is both. The picturesque is found "in the simplicity of nature" and in her most unusual forms. Even barren country produces pleasure: "When we have no opportunity of examining the grand scenery of nature, we have everywhere at least the means of observing with what a multiplicity of parts, and yet with what general simplicity, she covers every surface." In fact, the traveler is more often offended by what man has made—houses, towns, gardens, even paintings—than by the most barren stretch of landscape. "The more refined our taste grows from the study of nature, the more insipid are the works of art."

*1. *A Philosophical Inquiry into the Origins of Our Ideas of the Sublime and the Beautiful* [2nd ed., 1759], p. 213.

*2. Mr. Burke is probably not very accurate in what he farther says on the connection between beauty and diminutives. Beauty excites love, and a loved object is generally characterized by diminutives. But it does not follow that all objects characterized by diminutives, though they may be so because they are loved, are therefore beautiful. We often love them for their moral qualities, their affections, their gentleness, or their docility. Beauty, no doubt, awakens love, but also excites admiration and respect. This combination forms the sentiment which prevails when we look at the Apollo of Belvedere and the Niobe. No man of nice discernment would characterize these statues by diminutives. There is then a beauty between which and diminutives there is no relation, but which, on the contrary, excludes them, and in the description of figures possessed of that species of beauty, we seek for terms which recommend them more to our admiration than our love.

*3. The roughness which Virgil gives the hair of Venus and Ascanius we may suppose to be of a different kind from the squalid roughness which he attributes to Charon:

> terribile squalore Charon, cui plurima mento
> Portitor has horrendus aquas, et flumina servat
> canities inculta jacet.

[*Aeneid* vi. 298: "A grim warden guards these waters and streams, terrible in his squalor—Charon, on whose chin lies a mass of unkempt, hoary hair" (Fairclough).] Charon's roughness is, in its kind, picturesque also, but the roughness here intended, and which can only be introduced in elegant figures, is of that kind which is merely opposed to hair in nice order. In describing Venus, Virgil probably thought hair, when "streaming in the wind," both beautiful and picturesque, from its undulating form and varied tints, and from a kind of life which it assumes in motion, though perhaps its chief recommendation to him at the moment was that it was a feature of the character which Venus was then assuming.

*4. It is much more probable that the poet copied forms from the sculptor, who must be supposed to understand them better, from having studied them more, than that the sculptor should copy them from the poet. Artists however have taken advantage of the prepossession of the world for Homer to secure approbation to their works by acknowledging them to be reflected images of his conception. So Phidias assured his countrymen that he had taken his Jupiter from the description of that god in the first book of Homer. The fact is, none of the features contained in that image, except the brow, can be rendered by sculpture. But he knew what advantage such ideas as his art could express would receive from being connected in the mind of the spectator with those furnished by poetry, and from the just partiality of men for such a poet. He seems, therefore, to have been as well acquainted with the mind of man as with his shape and face. If by κυανέῃσιν ἐπ' ὀφρύσι we understand, as I think we may, "a projecting brow which casts a broad and deep shadow over the eye," Clarke has rendered it ill by *nigris superciliis*, which most people would construe into "black eyebrows." Nor has Pope, though he affected a knowledge of painting, translated it more happily by "sable eyebrows." But if Phidias had had nothing to recommend him except his having availed himself of the only feature in the poet which was accommodated to his art, we should not have heard of inquirers wondering from whence he had drawn his ideas, nor of the compliment which it gave him an opportunity of paying to Homer.

*5. Though there are only perhaps two or three of the first antique statues in very spirited action—the Laocoön, the Fighting Gladiator, and the Boxers— yet there are several others which are in action: the Apollo Belvedere, Michelangelo's Torso, Arria and Paetus, the Pietas Militaris (sometimes called the Ajax, of which the Pasquin at Rome is a part, and of which there is a repetition more entire, though still mutilated, at Florence), the Alexander Bucephalus, and perhaps some others, which occur not to my memory. The paucity, however of them, even if a longer catalogue could be produced, I think, shows that the ancient sculptors considered the representation of spirited action as an achievement. The moderns have been less daring in attempting it. But I believe connoisseurs universally give the preference to those statues in which the great masters have so successfully exhibited animated action.

*6. The idea of the ruffled "plumage of the eagle" is taken from the celebrated eagle of Pindar, in his first Pythian ode, which has exercised the pens of several poets, and is equally poetical and picturesque. He is introduced as an instance of the power of music. In Gray's Ode on the Progress of Poesy we have the following picture of him:

> Perching on the sceptered hand
> Of Jove, thy magic lulls the feathered king
> With ruffled plumes, and flagging wing;
> Quenched in dark clouds of slumber lie
> The terror of his beak, and lightning of his eye.

Akenside's picture of him, in his hymn to the Naiads, is rather a little stiffly painted.

> With slackened wings,
> While now the solemn concert breathes around,
> Incumbent on the sceptre of his lord
> Sleeps the stern eagle; by the numbered notes
> Possessed; and satiate with the melting tone;
> Sovereign of birds.

West's picture, especially the two last lines, is a very good one.

> The bird's fierce monarch drops his vengeful ire.
> Perched on the sceptre of th' Olympian king,
> The thrilling power of harmony he feels
> And indolently hangs his flagging wing;
> While gentle sleep his closing eyelid seals,
> And o'er his heaving limbs, in loose array,
> To every balmy gale the ruffling feathers play.

*7. A stroke may be called "free" when there is no appearance of constraint. It is "bold" when a part is given for the whole, which it cannot fail of suggesting. This is the laconism of genius. But sometimes it may be free and yet suggest only how easily a line which means nothing may be executed. Such a stroke is not bold, but impudent.

*8. Language, like light, is a medium, and the true philosophic style, like light from a north window, exhibits objects clearly and distinctly, without soliciting attention to itself. In subjects of amusement, indeed, language may gild somewhat more, and color with the dyes of fancy, but where information is of more importance than entertainment, though you cannot throw too strong a light, you should carefully avoid a colored one. The style of some writers resembles a bright light placed between the eye and the thing to be looked at. The light shows itself and hides the object; and, it must be allowed, the execution of some painters is as impertinent as the style of such writers.

*9. On all human flesh held between the eye and the light, there is a degree of polish. I speak not here of such a polish as this, which wrought marble always, in a degree, possesses, as well as human flesh; but of the highest polish which can be given to marble, and which has always a very bad effect. If I wanted an example, the bust of Archbishop Boulter in Westminster Abbey would afford a very glaring one.

*10. Sir Joshua Reynolds had seen this essay several years ago, through Mr. Mason, who showed it to him. He then made some objections to it: particularly, he thought that the term *picturesque* should be applied only to the works of nature. His concession here is an instance of that candor which is a very remarkable part of his character, and which is generally one of the distinguishing marks of true genius.

WALTER WHITER

Walter Whiter (1758–1832) lived in Clare College, Cambridge, as student and fellow, for twenty-one years. He was a friend of the great Porson and was himself an excellent scholar of the classics. His chief interest, however, was philology, and his chief works were two etymological dictionaries, *Etymologicon Magnum* (1800) and *Etymologicon Universale* (1811–25). For the last thirty-five years of his life he was a rector in Norfolk. In 1819 he published *A Dissertation on the Disorder of Death, or that State called Suspended Animation; to which remedies have been sometimes successfully applied, as in other disorders, in which it is recommended, that the same remedies of the resuscitative process should be applied to cases of natural death, drowning,* etc. London, "printed for the Author."

His *Specimen of a Commentary on Shakespeare. Containing I. Notes on As You Like It. II. An Attempt to Explain and Illustrate Various Passages, on a New Principle of Criticism, Derived from Mr. Locke's Doctrine of the Association of Ideas* (1794) became interesting to modern students of imagery when a leading article in the London *Times Literary Supplement* (Sept. 5, 1936) pointed out how Whiter had anticipated the work of Caroline Spurgeon, Wolfgang Clemen, and others. The first quarter of this book consists of about thirty notes on difficult passages in *As You Like It;* many of these show why the readings of the original text are superior to the emendations proposed by Shakespeare's editors. The longest note is the one here reprinted, in which Whiter anticipated the second part of his work by suggesting that the source of the imagery in a certain passage in the play was probably old tapestries or wall hangings representing figures from classical mythology.

In the second part of his book Whiter depends heavily upon his analysis of specific examples to elucidate his theory that Shakespeare's imagery is frequently the result of an unconscious process of association. In a brief introduction to the series of extended analyses Whiter defines association as the power to supply the poet "with words and with ideas which have been supplied to the mind by a principle of union unperceived by himself and independent of the subject to which they are applied." He outlines four ways in which this principle works: (a) The poet may use an unusual metaphor or expression because a subject previously discussed or referred to may be still lingering in his mind and thereby supply him with a term he would not otherwise have thought of. The first of the examples included in the present selection is an illustration of this kind of association. (b) Sometimes equivocal expressions or homonyms may introduce a new series of metaphorical variations (illustrated in the second example in the present abridgement). (c) One phrase or metaphor may suggest to the poet an associated, or similar, expression or subject which, though it does not get into the text, will supply him in turn, by way of a second process of association, with the term he finally uses. (d) Imagery may come in constellations all derived from some part of the poet's daily life or important experience. To this kind Whiter devotes several of his longest critiques, one showing how the words *hell, heaven, night, cave, fire, smoke, black, blanket,* and *blood* are all associated with theatrical presentations of tragedy. His references to Thomas Warton and Richard Hurd indicate his indebtedness to them for his examples of how masques and pageants also supplied Shakespeare with imagery.

The modernity of Whiter's attitude and method is apparent in his statement that "in the fictions, the thoughts, and the language of the poet, you may mark the deep and unequivocal traces of the age in which he lived, of the employments in which he was engaged, and of the various objects which excited his passions or arrested his attention."

I have omitted some of Whiter's notes, and I have edited some of those I have included.

1. Whiter used Malone's 1790 edition of Shakespeare, which included notes by all the preceding editors. George Tollet (1725–1779) had contributed notes to Johnson and Stevens' edition.

*2. Warton's *History of English Literature*, II, 215. ["We must acknowledge that all the picturesque invention which appears in this composition (Stephen Hawes's *Temple of Glass*) entirely belongs to Chaucer. . . . In the meantime, there is reason to believe that Chaucer himself copied these imageries from the romance of *Guigemar*, one of the metrical tales, or *lais*, of Bretagne translated from the Amorican original into French by Marie, a French poetess, about the thirteenth century, in which the walls of a chamber are painted with Venus and the *Art of Love* from Ovid. Although perhaps Chaucer might not look further than the temples in Boccaccio's *Thessid* for these ornaments. At the same time it is to be remembered that the imagination of these old poets must have been assisted in this respect from the mode which anciently prevailed of entirely covering the walls of the more magnificent apartments in castles and palaces with stories from Scripture, history, the classics, and romance."] See likewise I, 209; and his *Observations on the Fairy Queen*, I, 176–177, and II, 232. See too his notes on Milton, p. 277.

In many cases it is impossible to ascertain whether tradition, the legend, or the picture supplied the original materials. It is probable that these popular representations, which might be derived from the forgotten legends of one age, became themselves the original sources of the romances in another. *The Bard* of Gray, which was borrowed from a picture of Raphael, is itself the subject of another picture by West.

*3. See [Malone's edition of Shakespeare, 1790] IV, 122 ["Shakespeare has, more than once, taken his imagery from the prints with which the books of his time were ornamented. If my memory do not deceive me, he had his eye on a woodcut in Holinshed while writing the incantation of the weird sisters in *Macbeth*. There is also an allusion to a print of one of the Henrys holding a sword adorned with crowns. In this passage he refers to a device common in the title pages of old books, of two hands extended from opposite clouds, and joined as in token of friendship" (Henley)] and VIII, 579 ["The poet, as Mr. Mason has observed in a note on *The Tempest,* was here thinking of the common representations of the winds, which he might have found in many books of his own time"].

*4. See III, 204 [" 'I will weep for nothing, like *Diana in the fountain*.'— There being nothing in mythology to which these words could relate, I some years ago conjectured that the allusion must have been to some well-known conduit. Very soon after my note was printed, I found my conjecture confirmed, and observed in *A Second Appendix* to my *Supplement of Shakespeare,* printed in 1783, p. 13, that our author without doubt alluded to the ancient Cross in Cheapside, at the East side of which (says Stowe) 'a curious wrought tabernacle of gray marble was then set up (in the year 1596), and in the same an alabaster image of Diana, and water conveyed from the Thames, spilling from her naked breast.' *Survey of London,* p. 484, edit. 1618" (Malone)]; X, 154; IX, 123.

*5. See I (pt. 2), 213 ["A *Cain*-colour'd beard.—Cain and Judas, in the tapestries and pictures of old, were represented with *yellow* beards" (Theobold)]; III, 190.

*6.   And as mine eye doth his effigies witness
               Most truly limned and living in your face.
                        [*As You Like It,* II, vii, 193]

          All the pictures fairest lined
          Are but black to Rosalind. [III, ii, 97]

          The quintessence of every sprite
          Heaven would in little show. [III, ii, 147]

          Of many faces, eyes, and hearts,
          To have the touches dearest prized. [III, ii, 160]

> I do remember in this shepherd boy
> Some lively touches of my daughter's favor. [V, iv, 27]

The description which Phoebe afterwards gives us of Rosalind, if it be not derived from a picture, is at least admirably calculated to supply the painter with a subject. (See Malone, *Merchant of Venice*, 44.)

> There was a pretty redness in his lip,
> A little riper and more lusty red
> Than that mixed in his cheek, 'twas just the difference
> Betwixt the constant red and mingled damask.
>
> > [*As You Like It*, III, v, 123]

This surely is too definite and precise to be suddenly formed by the fleeting powers of the imagination unfixed and unassisted by any object.

> *Ros.* His very hair is of the dissembling color.
> *Cel.* Something browner than Judas's. [III, iv, 9]

"Judas," says Mr. Steevens, "was constantly represented in ancient painting or tapestry with red hair and beard."

*7. *History of English Poetry*, III, 361.

*8. It must not be forgotten by the reader that some portrait of this kind has likewise furnished our poet with a very elegant specimen of a poetical picture:

> In such a night
> Stood Dido with a willow in her hand
> Upon the wild sea banks and waft her love
> To come again to Carthage. [*The Merchant of Venice*, V, i, 9]

Our commentators seem to be embarrassed respecting the source from which this description is derived. Mr. Warton suggests that Shakespeare might perhaps have taken it from some ballad on the subject, and Mr. Steevens very gravely observes, "This passage contains a small instance out of many that might be brought to prove that Shakespeare was no reader of the classics." I fear that most of the instances relating to this subject, which have been produced as indisputable proofs, are precisely upon a level with the passage before us.

*9. I doubt not but that the idea of the eyes dropping millstones (which is familiar to our ancient poets) was suggested by the coarse imitation of tears in tapestry and paintings. So our author in *Troilus and Cressida*:

> *Pan.* Queen Hecuba laughed, that her eyes ran o'er.
> *Cres.* With millstones. [I, ii, 156]

And he again twice uses this expression in *Richard III*:

> Your eyes drop millstones when fools' eyes drop tears. [I, iii, 354]

> *Clar.* Bid Gloucester think of this, and he will weep.
> *1 Mur.* Aye, millstones, as he lessoned us to weep. [I, iv, 426]

*10. See a description of her picture in the *Arcadia*, I, iii.

*11. Everything that we read in our ancient authors respecting Lucretia appears to remind us of the source from which it is derived, and to point out how familiarly her picture or representation is impressed on the mind of the writer. She seems to have been a common subject for engraving on seals. So in the *Twelfth Night* (II, v, 103), "By your leave, wax. Soft, and the impressure her Lucrece, with which she uses to seal." She furnishes likewise another image for the verses contained in the letter:

> But silence, like a Lucrece knife,
> With bloodless stroke my heart doth gore. [II, v, 116]

Nay, so common were her portraits that she became the figure on the sign of the King's printer, Berthelette, in Fleet Street, who flourished about the year 1540. (Warton's *History of English Poetry*, III, 416). A cut of her is sometimes to be seen in his books. (See [Joseph] Ames, [*Typographical Antiquities: Being an Historical Account of Printing in England* 1471–1600 (1749),] I, 416, etc.) Let me add likewise that in our author's poem on this subject, Lucretia is sent for consolation to a piece of skillful painting which depicted "a thousand lamentable objects" in the history of Troy.

*12. Our poet appears to have caught the idea of Rosalind's cheek, and of all the graces being united by nature in her person, from the following passage in the original novel: "All in general applauded the admirable riches that nature bestowed on the face of Rosalind, for upon her cheeks there seemed a battle between the graces, who should bestow most favors to make her excellent." Her cheeks are again thus described:

> Her cheeks are like the blushing cloud
> That beautifies Aurora's face,
> Or like the silver crimson shroud
> That Phoebus' smiling looks doth grace.

And again,

> By those sweet cheeks, where love encamped lies
> To kiss the roses of the springing year.
> [Thomas Lodge, *Rosalynde*, ed. by E. C. Baldwin (Boston, 1910), pp. 13, 55]

She is thus described in her character of Ganymede, "In his cheeks the vermilion tincture of the rose flourished upon natural alabaster, the blush of the morn and Luna's silver show were so lively portrayed that the Trojan that fills out wine to Jupiter was not half so beautiful." Our poet has in this very play supposed the power of love to be seated in the cheek.

> *Sil.* O dear Phebe,
> If ever—as that ever may be near—
> You meet in some fresh cheek the power of fancy,
> Then shall you know the wounds invisible
> That love's keen arrows make. [*As You Like It*, III, v, 127]

*13. *In little show.*] The allusion is to a miniature *portrait:* "The current phrase in our author's time was *painted in little.*" (Malone.) So Hamlet: "It is not very strange, for my uncle is King of Denmark, and those that would make mows at him while my father lived give twenty, forty, fifty, a hundred ducats a piece for his *picture in little.*" [II, ii, 388]

*14. *The touches.*] The features; *les traits.* (Johnson.) I believe that *priz'd* is a word of this sort.

*15. Observe likewise that in the description which Phebe gives of Rosalind, her *tallness, leg,* and *cheek* are among the objects of Phebe's admiration:

> He is not very tall, yet for his years he's tall.
> His leg is but soso, and yet 'tis well.
> There was a pretty redness in his lip,
> A little riper and more lusty red
> Than that mixed in his cheek, 'twas just the difference
> Betwixt the constant red and mingled damask. [III, v, 118]

This very precise discrimination between the shades of color on the lip and the cheek will serve at once to confirm our hypothesis respecting the cheek of Helen, and at the same time to point out the source from which it is itself derived.

*16. In this note I have been barely able to give the reader a general notion of the subject: it would require and deserve a separate dissertation. It is from this source that our old writers were so intimately and personally acquainted with the illustrious characters in the Scripture. The very accurate description which the Venerable Bede has given us of the ages, figures, beards, hair, etc., of the wise men who brought their offerings to Christ "is now to be seen," says Mr. Warton, "in the old pictures and popular representations of the wise men's offerings." (Second Dissertation, "On the Introduction of Learning into England," in *The History of English Poetry,* Vol. I.) We cannot produce a more curious and convincing instance of the ancient prevalence and familiarity of these allusions than by showing that they still remain in the quaint language of the vulgar. The phrases *Nazarene foretop* and *Maudlin drunk* (if we may believe the *Classical Dictionary,* 2nd Edition) are to be referred to this origin. By the former indecent expression is denoted the foretop of a wig made in imitation of the hair of Christ as represented by painters and sculptors; and by the latter is meant one who is in that joyless state of uncomfortable intoxication as to resemble the tristful figure of Mary Magdalene, such as she was formerly represented in paintings and tapestry. There will be little reason to doubt the justness of this explanation when it is recollected that in this very play we find a familiar allusion to the "brown hair of Judas" [*As You Like It,* III, iv, 9] and in the *Merry Wives of Windsor* to the "yellow beard of Cain" [I, iv, 23]. (See Dodsley, *Old Plays,* III, 198.)

*17. This argument is fallacious if the poems under the name of Rowley are the productions of Chatterton. In this composition, the species of metaphysical forgery which I have described has been conceived, attempted, and successfully executed. I find in these poems all the effects of an ancient mind which my theory had taught me to expect.

*18. There is no reader of taste who will not on this occasion be reminded of the *Dialogue on the Age of Elizabeth* [by Richard Hurd, in *Moral and Political Dialogues* (1759)]

*19. These are not the only instances in Macbeth of allusions derived from the stage.

> *Macb.* Two truths are told
> As happy prologues to the swelling act
> Of the imperial theme. [I, iii, 127]

> *Macb.* Life's but a walking shadow, a poor player
> That struts and frets his hour upon the stage
> And then is heard no more. [V, v, 24]

> He died
> As one that had been studied in his death. [I, iv, 8]

Our author's profession, says Mr. Malone, furnished him with this phrase. "To be studied in a part, or to have studied it, is yet the technical term of the theater." I cannot help observing that this term (whatever might have been the reason) seems to be particularly applied to the art of dying. So in *Vittoria Corombona:*

> *Flam.* Then here's an end of me; farewell, daylight,
> And, O contemptible physic, that dost take
> So long a study, only to preserve
> So short a life. [*Old Plays,* Vol. VI, p. 346]

> *Flam.* I am in the way to study a long silence. [*Id.,* p. 369]

There is another allusion in *Macbeth* to the stage which the reader will find in the succeeding discussion.

*20. We know that the *Heroas,* the *Termagants,* and the *Tamburlaines* were the blustering heroes of our ancient plays and moralities, and that the bliss which so ravished the senses in this theatrical heaven consisted only in "big sounding sentences and words of state." To a mind therefore conversant with the objects of the stage, no association would be more obvious or natural than that of *lofty* language and a *low heaven.* Now it is remarkable that such a combination of ideas actually takes place in a passage of Shakespeare which has appeared so extraordinary to the commentators that the original reading has been rejected from the text. This singular passage occurs in *Love's Labor's Lost* [I, i, 316]:

> "*King.* A letter from the magnificent Armado.
> *Bir.* How low soever the matter, I hope in God for high words.
> *Long.* A high hope for a low heaven."

Such a reading of the old copies. The critics, however, appear to have thought the word *heaven* too remote and too solemn for so ludicrous an occasion, and they have accordingly, since the days of Theobald, rejected it from the text. *Having* is the word now read in all the editions of Shakespeare, which, I trust, will never again be inserted. There is an allusion likewise in this passage (as Mr. Steevens has observed) to the gradations of happiness in higher or lower heavens; and this judicious critic will be gratified by observing that his quotation in favor of the original reading from *Old Fortunatus* (1600),

> "Oh, how my soul is rapt to a third heaven,"

coincides with a line in Hall:

> "Rapt to the *three*-fold loft of heaven hight."

In the following passage the third heaven is applied, as in the quotation from Hall, to a person intoxicated:

"*Smug.* Mine host, my bully, my precious consul, my noble Holofernes, I have been drunk in thy house twenty times and ten; all's one for that: I was last night in the third heaven, my brain was poor, it had yeast in't, but now I am a man of action; is't not so, lad?"

This passage occurs in the elegant and entertaining play of the *Merry Devil of Edmonton (Old Plays, V, 285). . . .*

*21. I must beseech the reader not to be contented with a superficial reading of the passages on which I have founded the above discussion. On a careful review of these quotations, and of the note on the passage from *Troilus and Cressida,* he will perceive that the vein of sentiment and language which pervades them all is derived from the objects of the theater, partly from the *mechanical appendages,* and partly from the *allegorical personages* of scenical exhibition. On the whole, we may observe that the representation of *night* by the darkening of the stage, with the circumstances generally annexed to it, and the introduction of Night as a personified character, with the necessary peculiarities of her dress and figure, have caused all that variety, or sometimes that confusion, of imagery which we have seen abounding in the above quotations.

I cannot dismiss this remark without pointing out, under one view, that peculiarity of metaphor which exists in so many passages: I mean that *light* and its opposite, *darkness* or *night,* are connected with terms that belong to the language of *love,* and the qualities of the person. First, the damps of the night *ravish* the morning air; and the supreme *beauty* of light sickens at their *breath.* Second, night is represented with a black *bosom,* and though the imagery is extremely confused, we find Tarquin associated with Night that his character as a *ravisher* may be more fully displayed. Thirdly, the *jealous* day is called upon not to behold that *face,* which *immodestly* lies martyred under the cloak of night. Fourthly, living light should *kiss* the *face* which is covered by darkness. Fifthly, the *face* of the sun is to be *masked* in clouds, and dark vapors are to *embrace* his *front.* Sixthly, nature's *beauty,* the light of heaven, is choked by stifling clouds. Seventhly, the dark dwellings of fogs and misty damps are addressed as *lovely joys* and *darlings.* Eighthly, night is *hugged* as a *bride.* Ninthly, she is a *foul* and *ugly* witch. Tenthly, she flies the *grasps of love.* Eleventhly, light is the *fair* grandchild of the sun and shuns the *ugly* darkness which it embraced before.—These expressions are all certainly derived from scenical personifications.

I shall conclude the present investigation by observing that the circumstance which I have been desirous to establish has but recently impressed itself on my mind and that my conviction of its truth was formed by the consideration only of three or four passages. Since, therefore, the examples relative to this point which might occur in the course of my reading previous to this impression could avail me nothing, the reader must not wonder that I have passed by a cloud of witnesses which I am persuaded are everywhere to be found for the confirmation of my hypothesis. Some of the passages which I have now adduced presented themselves by accident even while I was employed in writing the discussion which they are intended to illustrate.

*22. Let it be remembered that if the name of *hell* at the lower part of the stage should not have escaped the knowledge of our critics, still, however, the passages from which I draw this conclusion are equally illustrative of the theory which I am discussing. They contain the same species of association, and many of them should be referred to the same principle of indirect allusion.

ALEXANDER KNOX

Alexander Knox (1757–1831), an Irish theological writer, was a friend of John Wesley and Hannah More. He wrote a great deal on the subject of Calvinism and the relationship of the Church of England to the Catholic Church. He was a good conversationalist. The three essays on Cowper here reprinted were attributed to him by Walter Graham (*N & Q*, CLXII [1932], 25) on the basis of a manuscript list of contributors found in a copy of the *Flapper* at the University of Illinois. Knox apparently contributed a total of ten essays to the paper. The *Flapper* was published twice a week in Dublin from Feb. 2, 1796, to Sept. 10, 1799. It was never reprinted.

I. The enthusiasm with which the public received the poetry of Cowper, Knox says, is proof that in a changing world common sense still prevails. The "common reader" is more often right than wrong in his judgments of poetry, even though Thomson's *Seasons* are more popular than Milton's *Paradise Lost*, which, because of the loftiness of its subject, the extent of its learning, and the literary quality of its style, "keeps the unlettered reader at an awful distance." Cowper is "accessible" for the same reasons that Thomson is—he writes about the common experiences of the mind and heart, in simple language. Like Thomson, he is a poet of nature, writing about familiar events and describing familiar scenes, but he is superior to Thomson because he describes not just what every man *may* see, but what he *must* see. He gives us "little domestic circumstances," and he describes them without the elaboration of Thomson; he uses only a "few masterly strokes." Thomson's descriptions are like Flemish paintings; Cowper's, like sketches of Raphael.

II. A poet who "impregnates the mind with seeds of a new conception" gives more pleasure than one who spells out all the details. In this respect Homer was better than his translator Pope. Cowper's descriptions, "in which nature and simplicity are the prevailing characters," "have a kind of mysterious power of captivating the human mind," and his homely scenes are "the means as well as the preservatives of innocence and tranquillity." In this respect the poet is a "benefactor of human kind" and a "minister of Heaven."

Cowper's humor is somewhat like Hogarth's.

III. All poetry depends upon the association of ideas, a faculty shared by all men, but one particularly vigorous in poets. One way in which the poet uses association is in finding "matters for humane and tender thought" in whatever he chooses to describe. In this Cowper is the equal of any of the greatest English poets. He writes from the heart. He may lack the sublimity of Milton, the "changeful excellence" of Shakespeare, the "majestic march" of Dryden, and the "melodious flow" of Pope, but above all of them he "claims this distinguished honor—that his muse is but the minister of his benevolence." Goldsmith is "a universal favorite" for the same reason—because he is "pathetic," because "his affections keep pace with his fancy."

1. In 1794 George III granted Cowper a pension of three hundred pounds a year.

2. Throughout the essay Knox alludes to Johnson's *Lives of the Poets*. The "common reader" is a term Johnson used in praising Gray's *Elegy*. See "Life of Gray" in *Lives of the Poets* (Oxford, 1952), II, 464.

3. See Johnson's "Life of Thomson," *Lives*, II, 358.

4. *Ars poet.* 360: "When a work is long, a drowsy mood may well creep over it" (Fairclough).

5. Jean-Baptiste-Louis Gresset (1709–1777), *Epître à ma muse.*

6. *Ars poet.* 311: "And when matter is in hand, words will not be loath to follow" (Fairclough).

7. *Ibid.* 99: "Not enough is it for poems to have beauty: they must have charm" (Fairclough).

8. Johnson in his "Life of Dryden" quoted Pope, *Imitations of Horace,* "Satire V," l. 269.

9. *Lives*, I, 323.

10. Knox abridged the last sentence of the "Life of Watts."

INDEX

Index

Addison, Joseph: critical essays by, 1-79;
on laughter, 377, 379; *Cato*, compared
with *Othello*, 664; *Cato*, J. Warton's
criticism of, 743-44; J. Warton on the
essays of, 745; mentioned, 276, 382,
383, 453-54, 455, 584, 602, 604, 636,
639, 645, 716, 717, 720, 735, 738, 756,
814
Aeschylus, 284, 703, 793, 918
Aesop: father of comedy, 91; mentioned,
97, 419
Afranius, Lucius, 346
Akenside, Mark, 718, 750, 1028, 1044
Alamanni, Luigi, 750
Alcaeus, 738, 878
Alcman, 878
Alcoran, the, 812
Alison, Archibald: on taste, 1011-46
Allegory: a species of wit, 13; Addison
on, 70; like tracks of light, 74; Homer's
use of, 260-61; in Spenser, 772-82; in
early English poetry, 778-82; in poetry
and painting, 1006-8
Allusions: a species of wit, 13
Amadis de Gaul, 921
Ammianus Marcellinus, 851
Anacreon, 413
Andrea, Giovanni Antonio, 684
Andreini, Giovanni Battista, 761
Antisthenes, 194
Antoninus, 751
Apelles, 572
Apollonius Rhodius, 260
Aratus, 2, 6
Archilochus, 444, 874
Archimedes, 894
Architecture: pleasures of imagination
in, 54-58
Ariosto, Lodovico: imitated by Spenser,
302; *Orlando Furioso*, criticized by
T. Warton, 769-71; mentioned, 35, 208,

305, 446, 718, 739, 761, 764, 765, 773-
74, 799, 800, 815, 887
Aristophanes, 91, 191
Aristotle: a regulated genius, 29; his rules
not immutable, 85; not qualified as
critic because not a poet, 86-90;
J. Warton's praise of, 736-37; author of
an elegy, 878; mentioned, 43, 77, 82,
84, 85, 96, 190-91, 193, 313, 419, 740,
764, 824, 940
— *Poetics:* only observations drawn from
works of Homer and Euripides, 87-90;
not applicable to Shakespeare, 281-82;
Ch. i, 872; v, 376; vi, 259, 363, 697;
vii, 620, 947; x, 33; xi, 34; xiii, 9, 893;
xxiv, 35; mentioned, 312, 317, 335,
865, 943
— *Rhetoric:* Bk. iii, 264, 464; mentioned,
37, 108
Aristoxenus, 876
Armstrong, John, 750
Art: works of compared with works of
nature, 51-53; its relation to nature,
258
Artist, the: his integrity, 197-98
Arts: how different from sciences, 932-
35; useful and fine distinguished, 935
Ascham, Roger, 663, 780, 795
Association of ideas: relation of to
genius, 882-95; influence of passions
on, 895-913; Alison on, 1025-36; applied to study of imagery, 1072-1103;
mentioned, 371-72
Augustine, St., 1014

Bacon, Francis, first Baron Verulam: a
regulated genius, 29; mentioned, 44,
417-18, 625, 756, 860, 866, 933, 937
Baillet, Adrien, 601
Ballads: Addison on, 17-27
Bandello, Matteo, 799